HAMMOND PUBLIC LIBRARY

3 1161 00642 7937

O9-AIG-881

WITHDRAWN BY THE
HAMMOND PUBLIC LIBRARY

# Holiday Symbols

# Holiday Symbols

A Guide to the Legend and Lore Behind the
People, Places, Food, Animals, and Other
Symbols Associated with Holidays and Holy Days,
Feasts and Fasts, and Other Celebrations,
Covering Popular, Ethnic, Religious, National,
and Ancient Events, as Observed in the
United States and Around the World

## 1998

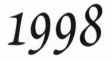

Sue Ellen Thompson, *Editor*

*Omnigraphics, Inc.*

Penobscot Building • Detroit, MI 48226

Hammond Public Library
Hammond, Ind.

Sue Ellen Thompson, *Editor*

Omnigraphics, Inc.

\* \* \*

Matt Barbour, *Production Manager*
Laurie Lanzen Harris, *Vice President, Editorial Director*
Peter E. Ruffner, *Vice President, Administration*
James A. Sellgren, *Vice President, Operations and Finance*
Jane Steele, *Marketing Consultant*

\* \* \*

Frederick G. Ruffner, Jr., Publisher

Copyright © 1998 Omnigraphics, Inc.

ISBN 0-7808-0072-9

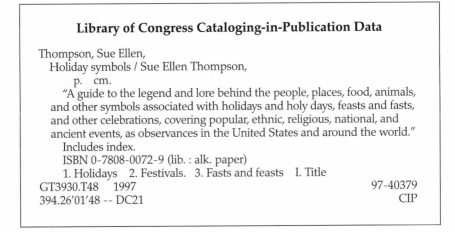

**Library of Congress Cataloging-in-Publication Data**

Thompson, Sue Ellen,
    Holiday symbols / Sue Ellen Thompson,
        p.   cm.
    "A guide to the legend and lore behind the people, places, food, animals,
and other symbols associated with holidays and holy days, feasts and fasts,
and other celebrations, covering popular, ethnic, religious, national, and
ancient events, as observances in the United States and around the world."
    Includes index.
    ISBN 0-7808-0072-9 (lib. : alk. paper)
    1. Holidays   2. Festivals.   3. Fasts and feasts    I. Title
GT3930.T48    1997                                                     97-40379
394.26'01'48 -- DC21                                                        CIP

The information in this publication was compiled from the sources cited and from
other sources considered reliable. While every possible effort has been made to
ensure reliability, the publisher will not assume liability for damages caused by inac-
curacies in the data, and makes no warranty, express or implied, on the accuracy of
the information contained herein.

This book is printed on acid-free paper meeting the ANSI Z39.48 Standard. The
infinity symbol that appears above indicates that the paper in this book meets that
standard.

Printed in the United States

R
394.2601
THOMPSO
1998

# *Contents*

# *Preface*

 olidays highlight the day-to-day lives of people of all cultures. People everywhere gather to celebrate many different types of holidays: religious holidays, such as Christmas or Ramadan; calendar holidays, such as New Year's or Leap Year Day; national holidays, such as Thanksgiving or the Fourth of July; as well as ancient and folkloric holidays, such as May Day and Halloween. The celebration of holidays is part of our history and our identity. Through the ritual of commemoration, we honor the past, mark the present, and anticipate the future.

The symbols associated with holidays are both timeless and timely. The exact history and original meaning of these symbols may be lost to time, but their resonance continues to our own day.

*Holiday Symbols: A Guide to the Legend and Lore Behind the People, Places, Food, Animals, and Other Symbols Associated with Holidays and Holy Days, Feasts and Fasts, and Other Celebrations, Covering Popular, Ethnic, Religious, National, and Ancient Events, as Observed in the United States and Around the World* presents the background of 174 of these holidays, and provides a historical survey of more than 750 symbols associated with them.

## The Plan of the Work

*Holiday Symbols* is arranged alphabetically by holiday name. Each holiday entry begins with bold-faced headings outlining:

- **Type of Holiday**, defining whether it is a religious, calendar, national, or ancient holiday
- **Date of Observation**, including any variants in different parts of the world

- **Where Celebrated,** outlining in which countries and for which religions a holiday is commemorated
- **Symbols** associated with each holiday, listing those that are described in the body of the text of the entry
- **Colors** associated with the holiday, if any, as well as their meaning
- **Related Holidays**, listing other holidays in the book associated with a specific celebration

This first section is followed by a brief essay on the **Origins** of each holiday, including historic and folkloric information on the background of the commemoration. This is followed by an alphabetically arranged section on the **Symbols** associated with the holiday. These sections focus on the origin and meaning of each holiday symbol. Each entry ends with a list of **Further Reading** for additional research.

Within the essays on each symbol, cross-references to symbols found in that specific holiday entry are set in small capital letters. Cross-references to symbols found in other holiday entries in the book appear in bold-faced capital letters.

The book ends with a General Index, listing all religions, countries, names, and other terms found in the text, and a Symbols Index listing all symbols covered in the text.

Because the study of holiday symbols is in no way an "exact" science, the basis for the essays are the legend, lore, and history of what is known about each holiday. These include information about celebrations that have occurred since the dawn of humankind, such as those commemorating the seasons and the harvest. Many of the essays trace how these most ancient celebrations have evolved in the modern era, and how some have been absorbed into modern religious or national festivals. As such, the essays delve into how symbols reflect on the evolution of society itself.

## Audience

*Holiday Symbols* is written to appeal to a wide range of readers. It can be used by students for class assignments, by general readers interested in the subject of holidays, and by teachers and librarians looking for information for units on holiday celebrations.

## Your Comments are Welcome

Readers are cordially invited to write the editor with comments and suggestions for future editions. Please direct your comments to:

Sue Ellen Thompson
Omnigraphics, Inc.
Penobscot Bldg.
Detroit, MI 48226

# *Advent*

**Type of Holiday:** Religious (Christian)

**Date of Observation:** Sunday closest to November 30 through December 24 in the West; November 15 through December 24 in the East

**Where Celebrated:** United States, Great Britain, Europe, and by Christians throughout the world

**Symbols:** Advent Calendar, Advent Candle, Advent Letters, Advent Plays, Advent Wreath

**Colors:** Advent is associated with blue, the color of the Virgin Mary's cloak. The liturgical color is purple, a reminder of the fact that Advent was originally a time for fasting and penance.

**Related Holidays:** Christmas, Christmas Eve

## ORIGINS

The name "Advent" comes from the Latin adventus, meaning "coming" or "arrival." Just as **LENT** is a period during which Christians prepare for **EASTER**, Advent is a period of preparation for **CHRISTMAS**. It was originally observed by Eastern and some Western churches as preparation for the feast of **EPIPHANY** (January 6), which at one time celebrated both the birth of Jesus Christ and His baptism. When Rome fixed December 25 as the commemoration of Christ's birth in the fourth century, however, Advent underwent a shift not only in time but in mood as well. No longer

1

a period of fasting and somber self-reflection, Advent became a time of joyous anticipation.

In the West, Advent Sunday is always the Sunday nearest the Feast of St. Andrew (November 30). The overall length of the Advent period may vary from 22 to 28 days, but it always ends on **CHRISTMAS EVE**. Although it is claimed that this holy season was instituted by St. Peter, no one has been able to determine the exact date when Advent was first observed. Up until the sixth century, Easter was considered the beginning of the Christian year, because the Jewish year began at approximately the same time. But when anti-Semitic Christian leaders persuaded their followers that the Christian calendar should be moved as far as possible from the Jewish dates, Advent was chosen as a convenient starting point. The Orthodox (Eastern) Christian year begins on September 1, and Advent is observed beginning on November 15.

## SYMBOLS

### Advent Calendar

The popular Advent calendar that parents give their children to help them count the days until Christmas originated in Germany, but quickly spread to other European countries. It usually consists of a "Christmas House" printed on cardboard with small cut-out windows that can be opened by folding them back, revealing a miniature picture or symbol associated with the feast of Christmas. The calendar is hung on a wall or window at the beginning of December, and one of the windows is opened each day. The last door or window is opened on Christmas Eve, and it shows the Nativity scene. Aside from this reference to the religious aspect of the season, however, Advent calendars are primarily a means of keeping children's minds occupied during the long wait for the arrival of Santa Claus.

### Advent Candle

The Advent candle may be a single large candle located in a central place in the home or four separate candles set in a special holder. The candles are usually white and may be hand-dipped. The holder is often decorated with moss and lichen. One candle is lit on Advent Sunday and allowed to burn down a little way. On the second Sunday, both the first and the second candles are lit for a while — and so on, until all four candles are burning at different levels on the Sunday preceding Christmas Eve. Like the Advent calendar, these candles serve as a reminder that Christmas is coming soon.

At pre-Christmas church services in Germany, children hold a decorated orange in which a small candle has been inserted. Originated by the Moravian Brethren in East Germany, the candle is called the Christingle, which might have derived from either *Christ-kindl*, meaning "Christ Child," or *Christ-engel*, referring to the angel who brings gifts to children.

## Advent Letters

An ancient custom popular in Europe, Canada, and South America, Advent letters are notes addressed to Baby Jesus that children leave on their window sills when they go to bed on December 5, the eve of St. Nicholas' Day. The notes contain lists of Christmas presents the children hope to receive and are supposedly taken to heaven by angels or by St. Nicholas himself. In South America, children write their notes to "Little Jesus" between December 16 and 24, leaving them in front of the crèche for the angels to pick up.

This is very similar to the American custom of sending Christmas letters to Santa Claus at the North Pole. These letters are dropped in specially decorated red mailboxes that are put out every year a few weeks before Christmas.

## Advent Plays

During Advent in Germany, it is popular to dramatize the *Herbergsuchen*, the Holy Family's fruitless search for shelter in Bethlehem on the night that Jesus was born. The performance is usually sung and is often followed by a "happy ending" tableau showing the Nativity scene.

A similar custom, popular in South America and particularly Mexico, is the Spanish **POSADAS**. Between December 16 and 24, several neighboring families gather in one house, where they prepare a shrine with a crib and traditional figures, but the manger itself is left empty. A procession moves through the house, pictures of Mary and Joseph are placed on the shrine, and a priest blesses everyone present. Sometimes a group of "pilgrims" will knock on the door and ask the owner of the house to let them in. This reenactment of Mary and Joseph's search for shelter (*posada* in Spanish) ends with a big party for the adults and an opportunity for the children to break a *piñata* filled with candy and suspended from the ceiling.

## Advent Wreath

The Advent wreath is made of yew, fir, or laurel and is suspended from the ceiling or placed on a table, usually in front of a family shrine. Four candles stand upright at equal distances around the circumference of the wreath,

3

representing the four weeks of Advent. One candle is lit each Sunday during the Advent season. On the fourth Sunday, the family gathers in the evening to say prayers and sing Advent hymns.

Symbols for light played an important role in late November and early December, the season during which the pre-Christian festival of Yule was observed with the burning of torches and bonfires. When Christianity came along, many of these light and fire symbols were kept alive. By the sixteenth century, the custom of using candles as a religious symbol of Advent had been established in Germany and was spreading rapidly among Protestants and Catholics alike.

In some parts of Europe, it is traditional for someone named John or Joan to light the candles on the Advent wreath, because the Gospel of John refers to Christ as the "Light of the World." Another possible reason for this custom is that John the Baptist was the first one to see the light of divinity shining around Jesus when he was baptized in the River Jordan.

The wreath itself is an ancient symbol whose eternal circle stands as a reminder of new beginnings at a time of apparent endings. While Advent falls near the end of the calendar year, it marks the beginning of the Christian year. Because the wreath is made of evergreens, it also serves as a symbol of eternal life in Christian terms and the life that goes on in nature despite the cold winter weather.

## Further Reading

Barz, Brigitte. *Festivals with Children,* 1989.

Brewster, H. Pomeroy. *Saints and Festivals of the Christian Church,* 1990.

Harper, Howard V. *Days and Customs of All Faiths,* 1990.

Hatch, Jane M. *The American Book of Days,* 1978.

Henderson, Helene and Sue Ellen Thompson. *Holidays, Festivals, and Celebrations of the World Dictionary,* 2nd ed., 1997.

MacDonald, Margaret R. *Folklore of World Holidays,* 1992.

Metford, J. C. J. *The Christian Year,* 1991.

Santino, Jack. *All Around the Year,* 1994.

Spicer, Dorothy Gladys. *Festivals of Western Europe,* 1994.

Weiser, Francis X. *Handbook of Christian Feasts and Customs,* 1952.

# All Souls' Day
## (*Día de los Muertos*)

**Type of Holiday:** Religious (Christian)

**Date of Observation:** November 2 in the West (November 3 if November 2 falls on a Sunday); three Saturdays prior to Lent and the day before Pentecost in the East

**Where Celebrated:** United States (particularly on Indian reservations in southwestern U.S.), Britain, Europe, Mexico, Central and South America, and by Roman Catholics, Anglicans, and Orthodox Christians throughout the world. Some Protestants informally observe All Souls' Day.

**Symbols:** Candles, Graves, Ofrenda, Skull or Skeleton, Soul Cakes

**Colors:** The liturgical color at all church services on November 2 is black. In parts of Europe, Roman Catholic services on this day are often referred to as "black vespers." In southern Europe, the churches are draped in black and worshippers wear black clothing.

## ORIGINS

All Saints' Day (November 1) was established in the ninth century as an attempt to Christianize the pagan festival of the dead, known as **SAM-HAIN**. St. Odilo, the abbot of Cluny in France, proposed that the day after be set aside to pray for the souls of the departed—especially those who were still in purgatory. All Souls' Day was well established by the end of the tenth century, and in the fourteenth century, Rome placed the day in the official books of the Western Church as November 2.

Many of the customs now associated with All Souls' Day—for example, laying out food for the dead, lighting candles on graves, and tolling the bells until midnight—can be traced back to the pagan celebration of Samhain. The pagans believed in pacifying the dead so they wouldn't haunt the living, while the Christian celebration of All Souls' Day is based on the belief that offering prayers for the dead will benefit the souls of the departed. It's interesting that while All Saints' Day was designed to displace the pagan festival of the dead, All Souls' Day comes very close to duplicating it.

In Mexico, Día de los Muertos (Day of the Dead) is a major celebration that blends European and Indian beliefs concerning the dead, whose spirits are believed to return to their families and communities at this time of year. The emphasis is on showing hospitality to these visiting spirits by giving them the opportunity to enjoy earthly pleasures. All Souls' Day is also observed by Native Americans on the Indian reservations of the western United States, particularly New Mexico.

## SYMBOLS

### Candles

Lighting candles is a symbolic attempt to illuminate the darkness for the returning souls of the dead. In Ireland, candles shine in the windows of Catholic homes on All Souls' Eve. In Belgium, a holy candle burns all night, and people walk in candlelight processions. In many Roman Catholic countries, the cemeteries are aglow with the candles that have been set on the graves, often protected by little glass lanterns, as symbols of the souls of the departed. The pueblo Indians of the southwestern United States place candles in their churches and houses in the belief that the dead will burn the fingertips of those who fail to light their way.

In Catholic sections of central Europe, it is the custom to ring church bells at the approach of dusk on November 1 to remind people to pray for the souls in purgatory. When they hear the bells, families gather in one room and extinguish all other lights except for the candle they have kept from the preceding **CANDLEMAS** (February 2).

### Graves

The cemetery is the focus of most All Souls' Day celebrations. The graves of the dead are thoroughly cleaned, raked, and weeded. Fresh flowers are set out, and other decorations—such as Styrofoam crosses, wreaths, and arrangements of silk or plastic flowers—are placed carefully on the grave.

The marigold is the traditional flower used to decorate graves in Mexico. The Aztecs observed two festivals for the dead, one for children and another for adults, in the belief that deceased relatives could serve as intermediaries between the living and the gods. Marigolds were a primary offering at these and other Aztec festivals, where flowers and butterflies were frequently substituted for human flesh. They still play an important role in the observation of Día de los Muertos and are often referred to by their ancient Aztec name, *Cempoalxochitl*.

The custom of decorating graves and praying in cemeteries on this day is widespread in Catholic Europe and America. In addition to flowers, candles or lanterns are often lit on the graves and left burning throughout the night on All Souls' Eve.

## Ofrenda

The *ofrenda* or domestic altar is central to the observance of Día de los Muertos in Mexico. It is set up at home, in the church, or outside the cemetery and serves as a "threshold" providing access between heaven and earth. Everything on the *ofrenda* — flowers, candles, incense, and the dead person's favorite foods — is chosen because it will promote communication with the spirit world. The sights, smells, and colors are regarded as signals that will draw the spirit of the deceased ancestor home.

Day of the Dead celebrations have become more common in the United States in recent decades. One of the more popular ways of observing it in cities with large Hispanic-American populations is to hold a Day of the Dead exhibit at a local museum or art gallery focusing on the Mexican *ofrenda* tradition. New York, Chicago, Houston, and Miami have all hosted such exhibitions.

## Skull or Skeleton

Although the skull and the skeleton are clearly symbols of death, they appear in a very lively form at Mexican and Hispanic-American celebrations of All Souls' Day. Toy skeletons can be seen dancing with beautiful young maidens, or laughing and playing the guitar while riding horseback. Candies made from sugar-based dough and shaped like skulls and tombstones are sold in bakeries and marketplaces as soon as the holiday approaches. *Pan de muerto* (bread of the dead) is baked in the shape of human figures, with a skull-and-crossbones design on top. In northern Spain and in Madrid, a special pastry called *Huesos de Santo* (Bones of the Holy) is sold on this day. Such edible treats are another way of inviting the spirits of the dead back to their homes, using food as a symbolic enticement. Skulls also appear — along with candles, flowers, crucifixes, and other icons — on the *ofrenda*.

Another Mexican Day of the Dead tradition is the composition of short poems known as *calaveras* (*calavera* means "skull" or "corpse"). This tradition began in Mexico City in the nineteenth century and still continues there today. Aimed at mocking police, government officials, the police, and even priests, writing and publishing these poems is primarily an urban tradition. Even those who excel at *calaveras* find that their fame is short-lived: Once the holiday is over, their taunts are usually forgotten. *Calaveras* are printed on large sheets of paper and are often illustrated with laughing skeletons dressed in fancy suits or gowns.

While the skeleton symbolizes death, primitive peoples regarded it as the source of life or the place where the soul lived. When the skeleton was destroyed, the soul vanished. The skull also functions as a "dual" symbol: It signifies mortality but stands as a receptacle for life and thought. At one time it was customary to open up charnel-houses (buildings where corpses or bones were deposited) during the All Souls' festival so that people could visit the bodies of their friends and relatives—usually skeletons dressed in robes and arranged in niches along the walls.

## Soul Cakes

In the Middle Ages, the custom of "souling" was widespread in the British Isles. On All Souls' Eve (November 1), "soulers" went from house to house offering prayers for the dead and begging alms in return. Eventually the alms took the form of "soul cakes." According to an old superstition, for each cake consumed, a soul would be released from the torments of Purgatory. This begging ritual, initially carried out by grown men, was eventually taken up by children who recited a rhyme or song requesting "mercy on all Christian souls for a soul cake."

Souling can be traced back to a heathen winter custom in England known as "hodening." A man wearing a white sheet and a wooden horse's head whose jaws were hinged in such a way that they could snap ferociously would go around the village with a band of men and boys, leaping and prancing as people opened their doors. Hodening usually took place at Christmas and on All Souls' Day or Eve. The horse-man and his followers were given ale and other gifts.

The pagan custom of hodening—probably derived from the ancient fertility rites and horse sacrifices of the Romans and Norsemen—was either combined with or replaced by the Christian custom of souling. The soul cakes used today are left out on All Souls' Eve for the dead to eat when they revisit their homes. In Italy, *fave dei morti* or "beans of the dead"—actually bean-shaped cakes—are served on this day. In some sections of central Europe, the boys receive All Souls' cakes in the shape of a hare, while the girls are given cakes in the shape of a hen—an interesting way of combining symbols for fertility with a symbol for the souls of the dead.

8

Soul cakes can still be found in Great Britain, Belgium, Southern Germany, and Austria. Some scholars think that the modern custom of begging for candy on **HALLOWEEN** is somehow linked to the medieval souling tradition.

## Further Reading

Chambers, Robert. *The Book of Days*, 1990.

Cirlot, J. E. *A Dictionary of Symbols*, 1962.

Ferguson, George. *Signs and Symbols in Christian Art*, 1954.

Hatch, Jane M. *The American Book of Days*, 1978.

Henderson, Helene and Sue Ellen Thompson. *Holidays, Festivals, and Celebrations of the World Dictionary*, 2nd ed., 1997.

Hole, Christina. *English Custom and Usage*, 1990.

James, E. O. *Seasonal Feasts and Festivals*, 1993.

Jobes, Gertrude. *Dictionary of Mythology, Folklore, and Symbols*, 1962.

Miles, Clement A. *Christmas in Ritual and Tradition, Christian and Pagan*, 1990.

Miller, Mary, and Karl Taube. *The Gods and Symbols of Ancient Mexico and the Maya*, 1993.

Pike, Royston. *Round the Year with the World's Religions*, 1993.

Santino, Jack. *All Around the Year*, 1994.

Santino, Jack. *Halloween and Other Festivals of Death and Life*, 1994.

Urlin, Ethel L. *Festivals, Holy Days, and Saints' Days*, 1992.

Weiser, Francis X. *Handbook of Christian Feasts and Customs*, 1952.

# *Annunciation of the Blessed Virgin Mary, Feast of the*
## *(Lady Day)*

**Type of Holiday:** Religious (Christian)

**Date of Observation:** March 25

**Where Celebrated:** Britain, Europe, United States, and by Roman Catholics and Anglicans around the world

**Symbols:** Dove, Lady Day Cakes, Lily

**Related Holidays:** Feast of the Assumption of the Blessed Virgin Mary

# ORIGINS

The Feast of the Annunciation celebrates the appearance of the Archangel Gabriel to the Virgin Mary, announcing that she was going to be the mother of Jesus Christ. Although the Christian church began commemorating this occasion early on, the exact date could not have been fixed until the date of **CHRISTMAS** was established in the late fourth century, since the two holidays obviously had to be nine months apart. Some scholars believe that the Feast of the Annunciation was established to curb the wild behavior associated with an ancient pagan spring festival held in Rome around this same time of year.

According to tradition, Mary of Nazareth was living in her parents' home at the time. Although she had made a vow that she would never marry, Jewish custom decreed that she and her sister should marry young Jewish men so the family wealth could be handed down. Distressed by the thought that she might be forced into a marriage she did not want, Mary was overjoyed to discover what lay in store for her. Not only could she keep her vow, but it would not prevent her from fulfilling her role as the most important mother in all of Christianity.

The English call March 25 "Lady Day of March," since there are four other feast days that qualify as Lady Days in the Christian calendar: The Purification of Mary (also known as **CANDLEMAS**), commemorating Mary's presentation of her son in the Temple at Jerusalem on February 2; the Visitation on July 2, commemorating Mary's visit to her cousin Elizabeth; the Nativity of Mary on September 8; and the Conception of the Blessed Virgin on December 8. According to an old tradition, the crucifixion of Jesus took place on March 25, and as a result it was considered unlucky if Easter and Lady Day coincided. The English had a rhyme that said, "If Our Lord falls in Our Lady's lap/ England will meet with great mishap." Those who cling to this belief point to 1910, when the two holidays coincided and King Edward VII died soon after.

In many European countries, the Feast of the Annunciation is a day for weather predictions. In Belgium, for example, it is believed that all seeds sown on this day are guaranteed to germinate. Although an Italian proverb says that frost on March 25 will do no harm, a French proverb says it will bring disaster to the fields. There is also a saying that rain on Lady Day will mean rain on all the other feast days dedicated to the Virgin Mary throughout the year.

# SYMBOLS

## Dove

For Christians, the white dove symbolizes purity because they believed that the Devil could transform himself into any bird except the dove. After observing the traditional 40-day period of purification following the birth of Jesus, Mary brought her son to the Temple at Jerusalem, where two doves were offered as a sacrifice. In Christian art, a dove also appears sometimes on the top of Joseph's rod to show that he was chosen to be Mary's husband. Because Jesus instructed his followers to be "innocent as doves," the doves often seen on gravestones symbolize the innocence of the person buried there.

The most important use of the dove, however, is as a symbol of the Holy Spirit. In medieval paintings of the Annunciation, the Virgin Mary is usually shown kneeling or seated at a table, reading. The Holy Spirit is seen descending toward her in the form of a dove. The dove usually appears within a beam of light striking Mary's ear. The light is symbolic of God, who separated light from darkness on the first day of Creation. In medieval times, the ear was believed to house the memory.

## Lady Day Cakes

In the English town of St. Albans, Lady Day is associated with the baking of special cakes. According to legend, a lady was travelling with her attendants when she lost her way near St. Albans. The lights from the monastery tower, located on a hill, guided her party to safety. To show her gratitude, she gave the monks of the abbey a sum of money to provide free cakes in the shape of ladies, to be distributed on March 25. The cakes were later called "Pope Ladies," a term that probably originated after the Reformation.

## Lily

The lily has traditionally symbolized purity, innocence, and virginity, and for Christians it became both a symbol and attribute of the Virgin Mary. Together with the DOVE, the lily is associated with the Annunciation. In Christian art Gabriel, the angel who appeared to Mary at the Annunciation, is usually shown holding a lily, as are Joseph and his parents, Anne and Joachim.

According to legend, the lily sprang from the tears of Eve when she was expelled from the Garden of Eden. The large white lily known as the Madonna Lily is sacred to the Virgin Mary and is said to have been yellow until she bent down to pick it.

11

## Further Reading

Biedermann, Hans. *Dictionary of Symbolism: Cultural Icons and the Meanings Behind Them,* 1989.

Chambers, Robert, ed. *The Book of Days,* 1864.

Cirlot, J. E. *A Dictionary of Symbols,* 1962.

Ferguson, George. *Signs and Symbols in Christian Art,* 1954.

Harper, Howard V. *Days and Customs of All Faiths,* 1957.

Henderson, Helene and Sue Ellen Thompson. *Holidays, Festivals, and Celebrations of the World Dictionary,* 2nd ed., 1997.

Hole, Christina. *English Custom and Usage,* 1941.

Leach, Maria, ed. *Funk & Wagnalls Standard Dictionary of Folklore, Mythology & Legend,* 1984.

Olderr, Steve. *Symbolism: A Comprehensive Dictionary,* 1986.

Rest, Friedrich. *Our Christian Symbols,* 1954.

Urlin, Ethel L. *Festivals, Holy Days, and Saints' Days,* 1915.

# *Aoi Matsuri*
## *(Hollyhock Festival)*

**Type of Holiday:** Folkloric, Religious (Shinto)
**Date of Observation:** May 15
**Where Celebrated:** Kyoto, Japan
**Symbols:** Hollyhock

## ORIGINS

One of the three major festivals of Kyoto, Japan, Aoi Matsuri dates back to the sixth century. It gets its name—the Hollyhock Festival—from the leaves used to decorate the headdresses worn by the participants. The festival takes place on May 15, when the cherry blossoms have fallen and the irises are not yet in flower. The heavy rains and gray skies that are common in Kyoto at this time of year are one reason, according to legend, that the festival was established. Flooding was so widespread during the sixth century that imperial messengers were sent to the Kyoto shrines of Shimogamo and Kamigamo to ask for the gods' help. When the floodwaters receded, the people held a celebration.

Today the festival, which was revived in 1884, consists of a recreation of the original procession to the shrines. The participants gather at the Imperial Palace at ten o'clock in the morning to begin the long, circuitous route to the shrines. Spectators may purchase seats at the palace to watch the parade, or they can choose their own viewing place along the route. The highlight of the procession is the imperial messenger and his courtiers, who are dressed in elaborate kimonos and the high-backed black hats known as *eboshi*. They surround a large, lacquered *gissha* or oxcart draped with *fuji* or artificial wisteria flowers and pulled by a black ox who is drawn through the streets by ropes of orange silk. Other participants in Heian-period costumes carry huge ceremonial umbrellas covered with large, artificial flowers—usually peonies, symbolic of wealth and distinction. A lady carried on a litter represents a princess who has been chosen to lead the difficult life of a Shinto priestess. Traditional Japanese music with flutes, gongs, and drums accompanies the procession. Spectators often need a program to help them identify the various warriors, courtiers, and other dignitaries in the parade.

## SYMBOLS

### *Hollyhock*

Aoi is usually translated to mean "hollyhock," but a different plant—probably a wild ginger—may originally have been used in the festival. When wild ginger became hard to find, other plants with heart-shaped leaves were substituted. At the end of the procession to the Kamigamo and Shimogamo shrines, the foliage is offered as a token of respect and appreciation to the gods.

The Japanese believed that hollyhocks could prevent storms and earthquakes. By bringing this plant with its heart-shaped leaves to the shrine, they are commemorating the heavy rains and flooding that plagued Kyoto during the sixth century.

## Further Reading

Bauer, Helen, and Sherwin Carlquist. *Japanese Festivals,* 1965.

Henderson, Helene and Sue Ellen Thompson. *Holidays, Festivals, and Celebrations of the World Dictionary,* 2nd ed., 1997.

Shemanski, Frances. *A Guide to World Fairs and Festivals,* 1985.

# *April Fools' Day*

**Type of Holiday:** Folkloric
**Date of Observation:** April 1
**Where Celebrated:** England, France, Scotland, United States
**Symbols:** Fish, Pranks and Practical Jokes

## ORIGINS

Children have been shouting "April Fool!" since the 1600s in England, shortly before the custom was brought to America by the first English settlers. But there are a number of theories as to how it got started. One explanation points to Noah as the first "April Fool." It is said that on this day Noah mistakenly sent the dove out to find dry land after the flood began to recede. Another possibility is that it had something to do with the change to the New Style or Gregorian calendar. Under the Old Style calendar, **NEW YEAR'S DAY** was celebrated around the time of the **VERNAL EQUINOX** in late March. Because this occasionally coincided with, or at least came close to, the celebration of **EASTER**, Church officials moved New Year's Day up to April 1. When the Gregorian calendar was officially adopted in 1582 and New Year's Day was shifted from April 1 to January 1, some people forgot about the change and continued to make their New Year visits on the old date. Others paid mock visits to friends and neighbors on April 1, shouting "April Fool!" at those who took them seriously.

April Fools' Day has been called by many other names—among them Huntigowk Day or Gowkie Day (in Scotland, where an April fool is called a "gowk"), All Fools' Day, and April Noddy Day (a fool in England is a "noddie"). But all of these names echo that of the Feast of Fools, a popular medieval festival during which social roles were reversed and rules were deliberately flouted. The men would dress up as women, eat and gamble at the altar, burn old leather sandals in the censors, and engage in other activities that would normally be unthinkable. The Feast of Fools was especially popular in France, where April Fools' Day is widely observed.

# SYMBOLS

## Fish

In France, the fish is the primary symbol of April Fools' Day. Chocolate candy shaped like fish is sold everywhere, and people often try to pin a paper fish on someone else's back without getting caught (for which the day is called Fooling the April Fish Day). The people known as "April fools" in English-speaking countries are called "April fish" (*poisson d'Avril*) in France. Since fish begin to run in the spring, it is likely that the April Fish is a symbol of rebirth and fertility.

## Pranks and Practical Jokes

There is a theory that the custom of pulling pranks and practical jokes on April 1 is a relic of the ancient Roman festival in honor of Ceres, the corn goddess, whose daughter Proserpine was carried off to the underworld by Pluto to be his queen. Ceres' day-and-night search for her daughter was considered a "fool's errand" because Pluto was a very powerful god. A similar connection exists between April Fools' Day and the Hindu spring festival of **HOLI**. Although there is no historical evidence of a connection between the two, it is interesting to note that one of the principal Holi customs is playing practical jokes and sending people on fools' errands.

A more modern explanation for the custom is that it accompanied the shift from the Old Style (or Julian) calendar to the New Style (Gregorian) calendar (see "Origins"). People in France who couldn't make the adjustment were often sent mock gifts and called "April fish" (see FISH) or April fools. The custom of April fooling spread quickly throughout France and Europe. In England, the custom had already taken root in the early eighteenth century, even though the change in the calendar was not official until 1752.

In England, an April fool was called an April gob, gawby, or noddie. In Scotland, it was an April gowk or cuckoo. A favorite prank in Scotland was to send someone to deliver a letter. Upon receiving it, the recipient would tell the carrier that he or she was mistaken; the letter was meant for someone who lived farther down the road. Unbeknownst to the carrier, what the letter really said was, "It's the first of April. Hunt the gowk another mile." When the gullible person was sent back to where he or she started, everyone involved in the prank would gather around him or her and shout, "April gowk!"

Pranking was brought to America by British and French settlers. Today, the classic April Fools' Day prank among children is to tell each other that their shoelaces are undone and then cry "April Fool!" when the victims glance at their feet. Sometimes the media get into the act, broadcasting fictitious news items designed to amuse or alarm the public. British television, for example, once showed Italian farmers "harvesting" spaghetti from trees. As other activities associated with the holiday—such as a Parade of Fools—have disappeared, pranking remains the only custom associated with this day.

## Further Reading

Henderson, Helene and Sue Ellen Thompson. *Holidays, Festivals, and Celebrations of the World Dictionary*, 2nd ed., 1997.

Purdy, Susan. *Festivals for You to Celebrate*, 1969.

Santino, Jack. *All Around the Year*, 1994.

Urlin, Ethel L. *Festivals, Holy Days, and Saints' Days*, 1915.

# *Arbor Day*

**Type of Holiday:** Promotional
**Date of Observation:** Varied, but usually last Friday in April
**Where Celebrated:** Puerto Rico, United States
**Symbols:** Trees

## ORIGINS

Known as the "Father of Arbor Day," Julius Sterling Morton settled on the treeless plains of Nebraska in 1855, where he edited the Nebraska city *News* and developed a lifelong interest in new agricultural methods. Believing that the prairie needed more TREES to serve as windbreaks, to hold moisture in the soil, and to provide lumber for housing, Morton began planting trees and urged his neighbors to do the same. When he joined the state board of agriculture, he proposed that a specific day be set aside for the planting of trees and that a prize be offered to the individual who planted the largest number of trees on that day. A million trees were planted in Nebraska on April 10, 1872, and 350 million more were planted within the next 16 years. In 1895 Nebraska became known as the Tree Planter's

State, although today it is more commonly referred to as the Cornhusker State or the Beef State. Nebraskans still honor Morton, who served as Secretary of Agriculture under President Grover Cleveland from 1893 to 1897, on April 22, the anniversary of his birth.

The observation of what came to be known as Arbor Day was widespread throughout the United States between the 1880s and World War II, when schools and communities would routinely hold tree-planting ceremonies. Although all 50 states still have an official Arbor Day—usually the last Friday in April—the custom of planting trees is not nearly as widespread as it was a couple of generations ago. A few states call it Arbor and Bird Day, emphasizing the planting of trees and shrubs that are attractive to birds. And every year on this day the President or the First Lady plants a special tree on the grounds of the White House in Washington, D.C. But most of the activities associated with Arbor Day take place in the public schools, where there are pageants, music, poetry, bulletin board displays, and discussions about the importance of trees. Although Girl Scouts, Boy Scouts, civic organizations, conservation groups, and service clubs occasionally hold tree-planting ceremonies on Arbor Day, for the most part the importance of trees has been replaced by concern for the environment in general. In fact, since 1970, Arbor Day has been eclipsed in many parts of the United States by Earth Day observances on April 22.

## SYMBOLS

### Trees

Trees are the original and most enduring symbol of Arbor Day. Although tree planting was widely associated with Johnny Appleseed, who planted thousands of apple seeds between 1801 and 1845 throughout Ohio and Indiana, there is no question that Julius Morton was the one who popularized the idea of planting trees and who established a special day for doing so.

Today, trees are symbolic of the conservation movement in general. On Arbor Day, trees are planted along roads and public highways, in parks and community forests, on the grounds of state capitols and school buildings, and on all types of public and private property for both ornamental and practical purposes. Trees have also been planted as memorials to outstanding Americans and in honor of various social causes, such as AIDS awareness. The National Arbor Day Foundation offers potential members ten free flowering trees if they join the organization.

## Further Reading

Cohen, Hennig, and Tristram Potter Coffin, eds. *The Folklore of American Holidays,* 2nd ed., 1991.

Hatch, Jane M. *The American Book of Days,* 1978.

Henderson, Helene and Sue Ellen Thompson. *Holidays, Festivals, and Celebrations of the World Dictionary,* 2nd ed., 1997.

Ickis, Marguerite. *The Book of Festivals and Holidays the World Over,* 1970.

Schaun, George and Virginia. *American Holidays and Special Days,* 1986.

Schmidt, Leigh Eric. *Consumer Rites: The Buying and Selling of American Holidays,* 1995.

# *Ascension Day*

**Type of Holiday:** Religious (Christian)

**Date of Observation:** Between April 30 and June 3; 40 days after Easter

**Where Celebrated:** Britain, Europe, United States, and by Roman Catholics and Anglicans around the world

**Symbols:** Ascension Plays, Beating the Bounds, Birds, Chasing the Devil, Crickets, Well-Dressing, Wheat

**Related Holidays:** Easter

## ORIGINS

After Jesus Christ was resurrected from the tomb, He spent 40 days with His disciples, instructing them on how to carry out His teachings. On the 40th day, He took them to the Mount of Olives near Jerusalem. As they watched, He raised His hands and was carried up to heaven.

Ascension Day, which has been observed since 68 C.E., is believed to be the oldest feast in the Christian Church. Although the Bible specifically mentions what happened on the 40th day after **EASTER**, the Ascension was not celebrated as a separate festival during the first three centuries following Christ's birth but was included in the celebration of **PENTECOST**. By the end of the fourth century, however, it was universally observed throughout the Roman Empire.

From the very beginning, Ascension Day observances included a procession that went outside the city, and usually to the top of a hill, in imitation of Christ's leading the Apostles "out towards Bethany," as described in the book of Luke. In Jerusalem, the procession followed the path that Christ took to the summit of the Mount of Olives. Although such processions were widespread during the eighth and ninth centuries, they were eventually replaced by the pageants or ASCENSION PLAYS of the Middle Ages. But processions are still held after Mass on Ascension Day in some parts of Germany and central Europe, with worshippers following clergymen carrying candles.

Ascension Day is also the day on which the Paschal candle (see **EASTER**) is extinguished.

# SYMBOLS

## Ascension Plays

From the eleventh century onwards, the processions that usually took place on Ascension Day were replaced by pageants performed in churches. By the thirteenth century, it was common practice to reenact the Ascension by hoisting a statue of Christ aloft until it disappeared through an opening in the church ceiling. As the image moved slowly upward, people rose and stretched out their arms toward the Christ figure. Huge pieces of silk or cloth were sometimes hung from the ceiling to represent clouds, and angels with lighted candles would come down from "heaven" to meet the Lord and accompany Him on His journey. A few minutes after He disappeared, a shower of roses, lilies, and other flowers would fall from the opening, symbolizing the gifts of the Holy Spirit.

Lutheran reformers attacked these plays for overdramatizing the story of the Ascension. But Martin Luther himself eventually decided that if such pageants were staged primarily as a way to teach schoolchildren about the life of Christ, they were permissible.

## Beating the Bounds

The three days preceding Ascension Day, which always falls on a Thursday, were known in the Church of England as the Rogation Days (from the Latin *rogare,* meaning "to pray" or "to ask"). The name refers to the ancient practice of having clergymen and members of the congregation walk around the boundaries of the parish and ask God's blessing on the fruits of the earth. Since maps were rare in those days, "beating the bounds" served a practical purpose as well: Greedy landlords often stole a corner of someone's property or made use of part of a neighbor's field without anyone noticing. At certain points in the procession, the people would stop. The clergyman would point out an example of God's goodness and lead them in singing a hymn of thanksgiving.

If a fence had been put up since the previous year, the processioners might take it down; if a canal had been cut across the boundary, someone had to strip off his clothes and dive in; if a house had been built on the boundary, the processioners would go in through a back door and out through a window. High walls had to be climbed, rivers and streams had to be crossed, and at the corners or boundary-crosses, small boys were whipped or bumped head downwards to help them remember the places better. The beating of young boys with willow switches was also a symbolic act designed to purify their souls.

The whole point of the Rogationtide ritual was to impress upon the younger generation the importance of keeping track of boundaries. It may have been a continuation of the ancient Roman festival known as the **TERMINALIA** (February 23), held in honor of Terminus, the god of boundary stones. Another theory is that it was a Christianization of the ancient Robigalia (April 25), held at the fifth milestone of the Via Claudi outside Rome to preserve the crops from mildew and other blights.

In many parts of England and Scotland, the custom of walking the parish boundaries is either still observed or has been revived after lapsing for many years. Choirboys and Boy Scouts are often stood on their heads at the most important places on the boundary, which in some cases has not changed since Anglo-Saxon times.

## Birds

In imitation of the way in which Christ "flew" up to heaven, it was common in many European countries at one time for people to eat a bird on Ascension Day. Pigeons, partridges, and even crows were served for dinner. In western Germany, bakers made special pastries in the shapes of various birds. Throughout Europe, it was a day for mountain climbing and picnicking in high places.

In Sweden, people rise at 3:00 or 4:00 in the morning on Ascension Day and go into the forest to hear the birds sing at sunrise. If a cuckoo is heard from the east or west, it means good luck. But it is a bad omen if the cuckoo is heard first from the north or south. According to an old Swedish saying, "Cuckoo in the west is the very best." After the sun rises, there is a picnic breakfast accompanied by music. These early morning outings are called *gök-otta* or "early cuckoo morning."

The cuckoo is a symbol of the future and of spring in particular. In modern Germany, the word for cuckoo (*kuckuck*) is a common euphemism for the Devil.

## Chasing the Devil

In some countries, a devil is chased through the streets on Ascension Day. When he is caught, he is dunked in a pond or burned in effigy—symbolic of Christ's triumph over evil when he ascended to heaven.

In Munich, Germany, it was customary up until the end of the eighteenth century for a man disguised as a demon to be chased through the streets on Ascension Eve by people dressed as witches and wizards. When he was caught, he was dunked in puddles and rolled in dung. Upon reaching the royal palace, he took off his disguise and was given a good meal as a reward. The costume he had worn was stuffed with straw and taken to the church, where it was hung in a window in the tower all night. Before vespers on Ascension Day, it was thrown down to the crowd that had assembled outside the church, and a tremendous struggle ensued. The effigy was finally carried out of town and burned on a nearby hill—a ritual intended to drive evil away from the city.

## Crickets

In Florence, Italy, people come to the Cascine Gardens on Ascension Day to pick up *grillos,* or crickets, and put them in cages with fresh lettuce leaves. If the cricket chirps within three days, it is believed that the family will have good luck. But if the cricket dies, the family dreads whatever ill fortune may befall them.

The cricket is traditionally a symbol of approaching summer. It also represents courage, making it an apt symbol for Ascension Day, when the Apostles watched their Lord leave them and ascend to heaven.

## Well-Dressing

There are a number of links between water and Ascension Day. In England, the rain that falls on this day is considered to be a remedy for sore eyes, because it falls straight from the heaven that opened up to let Christ enter. The water that is drawn from certain "holy wells" on Ascension Day is also believed to have curative powers. Well-dressing ceremonies, at one time popular throughout Great Britain, involved decorating the wells with flowers by building frames and trellises around them. After the morning church service, the priest and his congregation would form a procession and visit every well in the area, singing psalms and hymns as they went. The well-dressing ceremony at Tissington in Derbyshire dates back to 1615, when the town's wells continued to flow even during a terrible drought. People came from miles around to draw water, and the well-dressing celebration was instituted to commemorate the event.

Some believe that well-dressing is a Christian adaptation of the ancient Roman Fontanalia, a festival held in honor of the god of springs, streams, and fountains. Garlands were thrown into springs and placed around the tops of wells. But it was actually the **FLORALIA**—the festival in honor of Flora, goddess of flowers and gardens—that was held at this time of year.

## *Wheat*

In Portugal, Ascension Day is known as "Ear of Wheat Thursday" because peasants make bouquets from olive branches and sheaves of wheat with poppies and daisies. The olive and the wheat are symbolic of an abundant harvest; the poppy stands for peace, and the daisy represents money. A bit of wheat—a traditional symbol of prosperity—is usually kept in the house throughout the coming year.

## Further Reading

Biedermann, Hans. *Dictionary of Symbolism: Cultural Icons and the Meanings Behind Them,* 1994.

Brewster, H. Pomeroy. *Saints and Festivals of the Christian Church,* 1906.

Chambers, Robert, ed. *The Book of Days,* 1864.

Ferguson, George. *Signs and Symbols in Christian Art,* 1954.

Harper, Howard V. *Days and Customs of All Faiths,* 1957.

Henderson, Helene and Sue Ellen Thompson. *Holidays, Festivals, and Celebrations of the World Dictionary,* 2nd ed., 1997.

James, E. O. *Seasonal Feasts and Festivals,* 1961.

Kelly, Aidan. *Religious Holidays and Calendars,* 1993.

MacDonald, Margaret Read, ed. *The Folklore of World Holidays,* 1992.

Olderr, Steven. *Symbolism: A Comprehensive Dictionary,* 1986.

Pike, Royston. *Round the Year with the World's Religions,* 1993.

Urlin, Ethel L. *Festivals, Holy Days, and Saints' Days,* 1915.

Weiser, Francis X. *Handbook of Christian Feasts and Customs,* 1952.

# *Ashura*
## *(Husain Day)*

**Type of Holiday:** Religious (Shi'ite Muslim)

**Date of Observation:** First ten days of the Islamic lunar month of Muharram

**Where Celebrated:** India, Iraq, Jamaica, Trinidad, Turkey, West Africa, and by Shi'ite Muslims throughout Asia

**Symbols:** Ashura Pudding, Rawda-Khani, Self-flagellation, Sherbet, Ta'ziyah

## ORIGINS

The Islamic faith consists of two main branches: the intense, exclusive, and often fanatical Shi'ites, many of whom live in Iraq and India; and the more tolerant, moderate Sunnis. Shi'ites believe that the divine spirit manifests itself in the human "imam," who is the spiritual and political leader of the community. Today Shi'ites comprise less than ten percent of all Muslims, and their doctrines differ significantly from those of the orthodox Sunni majority. But it is among the Shi'ites that the most important rituals associated with the tenth of Muharram take place.

It was on this day in the year 680 that Husain, the third imam and grandson of the prophet Muhammad, was killed in a skirmish between Sunnis and the small group of Shi'ite supporters with whom he was travelling to Iraq. He was buried on the battlefield where he fell in Kerbela, about 60 miles from Baghdad, and the site almost immediately became a destination for Muslim pilgrimages. Even today, many Shi'ites come to Kerbela to die, or request that their bodies be brought there for burial. The town has become a devotional center for Shi'ite Muslims around the world and a vast burial ground.

Shi'ites begin the observation of Ashura, the commemoration of Husain's death, on the first day of Muharram, when they put on their mourning clothes and refrain from shaving or bathing. Black tents are pitched in the streets, adorned with draperies and candelabra. Wooden pulpits are erected, and speakers use them to tell the story of Husain's martyrdom with as much detail and elaboration as possible.

For the first nine days of the month, groups of half-naked men with their bodies dyed black or red roam the streets. Dragging chains and performing wild dances, they pull out their hair, inflict wounds on themselves with their swords, and occasionally engage in violent fights with Sunnis or other adversaries. On the tenth day there is a big funeral parade for Husain, featuring a coffin carried by eight men and accompanied by others holding banners. Horses and blood-smeared men march behind the coffin and sing battle songs.

While the tenth of Muharram procession has remained primarily a Shi'ite observance, the veneration of Husain has spread among Sunni Muslims as well. Modern-day Sunnis observe Ashura as an optional fast day, but in countries like Iraq they are not allowed to participate in the processions.

In Jamaica and Trinidad, the festival is called Hosay and is celebrated by Muslims and Hindus as a symbol of East Indian unity. In West Africa, the holy day is spent eating to ensure prosperity. In Senegal, Guinea, and Sierra Leone, the dried head and feet of the ram killed at **ID AL-ADHA** are cooked and served on this day. In addition to commemorating the death of Husain, the tenth of Muharram also celebrates the safe landing of Noah's ark (see ASHURA PUDDING).

## SYMBOLS

### *Ashura Pudding*

According to legend, Noah was so happy to stand on dry ground at the end of the floods described in the Bible that he asked his wife to prepare a pudding so they could celebrate. She gathered dates, figs, nuts, and currants to make the largest pudding ever made and named it "Ashura."

In Turkey, the tenth day of Muharram is called Yevmi Ashurer, or the "day of sweet soup or porridge." It commemorates Noah's departure from the Ark onto Mount Ararat. Everyone makes *ashurer,* a pudding made from boiled wheat, dried currants, grain, and nuts, similar to that prepared by Noah's wife.

### *Rawda-Khani*

One of the rituals associated with Ashura is the *rawda-khani,* or recital of the sufferings of the Imam Husain. An individual or a family will invite a group of friends to a private gathering, where a professional storyteller will recite the tale of Husain's martyrdom, playing upon the emotions of his listeners and often reducing them to tears or provoking them to cry out Husain's name. Sometimes these recitations take place in mosques, and they have been known to result in public frenzies where devout Shi'ites cut themselves with swords and knives, or beat themselves with chains in imitation of the torments to which Husain was subjected.

## Self-flagellation

The practice of self-flagellation, in which devout Shi'ite Muslims strike themselves with chains and knives while chanting the name of Husain, is symbolic of the pain and anger they felt when Husain was murdered by Umayyad soldiers. It also serves as a ritual punishment, because many Shi'ites stayed home rather than march out to join Husain in fighting the Umayyad rulers. It is during Ashura that the Shi'ite community expresses its guilt and anguish over the death of one of its most beloved leaders.

## Sherbet

Throughout the ten days of Ashura, Muslims eat a kind of sherbet in memory of the intense thirst that Husain experienced on the battlefield of Kerbela. He was surrounded by an army of 4,000 soldiers near the Euphrates River, where they cut off his water supply for eight days. When he finally mounted his horse and rode into battle, he was so weakened by thirst that he was killed.

## Ta'ziyah

The *ta'ziyah* or passion play performed during Ashura in every Shi'ite community is a detailed and emotional reenactment of Husain's martyrdom. The actors on stage portray not only the events surrounding the death of Husain but also the struggle of the Shi'ite community and its imams in their fight to overcome the Umayyad rulers. The play consists of 40 or 50 scenes, some of which are highly realistic. Perhaps the most realistic of all is the portrayal of the attack on Husain and his infant son.

Throughout the performance of the ta'ziyah, the audience is expected to participate. They shout their advice to the actors, laugh when the imams are doing well, and fall silent when events turn against the Shi'ite leaders. When the soldiers close in on Husain with their spears and swords, hacking away at his horse and finally beheading him, members of the audience have been known to weep out loud and hurl curses at the Umayyad soldiers. Sometimes they leap up on the stage to protect Husain and his family or to threaten the actor who plays Umar, the soldier who deals the fatal blow.

The ta'ziyah was first witnessed by a European in 1811, and it remains the only drama to be developed in either Persian or Arabic literature. The word *ta-ziyah* means "solace" or "condolence," and the play's underlying message is the salvation that was achieved through Husain's sacrificial death. In India, *ta-ziyah* refers to small replicas of Husain's tomb, which are carried and buried in the local "Kerbela" grounds, named after the place where Husain was killed.

## Further Reading

Gaer, Joseph. *Holidays Around the World,* 1953.

Glassé, Cyril. *The Concise Encylopedia of Islam,* 1989.

Gordon, Matthew S. *Islam,* 1991.

Henderson, Helene and Sue Ellen Thompson. *Holidays, Festivals, and Celebrations of the World Dictionary,* 2nd ed., 1997.

Smith, Huston. *The Illustrated World's Religions,* 1958.

Von Grunebaum, G. D. *Muhammadan Festivals,* 1988.

# *Ash Wednesday*

**Type of Holiday:** Religious (Christian)

**Date of Observation:** Between February 4 and March 11

**Where Celebrated:** Britain, Europe, United States, and throughout the Christian world

**Symbols:** Ashes, Burial of the Sardine, Jack-o-Lent

**Colors:** Violet or purple is the ecclesiastical color associated with this day.

**Related Holidays:** Easter, Lent, Palm Sunday, Shrove Tuesday

## ORIGINS

For Roman Catholic and some Protestant churches, Ash Wednesday marks the beginning of **LENT**, a 40-day period devoted to self-examination and penitence in preparation for **EASTER**. Lent originally began in the Western Church on a Sunday. But since Sundays were feast days, Pope Gregory I moved the beginning of Lent ahead four days in the latter part of the sixth century.

Gregory is also credited with having introduced the ceremony that gives this day its name. When penitents came to the church to ask forgiveness for their sins, the priest would take some ASHES and mark their foreheads with the sign of the cross while repeating what God said when He expelled Adam and Eve from the Garden of Eden: "Remember, man, dust thou art and to dust thou shalt return."

The American Dental Association has declared Ash Wednesday to be No Sugar Day. Since many Catholic children give up eating candy for Lent, this draws attention to the health benefits of eating less sugar.

## SYMBOLS

### *Ashes*

Ashes were a biblical symbol of repentance, based on the story of Job, who put on sackcloth and sat down in ashes to show how sorry he was that he had questioned the ways of God. According to the early medieval code of punishment, serious sinners who were ready to seek forgiveness had to come to the church barefoot on the first day of **LENT**. After they had expressed their sorrow, they had ashes sprinkled on their heads or were handed a sackcloth garment covered in ashes. As private confessions became more common, the practice of using sackcloth and ashes on individual sinners declined. Instead, ashes were distributed to the entire congregation.

Ashes are also a symbol of mortality and the shortness of earthly life. When churchgoers have ashes placed on their foreheads on Ash Wednesday, they are reminded of the penitential nature of the Lenten season and of their own human bodies, which will return to ashes when they die. The ashes used on this day are made by burning the palms used during the previous year's **PALM SUNDAY** celebration.

### *Burial of the Sardine*

The custom of burying a strip of meat as thin as a sardine on Ash Wednesday is common throughout Spain. It is thought to have originated in an old fertility custom symbolizing the burial of winter in early spring. The ceremony also symbolizes the burial of worldly pleasures and serves as a reminder to onlookers that they must abstain from eating meat throughout

Lent. In Seville, a strip of pork resembling a sardine is buried with considerable pomp and ceremony; in Madrid, a sausage link is used.

## Jack-o-Lent

The English used to dress a straw figure in old clothes and carry it through the streets on Ash Wednesday. Afterward, the effigy—known as Jack-o-Lent—was hanged. The figure was supposed to represent Judas Iscariot, who betrayed Jesus by identifying Him to His enemies as He left the garden of Gethsemane. But it may originally have been a symbol of the dying winter, similar to the Shrovetide Bear (see **SHROVE TUESDAY**).

### Further Reading

Ferguson, George. *Signs and Symbols in Christian Art,* 1954.

Henderson, Helene and Sue Ellen Thompson. *Holidays, Festivals, and Celebrations of the World Dictionary,* 2nd ed., 1997.

Hole, Christina. *English Custom and Usage,* 1941.

Ickis, Marguerite. *The Book of Festivals and Holidays the World Over,* 1970.

Ickis, Marguerite. *The Book of Religious Holidays and Celebrations,* 1966.

Metford, J. C. J. *The Christian Year,* 1991.

Santino, Jack. *All Around the Year,* 1994.

Tuleja, Tad. *Curious Customs: The Stories Behind 296 Popular American Rituals,* 1987.

# *Assumption of the Blessed Virgin Mary, Feast of the*

**Type of Holiday:** Religious (Christian)

**Date of Observation:** August 15

**Where Celebrated:** Britain, Europe, United States, and by Roman Catholics, Anglicans, and Orthodox Christians around the world

**Symbols:** Assumption Plays, Bowing Procession, Fruits of the Harvest

**Related Holidays:** Feast of the Annunciation of the Blessed Virgin Mary

# ORIGINS

The Feast of the Assumption represents a long tradition of speculation about how Mary died and what happened to her body. Legend says that after the Crucifixion of Jesus Christ, Mary lived with the Apostle John in Jerusalem, revisiting many of the places associated with her son's life. Finally she became so lonely that she prayed for death. An angel visited her and promised that within three days, she would enter heaven, where Jesus awaited her. The angel presented her with a palm branch, which Mary in turned handed to St. John, requesting that it be carried before her at her burial. Mary also requested that all the Apostles be present at her death, and the message reached them miraculously even though they were scattered all over the world. Only St. Thomas, who was late as usual, missed the final gathering at her deathbed. Arriving after the funeral was over, he was so filled with grief and regret that he asked to have the tomb reopened so that he might have one last look at her body. The tomb was empty—proof that rather than being subjected to the usual process of physical decay, it had been "assumed" into heaven, where it was reunited with her soul. The commemoration of this event is called the Dormition of the Most Holy Mother of God in the Eastern Church, a reference to Mary's "falling asleep."

The choice of August 15 as the date of this event is significant, since it roughly coincided with the gathering of the harvest in southern Europe. There is some evidence that the date might have been chosen to replace an old pagan harvest festival in honor of Diana, the Roman goddess of the hunt, on August 13 (see FRUITS OF THE HARVEST); in some parts of Europe, the feast is still called Our Lady of the Harvest. Farther north, where the harvest is delayed until autumn, the harvest rites dedicated to Mary were performed at the Feast of the Nativity on September 8.

Although belief in the Assumption was widespread by the fifth century and the feast was observed throughout Europe during the Middle Ages, it didn't become an official dogma of the Roman Catholic Church until Pope Pius XII ruled it so in 1950. The English suppressed the celebration of "Mary-Mass," as it was known in Medieval times, because it took laborers away from their work in the middle of the harvest; but in Catholic countries, the Assumption became one of the most popular festivals of the year.

In Christian art, Mary's body is usually shown being carried up to heaven by angels—in contrast to the **ASCENSION** of Christ, who rose up to heaven by His own power.

# SYMBOLS

## *Assumption Plays*

In the fourteenth century, miracle plays dramatizing the death, assumption, and coronation of the Virgin were common. They usually showed Mary as she summoned the Apostles to her deathbed from all parts of the world, and often reflected the legendary belief that St. Thomas was carried to her from India on a cloud. Similar plays in honor of the Dormition and the Coronation of Mary were a regular part of the popular play cycles performed in York, Towneley, and Chester, England at the time.

In France, a traditional pageant used to be performed in many places on Assumption Day. Figures of angels descended from the roof of the church to a flowery sepulcher or tomb and then reascended with the image of the Virgin Mary dressed in white. It was not uncommon for an image of the Virgin standing on a platform before the high altar to be drawn up through an opening in the roof—undoubtedly the same opening used to dramatize the Ascension of Christ (see ASCENSION PLAYS under **ASCENSION**) in the spring.

An assumption play is still performed at Elche in southern Spain, where the church is transformed into a theater for the annual event. A blue cloth is stretched across the dome to represent the sky, and there is a small trap door through which the angel makes his 60-yard descent on a golden pedestal called the *Ara Coeli*. The play, which is more like an operetta, concludes when Mary is raised from her tomb, and the Ara Coeli carries her to heaven.

## *Bowing Procession*

In rural areas outside Rome, the Feast of the Assumption is celebrated with an annual Bowing Procession, known as *L'Inchinata*. A statue of Mary is carried through town, symbolizing her journey to heaven. She meets a statue of Christ under a gaily decorated arch of branches and flowers representing the gate of heaven. Both images are inclined toward each other three times, after which Christ accompanies His mother back to the parish church, symbolic of their joint ascent to Paradise.

A similar procession in Sardinia is called *Candelieri* because seven huge candlesticks, each supporting a 100-pound candle, are carried to the Church of the Assumption. The candles are placed beside Mary's shrine, a tradition that dates back to 1580.

## *Fruits of the Harvest*

The ancient Roman festival in honor of the goddess Diana held at this same time of year was known as the Nemoralia, after her temple on the shores of Lake Nemi outside of Rome. In addition to celebrating Diana's power, the Nemoralia was observed to protect the vines and fruit trees. Other symbolic rites designed to ensure good weather for the reaping of fall fruits were carried out between mid-August and mid-September as well. According to popular legend, this 30-day period was a "blessed" time when animals and plants were believed to lose their harmful traits. Food produced during this period would remain fresh longer than at other times of year. The Christian Feast of the Assumption eventually incorporated the harvest-blessing element of this ancient festival, and many Assumption shrines show Mary wearing a robe covered in ears of grain. It is still common in the Orthodox Christian Church for worshippers to make offerings of new wheat, a symbol of prosperity and the bounty of the earth, on August 15.

Grapes are another harvest fruit associated with autumn. Along with wheat, they symbolize the consecrated bread and wine used in the celebration of the Eucharist. In Armenia, no one will taste the new crop of grapes until Assumption Day, when a trayful of grapes is blessed in the church. In Sicily, people abstain from eating fruit altogether during the first two weeks of August, in honor of the Virgin Mary. On the feast of her Assumption, they serve fruit that has been blessed in the church for dinner and present each other with baskets filled with a variety of fruits.

In Austria, Assumption Day is known as The Blessing of the Herbs. A statue of Mary is carried on a litter out to the fields, where four altars (representing the four Gospels) have been set up. Prayers are offered for good weather and crops, the Gospels are read, and the blessing is given. At one time in central Europe, the Feast of the Assumption was called Our Lady's Herb Day, based on the medieval belief that herbs picked in August had the power to heal.

In Latin countries, especially Portugal, where the primary "harvest" is fish, the ocean and fishing boats are blessed on Assumption Day. The Blessing of the Fleet also takes place in many coastal American towns on or around August 15.

## Further Reading

Ferguson, George. *Signs and Symbols in Christian Art*, 1954.
Frazer, Sir James G. *The Golden Bough: A Study in Magic and Religion*, 1931.
Harper, Howard V. *Days and Customs of All Faiths*, 1957.

Henderson, Helene and Sue Ellen Thompson. *Holidays, Festivals, and Celebrations of the World Dictionary*, 2nd ed., 1997.

James, E. O. *Seasonal Feasts and Festivals*, 1961.

MacDonald, Margaret R., ed. *The Folklore of World Holidays*, 1992.

Metford, J. C. J. *The Christian Year*, 1991.

Monks, James L. *Great Catholic Festivals*, 1951.

Weiser, Francis X. *Handbook of Christian Feasts and Customs*, 1952.

# *Awoojoh*

**Type of Holiday:** Ethnic (Yoruba)
**Date of Observation:** Various
**Where Celebrated:** Sierra Leone
**Symbols:** Kola Nuts

## ORIGINS

A thanksgiving feast observed in the West African nation of Sierra Leone, the Awoojoh honors the spirits of the dead, who are believed to have influence over the fortunes of the living. It may be held at any time of the year, and the guests include not only friends and relatives but, in a small community, the entire village. The day begins with a family visit to the cemetery, where a libation (usually water or liquor) is poured over the relatives' graves, and the dead are invited to join in the thanksgiving celebration. Afterward, everyone returns home to share in a feast. All family quarrels must be settled before the feasting begins.

Preparations for the feast begin days ahead of time. Sheep and chickens are slaughtered, and supplies of rice, beans, plantains, onions, peppers, tomatoes, sweet potatoes, and other vegetables are gathered. The most popular dish is "Awoojoh beans," made by simmering cooked beans in fried onion and red palm oil, then adding plantains and sweet potatoes. The centerpiece of the meal, however, is an elaborate stew, one portion of which is set out for the dead ancestors or thrown to the vultures, who are believed to embody the souls of the departed.

Although the practice of holding a thanksgiving feast originated with the Yoruba, who came to Sierra Leone from Nigeria, Christian Creoles and Muslim Akus hold such feasts as well.

## SYMBOLS

### *Kola Nuts*

Kola nuts symbolize the power exercised by the dead over the living. A popular custom on Awoojoh is to split in half two kola nuts, one red and one white, and then throw them up in the air over a dead relative's grave. The pattern in which they fall is believed to carry a message from the ancestors. For example, if two of the pieces fall with the hollow sides up and two with the hollow sides down, it is considered a very favorable message.

### Further Reading

Henderson, Helene and Sue Ellen Thompson. *Holidays, Festivals, and Celebrations of the World Dictionary,* 2nd ed., 1997.

MacDonald, Margaret R., ed. *The Folklore of World Holidays,* 1992.

# *Awuru Odo Festival*

**Type of Holiday:** Ethnic (Igbo)
**Date of Observation:** Biennially in April
**Where Celebrated:** Nigeria
**Symbols:** Odo Play

## ORIGINS

Among the Igbo people of Nigeria, the Odo are the spirits of the dead, who return to the earth to visit their families every two years. They arrive, in the form of costumed men wearing masks, sometime between September and November and depart in April. Before they leave, there is a big theatrical performance (see ODO PLAY) reenacting the story of their visit and the agony

33

of their departure, since many of them do not wish to return. The musical accompaniment featuring xylophones, drums, and rattles is known as *obilenu* music, meaning "that which lies above."

Preparations to receive the Odo are quite elaborate. Men prepare the shrines, surrounded by fences, where the returning spirits of the dead will worship. They also refurbish the masks that the Odo will wear or create new ones. All of these preparations must be conducted in secret, because women and non-initiates are not allowed to see what goes on. The women are primarily responsible for seeing that there is enough food to serve the Odo and any visitors who may come to watch the performance.

Although each family holds a welcoming ceremony for its particular Odo group, the big celebration in April features all of the Odo groups from all of the families. Immediately after the performance is over, the Odo climb the Ukehe hills and make their way back to the land of the dead. With them they take the prayers of the living, who appeal to them for abundant crops and for many children. Women who have recently given birth often bring gifts of thanks.

## SYMBOLS

### *Odo Play*

The Odo play, also known as the Awuru Odo performance, takes place in the Nwankwo market square in Ukehe, where the Odo shrine and the ritual stage are located. The performers include the Odo characters themselves and the people who accompany them. The characters are mostly concealed by masks, but sometimes their legs are visible. The elderly Odo are accompanied by middle-aged men who blow elephant tusks and horns, while the youthful Odo are accompanied by young men and the Odo children are either alone or in groups. The evil Odo, who were criminals when they were alive, wear black costumes and cover their bodies with thorns. The other performers wear costumes traditionally made from plant fiber, leaves, beads, and feathers, although more durable cloth costumes are becoming more common in contemporary Odo plays. The villagers serve as a chorus, with the women dressed in their most expensive clothing and jewelry and the men carrying long sticks, guns, and machetes.

The Odo play itself reenacts the end of the Odo's stay on earth. The story begins with their arrival, dramatizes their stay with the living, and finally portrays their agonizing journey away from their loved ones and back to the land of the dead. The spirits who await them there are anxious for their return and place many obstacles in their path to make them fall and be ashamed. But the Odo are very careful not to fall, knowing that it will bring bad luck to the living. When they have circled the marketplace successfully, there is great celebration and dancing.

## Further Reading

Henderson, Helene and Sue Ellen Thompson. *Holidays, Festivals, and Celebrations of the World Dictionary*, 2nd ed., 1997.

MacDonald, Margaret R., ed. *The Folklore of World Holidays*, 1992.

# *Bastille Day*

**Type of Holiday:** Historic, National

**Date of Observation:** July 14

**Where Celebrated:** France; New Caledonia, Tahiti, and other French territories

**Symbols:** Bastille

**Related Holidays:** Fourth of July

## ORIGINS

Bastille Day in France is the equivalent of the **FOURTH OF JULY** in the United States. It is the day on which the French celebrate their independence from the monarchy by commemorating the storming of Paris's Bastille prison on July 14, 1789—an event that marked the end of Louis XVI's rule and started the French Revolution. By freeing the political prisoners held there and dismantling the building stone by stone, the Parisians displayed their scorn for the Bourbon kings who had ruled France for so long. The Marquis de Lafayette, who had been named commander of the National Guard the day after the Bastille fell, later gave the key to the infamous prison to George Washington, under whom he had served during the American Revolution. It is still on display at Mount Vernon, Washington's home.

Americans were particularly happy to hear of the Parisians' revolutionary act, and they celebrated Bastille Day for a number of years, particularly in Philadelphia. But eventually the celebration diminished in this country, with the exception of the Bastille Day observance in Kaplan, Louisiana, an area with many ties to French traditions. Bastille Day is also observed in a number of French territories in the Pacific with parades, fireworks, and dancing in the streets. In Tahiti and the rest of French Polynesia, it is called Tiurai, and the celebration goes on throughout most of the month of July.

In France, Bastille Day continues to be celebrated as the great national holiday. There is usually a parade down the Champs-Élysées, street dancing, fireworks, and free theatrical performances.

## SYMBOLS

### *Bastille*

Built around 1369 at the order of King Charles V, the prison-fortress known as the Bastille had eight towers and 100-foot-high walls. Beginning in the seventeenth century, it was used to house primarily political prisoners, including many famous people — such as the French writers Voltaire and the Marquis de Sade — who had displeased the court or were considered a threat to the monarchy.

Although it was razed to the ground two days after it was stormed by the angry Parisians, the Bastille remains a symbol of the oppression of the monarchy to the French people.

## Further Reading

Chambers, Robert, ed. *The Book of Days,* 1864.

Dunkling, Leslie. *A Dictionary of Days,* 1988.

Hatch, Jane M. *The American Book of Days,* 1978.

Henderson, Helene and Sue Ellen Thompson. *Holidays, Festivals, and Celebrations of the World Dictionary,* 2nd ed., 1997.

MacDonald, Margaret R., ed. *The Folklore of World Holidays,* 1992.

Van Straalen, Alice. *The Book of Holidays Around the World,* 1986.

# *Beltane*
## *(Beltine)*

**Type of Holiday:** Ancient or pagan, Calendar
**Date of Observation:** April 30 or May 1
**Where Celebrated:** Brittany, Ireland, Isle of Man, Scotland, Wales
**Symbols:** Beltane Cake, Bonfires, Carline, Tree or Maypole
**Related Holidays:** Imbolc, Lughnasa, May Day, Samhain

## ORIGINS

Along with **IMBOLC** (February 1), **LUGHNASA** (August 1), and **SAM-HAIN** (November 1), Beltane was one of the four great Celtic festivals—the last to be celebrated before the Celtic year turned full circle back to midsummer and began all over again. It takes its name from the ancient god Bel, also known as Beli, Belin, or Belinus, and possibly associated with the Phoenician or Canaanite word *Ba'al*, which means "master." *Bellus* in Latin means "beautiful," and *tan* means "fire" in Cornish (*tine* in Irish or Gaelic), so it is not surprising that both the god Bel and the rituals associated with the festival involve fire.

Bel was the young sun god, counterpart of the older god Bran. His festival was the focal point of the second half of the Celtic year, just as the most important festival in the first half of the year was Lughnasa (Bran and Lugh were gods of the same type). Since the Celts believed that each day began with the setting of the sun the night before, Beltane was celebrated by lighting BONFIRES on the night of April 30 to honor the sun god. The fires were used for both purification and fertility rites, and a number of superstitions were attached to both flames and ashes.

Beltane is believed to be a survival of an even more ancient pastoral festival that accompanied the first turning of the herds out to wild pasture. It was a time of year when witches and fairies were said to be out in great numbers, and in Ireland it was said that whoever was foolish enough to join a fairy dance on Beltane Eve would not be set free until the following May 1. Beltane is still observed in Ireland, the Scottish highlands, Wales, Brittany, and the Isle of Man. In the United States, many of the customs originally associated with Beltane have survived in the modern observance of **MAY DAY**—including the making of flower garlands and dancing around a decorated MAYPOLE.

# SYMBOLS

## Beltane Cake

A large oatmeal or barley cake called the Beltane cake was typically served at village feasts on Beltane. The person in charge of the feast would divide the cake and give everyone a piece. One particular piece was called the Beltane CARLINE, and whoever got it was threatened with being thrown into the BONFIRE or subjected to various mock tortures.

Sometimes the carline piece was daubed with charcoal from the bonfire until it was completely black. Then all the pieces of cake were put in a bonnet, and everyone had to draw out their portion while wearing a blindfold. Whoever drew the black piece had to endure a mock sacrifice to Baal, whose good will was essential to a productive harvest. Instead of being thrown on the fire, the person would be allowed to leap three times through the flames.

In some areas of Scotland, oatmeal cakes were rolled down a hillside around noon on the first day of May. The superstition was that the person whose cake broke before reaching the bottom would die or have bad luck before the year was out. There is also some evidence that in rural areas, these Beltane cakes were kept for an entire year as a charm against spells that would ruin the cows' milk.

## Bonfires

In ancient times, the bonfires that were lit with great ceremony on the night of April 30 in the central highlands of Scotland were often accompanied by human sacrifices, which is perhaps why Beltane fires were called "bone-fires." Eventually the human victims were spared, but people still regarded the fires as possessing magical powers. Since contact with the fire was symbolic of contact with the life-giving sun, people would leap through the flames to forestall bad luck and to cure barrenness. On the Isle of Man, branches or twigs from the rowan tree were carried three times around the fire in the direction of the sun (i.e., turning to the right) and then taken home to protect the family and animals from evil. Even today in Ireland the rowan branch is often hung over the hearth as a good-luck charm.

The Beltane fires were also associated with purification. Farmers would drive their livestock between two fires — a practice that required a good deal of prodding and prompting from the entire community — to purge them of disease as they emerged from the rigors of winter. Then they would be taken out to new pastures, often on higher ground, where they would have access to nutritious spring grasses. The custom of driving cattle through or between fires on **MAY DAY** or the evening before persisted in Ireland until fairly recent times. The Irish expression *idir dá teine lae Bealtaine* ('between two Beltane fires") can be loosely translated as "in a dilemma."

According to Welsh folklore, the bonfires that are lit in early May protected the fields from witchcraft so that good crops would follow. Even the ashes from the fire were considered a valuable charm against bad luck, infertility, and disease.

It was common at one time to cut a trench in the turf, forming a kind of bench for spectators, and then build a pile of wood or other fuel in the center. The fire would be lit with an elaborate and primitive system for producing sparks by friction, as evidenced by the Irish term *teine éigin* (fire from rubbing sticks), which is used to refer to the Beltane bonfire. Sometimes the villagers would sit around this table of turf eating custard and oatmeal cakes (see BELTANE CAKE) that had been toasted in the fire's embers.

## Carline

The term *carline* refers to a hag or old woman. It was applied to the person who, after getting the blackened piece of the BELTANE CAKE, was routinely subjected to various mock tortures — including being nearly thrown in the BONFIRE or stretched out flat on the ground and "quartered." Once the carline had been through these torments, the rest of the villagers treated him as someone who was already dead. This treatment continued, not just for the duration of the celebration but for an entire year.

The whole idea of the Beltane carline probably goes back to ancient times, when human sacrifices were made on Beltane. The victim back then was usually a woman, perhaps indicating that the custom was part of a primitive female fertility cult.

## Tree or Maypole

The idea of a central tree or pole at the axis of the cosmos is actually a very ancient one that can be found in many cultures. The idea of dancing around a decorated Maypole may have been Celtic in origin and is believed to have been a part of the original Beltane celebration. It was obviously intended as a phallic symbol, as seen in the various fertility rituals involving young people and farm animals that were part of the festival (see BONFIRES). When the Maypole came to America as part of the celebration of **MAY DAY**, however, its phallic associations so upset the Puritan authorities that they tried to outlaw the custom.

## Further Reading

Frazer, Sir James G. *The Golden Bough: A Study in Magic and Religion,* 1931.

Heinberg, Richard. *Celebrate the Solstice: Honoring the Earth's Seasonal Rhythms through Festival and Ceremony,* 1993.

Henderson, Helene and Sue Ellen Thompson. *Holidays, Festivals, and Cele-brations of the World Dictionary,* 2nd ed., 1997.

King, John. *The Celtic Druids'Year: Seasonal Cycles of the Ancient Celts,* 1995.

Leach, Maria, ed. *Funk & Wagnalls Standard Dictionary of Folklore, Mytholo-gy, & Legend,* 1984.

# *Blessing of the Waters*
### *(Orthodox Epiphany)*

**Type of Holiday:** Religious (Christian)

**Date of Observation:** January 6

**Where Celebrated:** Greece, United States, and by Orthodox Christians around the world

**Symbols:** Basil, Cross, Dove

**Related Holidays:** Epiphany

## ORIGINS

While the Roman Catholic and Protestant churches emphasize the visit of the Magi when they celebrate **EPIPHANY**, the Orthodox Christian Churches celebrate the baptism of Jesus in the River Jordan on January 6. In honor of Christ's baptism, when the Holy Spirit descended in the form of a DOVE and proclaimed Him the Son of God, the church's baptismal water is blessed, and small bottles of holy water are given to worshippers to take home. In many American cities, priests lead their congregations to a local river, which they bless. Many countries throughout the world mark the day with the immersion of a CROSS in the sea, a lake, or a river.

In Palestine, it was the River Jordan that received a blessing on Epiphany. Thousands of pilgrims would gather on its shores to step into the water after the rites were held, submerging themselves three times to obtain the maximum blessing. In Egypt, the Nile was blessed for many centuries. Christians and Muslims alike would plunge into the waters three times, then drive their domestic animals into the river. In Rome, the water that was blessed in the church and taken home on this day was believed to stay fresh throughout the year and even longer.

In Greece, the Blessing of the Waters is still one of the country's most important church days, especially in seaport towns. Back when Greek ships depended on the wind to get from one place to another, most seamen tried to be home before **CHRISTMAS**. Believing it wasn't a good idea to be at sea during the Twelve Days of Christmas, they cast anchor and waited for the priest to bless the waters before they set out on their next journey. Even today, Greek seamen try to be back in their home ports for Epiphany. When the cross is thrown into the water, the ships blow their whistles or fire cannons. Young men dive in to retrieve the cross, and the one who brings it to the surface has the privilege of carrying it around town and receiving gifts from the townspeople.

In the United States, the best-known Blessing of the Waters celebration takes place in Tarpon Springs, Florida. The community's Greek roots can be traced back to the early twentieth century, when sponge divers from Greece came there to take part in the growing sponge industry. The Epiphany Day ceremonies begin with a religious service, during which the water in the church is blessed with special prayers and rituals. A long and colorful procession through the streets follows, ending at the Spring Bayou. There a priest reads the story of Christ's baptism from the New Testament and, at the stroke of noon, a white DOVE is released. The archbishop then throws a golden CROSS into the water and 100 young men from the local Greek Orthodox churches compete in diving for it. The one who retrieves it receives a blessing from the archbishop and is supposed to have good luck for the entire year. Afterward, a Greek dinner is served, bouzouki music is played, and Greek folk dances are performed.

## SYMBOLS

### Basil

In Greece, young girls sometimes sit up all night on Epiphany Eve to watch a pot of sweet basil, symbolic of good wishes, burst into flower when the heavens open up. They believe that wishes made on this night are more likely to be answered.

In Greek villages, the Blessing of the Waters often takes the form of having the local priest walk through the village after Mass and bless each home by sprinkling them with a sprig of basil dipped in holy water.

## Cross

The cross that is thrown into the water on Epiphany is a symbol of Christ, who died on the cross. It is also a symbol of salvation and redemption through Christianity. Although the cross occupied a prominent place in other religions long before Christianity, it has come to be regarded as a uniquely Christian symbol.

## Dove

In ancient and Christian art, the dove is a symbol of purity and peace. It also symbolizes the Holy Ghost, who appears in the story of Christ's baptism as told in the New Testament: "And John bore record, saying, I saw the Spirit descending from heaven like a dove, and it abode upon him." (John 1:32)

## Further Reading

Cirlot, J. E. *A Dictionary of Symbols,* 1962.

Cohen, Hennig, and Tristram Potter Coffin, eds. *The Folklore of American Holidays,* 2nd ed., 1991.

Ferguson, George. *Signs and Symbols in Christian Art,* 1954.

Henderson, Helene and Sue Ellen Thompson. *Holidays, Festivals, and Celebrations of the World Dictionary,* 2nd ed., 1997.

Ickis, Marguerite. *The Book of Festivals and Holidays the World Over,* 1970.

Johnson, F. Ernest, ed. *Religious Symbolism,* 1955.

MacDonald, Margaret R., ed. *The Folklore of World Holidays,* 1992.

Olderr, Steven. *Symbolism: A Comprehensive Dictionary,* 1986.

Santino, Jack. *All Around the Year,* 1994.

Weiser, Francis X. *Handbook of Christian Feasts and Customs,* 1952.

# *Boston Marathon*

**Type of Holiday:** Sporting
**Date of Observation:** Third Monday in April
**Where Celebrated:** Boston, Massachusetts
**Symbols:** Heartbreak Hill, Laurel Wreath
**Related Holidays:** Olympic Games

## ORIGINS

The oldest footrace in the United States was first held on Patriot's Day, April 19, in 1897. Organized by members of the Boston Athletic Association (BAA), the race involved only 15 runners. Nowadays the Boston Marathon, which has been held on the third Monday in April since 1969, draws anywhere from 7,000 to more than 9,000 official starters, who must meet established qualifying times. Several thousand additional runners participate on an unofficial basis. In 1972, it became the first marathon to officially admit women runners.

The 26.2-mile course begins in Hopkinton and ends in front of downtown Boston's Prudential Center. It is based on the long-distance footrace first held at the revival of the **OLYMPIC GAMES** in 1896, which commemorated the legendary feat of a Greek soldier who is supposed to have run from Marathon to Athens, a distance of about 25 miles, to bring news of the Athenian victory over the Persians in 490 B.C.E. Appropriately, the first modern marathon winner in 1896 was a Greek, Spiros Louis.

The Olympic marathon distance was standardized at 26 miles, 385 yards in 1924. The extra 385 yards was added to accommodate the distance from Windsor Castle, where the 1908 Olympic race began, to the royal box in the stadium at London.

Runners from all over the world come to Boston to compete in the marathon, which is considered one of the most prestigious running events in the world. Well-known American winners include the "old" John Kelley, who won twice and continued to complete the race well into his 80s; the "young" John Kelley (no relation), who was the first American victor in the post-World War II era; "Tarzan" Brown, who in 1938 took a break at the nine-mile mark for a quick swim in Lake Cochichuate; and Bill Rodgers, who won three consecutive marathons in 1978-80. Among the women, Rosa Mota of Portugal was the first to win three official Boston Marathon titles. And few people will forget the infamous Rosie Ruiz in 1980, who many believed tried to defraud the BAA by showing up at the end of the race to capture the women's LAUREL WREATH without having actually run the full distance. This was later substantiated by television coverage of certain checkpoints. Jackie Gareau of Canada was later declared the women's winner, although Ruiz continued to insist that she'd run the race fairly.

## SYMBOLS

### *Heartbreak Hill*

Probably the best-known stretch of the course covered by the Boston Marathon is located at the 21st mile. It is a section of Commonwealth Avenue in Newton Centre known as "Heartbreak Hill," and it has literally been the downfall of many marathon competitors. Occurring as it does more than two-thirds of the way to the finish line, when many runners have expended most of their energy, the incline poses more of a challenge than non-runners can appreciate.

### *Laurel Wreath*

The laurel wreath that is placed on the heads of the first male and female runners to cross the finish line in the Boston Marathon is a traditional symbol of victory that dates back to very ancient times. The laurel tree was sacred to Apollo, the ancient Greek and Roman god of light, healing, music, poetry, prophecy, and manly beauty. The leaves of the laurel were used to weave garlands and crowns for festivals, and the crowning of a poet, artist, or hero with laurel leaves signified that he had overcome many obstacles and negative influences—whether internal or external—to achieve his goal.

## Further Reading

Cirlot, J. E. *A Dictionary of Symbols,* 1962.

Hatch, Jane M. *The American Book of Days,* 1978.

Henderson, Helene and Sue Ellen Thompson. *Holidays, Festivals, and Celebrations of the World Dictionary,* 2nd ed., 1997.

# *Bouphonia*

**Type of Holiday:** Ancient or pagan
**Date of Observation:** Late June or early July
**Where Celebrated:** Athens, Greece
**Symbols:** Ox

## ORIGINS

The ancient Athenian ritual known as the "murder of the ox" or Bouphonia took place at the end of June or beginning of July, the time of year when the threshing of the grain was nearly over. According to legend, the custom of sacrificing an ox at the altar of Zeus on the Acropolis can be traced back to an incident in which a man named Sopatrus killed an ox who had eaten the grain he was offering as a sacrifice. He was so overcome by remorse afterward that he buried the animal and fled to Crete. But then a famine set in, and the people of Athens instituted the custom of sacrificing an ox to Zeus in the hope that it would bring the famine to an end.

Primitive people were reluctant to taste the first fruits of any crop until some kind of ceremony had been performed that made it safe for them to do so. Because they believed that the first fruits either belonged to or actually contained a divinity, any man or animal who appropriated these sacred fruits was regarded as the divinity himself in human or animal form taking possession of what belonged to him. When the ox ate the grain that had been left on the altar to Zeus, it may have been viewed as a symbol or embodiment of the corn god, which would explain why the Athenians attached so much importance to the killing of the ox.

The ritual that eventually became known as the Bouphonia has been described in great detail. Barley and wheat cakes were laid upon the altar of Zeus. Oxen were then driven around the altar, and the ox that went up and ate the offering was the one selected for sacrifice. The ax and the knife used to kill the beast were wetted with water, sharpened, and handed to butchers, one of whom struck the ox while the other cut its throat. As soon as the animal had been killed, both men dropped their weapons and fled. The ox was then skinned and everyone shared in eating its flesh. The ox-hide was later stuffed with straw and sewn up again, so that it stood upright and could be yoked to a plow — perhaps a means of bringing it "back to life."

After the ritual killing, a trial was held to see who had murdered the ox. The young maidens who carried the water used to wet the weapons accused the men who had sharpened the ax and the knife, who in turn blamed the men who had handed the implements to the butchers. The butchers themselves laid the blame on the ax and the knife, which were accordingly found guilty, condemned, and cast into the sea.

## SYMBOLS

### Ox

Because the ox is the domesticated (i.e., castrated) counterpart of the wild bull, it symbolizes patience and strength, representing all who bear their yoke while laboring in silence for the good of others. It was for this reason that the ox was popular as a sacrificial animal.

The Bouphonia was instituted because the Athenians believed that the ox embodied the corn spirit. The eagerness with which everyone tried to escape the blame for killing the ox, together with the formality of the trial and the severity of the punishment, supports the idea that the ox was regarded as a sacred creature rather than just a sacrificial victim. Eating the flesh of the ox who had consumed the sacred first fruits from the altar was an early form of the modern European harvest supper.

## Further Reading

Biedermann, Hans. *Dictionary of Symbolism: Cultural Icons and the Meanings Behind Them*, 1994.

Ferguson, George. *Signs and Symbols in Christian Art*, 1954.

Fowler, W. Warde. *The Roman Festivals of the Period of the Republic*, 1925.

Frazer, Sir James G. *The Golden Bough: A Study in Magic and Religion*, 1931.

Leach, Maria, ed. *Funk & Wagnalls Standard Dictionary of Folklore, Mythology, & Legend*, 1984.

Scullard, H. H. *Festivals and Ceremonies of the Roman Republic*, 1981.

# Candlemas
## (Groundhog Day)

**Type of Holiday:** Religious (Christian), Folkloric
**Date of Observation:** February 2
**Where Celebrated:** United States and throughout the Christian world
**Symbols:** Candles, Groundhog

## ORIGINS

According to the law of Moses, it was the parents' duty to bring their first-born son to the church and make an offering to God on his behalf. This usually took place on the 40th day following the child's birth. After observing the traditional 40-day period of purification following the birth of Jesus, therefore, Mary presented Him at the Temple in Jerusalem. An aged and devout Jew named Simeon held the baby in his arms and announced that He would be a "light to lighten the Gentiles" (Luke 2:32). This is why February 2 (which is 40 days after **CHRISTMAS**) came to be called Candlemas (Candelaria in Spanish-speaking countries) and has been celebrated by the blessing of CANDLES since the eleventh century. In the Eastern church, it is known as the Feast of the Presentation of Christ in the Temple, while in the Western church it is the Feast of the Purification of the Blessed Virgin Mary. But both festivals celebrate the same sequence of events and are characterized by the blessing of candles and candlelight processions.

Some think that the custom of forming a procession with lighted candles was not originally a Christian idea but was instead an attempt to Christianize an ancient Roman rite (see CANDLES) that took place in February and consisted of a procession around the city with lighted candles. Roman Christians borrowed the practice of using candles in religious services, and in 494 C.E. Pope Gelasius I established the Feast of the Purification of the Virgin Mary. The Feast of the Purification was also the time to kindle a "brand" left over from the Yule log at Christmas.

## SYMBOLS

### Candles

It was an ancient Roman tradition at the **LUPERCALIA**, observed on February 15, to hold a torchlight parade in honor of the corn goddess Ceres and her daughter Proserpine, who was carried off to the underworld by Pluto. Ceres searched for her daughter all over Sicily, lighting torches from the flames of Mount Aetna at night so she could continue her search. Some scholars believe that this is where the candlelight processions now associated with Candlemas originated.

Lamps and candles are a traditional symbol of rejoicing. During the Middle Ages, Candlemas was the day on which the church blessed candles for the entire year. There was a procession of worshippers holding candles in their hands, and people believed that wherever these candles were used, they would chase away the devil. The unused candle stubs were often preserved as good-luck charms. In many Roman Catholic countries today, the candles blessed on Candlemas are still regarded as possessing special powers. In Brittany, for example, they are lighted in times of storm or illness. In parts of Austria, they are lighted at important family occasions such as christenings and funerals. In Sicily, the Candlemas candles are brought out when there is an earthquake or when someone is dying.

The candles that are "purified" or blessed in the church on February 2 are also used to bless people's throats on St. Blaise's Day (February 3), protecting them from colds and from fishbones getting stuck.

### Groundhog

In the United States, February 2 is popularly known as Groundhog Day. There was a medieval superstition that all hibernating animals—not just groundhogs—came out of their caves and dens on Candlemas to check on the weather. If they could see their shadows, it meant that winter would go on for another six weeks and they could go back to sleep. A cloudy day meant that spring was just around the corner. Farmers in England, France, and Canada used to look for the stirring of the "Candlemas Bear" as a sign that spring was on its way; in Ireland, it was the hedgehog; and in Germany, it was the badger. The return of hibernating animals was one of several ways in which nature announced a change in the season, and those whose livelihood depended upon natural cycles were very attuned to such signs.

It was the early German settlers known as the Pennsylvania Dutch who brought this custom to the United States and chose the groundhog as their harbinger of spring. No one really knows why the weather on this day was believed to indicate the reverse of what was to come: Good weather meant prolonged winter, and cloudy weather meant an early spring. But the tradition took hold in America, giving rise to the legend of Punxsutawney Phil, a groundhog in Pennsylvania believed to be nearly a century old. There is a club in Punxsutawney whose members still trek up to Phil's burrow on February 2 and wait for him to emerge. Unfortunately, weather researchers have determined that the groundhog has been correct only 28 percent of the time.

If February 2 seems a little early to look for signs of spring, remember that before the adoption of the Gregorian calendar, Candlemas fell on February 14. Until recently, farmers in Mississippi and Arkansas observed Groundhog Day on the 14th because it was closer to the arrival of warm weather.

## Further Reading

Crippen, T. G. *Christmas and Christmas Lore,* 1990.

Henderson, Helene and Sue Ellen Thompson. *Holidays, Festivals, and Celebrations of the World Dictionary,* 2nd ed., 1997.

Ickis, Marguerite. *The Book of Festivals and Holidays the World Over,* 1970.

Miles, Clement A. *Christmas in Ritual and Tradition,* 1990.

Santino, Jack. *All Around the Year,* 1994.

Tuleja, Tad. *Curious Customs: The Stories Behind 296 Popular American Rituals,* 1987.

# *Carnival*
## *(Mardi Gras)*

**Type of Holiday:** Religious (Christian)

**Date of Observation:** Dates vary, between Epiphany and Shrove Tuesday (Ash Wednesday Eve)

**Where Celebrated:** Central America, Europe, South America, United States, Caribbean Islands, and throughout the Christian world

**Symbols:** Carnival King, Forty Hours' Devotion, Fried Dough, King Cakes, Krewes, Ox

**Colors:** Purple, green, and gold (see KING CAKES)

**Related Holidays:** Ash Wednesday, Lent, Shrove Tuesday

## ORIGINS

The season known to Christians as Carnival actually extends all the way from **EPIPHANY** (January 6) to **SHROVE TUESDAY**, or the day before **LENT**. The Latin *carne vale* means "farewell to meat," but it could also be a broader reference to the pleasures that are forbidden during the 40 days of Lent. Carnival in general is a time for feasting and self-indulgence, with the most intense period of celebration usually taking place the last three days before **ASH WEDNESDAY** and particularly on Shrove Tuesday. It features masked balls, lavish costume parades, torchlight processions, dancing, fireworks, and of course feasting on all the foods that will have to be given up for Lent. It is interesting to note that processions, feasting, and masquerades were also popular activities among the pagans during their spring festivals, which were designed to ensure the health and growth of their crops. Most of the features of the modern Carnival celebration are firmly rooted in a tradition that can be traced back to the fourteenth century.

One of the most famous Carnival celebrations in the world takes place in Rio de Janeiro, Brazil. The parades, pageants, and costume balls go on for four days, but the highlight of the festival is the parade of the samba schools, which takes place on the Sunday and Monday preceding Ash Wednesday. The competition among these neighborhood groups is fierce, and people spend months beforehand making costumes and learning special dances for the parade.

The most flamboyant Carnival celebration in the United States takes place during the two weeks preceding Ash Wednesday in New Orleans, Louisiana. Known among New Orleans' early French settlers as Mardi Gras

("Fat Tuesday") because the day before the start of Lent was traditionally a time to use up all the milk, butter, eggs, and animal fat left in the kitchen, this grand celebration culminates in a series of parades organized by groups known as KREWES. With marching jazz bands and elaborately decorated floats, the parades attract over a million spectators every year.

## SYMBOLS

### Carnival King

Carnival is an especially important season for Roman Catholics. In Italy, Spain, France, and other European countries where the influence of Rome has been the strongest, a popular feature of Carnival celebrations is a burlesque figure, often made out of straw and known as the Carnival King. When his brief reign over the Carnival festivities is over, the king is usually shot in public, burned, drowned, or otherwise destroyed while the onlookers cheer openly. This may be a symbolic act designed to rid the spectators of their folly and sinfulness.

One theory about the origin of the Carnival King is that he is a direct descendant of the old King of the **SATURNALIA**, the ancient Roman festival held in December. This pagan king was a man chosen to impersonate the Roman agricultural god Saturn for the duration of the celebration; but at the end, he suffered a real death rather than a make-believe one. The brutal custom of putting a mock king to death eventually faded, but the idea of appointing someone to reign over the festivities appears to have survived in the figure of the Carnival King.

### Forty Hours' Devotion

To encourage good Christians to compensate for the excessive behavior exhibited at Carnival time, Pope Benedict XIV in 1748 instituted a special devotion for the three days preceding Lent. Called the "Forty Hours of Carnival," it is still held in many American and European churches where carnival celebrations are a long-standing tradition. The Blessed Sacrament is exposed all day Monday and Tuesday, and devotions are held in the evening.

### Fried Dough

Most Carnival and Mardi Gras celebrations throughout the world include the preparation of some form of fried dough. In New Orleans, for example, the *beignet* is a square doughnut without a hole, similar to a fritter. In some areas of Germany, where Carnival is called Fastnacht, fried dough is served in the form of *Fastnachtkuchen*. This raised doughnut was brought to the United States by the Germans who settled in Pennsylvania, and such fried cakes can still be found in other German-settled areas of the country.

Since it was customary on Mardi Gras or "Fat Tuesday" to use up all the animal fat in the house before the start of Lent, food was often fried so the fat wouldn't go to waste.

## King Cakes

The round or oval cakes known as King Cakes are one of the primary foods associated with the Carnival season. They are frosted with alternating bands of sugar in the three colors that have become associated with Mardi Gras: purple, symbolizing justice; green, symbolizing faith; and gold, symbolizing power. There are tiny dolls — or sometimes a bean — hidden in the cakes, and whoever is served the piece containing the doll or bean is crowned king for a day. In New Orleans, where the Carnival season begins with the *Bal du Roi* (King's Ball), a Parisian tradition, the person who gets the doll has to hold the next ball. These balls continue throughout the season, with the final one being held on Mardi Gras.

## Krewes

The private clubs known as "krewes" that give parties, parades, and balls during the Mardi Gras celebration in New Orleans can be traced back to Mobile, Alabama, in 1831. A man named Michael Krafft had been out celebrating New Year's Eve with his friends when they decided to break into a hardware store. They stole some cowbells and rakes, and paraded through the streets making as much noise as possible. This incident led to the establishment of the Cowbellion de Rakin Society, which organized a rowdy costume parade the following year featuring tableaux and dancing. In 1857, six men from Mobile who had been members of the society and who now lived in New Orleans decided to introduce a similar organization there, which they called the Mystick Krewe of Comus — a reference both to the masque (a dramatic entertainment featuring elaborate costumes, scenery, music, and dancing) *Comus*, written by English poet John Milton, and to the Greek and Roman god of revelry, feasting, and nocturnal entertainment. The word "krewe" is supposed to have come from the Anglo-Saxon spelling of "crew."

By 1988, there were approximately 60 other krewes in New Orleans, and today they parade through the streets for nearly three weeks before Mardi Gras. Comus remains the most traditional krewe, producing floats for the parade similar to those seen a hundred years ago. The other krewes—with names like Rex, Zulu, Proteus, and Momus—are also private clubs, often linked to old-line Protestant or Catholic social networks. In addition, there are "maverick" krewes whose membership is open to anyone who can pay the required fee. The floats designed by the krewes range from the most traditional—small, delicate floats with a great deal of ornamental sculpture and extensive use of gold and silver foil—to considerably less formal processions of decorated vans and trucks.

Some think that the krewes and their parades go back to the *reynages* of medieval France—make-believe kingdoms established as part of the Carnival celebration. It is also possible that the floats seen in today's Mardi Gras parades were derived from religious tableaux originally performed in churches but moved outside when they became too rowdy.

## *Ox*

One theory regarding the origin of "Fat Tuesday" or Mardi Gras is that it was named after the practice of leading a fattened ox through the village streets before Lent. Afterward, it was slaughtered to provide the final meal before Lenten restrictions on meat and dairy products went into effect.

In many Carnival celebrations held in France today, a fattened ox plays a central role in the festivities. A child known as the "king of butchers" usually rides in a decorated car behind the ox, and people throw confetti or blow horns as the ox and the butcher pass by. In New Orleans, the Krewe of Rex (see KREWES) is credited with reintroducing the fattened ox to the Mardi Gras celebration by using it as the theme for a giant float.

## Further Reading

Dobler, Lavinia. *Customs and Holidays Around the World,* 1962.

Frazer, Sir James G. *The Golden Bough: A Study in Magic and Religion,* 1931.

Henderson, Helene and Sue Ellen Thompson. *Holidays, Festivals, and Celebrations of the World Dictionary,* 2nd ed., 1997.

Purdy, Susan. *Festivals for You to Celebrate,* 1969.

Santino, Jack. *All Around the Year,* 1994.

Urlin, Ethel L. *Festivals, Holy Days, and Saints' Days,* 1915.

Weiser, Francis X. *Handbook of Christian Feasts and Customs,* 1952.

# Chinese New Year
## (*Lunar New Year, Yuan Tan*)

**Type of Holiday:** Calendar

**Date of Observation:** First day of the first Chinese lunar month, between January 21 and February 19

**Where Celebrated:** China, and by Chinese communities in the United States and throughout the world

**Symbols:** Debt-paying, Firecrackers, Flowers, Gate Gods, Kitchen God, Lucky Phrases or Spring Couplets, New Year Prints, Nian Monster

**Colors:** The color red, associated with good luck, can be seen everywhere during the Chinese New Year celebration (see FIRECRACKERS, NIAN MONSTER). LUCKY PHRASES are printed on red paper, red luck candles are displayed in homes and offices, and at one time, doorways were painted red to frighten demons away.

**Related Holidays:** Lantern Festival, Li Ch'un

## ORIGINS

The Chinese New Year celebration is actually a two-week sequence of events, beginning with the ascent of the KITCHEN GOD to heaven near the end of the 12th lunar month and ending with the **LANTERN FESTIVAL** on the 15th day of the first month. On New Year's Eve (Moon 12, Day 30) all the doors to the house are sealed with strips of paper and the head of the household performs three important ceremonies: the offering to the God of Heaven and Earth, the offering to the Household Gods, and the worship of the ancestral tablets, usually strips of wood with the names and dates of deceased family members in raised or gilded characters. Then the entire family, putting aside their quarrels with one another, sits down to a special reunion meal. At midnight, everyone presents New Year wishes to one another in a very formal ceremony known as *K'o T'ou* (or kowtow, meaning to touch the ground with the forehead), observing strict rules about who should bow to whom. Between 3:00 and 5:00 a.m., the head of the household breaks the seals on the front door and greets the returning Household Gods, led by Tsao Wang, the Kitchen God.

New Year's Day itself is spent paying respects to elders, setting off FIRE-CRACKERS, burning incense, and calling on friends and relatives. No knives or sharp instruments may be used on this day, for fear of "cutting" good fortune, and brooms aren't used because they might sweep good fortune away. The first five days of the New Year, known as the Beginning of the New Spring, are devoted to the worship of the God of Wealth. Married women visit their family homes and sweep out their houses to fend off poverty. Most people return to work after the fourth or fifth day of celebration, and by the 13th and 14th days, they're busy getting ready for the Lantern Festival.

Telling fortunes based on the zodiac, an astrological diagram of the universe, is a popular New Year's custom in China. According to legend, the Chinese zodiac of 12 animals representing each year in succession came about in the sixth century B.C.E., when Buddha invited all the animals in creation to come to him. Only 12 responded: the tiger, rabbit, dragon, snake, horse, goat, monkey, rooster, dog, pig, rat, and ox. Buddha rewarded them by giving each one a year that would carry the animal's name as well as its traits: hence the "Year of the Rat," "Year of the Monkey," etc. By referring to the "eight characters" (which symbolize the hour, day, month, and year of a person's birth) and the 12 signs of the zodiac, fortunetellers can predict what events the coming year might hold.

New Year's Day is also a birthday celebration for all Chinese people, since birthdays are calculated according to the year in which a person is born rather than the day. Every new baby, in other words, is considered exactly a year old on New Year's Day. Some people, however, prefer to use the Western method of observing birthdays.

## SYMBOLS

### *Debt-paying*

Anyone who has not paid his debts before New Year's Day loses face, which in China means that he is disgraced. Shops are open and customers line up, waiting to settle their accounts. Paying off debts is a symbolic as well as a practical act, enabling people to face the New Year with a "clean slate."

The Chinese have three traditional dates for settling their debts: New Year's Day, the **DOUBLE FIFTH** (Dragon Boat Festival), and the **MID-AUTUMN FESTIVAL**. In between times, many people live on credit. There is a great deal of scurrying around as the Lunar New Year approaches and people try to raise cash to pay their debts. If someone can't pay up, he may try to hide until New Year's morning. Then he is safe until the next settlement day—unless the person he owes goes searching for him with a lantern, indicating that it is still dark and that the debt may be collected without violating the New Year.

Poor debtors often find refuge in the courtyard in front of the temple of the City of God. Comedy troupes give free performances here, and creditors who spy their debtors in the crowd are usually hesitant to demand payment in front of other people.

## Firecrackers

Firecrackers play an important role in many Chinese celebrations. Along with fire (or bright light) and the color red, loud noises are guaranteed to scare off evil spirits—particularly the NIAN monster, a legendary beast who appears at this time of year.

Firecrackers are first set off when the KITCHEN GOD departs for heaven, several days before the New Year actually begins. Intended to speed him on his way, the noise they make also keeps evil spirits out of the house until he returns. More firecrackers are set off during the **LANTERN FESTIVAL,** which concludes the New Year celebrations.

## Flowers

Flowers can be seen everywhere during the celebration of the Lunar New Year, particularly in southern China. They are used to decorate houses and public places, and each flower has a symbolic meaning. The white narcissus, for example, stands for good fortune and prosperity; the camellia, springtime; the peony, wealth; the peach (or plum), longevity. The quince, traditionally a symbol of fertility, is often used by the Chinese community in San Francisco.

Any plant with red flowers is considered a symbol of good luck and happiness. Blossoms that open on New Year's Day signify an extra dose of good fortune.

## Gate Gods

During the New Year celebration, the Chinese put up pictures of the Gate Gods, guardians of the home and protectors of mankind, on the panels of their front doors. These figures are often shown against a background of peach blossoms; according to legend, the Gate Gods were two brothers who lived under a peach tree so large that 5,000 men could not encircle it with their arms. Images of these traditional warriors have stood guard over Chinese households for 13 centuries.

The earliest "New Year pictures" of the Gate Gods date from the late second century and show Shentu and Yulu, guardians of the underworld, who protected families by tying up threatening demons and throwing them to the tigers. They are dressed in full armor, and their faces are painted with the bright makeup of the Chinese opera.

The most popular Gate Gods today are the Tang dynasty (618-907) generals Qin Qiong (or Qin Shubao) and Yuchi Jingde (or Hu Jingde). Legend says that when the Tang emperor Tai Zong was kept awake all night by evil demons, two of his ministers offered to stand guard outside the palace gates, but they never saw a sign of ghosts or goblins. After letting them spend several nights like this, the emperor decided to have their portraits painted and hung up on either side of the gate. His sleep was never disturbed again.

## Kitchen God

Tsao Wang, also known as the Kitchen God or Prince of the Oven, personifies the hearth or center of the home. He is one of the oldest gods worshipped in China, and he serves as a messenger between the inhabitants of the earth and the gods in heaven. Every Chinese kitchen has a shrine with a picture of Tsao Wang, usually in a small niche behind the cooking stove, which is considered the soul of the family and represents its fate. A good stove guarantees peace in the family, while a bad one brings strife.

The Kitchen God spends the entire year with the family, observing everything that goes on. Then, on the 23rd day (24th in the South of China) of the last month of the lunar year, he ascends to heaven to make his annual report on what he has seen and heard. Commonly called Little New Year, this occasion is marked with a farewell dinner given by the family and with offerings of sweet cakes and preserved fruits. Sometimes his picture is dipped in wine and his lips are smeared with honey so that he will be in a good mood when he reports on the family's behavior.

After the dinner is over, Tsao Wang's portrait is carried out into the courtyard and set up on an improvised altar with candles and incense. Prayers are offered, and the portrait is set on fire. The burning of the image releases Tsao Wang for his "ascent" to heaven. Paper spirit money (called *qianchang* or *yuanbao*) is thrown into the fire along with straw for the Kitchen God's horse. Peas and beans are tossed on the kitchen roof to imitate the clatter of the horse's hooves and to bring good luck in the coming year to the family's livestock.

The Kitchen God is usually shown sitting next to his wife. Sometimes a dog and a rooster, domestic symbols of a rural household, are shown with him. If the family is very poor and can't afford a woodblock print of Tsao Wang, his shrine may have nothing more than a plain sheet of red paper with his name written on it.

## Lucky Phrases or Spring Couplets

On the last day of the 12th lunar month, the gate posts and door panels of Chinese homes are decorated with images of the GATE GODS and "lucky phrases"—brief inscriptions printed on red paper (blue if the family is in mourning) with characters embossed in gold ink. Sometimes they are written in the form of "spring couplets" or two-line verses, and sometimes they consist of only a single character. "Fu," the character for good fortune, is often used because when it is printed upside down, it sounds the same as the word meaning "to arrive," thus implying that good fortune has arrived.

A popular custom for more than 1,000 years, lucky phrases are designed to bring good fortune of a particular kind. For example, a merchant might put up an inscription designed to attract success in his business; a farmer's lucky phrase might express the wish for a good harvest. In private households, lucky phrases usually concern wealth, longevity, the gift of sons, and official promotion—all traditional Chinese ideals.

The first spring couplets were composed to bring good fortune to the emperor Meng Zhang in the tenth century. It wasn't until the Ming dynasty (1368-1644) that the custom became a popular one. During the Qing dynasty (1644-1911), the composition of these brief verses was regarded as a means of measuring one's literary talent, education, and wit. They consist of two lines, called the "head" and the "tail," that correspond to and balance each other: for example, "By virtue united, heaven is strong;/Through compassion shared, earth is yielding." Many contemporary New Year couplets set political terminology against traditional descriptive elements. "Red flags," for example, might be paired with "fresh flowers." No longer composed by scholars, today's spring couplets are mass produced and can be purchased at stationery stores and magazine stands.

## New Year Prints

*Nianhua* or New Year prints are posted at the same time as the GATE GODS and SPRING COUPLETS, providing visual images of the wishes that the couplets describe. The desire for many children might be accompanied by a picture of a pomegranate, a symbol of fertility. Wishes for wealth and honor are often represented by full-blossomed peonies. The bat is another popular subject;

although associated with evil in European folklore, in China it is a common symbol for good luck and happiness. Plowing and weaving prints are popular, as are peaches (symbolizing longevity) and pictures of plump, healthy children holding pots of money (progeny and wealth). Some New Year prints portray scenes from historical novels and popular operas.

The subject matter of New Year prints has changed with the times. In the People's Republic of China, there was an increased demand for art with a socialist theme; prints often showed cooperative labor and bumper harvests. Since the Cultural Revolution (1966-76) ended, traditional New Year sentiments have been more acceptable. Some New Year prints try to combine both: for example, a picture of a communal fish pond may support the government's involvement in aquaculture, but it also symbolizes the traditional New Year wish for wealth. The word *yu,* meaning "fish," sounds the same in Chinese as the word meaning "affluence."

Like LUCKY PHRASES, New Year prints are purchased rather than created. Nianhua workshops throughout China produce more than 100 million of these prints each year.

## Nian Monster

According to Chinese legend, there was a frightening creature called *nian* (which is the same as the word meaning "year") who appeared at the end of the year, attacking villagers and their livestock. Nothing could destroy the *nian,* but people eventually discovered that it had three weaknesses: It was frightened by loud noises, it disliked sunshine, and it was terrified of the color red. So they built a huge bonfire outside the village, set off firecrackers, and painted the doors of their houses red. The *nian* covered its head in fear and ran away.

## Further Reading

Bredon, Juliet, and Igor Mitrophanow. *The Moon Year: A Record of Chinese Customs and Festivals,* 1966.

Frazer, Sir James G. *The Golden Bough: A Study in Magic and Religion,* 1931.

Gaer, Joseph. *Holidays Around the World,* 1953.

Henderson, Helene and Sue Ellen Thompson. *Holidays, Festivals, and Celebrations of the World Dictionary,* 2nd ed., 1997.

Purdy, Susan. *Festivals for You to Celebrate,* 1969.

Santino, Jack. *All Around the Year,* 1994.

Stepanchuk, Carol, and Charles Wong. *Mooncakes and Hungry Ghosts: Festivals of China,* 1991.

# Ch'ing Ming
## (Pure and Bright Festival, Spring Festival)

**Type of Holiday:** Calendar

**Date of Observation:** April 5 or 6; fourth or fifth day of the third lunar month

**Where Celebrated:** China, and by Chinese communities in the United States and throughout the world

**Symbols:** Ancestral Graves, Cold Food, Kites, Willow

**Related Holidays:** Li Ch'un, Winter Solstice

## ORIGINS

*Ch'ing Ming* means "Pure and Bright," an apt name for a Chinese festival that takes place at the beginning of spring. Although **LI CH'UN** celebrates the first day of spring, it usually occurs in February when the weather is still cold and the nights are long. Ch'ing Ming marks the *real* start of spring. It is always observed 106 days after the **WINTER SOLSTICE** and two weeks after the vernal equinox.

Ch'ing Ming was originally a festival of life renewal celebrated with dancing, singing, and picnicking. Eggs would be boiled and colored, then broken to symbolize the opening and dispersal of life. The emperor would plant trees on the palace grounds; villagers would place pine branches, a symbol of longevity, in front of their doors and hang sprigs of WILLOW under the eaves of their houses to ward off the forces of evil. Much like **ARBOR DAY** in the United States, this holiday was also known as the Tree Planting Festival (Chih Shu Chieh).

Over a period of several centuries, the Spring Festival changed from a celebration of new life to a commemoration of dead ancestors, similar to **ALL SOULS' DAY** in Europe and elsewhere. This transition is less puzzling to the Chinese, who regard the dead as intimately connected with life because they are responsible for ensuring fertility in the family as well as the fields. Nowadays Ch'ing Ming is observed with a ceremonial meal at the family tomb. Graves are cleaned and repaired, and offerings of food and "spirit money" are made to keep the ancestors happy and ensure a good harvest.

# SYMBOLS

## *Ancestral Graves*

The Chinese believe that one of the several souls belonging to each person remains near the grave where it can stay in contact with family members. Because this spirit has the power to cause harm or promote good, it must be offered food, music, and burnt sacrifices so it will be favorably disposed toward the living.

Chinese families at one time had private burial grounds outside the city walls, often in the midst of cultivated fields. But the shortage of land has made public cemeteries more common. Early on the morning of Ch'ing Ming, families carrying food, sticks of incense, and paper money tied up in cloth bundles go to visit their ancestral graves. They begin by cutting down any weeds that have grown up around the grave and sweeping away the dirt. The food is set out on stone altar-tables—with an emphasis on dishes the ancestor was fond of—and the paper money is usually left on the grave with a stone or lump of clay to hold it in place. After the spirits of the dead have been worshipped according to prescribed ritual, the family may dine near the graves or return home to feast on the food that was offered.

Those who can't visit their family graves at Ch'ing Ming offer prayers to their ancestors and make an offering of paper bags decorated with two human figures in flowery robes. Between the figures there is a space where the names of those buried in the family graveyard can be listed. The bags are then filled with paper money, placed on an altar with fruit, sweets, and tea, and burned before sundown because the ancestors must return to their graves before the city gates close at nightfall. Most Chinese, however, make a special effort to be home in time for the Spring Festival.

It is considered essential to visit the family graves at least once a year, because an unswept grave is considered an indication that the family has died out. Neglected tombs, especially those located in fields, might be plowed under, or the land might be sold. The punishment for damaging or tampering with graves—as long as they're obviously being cared for—is harsh.

## *Cold Food*

On the eve of Ch'ing Ming, some Chinese observe the Han Shih (Cold Food) Festival. No fires are lit and nothing hot is eaten for 24 hours. This custom can be traced back to an ancient tribal rite whereby a new fire could only be kindled once a year. Han Shih, which originally lasted three days, marked the interval between the extinction of the old fire and the lighting of the new one by rubbing two WILLOW sticks together. Courtiers' children were performing this fire-kindling ceremony in the open space before the Imperial Palace as late as the Tang dynasty (seventh to tenth centuries). The first to set his or her sticks alight received a golden cup and three pieces of silk. This custom is believed to be a survival of an ancient sun-worship and purification ritual practiced by the nomads of the Zhou dynasty, who burned the fields in order to rid them of evil influences and clear the way for spring planting. It may also be linked to the Roman Catholic custom of letting the hearth fire go out on Easter Sunday and rekindling it on Easter Monday.

A myth has also been devised to explain the custom. It involves a faithful servant travelling with his lord who, when misfortune fell and food supplies ran out, cut off a piece of his own flesh to feed his master. Afterward, he fled to the mountains. The lord set fire to the underbrush to chase him out of hiding so he could be properly rewarded, but the hero preferred to burn alive. After his death, the lord proclaimed that people would honor his example by not lighting any fire in their homes for three days and eating cold food.

Observance of the Cold Food feast is dying out in Beijing, but it is still practiced elsewhere in China.

## Kites

During the war between the states of Chu and Han in the third century B.C.E., a famous Han general by the name of Han Xin built a giant wooden kite for the great warrior Zhang Liang to ride in. The legend says that Zhang Liang flew above the Chu encampment singing traditional Chu songs, which made the enemy soldiers so homesick that they left their camp and were defeated. To this day Ch'ing Ming is a popular day to fly kites. There are informal kite competitions and formal exhibitions of kites with participants from all over the world.

After people have visited their family graves and paid their respects to the ancestors, they often picnic, play games, and fly kites in a variety of shapes and designs. Some kites illustrate plots from Chinese folk tales or historical legends; other convey good luck wishes. Many are designed to make sounds in the wind or to create special visual effects. This is why the common word in China for kite is *fengzheng* or "wind zither."

## *Willow*

Because it is the first tree to respond to the sun by putting out new leaves, the willow has always been an emblem of spring and erotic awakening. The Chinese phrase "willow feelings and flower wishes" refers to sexual desire. And the expression "looking for flowers and buying willows" means paying a visit to a prostitute. The willow is also a symbol of vitality because it is extremely hardy and will take root almost anywhere.

The origins of the willow's mystical connection to the Spring Festival are somewhat obscure, but according to a popular legend, a rebellious member of the Tang dynasty took the willow as his personal sign. Those willing to support him were asked to hang a willow branch outside their houses. When the signal for revolt was given on the day of the Ch'ing Ming festival, those who had the branch on their houses escaped massacre. Their descendants continued the custom, and to this day, sprigs of willow are hung under the eaves of houses to keep demons away. In some parts of China, women wear willow sprigs in their hair at Ch'ing Ming, and young people wear "willow dogs" (sprouts of willow) all day. There is a saying that "Those who wear no willow at the Ch'ing Ming will be re-born as yellow dogs in future life"—a sufficient threat to ensure that willow is seen everywhere.

In addition to repelling demons, willow also has the ability to attract good. It can draw the spirits of ancestors back to their homes, which is why it is so often used for decorating graves.

## Further Reading

Bredon, Juliet, and Igor Mitrophanow. *The Moon Year: A Record of Chinese Customs and Festivals*, 1966.

Eberhard, Wolfram. *A Dictionary of Chinese Symbols: Hidden Symbols in Chinese Life and Thought*, 1986.

Gaer, Joseph. *Holidays Around the World*, 1953.

Henderson, Helene and Sue Ellen Thompson. *Holidays, Festivals, and Celebrations of the World Dictionary*, 2nd ed., 1997.

Stepanchuk, Carol, and Charles Wong. *Mooncakes and Hungry Ghosts: Festivals of China*, 1991.

# *Christmas*

**Type of Holiday:** Religious (Christian)

**Date of Observation:** December 25

**Where Celebrated:** United States, Great Britain, Europe, and by Christians throughout the world

**Symbols:** Boar, Candy Cane, Christmas Card, Christmas Carols, Christmas Tree, Crèche, Gifts, Holly, Mistletoe, Poinsettia, Wassail, Wreath (see **CHRISTMAS EVE** for Candles, Reindeer, Santa Claus, Yule Log)

**Colors:** Christmas is traditionally associated with the colors red and green.

**Related Holidays:** Advent, Christmas Eve, Epiphany, St. Stephen's Day (Boxing Day)

## ORIGINS

The first celebration of the birth of Jesus Christ on December 25 took place in Rome about the middle of the fourth century, although the Eastern church was already observing January 6 as a joint commemoration of Christ's birth and baptism. Since the exact date of the Nativity is not known, there are a number of theories as to why December 25 was chosen. One is that it was designed to replace the ancient Roman winter festival known as the **SATURNALIA**, which was held on December 17-23. Another is that it was a replacement for the Brumalia, or Birthday of the Unconquered Sun, which was observed on December 25 because it followed the winter solstice, when the days began to grow longer. Christmas also coincided, more or less, with the Jewish Feast of Lights or **HANUKKAH**, the Egyptian Birthday of the Sun-God, and the Anglo-Saxon Feast of Yule. In any case, it must have seemed only natural to replace the birthday of the sun with the birthday of the Son of God. Many of the symbols associated with Christmas still reflect its twin roots in Christianity and pagan seasonal lore.

Even in pre-Christian times, the period between December 25 and January 6 was considered a special time of year. Now widely referred to as "The Twelve Days of Christmas," this was a time when spirits roamed the earth and were apt to cause mischief if certain precautions weren't taken. A number of the superstitions associated with this period concerned spinning. In England, for example, it was said that if any flax were left on the distaff, the Devil would come and cut it. In Denmark, it was believed that nothing characterized by a circular motion (such as a spinning wheel) should be used between Christmas and **NEW YEAR'S DAY**.

When the Gregorian calendar replaced the Julian calendar in 1582, 11 days were dropped to make up for the discrepancy that had accumulated over the centuries. Roman Catholic countries quickly accepted the new calendar, but in England and Scotland, people had trouble adjusting to the change. For almost 200 years, they continued to observe Christmas on what was now January 5. Even after the British adopted the Gregorian calendar in 1752, people living in rural areas continued to observe "Old Christmas Day" on January 5 (January 6 after 1800). The new calendar was never adopted by the Greek and other Eastern churches, where Christmas is still observed on January 6.

Xmas, the common abbreviation for Christmas, is regarded by many — especially those who are intent on preserving the holiday's religious roots and traditions — as an insult to Christ, if not a sacrilege. In fact, the abbreviation is entirely appropriate. The letter "X" (*chi*) is the first letter in the Greek word for Christ. According to the *Oxford English Dictionary*, there was an even longer abbreviation that came into use around 1550: *X-temmas.*

## SYMBOLS

### Boar

Perhaps because the ancient Celts supplied the rest of Europe with pork and bacon, the boar's association with the Yuletide feast goes back to prehistoric times. According to Norse folklore, boar was served in Valhalla, the mythical hall where Odin received the souls of heroes who had fallen in battle. Pork was highly prized in Ireland and Wales, where many preferred it to beef and mutton.

In eleventh- and twelfth-century England, hunting the wild boar became a traditional Christmas sport. Its head would be carried into the dining hall afterward with a great flourish, often to the accompaniment of "The Boar's Head Carol," the oldest printed Christmas carol in existence (1521). Queen's College, Oxford, was at one time known for its traditional Christmas ceremony of ushering in the boar's head. According to legend, a student of the college was attacked by a wild boar while walking in the country. He was reading Aristotle as he walked, and was able to escape injury by shoving the book down the boar's throat.

In Scandinavia, it is customary to use the last sheaf of corn from the harvest to bake a loaf in the form of a boar or pig at Christmas time. Throughout the festival of Yule *(Jul)*, the boar-shaped loaf remains on the table. It is often kept in the house until the crops are sown in the spring. Then part of it is mixed with seed-corn and part is given to the ploughman or his animals to eat. Scholars believe that the Yule boar represents the corn-spirit (a primitive deity who makes the crops grow) in pig form.

In Psalm 80, Satan is described as "the wild boar out of the wood" who has wasted the Lord's vineyards. Carrying the boar's head on a platter is symbolic of his final defeat by Jesus Christ, the newborn King.

## Candy Cane

The very earliest Christmas trees were decorated with symbols associated with the birth of Jesus. Candles were used to symbolize Christ, the Light of the World, and the star placed on the topmost branch recalled the Star of Bethlehem that shone over the manger. The shepherd's crook represented the shepherds in the fields near Bethlehem, who were the first to receive the news that a Savior had been born.

In Europe, the most popular Christmas tree decorations were edible. Cookies and candy not only provided a treat for children but symbolically expressed Christians' gratitude for the "daily bread" that the Lord provided. The red-and-white striped candy canes that are hung on the branches of Christmas trees today were once a symbol of the shepherds who came to Bethlehem to worship the Christ Child.

## Christmas Card

In ancient Rome, it was customary to exchange greetings and gifts on the first day of January. With the advent of Christianity, the giving and receiving of such tokens continued in some European countries, often taking the form of New Year cards. These contained no references to Christmas and were sent out after December 25 so they would arrive on **NEW YEAR'S DAY**. In England, however, seasonal greeting cards combined Christmas and the New Year—with the emphasis on Christmas. They were meant to be delivered on or before Christmas Day and to convey greetings for both holidays.

The invention of lithography at the end of the eighteenth century gave the production of New Year cards in Europe a real boost. But most stationery manufacturers looked upon these cards as a temporary fad that probably wouldn't last. People who didn't want to spend their money on manufactured cards often converted their printed calling cards for the purpose, decorating them with scraps of cloth or paper and adding a Christmas greeting.

The first printed Christmas card was produced in England in 1843. Designed by John Calcott Horsley, it sold for a shilling and looked like a postcard. It wasn't until the 1880s that cards became folders of four, eight, or more pages.

Cards became increasingly elaborate throughout the Victorian period, with "frosted" surfaces, fancy cut edges, layers of lace-paper, and other forms of decoration. Sometimes the top cover or flap was embossed, "jewelled" with sparkles, and edged with silk fringe or tassels.

Louis Prang started producing Christmas cards in the United States in 1875. His plant in Roxbury, Massachusetts, was the birthplace of what is now the American greeting card industry. The subject matter ranged from traditional midwinter and Nativity scenes to flowers, animals, birds, and insects; comic or serious illustrations of public figures or popular characters; and novelties—such as the bicycle and the telephone—, customs, and habits.

Christmas cards in America today are so much a part of the holiday tradition that people often regard sending them as a burden. And fear of offending the sensibilities of non-Christians has led many card manufacturers to omit the word "Christmas" altogether, substituting more secular messages focusing on world peace and understanding.

## Christmas Carols

Although it is difficult to imagine the holiday season without Christmas carols, Christmas was observed for more than 800 years before the first real "carols" were written. The term originally referred to a ring-dance accompanied by singing, without any religious overtones. Eventually it came to mean a merry song with a tune that could be danced to.

The Italian friars who lived with St. Francis of Assisi were the first to compose simple, uplifting songs based on the stories of the Gospel. Unlike hymns, the earliest carols treated religious subjects in a familiar, playful, or festive style. From Italy, the carol passed to Spain, France, and Germany, where it retained its cheerfulness, childish simplicity, and religious fervor. The earliest known English carol dates from about 1410 and describes the Virgin Mary singing a lullaby to her child.

Carols as they are known today typically describe scenes and events associated with the birth of Christ—for example, the shepherds watching over their flocks and seeing the Star of Bethlehem, the discovery of the infant Jesus in the stable, the journey of the Wise Men from the East, etc. The best-loved carols—including "Deck the Halls," "God Rest Ye Merry Gentlemen," and "Here We Come A-Wassailing"—were written before the Restoration (1660); those written later tend to lack the earlier carols' spontaneity and festive nature. The rise of Puritanism in England was nearly fatal to Christmas carols, and by 1800, the custom of singing carols had nearly died out. But people in rural areas kept the tradition alive, and a new generation of editors and publishers made sure that the best of the old carols survived.

Christmas caroling—the custom of singing carols in a group while moving from house to house—originally took place on **CHRISTMAS EVE** or early in the morning on Christmas Day. Today it is a popular Christmas Eve tradition. Since the nineteenth century, carols have been sung in place of hymns in most churches on Christmas Day. Although some very good carols have been written for holidays other than Christmas, no one ever seems to sing them.

## Christmas Tree

The decorated tree didn't really become a popular part of the Christmas celebration until the nineteenth century, but some scholars believe that the custom can be traced all the way back to ancient times. The Egyptians observed a midwinter festival in honor of the god Horus, son of Isis (goddess of motherhood and fertility). The symbol for this celebration was a palm tree with 12 shoots symbolizing the months of the year. The Romans decorated with candlelit trees during the **SATURNALIA** in December and brought laurel boughs and green trees into their houses at the kalends (first day) of January.

The Christmas tree as it is known today came to America from Germany in the early eighteenth century. The Germans had for some time been celebrating Christmas by setting up a wooden structure shaped like a pyramid and covering it with boughs of evergreen. The *Weihnachtspyramide* was probably derived from the "Paradise tree" used in Medieval mystery plays. A fir tree decorated with apples and surrounded by candles, it symbolized the story of Adam and Eve. According to legend, when Adam left Paradise, he took with him a sprig (or seed) from the Tree of Knowledge. From this grew the tree that later provided wood for the cross on which Jesus Christ was crucified.

There is also a legend concerning the miraculous transformation of nature at the moment of Christ's birth, when it is said that the rivers flowed with wine and the trees blossomed in the midst of ice and snow. The Christmas tree, which "blossoms" with light and ornaments at this time of year, may have been a symbolic representation of this legendary miracle.

Although Christmas trees can be seen everywhere in the United States—in homes, schools, office buildings, and shopping malls—they do not play the central role here that they do in the German celebration of Christmas. No one in Germany is too poor or too lonely to put up a tree. And unlike Americans, who tend to arrange their Christmas gifts around the base of the tree, the Germans consider their tree an object of wonder all by itself. It is decorated in secret behind closed doors and revealed to the assembled family and guests on Christmas Eve.

In the United States today a fir tree is traditionally placed at the highest point of a building under construction—even if it's a skyscraper. Just as Christmas celebrates the birth of Christ, the occupational symbol of the fir tree serves as a reminder of the work that goes into a new building and the people who make this modern "miracle" possible.

## Crèche

The crèche, a display of a stable with figures representing the Nativity scene, is usually attributed to St. Francis of Assisi, who used real people and live animals to reconstruct the birth of Jesus in a cave near the Italian village of Greccio in 1224. The "living pantomime" became a popular Italian custom and eventually spread throughout the Christian world.

But the idea goes back even further, to fourth-century Rome. The early observance of the festival of Christmas included three Masses, one of which was referred to as *Ad Praesepe* (the Crib). The "Crib" was a shrine that had been built in the basilica of Santa Maria Maggiore from some of the boards believed to have been saved from the original stable in Bethlehem. The custom of saying a Mass over the manger seems to have inspired other churches in Italy and throughout Europe to set up their own "cribs." But it was St. Francis of Assisi who took the crèche out of the church and popularized it, giving rise to the practice of setting up crèches in public squares and private homes.

In Italy today, every home has its *Presepio* at Christmas. It includes not only the immediate scene—with Mary and Joseph, the Christ child, the shepherds, the Three Kings, and assorted farm animals and worshipping angels—but the surrounding countryside of Bethlehem with its hills and streams. South America is also known for its elaborate Nativity scenes. An entire room is often filled with a reconstructed landscape representing the mountains, plains, and valleys surrounding Bethlehem. The shepherds can be seen leading their sheep across the hills, while the Wise Men are crossing the desert on their camels. Sometimes there are water mills, grottos, and sailboats on the sea.

In fourteenth-century Germany, there was a very popular Christmas custom known as *Kindelwiegen* or "cradle-rocking." People danced around the cradle containing an image of the Christ child and then took turns rocking it with their own hands. Sometimes the participants would get carried away, rocking and fondling the Christ Child and leaping around the cradle. Because cradle-rocking so often got out of hand, the practice was eventually discontinued in most German churches.

There has been some controversy in the United States about erecting crèches in public places, such as town halls. State and local governments have been under pressure to make their displays non-denominational by adding other symbolic elements. Vandalism and theft of the figures in the crèche are becoming increasingly common, prompting some cities and towns to do away with outdoor Nativity scenes altogether.

## Gifts

The custom of exchanging charms or small tokens of good luck at the end of the year goes back to very ancient times. The Egyptians used to give each other small, symbolic presents conveying good luck wishes at **NEW YEAR'S**. When the tombs of the Pharoahs were unearthed, small blue-glazed bottles (probably scent flasks) with messages about the approaching New Year were found intact. The Romans, too, exchanged gifts and New Year's greetings on the Kalends (or first day) of January. Originally laurel or olive branches picked from the holy groves dedicated to Strenia, the goddess of health, these gifts or *strenae* became more elaborate, often consisting of symbolic objects such as lamps (symbol of light) or silver and gold (wealth). Giving people such gifts was supposed to bring them luck in the coming year. The Roman roots of the gift-giving custom can still be seen in the French word for New Year's presents: *étrennes.*

St. Nicholas, the Bishop of Myra, has also been linked to the gift-giving tradition. Because he was not only wealthy but modest, he liked to help people in need without drawing attention to himself. Poor families would often find a gold piece or a well-filled purse without knowing where it had come from. His American successor, Santa Claus, carried on the tradition by delivering gifts in his sleigh on **CHRISTMAS EVE**.

In Russia, it is Babuska (the Grandmother) who brings gifts at Christmas. According to legend, this is the old woman who deliberately misdirected the Three Wise Men when they stopped to ask directions on their way to Bethlehem. Another version of the story says that they urged her to come with them, but she said she was too busy spinning. In any case, she later repented and tried to make amends by going around the world on Christmas Eve distributing gifts to good children.

The growing commercialism surrounding Christmas, particularly in the United States, has placed so much emphasis on shopping for Christmas gifts that many people feel it has robbed the holiday of its religious significance. A popular slogan reminds busy American consumers to "Put the 'Christ' back in Christmas."

## Holly

The *ilex* or holly oak is regarded as a symbol of the passion of Christ because its thorny leaves resemble the crown of thorns that Christ wore at His crucifixion. It is also said to have been the tree from which the Cross was made. All the other trees, according to legend, agreed not to allow their wood to be used for this purpose. When touched by an axe, they splintered into a million pieces. Only the ilex remained whole and permitted itself to be felled.

Today holly is used to decorate homes and churches at Christmas. Like ivy and MISTLETOE, holly bears its fruit in the wintertime, which is why it is considered a symbol of eternal life. Other evergreens used for decorating at Christmas include the laurel (or bay), symbolic of triumph, and the yew or cypress, which is also symbolic of immortality because it stays green.

## Mistletoe

The evergreen boughs and sprigs of holly, ivy, and mistletoe used to decorate homes during the Christmas holiday symbolize immortality because they retain their green color even after they've been cut. The custom of decorating indoors with evergreens dates back to the Roman **SATURNALIA**, where it may have been an offer of hospitality to the spirits that haunted the woods.

In ancient Britain, the Druids worshipped mistletoe, a semi-parasitic plant that draws its water and minerals from the tree on which it grows. According to legend, mistletoe was most likely to be found on trees that had been struck by lightning, particularly oaks. Although the Druids regarded mistletoe in general as a cure for almost any disease and a remedy against poisons, oak-mistletoe was considered the most powerful. It could heal ulcers or help a woman conceive; it was widely regarded as a cure for epilepsy (known as "the falling sickness") because it was rooted high in the branches of a tree and could not fall to the ground. Gathering it on the first day of the lunar month increased its power, and the Druids made sure that it was cut with a golden sickle and caught in a white cloth so it wouldn't touch the ground.

In Norse mythology Balder, the god of light and vegetation, dreamed that he was going to die. To protect him from every imaginable danger, the goddess Frigga made all of the beasts and birds, as well as the stones, the trees, fire, and water, swear an oath that they would not harm him. Once the other gods realized that Balder was invulnerable, they often amused themselves by shooting and throwing stones at him. But the mischievous Loki tricked Frigga into revealing that a plant called mistletoe had seemed too young at the time to participate in the oath. Loki gave a sprig of it to the blind god Hother and told him to shoot at Balder with the twig. The mistletoe struck Balder and he was killed.

Such legends contributed to mistletoe's reputation as a sacred and very powerful plant. The oak tree on which it grew became a Christian symbol when it was identified as the tree from which the Cross was made. Because of its solidity and endurance, it is also a symbol of the strength of the Christian faith. But because of its association with the ancient religion of the Druids, mistletoe is generally not allowed in church decorations.

The custom of hanging a sprig of mistletoe in a doorway at Christmas dates back to the ancient Scandinavian custom of having enemies who encountered each other under mistletoe in the forest lay down their arms and maintain a truce until the following day. Nowadays people who find themselves standing under the mistletoe in a doorway are expected to kiss each other—another way of making a pledge of peace and friendship.

In England, Christmas decorations were never simply thrown away; they were usually burned or allowed to stay up until **CANDLEMAS** (February 2). Mistletoe often stayed up until it was replaced by a new branch the following year.

## Poinsettia

Native to Central America, the red and green poinsettia has been a symbol of Christmas in the United States since the 1820s, when it was first shipped to North America by Joel Poinsett, the American minister to Mexico. The shape of the bright red blossoms has often been compared to the Star of Bethlehem.

## Wassail

The term *wassail* comes from the Middle English *waes haeil,* which means "be in good health." *Wassailing* was the old English custom of toasting the holiday and each other's health. From the thirteenth century onward the term referred not only to the toasts that were exchanged during the Christmas season but to a traditional beverage — a mixture of ale, roasted apples, sugar, and spices, sometimes with eggs or cream added. It was served from giant "wassail bowls" and remained the favorite holiday drink until the early eighteenth century, when the growing popularity of spirits led to the invention of punch. Today, liquor-based punches and egg nog—a nineteenth-century invention—have replaced the original wassail. But the custom of offering toasts remains.

## Wreath

The circular shape of the Christmas wreath makes it a symbol of eternity. Because the wreath remains green throughout the holiday season, it serves as a reminder that life is present even during the dead of winter.

The Christmas wreath is the logical continuation of the Advent wreath, an old Christian custom that originated with the Lutherans in Germany. It is a simple circle of greenery around which four candles, representing the four weeks of the **ADVENT** season, are equally spaced. One candle is lit the first Sunday and another is lit each week thereafter. Because of the burning candles, however, Advent wreaths were usually placed on a table or hung parallel to the floor. Christmas wreaths are traditionally hung on the doors, walls, or windows of homes and churches.

Many people leave their wreaths up all winter. When the wreath is taken down, it is symbolic of winter's end.

## Further Reading

Barz, Brigitte. *Festivals with Children,* 1989.

Biedermann, Hans. *Dictionary of Symbolism: Cultural Icons and the Meanings Behind Them,* 1994.

Buday, George. *The History of the Christmas Card,* 1971.

Crippen, T. G. *Christmas and Christmas Lore,* 1990.

Dawson, W. F. *Christmas: Its Origin and Associations,* 1990.

Ferguson, George. *Signs and Symbols in Christian Art,* 1954.

Frazer, Sir James G. *The Golden Bough: A Study in Magic and Religion,* 1931.

Henderson, Helene and Sue Ellen Thompson. *Holidays, Festivals, and Cele-brations of the World Dictionary,* 2nd ed., 1997.

Ickis, Marguerite. *The Book of Festivals and Holidays the World Over,* 1970.

Miles, Clement A. *Christmas in Ritual and Tradition, Christian and Pagan,* 1990.

Monks, James L. *Great Catholic Festivals,* 1951.

Purdy, Susan. *Festivals for You to Celebrate,* 1969.

Santino, Jack. *All Around the Year,* 1994.

Tuleja, Tad. *Curious Customs: The Stories Behind 296 Popular American Rituals,* 1987.

# *Christmas Eve*

**Type of Holiday:** Religious (Christian)

**Date of Observation:** December 24

**Where Celebrated:** United States, Great Britain, Europe, and by Christians throughout the world

**Symbols:** Candles and Fire; Reindeer; Santa Claus; Yule Log

**Colors:** Christmas Eve is traditionally associated with the colors red and green.

**Related Holidays:** Advent, Christmas, Epiphany, St. Stephen's Day (Boxing Day)

## ORIGINS

Christmas Eve marks the end of the **ADVENT** season, the period of preparation for **CHRISTMAS** that begins on November 30 (November 15 in the East). It was on this night that the shepherds keeping watch over their flocks outside Bethlehem saw the bright star in the sky that signaled the birth of Jesus Christ.

Despite its Christian significance, there are a number of pagan and super-natural beliefs connected with Christmas Eve. In Scandinavian countries, it is believed that the dead revisit their former homes on Christmas Eve. People make sure that their parlors are tidy and that a good fire is burning before they go to bed. They often light candles, set the table, and leave out plenty of food for their ghostly visitors. They also make sure that the seats of their chairs have been dusted. When they get up in the morning, they wipe the chairs again with a clean white towel. If they find any dirt on the seat, it means that a relative fresh from the grave sat there during the night.

In many parts of Europe, people believe that at midnight on Christmas Eve, animals briefly possess the power of speech. It might have been the traditional association of the ox and the ass with the Nativity scene that gave rise to such superstitions, but the concept of talking animals is probably pagan in origin. A closely related belief, widespread in England and Europe, is that cattle rise in their stalls at midnight on Christmas Eve, or kneel to worship the Christ Child.

The midnight church service celebrating the birth of Jesus Christ is the main Christmas Eve tradition for Christians of all denominations and even for non-believers, many of whom come to hear Christmas music performed.

# SYMBOLS

## Candles and Fire

Candles have always been symbolic of the sun's light and warmth, and in ancient times they were lit to dispel the darkness of winter at the time of the **WINTER SOLSTICE** (December 21 or 22). Early Christians preferred to see them as symbols of Christ's "light," which replaced the darkness of paganism. Some scholars think that the custom of lighting candles on Christmas Eve came from the Jewish "Feast of Lights" or **HANUKKAH**, which was held around the same time of year and featured the lighting of candles or lamps.

Throughout the Middle Ages, it was customary to light one large candle on Christmas Eve, in both the church and the home, to commemorate the Star of Bethlehem. The candle may also have been symbolic of the Holy Child, whom Simeon called "A Light to lighten the Gentiles." These giant candles burned continuously throughout the Christmas season, right up until **TWELFTH NIGHT**. In Scandinavian countries, keeping the "Yule candle" burning was very important. Sometimes there were two candles representing the head of the house and his wife. If one of them went out first, it meant that the other partner would live longer. A similar belief prevailed in Scotland before the Reformation. If the Christmas candle was extinguished before midnight, it meant that a great disaster would befall the family. In Ireland, the Christmas Eve candle is often so big that a large turnip must be carved out to serve as a candlestick.

In the nineteenth century in what is now New Mexico, bundles of branches were set ablaze along the roads and pathways so that travelers could find their way to people's homes on Christmas Eve. Called *luminarias* or "little lights," these small bonfires dated back to the time of the Spanish conquistadors, when they were used to light the way for the Christ Child. Eventually they were looked upon as a fire hazard and were replaced by small candles burning inside brown paper bags, weighted with sand to keep the candles from tipping over. The custom of lining roads and driveways with luminarias is very popular throughout the southwestern United States and is taking hold in other parts of the country as well. House and street lights in many neighborhoods are turned off on Christmas Eve, and motorists are asked to dim their headlights as they tour residential areas.

In Louisiana along the levees of the Mississippi River, bonfires built out of logs, cane reed, old tires, and bamboo are lit on Christmas Eve. Derived from the *feux de joie* (fires of joy) that burned in France on Epiphany Eve, the eve of **ASH WEDNESDAY**, and **NEW YEAR'S EVE**, these fires were brought to Louisiana after the Civil War by Marist priests. When Christmas became the predominant winter holiday, the bonfire tradition was shifted to December 24.

## Reindeer

More than 600 years after St. Nicholas' death, Russians carried his legend back from Constantinople, and he became Russia's patron saint. From there, his story spread to Lapland, home of the reindeer, which may explain why the modern Santa Claus lives at the North Pole and gets around in a sleigh pulled by eight reindeer. In reality, of course, he often arrives by car or helicopter at the local shopping mall.

Clement Moore's poem "A Visit from St. Nicholas" popularized the names of Santa's reindeer: "Now Dasher! Now Dancer! Now Prancer and Vixen! On Comet! On Cupid! On Donder and Blitzen!" But to children everywhere, Rudolph is the most beloved. He first appeared in a complimentary Christmas store souvenir given out by Montgomery Ward during the holidays in 1939. The little book was written by Robert May, a Montgomery Ward ad man known for his light verse. It tells the story of Rudolph the Red-Nosed Reindeer, a variation on the ugly duckling motif. Illustrated by May's friend Denver Gillen, the story of Rudolph sold 2.4 million copies in Montgomery Ward stores that first year. The poem appeared in book form in 1947, and when the singing cowboy star Gene Autry recorded a musical version of the tale in 1949, it reached the top of the Hit Parade. What began as an advertising gimmick soon became a popular emblem of the modern American Christmas. Nowadays Rudolph can be seen on television, in store window displays, and on front lawns and rooftops everywhere.

## Santa Claus

The original Santa Claus was Nicholas, the legendary saint who was bishop of Myra (Turkey) in the fourth century. He was usually shown wearing the fur-trimmed robes of a cleric, with a beehive (symbolizing industry) and a bulldog (fidelity) at his side. He was a gift-giver but also a disciplinarian, bringing switches and rods for children who misbehaved. December 6 was his feast day, and in many countries, it is on this day—not Christmas Eve—that St. Nicholas arrives to hand out his presents and punishments.

The Christian story of St. Nicholas was brought to Europe, where it got mixed up with the Germanic religion and its chief god, Woden (or Odin), who rode an eight-legged white horse. The Dutch *Sinter Klaas,* for example, wears bishop's robes and rides a white horse. In other northern European countries, St. Nicholas has been integrated with ancient gods to become a spirit of winter rather than a Christian saint.

Martin Luther substituted the Christ Child for St. Nicholas as a bearer of gifts, and moved the day of his arrival from December 6 to Christmas as part of an effort to remove the last vestiges of paganism from the Christian church. In some parts of Europe, it is still the Christ Child who brings gifts, which is why he is called Kriss Kringle (from the German *Christkindl*).

The American Santa Claus is actually a combination of three figures: (1) the English Father Christmas, a winter deity wearing a crown of holly who replaced St. Nicholas after the Reformation; (2) the German St. Nicholas, brought to the United States by German immigrants during the eighteenth and early nineteenth centuries; and (3) the Dutch Sinter Klaas, who was brought by Dutch settlers to New York. But it wasn't until the publication of Clement Moore's poem "A Visit from St. Nicholas" on December 23, 1823, that the American Santa Claus was transformed from a tall, thin bishop to a jolly, overweight, pipe-smoking figure wearing a fur-trimmed red suit. His elf-like image was reinforced by Thomas Nast, an editorial cartoonist who did numerous illustrations of Santa Claus based on Moore's poem. Washington Irving made his own contribution in *A History of New York,* when he described St. Nicholas as "laying a finger beside his nose" and dropping gifts down the chimney.

Most American children believe that Santa Claus comes down the chimney on Christmas Eve to fill the stockings they've left hanging on the mantle. This custom can be traced back to a folk legend in which three daughters decided to help their father escape poverty by selling themselves into prostitution. A wealthy man named Nicholas visited their house on three successive nights, and each time he tossed a ball of gold through an open window. The three gold balls, which landed in the stockings the girls had hung by the fire to dry, saved them from a life of sin.

Some scholars have traced this tradition back even farther, to the ancient Norsemen's winter solstice festival in honor of Herthe, goddess of the home. Before the holiday feast, a fire of fir boughs was laid on an altar of flat stones in the belief that Herthe would appear in the smoke to bring the family good fortune. The Norse altar stones became our modern hearth stones, and Santa's trip down the chimney was an updated version of Herthe's appearance in the smoke.

## Yule Log

Traditionally burned on Christmas Eve and throughout the Christmas season, the Yule log gets its name from the pagan Norsemen, who observed a 12-day winter celebration called *Jól,* which means "wheel" and probably refers to the turning of the sun at the winter solstice. There is also an old English word, *geol,* which means "feast." In pre-Christian times, the entire month of December was known as *geola,* or "feast-month." The name was later attached to the Christmas feast known as Yule in England and Jul in Scandinavia.

It was common in ancient times to light bonfires at the winter solstice to scare off winter's demons and to brighten the darkest time of the year. But the Yule log, which appears to be a survival of this custom, is burned indoors and is more of a domestic than a public celebration. In its purest form, the Yule log is a whole trunk of a tree, selected and cut on **CANDLE-MAS** (February 2) and dried throughout the year. The usual practice in England was to light the Yule log with a fragment of the previous year's log, which had been kept in the house throughout the year in the belief that it would offer protection against fire and especially lightning. Because it was usually an oak log, it's possible that this belief is a relic of the ancient Aryan religion, which associated the oak tree with the god of thunder.

The English Yule log is said to have come from the Druids, the ancient Celtic religious order. The Druid priests prayed that the oak or fruitwood log burned in their midwinter festival would flame, like the sun, forever. Both the log and its ashes were considered symbols of good luck and strength. Even in more recent times, bringing the Yule log into the house was often accompanied by great ceremony. The youngest child would pour wine on the log before it was thrown into the fire, and then a remnant of the log would be saved and used to kindle the new log on the following Christmas Eve. It was considered bad luck if the fire went out before New Year's Day.

Yule log ceremonies are most elaborate among the Serbs and Croats, where two or three young oaks are cut down for every house (sometimes one log for each male member of the family). As the logs are carried in, lighted candles are held on either side of the door, and as the father of the family crosses the threshold with the first log, someone throws corn at him or pours wine over the log. The log itself may be a symbol of the spirit of vegetation, and burning it may be symbolic of sunshine, whose influence is needed during the coming year. The corn and wine are probably symbols of the sun and rain the crops need to grow.

A number of superstitions surround the Yule log in Europe. In southern France, people put the log on the fire for the first time on Christmas Eve and then continue to burn it a little bit each day until **TWELFTH NIGHT** (January 5). If it is kept under the bed, it will protect the house from fire and thunder and will prevent those who live there from getting chilblains on their heels in winter. The unburned remains are also believed to cure cattle of many diseases and to help cows deliver their calves. If the ashes are scattered over the fields, it will save the wheat from mildew.

## Further Reading

Crippen, T. G. *Christmas and Christmas Lore,* 1990.

Frazer, Sir James G. *The Golden Bough: A Study in Magic and Religion,* 1931.

Henderson, Helene and Sue Ellen Thompson. *Holidays, Festivals, and Celebrations of the World Dictionary,* 2nd ed., 1997.

Miles, Clement A. *Christmas in Ritual and Tradition, Christian and Pagan,* 1990.

Purdy, Susan. *Festivals for You to Celebrate,* 1969.

Santino, Jack. *All Around the Year,* 1994.

Schmidt, Leigh Eric. *Consumer Rites: The Buying and Selling of American Holidays,* 1995.

Tuleja, Tad. *Curious Customs: The Stories Behind 296 Popular American Rituals,* 1987.

# *Chrysanthemum Festival*
## *(Jugoya)*

**Type of Holiday:** Calendar, Promotional

**Date of Observation:** Ninth month of the Buddhist lunar calendar

**Where Celebrated:** Japan, Korea, Okinawa

**Symbols:** Chrysanthemum, Chrysanthemum Dolls, Mounting the Heights, Number Nine

**Related Holidays:** Chung Yeung

## ORIGINS

The Chrysanthemum Festival was the last of the five sacred festivals of ancient Japan. It was observed throughout the ninth month and often into the tenth month of the Buddhist lunar calendar (September-October). The ninth day of the ninth moon, known as Chrysanthemum Day, was primarily an occasion for visiting one's superiors and expressing concern for their well-being during the cold months ahead. Chrysanthemums were planted in pots and gardens in anticipation of visitors.

For at least a thousand years, the Chrysanthemum Festival was basically a sun festival dedicated to assuring the health of the community by delaying the "decay" of the sun and of mankind's vital powers. Not only was the chrysanthemum an autumn-blooming flower, but its petals resembled the sun's rays. It wasn't until the late seventeenth century that this festival became a national holiday and a much more elaborate event. By that time feudal lords and other wealthy people had taken up the hobby of cultivating new varieties of the flower, especially very large ones. By the end of the Tokygawa period (seventeenth to eighteenth centuries), there were hundreds of varieties, and flower-viewing parties were popular. Depending upon the local climate, the festival might last a month or more.

Today, Chrysanthemum Day is observed in scattered locations throughout Japan, Korea, and Okinawa by eating chrysanthemum cakes (a dumpling made from yellow petals mixed with rice flower) and drinking chrysanthemum wine. Because the Double Ninth (ninth day of the ninth lunar month) is also associated with fear and death, it is considered by some to be a festival of the dead, a time to visit the graves of ancestors and tend their gravestones, similar to the **CH'ING MING** Festival in China.

# SYMBOLS

## *Chrysanthemum*

The chrysanthemum was imported to Japan from China in 386 C.E., after which its popularity spread rapidly. Because it bloomed in the autumn, it was associated with melancholy thoughts, reminding people of winter and of their own approaching deaths. The chrysanthemum was also regarded as a symbol of the sun, which it resembled in color and shape. The traditional Japanese sun emblem became a stylized chrysanthemum on the personal badge of the late twelfth century Emperor Go-Toba, at a time when individual signs or badges were used among the nobility to identify their carriages and attendants. It remained as a badge in the Imperial family, and after 1868 it was reserved exclusively for the ruler and his relatives.

The chrysanthemum is known as the *kunshi* or "nobleman" of flowers. It is held in higher esteem than even the cherry or plum blossom, and its dignity has been compared to the upright character of a true gentleman. Its strong smell and taste make it a good plant for guarding against the evils of the approaching winter, and it is widely regarded as a symbol of longevity and good health. Buddhist temples often use chrysanthemums as an ornamental theme, shopkeepers may have a pot of chrysanthemums on their balconies, and wealthy families sometimes have a separate chrysanthemum enclosure in their gardens.

## *Chrysanthemum Dolls*

In the latter part of the eighteenth century, the art of training small chrysanthemums to grow over a framework led to the popularity of *kiku ningyo* or chrysanthemum dolls. The plants were grown within a fragile network of woven bamboo or wire and trained so that the blossoms would only form on the surface, covering the entire structure with a smooth, velvety coat of flowers in varying sizes and colors. The frame was shaped and posed to resemble a human figure, with the head, hands, and feet made of wax or paste. The dolls were arranged in tableaux, with a background composed entirely of floral objects.

At one time, Edo (Tokyo) had more than 50 places where displays of *kiku ningyo* were held. Other large Japanese cities held such exhibitions in public parks. Eventually the cost of producing the figures became prohibitive, and by the early twentieth century such exhibitions had died out.

It is possible that these huge dolls descended from the primitive grass dolls known as *hammasama*. When thrown into a stream or swift-moving river, these ancient dolls were believed to carry the individual's sins with them as they floated away.

## Mounting the Heights

Chrysanthemum Day is a popular time for "mounting the heights"—going to the nearest mountain or hill for a picnic. According to a Han dynasty legend, a famous soothsayer named Fei Changfang warned his friend, a scholar named Huan Jing, that a disaster was about to occur. Fei recommended that Huan pack up his family, some food, and a jug of chrysanthemum wine and seek the shelter of a high hill. Huan did as he was told, and when he descended later that day, he discovered that all of his livestock were dead. He realized that if he had not taken the soothsayer's advice, he would have been killed as well.

Hillside picnics and chrysanthemum wine remain a popular way of ushering in the autumn and commemorating Huan's good fortune.

## Number Nine

The date of this festival—the ninth day of the ninth lunar month—was originally adopted from China (see **CHUNG YEUNG**), where the number nine was considered especially lucky. Since three is the universal "perfect number" and three times three equals nine, the "double ninth" can only bring the best possible fortune.

The ninth day of the ninth month is also a symbol of "yang," or the positive, masculine force in Chinese cosmology. According to the yin-yang theory, odd numbers are associated with the male principle and the occurrence of two yang numerals, especially when they are both nine, is particularly advantageous.

## Further Reading

Casal, U. A. *The Five Sacred Festivals of Ancient Japan,* 1967.

Eberhard, Wolfram. *A Dictionary of Chinese Symbols,* 1986.

Henderson, Helene and Sue Ellen Thompson. *Holidays, Festivals, and Celebrations of the World Dictionary,* 2nd ed., 1997.

Stepanchuk, Carol, and Charles Wong. *Mooncakes and Hungry Ghosts: Festivals of China,* 1991.

# *Chung Yeung*
### *(Chung Yang Chieh, Kite-flying Festival, Festival of High Places)*

**Type of Holiday:** Folkloric, Sporting
**Date of Observation:** Ninth day of the ninth Chinese lunar month
**Where Celebrated:** China
**Symbols:** Good-luck Charms, Kite-flying, Mounting the Heights, Têng Kao
**Related Holidays:** Chrysanthemum Festival

## ORIGINS

The festival known as Chung Yeung in China has much in common with Japan's Chrysanthemum Day (see **CHRYSANTHEMUM FESTIVAL**). The ninth Chinese lunar month is known as the "Chrysanthemum Moon" because it marks the season when these flowers are in bloom. Chrysanthemum-viewing parties were at one time held by the Imperial Court in the grounds of the Forbidden City on this day. But now the "Double Ninth" is primarily an occasion for picnicking in the hills (see MOUNTING THE HEIGHTS) and KITE-FLYING. In southern China, it is a day for visiting the family graves and performing ceremonies in honor of dead ancestors. It is a public holiday in Hong Kong and Macau.

## SYMBOLS
### *Good-luck Charms*

KITE-FLYING competitions are held throughout China on this day. It is primarily an activity involving boys and men; girls tend to watch from the sidelines, and the women are usually busy preparing the evening feast. Because maneuvering the kites, which are often quite large and elaborate, requires considerable skill, the kite-fliers come well prepared with their favorite good-luck amulet or charm. They may wear the claw of a tiger to make them brave, carry a peachstone to ward off misfortune, or wear a coffin nail tied to their ankle to protect them from accidents.

A jade amulet is considered the best good-luck charm of all. Jade is known as the "stone of the seven virtues," which include benevolence, knowledge, uprightness, power, purity, eternity, and moral principles. Best of all, it never wears out, no matter how often it is used. Before releasing their kites, the competitors rub the amulets in their hands. If they win the competition, they rub the charms again.

## *Kite-flying*

Kite-flying is such an important part of the Chung Yeung festival that huge crowds gather to watch the spectacle. The festival kites, made of silk or paper, are often so large that it takes four or five grown men to handle them. Shaped like butterflies (symbol of pleasure and a happy marriage), fish (health, wealth, and offspring), dragons (male vigor, fertility), and other symbolic creatures, some of the kites have movable eyes, limbs, and wings. As soon as they are in the air, the competition begins. Their operators try to cross each other's strings, pulling and vibrating their own string in such a way that it cuts the string of their opponent's kite. When someone's kite is downed, the spectators yell and cheer. The competition can be fierce, and sometimes the police are brought in to prevent fights. To add to the excitement, some kites have firecrackers attached, which are set to go off after the kite reaches a certain height.

Some of the kites give off eerie sounds as they flutter overhead. This is because they have tiny Aeolian harps (made from gourd-shaped frames of bamboo with slivers of the bamboo plant stretched across them to form "strings") attached. These "singing" kites are a reminder of the Han dynasty general who, when his army was trapped and about to be annihilated, frightened the enemy by flying kites overhead that had been fitted with metallic strings. They made such a strange noise that the enemy soldiers thought they were being attacked by supernatural powers and ran away.

Occasionally a kite-flier will set his kite adrift in the hope that when it falls to earth, the evil lurking within the family will fall with it. Some believe that if the kite flies higher than the string allows, it will bring the family great honor.

## *Mounting the Heights*

According to legend, the custom of climbing a nearby hill or mountain for a picnic on Chung Yeung goes back more than 2,000 years. A famous magician, Fei Chang-Fang, warned his student, Huan Ching, to immediately take his family away from the valley where they lived and up the nearest mountain. Huan heeded the warning, leaving all of his possessions behind. When he returned, he discovered that his house, his cattle, and everything else he owned had been destroyed as Fei had predicted. The Chinese commemorate Huan's escape by going to the highest places they can find and flying their kites. Those who, like Huan, are scholars often spend the day sitting in picturesque mountain settings, composing poems and discussing classical texts.

There is another theory about why people mount the heights on this festival. Because it was observed at a time of year when the harvest had just been brought in, enemies felt free to make war on each other. Groups of men with provisions were sent up to the mountains as lookouts, so they could warn their people of any advancing armies. Long after the need for these expeditions passed, people continued to mount the heights with food and wine.

## *Têng Kao*

Chung Yeung picnickers traditionally feast on chrysanthemum wine and special cakes called *têng kao,* made of glutinous rice, filled with meat, and steamed. The name of these cakes is a play on the Chinese words, which mean not only "cake" but "promotion." The individual who eats them is believed to secure his or her advancement in official life, just as the person who "climbs the heights" advances his or her scholarly knowledge.

## Further Reading

Bredon, Juliet, and Igor Mitrophanow. *The Moon Year: A Record of Chinese Customs and Festivals,* 1966.

Gaer, Joseph. *Holidays Around the World,* 1953.

Henderson, Helene and Sue Ellen Thompson. *Holidays, Festivals, and Celebrations of the World Dictionary,* 2nd ed., 1997.

MacDonald, Margaret R., ed. *The Folklore of World Holidays,* 1992.

# *Compitalia*

**Type of Holiday:** Ancient
**Date of Observation:** Early January
**Where Celebrated:** Rome
**Symbols:** Crossroads, Woolen Doll

## ORIGINS

The Compitalia were moveable feasts, held between the **SATURNALIA** (December 17) and January 5, although in the later Roman Empire, they were traditionally held on January 3-5. The history of their celebration spans 1,000 years, beginning with the primitive agricultural villages of early Rome and ending with the late Empire.

The festivals were held in honor of the *Lares* or spirits of the household and family. They were instituted by Tarquin the Proud, the seventh and last king of Rome, after an oracle told him to make an offering of human heads to the Lares. After the brutal king and his family were finally expelled from Rome in 244 C.E., it was decided that the heads of poppies and human figures made out of straw were a sufficient offering. The sacrifices were held at special shrines that had been built at rural or town CROSSROADS, and the men who prepared these sacrifices had to be slaves from whom all signs of servitude had been removed. Slaves, in fact, were allowed to participate fully in the festivities, just as they were at the Saturnalia. They would often join their master in the feasting, dancing, and merrymaking that followed.

The purpose of the Compitalia may have been purification before beginning the year's work, or it might have been to seek the *numen* or mysterious power of the Lares. In any case, it provided a good excuse for neighbors to get together and celebrate the New Year. In the country, the celebration centered on neighboring farms; in the city, it meant games and dancing that spilled out into the streets. The spirit of this ancient festival survived in the rustic English holiday known as Plough Monday, a time for farm workers to celebrate the completion of their plowing.

## SYMBOLS

### *Crossroads*

The *compita* or crossroads were originally places where the paths of farms crossed each other or where country roads met. Shrines resembling small towers were built there, with small altars facing in all four directions so that the *Lares* or deities who protected each farm would have access to them. When the agricultural villages of early Rome developed into towns, the compita were the crossing-points of the *vici*, or residential streets. *Sacella* or shrines were erected there just as they were in the countryside, and fattened pigs were sacrificed to the Lares. The shrines served as a religious center for the area's inhabitants, including slaves.

The belief that crossroads are holy, sometimes haunted, places is widespread in folklore. They stood as symbols of the place where people crossed from one realm to another and were likely to need guidance. In ancient Rome, the meeting of two or more roads symbolized the "navel" of the world. Statues of the god who protected travelers were often placed there to give direction to those who were in doubt. Sometimes farmers would hang a broken plow on the shrine as a sign that their work had been completed.

## Woolen Doll

On the night before the sacrifices were held at the crossroads shrines, woolen dolls or effigies of men and women—one for each member of the family, with a ball of wool for each slave—were hung on the doors of all the houses in Rome. The doll, of course, had a head, symbolic of a legal identity. The woolen balls representing slaves lacked heads, indicating that slaves were not considered full members of society.

Some scholars think that these effigies were substitutes for the original human victims sacrificed to the Lares. Given the fact that some Romans regarded the Lares as ghosts of the dead rather than benevolent deities of the house and farm, it might have been their hope that the ghosts would carry off the woolen dolls and spare the living.

## Further Reading

Fowler, W. Warde. *The Roman Festivals of the Period of the Republic,* 1925.

Frazer, Sir James G. *The Golden Bough: A Study in Magic and Religion,* 1931.

Henderson, Helene and Sue Ellen Thompson. *Holidays, Festivals, and Celebrations of the World Dictionary,* 2nd ed., 1997.

Jobes, Gertrude. *Dictionary of Mythology, Folklore, and Symbols,* 1962.

Scullard, H. H. *Festivals and Ceremonies of the Roman Republic,* 1981.

# Dewali
## (Divali, Deepavali, Festival of Lights)

**Type of Holiday:** Religious (Hindu)

**Date of Observation:** Last two days of the Hindu lunar month of Asvina and first two days of Kartika

**Where Celebrated:** India, Malaysia, Mauritius, Nepal, and by Hindus throughout Asia

**Symbols:** Games of Chance, Good Luck Designs, Lamps

## ORIGINS

The word *Dewali* is a corruption of the Sanskrit word *Deepawali*, which means "a row of lights." Also known as the Festival of Lights, Dewali is observed primarily in honor of Lakshmi, the goddess of wealth and prosperity. In northern India, it is believed that this is the time of year when Lakshmi returns from her summer home in the country. The special oil lamps that line the rooftops and windowsills of Hindu homes during the four-day festival are put there to help her find her way.

Because it is the most widely observed Hindu holiday, a number of legends concerning its origin have clustered around Dewali, and Hindus everywhere can find something in it to celebrate. It marks the beginning of the New Year for Hindus in northern India, where people whitewash their houses and businesses, open new account books, and pray for success and prosperity in the coming year. Even the poor put on new clothes, and employers sometimes buy clothes for their workers. In other parts of India, Dewali celebrates the destruction of a demon named Naraka by the god Vishnu. This demon might originally have symbolized the monsoon that floods a good part of the country, and Dewali marks the end of the monsoon season. In any case, Dewali celebrations often include burning effigies of Naraka.

In Bengal, Dewali is dedicated to the worship of Kali, the goddess of strength. Spectacular images of the goddess are decorated and worshipped before being immersed in a river, sea, or sacred tank. In Maharashtra, Dewali is a festival to ward off King Bali, the ruler of the underworld. In the Punjab and Mauritius, Dewali celebrates the coronation of Rama (a manifestation of Vishnu) after his conquest of Ravana, the ruler of Sri Lanka who had stolen his wife. The Jains (Jainism is a Hindu religion resembling Buddhism) commemorate the death of their great hero, Mahavira, on Deva Dewali, the tenth day after the Hindu Dewali. The Sikhs (a Hindu religious sect) regard this holiday as a time to celebrate the freeing of their Guru Hargobind Sahib by the Mughal emperor. In Nepal, it is called Tihar, a multiple holiday that celebrates the New Year and Lakshmi.

Dewali is as important to Hindus as **CHRISTMAS** is to Christians. In fact, there is a modern custom of sending greeting cards wishing friends and relatives a "Happy Dewali and a Prosperous New Year." It is a time for showing charity toward others and for making a fresh start at the beginning of the New Year.

# SYMBOLS

## *Games of Chance*

Gambling on Dewali is a traditional activity, certain to bring good luck. According to Hindu legend, the god Shiva played a game of chance with his wife, Parvati, and lost everything. When his son, Kartik, saw how depressed his father was over his losses, he was determined to win back his father's money and reconcile his parents. He studied the art of throwing dice, went to his mother and challenged her to a game, and ended up regaining his father's lost wealth. Now it was his mother who became melancholy. She taught her other son, Ganesh, how to throw dice, and Ganesh defeated Kartik. Deciding that the entire business had gone far enough, Shiva sent Ganesh to bring his mother back home. Instead,

Ganesh found her gambling with Narad and Ravana. Vishnu—who, along with Shiva, is one of the two most powerful Hindu gods—had taken the form of a pair of dice and caused Parvati to lose everything. She was about to curse Vishnu for cheating her when Ganesh intervened. Instead, she pronounced a blessing upon all those who play with dice on the first day of Kartika, assuring them that they will be successful in all of their dealings throughout the year.

## Good Luck Designs

In some parts of India and Malaysia, families draw elaborate designs called *alpanas* on the floors of their homes near the front door to welcome Lakshmi. These good luck designs are made from a special rice flour, symbolic of abundance and welcome. The flour may be left white or mixed with dry pigments to form different colors. The design is usually abstract or incorporates a traditional folk motif like the paisley. Some cities hold competitions to see who can make the most beautiful alpana.

## Lamps

The most outstanding feature of Dewali is the constant illumination by lamps, bonfires, and fireworks. People line their houses, courtyards, roofs, and gardens with oil-filled earthen lamps (called *dipas*), candles, or electric bulbs. Some buildings even use neon lights. But even where electric lights are used, it is customary to leave an open lamp of burnt clay filled with *ghee* or clarified butter burning throughout the night at the nearest place of worship so that Lakshmi will feel welcome and will be able to find her way home.

The custom of burning lamps originated with the Vaishnavas—those who worship Vishnu as the supreme god and who observe Dewali in honor of the coronation of Rama, the greatest of India's hero-kings and the seventh incarnation of Vishnu. On the night of the coronation, it is said that the entire countryside was illuminated by lights to symbolize Rama's role in leading the world from darkness to light.

In Bengal, Dewali lights take the form of lit torches held on long poles. Here it is believed that Dewali marks the beginning of the night of the *Pitris* (souls of the departed ancestors), and the torches are intended to guide them.

The best illuminations can be seen in Bombay and in Amritsar, where the famous Golden Temple is lit in the evening with thousands of glittering lamps placed along the steps of the huge tank or sacred pool.

## Further Reading

Gupte, Rai Bahadur B. A. *Hindu Holidays and Ceremonials*, 1916.

Henderson, Helene and Sue Ellen Thompson. *Holidays, Festivals, and Celebrations of the World Dictionary*, 2nd ed., 1997.

MacDonald, Margaret R., ed. *The Folklore of World Holidays*, 1992.

Oki, Morihiro. *India: Fairs and Festivals,* 1989.

Purdy, Susan. *Festivals for You to Celebrate*, 1969.

Sharma, Brijendra Nath. *Festivals of India*, 1978.

Sivananda, Swami. *Hindu Fasts and Festivals*, 1983.

Thomas, Paul. *Festivals and Holidays in India*, 1971.

# *Dionysia*
## *(Bacchanalia)*

**Type of Holiday:** Ancient or pagan
**Date of Observation:** Various
**Where Celebrated:** Greece
**Symbols:** Bull, Goat, Thyrsus, Winnowing Fan

## ORIGINS

There were actually a series of festivals in ancient Greece held in honor of Dionysus, the god of wine, fertility, and drama. In the fall there was the Oschophoria ("carrying of the grape cluster"), which included a footrace for young men. The rustic Dionysia was held in December or January at the first tasting of the new wine. The Lenaea, held in Athens in January or February (Dionysus was sometimes known as Lenaeus), included a procession of jesting citizens through the city. The Anthesteria, observed in February or March, celebrated the beginning of spring and the maturing of the wine stored during the previous year. Best known of all was the Great Dionysia, held in the spring (March-April) in Athens for five or six days. It featured the performance of new tragedies, comedies, and satiric dramas at the Theater of Dionysus on the side of the Acropolis.

According to mythology, Dionysus was the offspring of Zeus and Semele. When Semele died in the sixth or seventh month of her pregnancy, Zeus saved the infant by keeping him in his thigh until the full nine-month term was up. When the child was reborn from his father's thigh, he was given to Semele's sister, Ino, and her husband, Athamas, to rear. Hera, whose intense jealousy was originally responsible for Semele's death, drove Athamas mad, and the care of Dionysus was transferred to the nymphs on Mount Nysa. Roaming freely over the mountain, Dionysus tasted the wild vine and discovered how to extract its juice.

Like other vegetation gods, Dionysus was believed to have died a violent death. In one myth, he is attacked by the Titans with knives to punish him for mocking his father. He keeps changing form, appearing first as a young man, then a lion, a horse, and a serpent. It is finally in the form of a BULL that he is cut to pieces. In some versions of the myth, he is pieced together again, or rises from the dead and ascends to heaven. His resurrection was believed to ensure the regeneration of plants and the fertility of animals in springtime. At the festivals in his honor, Dionysus' death and resurrection were reenacted by killing a BULL (or GOAT) and then stuffing and setting up the slain animal, as was customary at the Athenian **BOUPHONIA**.

The Dionysia came to Greece by way of Egypt. Because the Greeks already had other fertility gods, the Dionysian rites there focused on wine and the exhilaration it produced. There were obscene songs and dances designed to magically stimulate plant growth, and sex orgies whose original purpose may have been to induce fertility in the fields. Peasants and shepherds dressed in animal skins and pretended they were Satyrs. The spring rituals in honor of Dionysus included a procession into the fields led by a maiden carrying a phallus and followed by the farmer, his wife, and his daughters, all of them singing bawdy songs. When the worship of Dionysus was introduced into Rome (where he was known as Bacchus, and his festival as the Bacchanalia), the debauchery eventually reached the point where it resulted in a wave of crime and immorality throughout Italy. The Roman authorities cracked down on such behavior and instituted a death penalty for anyone who failed to obey the new restrictions.

Just as wine could make people either high spirited or drunk and irresponsible, Dionysus was both a merry god who inspired great poetry and a cruel god. His festivals therefore combine elements of bloodshed and revelry. He is usually shown as an effeminate young man wearing a crown of vine and ivy and carrying a THYRSUS.

## SYMBOLS

### *Bull*

Although Dionysus was a god of vegetation, he was often represented in animal form, especially that of a bull. One theory as to why he is associated with the bull is that he was the first to yoke oxen to the plow, which had formerly been dragged along by hand. But whatever the reason, images of Dionysus frequently show him wearing a bull's hide with the head, horns, and hoofs hanging down behind him. Sometimes he is shown as a calf-headed child with clusters of grapes around his brow and horns sprouting from his head.

The tearing apart of live bulls and calves was a regular feature of Dionysiac rites. According to Greek mythology, it was when he had assumed the form of a bull that Dionysus was torn to pieces by the Titans. When his worshippers killed a bull and ate it, therefore, they were symbolically killing the god and partaking of his flesh and blood, thus securing for themselves a portion of the god's life-giving and fertilizing influence.

### *Goat*

To save him from the wrath of the jealous Hera, Zeus changed the youthful Dionysus into a kid. And when the gods fled to Egypt to escape the fury of Typhon, Dionysus was turned into a goat. But this is only part of the explanation for why worshippers of Dionysus often tore a live goat to pieces during his festival and ate its flesh raw. Although it may seem a strange practice to kill and eat an animal who embodies the god being worshipped, the custom of killing a deity in animal form can be traced back to a very primitive stage of human culture. Goats may also have been sacrificed during the Dionysia because they had a tendency to nibble away at grapevines, and Dionysus was the god who protected the vineyards.

Dionysus is closely associated with Pan, the Satyrs, and other minor deities who resemble goats. Pan is usually shown in painting and sculpture with the face and legs of a goat, while the Satyrs are depicted with pointed goat-ears, sprouting horns, and short tails. In early Greek drama, their parts were often played by men dressed in goatskins.

Whether it was a goat or a BULL that was sacrificed at the Dionysia, the purpose of eating the flesh raw was to physically ingest some of the positive force associated with the god of vegetation. Some worshippers carried pieces of goat home and buried them in their fields to convey to the earth some of the god's quickening influence.

## *Thyrsus*

The thyrsus, a staff tipped with a pine-cone and twined with ivy, is always associated with Dionysus, the Satyrs, and Dionysian revelers. In addition to being the god of the vine, Dionysus was also the god of trees in general, and cultivated trees in particular. Fruit farmers would often set up an image of him in the shape of a natural tree stump in their orchards.

Among the trees sacred to Dionysus was the pine tree. Like other evergreens, it was a symbol of immortality. Pinecones, because they contained so many seeds, symbolized fertility. So the thyrsus was not only a phallic symbol, in keeping with the wild sexual behavior that Dionysian revelers engaged in, but also an apt reminder of the fertility and regeneration in the natural world over which Dionysus was thought to have influence.

## *Winnowing Fan*

A winnowing fan is a large, open, shovel-shaped basket. Until modern times, it was used by farmers to separate the grain from the chaff by tossing the corn in the air and allowing the chaff to blow away. Dionysus is said to have been placed at birth in a winnowing fan, and in paintings he is often shown as an infant cradled in such a basket.

## Further Reading

Cirlot, J. E. *A Dictionary of Symbols*, 1962.

Fowler, W. Warde. *The Roman Festivals of the Period of the Republic*, 1925.

Frazer, Sir James G. *The Golden Bough: A Study in Magic and Religion*, 1931.

Henderson, Helene and Sue Ellen Thompson. *Holidays, Festivals, and Celebrations of the World Dictionary*, 2nd ed., 1997.

Jobes, Gertrude. *Dictionary of Mythology, Folklore, and Symbols*, 1962.

Leach, Maria, ed. *Funk & Wagnalls Standard Dictionary of Folklore, Mythology, & Legend*, 1984.

L'Empriere's Classical Dictionary, 3rd ed., 1984.

Scullard, H. H. *Festivals and Ceremonies of the Roman Republic*, 1981.

Whibley, Leonard. *A Companion of Greek Studies*, 1968.

# *Distaff Day*

**Type of Holiday:** Folkloric
**Date of Observation:** January 7
**Where Celebrated:** England
**Symbols:** Distaff

## ORIGINS

The DISTAFF and the spindle were used to spin flax or wool fibers before the invention of the spinning wheel in 1533. The flax was wound around a short staff known as the DISTAFF, which was fastened at the woman's waist by her girdle or tucked under her arm. The flax would be fed from the distaff through the woman's fingers to the spindle, which twisted it into yarn or thread. When women visited each other, they often carried their distaff and spindle with them to occupy them as they chatted. Sometimes the distaff was called the "rock"—from the German *rocken,* which described the spinning apparatus. When women gathered together to spin, it was often referred to as "rocking."

January 7 was traditionally the day on which women resumed their chores after the 12-day **CHRISTMAS** celebration, which ended on **EPIPHANY**, or January 6. Because spinning was such a basic and essential female activity at one time, it made sense to call the day on which women returned to their normal routine Distaff Day or Rock Day. Some people called it St. Distaff's Day, although the name was a medieval joke. There never was a St. Distaff, nor was Distaff Day really a church festival. But it was widely observed at one time in England.

Men apparently didn't feel the same compulsion to get back to work after Christmas. They often made fun of the women by setting fire to their flax, in return for which they had pails of water dumped on their heads.

## SYMBOLS

### *Distaff*

Because it was the women who did most of the spinning, the distaff became a symbol for the female sex. The "distaff side" was a legal term referring to the female branch of the family, while the "spear side" was the male branch. And a "spinster," of course, was an unmarried woman who had nothing better to do than spin all day.

The art of spinning was so essential and so completely identified with women that the Three Fates in Greek mythology were depicted as three women spinning the thread of human destiny.

### Further Reading

Brewster, H. Pomeroy. *Saints and Festivals of the Christian Church,* 1990.

Chambers, Robert, ed. *The Book of Days,* 1864.

Cirlot, J. E. *A Dictionary of Symbols,* 1962.

Dunkling, Leslie. *A Dictionary of Days,* 1988.

Harper, Howard V. *Days and Customs of All Faiths,* 1957.

Henderson, Helene and Sue Ellen Thompson. *Holidays, Festivals, and Celebrations of the World Dictionary,* 2nd ed., 1997.

# *Double Fifth*
## *(Dragon Boat Festival)*

**Type of Holiday:** Historic, Folkloric

**Date of Observation:** Fifth day of the fifth month of the Chinese lunar calendar

**Where Celebrated:** China, and by Chinese communities in the United States and throughout the world

**Symbols:** Dragon Boats, Five Poisonous Creatures, Hundred Grass Lotion, Mugwort, Red Threads, Rice Dumplings

**Colors:** Red, azure, yellow, white, black (see RED THREADS)

## ORIGINS

The fifth moon of the Chinese lunar calendar is known as the Evil or Wicked Moon. It arrives at a time of year when dry winds and droughts give way to hot, humid weather, creating ideal conditions for the appearance of the FIVE POISONOUS CREATURES. To ward off these and other evil influences, people offer special prayers to Yao Wang, the King of Remedies, whose image can be seen in every village shrine. Yao Wang has the power to save people who are sick, particularly those suffering from fever. Since hot, steamy weather encourages the growth of insects and the spread of infectious diseases, Yao Wang and the other Gods of Medicine are especially worshipped on the "Dangerous Fifth."

The Feast of the Fifth Month dates back at least 2,000 years, when ceremonies were held around the time of the summer solstice to ensure that there would be enough rain. In agricultural areas, these ceremonies were held right after the young rice plants had been transplanted and the torrential summer rains were about to begin. They included special rites in honor of the Dragon God, who controlled rivers and rainfall. Early summer was also a time when ancient people tried to please the alligators, who were believed to be possessed by the spirits of the people they'd eaten. If these spirits weren't satisfied, they might take their revenge by spoiling the crops or sending a plague. The Dragon God may have evolved from these earthly monsters.

The dragon boat races held on this day owe their origin not only to the Dragon God but to a more recent legend. A fourth-century statesman and poet named Ch'ü Yüan was an honest man who tried to expose the corruption of his government. When he realized there was nothing he could do to stop what was going on, he composed a poem cataloguing his worries. Then, clutching a huge rock in his arms, he threw himself into the T'ung Ting Lake in Hunan Province. The people organized search parties to go out on the river and search for Ch'ü Yüan, decorating their boats and striking gongs to ward off the evil spirits. But his body was never recovered. In honor of his sacrifice, the people threw rice on the water every year to feed his ghost. Although Chinese officials have often tried to discourage the dragon boat races, hoping that people will forget the hero who chose to die rather than tolerate corruption, they have never been successful in stamping out this popular holiday.

## SYMBOLS

### Dragon Boats

In ancient times, boats were believed to be guided by supernatural powers. The Romans raced boats at their **MIDSUMMER DAY** celebrations. In fact, water has played an important role in summer solstice rituals all over the world. Paper or rush boats were often brought down to the beach or riverbank and set on fire so that their "ghosts" would carry off evil influences. The notion that sin, illness, and even death could be loaded on a vessel and sent away was both appealing and widely accepted.

The dragon boat races held throughout South and Central China, Hong Kong, and Taiwan on the Double Fifth may originally have been an attempt to appease the Dragon God so that he would send rain for the crops. People may also have hoped that their battles on the water would induce the dragons of the air to do battle, thus triggering rainstorms. The drums and gongs that were sounded during the races were meant to imitate the rumbling of thunder.

The boats used in these races are long and narrow, suggesting the hollowed-out tree trunks from which they were originally made. They are brightly painted with dragon-like scales and decorated with flags, with a high prow shaped like a dragon's head and a raised stern resembling a tail. A single boat can have as many as 80 rowers, depending on its length. One man stands in the bow, as if searching for the body of Ch'ü Yüan, and pretends to cast rice upon the water. Each boat is accompanied by a small band or a drummer who strikes the beat for the rowers to follow.

The earliest dragon boat races were violent struggles where at least one person had to drown as an offering to the river gods—a human sacrifice to ensure the fertility of the fields. Even as recently as the early 1900s, the annual dragon boat competition was outlawed for a period of time because of the large number of fights and fatal accidents that occurred. Today, dragon boat regattas are rare in Northern China but popular in the south, where rivers and lakes are more numerous. Accidents continue to occur, since the boats themselves are so unstable.

The dragon is one of China's most complex symbols. The Chinese believe that the kingdoms of the world are controlled by dragons whose spheres of influence are re-distributed each year at the beginning of summer. They sleep during the cold, dry season, begin to stir with the first warm weather, and then rise up to the clouds, where they gather in groups and challenge their rivals. These battles result in rain showers. In Chinese art, two dragons are often seen playing together in the clouds with a ball or a pearl, the symbol for thunder.

## Five Poisonous Creatures

Many of the superstitions associated with the Double Fifth are designed to ward off the five poisonous creatures associated with this day and with midsummer in general: the snake, the scorpion, the lizard, the toad, and the centipede. Yellow paper charms with pictures of the five creatures are hung over doorways and windows, while young girls wear paper flowers in their hair with images of the creatures on each petal, or hang sachets filled with aromatic herbs (see MUGWORT) around their necks. Paper dolls representing each member of the family are burned in the hope that they will take away any misfortunes that might be coming their way. Sometimes a cloth boy doll is placed on the gatepost in front of the house as a way of warding off sickness.

Many Chinese burn realgar, a reddish mineral that gives off a yellow smoke and a foul odor that is believed to kill insects. In some areas, old women cut red paper into the shapes of the five creatures and place them, along with a cut-paper tiger, inside a gourd. The belief here is that by containing the poisonous creatures, they will not be able to cause any harm. Their evil influence can also be avoided by eating the cakes that are sold on this day—stamped, of course, with the image of the five poisonous animals. In fact, the *wudu* motif is so popular that it is embroidered on everything from vests and aprons to backpacks and shoulder bags.

It is interesting to note that the five creatures vary from one part of China to another, depending on the climate and which insects are considered the most bothersome. The spider, for example, often replaces the centipede or the scorpion.

## Hundred Grass Lotion

It is a well-known custom in China on the Double Fifth to get up early and walk exactly 100 paces into a field. One hundred blades of grass are picked and brought back to the house, where they are boiled thoroughly in water. The water, which is now believed to possess all the virtues of the grass, is strained, boiled a second time, and stored in bottles as a remedy for headaches, wounds, and nervous diseases. It is called the *pai tsao kao* or "hundred grass lotion."

This special medicine loses its effectiveness if any part of the ritual involved in gathering and preparing it is not observed exactly as prescribed. And it must be done of the fifth day of the fifth moon, because this is the only day on which ordinary grass posseses *ling*—spiritual or health-giving properties.

## Mugwort

According to legend, a famous Chinese rebel by the name of Huang Ch'ao gave orders to spare any family that hung mugwort (an aromatic plant whose scientific name is *artemisia vulgaris*) over its door. But the custom of hanging sprigs of garlic or other strong-smelling plants over doorways is an ancient method of repelling ghosts and demons. Leaves of sweet-flag, which are pointed and resemble swords, are also used to ward off summer odors and insects—a real problem in many Chinese cities lacking adequate drainage systems. Why are such odors considered so powerful? It's important to remember that Buddha himself was cured of sickness by the perfume of a lotus blossom.

The custom of hanging up fragrant herbs in midsummer is popular in the West as well. In Russia, Norway, Sweden, Belgium, and other European countries, artemisia is put up on houses and stables to protect them against evil on St. John's Day (June 24). According to an old French belief, such herbs must be gathered on Midsummer Eve (June 23) if they are to be effective.

On their way back from casting RICE DUMPLINGS on the water in a symbolic search for Ch'ü Yüan, people bring with them branches of mugwort, banyan tree leaves, and sword grass. When stuffed in the cracks of the wooden doorposts, these branches are believed to preserve the household from summer illnesses.

## Red Threads

Red is the color of the peach blossom, widely considered to be a powerful protector against demons. Red threads, symbolic of long life, are often tied to the wrists of young boys on the Double Fifth; girls wear these threads or silk ribbons in their hair. Sometimes threads of five colors are used, symbolizing the five elements: wood is azure, fire is red, earth is yellow, metal is white, and black stands for water. The five-colored threads also represent the FIVE POISONOUS CREATURES. The RICE DUMPLINGS thrown into the water in honor of Ch'ü Yüan were originally tied with five-colored threads.

Families give red or multicolored threads as gifts to each other's children. The mother ties them on, but takes them off again after noon on the Double Fifth—a symbolic gesture that represents "throwing away evil."

## Rice Dumplings

Sticky rice dumplings known in China as *zong zi* are associated with the legend of Ch'ü Yüan, whose spirit was not satisfied by the rice being thrown into the river because the river dragon kept eating it. So people started to wrap the rice in palm leaves (*zong* is a homonym of the written character for "palm") and tie up the opening with multicolored silk thread (see RED THREADS). Another method was to stuff the rice into tubes of bamboo so the river dragon couldn't eat it before Ch'ü Yüan found it. Nowadays the dumplings are usually wrapped in bamboo leaves and tied with a special grass.

## Further Reading

Bredon, Juliet, and Igor Mitrophanow. *The Moon Year: A Record of Chinese Customs and Festivals*, 1966.

Casal, U. A. *The Five Sacred Festivals of Ancient Japan*, 1967.

Eberhard, Wolfram. *A Dictionary of Chinese Symbols*, 1986.

Gaer, Joseph. *Holidays Around the World*, 1953.

Henderson, Helene and Sue Ellen Thompson. *Holidays, Festivals, and Celebrations of the World Dictionary*, 2nd ed., 1997.

MacDonald, Margaret R., ed. *The Folklore of World Holidays*, 1992.

Stepanchuk, Carol, and Charles Wong. *Mooncakes and Hungry Ghosts: Festivals of China*, 1991.

# *Durga Puja*
## *(Dussehra, Navaratri, Dasain)*

**Type of Holiday:** Religious (Hindu)
**Date of Observation:** Bright half of the Hindu lunar month of Asvina
**Where Celebrated:** India and Nepal
**Symbols:** Bathing in the Ganges, Durga Images, Ram Lila Pageant

## ORIGINS

This Hindu festival honors the Divine Mother Durga, wife of Siva and mother of the goddesses Sarasvati and Lakshmi. Since Durga has nine manifestations, the festival lasts for nine nights (ten days) during the month of Asvina (September-October). *Puja* means "worship," and the exact time to worship Durga is determined with great precision by Hindu astronomers. It is believed that her spirit lights upon her image for only as long "as a mustard seed can stand on the pointed edge of a cow's horn." This is the moment at which sacrifices must be made to Durga and worshipping must begin.

According to Hindu legend, Durga's mother longed to see her daughter, but Durga was only permitted by Siva to visit her mother for nine days a

year. The Durga Puja Festival commemorates this brief visit and ends with
Vijaya Dasami Day, when the goddess Durga departs. In Bengal particularly, this is a time for reunions between mothers and their daughters or sons,
similar to **MOTHER'S DAY** in the United States.

During the first three days of the festival, Hindus pray to Durga to destroy
all their sins and vices. Once they've rid themselves of their bad habits,
they spend the next three days trying to achieve a more spiritual personal-
ity by worshipping the goddess Lakshmi, who symbolizes purity. After the
worshippers have acquired Lakshmi's pure, divine qualities, they are ready
to attain wisdom. So during the final three days of the festival they worship Sarasvati, the Hindu goddess of divine knowledge. The tenth and
final day of the festival, known as Vijaya Dasami, marks the soul's attainment of liberation.

In southern India, this festival is known as Navaratri, which means "nine
nights." In addition to worshipping the goddesses Lakshmi and Sarasvati,
Hindus in the south take advantage of the holiday to visit their friends and
relatives. In other parts of India, the festival celebrates the victory of Lord
Rama over Ravana and is known as Dussehra (see BATHING IN THE GANGES).
During the ten days of the festival, scenes from the epic poem *Ramayana*
are dramatized (see RAM LILA PAGEANT). In Nepal, where the festival is called
Dasain (or Bada Dasain), the *Ramayana* story is modified to include the
Goddess Durga's victory over the forces of evil represented by the demon
Mahisasura. In the Katmandu Valley, there are masked dances and proces-
sions of priests carrying wooden swords, symbolic of the sword used to kill
the buffalo-headed demon.

Durga is usually depicted as a very tall woman whose skin is tinged with
the sacred color yellow. She has ten arms, each of which carries a weapon
with which to destroy evil, and she rides on a sacred lion.

## SYMBOLS

### *Bathing in the Ganges*

Every Hindu hopes to bathe in the Ganges River at least once before he or
she dies. The water is believed to cure various diseases, to ease the agony of
the dying, and to erase the sins of the living. The word "Dussehra," in fact,
is an abbreviation of the Sanskrit phrase *Dasa-bidha pap hara,* "The destroyer of the ten kinds of sin." A dip in the sacred waters of the Ganges is
therefore much more than a ritual bath; it is believed that merely uttering
the name *Ganga* will purify a person from sin.

Men, women, and children come to the Ganges, which flows from the Himalaya Mountains to the Bay of Bengal, to take a dip. The tanks (or pools) of the river are particularly crowded with bathers during the Durga Puja festival. Those who can't get to the Ganges go to the nearest river, tank, pond, or sea, chanting "Hara Hara Gangey" as they immerse themselves.

## Durga Images

During the holiday, Durga's image is everywhere, usually surrounded by images of her offspring. In Calcutta, craftsmen build huge clay figures of the goddess on her lion slaying demons and engaging in other characteristic activities. Often ten feet tall, with straw-and-bamboo frames, these figures are used in tableaux throughout the city during the festival. On the fourth night, the images are taken down, placed on bamboo stretchers, and carried — accompanied by bagpipers and other musicians — to the banks of the Hooghly River. After being stripped of their clothes and valuable ornaments, the figures are thrown into the water. As they float toward the mouth of the River Ganges, they dissolve back into clay, straw, and bamboo.

## Ram Lila Pageant

For two hours a day on each of the ten days of the Durga Puja festival, the Ram Lila Pageant is presented in every town, city, and village throughout northern India. The pageant portrays events described in the sacred Hindu epic *Ramayana,* based on the life of Rama, son of King Dasaratha. The story of Rama is as familiar to Hindus as the story of Jesus is to Christians, but the audience for this yearly spectacle respond as if they are watching the drama unfold for the very first time. Sometimes neighboring towns will compete with each other to see who can put on the most elaborate version of the pageant.

Audience participation is central to the pageant. In between battle scenes, a chorus sings passages from the *Ramayana,* and the people respond to certain passages by shouting, "Victory to Rama! Death to Ravana!"—Ravana being the cruel demon with ten faces and 20 hands who threatened to conquer the earth until he was killed by Rama. The ten-day pageant ends with the death of Ravana, who is burned in effigy. An image of the demon made of bamboo and colored paper and stuffed with fireworks is placed on a platform and exploded in a great show of flames and noise.

## Further Reading

Gaer, Joseph. *Holidays Around the World,* 1953.

Henderson, Helene and Sue Ellen Thompson. *Holidays, Festivals, and Celebrations of the World Dictionary,* 2nd ed., 1997.

Oki, Morihiro. *India: Fairs and Festivals,* 1989.

Sharma, Brijendra Nath. *Festivals of India,* 1978.

Sivananda, Swami. *Hindu Feasts and Festivals,* 1983.

Thomas, Paul. *Festivals and Holidays in India,* 1971.

# *Easter*

**Type of Holiday:** Religious (Christian). Principal feast of the Christian year.

**Date of Observation:** Between March 22 and April 25 in the West; between April 4 and May 8 in the East; first Sunday after the first full moon on or following the vernal equinox

**Where Celebrated:** Easter is celebrated worldwide, in over 80 nations

**Symbols:** Easter Bonnet, Easter Bunny, Easter Eggs, Easter Fires, Easter Lily, Paschal Candle, Paschal Lamb

**Colors:** Purple is the ecclesiastical color associated with Easter in the Christian Church. It symbolizes the union of love and pain in repentance. Purple or violet is used throughout Holy Week as well as on **ASH WEDNESDAY** and during **LENT** and **ADVENT**.

On Easter morning, the pope puts on his white vestments and lights a large white candle symbolizing the light of the world: the resurrected Christ. White is also the color of the EASTER LILY.

**Related Holidays:** Ash Wednesday, Carnival, Lent, Maundy Thursday, Good Friday

## ORIGINS

It was common during the early days of Christianity to try to attract new converts by blending specifically Christian observances with existing pagan festivals. Just as the observation of Christmas was moved from January 6 to December 25, where it would coincide with the pagan celebration of the winter solstice, the crucifixion of Jesus Christ was traditionally identified with March 25, perhaps in the hope that it would supplant the ancient pagan festival in honor of the vernal equinox.

Many of the symbols associated with Easter have their roots in the ancient rituals celebrating the arrival of spring. The delight that the pagans took in watching the land's rebirth at the end of winter has much in common with the Christian celebration of Christ's resurrection and triumph over death.

The name "Easter" may have come from the Anglo-Saxon goddess Eostre, whose feast was celebrated in the spring and who was associated with spring and fertility.

## SYMBOLS

### Easter Bonnet

Wearing a new hat to church on Easter Sunday was a common practice in the United States during the years when hats themselves were in vogue. American well-known songwriter Irving Berlin celebrated the custom in his song "Easter Parade," written in 1933. Now that women are less inclined to wear hats, the Easter bonnet is not the popular symbol it once was. But wearing new clothes on this day continues to symbolize spiritual rebirth — the new person each individual can become.

In some areas of the United States, the Easter bonnet has been transformed into a decoration for the home. Baskets of flowers, flower wreaths, and straw hats decorated with spring flowers can often be seen hanging on doors at this time of year.

### Easter Bunny

Rabbits were common in pre-Christian fertility lore, where they symbolized the abundance of new life associated with spring. The ancient German goddess Ostara, for whom the German spring festival Ostern was named, was always accompanied by a hare, who may have been the precursor of the modern Easter Bunny. In any case, the association of the rabbit with Easter is probably the vestige of an ancient spring fertility rite.

Although rabbits and hares (their European cousins, with shorter ears and longer hind legs) have never had any connection to Christian religious symbolism, the Easter Bunny's role in the celebration of Easter is an important one, particularly for children. It is the Easter Bunny who lays the eggs that children hunt for on Easter morning, and who fills their Easter baskets with candy. Bunnies made out of pastry and sugar are popular in many European countries, while American children look forward to receiving chocolate or marshmallow rabbits.

The Easter Bunny came to America by way of the eighteenth-century German settlers, who referred to him as "Oschter Haws." Pennsylvania Dutch children prepared nests for this shy creature in a secluded corner or sheltered place in the garden or barn. On Easter Eve, the rabbit would lay his colored eggs in these nests, or in the caps and bonnets that children left out for him. The custom of leaving out an empty Easter basket didn't come along until later.

In Germany, the Easter Bunny lays red eggs on **MAUNDY THURSDAY** (the Thursday before Easter) and eggs of other colors on Easter Eve. In Panama, it's the *conejo* or "painted" rabbit who lays the eggs. He has smaller ears than his U.S. counterpart and is brown with white spots, similar to the markings of a fawn.

Some religious purists believe that the Easter Bunny has done to Easter what the cult of Santa Claus has done to Christmas. Others prefer to regard the rabbit emerging from his underground burrow as akin to Christ rising from His tomb on Easter morning. But no one has yet come up with a good explanation for why a rabbit would lay eggs.

## *Easter Eggs*

As a symbol of fertility and immortality, the egg is an integral part of the mythology of all races, beginning with the ancient Egyptians and Hindus. Among Christians, the egg is associated with the rock tomb from which Christ emerged to begin His new life. Because the celebration of Easter is preceded by the 40 days of Lent, during which eggs and other dairy products are forbidden among Orthodox Christians, it is traditional to begin the Easter meal in Russia and eastern Europe by cutting up an egg that has been blessed and distributing the pieces to each family member and guest.

The custom of dyeing Easter eggs, usually with vegetable colors, is practiced throughout the United States and in northern and eastern Europe. It has become an art form in Poland and the Ukraine, where *pysanki* (from *pysac*, meaning to write or design) are decorated with geometrical or abstract patterns etched in wax (so as not to absorb the color) and applied with a needle or a small metal tube. Russians often exchange eggs that have been colored red, in honor of Christ's blood, on Easter Day. The elaborate jeweled Easter eggs created by Peter Carl Fabergé in St. Petersburg during the late nineteenth and early twentieth centuries were prized by the Russian royal family and other European aristocrats.

Games involving eggs are often played on Easter. In England, "Egg Saturday" marks the beginning of Shrovetide, or the last four days before Lent. Children used to go from door to door asking for eggs or meat, and hurling broken crockery at the doors of those who refused—a custom known as Lent-crocking. Egg shackling, another English custom, involves placing eggs in a sieve and shaking them until all but one are cracked. The owner of the uncracked egg gets a prize. Pace-egging (a corruption of Pasch) refers to the custom of going from house to house asking for gifts of Easter eggs.

Egg-cracking, egg-rolling, egg races, and Easter egg hunts are also popular games at Easter time. In Greece, an egg is suspended on a string from the ceiling while the guests who sit around the table start it swinging by hitting it with their heads, then try to catch it in their mouths. Egg-tapping, where children strike their eggs against one another to see whose survives without damage, is popular in many parts of the world. Egg-rolling is believed to symbolize the rolling away of the stone from Christ's tomb. Perhaps the most famous egg-rolling event takes place Easter Monday in Washington, D.C., on the White House lawn.

Where do Easter eggs come from? According to German folklore, the Easter Bunny lays the eggs and hides them in the garden, although other creatures have also been given credit for the laying of Easter eggs. In France, children are told that the Easter eggs are dropped by the church bells on their way back from Rome.

## Easter Fires

Primitive peoples believed that fire came from the sun and was capable of both giving life and destroying the forces of evil. It was a pagan custom to light bonfires around the time of the vernal equinox to celebrate the re-emergence of the sun after the long, dark winter and to harness its life-giving powers. Torches, embers, or ashes taken from these fires were believed to be capable of stimulating the growth of crops and protecting the health of family members and farm animals.

When Christianity arrived, the tradition of setting bonfires at the beginning of spring was frowned upon by the Church. In Ireland, however, St. Patrick started the custom of lighting and blessing bonfires outside the churches on Holy Saturday night as a way of reinforcing the relationship between fire and Christ, the Light of the World. The Irish bishops and monks who came to the European continent in the sixth and seventh centuries brought the custom with them, and by the ninth century it had become so popular that it was eventually incorporated into the liturgy of Rome. The "blessing of the fire" has now become the opening rite of the Easter Vigil service.

In many Roman Catholic countries, people extinguish their fires and all other sources of light in their homes before the vigil service begins on Easter Eve. A bonfire is built in front of the church, where the priest lights it and blesses the fire. Glowing embers from the fire are then taken home and used to re-light the stoves and the lamps. Sometimes sticks charred in the Easter bonfire are laid on the hearth, where they offer protection from fire, lightning, and hail. Others are placed in the fields or gardens to preserve them from blight. Ashes from the Easter bonfire, often mixed together with ashes from the consecrated palms distributed on Palm Sunday, are sometimes mixed with the seed at sowing time, or sprinkled in with the cattle's drinking water to protect them from disease. The many superstitions associated with the Easter fires is strong evidence of their link to the old pagan fires of spring.

In Holland, Luxembourg, and several other European countries, worshippers carry wax candles to church on Easter Eve. One by one, they light their candles from the great PASCHAL CANDLE on the altar, until the entire church is illuminated by their flames.

Easter bonfires are still common in the Alpine regions of Austria, where they can be seen burning on the mountaintops after sunset on Holy Saturday, and where they are accompanied by children carrying lighted torches and bands of musicians playing sacred hymns. In western Sweden, the fires are usually built near the center of the village, where the singing, dancing, and merrymaking can last all night.

The alchemists of the Middle Ages regarded fire as an agent of transformation, since all things derived from and returned to fire. Among Christians, the light from the candles or fires lit on Easter Eve symbolizes Christ's resurrection and rebirth.

## Easter Lily

The flower commonly referred to as the Easter lily was brought to the United States in the 1880s from Bermuda. Although it was not originally associated with Easter, it was so named because it flowered around this time of year. Lilies in general were a symbol of purity in medieval iconography, and the Bible mentions them frequently as representative of beauty, perfection, and goodness.

Americans were quick to attribute symbolic value to the fact that this particular plant produced its impressive white flowers at a time that more or less coincided with the celebration of the resurrection of Christ. And because it grows from a bulb that is "buried" and then "reborn," it serves as a perfect emblem of the death and rebirth of the Savior. With their trumpet-shaped blooms suggesting the angel Gabriel's horn, lilies herald both the coming of spring and the celebration of the greatest Christian feast. They can be seen decorating homes and churches throughout the Easter season.

## Paschal Candle

The earliest celebrations of Easter in Jerusalem featured a ceremony known as the "Illumination": the lighting of a candle at the beginning of the Easter Vigil or Night Watch on the eve of Easter Sunday. The blessing of the new fire (see EASTER FIRES) and the lighting of the Paschal candle is an adaptation of this ancient rite. As far back as the fourth century, a large candle decorated with five grains of incense (symbolizing the five wounds that Jesus received on the cross) was blessed on Easter Eve and lit with newly blessed fire to symbolize Christ and spiritual illumination.

In Roman Catholic and other Christian churches, the Paschal candle usually stands at the side of the altar during the Easter service. Placed there on Holy Saturday (the day before Easter), it is removed on **ASCENSION DAY** and brought back for a final appearance on **PENTECOST**.

In medieval times, parishes would compete with each other to see who could make the largest Paschal candle. One used at the altar in Salisbury, England, in 1517 measured more than 30 feet high. A giant candle made in 1558 for the altar at Westminster Abbey in London required 300 pounds of wax. After Pentecost, the huge candles were usually melted down and made into narrow tapers for funerals of the poor.

## Paschal Lamb

The name "Pasch," which means Easter, derives from the Hebrew *pesach* or **PASSOVER**, which commemorates the deliverance of the people of Israel the night before their departure from Egypt. The Angel of God killed the first-born sons of all the Egyptian families but passed over the houses of the Israelites, whose doors had been marked with the blood of a young lamb. That evening, the Israelite families roasted the lamb and ate it with unleavened bread and bitter herbs. Jews still repeat this rite every year on the night before Passover.

The fact that Christ died on Passover Day forged a strong link between the Jewish feast and the Christian observation of Easter. The lamb sacrificed on the eve of Passover was later identified with the "Lamb of God, who takes away the sins of the world" (John 1:29). As a symbol that can be traced back to the Book of Enoch, the lamb signifies purity, innocence, and meekness as well as unwarranted sacrifice—qualities closely identified with Christ.

Christians all over the world traditionally serve lamb for Easter dinner. In parts of Greece, the master of the house selects the Paschal lamb from among his own flock, usually choosing the male with the whitest fleece. It is common in many European countries to serve a cake or an ice in the shape of a Paschal lamb, and the Paschal lamb candies made in Palermo, Italy, are among the most elaborate and artistic of Easter delicacies.

In past centuries, it was considered a lucky omen to meet a lamb, especially around Easter time. According to superstition, the Devil could assume the form of any other animal but never the lamb, because of its deep religious significance.

## Further Reading

Chambers, Robert. *The Book of Days,* 1862; repr. 1990.

Cirlot, J. E. *A Dictionary of Symbols,* 1962.

Crim, Keith. *The Perennial Dictionary of World Religions,* 1981.

Dobler, Lavinia. *Customs and Holidays Around the World,* 1962.

Frazer, Sir James. *The Golden Bough* [abridged], 1959.

Hazeltine, Alice Isabel, and Elva Sophronia Smith. *The Easter Book of Legends and Stories,* 1947; repr. 1992.

Henderson, Helene and Sue Ellen Thompson. *Holidays, Festivals, and Celebrations of the World Dictionary,* 2nd ed., 1997.

James, E. O. *Seasonal Feasts and Festivals,* 1961; repr. 1993.

Lord, Priscilla S., and Daniel J. Foley. *Easter the World Over,* 1971.

Santino, Jack. *All Around the Year,* 1994.

Weiser, Francis X. *Handbook of Christian Feasts and Customs,* 1952.

# *Egungun Festival*

**Type of Holiday:** Ethnic (Yoruba)
**Date of Observation:** June
**Where Celebrated:** Nigeria, Brazil
**Symbols:** Masks, Yam

## ORIGINS

The Egungun is a secret society among the Yoruba people of Ede, Nigeria. A hereditary chief called the Alagba heads the society, which celebrates its most important festival in June. Members of the society come to the marketplace and perform dances for the Timi or chief, wearing MASKS that represent the spirits of deceased ancestors. Which spirits are worshipped each year is decided by the Ifa oracle. A man who is instructed by the oracle to worship his ancestor has a special mask made for the dance. Although he himself doesn't participate in the dance, he is considered the owner of the mask. He takes it to the Alagba, along with appropriate gifts, and the Alagba secretly appoints a member of the Egungun society to wear it during the festival.

About 30 masqueraders in long, colorful robes gather in a grove not far from town and then arrive as a group to perform their dance in the marketplace. Some Egungun dance in one place, while others make sudden movements toward the surrounding spectators. When one leaps forward, the young men acting as guards lash out with their whips to prevent anyone from coming near the masked figure. The high point of the festival is the appearance of Andu, the most important and powerful mask. The other masqueraders clear a path for him, and the drums beat louder and faster as Andu rushes into the marketplace.

It is the Egungun who listen to the requests of the living and carry their messages back to the ancestral community in heaven. Women who are having difficulty conceiving, for example, frequently ask the masked figures to grant them children. The responses of the Egungun can be fierce as well as generous. They expect their descendants to uphold the highest moral standards and are quick to expose the evil thoughts that neighbors harbor against one another. Even though the annual appearance of the Egungun in the streets of Yoruba towns and villages inspires a certain amount of fear, it also assures the people of their continued guidance.

The word "Egungun" is sometimes translated literally as "bone" or "skeleton." This is probably the result of a misunderstanding of the correct tone, since Yoruba is a tonal language. When the word is pronounced with the correct tone, it means "masqueraders." Today there is a thriving community of Egungun worshippers in Salvador da Bahia, Brazil, where they wear the colorful costumes of their Nigerian counterparts.

## SYMBOLS

### Masks

Some of the Egungun masks consist of colored cloth and leather that cover the entire body while the dancer looks out through a closely knitted net. Others are wooden masks worn in front of the face, and still others are carved heads worn on top of the dancer's own head. The mask-wearers are always accompanied by men holding sticks or whips who keep the crowd from getting too close. This is because it is considered extremely dangerous to approach the spirits of the deceased. According to an old Yoruban proverb, "Even a Prince cannot go near an Egungun with impunity." At one time, anyone who saw even part of the man who was wearing the mask could be put to death as a punishment.

Each mask represents the spirit of a particular ancestor. In reality, everyone knows that there is a human being beneath the mask. But it is believed that the spirit of the deceased may be persuaded to enter into the masquerader while he is dancing. At the height of the dance, every true Egungun enters into a trance-like state and speaks with a voice he has never used before.

### Yam

The Yoruba honor the annual return of the ancestors to the world of the living during the season of the yam harvest. Their arrival not only brings a blessing upon the crops, but stands as a reminder that it was the ancestors who first cultivated Yoruba land.

When a Yoruba man dies, the Egungun are especially concerned about the separation of the dead from their former life. So after a certain amount of time has elapsed, the widow is led to a mound of earth that represents her husband. From this she takes a yam, which symbolizes the last gift she will receive from him. Then, a week or so later, one of the Egungun visits her house and calls to the dead person in a high-pitched or nasal voice. This is a signal for the dead person to leave the earth and his family behind.

## Further Reading

Henderson, Helene and Sue Ellen Thompson. *Holidays, Festivals, and Celebrations of the World Dictionary*, 2nd ed., 1997.

King, Noel Q. *Religions of Africa: A Pilgrimage into Traditional Religions*, 1970.

MacDonald, Margaret R., ed. *The Folklore of World Holidays*, 1992.

Murphy, Joseph M. *Santería: African Spirits in America*, 1988.

# Epiphany, Feast of the
### (Twelfth Day, Three Kings' Day, Feast of Jordan)

**Type of Holiday:** Religious (Christian)

**Date of Observation:** January 6

**Where Celebrated:** Europe, Great Britain, Greece, South America, and throughout the Christian world

**Symbols:** Befana; Blessing of the Waters; Gold, Frankincense, and Myrrh; Kings' Cake; Magi

**Related Holidays:** Christmas, Twelfth Night

## ORIGINS

The word Epiphany means "manifestation" or "showing." In the ancient Greek and Roman world, the term *epiphaneia* referred to an occasion on which a king or emperor made an official state visit to a city, showing himself publicly to his people. Early Christians celebrated the birth of Jesus on this day—the day on which God manifested himself in human form. Nowadays Christians celebrate the Nativity on **CHRISTMAS**, December 25. But the original celebration took place on January 6, a date that coincided with an ancient Egyptian **WINTER SOLSTICE** festival held in honor of the sun god. As was often the case, early Church officials simply replaced this pagan festival with a Christian feast.

The feast of the Epiphany started out as a nativity celebration and stayed that way for more than 200 years. It came to Europe during the fourth century, at about the same time that the new feast of Christmas was being established in Rome. Once Christmas took hold, the purpose of Epiphany shifted. In the Western Church, it became a celebration of the adoration of the Magi—the day on which the three Wise Men reached the manger in Bethlehem and worshipped the Christ Child. In the East, it became a celebration of Christ's baptism in the River Jordan, when the Holy Spirit descended in the form of a dove and proclaimed him the Son of God. For this reason, it is sometimes referred to as either Three Kings' Day or the Feast of Jordan. Both represent occasions on which the divinity of Jesus was manifested or revealed to humankind.

For most of the Christian world today, Epiphany marks the end of the "Twelve Days of Christmas"—an appropriate time to take down Christmas decorations and greenery. In some countries, it is the day on which the last gift of the holiday season is exchanged.

## SYMBOLS

### Befana

According to an old Italian legend, Befana was sweeping her house when the Magi stopped by on their way to Bethlehem to bring gifts to the Christ Child. They invited her to come along with them, but she said she was too busy. She later regretted her decision and tried to catch up with them, but she got lost and never reached the manger. Every year she passes through Italy in her continuing search for the *Bambino*, hoping that each child to whom she brings gifts is the one she has been seeking.

The name Befana is actually a corruption of the Italian word for Epiphany. She is a cross between a witch and a fairy queen, and she plays much the same role in Italy as Santa Claus does in the United States. Children write letters to her, asking for specific presents. She slides down the chimney on Epiphany Eve and fills their socks and shoes with toys. If they misbehave, their parents threaten to tell La Befana to leave only pebbles, charcoal, or ashes. In most Italian cities and towns, young people gather in the streets on Epiphany to honor La Befana with trumpets, tambourines, drums, and tin horns—a survival, perhaps, of the pagan custom of scaring off demons with loud noises.

### Blessing of the Waters

In the East, the custom of blessing the waters on Epiphany goes back to the holiday's origins as a commemoration of Christ's baptism in the River Jordan. It is traditional there to bless both the baptismal water in the church and the waters of a nearby river or fountain. In Egypt, the Nile was blessed on this day for many centuries. The entire Christian population would plunge into its waters three times, then drive their cattle and other farm animals into the river. In Rome, the water that was blessed in the church on this day was believed to stay fresh all year.

The Blessing of the Waters remains an important symbolic act on Epiphany in all countries where the Greek Orthodox Church prevails. In Greece, the "Great Blessing" is an elaborate celebration in seaports and coastal towns, where people depend on the water for their livelihood. Sometimes a cross is thrown into the water and people dive after it, struggling to see who can bring it to the surface. After the cross has been recovered, the people take home some of the sanctified water to drink and to sprinkle around their homes and fields. The priest may bless a container of clean water before immersing a cross and raising it again, symbolizing the baptism of Christ. Holy water drawn on this day is used for baptisms and other sacraments throughout the year.

Some scholars believe that the practice of blessing the waters is actually a Christianized version of a primitive ritual designed to encourage rain by imitating a good drenching.

## Gold, Frankincense, and Myrrh

Although most of the details surrounding the story of Three Magi have been invented over the centuries, the three gifts that they bring to the Christ Child are specifically mentioned in the Bible as "gold, frankincense, and myrrh." Gold is symbolic of royalty and therefore a tribute to Christ's kingship. Frankincense, a gum used as incense, is a symbol of purification and stands for His divinity. Myrrh, a burial spice, is symbolic of death and represents Christ's eventual suffering and death on the cross.

## Kings' Cake

Serving a cake in which a bean or charm has been hidden is an old Epiphany tradition that can be traced back to the large plum cake served at the ancient Roman **SATURNALIA**. Whoever found the bean hidden in his piece of plum cake was dubbed "King of the Bean" and ruled over the festivities for the next 12 days. The bean was considered a sacred vegetable in ancient times.

In France, where Epiphany is called *Le Jour des Rois* (Day of the Kings), the *Galette des Rois* or Kings' Cake is a puff pastry cake in which a bean (*fève*)has been concealed. Whoever finds it is crowned *Roi de la Fève*. If it's a girl, she becomes the Queen and must choose a King. It is customary to save a portion of the cake and set it aside for the Magi, a particular saint, or the Lord himself. This portion, called *la part du bon Dieu,* was usually given to the poor after the feast was over. The French Kings' Cake goes back at least as far as the thirteenth century, and similar customs can be found in Austria, Germany, Holland, England, and Canada. Sometimes a bean and a pea are hidden in the cake. The person who finds the pea is crowned Queen, with the bean going to the King. In Macedonia, a "St. Basil's Cake" is served on New Year's Eve, with a coin and a cross of green twigs baked inside. Whoever finds either one will prosper during the coming year.

The first Kings' Cakes were made of flour, honey, ginger, and pepper; some were ordinary plum cakes. By the end of the eighteenth century, however, they were elaborately decorated confections with brightly colored figures made of sugar or plaster. In England under the reign of King George IV, these very expensive cakes were displayed in every confectioner's shop in London.

## *Magi*

The Three Kings or Magi who play such an important role in the story of Christ's birth are largely fictitious creations. They are believed to have been wise men famous for their knowledge of astrology and astronomy. On the night of Christ's birth, they noticed a star shining in the west, more brightly than any star they had ever seen before. They decided to follow it, and when it stood still over Bethlehem, they found the Christ Child in the manger.

The Bible doesn't say anything about how many Wise Men there were, what they were named, or where they came from. The word "Magi" comes from the Latin meaning "magician" or "astrologer," and the earliest pictures of the Wise Men show them dressed quite differently from the kings' robes in which they began to appear from the tenth century onward. Their names—Caspar, Melchior, and Balthasar—were not standardized until the Middle Ages, and in early Christian paintings and mosaics there are often as many as 12 of them. But the Bible says that they offered three gifts to the Christ Child, which is probably why their number was eventually fixed at three.

Caspar, who is young and beardless with a ruddy complexion, is said to have been the king of Tarsus (southern Turkey), the land of myrrh (see GOLD, FRANKINCENSE, AND MYRRH). Melchior, often depicted as an old man with white hair and a long beard, is said to have been the king of Arabia, the land of gold. Balthasar, of dark complexion with a heavy beard, came from Saba (near modern-day Yemen), a land where frankincense flowed from the trees. Together the Three Kings symbolize the three races of humankind, descended from Noah's sons Ham, Shem, and Japheth.

Legend has it that many years after their trip to Bethlehem, the Magi were visited by St. Thomas, who instructed them in the ways of Christianity and baptized them. They were then ordained to the priesthood and later made bishops. At the end of their lives, the Star of Bethlehem appeared one more time, and they were reunited. Their relics were brought to Constantinople in the fifth century, transferred to Milan a hundred years later, and eventually deposited in Cologne, Germany. Their shrine there is a popular destination for pilgrimages.

In Italy and Spanish-speaking countries, toy store employees can often be seen dressed up as the Magi on Epiphany Day, delivering gifts to children. In Madrid, groups of people roam about on Epiphany Eve with bells and pots and pans, carrying torches and tall ladders to help them see whether the Three Kings are on their way.

## Further Reading

Crippen, T. G. *Christmas and Christmas Lore,* 1990.

Ferguson, George. *Signs and Symbols in Christian Art,* 1954.

Harper, Howard V. *Days and Customs of All Faiths,* 1957.

Henderson, Helene and Sue Ellen Thompson. *Holidays, Festivals, and Celebrations of the World Dictionary,* 2nd ed., 1997.

Ickis, Marguerite. *The Book of Festivals and Holidays the World Over,* 1970.

Ickis, Marguerite. *The Book of Religious Holidays and Celebrations,* 1966.

Leach, Maria, ed. *Funk & Wagnalls Standard Dictionary of Folklore, Mythology & Legend,* 1984.

Metford, J. C. J. *The Christian Year,* 1991.

Miles, Clement A. *Christmas in Ritual and Tradition,* 1990.

Monks, James L. *Great Catholic Festivals,* 1951.

Purdy, Susan. *Festivals for You to Celebrate,* 1969.

Santino, Jack. *All Around the Year,* 1994.

Spicer, Dorothy Gladys. *Festivals of Western Europe,* 1994.

Urlin, Ethel L. *Festivals, Holy Days, and Saints' Days,* 1915.

Weiser, Francis X. *Handbook of Christian Feasts and Customs,* 1952.

# Esala Perahera
## *(Festival of the Sacred Tooth)*

**Type of Holiday:** Religious (Buddhist, Hindu), National
**Date of Observation:** Mid-June to mid-July for ten days
**Where Celebrated:** Kandy, Sri Lanka
**Symbols:** Raja the Tusker, Sacred Tooth, Water-Cutting Ceremony

## ORIGINS

Observed annually in the city of Kandy, Sri Lanka (formerly Ceylon), this ten-day festival originally honored the Hindu gods Natha, Vishnu, Kataragama, and Pattini. Since 1775 it has also honored the SACRED TOOTH believed to have come from Lord Buddha. Kandy, originally the capital of the independent kingdom of Kandy in the Sri Lankan highlands, is the site of the Dalada Maligava, or Temple of the Tooth, where the sacred relic is kept. The celebration originated in the fourth century, when the king of Kandy declared that the tooth be paraded annually through the city streets.

Although it appears that the roots of the festival were Hindu in origin, over the years the Buddhist celebration has merged with it. Today, it includes delegations from the four major Hindu temples as well as the Buddhist Temple of the Tooth. The highlight of the festival is a torchlight procession about a mile long, involving thousands of participants. Men snapping whips lead the parade, representing the whip-crackers who used to be special messengers to the king. They are followed by more than 200 elaborately decorated elephants, priests in flowing silver and gold robes, Kandyan dancers, flute players, and drummers. A huge elephant known as RAJA THE TUSKER carries the golden casket containing the sacred tooth, flanked on both sides by two other elephants. A canopy is held above the casket, and a white cloth is spread in the elephant's path as a symbol of respect. Spectators from Sri Lanka and other countries — not only Buddhists but Hindus, Muslims, and even some Christians — come to witness the spectacle. The procession is repeated every night for ten nights.

The largest and most important festival in Sri Lanka, the Esala Perahera is more of a nationalistic celebration than a religious one. The king, various government officials, and members of many different social castes in the community all participate in the Perahera or procession, which symbolizes the nation's victory over its enemies.

# SYMBOLS

## *Raja the Tusker*

The Raja (or senior) tusker is the elephant chosen to carry the golden casket containing the sacred tooth of Buddha. Everyone admires the elephant's stately walk, which appears to keep time with the beating of the drums and the rhythm of the Kandyan dancers.

In 1959 there was an elephant stampede during the Esala Perahera. Raja the Tusker was nearly opposite the Queen's Hotel when word was received to turn back. Rather than joining the other elephants in the stampede, Raja went right back to the temple, where it is reported that he assisted the custodians of the sacred relic in returning it to safekeeping.

## *Sacred Tooth*

The sacred tooth is supposed to have been brought to Ceylon in 311, concealed in the hair of an Indian princess, and kept in a temple at Anuradhapura. It was immediately recognized as the island's most precious possession, and the King of Lanka considered it the supreme symbol of his authority. It was stolen once or twice, but always recovered and put back in its shrine. Then in 1560 it was captured by the Portuguese and carried away to triumph to their stronghold of Goa on the western coast of India.

The tooth that belonged to Buddha was reportedly ground into powder, burned, and thrown into the sea by the Archbishop of Goa, a devoted Catholic who considered it a heathen idol. But many believe that it was only a copy of the tooth that was destroyed, and that the real tooth is still enshrined in the temple at Kandy. Those privileged enough to have seen the relic describe it as being nearly three inches high and about as thick as a man's little finger; if so, it could not have come from any human mouth. It is possible that the monks of Kandy found another tooth to replace the one they had lost.

The sacred tooth is housed in seven nesting caskets, carried on the back of RAJA THE TUSKER. When it is returned to the shrine at the end of the procession, a sacred dance is performed there.

## *Water-Cutting Ceremony*

On the tenth and final day of the festival, the Esala Perahera procession is held in the daytime. It ends up on the banks of the Mahawali River just outside the city of Kandy. The tooth is carried down to the river and lowered into a special shelter or decorated boat. There, the priests of the four Hindu temples draw their swords and strike the water. Then they fill four clay bowls with the water and take them back to their temples, where they are kept until the following year's celebration. Sacred dances are then performed to ward off evil spirits and to seek the blessings of the gods.

The Kandy water-cutting ceremony symbolizes the return of the Sinhalese to Sri Lanka in the second century C.E. with 12,000 enemy captives from southern India. Nila, a Herculean soldier, divided the ocean with a blow of his sword, enabling the entire Sinhalese force to walk back to Sri Lanka.

## Further Reading

Dobler, Lavinia. *Customs and Holidays Around the World,* 1962.

Henderson, Helene and Sue Ellen Thompson. *Holidays, Festivals, and Celebrations of the World Dictionary,* 2nd ed., 1997.

MacDonald, Margaret R., ed. *The Folklore of World Holidays,* 1992.

Pike, Royston. *Round the Year with the World's Religions,* 1993.

Van Straalen, Alice. *The Book of Holidays Around the World,* 1986.

Welbon, Guy R., and Glenn E. Yocum. *Religious Festivals in South India and Sri Lanka,* 1982.

# Father's Day

**Type of Holiday:** Promotional
**Date of Observation:** Third Sunday in June
**Where Celebrated:** United States
**Symbols:** Necktie, Rose
**Related Holidays:** Mother's Day

## ORIGINS

The idea of setting aside a day especially for fathers was at least partially inspired by the success of **MOTHER'S DAY**, established in 1914. Sonora Smart Dodd from Spokane, Washington, was listening to a Mother's Day sermon in church and decided that the nation's fathers deserved a similar day of recognition. One of six children raised by her father after her mother's death in 1898, Dodd began working through Protestant churches and local groups in Spokane to promote the holiday. She circulated a petition suggesting the third Sunday in June as an appropriate time and urging people to wear a ROSE that day in honor of their fathers.

Because the petition was originally circulated among ministers and church organizations, the earliest observances took place in churches and modeled themselves on Mother's Day rituals. Father's Day was also seen as a good opportunity to underscore the "masculine" side of Christianity and to remind fathers of their obligation to look after their families' spiritual welfare.

Dodd formed a committee to promote the new celebration by getting political endorsements, answering inquiries from around the country, and staging local celebrations, but the idea was slow to catch on. By the 1920s Father's Day had more or less died out as a local event, and Dodd herself moved on to other projects. But after studying at the Art Institute of Chicago and working as a fashion designer in Hollywood, she returned to Spokane in the early 1930s and resumed her campaign, focusing on the holiday's 25th anniversary observance in 1935. This time she had more success, and Father's Day enjoyed a resurgence — at least in eastern Washington.

The rest of the country, however, regarded it as just another excuse for a holiday. What did fathers want with sentimental gifts and greeting cards? But then the Associated Men's Wear Retailers of New York City took up the cause, recognizing its commercial potential. They set up the National Council for the Promotion of Father's Day in 1938. The council coordinated the efforts of florists, tobacconists, stationers, and men's clothiers across the country to promote Father's Day. "Give Dad Something to Wear" was its slogan, and its goal was to boost sales by increasing the demand for Father's Day gifts.

President Calvin Coolidge had recommended that Father's Day become a nationwide observance as early as 1924. But it wasn't until 1972 that President Richard Nixon signed a proclamation to that effect. By the time Dodd died in 1978 at the age of 96, the Father's Day Council estimated the holiday to be worth more than $1 billion in retail sales.

## SYMBOLS

### Necktie

What Mother's Day did for the florist industry, Father's Day did for the necktie industry. Along with tobacco, shirts, and other typically masculine gifts, neckties appeared on the earliest Father's Day greeting cards, and retailers wasted no time in turning the holiday to their advantage. Knowing that many people regarded Father's Day gifts as a joke, they designed ads showing fathers surrounded by ridiculous or tacky gifts, and then suggested the purchase of a classic silk necktie or pair of socks. Although their ploys were not difficult to see through, such advertising campaigns made it increasingly difficult to ignore Father's Day altogether.

As early as 1920 the custom of giving ties to fathers as a token of affection had already become a standing joke. The women who chose them often showed questionable taste, and everyone knew that it was usually the fathers themselves who ended up paying for the gifts. But the thought of giving flowers was even more laughable, and at least neckties were a more masculine, less sentimental gift. Along with socks, pipes, cigars, and shirts, neckties have somehow managed to retain their standing as the classic Father's Day gift.

## Rose

Just as the carnation became a symbol for **MOTHER'S DAY**, the rose was suggested as the official Father's Day flower by Sonora Dodd in her 1910 petition to the Spokane Ministerial Association. It would be appropriate, she thought, if people wore a white rose in remembrance of a father who had died and a red rose as a tribute to a living father. Although more than 60 years passed before the holiday was officially established, the rose never encountered any real competition as the symbolic flower of Father's Day. People used to joke, however, that the best flower to commemorate fathers would be a dandelion because—like father—"the more it is trampled on, the more it grows."

## Further Reading

Henderson, Helene and Sue Ellen Thompson. *Holidays, Festivals, and Celebrations of the World Dictionary*, 2nd ed., 1997.

Ickis, Marguerite. *The Book of Religious Holidays and Celebrations*, 1966.

Schmidt, Leigh Eric. *Consumer Rites: The Buying and Selling of American Holidays*, 1995.

Tuleja, Tad. *Curious Customs: The Stories Behind 296 Popular American Rituals*, 1987.

# *Feast of Fools*

**Type of Holiday:** Religious (Christian)

**Date of Observation:** Late December or early January

**Where Celebrated:** France, Germany, and other European countries. Observed less widely in England.

**Symbols:** Archbishop of Fools, Ass

**Related Holidays:** Holy Innocents' Day, Saturnalia

# ORIGINS

A mock-religious festival popular during the Middle Ages in Europe, particularly France, the Feast of Fools has much in common with the ancient Roman **SATURNALIA**, observed in late December. Shortly after **CHRISTMAS**, various lower-level clergy and church officials held a series of revels. The deacons held their celebration on **ST. STEPHEN'S DAY** (December 26), the choirboys on **HOLY INNOCENTS' DAY** (December 28), the priests on the Feast of the Circumcision (January 1), and the sub-deacons on **EPIPHANY** (January 6). Collectively, these festivals came to be known as the Feast of Fools because they usually involved irreverent and disorderly behavior. The group to whom the day belonged would nominate a bishop or ARCHBISHOP OF FOOLS, who was then ordained in a mock cere-mony and presented to the people. Wearing masks and dressed in women's clothing, the revelers would dance and sing obscene songs, play dice or eat black pudding at the altar while the Mass was being said, burn old shoes in the censers, and run around the church behaving in a way that would have been unthinkable under normal circumstances. The Feast of Fools eventually developed into a celebration for the poor and lower-class clergy in general, who undoubtedly had a great deal of fun mocking the sacred but tedious rites performed by their superiors.

The temporary reversal of authority associated with the Feast of Fools was characteristic of the ancient Roman observation of the *Kalends,* or first day of the month, as was the wearing of beast-like masks and dressing up in women's clothes. In fact, the Feast of Fools probably represents a combina-tion of the Roman feast of the Kalends of January with other Celtic pagan festivals. The lower clergy usually belonged to the peasant or bourgeois class and were not well educated, which made them more inclined to cling to superstitions and pagan folk rituals. The whole idea of setting aside cer-tain days for reveling and masquerading was probably designed to prevent them from misbehaving during Christmas week.

The Feast of Fools was most widely celebrated in France, although it was also observed in Germany and Bohemia, and to a lesser extent in England. During the twelfth to fifteenth centuries, Church reformers tried to crack down on some of the abuses and even to prohibit the celebration altogeth-er, but it was too popular to be suppressed entirely. Even after it was expelled from the churches of France in the fifteenth century, its traditions continued to be observed outside the church, often at times other than the Christmas season. In the cathedral at Amiens, France, the Feast of Fools was still being observed as late as 1721.

# SYMBOLS

## *Archbishop of Fools*

It was customary for a low-level clerk to preside over the services held throughout the Feast of Fools. He would be given the staff normally used by the official who directed the church's choral services and, dressed in the robes worn by his superiors, he would sit on the real bishop's throne, handing out benedictions and indulgences. He was referred to as the Archbishop (or sometimes cardinal or pope) of Fools.

Aside from being characteristic of the role reversal associated with the Kalends celebrations (see "Origins" above), the Archbishop of Fools may have been a survival of the tradition of crowning a mock king at the **SATURNALIA**.

## *Ass*

The traditions associated with the Feast of Fools were continued by, and eventually blended with, the Feast of the Asses (or Feast of the Ass), which was also observed on January 1, the Feast of the Circumcision. This festival involved a crude reenactment of the flight of Mary, Joseph, and Jesus into Egypt to escape King Herod's order that all the young boys in Bethlehem and the surrounding area be slaughtered (see **HOLY INNOCENTS' DAY**). A young girl holding a baby would ride into the church on an ass, and at the close of the service the priest would bray like a donkey three times, and the congregation would respond in the same manner.

In France during the fifteenth century and later, when the Feast of Fools celebration moved outside the church after being condemned by church authorities as too blasphemous and irreverent, the popular figure of the ARCHBISHOP OF FOOLS was replaced by a *Prince des Sots* (Prince of Fools), whose distinctive costume included a hood with asses' ears. This is believed to be a relic of primitive times, when the heads of sacrificed animals were often worn by festival worshippers.

The ass is frequently portrayed in Renaissance paintings, particularly when the subject is the Nativity, the Flight into Egypt, or the Entry of Christ into Jerusalem. Because the ass represents the humblest of animals, its presence at such pivotal events in the life of Christ not only underscore His divine humility but show that even the lowliest beings of creation recognized Him as the Son of God.

## Further Reading

Ferguson, George. *Signs and Symbols in Christian Art,* 1954.

Henderson, Helene and Sue Ellen Thompson. *Holidays, Festivals, and Celebrations of the World Dictionary,* 2nd ed., 1997.

James, E. O. *Seasonal Feasts and Festivals,* 1961.

Jobes, Gertrude. *Dictionary of Mythology, Folklore, and Symbols,* 1962.

Leach, Maria, ed. *Funk & Wagnalls Standard Dictionary of Folklore, Mythology, & Legend,* 1984.

Miles, Clement A. *Christmas in Ritual and Tradition,* 1990.

Urlin, Ethel L. *Festivals, Holy Days, and Saints' Days,* 1915.

Weiser, Francis X. *Handbook of Christian Feasts and Customs,* 1952.

# *Floralia*

**Type of Holiday:** Ancient or pagan
**Date of Observation:** April 28-May 3
**Where Celebrated:** Rome, Italy
**Symbols:** Beans, Hares or Goats
**Related Holidays:** May Day

## ORIGINS

An ancient Roman festival held in honor of Flora, the goddess of flowers and gardens, the Floralia was instituted in 238 B.C.E. It was originally a movable feast whose date depended on the conditions of the crops and flowers in any particular year at the end of April and beginning of May. In 173 B.C.E., after severe storms had brought disaster to the cornfields and vineyards, the Roman Senate made it an annual festival extending for six days—from April 28, the anniversary of the founding of Flora's temple, through May 3.

The events of the festival included games, dances, and theatrical performances. From the very beginning, the Floralia was characterized by wild and often indecent behavior. Prostitutes claimed it as their feast day, and courtesans are said to have performed mimes and dances in the nude. The obscene nature of the festivities was probably due to their roots in early pagan fertility rites designed to promote the earth's fruitfulness. But when the festival was introduced into Rome, it became a good excuse for excessive drinking and carrying on.

The Floralia, which originally featured small statues of Flora that children would decorate with flowers, is believed to have been the precedent for the Christian **MAY DAY** celebrations and their dolls or images of the Virgin Mary.

## SYMBOLS

### Beans

The temple dedicated to Flora was located on the lower slope of the Aventine, one of the seven hills of Rome, near the arena known as the Circus Maximus. Beans, lupines, and vetches were often scattered among the crowd that gathered there for the festival. It was a common practice at the time to throw all kinds of grain, including rice, peas, and beans, as part of the marriage rite and at the birth of children. Because legumes yield so many seeds, beans were a popular symbol of fertility and wealth. Given the fact that the Floralia was observed in April, the custom of throwing beans is probably a very ancient one rooted in beliefs about the fertility of the earth and of humans.

### Hares or Goats

Hares and goats, which had a reputation for being very fertile animals, were let loose in the Circus Maximus during the celebration of the Floralia. The hare (or rabbit, which is not distinguished from it in terms of symbolism) was known for multiplying rapidly, making it a popular symbol of fertility and sexuality. Since Flora was the patroness of gardens and fields, not of forests and wild animals, the hare and the goat were appropriate symbols of fertility in a domestic setting.

### Further Reading

Biedermann, Hans. *Dictionary of Symbolism: Cultural Icons and the Meanings Behind Them*, 1994.

Fowler, W. Warde. *The Roman Festivals of the Period of the Republic*, 1925.

Henderson, Helene and Sue Ellen Thompson. *Holidays, Festivals, and Celebrations of the World Dictionary*, 2nd ed., 1997.

Scullard, H. H. *Festivals and Ceremonies of the Roman Republic*, 1981.

# *Flute Ceremony*

**Type of Holiday:** Ethnic (Native American)
**Date of Observation:** Mid-August for nine days
**Where Celebrated:** Arizona
**Symbols:** Flute Altar, Sun Emblem, Tiponi
**Related Holidays:** Hopi Snake Dance

## ORIGINS

Like the **HOPI SNAKE DANCE**, the Flute Ceremony takes place over a nine-day period in the summer on the mesas of northeastern Arizona, where the Hopi Indians live. Although the Snake Dance attracts bigger crowds, the Flute Ceremony is just as central to the Hopi system of religion. Its purpose is to encourage rainfall and promote the growth of corn, the primary food of the Hopi nation.

Unlike other Hopi ceremonies, which are performed in the *kiva* or underground ceremonial room, this ceremony takes place in the ancestral rooms of the Flute clan. It begins with a procession into the pueblo led by the clan's chief, who is followed by the Flute boy, with a Flute girl on either side. Other members of the procession include men wrapped in white blankets, men carrying cornstalks, a warrior carrying a bullroarer (which makes a whizzing sound when swung in circles overhead), a man wearing a SUN EMBLEM on his back, a man carrying a rectangular "moisture tablet," and a number of small naked boys. The Flute girls each wear a feather in their hair and two white blankets, one of which serves as a skirt. The Flute boys wear white ceremonial kilts.

Once the procession has arrived at the pueblo, additional rites—which include ceremonial prayers for rain and corn, singing, and smoking—are conducted in the ancestral Flute room. Many of the rites involved in the Flute Ceremony are actually pantomimes of what the Hopis want their gods to do. For example, the priest may scatter meal on the ground or around the FLUTE ALTAR to imitate the falling rain. Pouring water into the medicine bowl that sits in front of the altar from the six cardinal directions of the world (north, south, east, west, up, down) shows the gods that he wants them to send rain from six different directions. Blowing clouds of smoke on the altar shows that he wants rain clouds to appear. And the bullroarer imitates the sound of thunder that often accompanies rain.

# SYMBOLS

## Flute Altar

A special altar is constructed in the ancestral room for the Flute ceremony. It includes a flat wooden arch, the upright members of which are carved or painted to represent rain clouds and falling rain. Ears of corn may be stacked up behind the altar. Other elements include rectangular tiles decorated with rain clouds and other symbols, and figurines representing the Flute Youth and the Flute Maid, the legendary ancestors of the Flute clan. These armless effigies are painted with symbolic representations of rain clouds and ears of corn. In front of them are short, thick, upright sticks rounded at the top and pierced with holes from which small wooden rods project like pins from a pincushion. These sticks, which are sometimes replaced by mounds of sand covered with cornmeal, symbolize the ancestral mounds of the underworld, and the wooden objects inserted in them represent flowers. There are also zigzag sticks (symbolic of lightning), cornstalks, and other symbolic objects arranged around the altar.

There is a zone of sand on the floor in front of the altar on which meal has been sprinkled. In the sand are placed roughly carved bird effigies and a medicine bowl from which one of the birds appears to be drinking. Other ceremonial items include rattles, a basket-tray of sacred meal, gourds of water, and a honey pot. Every element of the Flute altar symbolizes some aspect of the agricultural process, particularly the weather needed for corn to grow.

## Sun Emblem

A man bearing a large feathered disk impersonates the sun during the procession into the pueblo that precedes the ceremonies in the ancestral rooms of the Flute clan. The central part of the sun emblem is about a foot in diameter and made of buckskin stretched over a hoop, with a border of braided corn husks. Eagle feathers and red-stained horsehair are inserted into the border of the disk to represent the sun's rays. The sun shield is attached to the back of the bearer by a cord tied across his shoulders. He carries a flute, which he plays to entice the Corn maids (Flute maids) into the pueblo, just as the Sun, or father of the gods, is said to have drawn the maids toward him in Hopi legend.

## *Tiponi*

An important part of the Flute Ceremony is the unwrapping of the *tiponi*, which usually takes place on the sixth day. The tiponi is a wooden cup-shaped object in which an ear of corn has been inserted. The cup itself is divided into quadrants, each of which is decorated with symbols of corn and rain clouds. The corn that is safeguarded in the tiponi—either in the form of loose grains or on the ear—is a symbol of the seed that the early nomadic tribes carried with them during their migrations, when the danger of losing it might have meant starvation.

The tiponi, as well as the corn it holds, is called the "mother." It is unwrapped very carefully by the Flute priest in a ceremony that takes about an hour. After a new ear of corn is placed in the cup, the entire thing is rewrapped in cotton string and feathers and put away until the next year's ceremony. The old grains of corn are planted later.

### Further Reading

Fewkes, Jesse Walter. *Tusayan Katcinas and Hopi Altars,* 1990.

# *Fourth of July*
### *(Independence Day)*

**Type of Holiday:** Historic
**Date of Observation:** July 4
**Where Celebrated:** United States
**Symbols:** American Flag, Eagle, Fireworks, Liberty Bell, Parades, Picnics, Uncle Sam, "Yankee Doodle"
**Colors:** Red, white, and blue (see AMERICAN FLAG)
**Related Holidays:** Memorial Day

## ORIGINS

The chief festival of summer in the United States, the Fourth of July commemorates the day on which the Declaration of Independence was approved by the Continental Congress in Philadelphia in 1776. For more than two centuries, Americans have been celebrating this historic event with FIREWORKS, PARADES, and backyard barbecues. But it wasn't until 1941 that Congress officially established the Fourth of July as a legal holiday.

The date could just as well have been July 2, the day on which the Continental Congress approved a resolution for independence, or August 2, the day on which the members of Congress actually signed the document. But it was on July 4 that the final text of the Declaration, which had been drafted by Thomas Jefferson, was ratified. John Adams wrote to his wife that the event "ought to be solemnized with pomp and parade, with shows, games, sports, guns, bells, bonfires, and illuminations, from one end of this continent to the other." As it turned out, Adams managed to touch on almost every feature of the modern Fourth of July celebration.

The first celebration took place in 1777. Warships along the docks in Philadelphia fired a 13-gun salute in honor of the 13 United States, and the soldiers who were stationed there paraded through the streets. By 1788, the Fourth of July commemorated the U.S. Constitution as well, which had recently been approved by ten states. The celebration that year featured a parade with horse-drawn floats, one of which was a huge EAGLE carrying the justices of the U.S. Supreme Court.

In 1790 Washington, D.C., was chosen as the site of the nation's permanent capital. President Thomas Jefferson observed July 4, 1801, by opening the executive mansion to guests. This custom continued under subsequent presidents, but the burning of the White House by the British in 1814 put a damper on the practice. Other notable celebrations include the one held at the end of the Civil War in 1865 on the battlefield at Gettysburg, the procession of freed black slaves who paraded through the streets of Richmond, Virginia, in 1866, and the Bicentennial celebration in New York City on July 4, 1976.

Today, not every American greets the Fourth of July with enthusiasm. African Americans, many of whom celebrate **JUNETEENTH**—June 19, the day in 1865 when news that the slaves had been freed finally reached Galveston, Texas, by ship—have often felt that the freedom celebrated by white Americans on this day is not really theirs to share; and women's groups have often pointed out that the phrase, "All men are created equal" excludes half the country's population. Native Americans usually join in the celebration with dances and pow-wows, paying respect to their own ancestors rather than to the nation's founding fathers.

For most Americans, however, the Fourth of July is a day of national unification, a time when political, religious, and ethnic differences are put aside. In some parts of the United States—Maine, for example—the eve of the

Fourth was at one time a popular occasion for pulling pranks, such as stealing outhouses and removing porch steps. Toasts were also popular on July 4, but the Temperance movement in the early 1900s discouraged public drinking. Today the Fourth is usually celebrated by tolling bells (see LIBERTY BELL), listening to patriotic prayers and speeches, igniting fireworks, saluting flags, and watching parades.

It is a striking coincidence that Thomas Jefferson, the author of the Declaration of Independence, died quietly at his Virginia home at noon on July 4, 1826 — the 50th anniversary of the document's signing. John Adams of Massachusetts, another early supporter of independence and father of President John Quincy Adams, died just a few hours later on the same day.

## SYMBOLS

### American Flag

The red, white, and blue American flag can be seen everywhere on the Fourth of July, and its colors carry their own symbolic meanings: Red stands for courage, white for liberty, and blue for loyalty.

The first national flag was raised on a hill near Boston on January 4, 1776, by troops serving under General George Washington. It was called the Grand Union flag, and it had 13 red and blue stripes. Instead of stars, it had the crosses of St. Andrew and St. George, the symbols of Great Britain. After the Declaration of Independence was signed, however, the American people wanted a new flag that would symbolize their independence from Britain. The Second Continental Congress appointed a committee (whose members included George Washington) to come up with an appropriate design. The committee asked Betsy Ross, an expert seamstress and upholsterer, to make them a sample. She looked at the sketch they gave her and suggested only one change: that the number of points on each star be reduced from six to five. The 13 stars, representing the 13 colonies that fought for freedom, were placed in a circle to signify that the Union would be without end.

Each time a new state was added to the Union, a new star and a new stripe had to be added to the flag. By 1792, it had 15 stars and 15 stripes. Congress soon realized that if this practice continued, the flag would just keep getting larger. So they decided in 1818 that the number of stripes would remain fixed at 13, and that only the number of stars would change.

Since Hawaii became the 50th state in 1960, the American flag has had seven red stripes and six white ones, with 50 white stars on a blue background. The flag's colors and design have inspired many nicknames, among them the "Stars and Stripes," the "Star-Spangled Banner," and the "Red, White, and Blue."

## Eagle

The bald eagle is the national bird of the United States and one of the largest birds in the world. When the first English settlers in America saw the eagle they called it "bald" meaning "white"—not hairless.

Eagles have been a symbol of power since ancient times. One of the Egyptian pharoahs used the eagle as his emblem, and golden eagles were perched atop the banners that Roman armies carried into battle. In fact, many Americans felt that because it had represented kings and empires, the eagle wasn't an appropriate symbol for a young, democratic nation. Benjamin Franklin pointed out that the eagle was "a bird of bad moral character" because it was too lazy to fish for itself. He suggested the turkey, a true American native, as a better choice for the national bird.

America's eagle population dwindled as the popularity of hunting grew. In 1940 Congress passed a law forbidding the capture or killing of a bald eagle. Pesticides like DDT lowered the eagles' birth rate, but its use was banned in 1972. Since that time, biologists estimate that the eagle population of the United States has increased from 1,000 to 4,000-5,000.

The eagle appears on coins, postage stamps, dollar bills, and the Great Seal of the United States. On the Fourth of July it can be seen decorating banners, balloons, and Independence Day floats.

## Fireworks

The term "fireworks" was first used in 1777 in connection with the first Fourth of July celebration; before that, they were called "rockets." After 1820, those that were made to be heard rather than seen were called "firecrackers." And in the 1880s, "sparklers" appeared—thin wands that sent off a shower of sparks and could be safely used by children.

During the Middle Ages in Europe, experienced handlers called "firemasters" designed the elaborate fireworks displays used to celebrate military victories, religious festivals, and the crowning of kings or queens. By the 1700s, most firemasters had helpers known as "wild men" or "green men" because they wore caps made of green leaves. Like jesters, they would run through the crowds telling stories, cracking jokes, and warning people to stand back. Then they would set off the fireworks with lighted sticks called fire clubs. Many green men were injured or killed when their firecrackers went off too soon or failed to rise high enough in the air. The largest and most elaborate fireworks displays today—like those set off in celebration of the country's Bicentennial in New York Harbor—are staged by experts who have much in common with the old firemasters.

When fireworks were brought to America, they were used for domestic as well as public celebrations. By the 1870s, American companies were marketing fireworks for private use with names like Roman Candles, Flying Dragons, Sun Wheels, and Prismatic Fountains. The popularity of "at-home" fireworks displays meant that in many areas, the Fourth of July celebrations moved off the streets and into private back yards.

The danger involved in lighting fireworks led to restrictions on their purchase and use. They are legal for general use in only 35 of the 50 states today; even so, there are laws governing what kind of fireworks can be sold and when. Cherry bombs and other large firecrackers have been banned nationwide since 1966 due to the large number of injuries associated with them. The majority of the fireworks used in the United States today are imported from China, Japan, South Korea, and Taiwan.

## Liberty Bell

The bell that originally stood on top of the State House in Philadelphia is known today as the Liberty Bell. When it arrived from England in 1752, it was placed on a temporary stand so its ring could be tested. The bell developed a crack. Some people thought it should be sent back to England for replacement, but it was finally decided to recast the bell in Philadelphia. The original bell was broken into small pieces so the metal could be melted down. A new mold was prepared, the metal was poured in, and the bell was recast. But the new bell had a dull, muffled-sounding ring. So it was melted down again, this time with success.

From 1753 until 1776, the State House bell was used to summon public officials to meetings. There is no record of its having been rung on the day the Declaration of Independence was adopted, but it did ring on July 8, 1776, when Colonel John Nixon, commander of the city guard, read the document in public for the first time. The bell was hastily removed from the State House in September of 1777 because the British army was approaching and people were afraid they would melt it down for ammunition. It was hidden in a church basement in Allentown and shipped back to Philadelphia after the British left the city in June of 1778. It was tolling for the funeral procession of John Marshall, chief justice of the Supreme Court, on

July 8, 1835, when it suddenly cracked for the second time—exactly 59 years after it had summoned the people of Philadelphia to the first reading of the Declaration of Independence.

The bell remained silent until 1846. Then the edges of the crack were filed down so they wouldn't vibrate against each other. But when the bell was rung on George Washington's birthday that year, the crack spread. After that, it was never used again. It was put on display in the State House in 1852, the 100th anniversary of its arrival in the United States. It travelled to New Orleans in 1885, to Chicago in 1893, to Boston in 1903, and to St. Louis in 1904, riding on a flat, open railroad car surrounded by a protective railing. After a final trip to San Francisco in 1915, it was discovered that the crack had widened. The bell has remained in Philadelphia ever since, a symbol of the nation's independence.

At the Bicentennial celebration in 1976, the Liberty Bell was displayed in a modern pavilion on the grassy mall below Independence Hall. On July 4 that year, descendants of the original signers of the Declaration of Independence gathered at the Liberty Bell pavilion. Exactly at 2:00 p.m., they tapped the bell gently with rubber-tipped hammers.

## Parades

The first Fourth of July parade took place on the Potomac River in Washington, D.C., when President John Quincy Adams (1825-29) and a group of American and foreign dignitaries boarded a steamboat and led a procession of barges and other boats up the river to the site of what is known today as the Tidal Basin. Transferring to smaller boats, the entourage floated up the old Washington Canal to the place that had been selected for the new Chesapeake and Ohio Canal. There President Adams turned the first spade of dirt for the waterway that for many years cut through the heart of Washington, D.C., between the Capitol Building and the Washington Monument.

Today, parades are held in almost every city, town, and village on the Fourth of July. Marching bands, fife and drum corps, and members of organizations such as the Boy Scouts and Girl Scouts participate in the parades. Local veterans usually march in formation or ride in specially decorated cars, and floats are used to illustrate various patriotic themes.

## Picnics

Feasting has always been part of July Fourth celebrations. In 1777, grand banquets were held in Philadelphia and other cities to commemorate the first anniversary of the approval of the Declaration of Independence. Eventually the parties moved outdoors, and by the mid-nineteenth century, the Fourth of July picnic had become a national tradition. It usually included sports and games such as tug-of-war, potato races, watermelon-eating contests, and chasing after a greased pig. Favorite picnic foods included fried chicken, potato salad, lemonade, chocolate and angel food cakes, pickles, deviled eggs, and homemade ice cream.

By the late nineteenth century, it was customary for political campaigns to begin on the Fourth of July. Local politicians would often sponsor holiday picnics, offering free hotdogs, corn on the cob, and steamed clams to anyone willing to listen to long political speeches. Political campaigns today don't get under way until Labor Day, but families still pack picnic baskets on the Fourth of July and head to the nearest state park, picnic area, or beach. The games afterward are usually confined to softball, but in some places tugs of war, sack races, and watermelon-eating contests are still popular.

## Uncle Sam

Uncle Sam—the gray-bearded man on stilts wearing a top hat, tailcoat, and striped trousers—is a popular symbol of the United States. But he is not entirely imaginary. The real Uncle Sam was Samuel Wilson, born in Arlington, Massachusetts, in 1766. He ran away from home at the age of 14 to enlist in the army. After the Revolutionary War was over, he moved to Troy, New York, and started a meatpacking business.

Known for his honesty and common sense, Sam Wilson supplied meat to the U.S. Army during the War of 1812. When a group of officials visiting his meatpacking plant saw that all the barrels of beef were stamped with the initials "U.S.," they asked what it meant. A workman told them it stood for "Uncle Sam" Wilson. The story was picked up by the newspapers, and soon people were referring to everything supplied to the army as "Uncle Sam's." The soldiers themselves began saying that they were in "Uncle Sam's Army."

After the war was over, Uncle Sam began appearing as a political cartoon figure. In the 1830s he was portrayed as a young man with stars and stripes on his shirt but without the gray hair, chin whiskers, top hat, or tailcoat that later became his trademarks. Some say that the costume now associated with Uncle Sam was invented by Dan Rice, a clown in the 1840s. Rice also walked on stilts, to make Uncle Sam look taller.

Uncle Sam's appearance was actually derived from two earlier symbolic figures in American folklore: Brother Jonathan and Yankee Doodle. Both Uncle Sam and Brother Jonathan were used interchangeably to represent the United States by cartoonists from the early 1830s to 1861. The first political cartoonist to standardize the figure of Uncle Sam was Thomas Nast, beginning in the 1870s. It was Nast who gave Uncle Sam his chin whiskers. Perhaps the most famous portrait of this symbolic figure is the one used on an army recruiting poster painted by James Montgomery Flagg during World War I. Uncle Sam is looking straight out at the viewer with his finger pointed, saying, "I Want You."

In recent years, some people have criticized the use of Uncle Sam as a symbol for the United States because he no longer reflects the diversity of the American population. But in 1961 the U.S. Congress passed a special resolution recognizing "Uncle Sam" Wilson of Troy, New York, as the namesake of our national symbol. His birthday, September 13, has been proclaimed "Uncle Sam's Day" in New York State.

## *"Yankee Doodle"*

As the unofficial anthem of the United States, the simple melody known as "Yankee Doodle" is played in almost every Fourth of July parade, usually by fife and drum corps. "Yankee" (*Janke*) is a familiar nickname for the Dutch name Jan, just as Johnny is a nickname for John. The Dutch who settled in New York used the term to describe the English settlers of Connecticut, who were regarded during colonial times as people who were more interested in making money than they were in behaving morally. A "doodle" was a simpleton or a foolish person.

Dr. Richard Shuckburg, a British army doctor who was serving in the American colonies, is believed to have written the lyrics for the popular tune. "Stuck a feather in his hat" is probably a mocking reference to the Yankees' attempts to appear stylish and European when they were actually quite uncivilized. "Macaroni" was symbolic of all things Italian, and was used in eighteenth-century England to mean a fop—someone who dressed as if he were Italian. The British loved to make fun of the poorly dressed, poorly educated Americans.

Some scholars think that "Yankee Doodle" derived from a children's play song—possibly a slave song—in Surinam on the coast of South America, whose lyrics went like this:

> Mama Nanni go to town,
> Buy a little pony.
> Stick a feather in a ring
> Calling Masra Ranni.

"Masra" is the equivalent of "Massa"—the way American slaves were taught to address their white "Masters." It is possible that British soldiers heard the children's song and thought it would be a good way of mocking the upstart Americans. But the Americans liked the song so much that they adopted it as their own and, during the Revolutionary War, whistled it as they marched into battle.

"Yankee Doodle" was sung at the first Independence Day celebration in Philadelphia in 1777 and quickly became a July Fourth tradition. Other songs frequently played on this day include "Yankee Doodle Boy" (also known as "I'm a Yankee Doodle Dandy") by George M. Cohan, "America," and "The Star-Spangled Banner."

## Further Reading

Giblin, James Cross. *Fireworks, Picnics, and Flags: The Story of the Fourth of July Symbols*, 1983.

Hatch, Jane M. *The American Book of Days,* 1978.

Henderson, Helene and Sue Ellen Thompson. *Holidays, Festivals, and Celebrations of the World Dictionary*, 2nd ed., 1997.

Hoig, Stan. *It's the Fourth of July!,* 1995.

Ickis, Marguerite. *The Book of Patriotic Holidays*, 1962.

Santino, Jack. *All Around the Year*, 1994.

Tuleja, Tad. *Curious Customs: The Stories Behind 296 Popular American Rituals*, 1987.

# Ganesh Chaturthi

**Type of Holiday:** Religious (Hindu)

**Date of Observation:** Fourth day of the bright half of the Hindu month of Bhadrapada (August-September)

**Where Celebrated:** India

**Symbols:** Elephant, Modakas, Moon, Mouse

## ORIGINS

Ganesh Chaturthi celebrates the birthday of Ganesha, the eldest son of the gods Shiva and Parvati and one of the five major Hindu deities. With his pot belly and ELEPHANT head, Ganesha is the god who removes all obstacles in the paths of those struggling to achieve both spiritual and worldly success. Almost every Hindu home has Ganesha's image over the doorway, and he is worshipped at the beginning of every important undertaking, whether it is the building of a new house, the beginning of a marriage, or the opening of a new account book.

After taking a bath on the morning of Ganesha's birthday, devoted Hindus go to the temple and say prayers in his honor, accompanied by offerings of coconut and sweet pudding (see MODAKAS). The worshippers ask Ganesha to help them overcome the obstacles they are likely to encounter on the road to spiritual wisdom. Beautifully decorated images of the god are carried through the streets and later immersed in the waters of the sea or a nearby river. MODAKAS or sweet-balls are served to everyone in the house.

Bombay is the center for Ganesh Chaturthi celebrations, and thousands of images of the god are made and sold there. Small images are used in the home, but life-size ones are often set up on temporary altars in the streets. These images are worshipped for three days, at the end of which they are carried in procession to the nearest body of water. In some parts of India, Ganesha is the god of the harvest, and after the immersion ceremony is over, sand or clay from the riverbed is brought back to the farm and scattered around the barns and storerooms.

## SYMBOLS

### Elephant

According to Hindu legend, Parvati created her son out of clay and oil, and posted him outside her door to prevent anyone from entering the house while she was taking her bath. When Shiva himself was not allowed to enter, he became so angry he shattered the boy's head. Parvati was inconsolable when she discovered what had happened to the son she had created. His head was broken in so many pieces that no one could find them all. To make amends, Shiva set out in search of a suitable replacement head and came back with the head of an elephant. To this day, Ganesha is known as "the elephant-headed god."

Ganesha also represents *Om*, which is the chief mantra or chant-word among Hindus. The belief that nothing can be accomplished without uttering this sound explains why Ganesha is invoked before undertaking a project. The elephant head is significant because it is the only figure in nature that has the same form as the Sanskrit symbol for Om. Some scholars think that the elephant's head and snout are reminiscent of a farmer carrying a corn sheaf on his head, with the lowest ears swinging to and fro. This fits in well with Ganesha's reputation as the god of the harvest.

### Modakas

Modakas or sweet-balls are symbolic of the sweet puddings that Ganesha was so fond of as a child. On one of his birthdays, he ate so many puddings that when the MOUSE on which he was riding was startled by a snake, Ganesha fell off and his stomach burst open. He stuffed all the puddings back in and tied the snake around his belly to hold it together. As the god of plenty, Ganesha is always shown with a round belly, symbolic of a good appetite and a plentiful harvest.

Modakas are made of rice flour, raw sugar, and the kernel of the coconut, all of which are in season in India during the month of Bhadrapada (August-September).

## Moon

Hindus consider it bad luck to look at the moon on Ganesh Chaturthi because legend claims that the moon laughed when Ganesha fell off his MOUSE and his stomach burst open (see MODAKAS). The god cursed the moon, who was forced to hide himself in shame. After the moon apologized, Ganesha lifted the curse but declared that the moon would always be in disgrace on this day. Those who do look at the moon will earn a bad name or ruin their reputations. But if they do so inadvertently, they can forestall the consequences by making sure that their neighbors treat them badly, thus punishing them for their mistake.

## Mouse

Ganesha is usually depicted riding on a mouse, a symbol of the conquest over egoism. Because he possesses the head of an elephant, the largest animal, and yet rides on a mouse, the smallest, Ganesha embodies the process of evolution—from small animals to large animals and finally to human beings.

Some scholars see the mouse as a field rat, the destroyer of crops, and Ganesha as its conqueror. The snake wrapped around the god's belly, which represents a barn full of harvested crops, is also capable of destroying the field rat. The root of the Sanskrit word for "rat" means "thief," which implies that Ganesha is riding over the thief of the field, or the field rat.

## Further Reading

Gupte, Rai Bahadur B. A. *Hindu Holidays and Ceremonials*, 1916.

Henderson, Helene and Sue Ellen Thompson. *Holidays, Festivals, and Celebrations of the World Dictionary*, 2nd ed., 1997.

Sharma, Brijendra Nath. *Festivals of India*, 1978.

Sivananda, Swami. *Hindu Feasts and Festivals*, 1983.

Thomas, Paul. *Festivals and Holidays in India*, 1971.

# *Gauri Festival*

**Type of Holiday:** Religious (Hindu)

**Date of Observation:** Third day of Bhadrapada (August-September)

**Where Celebrated:** Southern India

**Symbols:** Cradle, Number Two, Winnowing Fan

**Colors:** Red, yellow, white, and black. Yellow is the color of wealth, beauty, and good fortune. In this festival, it appears in the color of turmeric powder, bananas, and the sour rice dish that is served. Red, the color of blood and vitality, can be seen in the vermilion powder, betel nuts, and bright red saris worn in some parts of India. White, the color of purity and continuity, can be seen in the rice and milk that are served. Black is symbolic of death, difficulty, and danger. Hindu women are given black bangles to protect them from misfortune. These four colors define the basic forces with which married women must contend.

## ORIGINS

Gauri is the Hindu goddess of married women as well as the goddess of daughters. She is a form of Parvati, the wife of Siva, and is often described as "the golden one" because Brahma gave her a golden complexion when her husband complained that her skin was too dark. Her festival, which is celebrated by women throughout southern India, involves a series of rituals associated with welcoming, worshipping, and sending the goddess back to her home. These rituals are designed to reflect the typical experience of a Hindu woman, who is born into her family, lives in her parents' home until shortly after her marriage, and finally leaves her family to become part of her husband's household.

The celebration begins on the third day of the Hindu lunar month of Bhadrapada. Women wash their faces, bathe themselves and their children in oil, and decorate their floors with elaborate white line drawings. Then they dress in their best saris and prepare to summon Gauri from her home in the river.

Men are not entirely excluded from the festival. A group of them go to the river with a large wooden CRADLE suspended from a long pole. The ball of sand they put in the cradle represents Gauri, who is taken into the village for everyone to worship. The women bring their trays filled with offerings, each of which has a symbolic meaning or color (see "Colors" above). A comb, for example, symbolizes good grooming, which is closely linked to sexuality and the sexual discipline that women are supposed to exhibit. The feast that follows the principal welcoming ceremony has two required dishes: white yogurt rice (white symbolizing purity, duty, and discipline) and sour yellow rice (wealth, good fortune), which are eaten together, along with various side dishes.

There is a lull of a day or two after the welcoming celebration, during which the goddess's son Ganesha is said to arrive in the village to tell his mother that his father, Siva, is lonely. Because it is taboo to send the goddess away on the second or fourth day of the month (even numbers being unlucky), the send-off ritual is performed on the third or fifth day. The sand ball representing the goddess is returned to the river, certain farewell rituals are carried out at the river's edge, and various foods and flowers are gathered to send with Gauri on her journey home.

The myth of Gauri symbolizes the transition a bride goes through when she leaves her family to live with her husband. The struggles that Gauri and Siva go through before assuming their life as a married couple have many parallels in the marriage negotiations that take place between Hindu families and in the struggles a bride must endure in her effort to be accepted by her husband's family. The women of the village who get together to celebrate the Gauri Festival often take advantage of the opportunity to discuss their own problems and the concerns of women in general, such as infertility, poverty, and desertion. They regard Gauri as married in a permanent way that stands as a model of stability. Since the fear of widowhood is intense among Hindu women, the fortunate women whose husbands are still living do everything in their power to honor the goddess who can help them remain in that favorable state.

## SYMBOLS

### *Cradle*

It is significant that Gauri is brought into the village in a cradle, not on a throne or some other conveyance befitting a goddess. The cradle is associated with pregnancy and childbearing, thus underscoring the festival's emphasis on a woman's experience.

## Number Two

Hindus generally consider even numbers unlucky because they convey the idea of finality. An even amount of money, for example, suggests finality and "no future;" therefore, Hindus in southern India will often pay 101 rupees for an item that is officially priced at only 100 rupees.

The numbers one and two contradict this cultural rule. Perhaps because two equals one plus one and symbolizes non-solitude, it is considered lucky even though it is even. Similarly, the number one is considered unlucky even though it is odd. In the context of the Gauri Festival, the number two symbolizes the fruitful partnership of the married couple. Women celebrating the festival always bring gifts and offerings that come in pairs, such as palm-leaf earrings. Even WINNOWING FANS are never sold as single items, but only in pairs.

## Winnowing Fan

The winnowing fan is used to separate grain from chaff, or useless husks. In India, it is used to produce clean, husked rice, which makes it a logical symbol of separation — the separation of the daughter from her family at marriage — and of purification. Used in the Gauri Festival to hold the gifts that women exchange with each other, the winnowing fans usually contain rice and other grains, salt, a cube of brown sugar, bananas, coconut, betel nuts, and turmeric root — everything that is needed for basic nutrition, with the exception of oil and spices. Such gifts are considered symbolic of nourishment and growth, and the women who exchange them are expressing the idea that each woman's wealth (symbolized by turmeric root, which is yellow) comes from another woman, both in the form of the dowry that is brought into a marriage and in the form of the gifts mothers give to their daughters.

Also known as "wealth-producing fans" or *bhagina mara,* the winnowing fans used in the festival are prepared in sets of four: a pair of fans is filled with gifts and covered with two more fans (see NUMBER TWO). A pair of doubled winnowing fans also rests in the CRADLE beside the ball of sand that represents the goddess Gauri.

## Further Reading

Hanchett, Suzanne. *Coloured Rice: Symbolic Structure in Hindu Family Festivals,* 1988.

Henderson, Helene and Sue Ellen Thompson. *Holidays, Festivals, and Celebrations of the World Dictionary,* 2nd ed., 1997.

# Good Friday

**Type of Holiday:** Religious (Christian)

**Date of Observation:** Between March 20 and April 23; the Friday before Easter

**Where Celebrated:** Throughout the Christian world

**Symbols:** Cock, Cross, Crown of Thorns, Hot Cross Buns, Kite-flying, Stations of the Cross, Tre Ore, Veil

**Colors:** Good Friday is traditionally associated with the color black, a symbol of death, despair, sorrow, and mourning. In many countries, churches are darkened and draped with black on this day, and religious processions often feature black-robed penitents or statues of Christ and the Virgin Mary draped in black.

**Related Holidays:** Easter, Maundy Thursday, Palm Sunday

## ORIGINS

There are several theories as to why the day commemorating Jesus Christ's crucifixion is called "Good" Friday. Some scholars think it's a corruption of "God's Friday," while others take "good" to mean "observed as holy." Although it may seem paradoxical, Christians regard the death of Jesus as "good" in the sense that it opened the gates of everlasting life. Orthodox Christians call it Great Friday, but it's not surprising that the Friday before **EASTER** is sometimes referred to as Black Friday or Sorrowful Friday.

Good Friday commemorates Jesus' journey to Calvary (see STATIONS OF THE CROSS) and His death on the CROSS, which took place on the Friday before Easter Sunday. Christians have been observing Good Friday even longer than Easter, although there was a period when it was neglected by Protestant churches. Nowadays it is observed almost universally by Christians around the world, who devote this day to remembering Christ's suffering and sacrifice.

## SYMBOLS

### Cock

As the bird of dawn, the cock is a sun symbol and stands for vigilance and resurrection. It became an important Christian image during the Middle

Ages, when it began to appear on weathervanes, cathedral towers, and domes.

In the context of Good Friday, the cock is symbolic of the denial of Peter, one of Christ's disciples. After Jesus had been seized by the servants of the high priest Caiaphas as He was leaving the Garden of Gethsemane, He was brought to the palace, where the council tried to find people who would bear witness against Him. Peter was there in the palace while Jesus was being accused. Some of the onlookers recognized him and accused him of being a follower of Christ. But just as Jesus had predicted would happen, Peter declared three times that he did not know the man who had been taken prisoner. When he heard the cock crow a second time, he remembered Christ's words: "Verily, I say unto thee, That this day, even in this night, before the cock crows twice, thou shalt deny me thrice" (Mark 14:30). Peter wept when he realized that he had been unfaithful to his beloved Master.

## Cross

Although the cross is even older than the Christian religion, the cross on which Christ died has become a symbol for salvation and redemption through Christianity. It can be seen in many different forms, but the so-called Latin cross (with a longer upright and shorter crossbar) is usually the symbol for the Passion of Christ. Five red marks or jewels are sometimes placed on the face of the cross to represent the five wounds Christ received when He was crucified. When the Latin cross stands on three steps—symbolizing faith, hope, and love (1 Cor. 13:13)—it is called the Calvary, or Graded, Cross.

## Crown of Thorns

The crown of thorns is an emblem of the Passion and the crucifixion of Christ. As described in the Gospel of Mark, chapter 15, verses 16-18, the soldiers into whose hands Jesus was delivered by Pontius Pilate dressed Him in purple and placed a crown of thorns on His head. Then, saluting Him with mock respect, they cried, "Hail, King of the Jews!" Christ is usually shown wearing the crown of thorns from this moment until He was taken down from the cross.

The way monks wear their hair—shaved on the top and with a short fringe all around—is designed to imitate Christ's crown of thorns.

## Hot Cross Buns

The pagans worshipped the goddess Eostre (after whom Easter was named) by serving tiny cakes, often decorated with a cross, at their annual spring festival. When archaeologists excavated the ancient city of Herculaneum in southwestern Italy, which had been buried under volcanic ash and lava since 79 C.E., they found two small loaves, each with a cross on it, among the ruins. The English word "bun" probably came from the Greek *boun*, which referred to a ceremonial cake of circular or crescent shape, made of flour and honey and offered to the gods.

Superstitions regarding bread that was baked on Good Friday date back to a very early period. In England particularly, people believed that bread baked on this day could be hardened in the oven and kept all year to protect the house from fire. Sailors took loaves of it on their voyages to prevent shipwreck, and a Good Friday loaf was often buried in a heap of corn to protect it from rats, mice, and weevils. Finely grated and mixed with water, it was sometimes used as a medicine.

In England nowadays, hot cross buns are served at breakfast on Good Friday morning. They are small, usually spiced buns whose sugary surface is marked with a cross. The English believe that hanging a hot cross bun in the house on this day offers protection from bad luck in the coming year. It's not unusual to see Good Friday buns or cakes hanging on a rack or in a wire basket for years, gathering dust and growing black with mold—although some people believe that if the ingredients are mixed, the dough prepared, and the buns baked on Good Friday itself, they will never get moldy.

## Kite-flying

On the island of Bermuda, the custom of flying kites is synonymous with Good Friday. It dates back to the nineteenth century, when a teacher who was having trouble explaining to his students how Jesus ascended into heaven took them to the highest hill on the island and launched a kite bearing an image of Jesus. When he ran out of string, he cut the line and let the kite fly out of sight. Flying kites has been a Good Friday tradition ever since.

## Stations of the Cross

Christ was crucified at Calvary, a place near Jerusalem also known as Golgotha, which means "skull." His journey there is usually divided into 14 scenes or "Stations:" (1) Jesus is condemned to death; (2) He receives His cross; (3) He falls the first time under His cross; (4) He meets His Mother; (5) Simon of Cyrene helps Jesus carry His cross; (6) Veronica wipes Jesus' face; (7) Jesus falls a second time; (8) He speaks to the women of Jerusalem; (9) He falls a third time; (10) He is stripped of His garments; (11) Jesus is nailed to the cross; (12) He dies on the cross; (13) He is taken down from the cross; and (14) He is laid in the Sepulchre. Although the number of stations was fixed at 14 in the eighteenth century, five of them have no basis in the Bible's account of Christ's Passion.

The original Stations of the Cross were the sites in Jerusalem and the surrounding area identified with these events. During the time of the Crusades, pilgrims to the Holy Land marked off these sites and, when they returned to their homes in Europe, they erected memorials of these stations in their churches and even their fields. Pictures of the Stations of the Cross can still be seen on the walls of Roman Catholic and Episcopal churches.

The form of worship that takes place at the Stations of the Cross has never been officially determined by any church authority. Sometimes groups of worshippers will pray together at each station and sing hymns as they pass from one station to the next. More often, individuals engage in private prayer and meditation.

## *Tre Ore*

The Tre Ore or "Three Hours" service takes place in many Protestant and Catholic churches on Good Friday. The name refers to the last three hours that Jesus hung on the cross, and the service itself is based on the last seven things that Jesus said before he died (also known as the "Seven Last Words"):

1. Father, forgive them, for they know not what they do.
2. Today shalt thou be with me in paradise.
3. Woman, behold thy son!
4. My God, my God, why has thou forsaken me?
5. I thirst.
6. It is finished.
7. Father, into Thy hands I commend my spirit.

The Tre Ore service is a devotional service that was first performed by Alonso Mexía, a Jesuit in Peru, after a devastating earthquake struck Lima in 1687. An Anglican priest named A. H. Mackonochie promoted it in England in the nineteenth century, and it eventually became the main Good Friday observance for many evangelical congregations. The words have been set to music by a number of composers, most notably Heinrich Schutz (c. 1645) and Charles François Gounod (1855). Brief speeches, hymns, and periods for meditation and prayer are usually interspersed throughout the musical score.

The Tre Ore service is held from noon until 3 p.m. to coincide with the period of time during which Jesus actually hung on the cross, which the Gospel of Matthew (chapter 27, verses 45-46) establishes as falling between the sixth and ninth hours of the day. In modern terms, this would be 12-3 p.m.

## *Veil*

When Jesus was on His way to be crucified, according to legend, a woman in the crowd named Veronica took pity on Him and wiped the sweat from His brow with her veil or handkerchief. Miraculously the cloth retained the likeness of Christ wearing his CROWN OF THORNS.

The veil passed through a series of adventures but finally ended up in Rome, where it has been kept for many centuries in St. Peter's Church.

## Further Reading

Brewster, H. Pomeroy. *Saints and Festivals of the Christian Church,* 1904.

Chambers, Robert, ed. *The Book of Days,* 1864.

Cirlot, J. E. *A Dictionary of Symbols,* 1962.

Dobler, Lavinia. *Customs and Holidays Around the World,* 1962.

Ferguson, George. *Signs and Symbols in Christian Art,* 1954.

Harper, Howard V. *Days and Customs of All Faiths,* 1957.

Henderson, Helene and Sue Ellen Thompson. *Holidays, Festivals, and Celebrations of the World Dictionary,* 2nd ed., 1997.

Ickis, Marguerite. *The Book of Festivals and Holidays the World Over,* 1970.

Ickis, Marguerite. *The Book of Religious Holidays and Celebrations,* 1966.

Kelly, Aidan, Peter Dresser, and Linda M. Ross. *Religious Holidays and Calendars,* 1993.

Lord, Priscilla Sawyer, and Daniel J. Foley. *Easter the World Over,* 1971.

Metford, J. C. J. *The Christian Year,* 1991.

Monks, James L. *Great Catholic Festivals,* 1951.

Rest, Friedrich. *Our Christian Symbols,* 1954.

Urlin, Ethel L. *Festivals, Holy Days, and Saints' Days,* 1915.

# Green Corn Dance

**Type of Holiday:** Ethnic (Native American)

**Date of Observation:** Various

**Where Celebrated:** Alabama, Florida, Mississippi, New Mexico, New York, and by Native American tribes throughout the United States

**Symbols:** Black Drink, Scratching

## ORIGINS

Most North American Indian tribes had three major corn ceremonies: a planting ceremony, a harvest ceremony, and most important of all, a green corn ceremony. Held several weeks before the main harvest, when the ears of corn were nearly ripe, it was an annual rite of purification and renewal involving ceremonial dances addressed to the god who controlled the growth of corn or maize. Up until the time the Green Corn Dance took place, it was considered a crime against the gods to eat or even touch the newly ripened corn. Among the southern American Indians in the eighteenth century, it was a time for getting new clothes, new pots, and new household utensils. They would collect their worn-out clothing and, along with all the leftover grain and other provisions, make a huge pile and set it on fire.

Although the Green Corn Dance was at one time observed by the Indians of the Prairies and Southwest as well as by Eastern tribes, it has died out in many areas. Today it is usually associated with the Seminole Indians of Florida, who hold their Green Corn Dance in May. The Seminole dance is derived from the Creek ceremony known as the busk (from the Creek word *boskita*, meaning "to fast"), which marked the end of the old year and the beginning of the new year. Aside from its ceremonial purpose, the Green Corn Dance is the time when the Seminoles hold their annual council meetings. It is also a time when the sins of the old year are forgiven and members of the tribe repent for anything they've done wrong. Events that take place during the festival include ball games, stomp dances, and special rites for young male members of the tribe who have come of age during the preceding year.

Among the eastern Cherokee and Creek Indians, the Green Corn Dance has died out as a vegetation rite but survives as a curative ceremony. The Iroquois celebrate their Green Corn Dance for four days in early September, during which they perform various thanksgiving rites including the Great Feather Dance and the Corn Dance itself. Almost every pueblo in New Mexico holds a corn dance on its saint's day, the most elaborate being the Santo Domingo Pueblo (New Mexico) Green Corn Dance held on St. Dominic's Day in August. *Koshares* or holy clowns who represent the spirits of pueblo ancestors weave among the dancers, all of whom carry evergreens, symbolic of growth.

## SYMBOLS

### Black Drink

Drinking an emetic or purgative, which induces vomiting, was a standard part of the rites that comprised the Green Corn Dance. It was usually cassine, from which a special tea was made, or *ilex vomitoria,* made from the holly shrub that was found along the coast of Carolina, Georgia, and northern Florida. The Indians believed that by drinking the so-called "Black Drink" on the evening of the festival's first day, they were purifying themselves physically and spiritually, emerging in a state of perfect innocence. The next day, they would eat the green corn, which they believed contained a divine spirit that must not be permitted to touch any common, unpurified food when it entered their stomachs. After fasting for an additional day, there would be a great feast.

There was a widespread belief that anyone who didn't take the Black Drink could not safely eat the new corn and would get sick during the year. The Indians also believed that the drink made them brave in war and cemented their bonds with one another.

### Scratching

Ceremonial scratching was a common practice during the Green Corn Dance among the Cherokee, Creek, Seminole, Yuchi, and Catawba tribes. It took place just before the Feather Dance on the second day. Those participating in the ceremony would use various methods to inflict deep scratches on their bodies, particularly their backs. Among the Cherokees, a bamboo brier with stout thorns was used, while the Seminoles used snake fangs inserted into a wooden holder. Ceremonial scratching was a symbolic act believed to cleanse the body from impurities. At other times of the year, it was used to punish children and to relieve fatigue.

## Further Reading

Cohen, Hennig, and Tristram Potter Coffin, eds. *The Folklore of American Holidays,* 2nd ed., 1991.

Dobler, Lavinia. *Customs and Holidays Around the World,* 1962.

Frazer, Sir James G. *The Golden Bough: A Study in Magic and Religion,* 1931.

Henderson, Helene and Sue Ellen Thompson. *Holidays, Festivals, and Celebrations of the World Dictionary,* 2nd ed., 1997.

Leach, Maria, ed. *Funk & Wagnalls Standard Dictionary of Folklore, Mythology, & Legend,* 1984.

Penner, Lucille Recht. *The Thanksgiving Book,* 1986.

# *Guy Fawkes Day*
### *(Bonfire Night)*

**Type of Holiday:** Historic

**Date of Observation:** November 5

**Where Celebrated:** England, New Zealand, and other countries with historical ties to England

**Symbols:** Bonfires, Fireworks, "Guys"

**Related Holidays:** Halloween, Samhain, Winter Solstice

## ORIGINS

This day commemorates the Gunpowder Plot of 1605, when a group of Roman Catholic dissidents tried to blow up King James I of England and his government officials, who had assembled for the opening of the Houses of Parliament. The reason for this bold attempt can be traced back to the persecution of English Catholics under Elizabeth I, James's predecessor. When James took the throne, the Catholics thought their problems would be resolved: He was, after all, the son of Mary, Queen of Scots, widely regarded by Catholics as a martyr, and the husband of Anne of Denmark, a Catholic convert. But James I failed to meet these expectations, and the persecution of Catholics continued.

Guy Fawkes was not the leader of the plot, but it was his job to light the train of gunpowder. He was found in the cellar beneath the Houses of Parliament on November 4, 1605, crouched in a corner amidst casks of explosives. He was arrested in the early morning hours of November 5 and taken to the Tower of London. The rest of the conspirators fled, but were eventually caught and made to stand trial. Fawkes, along with Robert Catesby, the leader of the plot, and several of the other conspirators were hung and then drawn and quartered. The executions took place on January 30 and 31 in St. Paul's Churchyard, London.

A year later, November 5 was declared a day of public thanksgiving. Since that time, it has become a popular holiday on which people remember the Gunpowder Plot and confirm their faith in the Anglican Church. It is still a tradition on this day for the Royal Yeomen of the Guard to prowl through the vaults beneath London's Houses of Parliament in a mock search for explosives. They are dressed in their traditional "beefeater" costumes (so called because they used to wear these uniforms when they attended the King and Queen at state banquets) and carry lanterns so they can peer into dark corners.

Guy Fawkes Day in England has been compared to **HALLOWEEN** in America. The begging, BONFIRES, and making of dummies (see "GUYS") are certainly similar to what goes on in the United States just a few days earlier. They also recall the ancient Celtic celebration of **SAMHAIN**. The celebration of Guy Fawkes Day was brought to America by British colonists, but it has since died out. As late as 1893, however, there were reports of its observation in the United States under the name of "Pope's Day."

## SYMBOLS

### *Bonfires*

Another name for Guy Fawkes Day is "Bonfire Night." The bonfires that are lit throughout England after dark on November 5 are considered symbolic of Guy Fawkes' execution, although he was not burned at the stake. They may also be a survival of the midwinter fires lit during pagan times to symbolize the sun's struggle to rise again in the sky after the **WINTER SOLSTICE**.

### *Fireworks*

For children, Guy Fawkes Day comes as a welcome break from the long, dreary spell between the end of summer and **CHRISTMAS**. They are allowed to stay up late on this night to watch the grown-ups set off fireworks symbolizing the Gunpowder Plot that was foiled. Fireworks fill the skies throughout Britain on the night of November 5, and children spend most of the money they've collected (see "GUYS") on fireworks for the display.

## "Guys"

Several days before Guy Fawkes Day, children in England build dummies referred to as "Guys." Sometimes these effigies are displayed on street corners, and children ask passersby for a "penny for the Guy." Then, on the night of November 5, the "Guys" are thrown on the BONFIRES and burned. It is ironic that these effigies represent a man whose only role in the plot was to make sure that the gunpowder was lit. The real leader, Robert Catesby, does not have a role in the celebration.

Burning effigies in BONFIRES was a popular folk custom throughout the British Isles. It is thought that these effigies originally represented the spirit of vegetation. By burning them in fires that symbolized the sun, people hoped to secure good weather and sunshine for their crops.

In the town of Ludlow in Shropshire, any well-known local man who has aroused the dislike or anger of the townspeople has his effigy substituted for (or added to) that of Guy Fawkes.

## Further Reading

Chambers, Robert, ed. *The Book of Days,* 1864.

Henderson, Helene and Sue Ellen Thompson. *Holidays, Festivals, and Celebrations of the World Dictionary,* 2nd ed., 1997.

Miles, Clement A. *Christmas in Ritual and Tradition,* 1990.

Purdy, Susan. *Festivals for You to Celebrate,* 1969.

Santino, Jack. *All Around the Year,* 1994.

# Hajj
## (Pilgrimage to Mecca)

**Type of Holiday:** Religious (Islamic)

**Date of Observation:** Eighth to the 13th day of Dhul-Hijjah, the 12th lunar month of the Islamic calendar

**Where Celebrated:** Mecca, Saudi Arabia

**Symbols:** Black Stone, Ihrâm (Pilgrim's Robe), Kaaba, Tawâf (Circumambulation), Ten Rites, Well of Zamzam

**Colors:** The Hajj is associated with white, the color of the IHRÂM or pilgrim's robe; with black, the color in which the walls of the KAABA are draped; and with green, the color of the scarf or turban worn by returning Muslims who have successfully completed the TEN RITES of the pilgrimage.

**Related Holidays:** Id al-Adha

## ORIGINS

Every year hundreds of thousands of Muslims make a pilgrimage to Mecca, the city in Saudi Arabia where the Prophet Muhammad was born in 570 C.E. Considered to be the religious center of the universe—the point at which heaven is nearest to the earth, and where prayers can therefore be more easily heard—Mecca is as sacred to Muslims as Rome is to Catholics and Jerusalem is to Orthodox Jews. Although Muslims may visit Mecca at any time of year, the Hajj may only be performed during the twelfth lunar month. Every pilgrim's goal is to reach Mecca by the seventh day of the month of Dhul-Hijja. Although the rituals associated with the Hajj do not begin until the eighth day, this is the day on which the pilgrims receive their instructions concerning the ceremonies in which they are about to take part.

Every Muslim capable of making the trip is expected to make a pilgrimage to Mecca at least once in his or her lifetime, although those who are too ill to travel or who simply cannot afford the expense are exempt from this requirement. The Hajj is considered one of the "five pillars" or fundamental duties of Islam, and the Koran (the sacred book of the Islamic religion) describes in great detail the rituals that must be followed when the pilgrim reaches the Holy City. Non-Muslims are forbidden not only to observe or participate in the pilgrimage but even to visit the city of Mecca. Any non-Muslim who is caught doing so faces the death penalty, although Westerners occasionally manage to sneak into the city disguised as Muslims.

Now that air travel is common, the journey to Mecca is not nearly the hardship it was for earlier pilgrims, who traveled on camels or horses — and sometimes barefoot across the burning desert sands — to fulfill their obligation. Because the Islamic calendar is lunar, the timing of the Hajj shifts back 11 days according to the Christian calendar each year. This means that sometimes it falls during the mild Saudi Arabian winter, but it also means that some pilgrims end up making their journey during the summer, when the heat can cause discomfort and serious health problems. The Saudi Arabian government does everything it can to keep the pilgrims comfortable, but the crowds can be so huge that simply moving about and getting sleep become a challenge. Pilgrims who arrive from the same country usually stay together and are looked after by a guide, who finds them accommodation and helps with their travel arrangements.

The custom of journeying to a sacred place to perform religious rites was common in pre-Islamic Arabia and among the Semitic peoples. But the real model for the Hajj comes from Muhammad's "farewell pilgrimage" from Medina, where he lived and ruled, to his birthplace several months before his death in 632 C.E.

## SYMBOLS

### Black Stone

Also known as the Ruby of Heaven, the Black Stone that is set into the eastern corner of the shrine in Mecca known as the KAABA is believed to have been brought by Adam from the Garden of Eden after he was banished. The stone itself is actually a dark reddish-brown. Because it was once split in a fire, it now consists of three large and several small pieces about 12 inches in diameter, held together by a silver band. As the pilgrims circumambulate the Kaaba (see TAWÂF), they are supposed to kiss the Black Stone or touch it with their fingers.

## Ihrâm (Pilgrim's Robe)

Pilgrims must be in a state of purity when they enter Mecca, so it is customary for them to stop about six miles outside the city and begin the purification process. After taking a ritual bath and reciting certain prayers, they put on a special garment known as the *ihrâm* or pilgrim's robe, which consists of two pieces of unsewn white cloth, usually linen or cotton. One piece is wrapped around the waist, and the other is flung over the left shoulder, leaving part of the right arm free. Although it is permissible to use an umbrella for protection from the hot sun, male pilgrims' heads must remain uncovered. Female pilgrims are covered from head to ankle, and their faces are often concealed by a mask that keeps the white fabric from touching their skin. Although bare feet are preferred, heelless slippers may be worn on the feet.

Uncomfortable as it must be when worn for several days in hot weather, the pilgrim's robe is rich in symbolism. It serves as a reminder that Muslims must be prepared to give up everything for Allah (God). When Muslims die, they leave all their clothes and belongings behind and are dressed for burial in simple pieces of cloth similar to those of the ihrâm. It is also symbolic of every Muslim's equality in Allah's eyes.

Most pilgrims put on their white robes several miles outside of Mecca at Miqat. Those arriving by air often change into the ihrâm on the plane so they don't arrive in Miqat wearing the wrong clothes.

## Kaaba

The Kaaba is a 15-foot-high square granite shrine in Mecca that contains the BLACK STONE believed to have been brought by Adam from the Garden of Eden. According to legend, Adam was so miserable after leaving the garden that God set up a red tent on the spot where the Kaaba now stands, and this is where Adam spent the remainder of his life. The Black Stone that he brought with him was later set into the eastern corner of the shrine built by Abraham at Allah's command. Some say that the footprint of Abraham, from whom Muhammad is believed to have descended, can still be seen in the stone.

The shrine itself—Kaaba means "cube"—is made of reddish granite and has only one door, which leads into an unfurnished room and is only opened on special occasions. The walls are draped in black brocade curtains, which are replaced every year. The old ones are cut up in small pieces and sold to pilgrims as precious souvenirs.

## *Tawâf (Circumambulation)*

As soon as possible after arriving in Mecca, the pilgrims enter the courtyard of the Great Mosque. They proceed toward the BLACK STONE, and with the KAABA on their left, they circle the shrine seven times. The first three circuits are done at a very fast pace, kissing or touching the Black Stone each time it is passed. Known as the *harwalah*, this quickened step is symbolic of what the Prophet Muhammad did on his "farewell pilgrimage" to show that he wasn't tired after his long journey. The last four circuits are walked at a more leisurely pace. After the seventh circuit, the pilgrims press their bodies against the *multazam,* a space between the eastern corner of the shrine and the door that is considered to be especially holy. In doing so they hope to absorb some of the *baraka*—the blessing of virtue—with which this holy building is endowed.

The root meaning of the word *hajj* is "to describe a circle." It is from this ritual circumambulation of the Kaaba, therefore, that the pilgrimage gets its name.

## *Ten Rites*

There are ten rites or ceremonies that must be performed by each pilgrim during the Hajj:

1. Entrance through the Gate of Peace. There are 19 gates leading to the courtyard of the Great Mosque of Mecca, which is 550 feet long and 360 feet wide. Pilgrims must enter through the Bab a-Salam or Gate of Peace.

2. Kissing of the Black Stone. The pilgrims make their way to the center of the courtyard, where the KAABA rises 50 feet into the air. They go directly to the BLACK STONE and kiss it with reverence.

3. Circumambulation. As described above (see TAWÂF), the pilgrims travel around the Kaaba seven times counterclockwise, always keeping the shrine on their left.

4. Prayer at the Mosque of Abraham. The next stop is the small, domed Mosque of Abraham, in which Ishmael (son of Abraham) and his mother Hagar are buried. Prayers are offered, and then the pilgrims walk over to drink from the sacred Well of Ishmael (see WELL OF ZAMZAM).

5. Ascent to Mount Safa and Mount Maret. Pilgrims leave the Mosque of Abraham with their left foot forward, going out of the courtyard through the Gate of Safa and following the road that leads from the hilltop of Safa to the top of Mount Maret (or Marwa), a distance of about one-seventh of a mile. The pilgrims must then run back and forth between these two points seven times, stopping at certain fixed points to offer prayers. This rite commemorates Hagar's search for water in the desert between the two mountains (see WELL OF ZAMZAM).

6. Journey to the Mountain of Mercy. The Hajj proper begins on the eighth day, as the pilgrims begin their long journey to Mount Arafat, also known as the Mountain of Mercy, several miles away. According to legend, exactly 700,000 pilgrims will reach Mount Arafat; if fewer than this number manage to do so, angels will come down and make up the difference.

7. Sermon on Arafat. Once they have gathered on Mount Arafat, the pilgrims listen to a sermon delivered by a religious leader, who addresses them while mounted on a camel.

8. Night in Muzdalifa. That evening, the pilgrims depart again for Mecca; but halfway between Arafat and the Holy City, they must spend a night in Muzdalifa. Huge crowds gather at the mosque there, and there is usually so much music and commotion that no one gets any sleep. Pilgrims also take advantage of this stop to gather the 70 pebbles they will need for the next day's rite.

9. Stoning of the Devils in Mina. On their way to Mecca the following day, the pilgrims stop in the village of Mina. Three pillars are there, and the pilgrims throw their pebbles at the pillars in a ceremony known as the Stoning of the Devils. This ritual is based on the story of how the devil tried three times to persuade Abraham to ignore God's command to sacrifice his son, Ishmael. Each time, Abraham threw pebbles at the devil in disgust and continued on his way. By throwing stones at the three pillars, the pilgrims are symbolically expressing their own ability to resist temptation. The stones that accumulate there are eventually taken to Mecca to be used as gravel on the floor of the Great Mosque. Animal sacrifices are also performed at Mina to commemorate God's provision of a ram to be sacrificed in Ishmael's place. The killing of so many animals has forced Saudi Arabian officials to explore new methods for freezing, preserving, and distributing the meat produced. After the sacrifice, male pilgrims' heads are shaved and women's hair is trimmed. The ihrâm is then taken off.

10. Visit to the Tomb of Muhammad. The pilgrims return to Mecca and try to get a bottle or tin of water from the WELL OF ZAMZAM, also known as

the Well of Ishmael. They then go to Medina, the city where the Prophet lived and was buried, to visit Muhammad's tomb. Although the visit to Medina, 200 miles away, is not compulsory, it is regarded as an act of great merit.

## *Well of Zamzam*

Also known as the Well of Ishmael, this sacred source of water is located just a few steps from the southeast corner of the KAABA beneath a domed building erected in 1661. The well itself is a shaft that goes down more than 100 feet and possesses the miraculous ability to maintain the same water level, no matter how much is drawn from it by pilgrims who believe in its curative powers. Some dip their robes in it or take some home to their relatives as gifts, to be used when someone is ill or to wash the body after death. Others drink as much of it as they possibly can.

Legend has it that when Hagar and Ishmael were abandoned in the desert near Mecca, they used up all the water in the goatskin that Abraham had given them. In a frantic search for more, Hagar ran back and forth between the two hills of Safa and Marwa seven times. God finally heard Ishmael's prayers, and the water gushed forth not far from where the KAABA now stands, making a sound like *zam-zam*.

Today the water is channeled to underground galleries that can be reached by a flight of stairs, where a number of faucets can supply many people at once. The well is fed by several springs and is visited by thousands of people daily.

## Further Reading

Ahsan, M. M. *Muslim Festivals*, 1987.

Crim, Keith, ed. *The Perennial Dictionary of World Religions*, 1989.

Gaer, Joseph. *Holidays Around the World*, 1953.

Glassé, Cyril. *The Concise Encylopedia of Islam*, 1989.

Henderson, Helene and Sue Ellen Thompson. *Holidays, Festivals, and Celebrations of the World Dictionary*, 2nd ed., 1997.

Pike, Royston. *Round the Year with the World's Religions*, 1993.

Von Grunebaum, G. D. *Muhammadan Festivals*, 1988.

# *Halashashti*

**Type of Holiday:** Religious (Hindu)

**Date of Observation:** August-September; sixth day of the waning half of the Hindu month of Bhadrapada

**Where Celebrated:** India

**Symbols:** Plough

## ORIGINS

This Hindu festival is often referred to as Balarama Shashti, after Krishna's older brother, Balarama, who was born on this day. According to the Hindu scriptures, Vishnu took two hairs, one white and one black, and these became Balarama and Krishna, the sons of Devaki. As soon as Balarama was born, he was taken to a safe place to preserve his life from the tyrant Kansa. He and Krishna grew up together, sharing many adventures, and Balarma's death while sitting under a banyan tree near Dwaraka was followed soon after by the death of his brother. Balarama's weapon was a PLOUGH, so this is also the day on which the farmers and peasants of India pay special tribute to the implement that helps them sow their crops.

Hindu women fast on this day, eating only buffalo milk and curds in the belief that it will ensure happiness, prosperity, and longevity for their sons. A fast may also be observed by farmers in rural areas, who hope that Lord Siva will bless their families' welfare and send them better crops in the coming year. Everyone shares in a huge feast in the evening.

## SYMBOLS

### *Plough*

The *hala* or plough that gives this festival its name is a symbol not only of Balarama but of farmers and farming in general. Hindu farmers show their reverence for the plough by applying powdered rice and turmeric to its iron blade and by decorating it with flowers.

## Further Reading

Henderson, Helene and Sue Ellen Thompson. *Holidays, Festivals, and Celebrations of the World Dictionary*, 2nd ed., 1997.

Kelly, Aidan. *Religious Holidays and Calendars*, 1993.

MacDonald, Margaret R., ed. *The Folklore of World Holidays*, 1992.

# *Halloween*

**Type of Holiday:** Ancient or pagan, Folkloric

**Date of Observation:** October 31

**Where Celebrated:** United States, British Isles

**Symbols:** Bat, Black Cat, Bonfires, Colcannon, Costumes, Goblins, Harvest Sheaves or Harvest Dummy, Jack-O-Lantern, Nuts or Apples, Trick-or-Treating, Witch

**Colors:** Black and orange. Orange, the color of the Jack-O-Lantern, is a symbol of strength and endurance. Along with gold and brown, it stands for autumn and the harvest. Black is primarily a symbol of death and darkness. The black of the witch's cloak and the black cat are a reminder that Halloween was once a festival of the dead.

**Related Holidays:** All Souls' Day, Samhain

## ORIGINS

Halloween can be traced directly back to **SAMHAIN**, the ancient Celtic harvest festival honoring the Lord of the Dead. Observed on November 1 in the British Isles and parts of what is now France, Samhain also marked the beginning of the Celtic New Year. Because it was a time of transition between the old and the new, the Celts believed that the souls of those who had died during the previous year gathered to travel together to the land of the dead. They lit BONFIRES and sacrificed fruits and vegetables, hoping to win the favor of the spirits of the deceased and to avoid their punishments. Sometimes the living disguised themselves in masks and COSTUMES so that the spirits of the dead wouldn't recognize them. Charms, spells, and predictions about the future seemed to carry special weight on the eve of Samhain (see NUTS OR APPLES).

By the fourth century, the Christian church was doing everything it could to stamp out pagan festivals like Samhain, but the Celts wouldn't give up their ancient rituals and symbols. So the Christian church gave them new names and meanings. November 1 became All Saints' Day (All Hallows' Day in England), a celebration of all the Christian saints. The night of October 31 became All Hallows' Eve (later Halloween). But its association with the supernatural persisted.

Halloween came to America with the Irish immigrants of the 1840s. Their folk customs and beliefs merged with existing agricultural traditions. The early American Halloween, therefore, was not only a time to foretell the future and dabble in the occult but to complete certain seasonal tasks associated with the fall harvest. Over the years the holiday's agricultural significance faded, and it became primarily a children's holiday—a time to dress up as the ghosts and GOBLINS their ancestors at one time feared.

# SYMBOLS

## Bat

Both positive and negative symbolic meanings have been associated with bats over the centuries. On the one hand, they are eerie creatures, winged mammals who fly around like ghosts at night and sleep hanging upside down during the day. On the other, they are regarded as particularly intelligent. The bat is a symbol of good fortune in China, and in ancient times, placing drops of bat's blood under a woman's pillow was believed to guarantee that she would bear many children.

Early pictures of WITCHES show them worshipping a horned figure with the wings of a bat—most likely the Devil. Before attending a Sabbath or witches' gathering, they would rub a special ointment containing bats' blood into their bodies. The wings and entrails of bats went into their brews. The fact that bats could fly around at night made it easy to believe that they possessed mysterious powers. And when they hung upside down to sleep, they draped their wings around their bodies like witches' cloaks.

Because of their association with witches, the black paper bats that can be seen in Halloween decorations today are symbols of evil and the supernatural.

## Black Cat

Long before they were associated with Halloween, cats were believed to have magical powers. The ancient Egyptians worshipped a cat-goddess named Pasht and used cats as a motif in their furniture and jewelry designs. The Celts believed that cats were human beings who had been changed into animals by evil powers. During the ancient celebration of **SAMHAIN** (see "Origins" above), it was customary to throw cats into the fire.

Back when people feared WITCHES and accused one another of witchcraft, cats were believed to assist witches in carrying out their magic. Since all cats looked black at night, the witch's cat was always thought of as being black. People were especially wary of cats at Halloween, when witches were known to be out riding the skies on their broomsticks. The fact that cats could see in the dark and move without making any noise added to their reputation as animals that couldn't be trusted.

With their links to the ancient festival of Samhain and later to witches, cats found a permanent place in the folklore of Halloween. Typically shown with their backs arched and their yellow eyes glaring, the cat is symbolic of the spirit of evil.

## Bonfires

Bonfires were an important part of the celebration of Samhain, the ancient festival from which Halloween derived. On a night when evil spirits were believed to be roaming about, a bonfire must have provided a reassuring source of light and comfort. Live animals and even men—usually criminals or prisoners of war—were often burned alive as sacrifices to Saman, the Lord of Death. Bonfires were also kindled on **MIDSUMMER DAY** and at other seasonal festivals to promote fertility, to protect the fields against thunder and lightning, and to ward off sickness.

Although not part of the American Halloween ritual, bonfires are still common in parts of Ireland on October 31. After the flames have subsided, young people often sit around the glowing embers and eat blackened potatoes that have been roasted on the coals.

## Colcannon

Colcannon is a traditional dish made of mashed potatoes, parsnips, and onions that is still served on Halloween in Ireland. Just as tiny figures or beans were hidden in Kings' Cakes on **EPIPHANY** and **CARNIVAL**, small objects are often concealed in the colcannon. If someone finds a coin, it means that he or she will be very wealthy. A ring stands for marriage, a doll for children, and a thimble for spinsterhood.

## Costumes

From ancient times, people have worn masks to frighten off demons and thus avoid droughts, epidemics, and other disasters. Even after the pagan festival of the dead known as Samhain became the Christian All Hallows' Eve, the people of Europe continued to feel uneasy at this time of year. If they left their homes after dark, they often disguised themselves with masks and costumes so they wouldn't be recognized by the evil spirits who were out roaming the earth. It was only natural for them to dress up as the ghosts, witches, and GOBLINS they were most fearful of meeting.

Trick-or-treaters in the United States are still apt to dress up in costumes that reflect their culture's most prevalent obsessions. During the Great Depression, for example, children often disguised themselves as hobos, burglars, pirates, and Indians — in other words, as economic and social outcasts, symbolic of the troubles from which their parents were struggling to escape. In contrast, during the 1980s children were dressing up as television and movie heroes and characters from television commercials, such as E.T., Ninja Turtles, or California Raisins. Witches and skeletons have always been popular costumes, representing the fear of death and evil; but nowadays it is not unusual to see children dressed up as Tylenol capsules (after the widely publicized deaths caused by swallowing capsules that had been tampered with), ax murderers, or nuclear waste materials. Although they may not do so consciously, children who disguise themselves as the agents of death and destruction are actually helping themselves (and their parents) defuse their deepest fears.

## Goblins

Goblins are symbolic of the evil spirits that were believed to emerge at Samhain and roam the earth at Halloween. They were ugly, menacing creatures who lived underground or in dark places. The word "goblin" is actually the French name for these fairy folk, who resembled leprechauns and pixies.

Some scholars say that during the Stone Age a small, dark-skinned people lived in Northern Europe and the British Isles. They wore green clothing so they could conceal themselves in the forests and fields, and they lived in low huts with turf as their roofs. They waylaid travelers, kidnapped children, and sometimes committed murder. Over the centuries, these real dwarf people were absorbed into the Celtic population around them. But they survived on a mythical level as the elves, goblins, and other fairy folk who also lived in low, mound-like houses and wore green clothing. They were symbols of the danger and evil that were believed to threaten people at this time of year.

## Harvest Sheaves or Harvest Dummy

Even in urban and suburban areas today, people tend to romanticize the tradition of the harvest and rural lifestyles by decorating their homes with sheaves of Indian corn, gourds, and pumpkins. Usually dried and attached to fence posts, outdoor lighting fixtures, or porch railings, these harvest decorations represent the approaching death of the natural world in the form of winter.

Dummies resembling scarecrows are often placed outside the house, sometimes in the midst of an arrangement that includes cornstalks and pumpkins, symbolizing the harvest that is being brought in from the garden or the fields. Unlike the scarecrow designed to protect the summer crops from hungry birds and animals, however, the Halloween dummy is usually placed near the house, perhaps to protect its inhabitants from the ravages of the approaching winter.

## *Jack-O-Lantern*

In England and Ireland, people often saw a pale, eerie light moving over bogs and marshes that resembled a lantern held in someone's hand. They referred to the phenomenon as "Lantern Men," "Hob-O'-Lantern," "Jack-O'-Lantern," or "Will-O'-the-Wisp." Similarly, the ghostly lights that seemed to hover over graves dug in marshy places were called "Corpse Candles." It's possible that these strange lights were the result of the spontaneous combustion of methane or marsh gas given off by rotting plant and animal life. But some people thought Jack-O-Lanterns were the souls of sinners condemned to walk the earth, or the souls of men who had been lost at sea.

Jack-O-Lantern became a legendary folk figure in Great Britain. He was the spirit of a blacksmith named Jack who was too evil to get into heaven but who was not allowed into hell because he had outwitted the devil. Doomed to wander the earth forever, he scooped up a glowing ember with the vegetable he happened to be eating at the time and used it as a lantern to light his way.

Jack-O-Lanterns, as they are known today — hollowed-out pumpkins with carved faces and lit candles burning inside — were originally made from turnips in Scotland, potatoes in Ireland, and "punkies" or large beets known as mangel-wurzels in England. When the Scottish and Irish immigrants who settled in the United States discovered pumpkins, they immediately recognized them as the ideal shape and size for Jack-O-Lanterns. Uncarved, they serve as a symbol of the harvest and are often displayed on front porches right up until **THANKSGIVING**. Carved and illuminated by a candle, they are symbolic of death and the spirit world.

## Nuts or Apples

The nuts and apples traditionally used to predict the future on Halloween in the British Isles were once symbols of the harvest. Nuts, symbolic of life and fertility, were so much a part of Halloween that in some parts of England, Scotland, and Ireland the night of October 31 was called "Nutcrack Night." Scottish young people put pairs of nuts named after certain couples into the fire. If the pair burned to ashes together, it meant that the couple could expect a happy life together. If they crackled or sprang apart, it meant that quarrels and separation were inevitable. In Wales, a brightly blazing nut meant prosperity, while one that smoldered or popped meant bad luck. Nuts may have taken the place of the live animal sacrifices performed during the ancient Celtic New Year celebration known as **SAMHAIN**.

Apples were also considered fertility symbols and were used to make predictions about love. At the first Halloween parties, people roasted apples and bobbed for them in tubs of water. If a boy came up with an apple in his teeth, it meant that the girl he loved wanted him as her boyfriend. In a traditional game known as Snap Apple, the boys took turns trying to bite an apple that was twirled on the end of a stick. The first to succeed would be the first to marry. For this reason, Halloween was sometimes referred to as Snap Apple Night.

Girls pared apples on Halloween, trying to keep the peel in a single unbroken strip. Then they would swing it three times around their head and throw it over their left shoulder. The fallen peel was supposed to form the initial of their future husband's name. Apple seeds were also used to foretell the identity of a girl's future mate. Seeds named for two different boys were stuck on the girl's eyelids. The seed that stayed on the longest was her true sweetheart—although skillful winking or twitching often gave one seed the advantage.

## Trick-or-Treating

The Halloween custom known as trick-or-treating—going from house to house begging for candy and threatening to cause mischief for those who don't cooperate—seems to have originated in the British Isles. It was customary for the poor to go begging on **ALL SOULS' DAY** in England, and children eventually took over the custom. In Ireland, legend has it that farmers used to go from house to house asking for food for their Halloween festivities in the name of the ancient god, Muck Olla. Good luck and wealth were promised to those who contributed; those who were stingy were threatened with bad luck.

Many believe that trick-or-treating is a relic of the Celtic New Year celebration known as Samhain. Since this was the time of year that the spirits of the dead returned to visit the living, people would unbolt their doors, keep their hearth fires burning, and set out gifts of food to appease these troublesome spirits. Later, they dressed up as spirits themselves (see COSTUMES) and demanded contributions from neighbors for communal feasts.

What "Trick or treat" really means is "Give me a treat or I'll play a trick on you." The phrase is American in origin, and it dates back to about the 1930s. It combines the food- and money-begging traditions of England and Ireland with the ancient belief in supernatural activity on this night. In fact, the "tricks" that are played on Halloween (or Mischief Night, October 30) often look as though supernatural forces were behind them. A favorite Halloween prank in rural areas, for example, involves disassembling a piece of farm equipment and reassembling it on a rooftop. Pranks characterized by a reversal of the usual order symbolize both the unpredictable weather at this time of year and the delicate balance between man and nature that can so easily be upset. In the nineteenth century, favorite Halloween pranks included "threshold tricks"—removing gates and fences, soaping or rattling windows, fixing bells so they rang constantly, and tying doors shut. The message behind these and other attacks on domestic security is the importance of exercising caution at a time of year when everyone is vulnerable to the forces of death and destruction. Just as Samhain was the time for the pagans to secure their farms and animals against the winter weather, Halloween pranks serve as a reminder that nature will not be kind to those who fail to take the necessary precautions.

In the 1930s, people who offered candy to Halloween visitors were genuinely concerned with protecting their homes against pranksters. But the custom of playing tricks on Halloween declined in popularity over the years, and by the 1950s, most children had no idea what kind of "tricks" they were expected to perform; all they wanted was the candy. Trick-or-treating rituals underwent a major shift in the 1970s and 1980s, when stories of razor blades or pins concealed in candy and apples began to surface. Suddenly symbolic fears were transformed into real ones, and children's freedom to roam the streets after dark was curtailed in many areas. Rather than being invited indoors for homemade treats, children now typically wait on the porch or doorstep while the host or hostess hands them their goodies. Young children are usually accompanied by their parents, who check the candy carefully for signs of tampering before allowing their children to eat it. In some areas, trick-or-treating is discouraged altogether. Instead, children attend organized Halloween parties.

## *Witch*

The witch is probably the most recognizable symbol of Halloween. The name comes from the Saxon word *wica,* meaning "wise one." Most witches were pagans, which explains why they fell out of favor as Christianity grew in popularity. Several times a year, witches from all over a certain region would gather in a sacred spot, such as the Hartz Mountains of Germany. Halloween was one of several dates on which these Witches' Sabbaths took place. They would perform marriages, initiate new witches, and participate in fertility dances. Sometimes the witches would gallop about on branches or broomsticks.

The early Americans' belief in witchcraft came from the European continent, particularly from Scottish and Irish immigrants. The GOBLINS and other evil spirits they feared at Halloween became identified with witches. Farmers in the Pennsylvania Dutch country painted hex signs on their barns to scare off witches. Iron and salt—two things that witches wouldn't touch—were often placed by the beds of newborn babies.

By the nineteenth century, few educated people took witchcraft very seriously. But those who were less educated, particularly those living in rural areas, went right on believing. Today, witches are usually depicted as old women with matted hair, black robes, and bony fingers, with BLACK CATS as their only companions. They are symbols of the evil spirits traditionally believed to be roaming the earth at Halloween.

## Further Reading

Barth, Edna. *Witches, Pumpkins, and Grinning Ghosts: The Story of Halloween Symbols,* 1972.

Biedermann, Hans. *Dictionary of Symbolism: Cultural Icons and the Meanings Behind Them,* 1994.

Henderson, Helene and Sue Ellen Thompson. *Holidays, Festivals, and Celebrations of the World Dictionary,* 2nd ed., 1997.

Ickis, Marguerite. *The Book of Festivals and Holidays the World Over,* 1970.

Purdy, Susan. *Festivals for You to Celebrate,* 1969.

Santino, Jack. *All Around the Year,* 1994.

Santino, Jack. *Halloween and Other Festivals of Death and Life,* 1994.

Tuleja, Tad. *Curious Customs: The Stories Behind 296 Popular American Rituals,* 1987.

# Hanukkah
### (Chanukah, Feast of Dedication, Festival of Lights)

**Type of Holiday:** Religious (Jewish)

**Date of Observation:** Between November 25 and December 26; from 25 Kislev to 2 Tevet

**Where Celebrated:** Europe, United States, and by Jews all over the world

**Symbols:** Dreidel, Latkes, Menorah

## ORIGINS

Hanukkah commemorates the successful rebellion of the Jews against the Syrian-Greek King Antiochus, who was determined to impose the Greek religion on all of his subjects. He forbid the Jews to read from their holy books, to pray to their god, or to celebrate their holidays. When Matthias, a Jewish priest of Modin (near Jerusalem) and his five sons heard about the king's decrees, they decided to fight back. They ran to the hills and organized a small army led by one of the sons, Judah (also known as Judas Maccabeus). They fought the Syrians for three years and finally succeeded in forcing the Syrian army out of their land in 162 B.C.E.

After the battle was over, the Jewish victors went into their Temple to get rid of the pagan altar and the statues of Zeus and other Greek gods. They wanted to rededicate the Temple to their own god by relighting the holy candelabrum known as the MENORAH. According to the story, they could only find enough consecrated (pure) oil to burn for one day, and it would take eight days to get more. Miraculously, the menorah burned continuously for eight days on its small supply of oil. The rededication ceremony took place on the 25th day of the Jewish month of Kislev—the anniversary of the Temple's desecration by the Greeks three years earlier. For this reason, the festival is sometimes called the Feast of Dedication (Hanukkah means "dedication" in Hebrew) or the Festival of Lights.

What Hanukkah really celebrates is the survival of Judaism. The Maccabees' primary goal was to preserve their own Jewish identity. So the holiday is not so much a commemoration of a military success as a celebration of Jewish independence and of religious freedom in general. Interestingly, it is the only major Jewish festival that is not mentioned in the Bible.

## SYMBOLS

### *Dreidel*

Known as a *sevivon* in Hebrew, the dreidel is a small, flat-sided top that spins on a central post or stem. Each of the four sides bears a Hebrew letter: Nun, Gimel, Hay, and Shin. Taken together, NGHS stands for the words *nes gadol hayeh sham,* which means "A great miracle happened there"—a reference to the miraculous burning of the MENORAH for eight days.

There is a theory that the game of dreidel was brought to Europe from India during the Middle Ages and eventually played by German Christians on **CHRISTMAS EVE**. The German letters H, G, H, and S stand for *Nichts* (nothing), *Ganz* (all), *Halb* (half), and *Stell ein* (put in). The Jews, according to this story, replaced the German letters with Hebrew ones that sounded similar, and made them into an acrostic of the Hebrew phrase, "A great miracle happened there."

The Hebrew letters found on the dreidel also carry numeric values: Nun=50, Gimel=3, Hay=5, and Shin=300. The players take turns spinning the dreidel and accumulating points. After an agreed-upon number of rounds, the person with the highest score wins. Sometimes small change, candy, or raisins and almonds are put in a pot. If the dreidel falls on Gimel, the player takes the entire pot; if Hay, the player takes half; if Nun, he or she takes nothing; and if it falls on Shin, he or she must put half of his or her pile in the pot. The game can be made more challenging by drawing a circle two feet in diameter and trying to keep the spinning dreidel inside the circle. The player whose spin travels outside the circle loses a turn.

The dreidel was often used in places where Jews were forbidden to practice their religion. They would meet, supposedly to play the dreidel, but in fact they would secretly pray together or study the Torah. Although early dreidels were carved from wood found in the forest, nowadays they can be purchased in many sizes, made from a variety of materials including redwood, silver, and plastic. In addition to recalling the miracle of the burning menorah, the spin of the dreidel also symbolizes the spinning of the earth on its axis and the cyclical nature of both the seasons and the fortunes of the Jews.

### *Latkes*

Latkes are potato pancakes served at Hanukkah in memory of the Maccabee women who cooked latkes for the Jewish soldiers when they were fighting the Syrians. Because they are fried in oil, latkes also symbolize the tiny jug of oil that miraculously lasted for eight days when the MENORAH in the Temple was first rekindled after the Syrians were driven out.

## *Menorah*

The original menorahs were made out of clay and burned oil. The design of today's menorah, which stands on a base from which nine branches sprout like the fingers of a hand, dates back to the Middle Ages. The Hanukkah menorah is called the *hanukkiyyah*. It has eight places for separate candles and a ninth place for the *shammesh* or "servant" candle, which is used to light the others. The shammesh is usually set apart by being higher than the other candles.

The lighting of the Hanukkah candles, which stand for spirit, courage, justice, and hope, is the festival's most important ritual. Using the shammesh, the first candle is lit at sundown on the 24th day of Kislev. On the second night, two candles are lit. On each night thereafter, one more candle is added until, on the eighth night of the festival, all eight (along with the shammesh) are burning together. Because Hebrew is read and written from right to left, the candles are set each night from right to left. But they are lit from left to right. The candles are left burning for at least a half hour and are allowed to extinguish themselves. The lighting ritual is accompanied by a blessing and a brief statement in Hebrew about what is being commemorated. The 30th Psalm, a kind of anthem for the festival, is then recited.

The lights associated with Hanukkah are not even mentioned in the Book of the Maccabees, which has led many scholars to conclude that they had nothing to do with the festival originally, but were adapted from the popular pagan custom of lighting candles, torches, or bonfires at the time of the WINTER SOLSTICE. But for most Jews today, the lighting of the candles in the menorah is symbolic of the rekindling of the Temple candelabrum by Judah and his followers.

## Further Reading

Cashman, Greer Fay. *Jewish Days and Holidays,* 1979.

Cuyler, Margery. *Jewish Holidays,* 1978.

Drucker, Malka. *Hanukkah,* 1980.

Gaer, Joseph. *Holidays Around the World,* 1953.

Gaster, Theodor H. *Festivals of the Jewish Year,* 1953.

Henderson, Helene and Sue Ellen Thompson. *Holidays, Festivals, and Celebrations of the World Dictionary,* 2nd ed., 1997.

Ickis, Marguerite. *The Book of Festivals and Holidays the World Over,* 1970.

Purdy, Susan. *Festivals for You to Celebrate,* 1969.

Renberg, Dalia Hardof. *The Complete Family Guide to Jewish Holidays,* 1985.

Santino, Jack. *All Around the Year,* 1994.

# *Hina Matsuri*
## *(Girls' Day, Dolls' Festival)*

**Type of Holiday:** Folkloric

**Date of Observation:** March 3

**Where Celebrated:** Japan

**Symbols:** Dolls, Peach Blossom

**Colors:** The dolls associated with Hina Matsuri are displayed on shelves covered in red cloth. Symbolizing the sun, red is the color of vigor and good fortune.

## ORIGINS

Sometimes referred to as Girls' Day, Hina Matsuri is observed by Japanese families with daughters by displaying sets of DOLLS, often with elaborate costumes and tiny utensils and furnishings, on elevated platforms. The practice originated 1,500 years ago during the Reign of Emperor Kenso. On the third day of the third month, the Emperor's household and guests would seat themselves along the banks of a stream. Lacquer *sake* cups (*sake* being an alcoholic drink made from fermented rice) were set adrift upstream. By the time a floating cup reached one of the guests, he or she had to have composed a special poem. If successful in doing so, he or she could pick up the cup, fill it with sake, and drink it.

Purification rituals were also associated with this day. Small paper dolls were thrown into the river in the belief that they would carry away sin and unhappiness. This custom gave rise to *amagatsu,* which were dolls made from two pieces of bamboo or wood, crossed in the middle and covered with a kimono. Buddhist verses were written on paper and tied to the doll's waist. The dolls were placed near children's beds as a charm to ward off evil and illness. Although boys usually gave up these charms at the age of 15, girls would continue to use them until they were married. In rural areas, dolls made of straw were often hung in a doorway or at the entrance to a village to protect against sickness, disaster, and other evil influences.

Skilled doll makers soon began to produce more sophisticated dolls. In the early seventeenth century, Emperor Gomizuno-o's daughter became Empress Meisho on her seventh birthday. Her mother celebrated the occasion by displaying dolls for her in their Kyoto palace. Eventually other wealthy families adopted the practice, and additional dolls were added to the display, along with miniature tables, chests of drawers, and other doll furnishings. Some of these doll sets became family heirlooms, handed down from one generation to the next.

By 1770, Hina Matsuri was a national holiday in Japan. It remained so until 1874, when its holiday status was removed. But the custom of displaying dolls on elevated platforms regained its popularity, and today the celebration is observed throughout Japan. It is primarily an opportunity for young girls to socialize, inviting their friends over to see their doll displays and serving them diamond-shaped cakes, fruit-shaped candies, and tiny bowls of rice boiled with red beans. The "utensils" that accompany the dolls have become extremely elaborate and refined: gold lacquer writing-boxes; racks for airing kimonos; tiny picnic chests complete with miniature lacquer plates and sake bottles; illustrated books only an inch tall; and everything needed for a formal Japanese tea ceremony. After the festival is over, the dolls and furnishings are wrapped up carefully, boxed, and put away for safekeeping.

## SYMBOLS

### Dolls

As described above, the earliest Japanese dolls were used as scapegoats. After the Japanese began to manufacture paper in the seventh century, paper dolls could be easily obtained from a priest. They were rubbed all over the body to absorb the person's evil thoughts and tendencies; then they were thrown into running water so the evil would be carried away. Later on, people got in the habit of placing these dolls on their *kamidana* or deity-shelf before using them. This may be where the custom of arranging the dolls on shelves or platforms originated.

Today the dolls displayed on Hina Matsuri are arranged on a *hinadan*, a five- to seven-tiered shelf covered with bright red fabric. The *Dairi-sama* (Court People) occupy the top shelf and consist of a male-female couple representing the Emperor and his Empress. On the second tier are three

*Kanjo* (Ladies-in-Waiting) who represent the three stages of life: youth, middle age, and old age. The third tier is filled with five Court Musicians who play the *taiko* (drum), *okawa* (lap drum), *kotsutsumi* (shoulder drum), and *fue* (flute). The fifth musician is usually the *utai* or singer, but there may also be dolls playing the gong, mouth organ, oboe, or *kaen taiko* (large standing drum). The fourth tier consists of two *Yadaijin* (Ministers) who function as guards rather than statesmen. Three *Jicho* (Footmen) occupy the fifth tier: one with a laughing face, one crying, and one angry. Sometimes they are called *Sannin Jogo* (the Three Drunks) because each face reflects a mood associated with drinking. The remaining lower tiers are for the miniature furniture, utensils, and other articles belonging to the dolls.

The dolls that were originally used to cleanse children from sin and protect them from illness now serve a cultural and educational purpose: to teach Japanese girls how to behave like young ladies and how to take care of their valuable belongings.

## Peach Blossom

Hina Matsuri originally took place a month later than it does now, after the warm spring weather had arrived. Sometimes it was called the Peach Blossom Festival (Momo-no-sekku), because it was a popular time for families to get out in the countryside and enjoy the blossoming trees. Part of the outdoor celebration was to cast crudely made paper dolls into the river and thus get rid of disease and misfortune.

The peach blossom remains a symbol for the traditionally feminine qualities of beauty, gentleness, and peacefulness that Japanese girls hope to acquire by the time they are married. It is customary to include a branch of peach blossoms, either real or artificial, as part of the doll display. Since the peach is also a symbol of fertility and happiness in marriage, a branch is often placed in each of two ritual sake bottles that stand between the Emperor and Empress on the top tier of the *hinadan* or doll stand.

## Further Reading

Araki, Nancy K., and Jane M. Horii. *Matsuri Festival: Japanese-American Celebrations and Activities,* 1978.

Bauer, Helen, and Sherwin Carlquist. *Japanese Festivals,* 1965.

Casal, U. A. *The Five Sacred Festivals of Ancient Japan,* 1967.

Dobler, Lavinia. *Customs and Holidays Around the World,* 1962.

Henderson, Helene and Sue Ellen Thompson. *Holidays, Festivals, and Celebrations of the World Dictionary,* 2nd ed., 1997.

# *Hogmanay*
## *(New Year's Eve in Scotland)*

**Type of Holiday:** Calendar

**Date of Observation:** December 31

**Where Celebrated:** Scotland

**Symbols:** Coullin, First-Footing, Last Sheaf or New Year's Wisp, Noise-making

**Related Holidays:** New Year's Eve

## ORIGINS

There are a number of theories about where Hogmanay, the Scottish New Year's Eve celebration, got its name. One is that it came from the Greek *hagi mene* (Holy Month), but this is considered unlikely. Another, equally unlikely, is that it came from the ancient Scandinavian Yuletide celebration known as Huggunott ("Hogg-night" or "Slaughter Night," since it was customary to sacrifice or slaughter cattle at this time of year), combined with "Mennie," the cup that was drained at the Yule feast. A more likely explanation is that it came from an old French Epiphany carol that began, "L'Homme est né, Troi rois là" ("A Man is born, Three Kings are there") which became "Hogmanay, Troleray" in Scotland. Yet another is that it came from *hagg*, an old Yorkshire word for a wood or coppice. A "hagman" was a woodcutter, and "Hogmanay" was what he called out when he appealed to his customers for some kind of seasonal tip or remembrance.

Scottish children, often wearing a sheet doubled up in front to form a huge pocket, used to call at the homes of the wealthy on this day and ask for the traditional gift of an oatmeal cake. They would call out "Hogmanay!" and recite traditional rhymes or sing songs, in return for which they'd be given their cakes to take home.

Hogmanay was celebrated at a time of year when people needed some assurance that the crops would return in the spring. Just as **NEW YEAR'S EVE** was an occasion to look both backward and forward, it represented a threshold between death and life in the natural world. The customs associated with Hogmanay (see below) suggest a relationship among the seasonal cycle, the agricultural cycle, and the human life cycle.

# SYMBOLS

## *Coullin*

In the ceremony known as *coullin* or *calluinn,* which was traditional in the Scottish Highlands as late as the nineteenth century, young men went from house to house carrying sticks with bits of rawhide attached. One of them wore a cow's hide on his back. Blowing a horn to announce their arrival, they would chase the man wearing the hide around the house three times, beating him on the back and making a sound like a drum. One of the men would then go into the house and pronounce a blessing upon it. Then each man would singe a small piece of the rawhide attached to his stick in the fire on the hearth and apply it to the nose of every person and animal living in the house. This was believed to protect them from diseases and other misfortunes, particularly witchcraft, during the coming year. They also gathered Hogmanay gifts, primarily food, in a bag made of animal skin.

Although it is not certain what the act of beating a cow's hide and making its wearer run around the house represented, many believe it symbolized the continuation of the past year's fertility into the next year. By always keeping the house on their right side as they circled it, the participants in the ceremony were believed to be imitating the course of the sun.

## *First-Footing*

The first visitor of the New Year was an important omen of what the coming year would be like. Many Scottish people living in rural areas still observe the old custom of opening all the doors in the house a minute or two before midnight on December 31 and leaving them open until the clocks have struck the hour—a practice known as "Letting the old year out and the new year in." The first visitor to cross the threshold after the stroke of midnight was known as a "first-foot." It was considered good luck if this first-footer was male, dark-haired, and did not have flat feet.

The first-footer would usually arrive with his or her arms filled with cakes, bread, and cheese for his or her hosts. One of the traditional foods shared with the first-footer was Hogmanay shortbread. The shortbread was baked in the shape of the sun—perhaps a survival of pagan sun worship. Wisps of straw (see LAST SHEAF OR NEW YEAR'S WISP) were another common first-footing gift.

## *Last Sheaf or New Year's Wisp*

Back when wheat, oats, and rye were harvested by hand using sickles, it was customary at the end of the harvest to keep a handful of stalks representing the last sheaf of the harvest. They were divided into three parts and braided, then fastened at the top. The result was often referred to as the *calliagh* (from the Gaelic meaning hag, old woman, or witch), the "hare" (an animal with supernatural associations, often believed to be an old woman in animal form), or the "churn." The witch or old woman "trapped" in the last sheaf may have represented a pre-Christian fertility goddess or corn spirit. Some clergymen were reluctant to allow these "corn dollies" or decorated calliaghs to be hung in the church as part of the harvest thanksgiving decorations.

At the end of the harvest, the last sheaf was brought back in triumph to the farmhouse and placed around the neck of the master or mistress of the house, who was then obligated to put on a feast. The worker who cut the last sheaf was the guest of honor at this harvest supper. Sometimes the calliagh was placed on the supper table, but more often it was hung over the hearth or door, or on the kitchen wall. If it was placed over the door, the first young woman to enter the house afterward could be kissed by the reapers in a custom similar to that associated with mistletoe at **CHRISTMAS**. Another superstition was that this young woman was destined to marry the man who had placed the last sheaf over the door.

Last sheaf traditions, which served as an important symbol linking agricultural life with the life of the community and the harvest with human fertility, were common at one time throughout the British Isles and Europe. Sometimes the sheaf would be fed to the livestock, or mixed with seeds to be sown the following spring in a gesture designed to symbolize the continuity of life in the midst of winter. If the sheaf was kept in the house, it was considered a charm against bad luck or witchcraft. The use of a braided straw wisp as a typical New Year's gift in Scotland is regarded as a symbolic gesture linking the previous year's harvest to the next year's planting. A sheaf of oats—whether or not it is actually the last sheaf of the harvest— was a common first-footing gift.

## Noisemaking

Blowing horns, beating drums, and firing shotguns is common on Hogmanay. The fact that these same noisemaking activities accompany weddings may indicate that they are related to an ancient fertility ritual. Noise was also believed to frighten off evil spirits, and New Year's Eve was a time when such spirits were believed to be very active.

## Further Reading

Chambers, Robert, ed. *The Book of Days,* 1864.

Crippen, T. G. *Christmas and Christmas Lore,* 1990.

Frazer, Sir James G. *The Golden Bough: A Study in Magic and Religion,* 1931.

Henderson, Helene and Sue Ellen Thompson. *Holidays, Festivals, and Cele-brations of the World Dictionary,* 2nd ed., 1997.

Hervey, Thomas K. *The Book of Christmas,* 1888.

Santino, Jack. *Halloween and Other Festivals of Death and Life,* 1994.

# *Holi*

**Type of Holiday:** Religious (Hindu)

**Date of Observation:** Full moon day of the Hindu month of Phalguna (February-March)

**Where Celebrated:** India

**Symbols:** Bonfires, Colored Water, Swing

**Colors:** Holi is associated with red and yellow, as seen in the colored water and powder that people sprinkle over each other. Sometimes Holi is referred to as the Fire Festival because the saffron and crimson that people smear or sprinkle on each other are the colors of fire.

**Related Holidays:** April Fools' Day, Valentine's Day, Vernal Equinox

## ORIGINS

The colorful Hindu spring festival known as Holi has much in common with both **VALENTINE'S DAY** and **APRIL FOOLS' DAY**. The spirit of the day is to make people look and feel ridiculous by spraying them with COLORED WATER and playing practical jokes on them. The presiding deity is Kama, the Hindu version of Cupid whose sugarcane bow is strung with a line of humming bees, and whose arrows are flower stems that have been tipped with passion to wound the heart. Kama is most active in the spring-time, when he wanders through the woodlands looking for victims. In southern India, Holi is known as Kamadahana, the day on which Kama was burned by Lord Shiva.

Although Holi is a two-day festival in some parts of India, in others the celebration goes on for up to ten days. During this period people often overindulge in an intoxicating drink known as *Bhang*, use foul language, and show little respect for their elders and masters. The usual distinctions of caste, sex, and age are ignored as they smear each other with red and yellow powder and shower each other with COLORED WATER shot from bamboo blowpipes or water pistols. The streets, parks, and public squares are filled with merrymakers and people painted in bright colors.

Holi gets its name from the wicked Holika. In Hindu legend there was an evil king who declared himself to be a god and ordered his subjects to worship him. His son, Prahlad, refused to do so because he believed only in Rama, one of the incarnations of the Hindu god Vishnu. To punish the child, the king tried to kill him with fire, but Prahlad was able to save himself merely by uttering Vishnu's name. Finally the king's evil sister, Holika, who believed that she was immune to fire, took the child in her lap and sat in the flames with him. When the fire had subsided, Prahlad was found safe. But his aunt Holika had perished.

Another legend says that Holi commemorates the destruction of a female demon named Putana. When Krishna was a baby, Kansa, his enemy and king of the realm, ordered a general massacre of all children so that he would be destroyed. Putana, one of Kansa's agents, assumed human form and went about the country offering her poisoned nipples to every baby she could find. The infant Krishna, knowing exactly who she was and what she represented, sucked so hard that he drained Putana of her life.

For children living in India, Holi is as exciting as **HALLOWEEN** is to children living in the West. They roam the streets with bamboo blowpipes, looking for people to spray with liquid or powdered colors. In western India, Holi is also a celebration of the **VERNAL EQUINOX** and the wheat harvest. Festivities among the lower classes in particular can get very boisterous. No women in western India dare to leave their houses during this festival for fear of having obscenities shouted at them in the streets.

## SYMBOLS

### *Bonfires*

Bonfires are a longstanding Holi tradition. Some light them to celebrate the cremation of Putana, who was eventually burned to death by the people whose children she'd poisoned. Others light bonfires in memory of the evil Holika, who was burned in the fire that Prahlad survived. Still another legend says that an old woman whose grandchild was about to be sacrificed to

Holika gathered as many children as she could find and made them abuse Holika with foul language. Holika fell dead, and the children made a bonfire of her remains.

For a week before Holi, boys in India go from door to door collecting fuel for the bonfires—everything from wood shavings from the floor of a carpenter's shop to broken furniture and old barrel staves. When the moon is high on the night before the festival, bonfires are lit all over the country, accompanied by the blowing of horns and the beating of drums. People dance and sing songs around the fire. At dawn, the embers are doused with water and people dip their fingers into the warm ashes and make a mark on their forehead to bring luck in the coming year.

Fire is also a purifying agent. People often take a little fire from the Holi bonfire and bring it home to make their houses pure and free from disease.

## Colored Water

According to legend, the small monkey god Hanuman managed to swallow the sun one day, plunging everyone into darkness. The other gods suggested that people squirt each other with colored water to make Hanuman laugh. The monkey god laughed so hard that the sun flew out of his mouth.

Because Holi falls just before the start of the wet season in India, water is an appropriate symbol of the coming rains. Hindus also regard water as protection against evil. At this and other festivals, they take ritual baths in the Ganges River or other sacred waters.

## Swing

Holi is sometimes referred to as *Dol Yatra* or the Swing Festival. Based on the legend of how the infant Krishna sucked the life out of Putana, an image of the god as a baby is placed in a small swing-cradle and decorated with flowers and colored powder. In Bengal, *dolas* or swings are made for Krishna instead of preparing BONFIRES. In other places, the fire is built in front of the swing. Women often celebrate Holi by sitting on swings and swaying back and forth to the accompaniment of music.

## Further Reading

Gaer, Joseph. *Holidays Around the World,* 1953.
Gupte, Rai Bahadur B. A. *Hindu Holidays and Ceremonials,* 1916.
Henderson, Helene and Sue Ellen Thompson. *Holidays, Festivals, and Celebrations of the World Dictionary,* 2nd ed., 1997.

Ickis, Marguerite. *The Book of Festivals and Holidays the World Over,* 1970.

MacDonald, Margaret R., ed. *The Folklore of World Holidays,* 1992.

Santino, Jack. *All Around the Year,* 1994.

Sharma, Brijendra Nath. *Festivals of India,* 1978.

Sivananda, Swami. *Hindu Feasts and Festivals,* 1983.

Thomas, Paul. *Festivals and Holidays in India,* 1971.

# *Holy Innocents' Day*
## *(Childermas)*

**Type of Holiday:** Religious (Christian)

**Date of Observation:** December 28

**Where Celebrated:** England, Germany, Ireland, Italy, Mexico, and throughout the Christian world

**Symbols:** Boy Bishop, Whipping

**Colors:** The liturgical color for Holy Innocents' Day is purple, the color of mourning, since the children commemorated on this day died without being baptized. But if this day falls on a Sunday, custom permits the use of red, an indication that the Innocents have been given their rightful place as martyrs "baptized in blood."

**Related Holidays:** Feast of Fools

## ORIGINS

Holy Innocents' Day commemorates the children slaughtered by King Herod in his attempt to destroy the infant Jesus (Matthew 2:16). When Herod heard that a child had been born who would become King of the Jews, he had every male child under the age of two in Bethlehem destroyed. But an angel appeared to Joseph, Mary's husband, and warned him to take his family and flee. Portrayals of this event, known as the Flight into Egypt, usually show the Virgin Mary riding an ass with the Infant Jesus in her arms (see **FEAST OF FOOLS**).

How many young boys were actually killed? Although their number has been wildly exaggerated, what is now known about the population of Bethlehem at the time would seem to indicate that only about 15-20 "Innocents" actually died. But in the Greek catalogues of saints' feasts, the number of Innocents is still officially recorded as 14,000.

The earliest recorded mention of this feast dates back to the end of the fourth century. Christians in Rome during the early celebrations of the feast were expected to observe it by abstaining from meat and from foods cooked in fat. In many religious communities, Holy Innocents' Day was the traditional feast of youth. Children were given the privilege of sitting at the head of the table, and in many convents and monasteries, the last one to have taken vows was allowed to act as superior for the day. The youngest member of the community was often given a holiday and served baby food at dinner.

In England, where Holy Innocents' Day was known as Childermas, the coronation of Edward IV was postponed because it fell on December 28.

Because the young martyrs died before they could be baptized, the day devoted to them was considered extremely unlucky. In Cornwall, no housewife would scour or scrub on Childermas, and in some areas it was considered unlucky to do any washing throughout the year on the day of the week on which the feast fell. In Ireland, it was known as "the cross day of the year," and any venture begun on this day was doomed to an unhappy ending. Despite the bad luck associated with Holy Innocents' Day, it was observed throughout the Middle Ages with extravagant festivities, similar to those of the Roman **SATURNALIA**.

# SYMBOLS

## *Boy Bishop*

In England, France, and Germany, Holy Innocents' Day was also the Feast of the Boy Bishop, a celebration instituted by Pope Gregory IV in 844 when he declared March 12, the feast day of St. Gregory I, a holy day for all students and choirboys. One of the choirboys would dress in pontifical robes and impersonate Saint Gregory. Sometimes he would preach a sermon or test his fellow students on their knowledge of religious doctrine. From the eleventh century onwards, the Feast of the Boy Bishop was moved to December 28, for by that time Holy Innocents' Day had become the official feast of students and choirboys. Unfortunately, it became identified with the **FEAST OF FOOLS** in some places, and for a long time it reflected the strange abuses of religious authority and decorum associated with this celebration. Choirboys would play at being bishops and call their self-appointed archbishop an "ass." Although the Feast of Fools was finally suppressed in the fifteenth century, the tradition of the boy bishop survived.

In England, the boy bishop's term of office extended from St. Nicholas' Day, December 6, until Holy Innocents' Day, when he would preach a sermon and be the guest of honor at a special dinner. If the boy bishop died during his term of office, he would be buried with full church honors. Although this cannot have been a very common event, in England's Salisbury Cathedral there is a small sarcophagus believed to have been made for a boy bishop who died between December 6 and 28.

## *Whipping*

Although the custom of whipping children on Holy Innocents' Day is believed by some to be a means of underscoring the Biblical account of Herod's slaughter of the Innocents, it is probably a survival of a pre-Christian custom. Similar ritual beating can be found in many countries at various seasons, and it was originally intended not as a punishment, but as a way of driving out harmful influences or evil spirits. In central Europe, Innocents' Day was one of the traditional "spanking days" observed by an ancient fertility cult. Groups of children would go from house to house with branches and twigs, gently stroking women and girls while reciting an old verse wishing them many children.

In south and central Germany, the custom of *pfeffern* ("peppering") was also common on St. John's Day and **ST. STEPHEN'S DAY**. In the Thuringian Forest, children would beat passers-by with birch boughs and be given apples, nuts, and other treats in return. In France, children who slept late on Innocents' Day were whipped by their parents. The practice even gave rise to a new verb: *innocenter,* meaning "to excuse or declare someone not guilty."

## Further Reading

Chambers, Robert, ed. *The Book of Days,* 1864.

Dunkling, Leslie. *A Dictionary of Days,* 1988.

Ferguson, George. *Signs and Symbols in Christian Art,* 1954.

Harper, Howard V. *Days and Customs of All Faiths,* 1957.

Henderson, Helene and Sue Ellen Thompson. *Holidays, Festivals, and Celebrations of the World Dictionary,* 2nd ed., 1997.

Leach, Maria, ed. *Funk & Wagnalls Standard Dictionary of Folklore, Mythology, & Legend,* 1984.

Miles, Clement A. *Christmas in Ritual and Tradition,* 1990.

Urlin, Ethel L. *Festivals, Holy Days, and Saints' Days,* 1915.

Weiser, Francis X. *Handbook of Christian Feasts and Customs,* 1952.

# Hopi Snake Dance

**Type of Holiday:** Ethnic (Native American)

**Date of Observation:** August (or early September) for 16 days

**Where Celebrated:** Arizona

**Symbols:** Kisi, Kiva, Pahos (Prayer Sticks), Sand Painting, Snake Youth or Antelope Maid

## ORIGINS

The Snake Dance held every two years by the Native American Hopi tribe dates back to the earliest era of human life in what is now the southwestern United States. Scholars believe that the dance was originally a water ceremony, because snakes were the traditional guardians of springs. Today it is primarily a rain ceremony, since the Hopis regard snakes as their "brothers" and rely on them to carry their prayers for rain to the underworld, where the gods and the spirits of the ancestors live. The tourists who flock to the Hopi villages to observe the ceremony, however, are usually more interested in the spectacle than they are in its power to influence the weather.

Performed by members of the Snake and Antelope clans on all three of the mesas in Arizona where the Hopis live, the dance represents the grand finale of a 16-day ceremony that begins a few days after the **NIMAN KATCHINA** or Going Away of the Gods. Preparations for the dance take place during the last nine days, and they include making the PAHOS or prayer sticks, designing the SAND PAINTING, and building an altar around the painting that includes bowls of water from a sacred spring, green cornstalks, and trailing vines of melons and beans—all symbolic of the rain that is needed for the survival of the Hopis and their crops.

During the last four days, the Snake priests leave their villages to gather snakes, often taking young boys with them. According to Hopi legend, boys of the Snake clan can capture and handle snakes without fear from the time they are born. They stroke the snakes with a feather to make them straighten out of their dangerous coils, then grab them behind the head.

The priests are usually armed with a digging stick to dig the snakes out of their holes and a snake whip, which is a rod with two eagle feathers attached.

Foot races are held on the last two mornings. The runners streak across the plain and up the steep slope of the mesa just before sunrise in a symbolic gesture representing the rain-gods bringing water to the village. Although the runners at one time were naked, with their hair worn loose in imitation of the falling rain, nowadays they usually wear underwear and cut their hair short. The winner of the first race is given a ring and a prayer-plume, which he plants in his field to ensure a good harvest. The trophy for the second race is a jar of sacred water, also poured over the fields to bring rain.

On the day of the dance itself, the snakes are washed in a large jar filled with water and herbs and then thrown on a bed of clean sand. Young boys guard the snakes to keep them from slithering away, and they use their snake whips to prevent them from coiling. Finally the snakes are gathered up in a huge bag, carried to the village plaza, and placed in the KISI or snake-shrine.

The highlight of the ceremony occurs when the Snake priests reach into the kisi and grab a snake, carrying it first in their hands and then in their mouths. Each priest is accompanied by an attendant who uses the snake whip to prevent the reptile from coiling. As the pairs dance around the plaza, each is followed by a third man called the gatherer, whose job it is to make sure that when the time comes for the dancer to drop his snake, it doesn't wander into the crowd. At just the right moment, the gatherer touches the snake with his feathered wand, drops meal on it, and catches it behind the head. Then he lays it over his arm and goes after another one. As many as 50 or 60 small whip-snakes, long bull-snakes, and even rattlesnakes can often be seen curling around the gatherers' arms and necks.

When the bag of snakes is empty, one of the Snake priests makes a large circle of meal on the ground. The gatherers throw all of their snakes into the circle, while women and girls scatter meal on the wriggling pile. Then the Snake priests dash in, scooping up armfuls of snakes, and rush out of the plaza. They carry them off to special shrines, where they are released so they can carry the prayer for rain from the mouths of the priests to the underworld, where the rain-gods live. The dance concludes with the drinking of an emetic, which makes the dancers vomit and thus purges them of any dangerous snake-charms. With a little luck, dark clouds will gather later in the afternoon and the rains will come.

# SYMBOLS

## *Kisi*

The kisi is a shrine built to hold the snakes used in the Hopi Snake Dance. It is supported on four sticks — usually fresh-cut cottonwood boughs — driven into the ground and tied together at the top to form a cone-shaped structure, open on one side and covered with a piece of canvas or animal skin. A hole about a foot deep is dug in front of this opening; a board is laid over the hole, and the ground around it is smoothed over until the board is barely visible. This is the *sipapu* or symbolic entrance to the underworld, where the spirits of the Hopi ancestors and the rain-gods dwell.

The kisi can be traced back to the ancient brush shelters in which the Hopis' ancestors, who were wandering tribes with no permanent homes, often lived. When they turned to agriculture and needed more permanent structures, they would dig a circular room into the ground, cover it with mud-daubed logs, and enter it from above by means of a ladder. Today such a structure serves as the KIVA or ceremonial lodge.

## *Kiva*

The original kiva was an underground home that could only be entered by climbing down a ladder through a hole in the ceiling. When Native Americans first joined together to form villages, they maintained their blood relationships through ceremonies conducted in the kiva, thus establishing the clans (such as the Hopi Snake and the Antelope clans) that are the basic unit of pueblo organization to this day.

The modern-day kiva is a ceremonial room that serves as the center of a tribe's clan and religious life. Until recently, male tribe members were expected to sleep in the kiva until they were married. While modern kivas may be either round or square and built either above or below ground, most retain the basic features of the original: a windowless room entered by a ladder through a hole that serves as a smoke-vent with a fire in the center and a *sipapu* or hole in the floor that represents the gateway to the underworld. All important clan and pueblo business is conducted in the kiva, and the preliminary rituals for every dance — including the Hopi Snake Dance — take place there.

## *Pahos (Prayer Sticks)*

Pahos or prayer sticks are usually no larger than a man's middle finger. One of the sticks has a flat side and is known as the "female" stick; the other is the "male" stick. Both have faces painted on one end.

At one time, according to Hopi legend, actual human sacrifices were part of the Snake Dance. But now it appears that the pahos serve as symbolic substitutes for human victims. The Aztecs used images made of dough as substitutes for human sacrifices to the gods, so there is good reason to assume that this practice was familiar to Native Americans.

Pahos are made by the Antelope priests and the Snake priests on the day before the Snake Dance. The male and female sticks are tied together in the middle along with a small bundle of herbs. Then the sticks are laid in front of the altar in the KIVA in tray-shaped baskets. Eventually they are used as offerings to the rain-gods, as rewards to the winner of the footraces, and in the arrangement of symbolic objects around the SAND PAINTING.

## Sand Painting

In the center of the altar erected in the KIVA before the Snake Dance begins is an elaborate picture made of colored sand. The border is usually composed of four bands: yellow, green, red, and white. These bands are separated by black lines and represent the cardinal points of north, south, east, and west. The rectangular space they enclose, which can be as large as three by four feet, is filled with rows of semicircles arranged to look like fish scales. These represent rain clouds, and the short parallel lines on the border behind them represent the falling rain.

There are zigzag designs that represent lightning in the form of snakes, also colored yellow, green, red, and white with black outlines. Each of these lightning symbols has a triangular head with two dots for eyes, parallel bands around the "neck," and a single horn attached. The upright sticks set in clay holders and lined up on either side of the sand picture probably represent arrows or weapons of war, and there may be other symbolic items arranged around the border as well, such as cornstalks and gourds.

The sand painting is more than a work of art to the Hopis. It symbolizes the forces that bring rain to the fields and provide the crops so essential to the tribe's survival.

## Snake Youth or Antelope Maid

A few days before the Snake Dance takes place, two children about 14 years old are selected to represent the Snake Youth and the Antelope Maid. The girl is dressed in white robes, with her hair worn loose and a great deal of jewelry. She holds a ceremonial jar filled with trailing bean and melon vines—symbolic of the crops that need rain to flourish. The boy wears a white kirtle (tunic) and sash, and he holds the *tiponi*, which is a hollow cottonwood root containing snake rattles and tied with the feathers of eagles and other birds symbolizing the directions of the compass.

The two young people stand at the head of the SAND PAINTING while the priests blow ceremonial smoke wreaths, sprinkle meal and water over the painting, and recite the legend of the Snake Youth and the Antelope Maid—a process that can take several hours. Because the Snake Dance is actually a form of ancestor worship—not snake worship, as many believe—the Snake Youth and the Antelope Maid represent the ancestors of the Snake and Antelope clans.

## Further Reading

Dobler, Lavinia. *Customs and Holidays Around the World,* 1962.

Fergusson, Erna. *Dancing Gods: Indian Ceremonials of New Mexico and Arizona,* 1931.

Fewkes, Jesse Walter. *Hopi Snake Ceremonies,* 1986.

Henderson, Helene and Sue Ellen Thompson. *Holidays, Festivals, and Celebrations of the World Dictionary,* 2nd ed., 1997.

# *Hungry Ghosts Festival*

**Type of Holiday:** Religious (Buddhist, Taoist)

**Date of Observation:** Fifteenth through the 30th day of the seventh Chinese lunar month (August-September)

**Where Celebrated:** China and throughout eastern Asia

**Symbols:** Ghost Money, Water Lanterns

**Related Holidays:** Ch'ing Ming

## ORIGINS

Dating back to the sixth century and Confucius, the Hungry Ghosts Festival is similar to the Christian **ALL SOULS' DAY**—a time when the souls of the dead roam the earth and, if they are not treated properly, cause trouble for the living. During the last 15 days of the seventh lunar month, therefore, families visit and repair graves and make offerings of food, GHOST MONEY, and paper reproductions of such useful items as cars, furniture, and clothing in the hope that when they are burned, these items will be freed for the dead souls' use. Although the roots of this festival can be traced to primitive spirit-worship, today it has become identified with the popular Buddhist belief that for one whole month, the souls of the dead are released from hell and permitted to enjoy earthly pleasures. According to the Buddhist calendar, the mouth of Hell opens on the last night of the sixth moon and closes again on the last night of the seventh moon. But it is on the 15th day of the seventh month that a community-wide celebration is usually held.

While the original Buddhist rite was designed to placate the spirits of ancestors, today the Hungry Ghosts Festival is devoted to the unhappy spirits of those who died an unnatural death (by accident or murder, for example) and those who have no human descendants to care for them. These discontented souls suffer from hunger and thirst and, if no one attends to their needs, are most likely to haunt the living. On the 15th day of the month, Buddhist and Taoist priests chant prayers, perform rituals on outdoor altars, and make offerings to the ghosts who have not yet attained the status of stable, contented spirits. Lantern processions (see WATER LANTERNS) guide these souls to their final resting place. The ceremony comes to a climax when the priest tosses candy to the "hungry ghosts" — and children rush in to gather whatever falls on the ground.

## SYMBOLS

### *Ghost Money*

People who live too far away to spend this holiday with their families and visit the local graveyard often fill paper bags with make-believe money. Each bag is labeled with a strip of red paper on which are written the name and death date of the individual for whom it is intended. The bags are laid on an improvised altar, a priest offers prayers, and then the bags are set on fire so that the "ghost money" will reach the spirits of those who died by accident or suicide, who died in childhood, or who died far away from home.

In addition to mock money, miniature paper reproductions of automobiles, horses, sedan-chairs, and other modes of travel may be burned so that the spirits of the dead can reach Heaven. Paper furniture, clothing, and other useful items are also burned for their benefit.

## *Water Lanterns*

Boats are supposed to convey the souls of Buddhist and Taoist monks across the Heavenly River to save the souls of those who are suffering in hell. During the Hungry Ghosts Festival paper boats—some with paper crew members and the images of various gods on board—are carried in procession either to the temple or the banks of a nearby river, lake, or canal. Priests conduct special ceremonies to invoke the blessings of the gods, and then, illuminated by candles, the boats are launched. Eventually they burn and their frames collapse, but not until they have served the purpose of guiding the hungry ghosts to their final resting place.

Because it is considered bad luck to meddle with these water lanterns, fishermen spend the day on shore and other boats are left at their moorings.

## **Further Reading**

Bredon, Juliet, and Igor Mitrophanow. *The Moon Year: A Record of Chinese Customs and Festivals*, 1966.

Henderson, Helene and Sue Ellen Thompson. *Holidays, Festivals, and Celebrations of the World Dictionary*, 2nd ed., 1997.

MacDonald, Margaret R., ed. *The Folklore of World Holidays*, 1992.

Stepanchuk, Carol, and Charles Wong. *Mooncakes and Hungry Ghosts: Festivals of China*, 1991.

# Id al-Adha
## (Feast of Sacrifice)

**Type of Holiday:** Religious (Islamic)

**Date of Observation:** Tenth day of Dhu al-Hijjah, the 12th Islamic month

**Where Celebrated:** Saudi Arabia, Turkey, Africa, and throughout the Muslim world

**Symbols:** Ram

**Related Holidays:** Hajj

## ORIGINS

Just as Muslims celebrate the safe landing of Noah after the flood (see **ASHURA**), they also commemorate Abraham, Adam, Joseph, David, Moses, and many other great Jewish leaders and prophets. The three-day festival known as Id al-Adha is held in honor of Abraham, from whom they believe that the prophet Mohammed is descended. According to the Koran or Islamic holy book, Abraham had two wives, Hagar and Sarah. With Hagar, he had a son named Ishmael; with Sarah, he had a son named Isaac. The descendants of Isaac eventually became the people known as Jews. The children of Ishmael became the Arabs.

Also known as Id al-Kabir or "the Great Feast," this festival celebrates a particular event in Abraham's life. God told Abraham to sacrifice his beloved son Ishmael as proof of his faith. Abraham was fully prepared to comply with God's request, but just as he raised the ax over the boy's head, a voice from heaven told him to stop. He was permitted to sacrifice a RAM instead. Within moments a ram miraculously appeared, his horns tangled up in a bush. So Abraham sacrificed the ram and his son was spared.

In the Old Testament, it is Isaac who is nearly killed. Muslims explain this and other discrepancies between the Koran and the Bible by saying that some of the stories told in the Bible were corrupted as they were handed down over the years and translated into different languages. They believe that the Koran is the final and infallible revelation of God's will. In any case, Abraham's willingness to sacrifice his then only son revealed the extent of his obedience to God. The birth of his second son, Isaac, was his reward.

It is customary during the festival to tell children the story of Ishmael's childhood, particularly how he saved his mother in the desert by kicking at the sand with his foot so that a spring of fresh water gushed out and how he founded the sacred city of Mecca. In fact, the Id al-Adha is the concluding ceremony of the **HAJJ** or Pilgrimage to Mecca. Pilgrims stop in the village of Mina outside Mecca and sacrifice an animal to commemorate Abraham's show of faith. Those who are not participating in the pilgrimage also carry out an animal sacrifice, usually in their backyard or garden. In countries where there is a large Muslim population, schools, universities, and government offices are closed during the three days of the festival, and the air is filled with the smell of roasting meat.

Although the Id al-Adha is primarily a festive occasion, it is also a time for remembering the dead—similar to **MEMORIAL DAY** in the United States. Muslims visit burial grounds, decorate the graves with palms, and recite passages from the Koran. The women often spend an entire day and most of the night in the cemetery, although the men usually go home after the ceremonies are over.

## SYMBOLS

### Ram

The ram—although it is sometimes a cow or a lamb—that is sacrificed at the Id al-Adha represents the story of Abraham and Ishmael. In commemorating the example set by Abraham, the ram also symbolizes Muslims' readiness to sacrifice their wealth and, if necessary, their lives for the cause of God.

The ram must be slaughtered according to Islamic rules, which means that the sacrifice is usually performed by the male head of the household. He faces Mecca, recites the appropriate ritual words, and then cuts the animal's throat in a single stroke so that it bleeds to death quickly. Women who head households usually ask a male relative or the Imam of the local mosque to perform the sacrifice for them, although it is permissible for them to perform the sacrifice themselves if no suitable male can be found.

There is no need for a special license to sacrifice animals in Muslim countries. In Western countries, however, a special license may be required. Sometimes a group of license holders will go to the slaughterhouse and sacrifice the animals on behalf of the Muslim community.

The meat from the sacrificed animal is normally divided into three portions, one of which is distributed to the poor. The second portion is given to friends and relatives, and the third portion is eaten at home by the family. In the West, where there may not be any poor Muslims who need the food, the meat is often given to nursing homes.

## Further Reading

Ahsan, M. M. *Muslim Festivals,* 1987.

Gaer, Joseph. *Holidays Around the World,* 1953.

Glassé, Cyril. *The Concise Encyclopedia of Islam,* 1989.

Henderson, Helene and Sue Ellen Thompson. *Holidays, Festivals, and Celebrations of the World Dictionary,* 2nd ed., 1997.

Smith, Huston. *The Illustrated World's Religions,* 1994.

# Id al-Fitr
## (Feast of Fast-Breaking, the Lesser Feast)

**Type of Holiday:** Religious (Islamic)

**Date of Observation:** First day of the tenth Islamic lunar month of Shawwal

**Where Celebrated:** Africa, Egypt, India, Indonesia, Iran, Iraq, Jordan, Lebanon, Malaya, Morocco, Pakistan, Saudi Arabia, Syria, Thailand, Turkey, and throughout the Muslim world

**Symbols:** Alms, 'Id Prayer, Moon

**Related Holidays:** Id al-Adha, Ramadan

# ORIGINS

Also known as the Little Festival or the Lesser Feast, the Id al-Fitr is the second most important major holiday (after the **ID AL-ADHA**, or Great Feast) in the Islamic calendar. It follows the sighting of the new MOON that signifies the end of the month-long fast of **RAMADAN** and the beginning of a three-day period of feasting and celebration. Sometimes it is called the "sugar" festival, because of the sweets that are exchanged as gifts on this occasion.

Because it marks the end of an entire month of fasting and devotion, the Little Festival is observed with even more enthusiasm than the Great Festival. Although both feasts last three to four days and involve special prayer services, the Id al-Fitr is characterized by more spontaneous shows of joy and generosity. Muslims dress in their newest or best clothes and begin the day by gathering to recite the 'ID PRAYER. When the prayers are over, everyone embraces, greeting each other with the words *'Id Mubarak* or "Happy 'Id." The day is often celebrated with camel races, puppet shows, and carnival rides.

*'Id* refers to a festival of great joy and never-ending happiness, a time when Muslim families get together to give thanks and forget their differences. Much like Christians preparing for **CHRISTMAS**, Muslims decorate their houses, buy gifts for their friends and relatives, and send out 'Id cards. Shopping is such a big part of the festival that stores in many Muslim countries stay open all night during Ramadan. Muslims living in Western countries usually take a day off work (as opposed to the three-day holiday observed in Muslim countries) and let their children stay home from school. In some countries, the Id al-Fitr is a popular time to invite non-Muslim friends over for a visit, to foster greater understanding among different ethnic and religious groups.

Foods traditionally served at the Lesser Feast include *shir khorma,* made from milk, vermicelli, sugar, dates, and nuts. In Pakistan, this special treat is known as *saween.*

# SYMBOLS

## *Alms*

A special offering, known as the *zakat al-fitr* and consisting of a measure of grain (or its equivalent) for each member of the household, is given to the poor during the Id al-Fitr. Every Muslim who can afford to do so is also asked to donate money to the poor in advance of the holiday, so that the poor have time to prepare for the celebration. In Western countries, money is often collected and sent to less wealthy Islamic countries, such as Bangladesh.

## 'Id Prayer

On the first morning of Id al-Fitr, Muslims wake up early and flock to mosques or outdoor prayer grounds—such as parks, fields, and play-grounds—to offer special 'Id prayers. Muslims living in London, for example, often hold their 'Id prayers in Regents' Park.

There are three different types of prayer in the Islamic religion. One is the spontaneous, individual prayer in which a worshipper expresses his personal feelings and petitions God. The second, known as *salah* ("worship"), is the ritual prayer that must be performed five times each day. Special forms of *salah* are prescribed for religious festivals, such as the 'Id al-Fitr, or to ask for guidance in particular circumstances. The third type of prayer is the inward prayer of "remembrance" of God, which often involves rhythmic chanting to induce a state of ecstasy.

Since Id al-Fitr is supposed to be a gathering for the entire Islamic community, women and children are also encouraged to come to the prayers. Many women, however, prefer to stay at home and prepare the foods that will be served during the three-day feast.

## Moon

Because it marks the end of the fast of **RAMADAN**, the first appearance of the new moon of Shawwal generates great excitement—even greater than that at the beginning of Ramadan. As soon as the moon is sighted, everyone rushes to congratulate each other and begin celebrating. If the moon can't be seen because of clouds, which often happens in Western countries, people consult their local mosque or Islamic center, which receives information from Muslim countries by radio and telephone about where and when the 'Id moon is due to appear. Because of the distance between the various Muslim countries, however, the 'Id al-Fitr does not always begin at the same time.

## Further Reading

Ahsan, M. M. *Muslim Festivals,* 1987.

Glassé, Cyril. *The Concise Encyclopedia of Islam,* 1989.

Henderson, Helene and Sue Ellen Thompson. *Holidays, Festivals, and Celebrations of the World Dictionary,* 2nd ed., 1997.

MacDonald, Margaret R., ed. *The Folklore of World Holidays,* 1992.

Von Grunebaum, G. D. *Muhammadan Festivals,* 1988.

# *Imbolc*
## *(Imbolg, Oimelg)*

**Type of Holiday:** Ancient or pagan

**Date of Observation:** February 1

**Where Celebrated:** British Isles

**Symbols:** Brigit, Lamb

**Colors:** Imbolc is identified with the worship of BRIGIT, with whom the color white is associated.

**Related Holidays:** Beltane, Candlemas (Groundhog Day), Lughnasa, St. Bridget's Day, Samhain.


## ORIGINS

Imbolc was an ancient Druidic festival dedicated to the mysteries of motherhood, which is why its ceremonies were usually carried out by Druid priestesses rather than by male members of the order. It was one of the "Greater Sabbats" of the Wiccan year ("Wicca" being the name used by believers in neo-pagan witchcraft to avoid the stigma attached to "witchcraft"), which were huge seasonal get-togethers for witches that involved all-night dancing, singing, and feasting. Like the other Sabbats (or Sabbaths) celebrated on April 30 (see **BELTANE**), July 31 (see **LUGHNASA**), and October 31 (see **SAMHAIN**), Imbolc revolved around the changing season and the breeding of animals (see LAMB).

Imbolc was dedicated to BRIGIT, the ancient Irish goddess whose name means "the shining one" (*breo* in Irish is a firebrand or torch, and *breoch* means glowing). Primarily a goddess of fertility, Brigit was frequently depicted as three goddesses in one: the virgin, the mother, and the crone. When Ireland became Roman Catholic, Brigit was transformed into a Christian saint, St. Brigid or Bridget, whose worship dates back to very early times.

As one of the four occasions during the year when witches gathered, often on mountaintops or at crossroads, to perform their black rites and reaffirm their obedience to the Devil, Imbolc was often characterized by wild sex orgies and other activities that can be traced to its origin as a pagan fertility celebration. It took place on the eve of February 2, later known to Christians as **CANDLEMAS.**

# SYMBOLS

## Brigit

Brigit was the archetypal mother-goddess, protectress of women in labor and childbirth. Because she stood as a symbol of motherhood and fertility in general, cows and their milk were dedicated to Brigit, as were ewes and their LAMBS. Although it is not certain exactly why, Brigit was also associated with brewing beer. According to a Christianized version of an old medieval tale, she presided over a brewing at **EASTER** in which she produced enough beer for 17 churches from a single measure of malt.

Brigit, with whom the color white is associated, is often shown carrying a white rod similar to the hazel rods carried by the Druid priests as symbols of their authority. The white rod symbolizes both the serpent and the swan, who is a bird with a serpent-like neck and a serpent's hiss.

Brigit has much in common with the Virgin Mary, and it is no coincidence that the Purification of the Virgin Mary and the Presentation of Jesus at the Temple in Jerusalem are commemorated on February 2 (see **CANDLE-MAS**). In fact, it is traditional on Candlemas to offer prayers to both St. Brigit and the Blessed Virgin, and to honor motherhood in general.

## Lamb

Imbolc took place at the beginning of the lambing season, so it was closely associated with the ewes and milking. This marked a vital turning point in the winter, since the first sheep's milk and cheese would have been very important at a time when stored meats and grains were beginning to run out and no other fresh foods were available.

Representing all things newborn and innocent, the lamb is a very ancient symbol. A real newborn lamb may have been paraded through the streets or worshipped during Imbolc, and there is also reason to believe that some of the ancient ceremonies held on this day involved drinking the first sheep's milk of the year. When Christianity arrived, of course, the lamb became a symbol of Christ, who was referred to as the "Lamb of God."

## Further Reading

Heinberg, Richard. *Celebrate the Solstice: Honoring the Earth's Seasonal Rhythms through Festival and Ceremony,* 1993.

Henderson, Helene and Sue Ellen Thompson. *Holidays, Festivals, and Celebrations of the World Dictionary,* 2nd ed., 1997.

Kelly, Aidan, Peter Dresser, and Linda M. Ross. *Religious Holidays and Calendars,* 1993.

King, John. *The Celtic Druids' Year: Seasonal Cycles of the Ancient Celts,* 1995.

Leach, Maria, ed. *Funk & Wagnalls Standard Dictionary of Folklore, Mythology, & Legend,* 1984.

# Incwala

**Type of Holiday:** Folkloric
**Date of Observation:** December-January
**Where Celebrated:** Swaziland
**Symbols:** Bull, Gourd

## ORIGINS

The most sacred national ceremony that takes place in the independent kingdom of Swaziland in southeast Africa is the annual kingship ceremony known as the Incwala. It is held around the time of the **SUMMER SOLSTICE**, which falls in late December in Africa, and lasts for about three weeks. In addition to marking the beginning of a new year, the Incwala features rites aimed at strengthening the king's authority and increasing the strength and cohesiveness of the nation as a whole.

The phase of the moon and the positions of the sun and stars are constant topics of conversation as everyone waits for the precise moment when the sun appears to stand still, rising and setting in the same place for several days. The Swazi believe that the full or waxing moon brings strength and health, while the waning moon is associated with weakness. It is important, therefore, that the ceremony coincide not only with the summer solstice but with a favorable phase of the moon. If the wrong day is chosen, it is considered a national calamity because it means the king will not be strong enough to endure the trials of the coming year. Since the new moon that marks the beginning of the festival rarely coincides with the solstice, special rituals have been devised to compensate for the unfavorable timing.

The Little Incwala, which lasts for two days, begins when the moon is dark and the king is at his weakest. Because one purpose of the ceremony is to temporarily separate him from society and make a symbolic break with the old year, the king is sequestered in a special enclosure — just as the sun is said to be "resting in its hut" at the solstice.

The Big Incwala, which begins on the night of the full moon and lasts for six days, marks the symbolic rebirth and revitalization of the king. On the first day, a group of young, unmarried (and therefore "pure") men is sent to gather branches from a magic tree and bring them back to the king's councilors, who use them to build the sanctuary in which the king's powers will be symbolically reborn. On the third day, the king strikes a black BULL with a rod that is believed to possess the power of fertility. The pure young men must catch the animal and kill it with their bare hands, after which it is dragged into the sanctuary and sacrificed. All of this is considered preparation for the fourth day, when the king symbolically overcomes his rivals and gets rid of the evils and pollution of the old year. He comes out of his enclosure dressed in a frightening costume of green grass and wild animal skins, his body gleaming with black ointments. While the people sing and dance in the background, the young men or princes alternately drive the king back and beg him to return. The climax occurs when the king throws a bright green GOURD toward his warriors. Then he is led back to his hut.

On the final day of the Incwala, all of the ritual implements that have been used in the ceremony are burned in a huge fire, symbolically ridding the kingdom of evil. The king is bathed, and the drops of water that fall from his body are believed to attract the coming rains, which will reenergize the forces of nature.

It was common in ancient cultures to associate the health and vitality of the king with the health of the kingdom. In some cases, old kings were removed at the time of the solstice. Getting rid of an old king was a common means of ridding the kingdom of bad influences and cleansing the country as a whole.

## SYMBOLS

### *Bull*

The main event of the third day of the Big Incwala is the killing of the bull, who symbolizes potency. Parts of the bull's body are used to prepare royal medicines, and the rest is given as an offering to the dead ancestors. The "Day of the Bull" is believed to fortify the king for the following day, when he appears in his terrifying costume and must "overcome" the young princes who symbolize his rivals.

### Gourd

The bright green gourd used in the climax of the Incwala ceremony is known as the "Gourd of Embo"—"Embo" meaning North, or the direction from which the royal clan originally came. The king throws the gourd carefully on the upturned shield of one of his subjects, who must not let the fruit touch the ground. The gourd symbolizes the continuity of the past. In discarding it, the king proves his strength and opens the way to the future.

### Further Reading

Heinberg, Richard. *Celebrate the Solstice: Honoring the Earth's Seasonal Rhythms through Festival and Ceremony,* 1993.
Henderson, Helene and Sue Ellen Thompson. *Holidays, Festivals, and Celebrations of the World Dictionary,* 2nd ed., 1997.
MacDonald, Margaret R., ed. *The Folklore of World Holidays,* 1992.

# Inti Raymi Festival
### (Inti Raymi Pageant, Sun Festival, Feast of the Sun)

**Type of Holiday:** Calendar
**Date of Observation:** June 24
**Where Celebrated:** Peru
**Symbols:** Golden Rod, Maize
**Related Holidays:** Winter Solstice

## ORIGINS

Inti Raymi is a **WINTER SOLSTICE** festival observed by the Incas in Peru. By the late fifteenth century their empire, which they believed lay at the center of the earth, extended along the Pacific coast of South America from northern Ecuador to central Chile. On the day of the solstice, the Incas would gather to honor Inti, their sun god, at the foot of the hill of La Marca, not far from where the equator is now known to be located. Just before dawn, the emperor and his entourage would go to a ceremonial plaza in central Cuzco, the empire's capital. They took off their shoes in deference to the sun, faced northeast, and waited for the sun to rise. When it appeared on the horizon, everyone crouched down and blew kisses in the sun's direction. Then the emperor lifted two golden cups of *chicha,* a sacred drink made of fermented MAIZE, and offered the cup in his left hand to the sun. It was poured into a basin that was designed to drain quickly. When the chicha disappeared, everyone thought the sun had consumed it. After sipping the chicha in the other cup, the emperor shared it with the others present and then proceeded to the Coricancha or Sun Temple. A fire was lit in the temple's innermost shrine, a room lined with magnificent gold "sun discs," by focusing the sun's rays with a convex mirror. Animal sacrifices and other ceremonies followed.

Today the main celebration still takes place in Cuzco, where there is a special procession and mock sacrifice to the sun, followed by a week-long celebration involving folk dances, tours of archaeological ruins, and displays of South American Indian arts and crafts. Bonfires are still lit in the Andes Mountains to celebrate the rebirth of the sun, and the Incas burn their old clothes as a symbolic way of destroying poverty and marking the end of the harvest cycle.

The Incas also observed a **SUMMER SOLSTICE** festival, known as Capac Raymi, in December.

## SYMBOLS

### Golden Rod

According to the Incas' creation myth, the first Incas were sent down to earth by their father, the Sun, to find the place where a golden rod he had given them could be plunged into the soil with one blow, indicating that the ground was good for planting. This mythical rod probably represents the vertical rays of the sun at noon on the solstice, when it stands directly overhead. The place where it sank into the ground was marked at first with a humble shrine, later expanded into the Temple of the Sun or Coricancha ("Golden Enclosure"). The Coricancha soon became a religious center and place of pilgrimage as well as a model for other sun temples throughout the vast Inca empire.

In 1600 Garcilaso de la Vega, the nephew of the 11th Inca ruler, document-ed the existence of a sacred group of gnomons or sunsticks near Quito, which is located very close to the Equator, where the sun passes through the zenith at noon on the equinox. According to Garcilaso, this was the seat that Inti, the sun god, liked best, because he sat straight up rather than leaning to the side. The Incas observed the equinoxes by watching their gnomons until the sun bathed all sides of the column equally, and there were no shadows cast. Then they decorated the gnomons with flowers and herbs and placed the Sun's throne on top.

## Maize

Maize (corn) and chicha (fermented maize drink) were specially prepared by a group of chosen women, referred to as the "wives of the sun," for the Inti Raymi Festival. Because maize was symbolic of the Sun's gifts, it was important to eat it during the Sun Festival. The maize used for the festival was grown in the garden of the Coricancha, and during major festivals like the Inti Raymi, maize plants made of gold were displayed there. Given the fact that the Incas' empire was situated primarily in high altitudes where frost and hail were common, it is not surprising that sun worship was so intimately connected to the growing of maize.

## Further Reading

Eliade, Mircea. *The Encyclopedia of Religion,* 1897.

Heinberg, Richard. *Celebrate the Solstice: Honoring the Earth's Seasonal Rhythms through Festival and Ceremony,* 1993.

Henderson, Helene and Sue Ellen Thompson. *Holidays, Festivals, and Cele-brations of the World Dictionary,* 2nd ed., 1997.

Leach, Maria, ed. *Funk & Wagnalls Standard Dictionary of Folklore, Mythology, & Legend,* 1984.

MacDonald, Margaret R., ed. *The Folklore of World Holidays,* 1992.

Shemanski, Frances. *A Guide to World Fairs and Festivals,* 1985.

# *Janmashtami*
### *(Krishna's Birthday)*

**Type of Holiday:** Religious (Hindu)

**Date of Observation:** Eighth day of the Hindu month of Bhadrapada (August-September)

**Where Celebrated:** India

**Symbols:** Curd Pots

## ORIGINS

The Hindu gods appeared in human or animal forms at certain times in history so they could perform great deeds. Each time a god went through another incarnation, it became the occasion for a new Hindu holiday. Vishnu, one of the three gods who make up the Hindu Trinity, appeared first as a fish, then as a tortoise and a boar. Later he appeared as a man-lion, a dwarf, the son of a great sage, and a prince. His most memorable incarnation, however, was when he appeared as Krishna, whose life and heroic deeds are described in the great Hindu epic, the *Mahabharata.*

The birthday of Lord Krishna, the eighth incarnation of Vishnu, is one of the most important Hindu festivals. Born at Mathura, in Uttar Pradesh, a state in northern India, Krishna's mission on earth was to get rid of the demon Kamsa, who had seized the throne, imprisoned the real king, and persecuted good people while making life easy for the wicked. His evil ways became so unbearable that Vishnu decided to incarnate himself as a man and bring about Kamsa's destruction.

Krishna grew up among the herdsmen of Gokul. As a child, he was adored for his mischievous pranks as well as his miracles. As a young cowherd, he became renowned as a lover, and the sound of his flute lured the wives and daughters of other cowherds to leave their homes to dance with him in the forest. When he finally returned to Mathura to slay the wicked Kamsa, he found the kingdom unsafe and led the people to the western coast of India, where he reestablished his court in what is today the state of Gujarat.

Janmashtami—the name comes from *Janma,* birth, and *ashtami,* the eighth—is celebrated on the eighth day of Bhadrapada by Hindus of all sects and castes throughout India, particularly in and around Mathura. The celebrations there include dancing, in imitation of the young Krishna's moonlight dances with the cow-girls, the singing of religious songs and hymns, and recitations from the great Hindu epics. Everyone, even children, fasts for 24 hours. The floor from the doorway to the inner meditation room of the house is often marked with a child's footprints, made by mixing flour and water, to create the impression that Krishna himself has walked through the house. Pilgrims from all over India visit the temple of Shri Rangji, where Krishna is known to have spent his childhood.

When the fast is broken at midnight, the ringing of temple bells, the jingling of cymbals, and the blowing of conch shells is ongoing. The image of Lord Krishna as a child is bathed in milk while his name is chanted, and, at the hour of his birth, the image is rocked in a cradle decorated with garlands of flowers.

## SYMBOLS

### Curd Pots

Dairy foods are usually served on Janmashtami because Krishna was very fond of milk and butter as a child. In some parts of India, the celebration includes the shattering of curd pots (unglazed ceramic pots containing sour milk), which are hung up high over the streets by young men forming human pyramids, or suspended from a pole supported by two uprights. The pots are knocked down and broken in imitation of the young Krishna, who was so fond of milk that he used to steal, with the help of his friends, curds and butter that had been hung in earthen pots from the kitchen ceiling to keep it out of children's hands. After the curd pots are broken, the celebrants dance as Krishna danced during his stay among the herdsmen of Gokul.

## Further Reading

Gaer, Joseph. *Holidays Around the World,* 1953.

Gupte, Rai Bahadur B. A. *Hindu Holidays and Ceremonials,* 1916.

Henderson, Helene and Sue Ellen Thompson. *Holidays, Festivals, and Cele-brations of the World Dictionary,* 2nd ed., 1997.

Sharma, Brijendra Nath. *Festivals of India,* 1978.

Sivananda, Swami. *Hindu Feasts and Festivals,* 1983.

Thomas, Paul. *Festivals and Holidays in India,* 1971.

# *John Canoe Festival*
### *(Jonkonnu Festival, Junkanoo Festival)*

**Type of Holiday:** Ethnic

**Date of Observation:** December 26, January 1

**Where Celebrated:** Bahamas, Belize, Guatemala, Jamaica

**Symbols:** Goombay, John Canoe

**Related Holidays:** Carnival (Mardi Gras)

## ORIGINS

Held on various Caribbean islands, the John Canoe Festival represents a combination of Mardi Gras (**CARNIVAL**), mummers' parades, and ancient African tribal rituals. Perhaps the best-known celebration is the one held in Nassau on December 26, Boxing Day (**ST. STEPHEN'S DAY**), and on January 1, **NEW YEAR'S DAY**. Masqueraded marchers wearing colorful headpieces and costumes that have taken months to prepare dance to the beat of an Afro-Bahamian rhythm called GOOMBAY. The Jonkonnu parade, which begins at four o'clock in the morning and contin-ues until sunrise, is followed by the judging of costumes and awarding of prizes. There are Jonkonnu parades in Freeport and elsewhere in the Bahamas as well.

When slaveholders in the American South observed holidays, their slaves would usually celebrate by holding their own parties and barbecues. In North Carolina, these celebrations always included the appearance of JOHN CANOE, dressed in a colorful costume made from many scraps of material and wearing a white mask that was frightening to children and adults alike. He would dance down the street with a jerking, gyrating motion, often accompanied by musicians. He sang songs, told stories, and accepted contributions from spectators. The procession would last all day, and the party that followed went on all night. It was a way for African-American slaves to have their own fun on holidays observed primarily by whites. The custom known as "Kunering" (John Canoe was sometimes known as John Kuner), which only took place between Christmas and the New Year, was outlawed by the North Carolina police around 1900 because educated blacks regarded it as degrading to members of their race.

Today, celebrations featuring John Canoe can be found primarily in the West Indies. In Belize and Guatemala, the John Canoe masqueraders dance from house to house, wearing wire-screen masks painted white or pink with staring eyes, red lips, black eyebrows, and thin mustaches. In Jamaica, the Jonkonnu procession includes a King and Queen with their courtiers; a Sailor Boy, who uses a whip to keep the audience in line; Babu, an East Indian cowboy with a long cattle prod; and Pitchy Patchy, another traditional figure. The Jonkonnu processions held in remote villages are even rowdier, featuring a Whore Girl who raises her skirts and a Belly Woman who shakes her belly in time with the music.

## SYMBOLS

### *Goombay*

Historically, "goombay" referred to the drumbeats and rhythms of Africa, which were brought to the Bahamas by slaves. The term was used during jump-in dances, when the drummer would shout "Gimbey!" at the beginning of each dance. The Ibo tribes in West Africa have a drum they called Gamby, from which the name "goombay" probably derived.

Today, Goombay refers to all Bahamian secular music, although it is particularly associated with the John Canoe Festival. It is played by a variety of unusual native instruments, including goat-skin drums, lignum vitae sticks, pebble-filled "shik-shaks," and steel drums.

## John Canoe

There are a number of theories as to where the name "John Canoe" came from. Some believe he is a symbol for John Conny, the West African tribal chief who outwitted Dutch merchantmen and maintained control of the Prussian Fort Brandenburg (later known as "Conny's Castle"), which he commanded during the early eighteenth century at Prince's Town. John Conny, who lived from 1660 to 1732, promoted trade between the Ashanti and the Germans for more than a decade and was sometimes called the "Last Prussian Negro Prince."

In the United States, John Canoe was a precursor of the unofficial governor chosen by African-American slaves in New England on Election Day. For about 100 years, beginning in 1750, New England slaves would hold an election of their own, which would be followed by a parade featuring their newly elected governor. Thousands of slaves participated in such parades throughout Massachusetts, Connecticut, and Rhode Island. Although the unofficial governor had no legal power, he was usually a very able man who exercised considerable authority over New England blacks.

Still another theory about the name John Canoe is that it came from the French *gens inconnus,* or "unknown people," referring to the masked dancers who appear at the John Canoe Festival.

### Further Reading

Anyike, James C. *African American Holidays,* 1991.
Cohen, Hennig, and Tristram Potter Coffin, eds. *The Folklore of American Holidays,* 2nd ed., 1991.
Henderson, Helene and Sue Ellen Thompson. *Holidays, Festivals, and Celebrations of the World Dictionary,* 2nd ed., 1997.
Shemanski, Frances. *A Guide to World Fairs and Festivals,* 1985.

# *Juneteenth*

**Type of Holiday:** Historic, Ethnic (African-American)
**Date of Observation:** June 19 and other dates
**Where Celebrated:** United States
**Symbols:** Singing and Dancing

# ORIGINS

Juneteenth—an abbreviation for June 19—is the oldest African-American observance in the United States. Also known as Emancipation Day, Freedom Day, and Jun-Jun, it is a celebration of freedom from slavery that began spontaneously and spread across the country.

Slavery was one of the major issues leading up to the Civil War in 1861. By 1862, laws abolishing slavery had been passed in the territories of Oklahoma, Nebraska, Colorado, and New Mexico. On September 22, 1862, President Abraham Lincoln issued a proclamation notifying the rebellious states that had seceded from the Union (Alabama, Florida, Georgia, Louisiana, Mississippi, South Carolina, and Texas, joined later by North Carolina, Arkansas, Virginia, and Tennessee) that if they didn't return to the Union by January 1, 1863, he would declare their slaves "forever free." This led to the Emancipation Proclamation, which declared that slaves in the 11 rebel states were free. Two years later, on January 31, 1865, Congress passed the 13th Amendment, abolishing slavery throughout the United States.

Even though slaves in the South were declared free in 1863, word didn't reach the slaves in Texas until June 19, 1865, the day General Gordon Granger and his federal troops arrived in Galveston with the intention of forcing slave owners to release their slaves. There are a number of theories as to why it took so long for the news of the Emancipation Proclamation to reach East Texas. Some people say that the news was delayed by mule travel, while others believe that the original messenger was murdered. The most popular explanation is that the news was deliberately withheld by wealthy landowners who wanted their slaves to bring in one last crop.

Juneteenth, the commemoration of General Granger's arrival, was originally celebrated not only in Texas but in Louisiana, perhaps because Granger left from New Orleans to begin his historic journey. Eventually the celebration spilled over into southwestern Arkansas. Then, as blacks began to migrate into the territory that was soon to become Oklahoma, they took their freedom festival with them.

In the late 1930s and early 1940s, there was a second migration of blacks from the southwestern states to California. These West Coast settlers continued to observe Juneteenth, but the celebration had dwindled to picnics sponsored by African Americans from the same state. For example, an "Oklahoma picnic" is still held in Los Angeles' Lincoln Heights Park every year on June 19. But what really emerged following these migrations was the idea of "homecoming:" West Coast blacks who originally came from east Texas and the surrounding area began to migrate back home for a visit on the weekend nearest the 19th—a practice that is still common today.

Juneteenth is observed on a number of different dates, due to the fact that enforcement of the slaves' liberation came about only after the defeat of local Confederate forces. It is observed on January 1 in New York City, Boston, Alabama, Georgia, North and South Carolina, Virginia, Tennessee, and Maryland; on February 1 in Philadelphia; on May 8 in eastern Mississippi; on May 20 in Florida; on August 1 in Ontario (Canada); on August 4 in northeastern Arkansas, north central Tennessee, central Oklahoma, southeastern Missouri, and southwestern Illinois; on August 8 in southwestern Kentucky; and on September 22 in Indiana, the rest of Illinois, and Ohio. East Texas, Oklahoma, Louisiana, southwestern Arkansas, southern Oklahoma, and California continue to observe it on June 19 with festivities that include parades, picnics, SINGING AND DANCING, and baseball games.

## SYMBOLS

## *Singing and Dancing*

Juneteenth is typically spent having fun. Games and picnics, beauty pageants, talent contests, and sporting events are common on this day, and almost every celebration includes singing and dancing. These expressions of joy are symbolic of the celebrations that took place on **NEW YEAR'S EVE** in 1862, as blacks awaited President Lincoln's official announcement that the slaves in the 11 southern states that had seceded from the Union were free.

## Further Reading

Anyike, James C. *African American Holidays,* 1991.

Cohen, Hennig, and Tristram Potter Coffin, eds. *The Folklore of American Holidays,* 2nd ed., 1991.

Dunkling, Leslie. *A Dictionary of Days,* 1988.

Henderson, Helene and Sue Ellen Thompson. *Holidays, Festivals, and Celebrations of the World Dictionary,* 2nd ed., 1997.

# *Kartika Snan*

**Type of Holiday:** Religious (Hindu)
**Date of Observation:** October-November; Hindu month of Kartika
**Where Celebrated:** India
**Symbols:** Lamps, Tulsi Plant
**Related Holidays:** Dewali

## ORIGINS

The Hindu months of Vaisakha (April-May), Kartika (October-November) and Magha (January-February) are regarded as especially holy and therefore suitable for acts of religious devotion. Throughout the month of Kartika, Hindus bathe in a sacred river, stream, pond, or well early in the morning. A month-long bathing festival is held on sacred rivers like the Ganges and the Yamuna. People set up tents on the riverbank, have regular morning baths, eat only a single meal each day, and spend their time in prayer and meditation.

Hindu women get up early in the morning and visit the sacred streams in groups, singing hymns along the way. After bathing, they visit a nearby temple. They also fast, keep sky LAMPS burning throughout the month, and worship the TULSI PLANT, which is considered sacred and is cultivated in homes and temples.

# SYMBOLS

## *Lamps*

Lamps hung in small baskets from the tops of poles or from bamboo plants growing along the riverbanks during Kartika are sometimes referred to as "sky lamps." They are kept burning throughout the holy month of Kartika because they are believed to light the path of departed souls across the sky.

In Madras, the capital of Tamil Nadu in southeastern India, the full moon day of the month of Kartika is celebrated in much the same way as **DEWALI** is observed in northern India—that is, by lighting lamps in temples and private homes.

## *Tulsi Plant*

Hindus believe that watering, cultivating, and worshipping the Tulsi plant ensures happiness. When Tulsi leaves are put into water, it becomes as holy as water from the Ganges. When placed in the mouth of those who are dying, along with some Ganges water, Tulsi leaves make their departure from this life easier. Tulsi leaves offered to Vishnu during Kartika are said to please him more than the gift of a thousand cows.

The Tulsi plant is a symbol for Vishnupriya (beloved of Vishnu), and their marriage is celebrated on the 11th day of the waxing half of Kartika.

## Further Reading

Henderson, Helene and Sue Ellen Thompson. *Holidays, Festivals, and Celebrations of the World Dictionary*, 2nd ed., 1997.

Kelly, Aidan. *Religious Holidays and Calendars*, 1993.

Welbon, Guy, and Glenn Yocum. *Religious Festivals in South India and Sri Lanka*, 1982.

# *Kataklysmos Day*
### *(Festival of the Flood)*

**Type of Holiday:** Religious (Orthodox Christian)

**Date of Observation:** Between May 10 and June 13; coincides with Pentecost

**Where Celebrated:** Cyprus

**Symbols:** Chattismata, Water

**Related Holidays:** Pentecost

## ORIGINS

Kataklysmos is a religious and popular festival celebrated on Cyprus, with its roots in both the Bible and Greek mythology. *Kataklysmos* is the Greek word meaning "flood," and it refers to the Bible's story about Noah in the book of Genesis as well as a Greek creation myth.

In the Bible story, God decides that all humankind is corrupt. He causes a flood that will destroy all life — except Noah, his wife, their sons and sons' wives, and a male and female pair of every kind of animal and bird. Noah builds an ark to hold this menagerie, and they all live on it while it rains for 40 days and 40 nights. They eventually land on what is now thought to be Mt. Ararat, and Noah and his family and animals replenish the earth's population.

In the Greek story, Zeus decides to destroy the earth because of human wickedness. Floods cover the earth, leaving only a small area of dry land on top of Mt. Parnassus. After nine days and nine nights of rain, a great wooden chest drifts to the spot. Inside are Deucalion and his wife, Pyrrha. Deucalion had been warned by his father, Prometheus, that the flood was coming and was able to save himself and his wife by building the chest. As they walked down the mountain into the flood-devastated world, Deucalion and Pyrrha heard a voice telling them to "cast behind you the bones of your mother." They realized that the earth was their mother and stones were her bones. They began to throw stones, and the stones took human form. His stones became men, while hers became women. To celebrate the end of the flood, Deucalion held a festival, which may have been the forerunner of today's Kataklysmos.

The celebration, which begins on a Friday and lasts until Monday, is usually held in seaside towns. Activities include games, folk dancing, boat races, swimming competitions, feasting, and listening to CHATTISMATA. The most popular custom is throwing water at one another, in memory of the flood that once destroyed nearly all life on earth.

## SYMBOLS

### *Chattismata*

*Chattismata* or "arguments in verse" are often held on Kataklysmos Day. The contestants exchange rhyming insults until one person can't think of a quick response, and his or her opponent wins. The responses must be immediate, appropriate, and clever. Skilled contestants can battle each other for hours.

### *Water*

Sprinkling water on each other is so much a part of the Kataklysmos festival that Cypriots consider it bad luck *not* to be sprinkled. Since they believe that the sea is blessed by the Holy Spirit on this day, having water sprinkled over one's head is symbolic of sharing in this blessing. It also symbolizes the purification of both body and soul.

In one of the traditional dances performed on Kataklysmos Day, a man balances a stack of six full glasses of water on top of his head.

## Further Reading

Henderson, Helene and Sue Ellen Thompson. *Holidays, Festivals, and Celebrations of the World Dictionary*, 2nd ed., 1997.
MacDonald, Margaret R., ed. *The Folklore of World Holidays,* 1992.
Van Straalen, Alice. *The Book of Holidays Around the World,* 1896.

# *Kentucky Derby*

**Type of Holiday:** Sporting
**Date of Observation:** First Saturday in May
**Where Celebrated:** Louisville, Kentucky
**Symbols:** Mint Julep, Red Roses

# ORIGINS

One of the top sporting events in the United States, the horse race known as the Kentucky Derby has been held at Churchill Downs racetrack in Louisville, Kentucky, since 1875. It was originally modeled on England's Epsom Derby, and the stylish clothes and parties associated with the race represent a deliberate attempt to recreate the social atmosphere of the English derby. The Kentucky Derby is unquestionably the most important social event of the year in Louisville, as evidenced by the more than 10,000 parties held there during Derby week.

Kentucky has a long tradition of horse racing and horse breeding. With its relatively mild climate, rich vegetation, and bluegrass meadows, Kentucky offers the ideal environment for raising thoroughbred horses. The first horse races in the state were held in Lexington in 1787, and the first jockey club was organized ten years later. Colonel Meriwether Lewis Clark, Jr., established Churchill Downs (named after the family that owned the land on which the track stands) as the home of the Louisville Jockey Club, and he served as the track's president from 1875 until 1894. He offered the Kentucky Derby as part of the Churchill Downs program, confining the race to three-year-old thoroughbreds carrying weight not in excess of 126 pounds.

On the day of the first Kentucky Derby, Colonel Clark gave a Derby breakfast for his friends — a custom that is still popular today. As soon as the race is over, the owner of the winning horse is invited to a private party given by the president of Churchill Downs, where he or she sips a MINT JULEP from a special sterling silver cup decorated with a wreath of roses (see RED ROSES) and a replica of a thoroughbred horse's shoe, authentic in every detail. The cup later becomes part of the collection of cups on display at the Downs.

The race is usually run in slightly over two minutes, although in 1964, Northern Dancer was the first to win the Derby in two minutes flat. The great Secretariat, fondly known as Big Red, is still the only horse who has run the Derby in less than two minutes — although only fractions of a second less. Ridden by jockey Ron Turcotte, Secretariat then went on to win the Triple Crown, which means that he also won the Belmont Stakes (run in June at Belmont Park, near New York City) and the Preakness (run in late May at the Pimlico Race Course near Baltimore). Only a horse that has won all three races in a single year, as Secretariat did in 1973, qualifies as a Triple Crown winner.

Although the race takes only a couple of minutes, the festivities surrounding it go on for the better part of a week and include parades, a steamboat race on the Ohio River, and countless dinner parties and balls.

## SYMBOLS

### Mint Julep

How the drink known as the mint julep came to be so closely associated with the Kentucky Derby is not really known. The julep has been a Kentucky tradition since before the Civil War, and most Kentuckians pride themselves on their own special recipes. The basic ingredients are fresh-picked mint, sugar, and Kentucky bourbon, served over crushed ice in a frosted silver cup or souvenir Derby glass. The drink symbolizes southern hospitality and social grace, both of which are on display throughout Derby week.

### Red Roses

Since 1932, it has been a Derby tradition for a group of Louisville women to sew hundreds of red rosebuds into a blanket to be worn by the winning horse. A wreath of red roses is also placed on the horse's neck in the winners' circle — an event that takes place in front of more than 115,000 spectators and millions of television viewers. Both are symbolic of victory, much like the victory wreath that crowns the winner of the **BOSTON MARATHON**.

### Further Reading

Cohen, Hennig, and Tristram Potter Coffin, eds. *The Folklore of American Holidays,* 2nd ed., 1991.

Hatch, Jane M. *The American Book of Days,* 1978.

Henderson, Helene and Sue Ellen Thompson. *Holidays, Festivals, and Celebrations of the World Dictionary,* 2nd ed., 1997.

Shemanski, Frances. *A Guide to Fairs and Festivals in the United States,* 1984.

# *King, Jr.'s Birthday, Martin Luther*

**Type of Holiday:** Historic
**Date of Observation:** Third Monday in January
**Where Celebrated:** Throughout the United States and four U.S. territories, and by more than 100 nations around the world
**Symbols:** "I Have a Dream" Speech

## ORIGINS

Born on January 15, 1929, Martin Luther King, Jr., was the son of Martin Luther King, Sr., the pastor of the Ebenezer Baptist Church in Atlanta, Georgia. He achieved national prominence in 1955, when he led the Montgomery, Alabama, bus boycott. The boycott was designed to end segregation in the city's transit system after Rosa Parks, a black seamstress, refused to obey a bus driver's order to give up her seat to a white male passenger and was fined $14. In 1960 King was chosen to head the Southern Christian Leadership Conference, giving him the organizational base he needed to extend his campaign for civil rights throughout the South. He organized many protests and marches, among them the August 1963 "March on Washington," at which he delivered his now famous "I HAVE A DREAM" SPEECH. Throughout his life he practiced nonviolent resistance and advocated peaceful protest against his country's segregationist practices. He received the Nobel Peace Prize in 1964.

Martin Luther King was assassinated in Memphis, Tennessee, by James Earl Ray on April 4, 1968. He had come to Memphis to help organize a strike of the city's sanitation workers, most of whom were black. He was shot while standing on the balcony outside his motel room. The assassination sparked riots in 120 American cities that year and led to a tremendous increase in the kind of violence that King had worked for more than a decade to prevent.

Eight days later, U.S. Representative John Conyers from Michigan called for a federal holiday honoring Dr. King. Atlanta was the first city to designate King's birthday as a paid holiday for city employees in 1971, and in 1973, Illinois became the first state to declare January 15 a statewide holiday. On January 15, 1981, which would have been King's 52nd birthday, more than 100,000 people gathered at the Washington Monument to rally for a national holiday. Legislation was finally passed by Congress in 1983 setting aside the third Monday in January to honor King. This day is only the tenth national holiday approved by Congress, and it is the only one honoring an American other than George Washington.

## SYMBOLS

### *"I Have a Dream" Speech*

Oratory was Martin Luther King's greatest talent. The speech he delivered at the Lincoln Memorial in Washington, D.C., on August 28, 1963, almost immediately became a symbol of the civil rights movement. It was heard by an audience of 250,000 who had assembled there during the famous March on Washington to win the support of Congress and the president for pending civil rights legislation. When King was assassinated five years later, the speech became a symbol of his lifelong effort to end segregation through nonviolent means.

King repeated the phrase "I have a dream" at several points during the speech, building intensity with each repetition. Those who were close to King at the time say that he spent days agonizing over each paragraph, sentence, and punctuation mark—as if he knew it would be the speech by which he is remembered. Excerpts from the "I have a dream" speech are still broadcast on television and radio around the time of the King holiday. It is often accompanied by the singing of "We Shall Overcome," widely regarded as the theme song of the civil rights movement.

## Further Reading

Anyike, James C. *African American Holidays,* 1991.

Hatch, Jane M. *The American Book of Days,* 1978.

Henderson, Helene and Sue Ellen Thompson. *Holidays, Festivals, and Celebrations of the World Dictionary,* 2nd ed., 1997.

Santino, Jack. *All Around the Year,* 1994.

Schaun, George and Virginia. *American Holidays and Special Days,* 1986.

# *Kupalo Festival*

**Type of Holiday:** Ancient or pagan, Calendar
**Date of Observation:** June 24
**Where Celebrated:** Ukraine, United States
**Symbols:** Fern, Tree
**Related Holidays:** Midsummer Day

## ORIGINS

This Ukrainian festival takes its name from Kupalo, the god of summer and fertility, who sleeps under a TREE during the winter and awakens in the spring. Many of the customs associated with this festival are directly linked to encouraging fertility in both the human and natural worlds. For example, young women often gather flowers to make a wreath that is tossed into a nearby river. Where the wreath touches the shore is believed to indicate what family the young woman will marry into. Another custom for girls is to make an effigy of Marena, the goddess of cold, death, and winter. After singing special holiday songs, they burn or drown the effigy to reduce the goddess's power over the coming winter. The Ukrainian winters are very harsh.

The Kupalo Festival dates back to pagan times, when people believed that the seasons were governed by supernatural forces. If certain yearly rituals were not carried out properly, the weather might not warm up in time to yield a good harvest. Today, the festival is still observed in parts of the Ukraine and in Ukrainian communities in the United States.

## SYMBOLS

### *Fern*

Young men go into the forest on Kupalo to look for a type of fern that, according to legend, blooms only on the night of **MIDSUMMER DAY**. They take with them a special cloth, white powder, and a knife. If they find the fern and are strong enough to ward off the enticements of the wood nymphs, they draw a circle with the white powder and sit down in the middle to wait for the fern to bloom. When it does, they cut off the blossom with the knife and wrap the flower in the special cloth. They must never tell anyone that they have found the fern, or they will lose the luck and power it is believed to symbolize. This story explains why some people have more luck and talent than others.

### *Tree*

A young sapling decorated with flowers, seeds, and fruit is probably the most recognizable symbol of the Kupalo Festival. It represents Kupalo himself, who awakens in the spring and shakes the tree he's been sleeping under, making the seeds fall and symbolically making the earth fertile again. During the festival young boys and girls dance around the tree and sing special songs to please this image of the fertility god.

## Further Reading

Henderson, Helene and Sue Ellen Thompson. *Holidays, Festivals, and Celebrations of the World Dictionary*, 2nd ed., 1997.

# *Kwanzaa*

**Type of Holiday:** Cultural

**Date of Observation:** December 26 - January 1

**Where Celebrated:** United States, Canada, Caribbean, and parts of Europe

**Symbols:** Candle Holder (Kinara), Corn (Muhindi), Crops (Mazao), Gifts (Zawadi), Mat (Mkeka), Seven Candles (Mishumaa Saba), Seven Principles (Nguzo Saba), Unity Cup (Kikombe Cha Umoja)

**Colors:** Kwanzaa is associated with red, black, and green—the colors of the national flag or *bendara* of the African-American people as designed by Marcus Garvey, father of the modern Black nationalist movement. Red symbolizes the continuing struggle of the African-American people, black is symbolic of their faces, and green stands for their hopes and aspirations for the future.

**Related Holidays:** Christmas, Hanukkah

## ORIGINS

The name of this holiday comes from the Swahili phrase *matunda ya kwanza*, which means "first fruits." It was established in 1966 by Dr. Maulana "Ron" Karenga, a UCLA professor from Nigeria. After the August 1965 Watts riots in Los Angeles, Dr. Karenga, at that time a graduate student, felt that his people had lost touch with their African heritage. After completing his Ph.D., he began teaching African-American history and studied the culture of the Yorubas, Ibos, Ashantis, Zulus, and other African tribes. All of these tribes celebrated some type of harvest festival (see NEW YAM FESTIVAL), during which they remembered their ancestors, celebrated their good fortune, and made their plans for the coming year. Using this as his model, Dr. Karenga decided to create a cultural holiday that African Americans of all faiths could celebrate and that would shift their attention away from CHRISTMAS and other traditional "white" holidays. Dr. Karenga added a second "a" to the Swahili word meaning "first" so that the name of this newly created holiday would have seven letters—a number possessing great symbolic value in the African culture. He also made it a seven-day celebration, not only because most of the other first fruits festivals lasted between seven and nine days, but because each day could then be dedicated to one of the SEVEN PRINCIPLES.

Among the activities associated with the celebration of Kwanzaa is the pouring of the *tambiko* or libation for the ancestors; the *Harambee*, which is a raised-arm gesture combined with a verbal call, the general meaning of which is "Let's all pull together"; and the lighting of the *mishumaa saba* or SEVEN CANDLES. Central to every Kwanzaa celebration is the *mkeka* or MAT, on which are arranged various symbolic items such as CORN, CROPS, a CAN-DLE HOLDER, and the UNITY CUP.

A communal feast or *Karamu* is held on the night of December 31, to which each participating family contributes a particular dish—usually made from okra, sesame seeds, black-eyed peas, peanuts, or other foods that African slaves brought to the United States. Before and during the feast, there is a program that combines information about African customs, traditions, and symbols with entertainment. The seventh and last day of Kwanzaa is also a time for opening GIFTS and thinking of ways to make the coming year better—not unlike the resolutions that other Americans make on **NEW YEAR'S DAY**.

Many African Americans wear African-style clothing during the Kwanzaa celebration. The women may wear a *buba* or loose-fitting gown, or a robe with a scarf at the waist called a *busuti*. Some women cover their hair with a *gele* or head wrap. Men may wear a shirt called a *dashiki*, or a long robe known as a *kanza*.

Kwanzaa shares many values and customs with the African harvest festivals from which it was derived. It is a time to strengthen the bonds among people, just as the harvest was an occasion to gather together, and to give thanks to the Creator for a bountiful life. It is also a time for African Americans to honor their roots and heritage, and to commemorate the struggles and survival of their people. Above all, it is a time to reassess their own lives and the lives of their communities, and to recommit themselves to certain cultural ideals.

# SYMBOLS

## Candle Holder (Kinara)

The *kinara* or seven-branched candle holder used in the celebration of Kwanzaa started out as a symbol of Nkulunkulu, the first ancestor and father of the African people. Nkulunkulu was referred to as the "corn stalk" that produced the "corn"—i.e., that went on to multiply as the African people. But now it has come to symbolize the African ancestors as a collective whole.

## Corn (Muhindi)

As one of the fundamental foods grown in Africa, corn has always been central to African agriculture and society. The life cycle of corn is regarded as a symbol of the human life cycle. Along with the "stalk" or *kinara* (see CANDLE HOLDER), therefore, the corn used in Kwanzaa celebrations symbolizes the relationship between parents and children, and between ancestors and their descendants.

Each family places as many ears of corn in the Kwanzaa display as there are children in the family. But even in households where there are no children, there is always at least one ear of corn. This is because in African society, parenthood is both biological and social. In other words, even individuals who are not personally responsible for children have a social responsibility for the children of the community. Kwanzaa is a time for reaffirming this responsibility.

## Crops (Mazao)

The *mazao* is a bowl of fruits and vegetables that represents the harvest. Because it refers back to the roots of the celebration in African agricultural festivals, it is considered the most important of the symbols displayed on the Kwanzaa MAT or *mkeka*. It symbolizes the rewards of collective and productive labor.

## Gifts (Zawadi)

When Kwanzaa was first established, there was some discussion over whether gift-giving should be a part of the celebration. There was a strong feeling that the kind of gift-giving associated with **CHRISTMAS**—which often involves spending money to impress or punish the receiver rather than to express love and bring pleasure—should be avoided. At the same time, it was recognized that gifts were symbolic of the fruits of labor, and that African gift-giving traditionally focused on items that were either made or grown.

In the end, it was decided that Kwanzaa gifts would be different. They would be instructive and inspirational, and would be linked to the needs of the African people and their struggle. Rather than relying on a Santa Claus-like figure who promises things that parents cannot always deliver, Kwanzaa gift-giving would underscore the hard work and sacrifice involved in providing children with gifts. The presents would not be purchased until after Christmas was over, and they would be given only to children. To avoid the shopping frenzy and undisciplined spending associated with Christmas, the gifts would be equal in value to the children's achievements.

Kwanzaa gifts may be exchanged at any time, but they are usually opened on January 1, the last day of the celebration. Most are educational or inspirational items—for example, books by or about Africa or African Americans, tickets to African-American cultural events, or works by African-American artists. Favorite gifts include African games and toys, handmade clothes and accessories, and ethnic dolls. No gift should be purchased if it causes financial hardship for the giver, and the emphasis is on homemade rather than store-bought items.

Despite all the efforts that have been made to avoid the commercialization associated with Christmas, today Kwanzaa cards and wrapping paper are sold in the stores, along with specially manufactured Kwanzaa gifts such as teddy bears dressed in African costumes.

## Mat (Mkeka)

The woven straw mat or *mkeka* on which all of the other Kwanzaa symbols are placed serves as a "foundation" for these items, just as tradition and history are the foundations necessary for self-knowledge and understanding of the African-American people. There is an old African proverb that says "No matter how high a house is built, it must stand on a something." In a symbolic sense, the *mkeka* provides such a foundation.

## Seven Candles (Mishumaa Saba)

Seven candles are placed in the *kinara* or candle holder: one black, three red, and three green—the colors of the national flag of the African-American people. The black candle is placed in the center of the kinara, while the red ones are places on the left and the green ones on the right. Each day, a candle is lit to symbolize one of the SEVEN PRINCIPLES. The person who lights it then explains what it stands for, and this becomes the main topic of discussion for that day.

The black candle in the center represents the unity of the African-American people, which is the first of the Seven Principles. Beginning with the second day, candles are lit on the left and right alternately. Because red symbolizes struggle and green represents hope for the future, this method of lighting the candles underscores the message that there can be no future without a struggle. Each candle that has been lit before is relit along with the candle of the day, until all seven are burning on the last day of the festival.

The lighting of the seven candles is a daily ritual, similar to that of lighting the menorah during **HANUKKAH**, that symbolizes both the illumination of the Seven Principles and the ancient African concept of "raising up light" to dispel the darkness in both a spiritual and intellectual sense.

## Seven Principles (Nguzo Saba)

One of the reasons that Dr. Karenga created Kwanzaa was to introduce and reinforce what are known as the Seven Principles or *Nguzo Saba*, defined as the values needed to build and sustain the African-American family, community, and culture. These principles are as follows: (1) Unity (*umoja*), (2) Self-determination (*kujichagulia*), (3) Collective work and responsibility (*ujima*), (4) Cooperative economics (*ujamma*), (5) Purpose (*nia*), (6) Creativity (*kuumba*), and (7) Faith (*imani*).

Each of the seven days of Kwanzaa is dedicated to one of the seven principles. Every evening during the festival, families gather together to discuss the principle to which that day has been dedicated and to light the candle (see SEVEN CANDLES) that symbolizes that principle. The Seven Principles are also described on a poster that is displayed during the celebration of Kwanzaa.

## Unity Cup (Kikombe Cha Umoja)

The Unity Cup is part of the arrangement of symbolic objects displayed on the MAT or *mkeka* throughout the seven days of Kwanzaa. It serves two basic functions: (1) It is used to pour the *tambiko*, which is usually wine or grape juice accompanied by a "libation statement" or *tamshi la tambiko* in honor of the ancestors; (2) It is passed around so that everyone can drink from it, a symbolic ritual designed to reinforce unity in the family and the African-American community. Pouring the *tambiko* and making a libation statement is a way of honoring the ancestors and reaffirming the link between them and their living African-American descendants.

After the cup has been passed around and is placed back on the table, the *kutoa majina* begins, which is the calling-out of the names of family ancestors. When the last name has been called, a drummer plays African-style rhythms, which is the signal for the start of the feast or *karamu*. The feast is followed by singing, dancing, and storytelling. The final evening of the celebration concludes with a Farewell Statement (*tamshi la tutaonana*) composed by Dr. Karenga. Then everyone shouts "Harambee!" seven times, and Kwanzaa is over.

# Further Reading

Henderson, Helene and Sue Ellen Thompson. *Holidays, Festivals, and Celebrations of the World Dictionary*, 2nd ed., 1997.

Karenga, Maulana. *The African American Holiday of Kwanzaa*, 1988.

McClester, Cedric. *Kwanzaa: Everything You Always Wanted to Know but Didn't Know Where to Ask*, 1985.

Medearis, Angela S. *The Seven Days of Kwanzaa*, 1994.

Santino, Jack. *All Around the Year*, 1994.

Schmidt, Leigh Eric. *Consumer Rites: The Buying and Selling of American Holidays*, 1995.

# *Lag Ba-Omer*

**Type of Holiday:** Religious (Jewish)

**Date of Observation:** Eighteenth day of the Jewish lunar month of Iyar (usually falls in May), or the 33rd of the 50 days separating Passover and Shavuot

**Where Celebrated:** United States, Israel, Palestine, and by Jews throughout the world

**Symbols:** Bonfires, Bow and Arrow

**Related Holidays:** Passover, Shavuot

## ORIGINS

The name of this Jewish holiday means "33 omer," *omer* being the Hebrew word for a sheaf of barley or wheat. According to the book of Leviticus, God told the Jews to make an offering of a sheaf of barley on each of the 50 days between **PASSOVER** and **SHAVUOT**. After the evening service, the number of the day was solemnly announced, and this ceremony was known as "the counting of the omer." When the 50 days were over, it was time to celebrate the harvest and to bring to the Temple two loaves of bread made from the new wheat.

Why the 33rd day of this period was singled out may have something to do with an ancient pagan festival that was celebrated around the same time of year. The Romans believed that it was unlucky to marry in May before the harvest because this was the season when the souls of the dead came back to earth to haunt the living, and they could only be appeased by funerals, not weddings. This unlucky period lasted 32 days and ended with a festival on the 33rd day, which was an occasion for celebration because the prohibition on joyful events had been lifted.

Why the seven weeks between Passover and the harvest came to be regarded as a period of semi-mourning for the Jews is not entirely clear. No doubt the character of this period changed after the destruction of the second Temple, when people realized they could no longer bring the season's first barley and the two loaves of bread there as offerings. It was also natural for farmers to feel some anxiety at this time of year, when the success or failure of the crops depended on the weather and other factors beyond their control. The 33rd day may have been intended as a much-needed break from the otherwise anxious and somber *omer* period.

There are other theories about the origins of this holiday as well. One is that it was the anniversary of the day when Bar Kochva and his Jewish warriors temporarily captured Jerusalem from the Romans in their fight to reestablish the Jewish nation. Another is that it marked the end of the epidemic that killed 24,000 students of the famous Rabbi Akiva during the first century. Still another links the holiday to the anniversary of the death of Rabbi Bar Yohai, a great Hebrew scholar who refused to obey the Romans when they forbade him to teach or to study the Torah.

Like the Christian **LENT**, the *omer* days are associated with certain restrictions. It is forbidden to get married, to shave or cut hair, to wear new clothes, to listen to music, or to attend any kind of public entertainment during the seven weeks. Whether this is because it was originally a period of mourning for certain historical events or because the weeks preceding the harvest were regarded as a time of "suspended animation," the fact remains that these prohibitions are lifted for a 24-hour period on the 33rd day. It is a popular day for Jewish weddings, for concerts and musical events, for wearing new clothes, and for lighting BONFIRES. In many American cities, Lag Ba-Omer is observed as Jewish Book Day or Scholars' Day in memory of Rabbi Akiva, Bar Yohai, and other scholars who upheld the right of Jews to follow the dictates of their religion and culture. Jewish books are exhibited in public libraries and lectures on Jewish literature are held. At Meron, the burial place of Bar Yohai, Hasidic Jews from all over Palestine and neighboring countries gather in his honor.

For children, particularly in Israel, Lag Ba-Omer is a day for outings and picnics. Armed with BOWS AND ARROWS, they go with their teachers out in the woods, where a picnic lunch is followed by archery contests. Hebrew schools usually arrange their annual outings to coincide with this holiday. Pageants and plays depicting the historical events associated with the 18th day of Iyar are also popular.

Lag Ba-Omer is not regarded as a sacred holiday, nor is it distinguished by any special service or prayer in the synagogue.

## SYMBOLS

### Bonfires

According to legend, the war hero Bar Kochva and his men lit fires in Jerusalem as a way of signaling villages far away that they had captured the city from the powerful Roman army. These villages, in turn, lit more fires — until the whole country knew about the victory. To commemorate this event, children throughout Israel start gathering scraps of wood, dry branches, rags, and other burnable items a few days before Lag Ba-Omer. They light huge bonfires on every empty lot they can find, sing songs, dance around the fire, and eat potatoes that have been baked in the hot embers.

Another Lag Ba-Omer custom associated with bonfires dates back to the sixteenth century. Orthodox Jewish parents bring their three-year-old boys to Meron, the village in Galilee where Rabbi Bar Yohai, the father of Jewish mysticism, and his son are buried. There a rabbi or other Jewish dignitary gives the young boys their first haircut, and the locks of hair are thrown into a bonfire. As a result of the Meron celebration, this custom has spread throughout Palestine.

It has long been traditional in many parts of the world to light bonfires at the end of April or the beginning of May to scare off witches and demons. In ancient Rome, fires were lit at the **PARILIA** on April 21; in England, fires are still kindled at crossroads on **ST. GEORGE'S DAY**, April 23. The ancient Celtic festival of **BELTANE** (May 1) was also marked with bonfires, a custom that still survives in the Scottish Highlands and parts of Ireland. In fact, this Jewish holiday has much in common with the European **MAY DAY**, which would appear to support the theory that it originated as a rustic festival linked to the harvest.

## *Bow and Arrow*

The Israeli custom of sending children out in the woods on Lag Ba-Omer to shoot with bows and arrows has its roots in both legend and folklore. In Germany, April 30 was **WALPURGIS NIGHT**, a time when demons and evil spirits were believed to roam the earth. It was common at one time to shoot arrows at these troublesome spirits, and in Germany, it is still common for rural people to go out in the woods and shoot arrows on the morning of May 1. In England, it is a popular day for archery contests — the bow and arrow being associated with Robin Hood, who is derived from the chief of the goblins and mischievous spirits, Robin o' the Wood. It is interesting to note that Israeli children take their bows and arrows to the cemetery as well as the forest. This might represent another link with ancient May Day customs (see BONFIRES), which often included dances and gatherings in graveyards.

There are other explanations for the custom in Israel. After the destruction of the Temple in Jerusalem by Titus, the Roman general, Rabbi Akiva decided that the best way to get rid of the Roman conquerors was to teach his students how to fight. To avoid arousing suspicion, they dressed up as hunters with bows and arrows, and went out in the woods to practice.

Another tradition links the bow and arrow to Rabbi Bar Yohai. Because he refused to obey the Roman decree against the study of the Torah and continued to teach his students, his life was perpetually in danger. He finally escaped to a cave in the mountains of Galilee, where he lived for 13 years by eating the fruit of the carob tree and drinking from a nearby spring. His students visited him each year on Lag Ba-Omer, disguising themselves as hunters by carrying bows and arrows.

## Further Reading

Edidin, Ben. *Jewish Holidays and Festivals*, 1993.

Gaer, Joseph. *Holidays Around the World*, 1953.

Gaster, Theodor H. *Festivals of the Jewish Year*, 1953.

Henderson, Helene and Sue Ellen Thompson. *Holidays, Festivals, and Celebrations of the World Dictionary*, 2nd ed., 1997.

Renberg, Dalia H. *The Complete Family Guide to Jewish Holidays*, 1985.

# *Lammas*

**Type of Holiday:** Religious (Christian)
**Date of Observation:** August 1
**Where Celebrated:** British Isles
**Symbols:** Loaf of Bread
**Related Holidays:** Candlemas, Martinmas, Pentecost

## ORIGINS

Originally called the Gule of August, Lammas was a celebration of the grain harvest and one of the four great pagan festivals of Britain. When Christianity was introduced, the day continued to be celebrated, and a LOAF OF BREAD made from the newly harvested grain was the usual offering at church. For this reason it was called *Hlaf-mass* (loaf mass), subsequently shortened to Lammas. Another theory about the name's origin is that it came from **LUGHNASA**, the ancient autumn festival in honor of Lugh, the Celtic sun god. Yet another explanation, although based on a custom apparently confined to the cathedral at York, is that it was called Lammas because it was traditional to bring a lamb to church as an offering on this day.

Although it is no longer observed, Lammas is important as an ancestor of other special days that are still celebrated. It was the forerunner of England's and Canada's modern Harvest Festival and of America's **THANKSGIVING**. Nowadays, harvest festivals tend to be observed later in the year, usually between September and November, when all of the autumn crops are in instead of just the early ones, like grain.

Up until the mid-eighteenth century, young herdsmen would band together in different companies and build towers out of stones or sod. On Lammas morning, the bands would assemble, waving flags and blowing horns, and set out to tear down one another's sod towers. Each carried a club or a cudgel, and victory was seldom gained without bloodshed. The day's activities usually ended with footraces.

In Scotland, Lammas was also one of the four cross-quarter days (along with **CANDLEMAS,** Whitsunday [see **PENTECOST**], and **MARTINMAS**) when tenants paid their rents — originally in the form of newly harvested grain — to their landlords. The phrase "at the Latter Lammas" meant "never" or "not in this lifetime." Tenants would often say, "I will pay him at the Latter Lammas," by which they meant, "I'll pay him when I get good and ready." In the Highlands, people sprinkled their cows and the floors of their houses with menstrual blood, which was believed to be especially potent against evil on May 1 and August 1.

## SYMBOLS

### *Loaf of Bread*

As a symbol of the harvest and therefore of God's bounty, the loaf of bread has always played a part in the celebration of Lammas. It was made from grain that had just been harvested and brought to the church as an offering. Scholars believe that Lammas was closely related to the Jewish **SHAVUOT** or Feast of Weeks, which also came at the end of the grain harvest and entailed offering two loaves of bread at the Temple in Jerusalem.

## Further Reading

Brewster, H. Pomeroy. *Saints and Festivals of the Christian Church,* 1990.

Chambers, Robert, ed. *The Book of Days,* 1864.

Dunkling, Leslie. *A Dictionary of Days,* 1988.

Harper, Howard V. *Days and Customs of All Faiths,* 1957.

Henderson, Helene and Sue Ellen Thompson. *Holidays, Festivals, and Celebrations of the World Dictionary,* 2nd ed., 1997.

Kelly, Aidan. *Religious Holidays and Calendars,* 1993.

Leach, Maria, ed. *Funk & Wagnalls Standard Dictionary of Folklore, Mythology, & Legend,* 1984.

MacDonald, Margaret R., ed. *The Folklore of World Holidays,* 1992.

Urlin, Ethel L. *Festivals, Holy Days, and Saints' Days,* 1915.

# *Lantern Festival*
## *(Teng Chieh, Feast of the First Full Moon)*

**Type of Holiday:** Folkloric

**Date of Observation:** Fifteenth through the 18th day of the first Chinese lunar month (usually February)

**Where Celebrated:** China, Malaysia, Taiwan, Tibet

**Symbols:** Dragon Parade, Lanterns, Lantern Riddles, Lion Dance, Rice Flour Dumplings (Yuanxiao)

**Related Holidays:** Chinese New Year

## ORIGINS

The Lantern Festival is believed to have originated with the emperors of China's Han Dynasty (206 B.C.E. - 221 C.E.), who paid tribute to the First Cause or origins of the universe on this night. Because the ceremony was held in the evening, lanterns were used to light the palace. Normally the Han rulers imposed a curfew on their subjects; but on this night, the curfew was lifted so that everyone could see the illuminated palace.

Today, whatever cosmic or religious significance the festival may originally have had is lost. The three-day Lantern Festival marks the end of the **CHINESE NEW YEAR** celebration and is primarily an occasion for hanging out lanterns, eating RICE FLOUR DUMPLINGS, and solving LANTERN RIDDLES. Merchants hang paper lanterns outside their shops for several days before the full-moon day, and homeowners hang them from their porches and in their gardens. On the night of the festival, people throng the streets to see the lantern displays. The most popular lanterns are cutouts of running horses that revolve with the heat of the candles that burn under them. In Taipei, Taiwan's capital city, high-tech lanterns with mechanical animation, dry-ice "smoke," and laser beams take the form of fire-spewing dragons and other fantastic creatures. In Hong Kong, it is traditional for any man who has had a son born during the year to bring a lantern to the Ancestral Hall, where the fathers gather for a meal. There are processions of clowns, stilt-walkers, and actors in costume, and the popular LION DANCE is performed in the streets.

## SYMBOLS

### Dragon Parade

The dragon is a mythical creature symbolic of vigor, fertility, and spring rain. It has been described as having the head of a camel, the horns of a deer, the eyes of a rabbit, the ears of a cow, the neck of a serpent, the scales of a fish, and the talons of a hawk. On the last day of the Lantern Festival, a huge dragon made of bamboo rods and satin cloth in sections three to four feet long and traditionally illuminated by candles is carried through the streets by dozens of men and boys. Strings of firecrackers are set off wherever the dragon parade goes.

The Golden Dragon Parade in San Francisco, where there is a large Chinese population, has been an annual event since 1953. The dragon is 160 feet long and is accompanied by floats, marching bands, dance troupes, bell-and-drum corps, and various carnival-like characters. The San Francisco parade is considered the largest event of its kind in the world.

## Lanterns

The lanterns for which this festival is named probably date back to an ancient ceremony welcoming spring. The lantern, a source of light, was symbolic of the lengthening days of spring, and willow branches were used to symbolize spring rains. Another explanation is that evil spirits were believed to roam the earth on this night, and lanterns were used to scare them off. According to legend, a Ming Dynasty emperor ordered 10,000 lanterns to be set afloat on the lake at Nanking, and the sight was so beautiful that Buddha himself came down from Heaven to see it.

In rural areas of China, people hang lanterns at crossroads, near wells, and by marshes and rivers—places where the spirits of those who have died before their time and are therefore doomed to wander the earth are most likely to be found—in the hope that the light will lead these spirits to judgment and reincarnation. In the industrial city of Harbin in northeast China, fantastic lanterns have been carved from huge blocks of river ice for centuries. Now they are illuminated with colored electric lights and left standing until spring comes and the ice melts.

Chinese children make or buy lanterns in all shapes and put candles inside. The most popular shapes are those of whatever animal is the patron protector of that particular Chinese year—the rabbit, the tiger, the rat, the monkey, the horse, etc. Older children may take sticks of bamboo and stuff the hollow center with paper and oil-soaked rags to form a torch that will burn for several hours. Couples without children may purchase lanterns in the shape of little boys, and extra lanterns are often hung outside the house to indicate a desire for more children.

## Lantern Riddles

The 15th day of the first month is also associated with a literary game that was popular at one time among elderly, educated people. Known as *Cai Deng Mi* or "Guessing the Lantern's Riddle," it consisted of writing riddles on slips of paper and pasting them lightly on lanterns hung either inside or outside the house. There might be hints in the form of objects hung from the lanterns with a written clue—a Chinese character, a line of verse, someone's name, etc.—pointing to the correct answer. Anyone who guessed the correct answer was rewarded on the spot.

Although lantern riddles are not as popular anymore, crossword puzzle lanterns with riddles pasted on their sides are still hung outside scholars' homes for the amusement of their literary friends.

## Lion Dance

Songs, dances, plays, and variety acts are performed throughout the Lantern Festival, but the Lion Dance is perhaps the most popular entertainment. Two men are concealed inside a huge papier-maché lion. One operates the moving jaws and lolling tongue of the head, which is decorated with bells. The other manipulates the lion's hindquarters. Accompanied by drums and gongs, the lion dances through the streets, crouching and leaping or bowing and hunching its back. Sometimes a "lion tamer" teases the lion. In some areas, the lion chases after a "pearl" or ball.

The Lion Dance reached its peak during the Tang dynasty (618-907 C.E.), when it featured five lions more than nine feet tall dressed in different colors. With wooden heads, silk tails, gilded eyes, and silver-plated teeth, the lions performed the Dance of the Five Directions while "lion boys" teased them with red whisks.

Because the lion is not indigenous to China, it took on a mythical aura. Sometimes lions were brought from Persia to the emperor as a form of tribute. They were highly valued and became symbolically associated with purity and protection.

## Rice Flour Dumplings (Yuanxiao)

Sweet-tasting glutinous rice flour balls known as *yuanxiao* are traditionally served during the Lantern Festival. They are symbolic of the first full moon of the year and, because of their perfectly round shape, of the family as well. They may be filled with hawthorn, black bean, date, or sesame paste; in the southern part of China, pork, chicken, and vegetable fillings are popular. They are cooked just long enough to make the outer skin slippery.

How did the rice flour dumplings get their name? According to legend, the Lantern Festival originated because a young woman living in the emperor's household by the name of Yuan Xiao longed to see her parents. To help her out, a resourceful friend named Dongfang Shuo spread a rumor that the god of fire was going to burn down the city of Chang-an. The ensuing panic was widespread, and when he was summoned by the emperor, Dongfang Shuo advised him to have everyone leave the palace and hang lanterns on every streetcorner and building. This would make the fire god think that the city was already burning. The emperor followed his advice, and Yuan Xiao was able to go off and see her family.

In the north, it is customary to make the rice flour dumplings on the seventh day of the New Year and sell them on the eighth. They are served in restaurants throughout the three days of the Lantern Festival.

## Further Reading

Bredon, Juliet, and Igor Mitrophanow. *The Moon Year: A Record of Chinese Customs and Festivals,* 1966.

Gaer, Joseph. *Holidays Around the World,* 1953.

Henderson, Helene and Sue Ellen Thompson. *Holidays, Festivals, and Celebrations of the World Dictionary,* 2nd ed., 1997.

Ickis, Marguerite. *The Book of Festivals and Holidays the World Over,* 1970.

MacDonald, Margaret R., ed. *The Folklore of World Holidays,* 1992.

Stepanchuk, Carol, and Charles Wong. *Mooncakes and Hungry Ghosts: Festivals of China,* 1991.

Van Straalen, Alice. *Book of Holidays Around the World,* 1986.

# *Laylat al-Miraj*
### *(The Ascent, The Night Journey)*

**Type of Holiday:** Religious (Islamic)

**Date of Observation:** Twenty-seventh day of the seventh Islamic lunar month of Rajab

**Where Celebrated:** Africa, Egypt, India, Indonesia, Iran, Iraq, Jordan, Lebanon, Malaya, Morocco, Pakistan, Saudi Arabia, Syria, Thailand, Turkey, and throughout the Muslim world

**Symbols:** Dome of the Rock, Seven Heavens

**Related Holidays:** Laylat al-Qadr

# ORIGINS

Laylat al-Miraj commemorates the ascent of the Prophet Muhammad into heaven, which is why it is often referred to as the Night Journey or the Ascent. The original account of this event is sketchy, and most of the details have been supplied by tradition. But according to the legend, the Prophet was sleeping in the sanctuary next to the Kaaba (see **HAJJ**) one night when the Angel Gabriel woke him and traveled with him to Jerusalem on the winged horse Buraq. There he prayed at the site of the Temple of Solomon (which lay in ruins after being destroyed by the Romans) with Abraham, Moses, Jesus, and other prophets. Muhammad was offered two vessels from which to drink, one of which contained wine and the other milk. He chose the milk, which Gabriel interpreted as his selecting "the primordial path" for himself and his followers. Then he was carried by Gabriel up to heaven from the rock of the Temple Mount, also known as Mt. Moriah, where it was believed that Abraham built the altar on which to sacrifice his son, Isaac. The DOME OF THE ROCK sanctuary stands at this site today, and nearby is the al-Aqsa mosque, which takes its name from the Koranic word for the Temple Mount.

The Prophet ascended through the SEVEN HEAVENS and as he did so, the Angel Gabriel and the prophets with whom he had prayed assumed their spiritual forms. At the summit of the ascent was the Lote Tree of the Uttermost Limit (see SEVEN HEAVENS), where Muhammad received the command from God that men should pray 50 times a day. When he descended, Moses advised him to go back and request that the number be reduced to something more realistic. He did, and the prayer requirement was finally reduced to five.

As he was returning from Jerusalem to Mecca, Muhammad saw caravans crossing the desert. When he told people that he had visited Jerusalem during the night and they didn't believe him, he described the caravans he'd seen on his return journey as proof that he was telling the truth. When the caravans arrived in Mecca, it confirmed his version of the night's events.

The journey from Mecca to Jerusalem is called the *Isra,* and the ascent from Jerusalem to heaven is called the *Mi'raj.* Together these two events are known as the Night Journey, which has often been portrayed in books of Persian miniatures. Although the exact date of the Mi'raj is not known, the event is usually celebrated on the 27th of Rajab.

# SYMBOLS

## *Dome of the Rock*

The Dome of the Rock is a shrine in Jerusalem, built between 685 and 691 C.E., which is the oldest existing Islamic monument. The Dome stands over the rock on the Temple Mount from which the Prophet is believed to have ascended to heaven. The rock is sacred not only to Muslims but to Jews, because it was here that Abraham, the first patriarch of the Jewish people, is said to have prepared to sacrifice his son Isaac. It may also have been the site of the Holy of Holies, the innermost sanctuary of the Temple of Solomon, where the Ark of the Covenant was kept. After Mecca and Medina, the Temple Mount was the third holiest place in Islam. The early Muslims prayed in the direction of the Temple Mount, although later on they prayed facing Mecca. It was also the goal of the **HAJJ**, later supplanted by Mecca as well.

The rock itself is oblong, approximately 56 by 42 feet. Below it is a small chamber, reached by a stairway, in which worshippers can pray, although a larger area has been set aside for this purpose on the ground level above. A crack in the rock, which is visible from the grotto below, is supposed to have appeared when the Prophet ascended to heaven. The rock, according to legend, wanted to follow and split in its effort to do so.

The sanctuary above the rock, with its golden dome dominating the skyline of old Jerusalem, was built by the Caliph 'Abd al-Malik ibn Arwan. The wooden dome, approximately 60 feet in diameter, is decorated with calligraphic designs typical of Islamic art and there are 240 yards of inscriptions from the Koran. The Dome of the Rock's octagonal structure became the model for domed sanctuaries and saints' tombs from Morocco to China. The dome itself is a symbol: one step in the mathematical sequence leading from the square, representing the earth, to the circle, representing the perfection of heaven. The architecuture of the Dome of the Rock therefore symbolizes the Prophet's ascent to heaven.

## *Seven Heavens*

The degrees of Being that separate creation from the Absolute in Islam are described symbolically in the Koran as the seven spheres, skies, or heavens. The seventh heaven is the furthest from the material world and the nearest to the state known as Beyond-Being. The final gulf between the two is marked by the Lote Tree of the Uttermost Limit, which is considered the limit of Being itself.

The concept of the seven heavens appears in early Jewish mysticism. It is probably of Babylonian or Persian origin, with the seven heavens being the spheres of the seven planets visible to the human eye.

## Further Reading

Ahsan, M. M. *Muslim Festivals,* 1987.

Crim, Keith, ed. *The Perennial Dictionary of World Religions,* 1989.

Glassé, Cyril. *The Concise Encyclopedia of Islam,* 1989.

Henderson, Helene and Sue Ellen Thompson. *Holidays, Festivals, and Celebrations of the World Dictionary,* 2nd ed., 1997.

MacDonald, Margaret R., ed. *The Folklore of World Holidays,* 1992.

# *Laylat al-Qadr*
### *(Night of Destiny, Night of Power)*

**Type of Holiday:** Religious (Islamic)

**Date of Observation:** One of the last ten days of Ramadan, the ninth month of the Islamic lunar calendar; usually the 27th

**Where Celebrated:** Africa, Egypt, India, Indonesia, Iran, Iraq, Jordan, Lebanon, Malaya, Morocco, Pakistan, Saudi Arabia, Syria, Thailand, Turkey, and throughout the Muslim world

**Symbols:** Koran

**Related Holidays:** Laylat al-Miraj

## ORIGINS

Also known as the "Night of Power" or "Night of Destiny," Laylat al-Qadr celebrates the night on which, in 610 C.E., the KORAN, or holy book of the Islamic religion, was first revealed to the Prophet Muhammad. While Muhammad was engaged in meditation in the cave of Hira, near the summit of the mountain Jabal Nur, the Angel Gabriel appeared to him with the first of the revelations that would continue on a sporadic basis for 23 years. The Prophet had no control over when Gabriel would speak, but when this occurred, Muhammad's state would visibly change. Once, for example, he was addressed by Gabriel while riding a camel. By the time the revelation was over, the camel was lying flat on the ground with its legs splayed out. Gabriel's words, according to Muhammad, physically assaulted him as if they were solid, heavy objects. In a trancelike state, Muhammad would repeat the words that Gabriel spoke, and his followers would record them on whatever was available — bones, bark, leaves, or scraps of parchment.

The first revelation is believed to have taken place during the last ten days of the holy month of **RAMADAN**. The widespread belief that the Koran was revealed on the 27th day of the month originated with Manicheism, a religion founded in the third century C.E. by Mani, who died on the 27th of Ramadan. Because no one is certain of the exact date, Muslims are asked to spend the last ten nights of Ramadan praying and reading the Koran. Some spend the entire night in the mosque during this period, or go out of their way to provide food and help for the poor.

In Freetown, Sierra Leone, Laylat al-Qadr is known as the Day of Light or the Lanterns Festival. The custom of parading through the streets carrying lanterns on the 26th of Ramadan was introduced by a trader known as Daddy Maggay in the 1930s. Originally simple paper boxes, the lanterns were meant to symbolize the divine light of the Koran, sent down to earth by God (Allah). But as they grew into elaborate, floatlike structures, the competition among lanternbuilders grew fierce, often erupting in violence. The Young Men's Muslim Association took control of the festival in the 1950s, in the hope that they could reduce the violence through better organization of the lantern-building competition.

## SYMBOLS

### *Koran*

The Koran — from the Arabic word *qur'an,* meaning "recitation" — contains the laws for Islamic society, warnings about the end of the world, descriptions of heaven and hell, and stories about both Biblical figures and events that do not appear in the Bible. Muslims regard the Koran as a continuation of God's revelations to the Jews and the Christians, whose Bibles record only portions of the truth. Many of the stories found in the Bible were partially corrupted in transmission, according to Muslim scholars, which explains why the Koran's version of certain Bible stories often differs considerably from those found in the Hebrew scripture.

The Koran is divided into 114 chapters known as Surahs. The longer Surahs precede the shorter ones, and the whole is divided into 30 sections of approximately equal length known as *ajza'* (singular *juz'*) to make it easier to read the Koran on a regular basis. One *juz'* is supposed to be read every day of the month, and these divisions are usually indicated in the margins. Although parts of the Koran were written down during its revelation, large portions of it were also committed to memory, as was the custom in preliterate cultures. Until recently, the first step in a Muslim's education was to memorize the entire Koran. Even today, many Muslims know the book by heart.

Reciting passages from the Koran is the primary activity associated with Laylat al-Qadr. The written book is considered by Muslims to be the earthly or material manifestation of the Uncreated Koran in much the same way that Christians regard Jesus as the human incarnation of God.

## Further Reading

Ahsan, M. M. *Muslim Festivals,* 1987.
Glassé, Cyril. *The Concise Encyclopedia of Islam,* 1989.
Henderson, Helene and Sue Ellen Thompson. *Holidays, Festivals, and Celebrations of the World Dictionary*, 2nd ed., 1997.
Ickis, Marguerite. *The Book of Festivals and Holidays the World Over,* 1970.
MacDonald, Margaret R., ed. *The Folklore of World Holidays,* 1992.
Smith, Huston. *The Illustrated World's Religions,* 1994.
Von Grunebaum, G. D. *Muhammadan Festivals,* 1988.

# Lazarus Saturday

**Type of Holiday:** Religious (Orthodox Christian)
**Date of Observation:** Between March 27 and April 30; Saturday before Palm Sunday
**Where Celebrated:** Eastern Europe, Greece, Russia
**Symbols:** Willow
**Related Holidays:** Easter, Palm Sunday

# ORIGINS

In the Russian and other Orthodox churches, the Saturday before **PALM SUNDAY** is set aside to honor Lazarus, the brother of Martha and Mary, the mother of Jesus. According to the Gospel of St. John, Jesus went to see Mary and Martha in Bethany when He heard that their brother was ill. But by the time He arrived, Lazarus had already been dead in his grave for four days. Jesus told Martha to take the stone away from the tomb where Lazarus had been buried. When she did, Jesus called out, "Lazarus, come forth." Lazarus walked out of the tomb, still wearing his graveclothes.

Lazarus Saturday was an important holiday in Bulgaria up until the early twentieth century. Young girls dressed up in bridal costumes went from house to house singing songs they had learned especially for this day and receiving eggs and sometimes small coins in return. On Palm Sunday, the older girls did the same thing, singing songs that dealt with various aspects of love, marriage, and family life. They made small wreaths out of WILLOW twigs and floated them on a river or in the village fountain. The girl whose wreath was the first to float after being submerged was given the title of *kumitsa.* The other girls were not allowed to speak to the kumitsa from Palm Sunday until **EASTER**. Then, on Easter Day, they would bring her presents of Easter eggs and a special kind of bread, in return for which the kumitsa would forgive them for their enforced silence.

In Greece, children still go from house to house singing songs about the resurrection of Lazarus on the day before Palm Sunday, usually carrying a picture of the story with them. Sometimes Lazarus is represented by a doll or a staff decorated with ribbons and cloth. In Cyprus, a boy covered with yellow flowers impersonates Lazarus. As he is led from house to house, he pretends to be dead and then rises when the girls say, "Lazarus! Come out!" This ritual so closely resembles the resurrection of Christ that it is often referred to as the "first Easter."

In Russia, the morning church service on this day is devoted to the memory of Lazarus. At the evening service, pussy willows are brought into the church to be blessed (see WILLOW). In Greece, Rumania, and the former Yugoslavia, groups of children carry willow branches from house to house and act out the story of Christ raising Lazarus from the dead. In return, they receive gifts of fruit and candy. They believe that the resurrection of Lazarus is symbolic of the renewal of spring.

## SYMBOLS

### Willow

Because the willow flourishes no matter how many of its branches are cut off, it stands as a symbol for the gospel of Christ, which remains intact no matter how widely it is spread over the world.

The willow is also known for its strength and flexibility. In Russia, the willow branches (or pussy willows) that are blessed in the church on Lazarus Saturday are never thrown out, but are later burned as sacred objects. According to an ancient folk belief, people who beat their children with willow branches are merely trying to impart the virtues of the willow tree — which is tall, healthy, and resilient — to the child.

### Further Reading

Ferguson, George. *Signs and Symbols in Christian Art,* 1954.

Harper, Howard V. *Days and Customs of All Faiths,* 1957.

Henderson, Helene and Sue Ellen Thompson. *Holidays, Festivals, and Celebrations of the World Dictionary,* 2nd ed., 1997.

MacDonald, Margaret R., ed. *The Folklore of World Holidays,* 1992.

Spicer, Dorothy G. *The Book of Festivals,* 1990.

# *Leap Year Day*
## *(Leap Day)*

**Type of Holiday:** Calendar
**Date of Observation:** Every four years on February 29
**Where Celebrated:** British Isles, Europe, United States
**Symbols:** Proposals of Marriage

## ORIGINS

Although a calendar year is thought of as being 365 days long, it actually takes the earth an additional five hours, 48 minutes, and 45 seconds longer than that to complete its trip around the sun. When Julius Caesar initiated his calendar reform in 45 B.C.E., he tried to accommodate this discrepancy by fixing the solar year at 365 days, six hours—or 365 1/4 days. Every four years, the extra six hours per year added up to a whole day, which was added to February because it was the shortest month.

The calendar year still didn't correspond exactly to the astronomical year, however, and the discrepancy between the Julian calendar and the seasons of the year continued to increase—about three days every 400 years. In March of 1582, Pope Gregory XIII abolished the use of the Julian or Old Style calendar and instituted the Gregorian or New Style calendar. In doing so, he not only canceled ten days but corrected the discrepancy in the length of the year. Pope Gregory decided that from this point on, Leap Year should be omitted in all centenary years, except those that are divisible by 400. 1600 was a Leap Year, therefore, but 1700, 1800, and 1900 were not. The Gregorian calendar managed to bring the solar year much closer to the astronomical year, reducing the discrepancy to only 26 seconds a year—which won't add up to a full day until 3,323 years have passed.

Why is it called Leap Year? One explanation is that the additional day did not have any legal status in the English courts. February 29 was therefore "leaped over" in the records, and whatever happened on that day was dated February 28.

## SYMBOLS

### *Proposals of Marriage*

Leap Year Day is sometimes referred to as Ladies' Day. There is an old tradition that women can propose marriage to men not only on Leap Day (February 29) but throughout Leap Year. It can be traced back to an ancient Irish legend concerning St. Patrick and St. Bridget in the fifth century. Bridget complained that her nuns were unhappy because they never had a chance to propose marriage—at the time, celibacy in religious orders was based on private vows and not required by the church. Patrick suggested that women be given this privilege every seven years, but that wasn't good enough for Bridget. She pleaded for granting it every four years, and Patrick obliged by offering them Leap Year—a so-called "compromise" that shows how passive women were expected to be in such matters. Bridget then proposed to Patrick, who declined—promising her instead a kiss and a silk gown.

In the British Isles during the Middle Ages, there was an unwritten law stating that any single man who declined a woman's proposal during Leap Year had to compensate her with a kiss and either a silk dress or a pair of gloves. Any woman who intended to propose to a man during Leap Year was expected to let a red petticoat show beneath the hem of her skirt. Similar laws were soon introduced in Europe, and the custom was legalized throughout France and in parts of Italy by the fifteenth century. It eventually spread to the United States, where it is no longer taken seriously. The tradition of having a man soften his refusal of a woman's proposal with a silk gown continued in Europe and the British Isles until its demise in the nineteenth century.

## Further Reading

Cohen, Hennig, and Tristram Potter Coffin, eds. *The Folklore of American Holidays,* 2nd ed., 1991.

Hatch, Jane M. *The American Book of Days,* 1978.

Henderson, Helene and Sue Ellen Thompson. *Holidays, Festivals, and Celebrations of the World Dictionary,* 2nd ed., 1997.

Kelly, Aidan. *Religious Holidays and Calendars,* 1993.

Tuleja, Tad. *Curious Customs: The Stories Behind 296 Popular American Rituals,* 1987.

Van Straalen, Alice. *The Book of Holidays Around the World,* 1986.

# *Lemuralia*
### *(Lemuria)*

**Type of Holiday:** Ancient or pagan
**Date of Observation:** May 9, 11, 13
**Where Celebrated:** Rome, Italy
**Symbols:** Beans, Lemures
**Related Holidays:** All Souls' Day

## ORIGINS

In ancient Rome, where even-numbered days were considered unlucky, the festival of the dead known as the Lemuralia was held on May 9, 11, and 13. It was established by Romulus, one of the legendary founders of Rome, to atone for killing his twin brother, Remus. Legend has it that when Romulus was raising the walls of Rome, Remus—who had been defeated in choosing the city's location—jumped over the wall in a gesture of scorn, for which his brother killed him.

The Lemures were the wandering spirits of the dead, who returned to visit and sometimes to threaten their kinfolk. To ward them off, the father or head of the household would get up at midnight, make a special gesture (holding his thumb between his closed fingers), wash his hands in pure water, and walk through the house spitting black BEANS from his mouth. He would repeat this ritual nine times without looking back, assuming that the ghosts of the dead would pick up the beans he left behind. Then he would wash his hands again and repeat the phrase "Ghosts of my fathers, be gone" nine times. After this, it was considered safe for him to look back, and all the ghosts would be gone.

The Lemuralia was a private and domestic rite rather than a public celebration. It was similar to the Parentalia observed in February, but probably descended from a more ancient, superstitious period in Roman history. The February celebration in honor of the dead was more cheerful and civilized, while the Lemuralia was rooted in a time when fear of the dead was a powerful factor in most people's minds. The custom of ridding the house of spirits may have evolved from the periodic expulsion of demons performed on behalf of the community. May was considered an appropriate time to get rid of these demons because they were more likely to be rampant at the turn of the year in spring.

Temples were closed and marriages were prohibited during the three days of the Lemuralia. On the third day, a merchants' festival was held to ensure a prosperous year for business.

## SYMBOLS

### *Beans*

Beans were associated with ghosts, witches, and supernatural spirits in ancient times. If a person dreamed about black beans, it was supposed to mean that grave danger awaited him or her. Sometimes beans were regarded as taboo, and priests would not touch them or even mention them—probably because of their association with the powers of the underworld. But their significance is uncertain; they may have been fertility symbols, or possibly surrogates for living family members, whom ghosts might try to snatch away.

Why would the ghosts of the dead pick up the beans scattered through the house at the Lemuralia? There is some reason to believe that by eating this traditional symbol of fertility, the ghosts hoped to obtain a new lease on life. It is also possible that people believed the souls of the dead resided in the beans. In any case, spitting beans was a widely used remedy against ghosts among the ancient Greeks and Romans. People often threw black beans on the graves of the deceased or burned them, as the dead were supposed to be unable to tolerate the smell.

The Japanese have a similar ceremony for driving out demons. On **NEW YEAR'S EVE**, the head of the household puts on his best clothes and goes through all the rooms at midnight, scattering roasted beans and saying, "Out, demons! In, luck!"

## Lemures

*Lemures* is a general term for spirits after they have left the body, while those who haunt houses are called *larvae.* Both are considered hostile ghosts, unlike the *manes,* who were the benign spirits honored at the Parentalia in February. Both the lemures and the larvae terrified the good and haunted the wicked. The custom of celebrating festivals in their honor appears to have been instituted by Romulus, who wanted to appease the ghost of his twin brother, Remus. In fact, the Lemuralia (or Lemuria) was originally known as the Remuria.

The Lemures were believed to be particularly restless in May, which is probably why this month was considered an unlucky time to get married.

## Further Reading

Bell, Robert E. *Dictionary of Classical Mythology,* 1992.

Fowler, W. Warde. *The Roman Festivals of the Period of the Republic,* 1925.

Henderson, Helene and Sue Ellen Thompson. *Holidays, Festivals, and Celebrations of the World Dictionary,* 2nd ed., 1997.

James, E. O. *Seasonal Feasts and Festivals,* 1961.

Leach, Maria, ed. *Funk & Wagnalls Standard Dictionary of Folklore, Mythology, & Legend,* 1984.

*L'Empriere's Classical Dictionary,* 3rd ed., 1984.

Scullard, H. H. *Festivals and Ceremonies of the Roman Republic,* 1981.

# *Lent*

**Type of Holiday:** Religious (Christian)

**Date of Observation:** Forty days, beginning on Ash Wednesday and ending on Easter eve

**Where Celebrated:** By Christians all over the world

**Symbols:** Birch Branches, Fasting, Lenten Fires

**Colors:** Lent is associated with the color purple, which symbolizes penance.

**Related Holidays:** Ash Wednesday, Carnival, Easter, Good Friday, Shrove Tuesday

## ORIGINS

Self-denial during a period of intense religious devotion is a long-standing tradition in both the Eastern and Western churches. In the early days, Christians prepared for **EASTER** by fasting from **GOOD FRIDAY** until Easter morning. It wasn't until the ninth century that the Lenten season was fixed at 40 days (with Sundays omitted), perhaps reflecting the importance attached to the number: Moses went without food for 40 days on Mt. Sinai, the children of Israel wandered for 40 years, Elijah fasted for 40 days, and so did Jesus, who also spent 40 hours in his tomb.

"Lent" comes from an Anglo-Saxon word meaning "spring" or "lengthening days." It is a period of self-examination and repentance in preparation for Easter and a time to strengthen one's faith in God through repentance and prayer. Lent has been observed for centuries with periods of strict fasting, abstinence from meat (and in the East, from dairy products, wine, and olive oil as well), additional prayer services, and other penitential activities. It is customary for modern-day Christians to "give up something for Lent"—a favorite food or other worldly pleasure. It is also customary for the church organs to remain silent during this period, and for weddings and other celebrations to be prohibited.

Although the observation of Lent is usually associated with Roman Catholics, Protestant churches also observe Lent. Most offer Holy Communion on each of the Sundays during Lent, and some organize special Bible study classes for children and adults. Almost every church sets aside Sunday evenings during Lent for performances of cantatas, oratorios, and other Lenten music.

# SYMBOLS

## Birch Branches

In Sweden, the Lenten season is called *Fastlagen*. It falls at a time of year when the ground is still frozen and the trees are bare. People cut birch branches and tie colored chicken or rooster feathers to the boughs. At one time, the decorated branches were used to beat one another, a cleansing ritual designed to get rid of anything evil or unholy. The custom of "birching" also served as a symbolic reminder of the beatings that Jesus received on His way to be crucified. Today, the branches are used to decorate windowsills.

## Fasting

From the time of the Apostles, the church had singled out Friday as a weekly day of fast. In addition, many early Christians observed a strict two-day fast from Good Friday to Easter Sunday. Eventually a longer period of fasting was introduced in preparation for Easter, although its observance varied widely. Some churches fasted only during Holy Week, while others extended the fast for two or more weeks. Sunday was always an exception, and, in the Eastern church, so was Saturday. During the third and fourth centuries most churches adopted a 40-day fast in imitation of Christ, who had fasted for 40 days in the wilderness after He was baptized.

Back in the days when there were no calendars to tell people how close they were to the end of the fasting period, they invented their own methods of keeping track of the time. One of these primitive calendars looked like a nun cut out of paper, with no mouth (symbolizing the abstention from food) and with her hands crossed in prayer. She had seven feet, all facing in the same direction. Every Saturday one of the feet was torn off, until the fast was over. Another approach, used in Greece, was to stick seven chicken feathers in a boiled potato or onion hanging from the ceiling by a string. A feather was removed as each week passed.

For nearly 1,000 years, the Catholic Church followed the fasting rules laid down by Pope Gregory the Great: no meat or animal products, such as milk, cheese, eggs, or butter. This is still the routine among members of the Eastern Catholic Church and the Greek Orthodox Church in the United

States. But a new ruling of the Ecumenical Council in Rome says that Catholics are obligated to fast on only two days during Lent: Ash Wednesday and Good Friday.

## Lenten Fires

The custom of lighting fires on the first Sunday in Lent was widespread in Europe at one time and is still common in parts of Belgium, northern France, and Germany. Children go around collecting fuel and cutting down bushes for days in advance. The fires are lit in the evening, often by the individual who has most recently married. Young people sing and dance around the bonfire, leaping over the embers to guarantee a good harvest or a happy marriage within the year, or to guard themselves against colic. In some areas, torches are lit from the fire and carried into the surrounding orchards, gardens, and fields. Ashes from the torches may be shaken on the ground or put in hens' nests so there will be plenty of eggs. In Switzerland, where the first Sunday in Lent is known as Spark Sunday, a "witch"—usually made from old clothes and fastened to a pole—is stuck in the middle of the fire. Sometimes old wheels are wrapped in straw and thorns, lit on fire, and sent rolling down a nearby hill.

There is an old peasant saying that neglecting to kindle the fire on the first Sunday in Lent means that God will light it Himself—i.e., that He will burn the house down. It was common at one time to roast cats alive over the Lenten fires. The cats symbolized the Devil, who could never be put through too much suffering.

## Further Reading

Dobler, Lavinia. *Customs and Holidays Around the World,* 1962.

Frazer, Sir James G. *The Golden Bough: A Study in Magic and Religion,* 1931.

Harper, Howard V. *Days and Customs of All Faiths,* 1957.

Henderson, Helene and Sue Ellen Thompson. *Holidays, Festivals, and Celebrations of the World Dictionary,* 2nd ed., 1997.

Ickis, Marguerite. *The Book of Festivals and Holidays the World Over,* 1970.

Ickis, Marguerite. *The Book of Religious Holidays and Celebrations,* 1966.

Santino, Jack. *All Around the Year,* 1994.

Spicer, Dorothy Gladys. *The Book of Festivals,* 1990.

Spicer, Dorothy Gladys. *Festivals of Western Europe,* 1994.

Urlin, Ethel L. *Festivals, Holy Days, and Saints' Days,* 1915.

Weiser, Francis X. *Handbook of Christian Feasts and Customs,* 1952.

# *Li Ch'un*

**Type of Holiday:** Calendar

**Date of Observation:** Early February

**Where Celebrated:** China, and by Chinese communities throughout the world

**Symbols:** Meng Shan, Ox

**Colors:** Five colors are associated with Li Ch'un: black, white, red, green, and yellow. They represent the five elements (fire, water, metal, wood, earth), the five planets that rule the elements (Mercury, Venus, Mars, Jupiter, and Saturn), the five kinds of grain grown in China, and the five kinds of weather conditions (see OX).

**Related Holidays:** Chinese New Year, Ch'ing Ming

## ORIGINS

Li Ch'un is the Chinese festival welcoming the start of spring. At one time it marked the traditional beginning of the farmer's agricultural year, which consisted of 24 "solar breaths" or "joints"—15-day periods calculated according to the solar rather than the lunar calendar and named after the characteristics of each season. Li Ch'un means "Spring is here."

In rural areas, Li Ch'un is still observed with plowing ceremonies. A government representative dressed in his official robes arrives early in the morning at an appointed field, where a plow and oxen (or water buffaloes) are waiting near a small shrine. He makes an offering of fruit and sweets to the god of spring and the god of husbandry. After burning incense on the altar, he plows the first furrow in the field.

In towns and urban areas, long and colorful processions are held to welcome spring. There are usually more participants in these processions than spectators. Only soldiers and military officers are prohibited from joining the procession because the gods who dwell in the heavens consider it a bad omen to see soldiers in the spring. The most prominent figure in the procession is the OX, made of paper and bamboo. When the procession reaches the temple, the image of the ox is burned so that its spirit will ascend to heaven and plead for a prosperous growing season.

The first day of spring is considered an auspicious time for weddings, and many people attend marriage ceremonies on the evening of Li Ch'un.

## SYMBOLS

### *Meng Shan*

Meng Shan or the "spirit driver" plays a prominent part in the spring processions held on Li Ch'un. Made out of stiff paper, he is dressed in a way that is believed to foretell the weather for the coming year. If he is wearing a hat, it will be a dry year; no hat means rain. If he is wearing lots of clothing, it is considered an indication that weather will be hot; little clothing means cold weather. Since Meng Shan is a spirit, he dresses exactly opposite to the way a living man would dress for certain types of weather. If he wears a red belt, there will be a great deal of sickness and many deaths in the coming year; if he wears his white one, good health will be widespread. He drives before him the paper effigy of the OX.

### *Ox*

The ox or water buffalo is the Chinese symbol for spring, because it is the animal that pulls the plow and draws new life out of the fields. In early observances of Li Ch'un, a live ox was slaughtered, but it was later replaced by a clay effigy. Nowadays the ceremonial ox is made of bamboo (symbolic of long life) covered with strips of paper in five colors: black, white, red, green, and yellow. After the bamboo frame for the ox is built, it is taken to a blind man (or a man who has been blindfolded). He is given an equal number of pieces of each of the five colors, all mixed together, and he pastes them on the framework at random. When the ox is taken out in the streets for the Li Ch'un procession, people study the colors carefully to see which one predominates. If there is more red than any other color, it means that the summer will be hot and dry; yellow means that it will be very windy; green means rain, and so forth.

The ox is prodded and beaten with bamboo poles decorated with strips of colored paper. Sometimes the effigy is filled with grain, which spills out when the ox is beaten. The grain-filled ox is probably a representation of the ancient corn-spirit, responsible for bringing fertility to the fields. The Chinese often put stalks of bamboo stuffed with chicken feathers in the ground in front of their houses on Li Ch'un. The first spring breeze is supposed to blow at the exact moment when the ox is being beaten, and it carries the feathers up into the sky. Sometimes the ox is whipped with willow twigs—willow being a traditional symbol of springtime. This "beating of the spring" is believed to hasten the season's arrival and promote fertilization of the soil.

After the procession is over, both the ox and the spirit driver are burned, and the pieces of charred paper that drift down are kept as good luck charms.

## Further Reading

Bredon, Juliet, and Igor Mitrophanow. *The Moon Year: A Record of Chinese Customs and Festivals*, 1966.

Frazer, Sir James G. *The Golden Bough: A Study in Magic and Religion*, 1931.

Gaer, Joseph. *Holidays Around the World*, 1953.

Henderson, Helene and Sue Ellen Thompson. *Holidays, Festivals, and Celebrations of the World Dictionary*, 2nd ed., 1997.

Ickis, Marguerite. *The Book of Festivals and Holidays the World Over*, 1970.

Stepanchuk, Carol, and Charles Wong. *Mooncakes and Hungry Ghosts: Festivals of China*, 1991.

# *Loi Krathong*

**Type of Holiday:** Religious (Buddhist)

**Date of Observation:** Fifteenth day of waxing moon in 12th lunar month; November

**Where Celebrated:** Thailand

**Symbols:** Krathong, Lotus

## ORIGINS

Considered the most beautiful festival in Thailand, Loi Krathong is said to have originated more than 800 years ago, when King Ramakhamhaeng of Sukhotai, the first capital of Thailand, was making a pilgrimage on the river from temple to temple. One of his wives, Nang Nophames, wanted to please both her husband and Lord Buddha, so she made a KRATHONG or paper lantern resembling a LOTUS flower, put a candle in it, and set it afloat. The king was so delighted he decreed that his subjects should follow this custom every year.

Another theory about the origin of Loi Krathong claims that it goes back even further, to the ancient practice of paying tribute to Me Khongkha, the Mother of Water. The small coins and other items placed in the bottom of the krathong are meant as tokens to ask forgiveness for the ways in which humankind has abused its most precious natural resource. Yet another theory claims that the festival celebrates the lotus blossoms that sprang up when the Buddha took his first baby steps, or that it atones for the sin of passing in boats over the footprints of Buddha, which may be imbedded in the riverbottom.

Thais celebrate the "Festival of the Floating Leaf Cups" by going down to the nearest river or canal and floating small lamps or lanterns in the shape of animals, birds, dragons, airplanes, battleships, or other objects on the water. If there is no moving water nearby, the lanterns are set afloat on irrigation ditches. They are usually made out of banana leaves or paper. As they float out of sight, the individuals who launched them make a wish. If the candle stays lit until the krathong disappears, it is believed that the wish will come true.

Houses and temples are decorated with colored streamers and lights throughout the three days of the festival, particularly in villages that are not located on rivers or canals. The monks, who are forbidden to take part in the floating of the krathong, conduct services three times a day in the *wat* or temple. The women and girls attend all three services, but the men and boys usually attend only the evening service, after which drums and gongs are beaten, firecrackers are exploded, and the festivities continue until dawn.

Although Loi Krathong is celebrated throughout the country, it is especially significant in Sukhotai, which is where lady Nophames set the first krathong afloat. A beauty contest is usually part of the celebration, and the winner gets to represent Nophames throughout the three days of the festival.

## SYMBOLS

### *Krathong*

*Loi* means "to float" and *krathong* is a "leaf cup" or "bowl." On the evening of the festival, Thais gather at the water after sunset to launch small lotus-shaped banana leaf or paper boats, each of which holds a lighted candle, a flower, and a small coin to honor the water spirits. Some say that the krathong is also a tribute to the snake named Phrajanag who lives at the bottom of the river or canal. According to legend, Phrajanag literally followed in the Buddha's footsteps and succeeded in reaching Nirvana.

Krathong or leaf cups, usually in the shape of a boat or a bird, go on sale several days before the festival. These commercially made krathong are really more like toys, and the stalls selling them are confined largely to cities and towns. In rural areas, people still make their own by hand.

The individual who has set the krathong afloat makes a wish as it drifts out of sight. If the candle is still burning when it disappears from view, it is believed that the wish will come true.

The paper or banana-leaf krathong are both an offering to appease the spirits of the river and a way of freeing oneself of the sins of the preceding year.

## Lotus

Krathong are often made in the shape of a lotus blossom, which symbolizes the flowering of the human spirit under Buddhism. As a symbol, the lotus was adopted from the Hindus by the Buddhists in India, who introduced it into their sculpture, painting, and literature. It is identified with purity and perfection because it grows out of the mud and yet is not defiled by it. In much the same way, humankind should be able to live in an evil and impure world without being influenced by it.

## Further Reading

Dobler, Lavinia. *Customs and Holidays Around the World,* 1962.

Henderson, Helene and Sue Ellen Thompson. *Holidays, Festivals, and Celebrations of the World Dictionary,* 2nd ed., 1997.

Kelly, Aidan. *Religious Holidays and Calendars,* 1993.

MacDonald, Margaret R., ed. *The Folklore of World Holidays,* 1992.

Shemanski, Frances. *A Guide to World Fairs and Festivals,* 1985.

Van Straalen, Alice. *The Book of Holidays Around the World,* 1986.

# *Lotus, Birthday of the*

**Type of Holiday:** Religious (Buddhist)
**Date of Observation:** Twenty-fourth day of the sixth Chinese lunar month
**Where Celebrated:** Beijing, China
**Symbols:** Lotus

## ORIGINS

Although the Chinese celebrate the birthday of flowers in general (Moon 2, Day 12 or 15) and honor Wei Shen, the protectress of flowers (Moon 4, Day 19), the LOTUS is singled out for special attention because of its importance to Buddhism. Gautama Buddha is described, in fact, as having "lotus eyes, lotus feet, and lotus thighs." His image is often shown seated or standing on a lotus.

The Birthday of the Lotus is observed at the time of year when lotuses bloom in the ponds and moats around Beijing, and people flock to the city to see them—much as they do in Japan and Washington, D.C., during cherry blossom time. The sixth moon of the Chinese calendar is called the "Lotus Moon" for this reason. Their blooms are a sign that prayers to the Dragon Prince have been answered and that the summer rains will start soon. Special lanes for rowboats are cut through the thick layer of lotus blossoms that cover the lakes of Beijing's Winter Palace.

## SYMBOLS

### Lotus

As a symbol, the lotus has been sacred to many cultures and religions. It was adopted from the Hindus by the Buddhists in India, who introduced it into their sculpture, painting, and literature. From India, it went with the Buddhists to Nepal, Burma, China—where it is held sacred above all other flowers—and finally Japan.

The lotus symbolizes purity and perfection because it grows out of the mud and yet is not defiled by it. In much the same way, humankind should be able to live in an evil and impure world without being influenced by it. The open flower resting quietly on the water signifies meditation; in full bloom, it symbolizes spiritual enlightenment. Just as the lotus has its roots in the mud but its flower rises to achieve great beauty, devout Buddhists expected to rise above passion and selfish striving.

The many-petaled spread of the lotus blossom also has a more cosmic significance. It symbolizes the space in which all existence is supported and passes away. It is also a symbol of knowledge, which leads believers out of the cycle of reincarnation to Nirvana.

## Further Reading

Biedermann, Hans. *Dictionary of Symbolism: Cultural Icons and the Meanings Behind Them,* 1994.

Bredon, Juliet, and Igor Mitrophanow. *The Moon Year: A Record of Chinese Customs and Festivals,* 1966.

Henderson, Helene and Sue Ellen Thompson. *Holidays, Festivals, and Celebrations of the World Dictionary,* 2nd ed., 1997.

Johnson, F. Ernest, ed. *Religious Symbolism,* 1955.

# *Lughnasa*
### (Lammas)

**Type of Holiday:** Ancient or pagan
**Date of Observation:** August 1
**Where Celebrated:** England, Scotland, Ireland
**Symbols:** Funeral Processions, Hilltops, Oak Tree, Teltown Marriage

## ORIGINS

Along with **BELTANE, SAMHAIN,** and **IMBOLC,** Lughnasa was one of the four major Celtic festivals observed in the British Isles during pre-Christian times. It takes its name from the ancient sun-god Lugh and the Celtic *nasadh,* meaning "commemoration." August 1 marked the midpoint of the warm or "summer" half of the year, which extended from May through October. Since the Celts measured their year from midsummer to midsummer, this festival was both a commemoration of the passing of the old year, as symbolized by FUNERAL PROCESSIONS for the sun-god Lugh, and a celebration of the arrival of the new year with games, feasting, and magic shows.

In Ireland, two important gatherings took place during Lughnasa: the assembly of Tailte, named after the goddess who was also the foster-mother of Lugh; and the assembly of Carman, which commemorated the grief of the mother-goddess Carman when her sons were expelled from Ireland. It was therefore an important gathering time for Celtic women, and there is evidence that ceremonies associated with marriage (see TELTOWN MARRIAGE), fertility, childbirth, and other female rites of passage took place during the festival.

In England, August 1 was called the festival of the Gule of August, a harvest celebration that was the forerunner of the American **THANKSGIVING**. When Christianity arrived, it was called Lammas, which may have come either from Lugh-mass or from "loaf-mass," since it was customary for loaves made from the first ripe grain to be blessed in the church on this day. Another theory is that the name derived from "lamb-mass," because it was the time of year when worshippers would bring a live lamb as an offering to the church.

While Beltane remained a pagan holiday and Samhain was largely replaced by the Christian festival of All Saints' Day, Lughnasa retained a mixture of pagan and Christian customs. In the Scottish Highlands, people used to sprinkle their cows and the floors of their houses with menstrual blood, which they believed would ward off evil on this day. Elsewhere in Scotland, Lammas was one of the so-called Quarter Days, when tenants paid their rents — an obvious Christianization of the harvest festival custom of having tenants bring the first new grain to their landlords. In Ireland, where the celebration of Lughnasa waned during the late nineteenth century and then was revived in the twentieth, it has survived primarily as a seasonal celebration.

# SYMBOLS

## *Funeral Processions*

Because Lughnasa was originally a festival of mourning for the death of the sun-god Lugh, funerary rites and processions were a common practice. It is possible that at one time the victims were real, and that eventually they were replaced by effigies of the dead, carried in procession and buried in symbolic graves. Some scholars believe that in ancient times, when the Celtic kings reigned for only a year, the old king allowed himself to be put to death so that a new king could take his place. Since the Celts normally crowned their kings at midsummer, this would explain the necessity for funeral processions at Lughnasa.

In any case, the festival was an occasion for paying homage to the dead—particularly warriors and heroes in the style of Lugh—and eulogies or poems praising ancient gods and heroes were often recited. Even today, mock-funeral processions are occasionally held in Yorkshire and Lancashire, England, with groups of young men carrying an empty coffin for many miles along an ancient path.

## Hilltops

Lughnasa was a popular time for gathering berries, particularly bilberries. In Ireland, where Lughnasa began in mid-July and lasted until mid-August, the first Sunday of this four-week period was known as Bilberry Sunday. Young people would go off to the hilltops, where berries were plentiful, and not return until dusk. The boys would make bilberry bracelets for the girls by stringing the berries along short pieces of thread, competing with each other to see who could make the most beautiful bracelet for his girlfriend.

Many of the hilltop sights originally visited for berrypicking were later taken over by the Catholic Church and turned into pilgrimage sights. Croagh Patrick in County Mayo, Ireland, is a good example. Also known as The Reek, it is Ireland's holiest mountain, and pilgrims flock to it on the last Sunday in July, which is known as Reek Sunday. Although the Christians who climb Croagh Patrick do so because they want to pray on the spot where Ireland's patron saint is believed to have started his ministry, this hilltop's fame may also be rooted in pagan celebrations.

As recently as the nineteenth century, people in Ireland were still visiting more than 100 hilltop sites on August 1 for berrypicking and pilgrimages.

## Oak Tree

It is a well-known fact that the Druids or priests of the ancient Celtic religion worshipped the oak. They were not, however, the first to do so. There were oak cults in ancient Greece and Libya, and scholars believe that the oak cult came to Britain somewhere between 1600 and 1400 B.C.E., at least 500 years before the Celts. In the ancient Druid alphabet, each letter stands for a tree or shrub with many mythological associations. The letter D or *Duir* means "oak."

The trees associated with the midsummer months are oak and holly, with the oak representing the god of the old year and the holly the god of the new year. The sun-god Lugh is associated with the oak in Celtic mythology because he symbolizes the old year (or the old king) who must yield to the new year (or new king) on August 1.

## *Teltown Marriage*

Lughnasa was a time for the king to reconfirm his divine "marriage" to the well-being of his kingdom. Midsummer was also a popular time for real marriages, since the harvest was in, food was abundant, and agricultural chores were less demanding. In many ways, it was the most relaxed time of year, when people had the leisure to celebrate.

In medieval Ireland, there was a special kind of "trial" marriage that could only take place at Lughnasa. Called a Tailtean or Teltown marriage — after Tailte, a powerful goddess and the foster-mother of Lugh — it lasted only a year and a day. It could be dissolved without any social stigma, but only if both individuals returned on the next Lughnasa and went through a ritual in which they walked away from each other — one heading north and the other south.

Teltown, located in Ireland's County Meath, was also the scene of one of the most important gatherings that took place on August 1: the assembly of Tailte (see "Origins").

## **Further Reading**

Chambers, Robert, ed. *The Book of Days*, 1864.

Heinberg, Richard. *Celebrate the Solstice: Honoring the Earth's Seasonal Rhythms through Festival and Ceremony*, 1993.

Henderson, Helene and Sue Ellen Thompson. *Holidays, Festivals, and Celebrations of the World Dictionary*, 2nd ed., 1997.

Kelly, Aidan, Peter Dresser, and Linda M. Ross. *Religious Holidays and Calendars: An Encyclopaedic Handbook*, 1993.

King, John. *The Celtic Druids' Year: Seasonal Cycles of the Ancient Celts*, 1994.

Leach, Maria, ed. *Funk & Wagnalls Standard Dictionary of Folklore, Mythology & Legend*, 1984.

MacDonald, Margaret R., ed. *The Folklore of World Holidays*, 1992.

Urlin, Ethel L. *Festivals, Holy Days, and Saints' Days*, 1915.

# *Luilak*
## *(Lazybones Day)*

**Type of Holiday:** Folkloric

**Date of Observation:** Between May 9 and June 12; Saturday before Pentecost

**Where Celebrated:** Netherlands

**Symbols:** Branches, Wagons

**Related Holidays:** Pentecost

## ORIGINS

Luilak or Lazybones Day is a youth festival celebrated in Zaandam, Haarlem, Amsterdam, and other towns in the western Netherlands. The holiday begins at four o'clock in the morning on the Saturday before **PENTECOST**, when groups of young people awaken their neighbors by whistling, banging on pots and pans, and ringing doorbells. Any boy or girl who refuses to get up and join in the noisemaking is referred to as *Luilak* or "Lazybones" throughout the coming year. The Lazybones must also treat their companions to candy or cakes, and they are the butt of all sorts of jokes and teasing.

According to legend, the holiday originated in 1672 when a watchman named Piet Lak fell asleep while French invaders entered the country. He was known thereafter as *Luie-Lak,* or "Lazy Lak." In many parts of the country, *Luilakbollen* or "Lazybones Cakes," traditionally baked in the shape of fat double rolls and served hot with syrup, are a specialty of the season.

## SYMBOLS

### *Branches*

In some parts of the Netherlands, boys and girls get up early on the Saturday before Whitsunday (**PENTECOST**) and gather green branches from the woods. Then they dip the branches in water and fasten them over the doors of late-sleepers in such a way that when the door is opened, the branches fall on the unsuspecting "Lazybones" and give them a drenching. Then the children, who are usually lurking nearby, chase the Lazybones and beat them with the branches.

The custom of beating each other with branches as a way of welcoming spring dates back to very ancient times, when it was probably intended as a purification rite.

## *Wagons*

Children often celebrate Luilak by making little wagons shaped like boots and decorated with branches and thistles, known as *luilakken.* Pulling the wagons over the cobblestone streets often generates enough friction to set the wheels smoking. The children then either watch their wagons go up in flames or douse them in the nearest canal.

Although the exact origin of the smoking wagons is not known, they are believed to be connected to an ancient spring fertility ceremony.

### Further Reading

Henderson, Helene and Sue Ellen Thompson. *Holidays, Festivals, and Celebrations of the World Dictionary,* 2nd ed., 1997.

Ickis, Marguerite. *The Book of Festivals and Holidays the World Over,* 1970.

MacDonald, Margaret R., ed. *The Folklore of World Holidays,* 1992.

Spicer, Dorothy G. *The Book of Festivals,* 1937.

Spicer, Dorothy G. *Festivals of Western Europe,* 1958.

# *Lupercalia*

**Type of Holiday:** Ancient or pagan

**Date of Observation:** February 15

**Where Celebrated:** Rome

**Symbols:** Blood, Februa, Goat, Milk, Wolf

**Colors:** Red and white, in the form of BLOOD and MILK, both played a part in the earliest observance of the Lupercalia. Nowadays these are the colors associated with **VALENTINE'S DAY**, to which this ancient festival has been linked.

**Related Holidays:** Candlemas, Valentine's Day

# ORIGINS

The Lupercalia was an ancient Roman festival held in honor of the WOLF who mothered Romulus and Remus, the legendary twin founders of Rome. During the original Roman celebration, members from two colleges of priests gathered at a cave on the Palatine Hill called the Lupercal—supposedly the cave where Romulus and Remus had been suckled by a she-wolf—and sacrificed a GOAT and a dog. The animals' BLOOD was smeared on the foreheads of two young priests and then wiped away with wool dipped in MILK. The two young men stripped down to a goatskin loincloth and ran around the Palatine, striking everyone who approached them, especially the women, with thongs of goat skin called FEBRUA. It is believed that this was both a fertility ritual and a purification rite. It may also have been a very early example of "beating the bounds" (see **ASCENSION DAY**), or reestablishing the borders of the early Palatine settlement.

There is some confusion over which god the Luperci or priests served; some say it was Faunus, a rural deity, and some say it was Pan, the god of shepherds who protected sheep from the danger of wolves. All that is certain is that by Caesar's time, the annual ceremony had become a spectacular public sight, with young men running half-naked through the streets and provoking much good-natured hysteria among the women. February 15 was also the day when Mark Anthony offered Julius Caesar the crown. Thanks to this historic event, and Shakespeare's account of it in his play *Julius Caesar,* the Lupercalia is one of the best known of all Roman festivals.

It is interesting that such a rustic festival continued to be celebrated in Rome for centuries after it had been Christianized. Its survival can be partially credited to Augustus, who rebuilt the Lupercal in the first century B.C.E., thus giving the celebration a boost. It continued to be observed until 494 C.E., when Pope Gelasius I changed the day to the Feast of the Purification of the Virgin Mary. There is some reason to believe that the Lupercalia was a forerunner of the modern **VALENTINE'S DAY**: Part of the ceremony involved putting girls' names in a box and letting boys draw them out, thus pairing them off until the next Lupercalia.

# SYMBOLS

## *Blood*

Blood played an important role in the observation of the Lupercalia. The blood of the animals sacrificed at the festival was smeared across the foreheads of two young priests with a knife—perhaps to symbolize death without actually killing anyone. Some accounts of the early observation of this festival say that the youths had to laugh after the blood had been wiped off (see MILK), which may have been another symbolic act designed to prove that they had been reborn or revived.

Red, the color of blood, is still closely identified with the celebration of **VALENTINE'S DAY** on February 14. There is reason to believe that what started out as a pagan fertility ritual was eventually transformed into a Christian feast in honor of St. Valentine. Then the Christian festival gradually turned into a secular celebration of young lovers. If this is the case, then the red that dominates so many modern Valentine cards may have derived from the sacrificial blood of the Lupercalia.

## Februa

The skins of the goats sacrificed at the Lupercalia were cut into long, thin strips, from which whips were made. The loinskin-clad youths ran through the streets, whipping everyone they met. Women in particular were eager to receive these lashes, as they believed that the whipping would cure infertility and ease the pains of childbirth.

The goatskin thongs used as whips were called *februa*. Both this name and the name of the month in which the festival was observed, February, were derived from the word *februum*, which was an ancient instrument of purification. Whipping certain parts of the body with an instrument believed to possess magical powers was considered an effective way of driving off the evil spirits that interfered with human fertilization. The goatskin thongs were believed to possess such powers.

Running around the settlement on the Palatine Hill in Rome wearing the skins and carrying the februa appears to have been an attempt to trace a magic circle around the city to shut out evil influences. This would make the Lupercalia a precursor of the ceremony that came to be known as "beating the bounds."

## Goat

In pre-Christian times, the goat was a symbol of virility and unbridled lust. Christians saw the goat as an "impure, stinking" creature in search of gratification. In portrayals of the Last Judgment, the goat is the creature who is eternally condemned to the fires of Hell, and it's no coincidence that the Devil has many goat-like characteristics. In the Middle Ages, witches were often shown riding through the air on goats, and the Devil appears as a male goat whose rump the witches kiss.

If the Lupercalia was primarily a fertility ritual, it makes sense that the women were whipped with thongs made from the skins of an animal identified with lust and virility. But why was a dog sacrificed as well? It is important to remember here that the Lupercalia was both a fertility rite and a purification rite, held to protect the fields and herds from evil. Perhaps dogs were involved in the sacrifice because they are the traditional guardians of the sheepfold.

Goats today are considered a symbol of sexual drive, and February is the month during which they mate.

## Milk

After the Luperci were smeared with the blood of the sacrifice, the blood was wiped from their foreheads with wool dipped in milk. Just as the blood symbolized death, the milky wool was symbolic of new life, because milk represents the source of life. Some scholars have theorized that the milk was a symbol of sperm and the red symbolized menstrual blood. According to an ancient theory of procreation, new life came from the union of white sperm with red menses.

Today, red and white are the colors associated with **VALENTINE'S DAY**.

## Wolf

The Latin word for wolf is *lupus,* from which both the Lupercal (cave) and the Lupercalia derived their names. While the festival may originally have been held in honor of the she-wolf who cared for Romulus and Remus, wolves also represented a threat to the herds on which the early Romans depended for food. The wolf is therefore a symbol not only for the wild, unrestrained forces of nature but also for the benevolent guardian of helpless creatures like Romulus and Remus.

Why were the priests called Luperci? The word *Lupercus* might have come from a phrase meaning "to purify by means of a goat"; or it might have come from a combination of *lupus* and *arcere,* meaning "he who wards off wolves." Whether the Luperci were protectors from wolves or wolf-priests who took the form of wolves as a means of bringing them under control is a question that has never been satisfactorily answered. Some scholars suggest that the dead revealed themselves in the form of wolves, against whom the community had to be defended.

## Further Reading

Biedermann, Hans. *Dictionary of Symbolism: Cultural Icons and the Meanings Behind Them*, 1994.

Fowler, W. Warde. *The Roman Festivals of the Period of the Republic*, 1925.

Henderson, Helene and Sue Ellen Thompson. *Holidays, Festivals, and Celebrations of the World Dictionary*, 2nd ed., 1997.

James, E. O. *Seasonal Feasts and Festivals*, 1961.

*L'Empriere's Classical Dictionary*, 3rd ed., 1984.

Santino, Jack. *All Around the Year*, 1994.

Scullard, H. H. *Festivals and Ceremonies of the Roman Republic*, 1981.

# *Martenitza*

**Type of Holiday:** Calendar, Folkloric

**Date of Observation:** March 1

**Where Celebrated:** Albania, Bulgaria, Canada, Cyprus, Greece, Macedonia, Romania

**Symbols:** Martenitza

**Colors:** This festival is associated with the colors red and white. Red, symbolizing life, is believed to possess the power to drive away evil. White symbolizes the sun and purity.

**Related Holidays:** Procession of the Swallow

## ORIGINS

The first day of March marks the beginning of spring in Bulgaria and the beginning of summer in Greece. The custom of exchanging MARTENITZAS, or tassels made of red and white threads, on this day is most widespread in Bulgaria, although it is common in southern Romania, Albania, Greece, and Cyprus as well.

The rites associated with the holiday are varied. In some regions, the women dress completely in red on this day. In northeastern Bulgaria, the lady of the house tosses a red cloth over a fruit tree, or spreads a red woolen cloth on the fields to improve their fertility. In stock-breeding areas, a red-and-white thread is tied to the cattle. In Greece, the martenitza (which means "March") is tied to the wrist or big toe of children to protect them from the intense March sun. There is a widespread folk belief that children should wear their martenitza until they see the first swallow of the year. Then they should hide it under a stone. When the stone is lifted 40 days later, ants indicate that wealth and happiness will come to the owner of the martenitza; but if there are worms, it means bad luck. Sometimes the martenitza is thrown on a rosebush in the garden, or tossed in the air when the first swallow is sighted. How these customs originated has been forgotten, but it is likely that the fate of the martenitza and of the person who wore it were somehow connected.

Bulgarians and Macedonians living in Canada exchange twists of red and white thread, known as *marteniki,* on the first day of March. When they see the first robins, they toss down the threads for the birds to use in their nest-building.

## SYMBOLS

### *Martenitza*

The red-and-white thread tassel that gives this holiday its name can be traced back to the ancient Thracians, who attached silver or gold coins to their martenitzas. March was the first month of the year in ancient Greece, and it is believed that the martenitza was originally a means of wishing each other good luck in the coming year. Since that time it has remained a symbol of good health and happiness, an appropriate token to exchange at a time of year when life is renewing itself.

### Further Reading

Henderson, Helene and Sue Ellen Thompson. *Holidays, Festivals, and Celebrations of the World Dictionary*, 2nd ed., 1997.

MacDonald, Margaret R., ed. *The Folklore of World Holidays*, 1992.

# *Martinmas*

**Type of Holiday:** Religious (Christian), Folkloric
**Date of Observation:** November 11
**Where Celebrated:** British Isles, Western Europe, Scandinavia
**Symbols:** Bonfires, Goose, Rod

## ORIGINS

Martinmas is the popular name for the feast day of St. Martin of Tours (316-397 C.E.), the patron saint of France. Pope Martin I (649-654 C.E.) made it a great church festival, probably in an attempt to Christianize the old Teutonic custom of slaughtering animals in mid-November because they couldn't be kept alive throughout the long winter.

During the Middle Ages, November 11 was regarded as both the beginning of the year and the beginning of winter, a time when rents for pastures were paid and farm servants changed jobs. It was called the Martinalia because it took the place of the Vinalia or vintage feast of ancient Rome and was observed by opening the first cask of the year's vintage.

In addition to giving thanks for the new wine, Martinmas was also a day of thanksgiving for the harvest. For rural people, Martinmas came at a happy time of year: The crops were in, the new wine was ready, the animals had been slaughtered, and it was time to relax. Not surprisingly, St. Martin became the patron saint of tavern keepers, wine-growers, and drunkards. The Feast of St. Martin is still observed as a harvest festival in Scandinavia and rural parts of Europe, with roast GOOSE being the traditional dish of the harvest feast.

Over the centuries, Martinmas has shifted from a religious feast to a folk festival. In Belgium and other western European countries, St. Martin's role is much like that of St. Nicholas. He appears dressed as a bishop in red robes, riding on a white horse. To children who have behaved well, he throws apples, nuts, and cakes; an ill-behaved child receives a ROD. Sometimes children fill their stockings with hay for St. Martin's horse and find them full of gifts the next morning.

Martinmas is also associated with the weather. In fact, the mild weather that often occurs in Europe in early November is referred to as "St. Martin's summer"—much like Indian Summer in the United States. This goes back to an old legend that says St. Martin cut his cloak in two and gave half to a beggar who was nearly frozen with the cold. God sent warm weather so that the saint would be comfortable until he was able to find another cloak.

## SYMBOLS

### *Bonfires*

The bonfires that can still be seen in Belgium, Holland, and parts of Germany on St. Martin's Day (or the night before) can be traced back to pagan times, when they were lit to ward off evil spirits and promote fertility. During the fifteenth century, so many fires were lit in Germany on this day that the festival was called Funkentag (Spark Day).

In northwestern Germany today, the fire is often contained in lanterns made of paper or carved-out turnips (see **HALLOWEEN**), carried through the streets by processions of children on St. Martin's Eve. Jumping over lighted candles set in the floor is another popular German fire custom. Elsewhere, young people dance around bonfires and leap through the flames. Later, the ashes are scattered over the fields to make them fertile.

### *Goose*

As mentioned above, mid-November was the season for slaughtering farm animals among the Teutonic peoples. In fact, the original Anglo-Saxon name for November was *Blot-monath* or "blood month," associated not only with animal sacrifices but with feasting on meat. The tradition of slaughter has been preserved in the British custom of killing cattle on St. Martin's Day—referred to as "Martlemas beef"—and in the German custom of eating "St. Martin's Goose."

Why goose? According to an old legend, when St. Martin heard that he had been elected Bishop of Tours, the thought so intimidated him that he hid in a barn. But a goose found him there and made such a racket that his whereabouts were soon discovered.

In Denmark, a goose is eaten for the Martinmas meal and then its breastbone is examined for clues regarding the approaching winter. A very white bone is a sign of snow, while brown means extreme cold.

In parts of Ireland, it was common in the nineteenth century to kill an animal on Martinmas and sprinkle its blood over the threshold. Neglecting this custom—which may have been a holdover from the old Celtic festival of **SAMHAIN**—would bring bad luck.

271

## Rod

In Bavaria and Austria, a *gerte* or rod is associated with St. Martin's Day. Used to promote fertility among cattle and prosperity in general, the rods are given to farmers, to be used in the springtime when they drive the cattle out to pasture for the first time. In Bavaria, the rods are made from birch boughs with all the leaves and twigs stripped off — except at the top, where oak leaves and juniper twigs are fastened. Flogging is common in folk rituals, and in this case its purpose is to drive away evil influences and transfer the life-giving virtues of the tree from which the rod is made.

There is some connection between the custom of flogging and St. Martin's role as a European Santa Claus. In Antwerp, Belgium, St. Martin throws down rods for naughty children as well as nuts and apples for good ones — just as Santa Claus leaves gifts for good children and a lump of coal for those who have misbehaved. In ancient times, beating someone didn't have the negative connotations it has today, but was instead a positive gesture meant to bestow virtue and vitality. In any case, it is interesting to note that so many pagan customs have gathered about the festival of a Christian saint.

### Further Reading

Harper, Howard V. *Days and Customs of All Faiths*, 1957.

Henderson, Helene and Sue Ellen Thompson. *Holidays, Festivals, and Celebrations of the World Dictionary*, 2nd ed., 1997.

Miles, Clement A. *Christmas in Ritual and Tradition*, 1990.

Pike, Royston. *Round the Year with the World's Religions*, 1993.

Purdy, Susan. *Festivals for You to Celebrate*, 1969.

Urlin, Ethel L. *Festivals, Holy Days, and Saints' Days*, 1915.

Weiser, Francis X. *Handbook of Christian Feasts and Customs*, 1952.

# *Maskal*
### *(Masqual, Meskel)*

**Type of Holiday:** Religious (Christian)
**Date of Observation:** September 27
**Where Celebrated:** Ethiopia
**Symbols:** Cross, Demara, Maskal Flowers

# ORIGINS

Maskal is primarily a Christian festival observed in Ethiopia to commemorate the finding of the True Cross (i.e., the cross on which Christ was crucified). According to legend, the CROSS was found by Queen (later Saint) Helena—mother of the Roman emperor, Constantine—while she was on a religious pilgrimage to Jerusalem in the fourth century. She was very interested in the Mount of Calvary, where Jesus Christ had been crucified, and she organized an excavation there. Although all three crosses that had originally stood on Calvary were unearthed, St. Helena was able to determine which one was the True Cross by asking a man who was very ill to touch each of them. When he touched the True Cross, he was miraculously cured.

A relic or fragment of the True Cross was brought to Ethiopia during the Middle Ages as a reward to the Christian kings who had protected Coptic minorities from invaders. They received the relic a week before Maskal, which at that time was primarily a festival celebrating the arrival of spring. Since that time, the holiday has combined both Christian and pagan traditions.

Because Maskal comes at the end of the rainy season in Ethiopia, the fields are usually blooming with small yellow daisies known as MASKAL FLOWERS. The flowers are cut and fastened to special poles (see DEMARA) that each family brings to a central clearing. The poles are used to build a bonfire, around which young men dance, shouting war chants. On the following day, people draw a cross on their foreheads with the charcoal from the fire.

# SYMBOLS

## Cross

The cross is one of the oldest and most universal of all symbols. It stands for Christ, who was sacrificed on a cross, as well as for the Christian religion and the idea of redemption or salvation through Christianity.

Maskal celebrates the finding of the True Cross by St. Helena, who is often depicted carrying a cross, along with a hammer and nails. Sometimes she is shown with the Cross borned by angels who are appearing to her in a vision.

## Demara

On the eve of Maskal, every town and village erects its own *demara*, which is a tall, conical arrangement of wooden poles decorated with maskal flowers and with a cross on top. The demara is blessed with incense, after which a procession of villagers or townspeople, led by the priests and local clergy, circle it three times in honor of the Trinity. When nightfall comes, the demara is set aflame to symbolize the burning incense that guided St. Helena to the exact location of the True Cross in Jerusalem.

## Maskal Flowers

The yellow daisies known as maskal flowers are usually in full bloom at the time of year when this festival is observed. They are symbolic of the arrival of spring, since Maskal used to be a pagan festival celebrating the end of the rainy season—known as "winter" even though Ethiopia lies north of the equator.

## Further Reading

Ferguson, George. *Signs and Symbols in Christian Art,* 1954.

Henderson, Helene and Sue Ellen Thompson. *Holidays, Festivals, and Celebrations of the World Dictionary,* 2nd ed., 1997.

MacDonald, Margaret R., ed. *The Folklore of World Holidays,* 1992.

Shemanski, Frances. *A Guide to World Fairs and Festivals,* 1985.

Van Straalen, Alice. *The Book of Holidays Around the World,* 1986.

# *Maundy Thursday*
## *(Holy Thursday)*

**Type of Holiday:** Religious (Christian)

**Date of Observation:** Between March 19 and April 22 in the West; between April 1 and May 5 in the East; Thursday before Easter

**Where Celebrated:** England, Europe, United States, South America, and throughout the Christian world

**Symbols:** Blessing the Oils, Foot Washing, Maundy Money, Silencing the Bells

**Colors:** The liturgical color for this day is white, the symbol of joy.

**Related Holidays:** Easter, Good Friday

# ORIGINS

The day before **GOOD FRIDAY** has been observed since very early times with acts of humility in imitation of Jesus Christ, who washed the feet of His disciples on the eve of His crucifixion. The name "Maundy" probably came from the Latin *mandatum*, meaning "commandment." After the FOOT WASHING took place, Christ said, "A new commandment I give unto you, that you love one another as I have loved you." (John 13:34) Some say that "Maundy" came from an old word meaning "basket" in England, where the poor used baskets to carry the food and money distributed to them on this day (see MAUNDY MONEY).

The real significance of Maundy Thursday lies in the fact that it was the day of the Last Supper, when Jesus and his 12 apostles gathered to share the traditional Passover meal, as many others were doing all over Jerusalem. Jesus took the bread and the wine and described them in symbolic terms as His body and His blood, thus instituting the ceremony known as the Eucharist. He was trying to tell his disciples that just as the Jews had been saved from bondage in Egypt by the blood of a lamb smeared on their doors (see **PASSOVER**), all of mankind would be saved from the bondage of sin by the sacrifice He was about to make. He wanted His disciples to use this ceremony as a pattern for a memorial service they could hold later in His memory.

In some western European countries, the Thursday before **EASTER** is called Green Thursday. In Germany it's called *Gründonnerstag*, a name that is thought to have derived from *grunen* or *greinen*, meaning "to mourn," later corrupted into *grün* (green). In Austria and Hungary, it is customary to eat spinach and green salad on this day—perhaps because the Jews ate green vegetables or herbs at their Passover feast.

At one time, this day was known as Pure or Clean Thursday, from the ancient tradition of cleansing the soul as well as the body in preparation for Easter. The Old English name Shere (or Shier) Thursday referred to the practice of men shaving their beards on this day.

# SYMBOLS

## *Blessing the Oils*

The ceremony performed on the morning of Maundy Thursday and known as the Blessing of the Oils takes place at St. Peter's in Rome and in cathedrals elsewhere. It dates back to an ancient rite, the renewal of the supply of oils used to anoint people who are baptized at **EASTER.** There are actually three types of oils that are blessed: (1) the oil of catechumens, used in baptizing people, consecrating churches, ordaining priests, and crowning sovereigns; (2) the oil used in administering extreme unction to those who are dying; and (3) the oil of chrism, used in confirmation, the consecration of bishops, and the blessing of bells. These oils are kept in a chrismatory or casket made of silver or brass.

Two of the oils blessed on Maundy Thursday are actually olive oil. But the chrism is an ointment based on olive oil to which balsam or a perfume has been added, symbolizing "the sweet savor of Christ." In the morning service, the bishop not only blesses the oils but invites his priests to renew their commitment to their calling.

## Foot Washing

The act of washing someone's feet was a courtesy offered to a guest and usually performed by a female servant, or by the women of the family if there were no servants. When Jesus washed the feet of His 12 disciples at the Last Supper, it was more than a dramatic gesture on the eve of His crucifixion: He was teaching them that by humbling themselves, they could show their love for one another.

Foot washing has been a Maundy Thursday custom since the early days of the Church. Bishops, abbots, prelates, and other religious officials participated in the ceremony, as did the popes. In medieval times—and in some countries up to the present century—Christian emperors, kings, and lords washed the feet of poor men on Holy Thursday, after which they were given money and provided with a meal. The king of England used to have poor men brought to him—one man for each year of his age. Then he washed their feet and gave them food, money, and clothing. The last British monarch to perform the foot-washing ceremony was James II (1685-88). Today, British rulers attend a special Maundy service and distribute MAUNDY MONEY to the poor afterward.

At St. Peter's Cathedral in Rome, it used to be the custom for the Pope to wash the feet of subdeacons on Maundy Thursday. He no longer takes part in the ceremony, which is performed at the Church of the Ara Caeli. The Biblical account of the event is chanted and then the bishop, who wears a linen cloth at his waist, kneels to wash the right foot of each of the 13 men selected for the occasion. Twelve of them represent the apostles and the 13th represents the angel who, according to legend, appeared to Gregory the Great when he was performing an act of charity on this day in the late sixth century. Some say the 13th man represents St. Matthias, who replaced Judas Iscariot after he betrayed Jesus.

Some Roman Catholic churches still carry out the foot-washing ceremony on the Thursday preceding Easter. It symbolizes Christ's commandment that His followers show humility.

## Maundy Money

At one time in England, the king would have as many men brought before him as he was years old. Then he would wash their feet with his own hands and distribute *maunds,* which consisted of meat, clothing, and money. Queen Elizabeth in 1572 gave each person enough cloth for a gown, half a side of salmon, six red herring, bread, and wine. In 1838 Queen Victoria gave out woolen and linen clothing, shoes and stockings, and new coins minted specially for the occasion, which were referred to as "Maundy money."

Today, it is the Archbishop of Canterbury who distributes the Maundy money, which is carried into London's Westminster Abbey on a huge platter by the Yeoman of the Guard. The Archbishop and the Dean of Westminster wear only plain white instead of their usual elaborate robes, and they carry linen towels on their shoulders to commemorate the FOOT WASHING ceremony, which is no longer performed. The Maundy money, contained in red and white purses, consists of specially minted silver coins that total in value the monarch's age. Although they are considered legal tender, most recipients keep the coins as souvenirs.

England is one of very few countries where the ancient custom of distributing Royal Maundy gifts is still continued.

## Silencing the Bells

There is a universal legend among children that all the church bells "fly to Rome" after the Gloria of the Mass is sung on Holy Thursday. In Germany and central Europe, children are told that the bells make a pilgrimage to the tomb of the apostles, or that they go to the pope to be blessed and then sleep on the roof of St. Peter's Cathedral until Easter. In France, they are told that the bells fly to Rome to fetch the Easter eggs.

Whatever the reason for their departure, the silencing of the bells after the Gloria on Maundy Thursday has produced the popular expression that "the bells have gone to Rome" and will return after the Gloria is sung on Holy Saturday. Children run through the streets shaking various types of rattles and clappers to communicate the great sorrow associated with this period. In rural parts of Austria, boys with wooden clappers go through the villages announcing the time, because even the church clock is stopped.

After the Holy Thursday Mass is sung in Rome's Sistine Chapel, no bells are allowed to ring in the city until the following Saturday morning. This means that all the bells in Rome are silent from about 11:30 a.m. Thursday until the same time on Holy Saturday. Even the hand-held bells used to summon hotel guests to dinner are silent, although occasionally wooden clappers are used instead. Since the ringing of bells symbolizes a joyous event, their silence is an appropriate symbol for the sorrow associated with Christ's suffering and death on the cross.

## Further Reading

Chambers, Robert, ed. *The Book of Days*, 1864.

Dobler, Lavinia. *Customs and Holidays Around the World*, 1962.

Ferguson, George. *Signs and Symbols in Christian Art*, 1954.

Harper, Howard V. *Days and Customs of All Faiths*, 1957.

Henderson, Helene and Sue Ellen Thompson. *Holidays, Festivals, and Celebrations of the World Dictionary*, 2nd ed., 1997.

Hole, Christina. *English Custom and Usage*, 1941.

Ickis, Marguerite. *The Book of Religious Holidays and Celebrations*, 1966.

James, E. O. *Seasonal Feasts and Festivals*, 1961.

Metford, J. C. J. *The Christian Year*, 1991.

Monks, James L. *Great Catholic Festivals*, 1951.

Pike, Royston. *Round the Year with the World's Religions*, 1993.

Urlin, Ethel L. *Festivals, Holy Days, and Saints' Days*, 1915.

Weiser, Francis X. *Handbook of Christian Feasts and Customs*, 1952.

# *Mawlid al-Nabi*
## *(Muhammad's Birthday, Birthday of the Prophet)*

**Type of Holiday:** Religious (Islamic)

**Date of Observation:** 12th day of the Islamic lunar month of Rabi al-Awwal (usually August or September)

**Where Celebrated:** Egypt, Indonesia, Iran, Kenya, Lebanon, Libya, West Africa, South Africa, Turkey, and throughout the Islamic world

**Symbols:** Burdah, Dhikr, Recitations

**Related Holidays:** Laylat al-Miraj, Laylat al-Qadr

# ORIGINS

Mawlid al-Nabi (Birthday of the Prophet) celebrates the birth of the Prophet Muhammad, the founder of Islam. Born in Mecca on August 20, 570 C.E., he was a shepherd and a trader who began to receive revelations from God when he was 40 years old. Over the next 23 years, he not only established the Islamic religion but brought an unprecedented degree of political unity to the Arab tribes. His birth is considered an event of major importance in the Muslim world because he was the last of the prophets and the one to whom the Koran or Qur'an (the holy book of the Islamic faith) was revealed.

The first Mawlid celebration took place in Upper Mesopotamia in 1207. Eventually it took root in Egypt and spread fairly quickly throughout the Muslim world. Nowadays Mawlid al-Nabi is observed largely according to local custom. In Lebanon, for example, the celebration includes nine days of fairs and parades. Children are told stories about the night when Muhammad was born in Mecca—particularly about the 7,000 angels who brought Muhammad's mother a golden vessel filled with dew to bathe the holy infant. In Egypt, Muhammad's birthday is celebrated by illuminating the city of Cairo and with special ceremonies and performances, including a DHIKR. Elsewhere, it is observed with RECITATIONS in mosques, gift-giving, and the lighting of firecrackers.

Feasting is an important part of Mawlid al-Nabi. Favorite foods served on this day include *tabboul,* made from grains of wheat that have been boiled and mixed with chopped mint, onions, parsley, and tomatoes, then mixed again with olive oil and lemon juice. A popular main course is *djaje mihshi,* or roast chicken filled with rice, spices, and ground lamb. *Baclava* is a typical Mawlid dessert, made from thin layers of pastry with crushed nuts and honey in between.

Muslims gather together in groups to remember Muhammad on his birthday. They tell each other the story of his life, his character, and his sufferings. These so-called "Mawlid gatherings" take place throughout the month of Rabi al-Awwal. Another popular way of celebrating this day is to take part in large processions, often led by colorfully decorated elephants.

# SYMBOLS

## *Burdah*

*Burdah* refers to one of the Prophet's cloaks or mantles, which was made out of goat hair. It was the inspiration for two famous poems—one by a contemporary of Muhammad named Ka'b ibn Zuhayr and the other by the thirteenth-century poet al-Busiri. In the first poem, the Prophet gives away one of his many cloaks to Ka'b ibn Zuhayr, an outlaw who repents and asks for Muhammad's pardon. The mantle given to Ka'b became part of the national treasury after the poet's death, and today it is kept in the Topkapi Museum in Istanbul.

It is al-Busiri's poem, however, that is particularly associated with the Mawlid celebration. The poet was suffering from paralysis. In a dream, he saw the Prophet lay his own mantle over him, and when he woke up, he was cured. The poem known as "The Burdah" describes the nature of the Prophet and praises him for his virtues. It is customary to recite this "Mantle Poem" during the celebration of the Prophet's birthday.

## Dhikr

The word *dhikr* means "remembrance" in Arabic. Among Sufi Muslims, *dhikr* refers to the chanting of certain words or phrases in praise of God. Its purpose is to induce an ecstatic experience or momentary union with God. Although the actual sequence of phrases can vary, the pattern is always the same. Such phrases as "There is no god but Allah," or "God is greatest" are repeated innumerable times to a certain rhythm, sometimes to the accompaniment of drums or pipes. Although *dhikr* meetings are held frequently by the Sufi, or dervish, fraternities, these litanies are particularly associated with the celebration of Mawlid al-Nabi.

## Recitations

The celebration of the Prophet's birthday usually includes a recitation of the Koran and stories about the life of the Prophet, often in verse or in a combination of poetry and prose. These recitations, called *maulids*, may have been inspired by the sermons given at the festivals of Christian saints. They trace the major events of the Prophet's life and emphasize his virtues. Maulid poems, of which many have been written in both Turkish and Arabic, have become so popular that they are sometimes recited on other festive occasions as well (see BURDAH).

## Further Reading

Ahsan, M. M. *Muslim Festivals*, 1987.
Dobler, Lavinia. *Customs and Holidays Around the World*, 1962.
Glassé, Cyril. *The Concise Encyclopedia of Islam*, 1989.

Henderson, Helene and Sue Ellen Thompson. *Holidays, Festivals, and Cele-brations of the World Dictionary*, 2nd ed., 1997.

MacDonald, Margaret R., ed. *The Folklore of World Holidays*, 1992.

Von Grunebaum, G. D. *Muhammadan Festivals*, 1988.

# *May Day*

**Type of Holiday:** Ancient or pagan

**Date of Observation:** May 1

**Where Celebrated:** England, Europe, United States, former Soviet Union

**Symbols:** Flowers, Jack in the Green, May Baskets, May Dolls, Maypole, Queen of the May

**Related Holidays:** Beltane, Floralia

## ORIGINS

May Day is a festival of purely pagan origin. The Celts observed **BELTANE** on May 1 by lighting bonfires to honor the sun god and welcome the return of spring. The Romans observed their festival of flowers, the **FLORALIA**, for six days at the end of April and beginning of May, and many of the customs associated with May Day—such as gathering FLOWERS and weaving them into garlands or wreaths—can be traced back to ancient Greece and Rome.

European communities celebrated the arrival of spring by decorating their homes with early-blooming flowers, selecting a QUEEN OF THE MAY, and dancing around the MAYPOLE. Women washed their faces in the early morning dew on May 1, believing that it would improve their complexions and bring them eternal youthfulness. Throughout the Middle Ages, the Renaissance, and even into the nineteenth century, May Day was widely observed throughout Europe and America—although the Puritans persecuted those who participated in the "heathen" customs associated with May Day and urged their children to spend the day reading the Bible.

Although May Day is primarily a festival to welcome spring, it also has political significance in some countries. At an international meeting of

Socialists in 1889, it was decided that May Day should be renamed Labor Day and turned into a holiday honoring the working man. Countries with Socialist or Communist forms of government still celebrate May 1 with speeches and displays of military strength. The May Day Parade in Moscow's Red Square is one of the better known examples, although it has been toned down somewhat since the dissolution of the Soviet Union. The United States observes its Labor Day in early September. Ironically, May 1 marks the anniversary of the 1886 Chicago labor rally that resulted in the infamous Haymarket Riot and the subsequent decline of the labor anarchist movement.

Although May Day is not a national holiday in the United States, people in Hawaii observe it as Lei Day by exchanging the traditional Hawaiian flower necklaces as symbols of friendship and good luck.

## SYMBOLS

### *Flowers*

As the quintessential symbol of spring, flowers have played a central role in May Day celebrations since the time of the Roman **FLORALIA**. Garlands of flowers were such an important part of the May Day ceremonies in England that it was often called Garland Day. The custom of "bringing in the May"—going out to the field or woods early in the morning on May 1 and returning with baskets full of flowers—was widespread throughout Europe and America. Sometimes the flowers would be strung together in long chains. Another popular custom was tying a single blossom to the end of a long wand. Sometimes the flowers were used to make a crown for the May Queen (see QUEEN OF THE MAY) or to fill MAY BASKETS. In Greece, wild flowers are still gathered and woven into May Day wreaths. The wreaths are then hung up to dry until St. John's Eve (June 23), when they are burned in the midsummer bonfires (see **MIDSUMMER DAY**).

Up until the mid-nineteenth century in England, the "May Birchers" would go from house to house on May Day Eve and decorate the doors with boughs of trees or flowers that expressed their opinion of the person who lived there. In some areas, the plants were chosen because they rhymed with the word describing the person. For example, the "fair" of face might find a pear bough placed over her door, while someone who was "glum" might find a branch of plum. Not surprisingly, this custom caused so much ill feeling that it was eventually discontinued.

## Jack in the Green

Until recently, a leaf-covered figure known as Jack in the Green was an important part of May Day celebrations in England. He was usually a young chimney sweep concealed inside a six-to-ten-foot-high wicker framework made of hoops and completely covered in holly and ivy. This leafy green figure danced at the head of a procession of chimney sweeps that meandered through the village, singing songs and collecting pennies.

Along with the QUEEN OF THE MAY, Jack in the Green is believed to be a relic of ancient European tree worship. The Gypsies of Rumania and Transylvania still observe their Green George Festival on April 23—Green George being a tree-spirit represented by a boy dressed in branches, leaves, and flowers. These humans disguised as trees are another example of May Day's pagan origins.

## May Baskets

The custom of hanging up small baskets filled with flowers became popular in the United States during the nineteenth century, and is still enjoyed in some areas by children today. The baskets are often made from woven strips of colored paper decorated with lace-paper doilies and ribbons. They're filled with flowers, candy, perhaps a short poem, and the name of the person for whom they are intended. The usual practice is to hang the basket on the person's front door, ring the bell, and then run away before the door is opened—much like trick-or-treating at **HALLOWEEN**. In Iowa, school-age children leave May baskets at the doors of those they have crushes on, flowers being symbolic of love, fertility, and the arrival of spring.

## May Dolls

The Romans welcomed the month of May by dedicating it to Flora, the goddess of flowers. They spent the first day of the month gathering flowers as offerings to the goddess. Sometimes Roman children made small images of Flora and decorated them with flowers. After Christianity was introduced and the Church tried to replace some of the pagan customs associated with May Day, these May dolls were turned into likenesses of the Virgin Mary. (See also QUEEN OF THE MAY)

## Maypole

The Maypole is probably the best known of the symbols associated with May Day. The earliest Maypoles were trees (usually fir or birch) brought in solemn procession to the village square. But in the sixteenth and seventeenth centuries, many towns in England and Europe erected permanent poles that were left standing throughout the year and could be decorated for May Day. The shaft was sometimes painted with stripes, and a flower doll (see MAY DOLLS) was frequently fastened to the top. A tuft of greenery was always left on the end of the pole as a reminder that it was a symbol of the newly awakened spirit of fertility and vegetation.

Colorful ribbons or streamers were hung from the pole, and people would dance around it holding the ends of the streamers in such a way that they were woven into a pattern as the dancers progressed. Today, the Maypole dance is often performed by traditional English Morris dancers—men wearing hats decorated with ribbons and flowers, streamers on their wrists and elbows, bells strapped to their shins, and holding white handkerchiefs and clacking wooden sticks. The bells and sticks were originally used to frighten off evil spirits, and the dancers' high leaps were believed to encourage the crops to grow tall.

The Puritans hated the idea of dancing around the Maypole because they saw the pole as a phallic symbol and the dance as a pagan fertility ritual that had no place in a civilized Christian society. Although they tried to stamp out the custom, they were never altogether successful in repressing this and other May Day ceremonies that obviously had their roots in very primitive human instincts.

## Queen of the May

The custom of crowning a Queen of the May commemorates Maia, the ancient Roman mother goddess associated with growth and the spring season, as well as Flora, the goddess of flowers. The Queen is usually chosen from the girls of the town or village, and at one time she was accompanied by a May King, their court, and villagers dressed up as shepherds, jesters, chimney sweeps, Morris dancers, and JACK IN THE GREEN, a mythical figure who symbolized the spirit of seasonal growth. Nowadays the May King has largely disappeared, but schoolchildren in London still choose their own May Queen.

In the United States, attempts to Christianize May Day focused on Mary, the mother of Jesus. In many places where May Day is celebrated with the crowning of a May Queen, there is often a procession to a local church, where the Queen places a crown of flowers on the statue of Mary.

## Further Reading

Dobler, Lavinia. *Customs and Holidays Around the World*, 1962.

Frazer, Sir James G. *The Golden Bough: A Study in Magic and Religion*, 1931.

Gaer, Joseph. *Holidays Around the World*, 1953.

Henderson, Helene and Sue Ellen Thompson. *Holidays, Festivals, and Celebrations of the World Dictionary*, 2nd ed., 1997.

Hole, Christina. *English Custom and Usage*, 1941.

Ickis, Marguerite. *The Book of Festivals and Holidays the World Over*, 1970.

Leach, Maria, ed. *Funk & Wagnalls Standard Dictionary of Folklore, Mythology & Legend*, 1984.

Long, George. *The Folklore Calendar*, 1990.

Purdy, Susan. *Festivals for You to Celebrate*, 1969.

Santino, Jack. *All Around the Year*, 1994.

Tuleja, Tad. *Curious Customs: The Stories Behind 296 Popular American Rituals*, 1987.

# *Memorial Day*

**Type of Holiday:** National or patriotic

**Date of Observation:** Last Monday in May

**Where Celebrated:** United States

**Symbols:** American Flag, Decoration of Graves, Poppy

**Colors:** Memorial Day is associated with the colors of the AMERICAN FLAG: red, symbolizing courage; white, symbolizing liberty; and blue, symbolizing loyalty.

## ORIGINS

Memorial Day was originally a day set aside to honor the northern Civil War dead by decorating their graves with flowers (see DECORATION OF GRAVES). Waterloo, New York, is generally credited with having held the first Memorial Day observance on May 5, 1866. Henry C. Welles, a Waterloo pharmacist, suggested to veterans' organizations that the graves of the dead be decorated with flowers. Referred to at the time as "Decoration Day," this early celebration included flying AMERICAN FLAGS at half-staff, a veterans' parade, and a march to the village cemetery to hear patriotic speeches.

The first nationwide Decoration Day was held on May 30, 1868, by a group of Union Army veterans known as the Grand Army of the Republic. The May 30 date had no real significance, although it roughly coincided with the anniversary of the surrender of the last Confederate army on May 26, 1865. Many southern states felt that Decoration Day was really observed in honor of Union soldiers, so in 1891, Florida designated the birthday of Confederate president Jefferson Davis as Confederate Memorial Day. Nine other states followed suit, with dates ranging from April 26, the anniversary of the surrender of General George Johnson at Durham Station (North Carolina) to June 3, Jefferson Davis's birthday. After World War I, the American Legion took over the task of planning the observance, which became known as Memorial Day and honored American servicepeople from all wars. It is now observed by every state but Alabama, which still celebrates Confederate Memorial Day on the fourth Monday in April.

Both religious services and patriotic parades mark the modern-day observation of Memorial Day. In the national official observance, a wreath is placed on the Tomb of the Unknown Soldier in Arlington National Cemetery in Virginia. One of the more moving observances is held in the Gettysburg National Cemetery in Pennsylvania, where schoolchildren scatter flowers over the graves of unknown Civil War soldiers. In 1986, Hands Across America—originally an effort to raise money for the homeless— was held on Sunday of Memorial Day weekend. The idea was to have an unbroken chain of people holding hands across the entire continent, but not enough people pledged to participate. They were urged to celebrate America anyway, and the event ended up merging with the observation of Memorial Day.

## SYMBOLS

### *American Flag*

There are many theories about the origin of the American flag. Best known is the story of Betsy Ross, an expert seamstress and upholsterer, who based her design on a sketch given to her by a committee appointed by Congress, one of whose members happened to be her deceased husband's uncle. It had 13 stars, symbolic of the 13 colonies, placed in a circle on a sky blue background to signify that the Union would be "without end." There were also 13 red and white stripes, the red symbolizing the Mother Country (Great Britain), and the white symbolizing liberty. They were carefully arranged so that red would appear at the top and bottom edge, making the flag easier to see from a great distance. The separation of red stripes by white stripes was also supposed to symbolize America's separation from England.

On Memorial Day the flag is displayed at half-mast, a symbol of mourning, from sunrise until noon, and at full staff from noon until sunset. This rule does not apply, however, to the millions of smaller flags that line American streets and sidewalks. There are also very specific rules governing how the flag should be displayed in churches.

## Decoration of Graves

The practice of decorating graves with flowers and wreaths on Memorial Day officially dates back to the first observance in Waterloo, New York, in 1866, although the town of Boalsburg, Pennsylvania, has proclaimed itself the "Birthplace of Memorial Day" because it was decorating soldiers' graves two years earlier. Both of these towns may have gotten the idea from a paragraph in the Troy, New York, *Tribune* two years after the Civil War ended. It described how the women of Columbus, Mississippi, strewed flowers on the graves of both Confederate and Union soldiers, an act that quickly became a symbol of friendship and understanding between the North and the South.

Visiting cemeteries and decorating graves was hardly an American invention. Festivals in both Europe and Asia have featured this custom since very ancient times. In China and Japan, for example, people decorate graves at the **LANTERN FESTIVAL, OBON FESTIVAL,** and **CH'ING MING. ALL SOULS' DAY** and Day of the Dead observances usually involve visiting and decorating graves as well.

## Poppy

Red paper poppies, symbolic of the war dead because real poppies bloomed everywhere in the battlefield graveyards of France, are traditionally sold by veterans on Memorial Day. The Veterans of Foreign Wars conducted the first nationwide "poppy sale" to raise money for disabled and destitute veterans in 1922. At one time, people referred to Memorial Day as Poppy Day.

## Further Reading

Cohen, Hennig, and Tristram Potter Coffin, eds. *The Folklore of American Holidays,* 2nd ed., 1991.

Hatch, Jane M. *The American Book of Days,* 1978.

Henderson, Helene and Sue Ellen Thompson. *Holidays, Festivals, and Celebrations of the World Dictionary,* 2nd ed., 1997.

Ickis, Marguerite. *The Book of Patriotic Holidays,* 1962.

Santino, Jack. *All Around the Year,* 1994.

Tuleja, Tad. *Curious Customs: The Stories Behind 296 Popular American Rituals,* 1987.

# *Michaelmas*
## *(St. Michael's Day, Feast of St. Michael and All Angels)*

**Type of Holiday:** Religious (Christian)

**Date of Observation:** September 29 in the West, November 8 in the East

**Where Celebrated:** Europe, Norway, Russia, United States, and by Christians all over the world

**Symbols:** Blackberries, Dragon, Goose, Scales

## ORIGINS

Michael, the leader of the heavenly host of angels, is an important figure in the Christian, Jewish, and Muslim religious traditions; he even has a counterpart among the Babylonian and Persian angels. The Jews think of Michael as the special guardian of Israel. In Christianity, it is Michael who will sound the last trumpet on Judgment Day and escort the souls of the faithful departed into the presence of God. Sometimes he is represented as the only archangel, and sometimes as the head of a fraternity of archangels that includes Gabriel, Raphael, and others.

The veneration of St. Michael the Archangel dates back to very early times. He was the patron saint of the sick among the early Christians, and a church bearing his name existed in fourth-century Constantinople (for which reason the Eastern Church celebrates the Feast of St. Michael on November 8). In the fifth century, a basilica was dedicated to St. Michael on

September 29 in the Via Salaria, about six miles from Rome. His feast day, originally celebrated only at this church, gradually spread to a number of holy places under his patronage. By the Middle Ages, the archangel Michael was widely revered throughout the Christian world, including Russia. He became even more popular after supposedly appearing in a vision on the top of Monte Gargano in Apulia, southern Italy, during the reign of Pope Gelasius I in the late fifth century. It is probably because of this that he came to be regarded as the angel of mountains. Many of the churches and chapels dedicated to him were erected on the tops of hills or mountains in western Europe. The French monastery known as Mont-Saint-Michel, located off the Normandy coast, is probably the most famous. Up until the seventeenth century, the red velvet buckler worn by Michael in his fight against Satan was displayed there (see DRAGON).

In England, where it is known as Michaelmas, St. Michael's Day was one of the four "quarter days" on which rents were due and contracts affecting houses and property were assumed or terminated. It is also associated with the opening of the fall term at public schools and universities.

In the mountains of Norway, *Mikkelsmesse* is the time of year when cows and goats are herded down from the mountain pastures to the valley farms. Dancing, singing, and feasting generally follow.

## SYMBOLS

### Blackberries

Arriving as it did at the end of the harvest season, St. Michael's Day was a natural time to overindulge in eating and drinking. Perhaps to give people something to blame for the way they felt the next morning, a legend developed that blackberries were poisoned on the eve of this day because Satan stepped on them. Anyone who felt ill after a St. Michael's Day feast could always lay the blame on eating the poisoned berries.

In some places it is still considered very unlucky to eat blackberries on or after Michaelmas because the Devil spits on them to get even with St. Michael, who was responsible for getting him thrown out of heaven (see DRAGON).

### Dragon

Perhaps the best-known story concerning St. Michael the archangel comes from the Book of Revelations. There was a war in heaven during which

Michael and the other angels fought against a dragon with seven heads, also known as Satan or the Devil. Michael won, and the dragon was cast out, along with the angels who had fought beside him.

In Renaissance paintings, St. Michael is often shown dressed as a warrior, with wings on his shoulders and a dragon under his foot, symbolic of his victory over the powers of evil and darkness.

## Goose

In rural England, where Michaelmas was the day on which tenant farmers paid their rents, it was customary to include in the payment "one goose fit for the lord's dinner." Although there is no question that geese were plentiful at this time of year, the goose has always played an important role in folklore and mythology. There were sacred geese in the Greek temples, and the geese from the Roman temple of Juno are credited with saving Rome from the invasion of the Gauls in the fourth century B.C.E. The Chinese, the Hindus, and the North American Indians also held the goose in high regard.

The custom of bringing a goose to the landlord at Michaelmas in hopes of making him more lenient gave rise to the superstition that eating goose on this day will prevent worries about money for an entire year. Goose is also eaten in Ireland on St. Michael's Day, supposedly as an act of gratitude for a miracle of St. Patrick's that was performed with the help of the archangel. Queen Elizabeth I is said to have been eating her Michaelmas goose when she received the good news about the defeat of the Spanish Armada.

## Scales

The archangel Michael is frequently shown carrying a pair of scales, a symbol of his responsibility for "weighing" souls after they are released from death.

# Further Reading

Brewster, H. Pomeroy. *Saints and Festivals of the Christian Church,* 1990.

Chambers, Robert, ed. *The Book of Days,* 1864.

Dunkling, Leslie. *A Dictionary of Days,* 1988.

Harper, Howard V. *Days and Customs of All Faiths,* 1957.

Hatch, Jane M. *The American Book of Days,* 1978.

Henderson, Helene and Sue Ellen Thompson. *Holidays, Festivals, and Celebrations of the World Dictionary,* 2nd ed., 1997.

Kelly, Aidan. *Religious Holidays and Calendars,* 1993.

Leach, Maria, ed. *Funk & Wagnalls Standard Dictionary of Folklore, Mythology, & Legend,* 1984.

MacDonald, Margaret R., ed. *The Folklore of World Holidays,* 1992.

Urlin, Ethel L. *Festivals, Holy Days, and Saints' Days,* 1915.

# Mid-Autumn Festival
## *(Birthday of the Moon)*

**Type of Holiday:** Calendar, Folkloric

**Date of Observation:** Full moon nearest September 15; 15th day of the eighth Chinese lunar month

**Where Celebrated:** China and throughout the Far East; in Asian communities all over the world

**Symbols:** Moon Cakes (Yueh Ping), Moon Hare, Moon Toad, Moon Viewing, Round Fruit

## ORIGINS

According to the Chinese lunar calendar, the autumn season extends throughout the seventh, eighth, and ninth months. This makes the 15th day of the eighth lunar month the season's midpoint. From this point onward, the power of the sun begins to wane; the days grow shorter and cooler, and the nights grow longer. According to the Gregorian calendar, mid-September marks the time when the full moon—commonly called the Harvest Moon or Hunter's Moon—is at its lowest angle to the horizon, making it appear larger and brighter than usual. The Chinese celebrate the moon's birthday on this day, believing that it is the only night of the year when the moon is perfectly round. The Mid-Autumn Festival is therefore a double feast—a time for worshipping the moon goddess and for expressing gratitude for the harvest.

The Mid-Autumn Festival has been compared to the American **THANKS-GIVING**, and there are some similarities. Family reunions are common, with family members often travelling long distances to be together. They

291

feast, exchange gifts, and eat MOON CAKES. Many of these reunions take place out-of-doors in the evening, where the size and brightness of the moon can be admired.

Village theatricals are a popular way of entertaining the gods on this day. They are usually held in open-air theaters attached to temples, or in special sheds erected for the purpose. These temple-dramas are similar to the medieval miracle plays in Europe, which were performed on the porches of cathedrals. But they tend to avoid religious messages and focus instead on plots taken from legend or history, or from episodes in famous novels. Other popular entertainments include lion dancers and stilt walkers.

The Mid-Autumn Festival continues for three days. The evenings are devoted to MOON VIEWING parties, and the days are usually spent hiking and picnicking in the mountains. In addition to being a harvest festival and a celebration of the moon's birthday, it is also a festival of liberation, commemorating the day on which the ancient Chinese people overthrew the Mongol overlords and brought Mongolia under Chinese rule (see MOON CAKES).

## SYMBOLS

### *Moon Cakes (Yüeh Ping)*

Made of grayish flour to resemble the color of the moon and often stacked in a pyramid 13-cakes high to represent the 13 months of the Chinese lunar year, moon cakes are the most distinctive offering of the Mid-Autumn Festival. They are round like the moon and filled with melon seeds, cassia blossoms, orange peel, walnuts, date paste, or smashed bean. They are sent from neighbor to neighbor and exchanged among friends during the festival. In cities, confectioners make moon cakes and donate them to the poor. In rural villages, "moon cake societies" are formed to make sure that everyone has an adequate supply of cakes when the festival arrives. While most moon cakes are only a few inches in diameter, imperial chefs have made them as large as several feet across, decorated with images of the moon palace, the cassia tree, or the rabbit (see MOON HARE).

Legend says that during the Yuan dynasty (1279-1368), these cakes were used to convey secret instructions to Chinese patriots concerning the overthrow of their Mongol rulers. There was a Mongol spy living in every household, and the only way the Chinese people could communicate with each other was to conceal their messages in moon cakes. Information about the time and place of the revolution was spread by hiding it on small squares of paper inside the moon cakes that were sent to friends and relatives during the Mid-Autumn Festival in 1353. The midnight attack came as a complete surprise and hastened the dynasty's downfall.

Today there are 20 to 30 varieties of moon cakes. Their roundness makes them a perfect symbol not only for the moon, but for family unity.

## *Moon Hare*

In China, the association between the hare and the moon is very ancient. Shepherds or nomads who slept under the open sky would see figures outlined on the face of the moon and make up stories about how they came to be there. The hare and the frog (see MOON TOAD) are probably the best-known inhabitants of the moon, which Chinese mythology says is populated by both humans and animals. There is an old superstition that the hare, who never closes her eyes, gives birth with her eyes fixed on the moon. How brightly the moon shines on the night of this festival determines how many hares will be born during the coming year.

Images of the Moon Hare appear everywhere during the Mid-Autumn Festival, usually in the form of small clay statues. This legendary rabbit comes from an old Buddhist tale brought to China from India. The animals of the forest were scrambling to prepare offerings to the Buddha, who had taken the form of a Brahman (or saint) and asked for food and water. The rabbit, embarassed by the meager collection of herbs and grasses he'd managed to gather, caught sight of the cooking fire and leaped into it, offering himself to the Buddha but pausing first to remove any small creatures who had lodged in his fur. He was rewarded by having his image appear on the face of the moon where everyone could admire the example of his self-sacrifice.

The moon is a symbol of longevity in Chinese mythology because it is the dwelling place of the immortals. The Moon Hare is traditionally pictured under the Sacred Cassia Tree, pounding the Pill of Immortality with his mortar and pestle. The cassia tree blooms just in time for the moon's birthday, and Chinese physicians believe that its aromatic bark cures disease. Next to the hare is the woodcutter Wu Gang, who is doomed to continually chop down a cassia tree as punishment for a mistake he made while studying to become an immortal. Every time the axe makes a cut, the tree miraculously heals itself and the cut closes up.

## *Moon Toad*

The Moon Toad (or frog) comes from the legend of Chang E, the goddess who inhabits the moon and who was changed into a three-legged toad because she found her husband's supply of the elixir of life and drank it all. When her misdeed was discovered, she fled to the moon, where she has lived ever since. Once a month, on the 15th day, her husband leaves his palace on the sun and comes to visit her. This explains why the moon is at its most beautiful on this day.

Just as the MOON HARE promises long life to those who are virtuous, the three-legged Moon Toad offers wealth to those who please the Moon Queen. He is often depicted with a string of gold coins.

## *Moon Viewing*

In Japan, the custom of *tsukimi* or "moon viewing" is observed at the same time as the Chinese Mid-Autumn Festival. People set up a table facing the horizon where the moon will rise and place offerings on the table for the spirit of the moon. These offerings might include a vase holding the seven grasses of autumn, cooked vegetables, and *tsukimi dango* or "moon-viewing dumplings" made of rice flour. Moon-viewing festivals are particularly popular in Tokyo and in Kyoto, where people watch the moon from boats with dragons on their bows.

## *Round Fruit*

The fruits associated with the Mid-Autumn Festival include apples, pomegranates, honey peaches, crab apples, sour betel nuts, and grapes—round fruits whose shape symbolizes the fullness of the moon and family harmony. Pears are excluded—not only because they are not perfectly round, but because the word for pear is *li*, which is pronounced the same as the word meaning "separation." On a day set aside for family reunions, pears would be considered an unlucky offering.

Chinese women set up an altar in the courtyard with five round plates filled with the fruits listed above. In the center are MOON CAKES baked especially for the holiday, and nearby are red candles and bundles of incense. Behind the family altar is a large paper scroll on which the MOON HARE appears, sitting under the Sacred Cassia Tree. Sometimes the scroll will show the MOON TOAD entangled in a string of coins. After a brief service in honor of the Moon Queen at midnight, the festival meal is eaten outdoors under the full moon.

## Further Reading

Bredon, Juliet, and Igor Mitrophanow. *The Moon Year: A Record of Chinese Customs and Festivals*, 1966.

Eberhard, Wolfram. *A Dictionary of Chinese Symbols: Hidden Symbols in Chinese Life and Thought*, 1986.

Gaer, Joseph. *Holidays Around the World*, 1953.

Henderson, Helene and Sue Ellen Thompson. *Holidays, Festivals, and Celebrations of the World Dictionary*, 2nd ed., 1997.

Stepanchuk, Carol, and Charles Wong. *Mooncakes and Hungry Ghosts: Festivals of China*, 1991.

# *Mid-Lent Sunday*
### *(Laetare Sunday, Mothering Sunday, Rose Sunday)*

**Type of Holiday:** Religious (Christian: Roman Catholic, Anglican, Episcopalian)

**Date of Observation:** Fourth Sunday in Lent (March-April)

**Where Celebrated:** England, Scotland, United States

**Symbols:** Golden Rose, Simnel Cakes

**Colors:** Rose-colored vestments are worn in Roman Catholic churches on this day, in place of the purple vestments worn on the other Sundays in Lent.

**Related Holidays:** Ash Wednesday, Easter, Lent

## ORIGINS

The name "Mid-Lent Sunday" is not really accurate, since the halfway point in the 40 days of **LENT** falls several days before the fourth Sunday. This may reflect an earlier method of computing the duration of Lent, but it is more likely that this holiday was moved up to a Sunday because Sundays were generally exempt from the Lenten fast, and breaking the fast on a weekday represented too great a departure from the restrictions of the season. In any case, there is no shortage of alternate names for this day. In the Roman Catholic Church it is called Laetare Sunday, from the Latin word meaning "rejoice," which begins the Introit of the Mass. Up until 1969, when Roman Catholic reforms reinstated all Sundays as festivals, it was also known as Refreshment Sunday because the usual Lenten restrictions were relaxed.

In the Church of England, as well as in the Episcopal Church in the United States, the fourth Sunday in Lent is known as Mothering Sunday. This designation goes back to the ancient Roman Hilaria, held on the Ides of March (March 15) in honor of Cybele, mother of the gods. The Christians took this pagan festival, symbolic of the high esteem in which motherhood was held, and turned it into a day on which offerings were brought to the "Mother Church" instead of to private chapels. As the Christian calendar took shape, this Sunday festival was shifted from mid-March to mid-Lent, and the idea of visiting the Mother Church spilled over into the family. Children living away from home returned to visit their parents, and servants were given a day off so they could do the same. They brought gifts for their mothers, typically flowers and a SIMNEL CAKE. The fourth Sunday in Lent became a popular time for family reunions throughout England, and a young person who made such a visit was said to go "a-mothering."

A popular dish served at these family get-togethers was furmety, a kind of sweet porridge made from wheat grains boiled in milk and spiced. In northern England and Scotland, the preferred dish was peas that had been fried in butter with salt and pepper and made into pancakes known as "carlings." For this reason, the day was sometimes referred to as Carling Sunday.

## SYMBOLS

### *Golden Rose*

Mid-Lent Sunday is also known as Rose Sunday. Beginning in the eleventh century, it was the custom for the Pope to carry a golden rose in his hand while celebrating Mass on this day. Although it was originally a single rose of normal size, since the fifteenth century it has been a cluster or branch of roses made of pure gold and set with precious stones. This custom may originally have been connected with the arrival of spring, when flowering branches were carried by the Pope from the Lateran Palace, his official residence in Rome, to Santa Croce in Gerusalemme, where he celebrated the Mass. It may also have something to do with the medieval devotion to the Virgin Mary, known as the "Rose of Sharon." The rose itself is considered a symbol of spiritual joy.

After being blessed by the Pope, the rose is sometimes sent to a particular parish in recognition of its special devotion to the Church, or to a distinguished person who has shown an unusual degree of religious spirit and loyalty. Then a new rose is made for the following year.

According to an old superstition, the Golden Rose brings bad luck to its owner. This probably dates back to the story of Joanna of Sicily, the first queen to whom the rose was sent. She was dethroned soon afterward and strangled by her nephew.

## Simnel Cakes

The earliest simnel cakes were unleavened cakes or buns made of wheat flour and boiled. Sometimes they were marked with a figure of Christ or the Virgin Mary, which would seem to indicate that they were originally linked to a pagan celebration and then Christianized—like the hot cross buns originally eaten in honor of the pagan goddess Eostre, then later marked with a cross to make them more acceptable to the Christian clergy (see **EASTER**).

Over the years, the simple flat cake with currants and spices evolved into an elaborate raised cake with a saffron-flavored crust and a ring of almond paste on the top. The center was filled with plums, candied lemon peel, and other fruits, and the entire cake was tied up in a cloth and boiled for several hours. Then it was brushed with egg and baked, giving the crust a consistency not unlike that of wood, with an ornamental border that made it look like a crown. As early as the fourteenth century, it was the custom for young people to carry simnels as gifts for their mothers on Mid-Lent (or Mothering) Sunday. Simnel cakes were made at Easter and **CHRISTMAS** as well.

There are a number of theories about the origin of the name "simnel." It may have come from the Latin *simila,* a very fine flour. Another theory is that the cakes were named after Lambert Simnel, a baker during the reign of Henry VII. There is also a legend about an elderly couple named Simon and Nelly. They combined the unleavened dough left over at the end of Lent with the plum pudding left over from Christmas. Then they got into an argument over whether the cake should be boiled or baked. They finally compromised and decided to do both. The result was the "Simon-Nelly" cake.

These cakes are still made in England and sent all over the world during Lent. In the towns of Devizes and Bury, the baking begins right after Christmas to allow time for delivery of cakes to people living abroad. Many emigrants left standing orders many years ago for simnels to be sent to them, and these orders have been renewed by their children and grandchildren.

### Further Reading

Brester, H. Pomeroy. *Saints and Festivals of the Christian Church*, 1990.

Chambers, Robert, ed. *The Book of Days*, 1864.

Harper, Howard V. *Days and Customs of All Faiths*, 1957.

Henderson, Helene and Sue Ellen Thompson. *Holidays, Festivals, and Celebrations of the World Dictionary*, 2nd ed., 1997.

Hole, Christina. *English Custom and Usage*, 1941.

Ickis, Marguerite. *The Book of Religious Holidays and Celebrations*, 1966.

Leach, Maria, ed. *Funk & Wagnalls Standard Dictionary of Folklore, Mythology & Legend*, 1984.

Metford, J. C. J. *The Christian Year*, 1991.

Urlin, Ethel L. *Festivals, Holy Days, and Saints' Days*, 1915.

# Midsummer Day
## (St. John's Day)

**Type of Holiday:** Calendar, Folkloric, Religious (Christian, Islamic)
**Date of Observation:** June 24, or nearest Friday
**Where Celebrated:** Brazil, Europe, Scandinavia
**Symbols:** Bonfires, Wheel
**Related Holidays:** Beltane, Inti Raymi Festival, Summer Solstice

## ORIGINS

This ancient pagan festival celebrating the **SUMMER SOLSTICE** was originally observed on June 21, the longest day of the year. Like **BELTANE** in Ireland, Midsummer Day in Europe and the Scandinavian countries was a time to light BONFIRES and drive out evil. At one time it was believed that all natural waters had medicinal powers on this day, and people bathed in rivers and streams to cure their illnesses.

When Christianity spread throughout the pagan world, the Midsummer festival on June 24 became St. John's Day, in honor of St. John the Baptist. Christian symbolism was attached to many of the pre-Christian rites associated with this day. The bonfires, for example, were renamed "St. John's Fires," and the herbs that were picked on this day for their healing powers were called "St. John's herbs." But the pagan customs and beliefs surrounding Midsummer Day never really disappeared, and the Feast of St. John is still associated with the solstice and solstitial rites.

In Sweden, the *Midsommar* celebration begins on a Friday and lasts through Sunday. Every town and village sets up a maypole (see **MAY DAY**), which is decorated with flowers, leaves, and flags. One of the most popular places to spend the Midsommar weekend is in the province of Dalarna, where some of Sweden's oldest wooden cottages have been preserved. Because Sweden is located so far north, Midsommar is called "the day that never ends." The sun doesn't begin to set until 10:00 p.m., and it rises again at 2:00 a.m. In areas of Norway and Sweden that lie above the Arctic Circle, the sun shines 24 hours a day in the summer.

## SYMBOLS

### *Bonfires*

Fire festivals were held all over Europe on June 23 (the **SUMMER SOLSTICE**) or on Midsummer Day (June 24) during pre-Christian times. The solstice is the turning point in the sun's journey across the sky: After climbing higher and higher, it stops and begins to retrace its steps. Ancient peoples believed they could stop the sun's decline by kindling their own "suns" in the form of bonfires.

Bonfires were originally called "bone fires," because young boys would often throw bones and other noxious-smelling things on the fire to drive away monsters and evil spirits. Over the centuries, these fires attracted many folk beliefs and rituals. For example, people believed that their crops would grow as high as the flames reached, or as high as they could jump over the burning embers. Farmers drove their cattle through the fires to guard them against disease and to promote their fertility. Sometimes ashes from the bonfires were scattered over the fields to protect the crops from blight and to ensure a good harvest.

Midsummer bonfires were associated with courtship and fertility rituals as well. Young girls would often make wreaths out of leaves and ribbons, then hang them in a tall fir tree that had been cut down and erected in the middle of the fire. As the flames licked at their heels, young boys would climb the tree, take down the wreaths, and stand on one side of the fire while their girlfriends stood on the other. Sometimes the girls would throw the wreaths across the fire to the boys they wanted to marry. Then, as the flames died down, the couples would join hands and leap over the fire three times for good luck.

In Bohemia, a region in the western Czech Republic, young boys would collect all the worn-out brooms they could find, dip them in pitch, and after setting them on fire, wave them around or throw them up in the air. Sometimes they would run headlong down a hillside, brandishing their torches and shouting. The burned stumps of the brooms would then be stuck in their families' gardens to protect them from caterpillars and gnats. Some people put them in their fields or on the roofs of their houses as a charm against lightning, fire, and bad weather.

In Sweden, Denmark, and Norway, midsummer bonfires were known as "Balder's balefires." Lighting them was a way of reenacting the myth of Balder, the Scandinavian god of poetry who was killed when Loki, a divine mischief-maker, struck him with a bough of mistletoe. His body was burned on a pyre at the time of the summer solstice. Later on, effigies of Balder were thrown into the midsummer bonfires.

When Midsummer Day became St. John's Day, the Church gave new meaning to the bonfires. Since Jesus had once called John the Baptist "a burning and a shining light" (John 5:35), church officials decided that the fires should stand for St. John instead of the sun. The fact that it was St. John who baptized Jesus in the River Jordan dovetailed nicely with the pagan belief in the medicinal powers of water on Midsummer Day.

Although at one time midsummer bonfires were popular from Ireland in the west to Russia in the east, and from Norway and Sweden all the way south to Greece and Spain, today the bonfire tradition is still alive in only a few countries—primarily Sweden, Finland, and Lithuania. Roman Catholics in Brazil build large bonfires in front of their houses on St. John's Day to commemorate Elizabeth, St. John's mother and a cousin of the Virgin Mary. According to legend, Elizabeth promised to notify Mary of the birth of her child by building a bonfire in front of her house and setting off fireworks. In the United States, midsummer bonfires have been moved to the **FOURTH OF JULY**.

## Wheel

Sometimes the straw that had been collected for the Midsummer BONFIRE was attached to a wheel and set on fire. As the wheel burned, two young men would grab the handles that projected from the axle and run downhill with it, often extinguishing the flames in a river or stream at the bottom of the hill. The wheel, of course, represented the sun, and letting it roll downhill was a demonstration of the fact that having reached its highest point in the sky, the sun was now beginning its descent. In Germany, the sun's "falling" is still celebrated on St. John's Day with burning wheels rolled down hills. It is considered good luck if a wheel burns all the way to the bottom of the hill.

In some European countries, burning discs were hurled into the night sky after being kindled in bonfires. Their flight made them resemble fiery dragons, symbolic of the monsters believed to roam the earth on this night.

### Further Reading

Dobler, Lavinia. *Customs and Holidays Around the World,* 1962.

Frazer, Sir James G. *The Golden Bough: A Study in Magic and Religion,* 1931.

Heinberg, Richard. *Celebrate the Solstice: Honoring the Earth's Seasonal Rhythms through Festival and Ceremony,* 1993.

Henderson, Helene and Sue Ellen Thompson. *Holidays, Festivals, and Celebrations of the World Dictionary,* 2nd ed., 1997.

Ickis, Marguerite. *The Book of Festivals and Holidays the World Over,* 1970.

Purdy, Susan. *Festivals for You to Celebrate,* 1969.

Santino, Jack. *All Around the Year,* 1994.

# Mother's Day

**Type of Holiday:** Promotional

**Date of Observation:** Second Sunday in May

**Where Celebrated:** United States, England

**Symbols:** Carnation

**Colors:** Mother's Day is associated with the colors red and white. Some people wear white CARNATIONS on this day to honor mothers who have died and red or pink carnations for those who are living.

**Related Holidays:** Father's Day, Mid-Lent Sunday

# ORIGINS

The observation of a national holiday in honor of mothers is due largely to the efforts of Anna Jarvis, who was born in Grafton, West Virginia, in 1864 and spent most of her adult life in Philadelphia. Her constant longing for the West Virginia countryside and for the family and friends she'd grown up with provided her with the theme for her Mother's Day movement, and it struck a familiar chord with other sons and daughters who had moved away from their home towns.

Jarvis's own mother was a model of domestic nurturing and responsibility. Although she had lived through many tragedies, including the deaths of seven of her eleven children, she never lost her faith in God. She cared for her children when they were ill, looked after a husband who was considerably older than she, and gave up her own dream of a college education. After she died, Jarvis helped arrange a special service at the church in Grafton to commemorate the work her mother had done there.

Eventually Jarvis decided that she wanted to honor her mother on a much larger scale — by honoring all mothers with their own special day on the second Sunday in May. She wrote letters to politicians, newspaper editors, and church leaders, and organized a committee, known as the Mother's Day International Association, to promote the new holiday. As a church organist and Sunday school teacher herself, Jarvis was familiar with Children's Day (the second Sunday in June), which had been observed since the 1870s. She wanted Mother's Day to stand closer to **MEMORIAL DAY**, so that people would remember the sacrifices their mothers had made for their families, just as they remembered the sacrifices their sons had made for their country.

The first official Mother's Day services were held in May of 1908. President Woodrow Wilson gave the day national recognition in 1914, and by the late 1920s, Mother's Day was one of the more prominent American holidays. But what Jarvis had originally envisioned as a church-based celebration of maternal love and sacrifice gradually came to embody the mounting tension in American culture between Christianity and commercialism. Greeting card manufacturers were quick to jump on the Mother's Day bandwagon, and the new holiday soon became the fourth largest card-buying occasion in the United States—after **CHRISTMAS, VALENTINE'S DAY,** and **EASTER.**

Mother's Day has also served as a focal point for various cultural debates involving women, justice, and inequality. Coretta Scott King, the wife of slain civil rights leader Martin Luther King, Jr., led a Mother's Day march in 1968 to rally support for poor mothers and their children. In the 1970s the National Organization for Women used Mother's Day to stage rallies for the Equal Rights Amendment, to promote access to child care, and to stage banquets supporting equality for women. In the 1980s, the Women's Party for Survival, founded by Helen Caldicott, used the holiday to stage antinuclear demonstrations.

Sometimes Mother's Day is confused with Mothering Sunday (see **MID-LENT SUNDAY**), an English holiday that falls on the fourth Sunday in **LENT.** But Mother's Day is now observed in England as well, and the traditions associated with Mothering Sunday have been largely forgotten. A growing number of Protestant churches celebrate the second Sunday in May as the Festival of the Christian Home, an attempt to emphasize the role of the family as a whole, rather than just mothers.

## SYMBOLS

### *Carnation*

During Victorian times, specific flowers had served as symbols for such complex emotions as sorrow, remembrance, hope, faith, longing, and love. Because they were associated with women and the home, flowers were a natural symbol of femininity and domestic happiness. Commercial florists in the United States reinforced these symbolic associations with great effectiveness. By 1918, the advertising slogan of the Society of American Florists was "Say It With Flowers."

Because her own mother had loved white carnations, Anna Jarvis urged people to wear them in honor of their mothers on the first national observance of Mother's Day. The unprecedented demand for white carnations boosted prices and caused shortages in some areas. To avoid similar problems in subsequent years, the floral industry tried to shift the focus from white carnations to flowers in general, encouraging people to decorate their homes, churches, and cemeteries with flowers and offering special Mother's Day bouquets. Year after year, the industry came up with elaborate campaigns urging people to buy roses, potted plants, corsages, spring flowers in baskets, and other floral arrangements for their mothers.

Jarvis lobbied hard against the floral industry's "profiteering." She even proposed substituting celluloid buttons for white carnations as the official badge of the holiday, and urged people to stop buying flowers or any other gifts for the occasion. Although she was not able to rid the holiday of its commercial aspects, it was the carnation—her mother's favorite—that survived as the main symbol for maternal purity, faithfulness, and love. Chronic shortages in the supply of white carnations led florists to promote the idea of wearing red (or pink) carnations to honor living mothers and white flowers to honor the deceased.

## Further Reading

Henderson, Helene and Sue Ellen Thompson. *Holidays, Festivals, and Celebrations of the World Dictionary*, 2nd ed., 1997.

Ickis, Marguerite. *The Book of Religious Holidays and Celebrations*, 1966.

Schmidt, Leigh Eric. *Consumer Rites: The Buying and Selling of American Holidays*, 1995.

# Naga Panchami
## (Naag Panchami)

**Type of Holiday:** Religious (Hindu)
**Date of Observation:** Fifth day of Sravana (July-August)
**Where Celebrated:** India and Nepal
**Symbols:** Snake

## ORIGINS

*Panchami* means "fifth," the day on which this Hindu festival is celebrated, and *Naga* refers to a group of serpent deities in Indian mythology. The mythical Nagas were semi-divine beings said to have sprung from Kadru, the wife of Rishi Kashyapa. Although they live and rule below the earth, the Nagas were believed to roam the earth wearing jewels and ornaments. SNAKE worship was fairly widespread in India at one time, and is still an important part of popular religious practice in some regions.

When Naga culture was incorporated into Hinduism, many of the snake deities were accepted by the Hindus into their mythology. The thousand-headed serpent Ananta, for example, is the most powerful of the Nagas. It is on the coils of Ananta that the Hindu god Vishnu is often seen resting. Shrines to the nagas can be found throughout India, and Hindu women often worship at "snake-stones" when they want to bear sons or avoid illness.

As a festival in honor of the snake deities, Naga Panchami goes back to very ancient times. It is an occasion for fasting and worshipping cobras, since the Nagas were often depicted as cobras with extended hoods. If cobras are not available, huge cloth effigies of serpents are made and displayed in public, as are snakes made from metal, stone, and clay. Images of snake deities are often painted on walls as well. Worshippers offer milk and flowers to the cobras and coins to the snake charmers who gather in town for the festival. Because serpents live underground, digging in the earth is prohibited on this day.

The Hindu god Siva is also worshipped at this festival, since he is traditionally shown wearing snakes as ornaments. In temples dedicated to Siva, particularly those in Ujjain and Varanasi, hundreds of cobras are brought in by trappers and released before the god's image. Worshippers then empty their pots of milk over the snakes' heads to protect themselves against snakebite throughout their lives. At the end of the day, there are serpent dances in open fields, and the snakes are freed.

## SYMBOLS

### Snake

Because the snake sheds its skin, it is regarded by Hindus as a symbol of immortality. In Hindu art, eternity is often represented by a serpent eating its own tail. The cobras worshipped on Naga Panchami are raised at special snake shrines. In places that are frequented by wild snakes, worshippers often leave out dishes of milk to feed them.

## Further Reading

Crim, Keith, ed. *The Perennial Dictionary of World Religions,* 1989.

Henderson, Helene and Sue Ellen Thompson. *Holidays, Festivals, and Celebrations of the World Dictionary,* 2nd ed., 1997.

Kelly, Aidan. *Religious Holidays and Calendars,* 1993.

Sharma, Brijendra Nath. *Festivals of India,* 1978.

Thomas, Paul. *Festivals and Holidays in India,* 1971.

# Navajo Mountain Chant

**Type of Holiday:** Ethnic (Native American)

**Date of Observation:** Nine days at the end of winter

**Where Celebrated:** Arizona

**Symbols:** Circle of Evergreens, Fire, Plumed Arrow, Sandpaintings

**Colors:** Blue and black play an important symbolic role in the Mountain Chant (see CIRCLE OF EVERGREENS below).

**Related Holidays:** Navajo Night Chant

## ORIGINS

The nine-day Mountain Chant marks a transition in the seasons. It takes place in late winter, at the end of the thunderstorms but before the spring winds arrive. Members of the Navajo Nation believe that if this ceremony were to be held at any other time of year, the result would be death from lightning or snake-bite. The chant is also considered a curing ceremony, performed not only for individuals who are sick but to restore order and balance in human relationships.

The legend on which the Mountain Chant is based chronicles the adventures of Dsilyi Neyani, the eldest son of a wandering Navajo family. He is captured by the Utes while hunting one day, but he manages to escape with the help of the gods (known as the Yei). During his long journey to rejoin his family, he encounters many hazards and learns a great deal about magic and ceremonial acts. For example, he learns how to make the SANDPAINTINGS that are used in the Mountain Chant, how to make the feathers dance, how to swallow swords (see PLUMED ARROW), how to make a weasel appear and do magic, how to handle FIRE without getting burned, and how to make the mystical "hu-hu-hu-hu" cry used in the Mountain Chant dance.

When Dsilyi Neyani returns to his family, he discovers that they have grown into an entire tribe during his long absence. It takes him four days and four nights to tell the story of his wanderings, but the rituals he brings back are so compelling that messengers are immediately sent out to invite guests to witness what he has learned. Even today, the Mountain Chant remains an event to which visitors from outside the Navajo Nation are especially welcome.

The Mountain Chant consists of four ceremonies, all based on the same legend but differing considerably in terms of their presentation and the wording of the songs that are sung. Perhaps the most moving ceremony takes place on the final day. The medicine man emerges from the lodge or hogan at sunset and begins to chant, while a CIRCLE OF EVERGREENS eight to ten feet tall—each concealing the man who handles it—rises as if by magic and forms a circular enclosure about 100 feet in diameter with only one opening, facing east. The ground within this circle is considered sacred, and there is a cone-shaped bonfire in the center.

The final ceremony begins when the central bonfire is lit. Dancers with their bodies whitened by clay rush into the circle, leaping wildly and waving their arms and legs. They circle the fire from south to west to north and then south again, the white clay on their bodies protecting them from the heat of the flames (see FIRE). Sometimes they throw sumac wands tipped with rings of fluffy eagle down into the fire. The down flares briefly and burns away, but the dancer conceals a second ring of fluff, which he then shakes to the end of the wand, creating the impression that the fluffy ball has been magically restored. A similar illusion is involved in the "yucca trick," in which a yucca plant appears to grow miraculously from a bare root, then blossoms, and finally reveals its fruit.

The Fire Dance takes place just before dawn, when the central bonfire has burned down to embers. Young men drag in huge trees to feed the central fire, and the dancers make a sound with their tongues that imitates the sound of a hot fire. They carry large bundles of shredded cedar bark, which are ignited with coals from the base of the fire. Once they are burning, the bundles are thrown over the fence to the east first and then in the other three directions. The men dance in a circle around the fire, beating their own and each others' bodies with the flaming brands. Spectators later gather up bits of the burned cedar, which is believed to offer protection against fire for the coming year.

In 1926 the Mountain Chant was made into a film, directed by Roman Hubbell. The star of the film was named "Crawler" because his lower limbs were paralyzed—supposedly while attempting to learn the **NAVAJO NIGHT CHANT**. But his disability did not prevent him from learning and practicing the Mountain Chant.

# SYMBOLS

## *Circle of Evergreens*

The first time the Mountain Chant was performed, the circle of trees within which it took place was six miles in diameter and crowded with people. Today it is no longer this large a celebration, but the dark circle formed by the branches continues to play an important part in the ceremony. The trees represent the black and the blue spruce, both of which are mentioned in the legend of Dsilyi Neyani. In the songs sung during the Mountain Chant, black symbolizes the male principle and blue is the female.

The pairing of blue and black is common in Navajo legend. Black is usually associated with the north, the direction where evil and danger dwell. Blue is associated with the south. The home of the mountain sheep, as described in the Mountain Chant, consists of two black rooms and two blue rooms.

## Fire

Fire is a symbol of annihilation among the Navajo, as it is among most Native American tribes who believe in magic. Fire is said to burn evil, and the exposure to intense heat that takes place during the Fire Dance on the final night of the Mountain Chant symbolizes the ability to control fire, which in turn controls evil.

## Plumed Arrow

One of the dances performed during the Navajo Mountain Chant is the Dance of the Great Plumed Arrows. Plumed arrows are considered the most sacred of healing devices, although there is a trick involved in this particular dance. Each dancer holds his arrow up over the "patient" who is being cured by the ceremony and then thrusts it down his own throat, causing the spectators to gag in sympathy. In reality, however, this "sword-swallowing" is made possible by holding the arrowhead between the teeth and running the shaft of the arrow into a hollow casing. The patient is then touched with the arrows, which are believed to chase evil from the body.

## Sandpaintings

The preparation of sandpaintings takes place before the Mountain Chant begins. A large space is covered with fine sand, smoothed out as flat as a canvas. As many as 12 men may work on the sandpainting at one time, letting colored sand—normally red, blue, yellow, and white—dribble through their fingers to form the desired pattern. The medicine man oversees the process and is quick to catch any errors, since a single mistake can undermine the effectiveness of the entire ceremony.

The sandpainting plays an important role in the healing process. When the patient is admitted to the hogan or lodge—a typical Navajo building with earth walls reinforced by timbers—the medicine man begins to chant.

When the chanting is over, he sprinkles the patient and the sandpainting with a feather dipped in water. He then takes sand from various parts of the painting and applies it to parts of the patient's body. Spectators in the hogan may take sand and touch their own bodies with it, so they can share in the "cure." Afterward, the sandpainting is destroyed, and the sand is taken away.

The sandpaintings typically illustrate events in the legend of Dsilyi Neyani. In one sandpainting, for example, there are four figures known as the Long Bodies, who helped Dsilyi during his long journey home. The black Long Body is said to belong to the north, the one under it (white) to the east, the next (blue) to the south, and the bottom one (yellow) to the west. (See discussion of sandpaintings under **NAVAJO NIGHT CHANT.**)

## Further Reading

Fergusson, Erna. *Dancing Gods: Indian Ceremonials of New Mexico and Arizona*, 1931.

Reichard, Gladys. *Navajo Religion: A Study of Symbolism*, 1950.

# Navajo Night Chant
## (Nightway)

**Type of Holiday:** Ethnic (Native American)
**Date of Observation:** Late fall or winter for nine days
**Where Celebrated:** Arizona
**Symbols:** Masks, Sacred Bundle, Sandpaintings
**Related Holidays:** Navajo Mountain Chant

## ORIGINS

The nine-night ceremony known as the Night Chant or Nightway is believed to date from around 1000 B.C.E., when it was first performed by the Indians who lived in Canyon de Chelly (now eastern Arizona). It is considered to be the most sacred of all Navajo ceremonies and one of the most difficult and demanding to learn, involving the memorization of hundreds of songs, dozens of prayers, and several very complicated SANDPAINTINGS. And yet the demand for Night Chants is so great that as many as 50 such ceremonies might be held during a single season, which lasts 18-20 weeks.

Like the **NAVAJO MOUNTAIN CHANT**, the Night Chant is basically a healing ritual, designed both to cure people who are sick and to restore the order and balance of human relationships within the Navajo universe. Led by a trained medicine man—a combination doctor-priest—who has served a long apprenticeship and learned the intricate and detailed practices that are essential to the chant, the ceremony itself is capable of scaring off sickness and ugliness through the use of techniques that shock or arouse. Once disorder has been removed, order and balance are restored through song, prayer, sandpainting, and other aspects of the ceremony.

Before the chant itself takes place, young children undergo a tribal initiation. After being stripped of their clothing and then struck with a yucca whip, young boys are allowed to see the "gods" (i.e., the dancers who impersonate the gods) without their masks for the first time. Girls are not whipped but rather touched with ears of corn covered with sprays of spruce.

On the day of the chant, crowds gather expectantly outside the lodge where rehearsals have been taking place. The outdoor area in which the ceremony will be held is cleared of spectators, and many fires are lit to take the chill out of the night air. The dancers, who represent the gods, are led in by the medicine man and Hastse-yalti, the maternal grandfather of the gods, along a path of meal that has been laid down for them to follow. The patient emerges from the lodge, sprinkles the gods with meal from his or her basket, and gives each one a sacrificial cigarette. The medicine man intones a long prayer for the patient, repeating each phrase four times. Then the four gods dance, with Hastse-yalti moving rhythmically back and forth and hooting at the end of every verse to show his approval.

The original Night Chant involved four teams who danced 12 times each with half-hour intervals in between—a total of ten hours. Today, however, there are often so many teams dancing that there is no time for intermissions. The dance movements resemble a Virginia Reel, with two lines facing each other. Each of the six male dancers takes his female partner, dances with her to the end of the line, drops her there, and moves back to his own side. The chant itself is performed without variation and has a hypnotic effect on the listeners. The only relief is provided by the rainmaker-clown named Tonenili, who sprinkles water around and engages in other playful antics.

The medicine men who supervise the Night Chant insist that everything—
each dot and line in every sandpainting, each verse in every song, each
feather on each mask—be arranged in exactly the same way each time the
curing ceremony is performed or it will not bring about the desired result.
There are probably as many active Night Chant medicine men today as at
any time in Navajo history, due to the general increase in the Navajo population, the popularity of the ceremony, and the central role it plays in Navajo life and health. But it is getting more difficult to find apprentices willing
to learn the elaborate rituals. Although a medicine man typically earns
between $500 and $1,000 for a nine-day Night Chant, compensation often
comes in the form of livestock, baskets, cloth, jewelry, blankets, buckskin,
and food for the duration of the ceremony.

## SYMBOLS

### Masks

There are typically 24 Nightway masks, although the ceremony can be performed with fewer. These masks are worn by the God Impersonators who
perform the ritual dances. Some of these impersonators—Calling God,
Gray God, Whistling God, Whipping God, and Humpedback God among
them—wear the masks of ordinary male gods with special ornaments
attached at the time of the ceremony. Other masks include the yellow and
blue Fringed Mouth of the Water mask, the Black and Red God masks, the
Monster Slayer mask, the Talking God mask, and the Born for Water mask.

In addition to being worn by the God Impersonators who dance on the
dramatic final night of the nine-day ceremony, the masks are vital to the
application of many "medicines" (including the SANDPAINTINGS) to the
patient. They also play a vital role in the initiation of the young. The masks
of the female goddesses are actually worn by men, since women are not
allowed to minister to the person for whom the chant is being sung.

The masks used in the Nightway ceremony are made of sacred buckskin,
which must be obtained without shedding the animal's blood. The usual
method consists of chasing the deer into a blind, throwing it to the ground,
and smothering it by stuffing sacred meal into its nostrils. Buckskin is a
symbol of life to the Navajo people.

### Sacred Bundle

The medicine man's sacred bundle or *jish* is made up of ceremonial items
such as bags of pollen, feathers, stones, skins, pieces of mountain sheep
horn, and a flint blade believed to belong to the god known as the Monster

Slayer. The sacred bundle also includes gourd rattles and the sacred buck-skin MASKS worn by the God Impersonators.

Although the medicine man might carry other necessary items in his jish—such as incense, spruce collars, and the ground pigments used in SANDPAINTING—they are not considered part of the sacred bundle. Most of the items in the jish are permanent; they are not used up during the ceremony itself.

## Sandpaintings

As in the **NAVAJO MOUNTAIN CHANT**, sandpaintings play an important role in the healing rituals of the Night Chant. Twelve different sandpaintings are considered appropriate for the Nightway, of which a maximum of six are usually chosen: four large and two small. The patient and his or her family normally have a say in which sandpaintings are used. Each one is associated with a particular story and is accompanied by specific songs, prayers, and ceremonial procedures.

It is rarely the medicine man himself who makes the sandpaintings, although he is responsible for overseeing their preparation. Usually his assistants do the actual painting, dribbling small amounts of colored sand through their fingers onto a smooth sand surface. The resulting works of art must be perfect; in other words, there can be no deviations from the design set down by the gods.

Every detail in each sandpainting has a special meaning. If the plumes on the heads of the figures are on the same side as the rattle, for example, it means that rain is desired. If they are on the opposite side from the hand holding the rattle, it means that the growth of corn is the desired outcome. Standard Nightway sandpainting designs include First Dancers, Whirling Logs, Water Sprinklers, Fringed Mouth Gods, Black Gods, and Corn People.

The purpose of the sandpaintings is to allow the patient to absorb the powers depicted in the painting, often by sitting or sleeping on it. The medicine man applies items from the *jish* or SACRED BUNDLE to the gods depicted in the sandpainting and then to the corresponding part of the patient's body. It is considered wrong—if not downright dangerous—to reproduce these sandpaintings in any way, since they might attract the attention of the gods to a situation where no real healing is intended. Sketching and photographing them is therefore prohibited, although sometimes this prohibition can be sidestepped by removing the prayer-plumes set around the painting or omitting some other detail, so that the painting itself is not really "finished."

## Further Reading

Faris, James C. *The Nightway: A History and a History of Documentation of a Navajo Ceremonial*, 1990.

Fergusson, Erna. *Dancing Gods: Indian Ceremonials of New Mexico and Arizona*, 1931.

Reichard, Gladys. *Navajo Religion: A Study of Symbolism*, 1950.

# Nawruz

## (Naw Roz, Navroz, No Ruz, Islamic New Year)

**Type of Holiday:** Calendar

**Date of Observation:** Beginning March 21 for 13 days

**Where Celebrated:** Afghanistan, India, Iran

**Symbols:** Egg and Mirror, Gardens of Adonis, Seven S's (Haft-sin), Water Sprinkling, Wheat Cakes

## ORIGINS

Nawruz, which means "new day" in Persian, celebrates the beginning of spring and the start of the Islamic New Year. It is observed by all religious groups in Iran and Afghanistan; in India, it is celebrated by the Parsis as Jamshed Navroz. This holiday dates back further than Islam and is believed to have come from Zoroastrian Persia, where it coincided with the **VERNAL EQUINOX** and was observed in honor of the solar new year.

In fifteenth-century Egypt, Persian Nawruz customs were combined with those of a typical **SATURNALIA** or **CARNIVAL** celebration. People crowned a "Prince of the New Year," who smeared flour all over his face, rode through the streets on a donkey, and collected money. Anyone who failed to make a suitable contribution was doused with water or dirt. Sometimes teachers were attacked by their students and thrown into a fountain, from which they had to "buy" their way out. Eventually the government succeeded in suppressing the more outrageous festival customs.

In modern Iran, houses are cleaned and children are given new clothes in preparation for the 13-day New Year's celebration. The evening before

Nawruz begins, a traditional omelette made with greens is served, along with pilaf, a rice dish symbolizing the wish for an abundant year. Friends and relatives visit each other and exchange gifts that include colored eggs (see EGG AND MIRROR), fruit, and bunches of narcissus. Banquets featuring seven foods beginning with the letter S (see SEVEN S'S) are held, and the New Year's dinner is typically eaten sitting around a tablecloth spread out on the floor. In Muslim homes, it is customary to pop a piece of candy into someone's mouth on Nawruz while reciting a brief passage from the Koran or holy book of Islam. Sometimes each member of the family will eat a piece of candy while a passage is read from the Koran. Then they embrace each other and say, "May you live a hundred years."

The 13th day of Nawruz is called Sizdan-Bedar or "Thirteenth Day Out." It is considered unlucky to remain at home on this day, so the entire family usually goes to the country or a city park to spend the day picnicking and to welcome the arrival of spring. Folk singers, dancers, clowns, and costumed actors wander about entertaining people on this day. Children bring their GARDENS OF ADONIS with them and throw them into a stream of running water.

In Afghanistan, Nawruz is a favorite time to play *buzkashi* or "goat-grabbing." The object of the game is for a team of horse riders to grab the carcass of a goat that has been placed in a pit, carry it around a goal post, and put it back in the pit. The game is believed to have developed on the plains of Mongolia and Central Asia, using a prisoner-of-war instead of a goat. Since there are several hundred horsemen on each team galloping at breakneck speed and lashing at each other with buzkashi whips, the game often results in fatalities.

## SYMBOLS

### Egg and Mirror

Muslim families observe Nawruz with a dinner consisting of foods that begin with the letter S (see SEVEN S'S). These dishes are laid out on a tablecloth on the floor, along with a colored egg, a mirror, and a candle for each family member. At the precise moment when the new year begins, the egg is placed on the mirror. To everyone's delight, the egg usually trembles a bit—probably because of all the cannons that are fired at midnight.

Eggs are a traditional symbol of fertility and new life, and their use at the new year festival may date back to the time when it was a pastoral festival marking the change from winter to summer. The light reflected in the mirror symbolizes the brightness of the future.

## Gardens of Adonis

A couple of weeks before Nawruz arrives, Iranian families plant quick-growing seeds such as wheat, celery, and lentils in shallow bowls containing a little dirt and water. They soon turn into masses of green, symbolizing life and good fortune. Then, on the 13th day of the festival, children take the sprouted seeds and throw them over the garden wall or into a stream of running water. This act is symbolic of doing away with family quarrels so that the new year can begin in friendliness and peace. (See WHEAT CAKES)

The name for these miniature gardens dates back to ancient mythology. Adonis—originally the Babylonian god Tammuz—was a young Greek god beloved by Aphrodite. He was killed by a wild boar while hunting in the mountains, and Aphrodite was so grief-stricken that the gods arranged to let him spend half the year on earth with her and the other half in the underworld. The story of the dying god who was resurrected each year became a symbol for the seasonal shift from winter to spring. A funeral cult was founded in his honor, and each spring the women of Greece and western Asia would plant seeds in vases and sprinkle them with warm water. These Gardens of Adonis, as they were called, would be cast into the sea along with images of the young god. The blooming of the red anemone seven days later was considered to be symbolic of his return.

## Seven S's (Haft-sin)

The most outstanding feature of the Nawruz celebration is the festival table, a cloth spread out on the floor containing the *Haft-sin* or "Seven S's," all food items that represent happiness in the new year: *sabyeh* or green sprouts grown from seed; *sonbul* or hyacinth; *samanoo* or sweet wheat pudding; *serkeh* or vinegar; *sumac* from the sumac plant; *seeb* or apple; and *senjed* or Bohemian olives. The Haft-sin represent the seven archangels of God who embody the principles of ethical behavior in the Zoroastrian religion.

Other foods served at the festival include roast chicken, fruit, bread, sweets, and rose water. After the feast is over, candy is passed around while passages from the Koran or Muslim holy book are read aloud.

## Water Sprinkling

In ancient Persia, Syria, and Egypt, Nawruz was originally a celebration of the arrival of spring. People woke up early, drew running water in a vase, and then poured it over themselves in a symbolic act designed to stave off bad luck and harm.

There are a number of theories as to where this custom originated. Legend has it that once, after a very long drought, rain fell on New Year's Day. From that time onward, rain was considered a good omen, and pouring water over each other became a new year's tradition. Another theory is that it is simply an act of purification designed to cleanse the body of the smoke and dirt associated with tending the winter fires.

Yet another explanation is that when the prophet Solomon lost his kingdom and his powers—symbolized by the loss of his signet ring—because one of his wives had returned to the worship of her old idols, he was forced to wander unrecognized through Jerusalem and beg for his food. According to the Koran, Solomon was not really at fault for this lapse, and as soon as he realized why he was being punished, he sought God's forgiveness. His signet ring was restored to him and with it, his sovereignty. The swallows were so overjoyed that they celebrated by splashing each other with water.

## Wheat Cakes

The wheat cakes associated with Nawruz are not ordinary cakes for eating. They are uncooked, and they contain whole grains of wheat. The cake is kept moist until the wheat sprouts and turns into a miniature garden. In many homes, there is a layer of the cake for each member of the family, and the children wait anxiously for the wheat to sprout on their layer. On the 13th day of the new year festival, the family takes the cake out into the fields and throws it away. Like GARDENS OF ADONIS, the wheat cakes take with them all the bad feelings and quarrels that have accumulated within the family, clearing the way for a peaceful new year.

## Further Reading

Dobler, Lavinia. *Customs and Holidays Around the World,* 1962.

Gaer, Joseph. *Holidays Around the World,* 1953.

Glassé, Cyril. *The Concise Encyclopedia of Islam,* 1989.

Henderson, Helene and Sue Ellen Thompson. *Holidays, Festivals, and Celebrations of the World Dictionary,* 2nd ed., 1997.

Ickis, Marguerite. *The Book of Festivals and Holidays the World Over,* 1970.

Ickis, Marguerite. *The Book of Religious Holidays and Celebrations,* 1966.

Leach, Maria, ed. *Funk & Wagnalls Standard Dictionary of Folklore, Mythology, & Legend,* 1984.

MacDonald, Margaret R., ed. *The Folklore of World Holidays,* 1992.

Purdy, Susan. *Festivals for You to Celebrate,* 1969.

Von Grunebaum, G. D. *Muhammadan Festivals,* 1988.

# New Yam Festival

**Type of Holiday:** Ethnic (Ibo, Igbo, Yoruba)
**Date of Observation:** Late June
**Where Celebrated:** Nigeria
**Symbols**: Divination Rites, Yam

## ORIGINS

The New Yam Festival is a public holiday celebrated annually by almost all of the ethnic groups in Nigeria. It usually takes place around the end of June, and it is considered taboo to eat the newly harvested YAM before this date. The high priest sacrifices a goat and pours its blood over a symbol representing the god of the harvest. Then the carcass is cooked and a soup is made from it, while the yams are boiled and pounded to make *foofoo*. After the priest has prayed for a better harvest in the coming year, he declares the feast open by eating the pounded yam and the soup. Then everyone joins in, and there is dancing, drinking, and merrymaking. After the festival is over, it is permissible for anyone in the community to eat the new yam.

Why is the yam so important? An old Igbo myth says that during a severe famine Igbo (from whom the tribe takes its name) was told that he must sacrifice his son, Ahiajoku, and his daughter, Ada, in order to save his other children. After they were killed, their flesh was cut into pieces and buried in several different mounds. A few days later, yams sprouted from the flesh of Ahiajoku, while cocoyams sprouted from the flesh of Ada. Igbo and his other children survived the famine by eating them. The spirit of Ahiajoku became the God of Yam.

The myth of Ahiajoku is reenacted during the New Yam Festival each year. Each householder places four or eight new yams on the ground near a shrine. After saying some prayers, he cuts small portions off each end of the yams to symbolize the sacrifice of Ahiajoku. The yams are then cooked with palm oil, water, and chicken to make a dish that symbolizes the body and blood of Ahiajoku. The Igbo people consider the yam to be so sacred that at one time, anyone caught stealing it would be put to death. Today, such thieves are banished.

The Yoruba people celebrate the New Yam Festival, known to them as Eje, for two days around the time of the harvest. They fast, give thanks for the harvest, and carry out special DIVINATION RITES to determine the fate of the community, and particularly its crops, in the coming year. Most of the festival activities take place in a sacred grove and at a sacred shrine, both of which are purified for the occasion. There are very specific rules governing how the new yams must be presented to the appropriate religious authorities.

The Ibo people celebrate what they call the Onwasato Festival in August, which marks the beginning of the harvest. There is a thanksgiving ritual in which the senior member of every family kills at least one fowl and sprinkles its blood on the *Okpensi* (symbol of the family), giving thanks to the family's ancestors. The feathers are removed and spread on the threshold to demonstrate the family's determination to forsake evil. One of the fowls is roasted and put aside, while the others are consumed during the day's feasting. On the second day, the roasted fowls are shared by members of the extended family.

## SYMBOLS

### *Divination Rites*

A highlight of the New Yam Festival, particularly among the Yoruba people, is the divination rite that determines the destiny of the community and the likelihood of an abundant harvest. One of the recently harvested yams is taken and divided in two. The two parts are thrown up in the air, and if one part lands face up and the other face down, it is considered a very promising sign. If both fall either face up or face down, it is taken as a bad omen.

### *Yam*

Yams are a staple of life in Nigeria, and a great deal depends on the success of the crop. Since it can be affected by many different religious powers, from the ancestors to the gods, it is essential that these powers be treated with respect and offered special prayers and sacrifices at the time of the yam harvest.

Among the Igbo, the yam is symbolic of a human being who was sacrificed so that other humans might survive. Ahiajoku (see "Origins") is the only example of a human hero who is deified in Igbo mythology, since his spirit became the God of Yam.

319

## Further Reading

Henderson, Helene and Sue Ellen Thompson. *Holidays, Festivals, and Celebrations of the World Dictionary,* 2nd ed., 1997.

MacDonald, Margaret R., ed. *The Folklore of World Holidays,* 1992.

# *New Year's Day*

**Type of Holiday:** Calendar

**Date of Observation:** January 1

**Where Celebrated:** Australia, British Isles, North and South America, Europe, Scandinavia, and in all countries using the Gregorian calendar

**Symbols:** Baby, First-footing, Football Games, Gifts, Pig, Resolutions

**Related Holidays:** Chinese New Year, Dewali, Nawruz, New Year's Eve, Oshogatsu, Rosh Hashanah, Saturnalia, Tet

## ORIGINS

Celebrating the first day of the year on January 1 is a relatively modern practice. Up until the time of Julius Caesar, the Romans generally celebrated New Year's Day in March, the first month of the Roman year. January 1 marked the beginning of the civil year for the ancient Romans, a time when new consuls were inducted into office. Although there were games and feasting at this time, March 1 was still observed as New Year's Day with a festival to Mars, the Roman god of war.

Caesar changed the Roman New Year's Day to January 1 in honor of Janus, the god of all beginnings and the keeper of the gates of heaven and earth. Janus was always represented with two faces, one looking back to the old year and the other looking forward to the new year. It was customary to celebrate the festival in his honor by exchanging GIFTS and making RESOLUTIONS to be friendly and good to one another.

When the Romans under Constantine accepted Christianity as their new faith, they retained the Festival of Janus as their New Year's Day but turned it into a day of fasting and prayer. It was a time for all good Christians to turn over a new leaf, but not all Christians observed it. Even after the Gregorian calendar was adopted by Roman Catholic countries in 1582, Great Britain and the English colonies in America continued to begin the year in March. It wasn't until 1752 that Britain and its possessions adopted the so-called New Style calendar (Gregorian) and accepted January 1 as the beginning of the year. But among the Puritans in New England, the old associations with the pagan god Janus were offensive enough to persuade many of them to ignore the day altogether and refer to January simply as "First Month."

The modern New Year's Day is geared toward feasting rather than fasting. Almost everywhere it is a day for receiving visitors (see FIRST-FOOTING) and recovering from **NEW YEAR'S EVE** festivities.

## SYMBOLS

### Baby

Just as the old man is a traditional symbol of the year that is ending, the image of the newborn baby is both a religious symbol of the Christ Child as well as a secular symbol of rebirth and renewal at the beginning of a new year. The "New Year Baby" that appears on holiday greeting cards and in New Year's decorations is usually a playful rather than a solemn child and is often shown wearing a party hat.

### First-footing

Many modern New Year's Day customs originated in Scotland and England. First-footing is a good example. It is still observed in Scotland, where a family's fortunes in the coming year are believed to be influenced by the first guest who sets foot in the door after the New Year strikes. If it's a woman, a light-haired man, an undertaker, or anyone who walks with his toes pointing inward, it is considered a bad omen. A dark-haired man, on the other hand, brings good luck. In some villages, dark-haired men hire themselves out as professional first footers whose job it is to go from house to house immediately after the New Year arrives. Female first-footers are considered to be such bad luck that male restaurant owners will sometimes make a point of opening the restaurant themselves before the waitresses arrive on New Year's Day.

Just as it is bad luck for a fair-haired or red-haired person to "let in" the New Year, there are folk beliefs surrounding what the first footer brings with him or her. When entering the house, he or she must bring a *handsel* — a piece of bread, an orange, or an ear of corn carried in his or her hand for good luck. Sometimes the first footer brings cheese or cakes to share with the family being visited. The Scottish name for New Year's Eve is "Hogmanay," and one of the traditional foods shared with the first footer is Hogmanay shortbread, baked in the shape of a sun — perhaps a survival of pagan sun worship at the **WINTER SOLSTICE**.

The Dutch who came to settle in New York introduced the custom of making calls on New Year's Day, and by the 1840s, visiting on New Year's Day was a widespread practice among the middle classes in America. Gentlemen arrived with engraved calling cards, and women set out beautifully decorated tables full of food and served coffee or whiskey punch. This custom continues in the popular "open house" parties held on New Year's today.

## Football Games

Perhaps no pastime is as closely identified with New Year's Day in the United States as watching football games on television — especially the Rose Bowl game in Pasadena, California; the Cotton Bowl in Dallas, Texas; the Sugar Bowl in New Orleans, Louisiana; and the Orange Bowl in Miami, Florida. In many homes, having friends over to watch football has replaced the more social visits paid on this day in past centuries.

## Gifts

The ancient Romans exchanged gifts on New Year's Day — usually coins bearing the portrait of the two-faced god, Janus. These gifts were called *strenae*, a name that survives in the French word *étrennes*, meaning New Year's presents. They were the precursor to our modern Christmas presents, and they were based on the belief that acting wealthy (i.e., by spending money on gifts) would attract good financial luck in the coming year. Feasting and drinking were popular for the same reason, serving as a kind of charm to guarantee abundance. In fact, many of the customs now associated with New Year's Day were based on the principle that whatever happened on the first day of the year would affect one's fortunes throughout the year.

Although gift-giving at New Year's is rare in the United States, it remains popular in France, Italy, and some other European countries.

## Pig

Roast pork or suckling pig is a favorite dish to serve at New Year's dinner. The pig is a symbol of good luck in many countries. But in this case the custom arose because the pig roots in a forward direction, making it an apt symbol of a prosperous future. Eating turkey, goose, or any other fowl is equivalent to inviting bad luck, since all fowl scratch backward in their search for food.

## Resolutions

Ancient peoples indulged themselves in alcoholic and sexual excess at New Year's as a way of acting out the chaos that they hoped the new year would banish. The New Year's festival was an attempt to start over, and it was customary to purge oneself of excess energy and to confess one's sins in the hope that the New Year would somehow be different.

The Puritans, who were never in favor of New Year's revelry, thought that this was a good time for religious renewal and spiritual resolve. They urged young people not to waste the holiday on vain and foolish amusements but to make New Year's an occasion for changing the way they lived their lives. Like Christians elsewhere, they often made New Year's vows or pledges designed to conquer their own weaknesses, to capitalize on their God-given talents, or to make themselves more useful to others.

The custom of making more secular New Year's resolutions came into vogue at the turn of the twentieth century. People started promising to be more moderate in their eating and drinking habits and to patch up their quarrels with friends, family, and business associates. But it was always understood that most of these vows would not be kept — at least not for long — since humans were backsliders by nature.

The New Year's resolutions that are so widely encouraged and talked about today are a secularized version of the vows that more religious individuals once made in their never-ending journey toward spiritual perfection. Although often made with the best of intentions, such pledges are rarely carried out and must be renewed on an annual basis.

## Further Reading

Gaer, Joseph. *Holidays Around the World*, 1953.

Henderson, Helene and Sue Ellen Thompson. *Holidays, Festivals, and Celebrations of the World Dictionary*, 2nd ed., 1997.

Ickis, Marguerite. *The Book of Festivals and Holidays the World Over*, 1970.

Miles, Clement A. *Christmas in Ritual and Tradition*, 1990.

Purdy, Susan. *Festivals for You to Celebrate*, 1969.

Santino, Jack. *All Around the Year*, 1994.

Schmidt, Leigh Eric. *Consumer Rites: The Buying and Selling of American Holidays*, 1995.

Scullard, H. H. *Festivals and Ceremonies of the Roman Republic*, 1981.

Spicer, Dorothy Gladys. *The Book of Festivals*, 1990.

Tuleja, Tad. *Curious Customs: The Stories Behind 296 Popular American Rituals*, 1987.

# New Year's Eve

**Type of Holiday:** Calendar

**Date of Observation:** December 31

**Where Celebrated:** Australia, British Isles, North and South America, Europe, Scandinavia, former Soviet Union, and in all countries using the Gregorian calendar

**Symbols:** Auld Lang Syne, Noisemaking, Old Man, Wassail Bowl

**Related Holidays:** Chinese New Year, Dewali, Nawruz, New Year's Day, Oshogatsu, Rosh Hashanah, Saturnalia, Tet

## ORIGINS

Midnight on December 31 marks the transition between the Old Year and the New Year, an occasion that is celebrated with everything from prayer to parties. Some people wear silly hats, drink champagne, and use NOISEMAK-ERS; they're apt to kiss their bosses, throw their arms around strangers on the street, and generally engage in behavior that would be considered scandalous at other times of the year. Others attend midnight church services, while still others congregate in public places like New York City's Times Square or London's Trafalgar Square to count down the closing seconds of the old year.

It is likely that our New Year's Eve customs are related, if only indirectly, to the ancient Roman **SATURNALIA**, which was observed around the time of the **WINTER SOLSTICE** in December. This pagan holiday was characterized by the suspension of discipline and rules governing behavior, and like New Year's Eve celebrations today, it occasionally got out of hand. In eighteenth- century America, the New Year's Eve revelry in such cities as Philadelphia, New York, and Baltimore often ended in street demonstrations and violence. Groups of men and boys would blow tin horns, set off firecrackers, knock down gates and fences, shatter windows, and even break into the homes of the wealthy, demanding money or hospitality.

Unlike **CHRISTMAS**, which is traditionally celebrated indoors, New Year's Eve festivities frequently take place in the out-of-doors, particularly in urban areas. A popular trend that has emerged in recent years is attending "First Night" celebrations. These originated in Boston in 1976 and are now held in more than 65 American cities. They represent a deliberate attempt to replace the partying and drinking that have traditionally marked New Year's Eve with a wide variety of cultural events and performances in both indoor and outdoor settings. Those who prefer a quiet New Year's Eve at home often get their outdoor experience vicariously by watching the illuminated ball that descends on Times Square during the closing minutes of the old year.

## SYMBOLS

### *Auld Lang Syne*

The custom of singing "Auld Lang Syne" on New Year's Eve is all that remains of a much broader custom that originated in the British Isles in the late eighteenth century, when all parties ended with the guests standing in a circle singing this traditional song. The custom first took hold in Scotland, probably because the lyrics were written in 1788 by Robert Burns, the country's favorite folk poet. There were other versions of the song, however, one of which was used in the 1783 opera *Rosina* by composer William Shield. Most musicologists agree that the tune came from a traditional Scottish folk melody, and that Burns and others merely tinkered with the words.

In the Scots dialect, *auld lang syne* means "old long since"—in other words, the good old days. Even the rowdiest New Year's Eve parties often end with a relatively quiet, if drunken, rendition of this simple tribute to times past.

### *Noisemaking*

The custom of using noise to welcome in the New Year dates back to ancient times, when noise was believed to scare off evil spirits. Although few people today link New Year's Eve with any kind of evil influence, noise-making still plays a prominent role in their celebrations. In Denmark, young people "smash in the New Year" by banging on their friends' doors and throwing pieces of broken pottery against the sides of houses. In Japan, dancers go from house to house at **OSHOGATSU** making strange noises by rattling bamboo sticks and pounding drums. In Vietnam, Hawaii, and South America, New Year's Eve is celebrated by setting off firecrackers. And in the United States, New Year's Eve parties almost always feature the inexpensive plastic, paper, or tin noisemakers normally associated with children's birthday parties.

## Old Man

If the baby is often used to symbolize the New Year, the old man is the classic symbol of the year that is drawing to an end. Holiday greeting cards used to feature these symbols regularly, although they are less common today. In some ways, Santa Claus (see **CHRISTMAS**) is the old man we now associate with the passing year. In any case, the baby and the old man serve as a useful metaphor for the birth and death of a calendar year.

## Wassail Bowl

In England at one time, New Year's Eve was an occasion for feasting and celebrating. Family and friends would gather around a bowl of hot ale spiced with cloves, nutmeg, and ginger, from which the head of the house would drink to their health. Then each family member or friend would drink from the bowl and pass it on, saying "Waes Hael!" as they drank — an Anglo-Saxon expression meaning, "May you be in good health." The bowl came to be known as the "wassail" bowl, and "wassailing" became a general term for merrymaking during the holiday season.

## Further Reading

Henderson, Helene and Sue Ellen Thompson. *Holidays, Festivals, and Celebrations of the World Dictionary*, 2nd ed., 1997.

Ickis, Marguerite. *The Book of Festivals and Holidays the World Over*, 1970.

Pike, Royston. *Round the Year with the World's Religions*, 1993.

Santino, Jack. *All Around the Year*, 1994.

Schmidt, Leigh Eric. *Consumer Rites: The Buying and Selling of American Holidays*, 1995.

Tuleja, Tad. *Curious Customs: The Stories Behind 296 Popular American Rituals*, 1987.

# *Niman Katchina*
### *(Niman Festival, Going-Away of the Gods,*
### *Going Home Ceremony)*

**Type of Holiday:** Ethnic (Native American)

**Date of Observation:** July

**Where Celebrated:** Arizona

**Symbols:** Katchinas, Masks

**Related Holidays:** Powamû Festival

## ORIGINS

The KATCHINAS are the ancestral spirits of the Hopi Indians. For six months of the year, they leave their home in the mountains and visit the tribe, bringing health to the people and rain to their crops. Their arrival in January or February is celebrated as the **POWAMÛ FESTIVAL**, and their departure in July is observed as the Niman Katchina Festival, with ceremonial dances at all four Hopi pueblos. These dances are actually the last in a series that take place throughout the six months when the katchinas are present in the pueblo.

The masked dancers who represent the katchinas perform their dances in the plaza, pounding their feet rhythmically, chanting, and sprinkling sacred meal on the ground. Their arms are filled with green cornstalks — symbolic of the crops for which the tribe is so thankful — and some carry musical instruments made from hollow gourds painted yellow and green. Notched sticks are laid across the gourds, and the scapulae (shoulder blades) of deer serve as bows for these primitive fiddles. The dance is repeated at intervals throughout the day.

During the dance, a procession of men and women emerges from the kiva — a large underground room used for ceremonial purposes. These are the Hopi priests and priestesses. One carries an ancient water bowl from which he flings drops of water, symbolic of rain, with an eagle feather; one has a ceremonial pipe, from which he blows smoke, symbolic of clouds. The women place meal in each dancer's hand — another indication that the

Niman Katchina is a ceremony of gratitude for the harvest as well as a going-away party for the ancestral spirits.

The dancers hand out gifts to the children: gourd rattles and bows and arrows for the boys, and katchina dolls for the girls. They also distribute baskets, bowls, or wash-pans filled with foods symbolic of the harvest— small ears of corn, peaches, melon, and other first fruits.

Young Hopi women who have married during the year are barred from observing any ceremonial dances until the Niman Katchina, at which their attendance is required. They all wear the pure white wedding blanket made by the groom from native cotton and wool. This blanket is worn at all ceremonial occasions after the wedding, and when the woman dies, it serves as her burial shroud.

The katchinas don't actually depart until the second morning of the festival. There is a brief ceremony at sunrise that involves throwing meal, pouring water, and other symbolic acts. The priest stands at the top of the ladder that leads down into the kiva and offers a prayer. The masked katchinas leave the village by way of a trail leading west, disappearing just as the sun appears over the horizon.

## SYMBOLS

### *Katchinas*

The word *katchina* means "spirit." It applies both to the ancestral spirits whose arrival and departure are celebrated each year and to the men wearing MASKS who impersonate these supernatural beings. Like all primitive peoples, the Hopis personify everything. Men, animals, plants, stones, mountains, storms, the sky, and the underground all have spirits personified as katchinas, who come into the modern world carrying the legends of the Hopi past. Although the katchinas themselves are not gods, they act as intermediaries between mortals and the Hopi deities. Prayers for sun and rain, or for more children, are made to the katchinas in the belief that they will bring these appeals to the gods' attention.

*Katchina* also applies to the dolls carved out of cottonwood and painted, dressed, and feathered to look exactly like the Niman Katchina dancers. Children play with katchina dolls, which can also be seen standing on special altars erected around the time of the festival.

There are a number of legends concerning the katchinas' origin, most of which agree that the chief katchina was a badger who came from the underworld. Many of the ceremonies featuring katchinas are conducted in a language so ancient that even the participants do not understand it.

## *Masks*

The katchina's most distinguishing feature is his mask or ceremonial helmet. The face may represent a bird, beast, monster, or man — or a combination thereof, with many variations in color. These masks usually bear symbols representing clouds, rain, or rainbows, since the Niman Katchina Festival takes place at a time of year when rain is apt to be scarce. The male katchinas often carry an object associated with the spirits they represent — for example, a bow and arrow, yucca whip, pine branch, or feathers. The women katchinas, known as *katchinamana*, are represented by men as well. They wear wigs with their hair styled in flat swirls over the ears known as squash-blossoms, a symbol of virginity.

Before the final katchina dance takes place, the masks are repainted and refinished with a ruff of feathers, fur, or spruce at the neck — spruce, according to the Hopis, having a magnetic attraction for rain. The remainder of the costume consists of a white ceremonial kirtle (kilt) and sash, with a turtle-shell rattle under the knee, moccasins, and jewelry. A fox skin hangs from the rear of the belt or sash — all that remains of the animal skins in which the Hopi katchinas once clothed their entire bodies.

## Further Reading

Fergusson, Erna. *Dancing Gods: Indian Ceremonials of New Mexico and Arizona*, 1931.

Fewkes, Jesse Walter. *Tusayan Katcinas and Hopi Altars*, 1990.

Heinberg, Richard. *Celebrate the Solstice: Honoring the Earth's Seasonal Rhythms through Festival and Ceremony*, 1993.

Henderson, Helene and Sue Ellen Thompson. *Holidays, Festivals, and Celebrations of the World Dictionary*, 2nd ed., 1997.

# Obon Festival
## (Bon Festival, Festival of Lanterns, Festival of the Dead)

**Type of Holiday:** Religious (Buddhist)

**Date of Observation:** July 13-15 or August 13-15

**Where Celebrated:** Japan, and by Japanese Buddhists throughout the world

**Symbols:** Bonfires, Bon-Odori, Lanterns

**Related Holidays:** All Souls' Day, Ch'ing Ming, Hungry Ghosts Festival

## ORIGINS

The Obon Festival has been observed by Buddhist families in Japan ever since Buddhism was introduced there around 552 B.C.E. Although it was originally celebrated only by the court and noblemen, the celebration eventually spread to the general population. It was a festival in honor of the dead, similar to the Christian **ALL SOULS' DAY**.

Although the Obon Festival is still a fairly solemn occasion, people take joy in the knowledge that their dead relatives can return to earth for a visit. Preparations include cleaning houses and graveyards, and lighting small BONFIRES to welcome the spirits home. The graves of the deceased are often decorated with the branches of the Japanese umbrella pine (*koya-maki*), rice balls (*mochi*), fruit, and incense. In the main room of the house, where the altar is located, a small mat is spread on the floor. The *ihai* or record of ancestry is placed on the mat, along with appropriate decorations. A miniature fence made of leaves surrounds this arrangement, and a table is set with foods that the dead particularly enjoy, which include potatoes cooked with sesame seeds, eggplant or gourds, sweets, fruits, and cakes. Throughout the three days of the festival, the dead are spoken to as if they were alive and present. On the final day, they are offered special "farewell rice balls" to sustain them on their return journey.

The purpose of the Obon Festival is to keep the memory of the deceased alive and to encourage obedience from sons and daughters. Obon celebrations are held not only in Japan, but in other countries where there is a large Japanese Buddhist population. In the United States, for example, there is a big Obon celebration in Chicago as well as in several California cities. Obon celebrations take place in either July or August, depending upon the location.

## SYMBOLS

### Bonfires

Bonfires are lit outside Japanese homes twice during Obon. At the start of the festival, they are lit to welcome the spirits of the dead as they return to earth to visit the living. On the third and final day of the festival, they are lit to guide the spirits back to their celestial home. Just as certain foods are prepared to satisfy the spirits' appetites, the light of the bonfires is regarded as necessary to help them find their way around.

In Kyoto, Japan, giant bonfires are lit on the mountainsides. They are made in the shape of the character that means "large."

### Bon-Odori

The climax of the Obon Festival is the Bon-Odori, or "Dance of Rejoicing," a folk dance that is held in every town, by the light of paper LANTERNS, to comfort the souls of the dead. It was originally a dance of lamentation in which close relatives of the deceased would dance and sing to the music of a flute and a drum. The early Bon dances were performed at a variety of local festivals, many of which coincided with Obon. These other festivals eventually merged, and what began as a religious celebration for the spirits of the dead evolved into a gala festival of dancing.

In Buddhist temples during Obon, dancers perform to the beat of a huge *taiko* (drum) mounted on a platform. Both men and women wear a light summer kimono known as a *yukata,* and most carry large sandalwood fans. Sometimes their steps are slow and graceful as they assume postures that resemble living statues. At other times, their bodies sway in unison and spin faster and faster as the tempo of the drumbeat increases. Although some people practice the traditional steps with instructors for weeks in advance, almost anyone can join in simply by following the person in front of him or her. Bon dances, which can continue throughout the night, express the joyous side of the Obon Festival, just as the lantern ceremonies (see LANTERNS) reflect its more serious side.

## Lanterns

Lanterns play an important role throughout the three days of Obon. At night, families go to the cemetery carrying lanterns designed to light the path for the ancestral spirits. Sometimes lanterns are left burning on the graves, casting an eery glow over the otherwise dark cemetery. Lanterns are often left burning in front of each house as well, serving as signposts for both guests and the souls of the departed. Then, on the final day of the festival, little boats with paper lanterns on the bow are set adrift on lakes and rivers. The boats contain the names of the ancestors who are being honored.

The Todaji Temple in Honolulu, which is the only member of Buddhism's oldest sect in the United States, holds a procession of floating spirits in Ala Moana Park during Obon. After a short service in the temple, its members launch several hundred wooden boats, each about three feet long, decorated with colored lanterns and filled with offerings of food and incense and memorial tablets with the names of ancestors written on them. Each family launches one boat—even if it's only a waxed paper carton. The fleet is led by the mother boat or *oyabune,* which is usually five feet long.

## Further Reading

Araki, Nancy K., and Jane M. Horii. *Matsuri: Festival: Japanese-American Celebrations and Activities,* 1978.

Bauer, Helen, and Sherwin Carlquist. *Japanese Festivals,* 1965.

Dobler, Lavinia. *Customs and Holidays Around the World,* 1962.

Eberhard, Wolfram. *A Dictionary of Chinese Symbols: Hidden Symbols in Chinese Life and Thought,* 1986.

Henderson, Helene and Sue Ellen Thompson. *Holidays, Festivals, and Celebrations of the World Dictionary,* 2nd ed., 1997.

# *Obzinky*

**Type of Holiday:** Calendar
**Date of Observation:** Late August to mid-September
**Where Celebrated:** Czech Republic
**Symbols:** Baba, Wreath

## ORIGINS

There are actually two harvest celebrations in the Czech and Slovak Republics. One of them, known as Posviceni, is the church consecration of the harvest. The other, Obzinky, is a secular festival where the field workers celebrate the end of the harvest by making a WREATH out of corn, wheat, or rye and wildflowers. Sometimes the wreath is placed on the head of a pretty young girl, and sometimes it is placed in a wagon along with decorated rakes and scythes and pulled in procession to the home of the landowner. Ribbons are braided into the horses' manes and tails, and the reapers wear their most colorful clothes. The laborers present the wreath and congratulate their employers on a good harvest, after which they are invited to participate in dancing, singing, and feasting at the farmowner's expense. Foods served at this feast traditionally include roast pig, roast goose, and *Kolace*—square cakes filled with plum jam or a stuffing made from sweetened cheese or poppy seed. Beer and slivovice, a prune liquor, accompany the food.

## SYMBOLS

### *Baba*

The woman who binds the last sheaf of corn or wheat in the harvest is known as the *Baba* or "old woman." In some areas, the Baba is a doll made from the last sheaf of grain and decorated with ribbons and flowers. Like the WREATH, the Baba is carried in procession to the landowner's home, where it occupies a place of honor until the next harvest.

The custom of making a "corn dolly" or puppet representing the corn goddess or spirit of the harvest is a very ancient one. Sometimes the reaper herself was wrapped up in cornstalks and brought to the farmhouse, where she was often the object of ridicule and teasing. The general belief behind all of these customs was that the spirit of the corn was driven out with the cutting of the last sheaf. After spending the winter in the barn, the corn spirit would go out again to the fields to resume her activity as the force that made the corn grow.

## Wreath

The wreath made of corn, wheat, or rye and brought to the landowner's house at the completion of the harvest serves much the same purpose as the BABA. It symbolizes the fruits of the fields, and presenting it to the landowner is a way of presenting him with the bounty of the harvest.

### Further Reading

Frazer, Sir James G. *The Golden Bough: A Study in Magic and Religion,* 1931.

Henderson, Helene and Sue Ellen Thompson. *Holidays, Festivals, and Celebrations of the World Dictionary,* 2nd ed., 1997.

MacDonald, Margaret R., ed. *The Folklore of World Holidays,* 1992.

Spicer, Dorothy G. *The Book of Festivals,* 1990.

# *October Horse Sacrifice*

**Type of Holiday:** Ancient or Pagan
**Date of Observation:** October 15
**Where Celebrated:** Rome, Italy
**Symbols:** Blood, Horse's Head
**Related Holidays:** Parilia

## ORIGINS

In ancient Rome, a two-horse chariot race was held in the Campus Martius (Field of Mars) on October 15. After the race was over, the right-hand horse of the winning chariot was killed with a spear as a sacrifice to Mars, the god of war. The HORSE'S HEAD was cut off first, and decorated with a necklace of loaves or cakes. Then there was a battle between the inhabitants of two different quarters of the city to see who could seize the head and hang it up in a place where everyone could see it. Meanwhile, the horse's tail, still dripping with BLOOD, was rushed to the king's house, where the blood was allowed to drip on the sacred hearth. The rest of the blood was preserved until April 21, when the **PARILIA** (a festival in honor of Pales, the protector of shepherds and their flocks) was held. It would then be burned as part of a purifying ceremony, and both men and animals would leap over the fire.

Many of the rituals associated with the October Horse Sacrifice have their roots in ancient agricultural customs. Horse racing was a common activity on farms at certain seasons of the year, and a wreath — similar to the necklace of loaves—was often hung around the neck of the winning horse. The men and women who worked on the farm also raced against each other in pursuit of a calf, a kid, a sheep, or some other animal believed to represent the corn-spirit or goddess of vegetation.

While there is strong evidence that the October Horse Sacrifice was originally an agricultural fertility rite, some scholars believe that it was more of a military rite, designed to purify the army when it returned from its summer campaign. The fact that a horse was sacrificed (as opposed to an ox or some other farm animal) would seem to support this theory, since horses were closely linked to war in ancient times. It is also possible that what started out as a fertility rite later developed into a martial one, with army horses taking the place of farm horses. In any case, the blood, the hearth, and the necklace of loaves hung around the horse's head all have strong associations with the fertility of the fields.

## SYMBOLS

### *Blood*

The blood of the sacrificed horse was a symbol of life. When dripped on the sacred hearth or burned in the fires of the **PARILIA**, it was believed to purify and ward off evil. Anyone who breathed in the smoke of the fire in which the blood had been scattered would therefore gain new life and strength, and avoid the evil forces that might otherwise hinder survival.

### *Horse's Head*

The horse's head represents the corn-spirit. In ancient times, it was common after the harvest was over to hang up some object in a prominent place on the farm or in the village — usually a bunch of corn or flowers —

and call it by the name of an animal. Eventually a real animal's head was used for the same purpose. Hanging a necklace of loaves around the horse's head showed that it was an object that possessed the power to make the fields more fertile.

### Further Reading

Fowler, W. Warde. *The Roman Festivals of the Period of the Republic,* 1925.

Henderson, Helene and Sue Ellen Thompson. *Holidays, Festivals, and Celebrations of the World Dictionary,* 2nd ed., 1997.

Leach, Maria, ed. *Funk & Wagnalls Standard Dictionary of Folklore, Mythology, & Legend,* 1984.

Scullard, H. H. *Festivals and Ceremonies of the Roman Republic,* 1981.

# *Ogun Festival*
## *(Olojo Festival)*

**Type of Holiday:** Ethnic (Yoruba)
**Date of Observation:** July
**Where Celebrated:** Ife, Oyo State (Nigeria)
**Symbols:** Crown, Iron
**Related Holidays:** Egungun Festival

## ORIGINS

The Ogun Festival, observed by the Yoruba people of Nigeria, commemorates the god Ogun, a mythical warrior, and the birth of his son, Oranmiyan, who later became king of Yorubaland. Ogun is the god of IRON and of war as well as the patron of blacksmiths and hunters. He was the first god to descend to earth while it was still a marshy wasteland. Since he was the only one who possessed a tool—an iron cutlass—that could penetrate the dense vegetation, he cleared the way for the other deities to descend. When Obatala had finished molding the physical form of the first ancestors, it was Ogun who added the finishing touches—a role he played throughout all of creation. He continues to preside over the "finishing touches" of culture, such as circumcisions and the cutting of tribal marks.

The Ogun Festival lasts for three days. It begins with the vigil known as the *Ilagun* or *Asoro,* which takes place at midnight. On behalf of its blacksmiths, the city of Ife donates two new hoes and several iron bell-gongs needed for the ritual. The Ogun shrine in Ife is decorated with palm fronds, and two dogs are prepared for sacrifice. A libation is poured, prayers to the god are offered, and a ritual dance is held around the shrine.

The city is in a festive mood for the remainder of the festival, when the war chiefs in full regalia dance to the tune of the *ibembe* drums and bell-gongs made of iron while traditional Ogun songs are sung. The highlight is the procession from the palace to Oke Mogun, where Ogun finally settled after abdicating the throne. The chief, who wears the royal CROWN of Ife, is accompanied by priests and priestesses of the various other gods and goddesses worshipped by the Yoruba. Guns are fired when they arrive at the shrine. Special rituals are carried out there, and a ram is sacrificed to the dead ancestors or *Oonis.*

The dances performed at the Ogun Festival reenact mythical themes and are choreographed according to traditional models. Sometimes they consist of simple gestures—such as swinging a machete—that recall the god's powers. Although Ogun is traditionally regarded as the patron of blacksmiths, who unlock the secrets of the earth and forge them into tools, nowadays he is worshipped by drivers and surgeons as the god of automobiles, trucks, and the operating room. Since metal makes the creation and expansion of civilization possible, Ogun is seen as the god who "opens the way;" that is, he makes it possible for the powers of other gods to be effective.

## SYMBOLS

### Crown

In the procession that is the highlight of the Ogun Festival, the chief wears the beaded crown known as *Are,* which is supposed to be as heavy as the load that an average man can carry. The crown symbolizes a living deity and therefore attracts many invisible spirits when it is brought out for the annual event. The people of Ife believe that it is the power of the crown that usually causes rain to fall on this day.

### Iron

Ogun is the god or *orisha* of iron, which can be transformed into the peaceful tools of agriculture as well as the terrible weapons of war. His iron cutlass stands as a symbol of his power, which can be channeled toward both creative and destructive ends. People who are asked to swear to tell the truth in a court of law and who will not swear on the Bible or the Koran are sometimes asked to put their tongue and lips on a cutlass made of iron. In one of the palaces of Ife, there is a large lump of iron that people touch to guarantee that they're telling the truth.

As the one who shapes iron, the blacksmith plays an important role in African mythology. The ability to turn fire and earthy substances into the products of civilization is seen as a parallel to the creation of the world. The smith is regarded as the chief agent of God on earth, the one who shapes the world.

## Further Reading

Eliade, Mircea. *The Encyclopedia of Religion,* 1897.
King, Noel Q. *Religions of Africa: A Pilgrimage into Traditional Religions,* 1970.
MacDonald, Margaret R., ed. *The Folklore of World Holidays,* 1992.
Murphy, Joseph M. *Santería: African Spirits in America,* 1988.

# *Olympic Games*

**Type of Holiday:** Sporting
**Date of Observation:** Every four years
**Where Celebrated:** Various countries around the world
**Symbols:** Olympic Flame

## ORIGINS

There were four major religious festivals in ancient Greece that entailed athletic competitions: the Olympic Games, the Pythian Games, the Nemean Games, and the Isthmian Games. The Olympic Games, held in honor of Zeus, were especially popular. First held in 776 B.C.E. at Olympia, Greece, they continued to be held once every four years for 1,168 years. Then Greece came under Roman rule, and the games declined. They were finally abolished in 393 C.E. by the Christian Roman emperor, Theodosius I, who probably objected to some of the pagan rites associated with the games.

At first the Olympic Games were confined to a single day and a single event: a footrace the length of the stadium. Additional races were added later, along with the discus throw, javelin throw, broad (or long) jump, boxing, wrestling, pentathlon (consisting of five different track and field events), chariot racing, and other contests. There were competitions for poets, orators, and dramatists as well. The length of the games was later extended to five days, and the winners were celebrated as national heroes.

It wasn't until the late nineteenth century that the games were revived, largely through the efforts of Baron Pierre de Coubertin of France, an educator and scholar who wanted to discourage professionalism in sports by holding amateur world championships. The first Olympiad of modern times was held under the royal patronage of the King of Greece in 1896 in a new stadium built for the purpose in Athens. Since that time, the games have been held in cities all over the world at four-year intervals, except for lapses during the First and Second World Wars. A separate cycle of winter games was initiated in 1924.

The modern Olympic Games consist of the Summer Games, held in a large city, and the Winter Games, held at a winter resort. Since 1994, the games have been held on a four-year cycle, but two years apart (i.e., Winter Games in 1994 and 1998, Summer Games in 1996 and 2000). There are 23 approved sports for the Summer Games, which include archery, basketball, boxing, canoeing, cycling, equestrian events, fencing, football (soccer), gymnastics, modern pentathlon, rowing, swimming, diving, volleyball, water polo, weight lifting, wrestling, and yachting. The Winter Games offer competition in biathlon (skiing and shooting), bobsled, ice hockey, luge, ice skating, and skiing, plus two demonstration sports. New sports, such as snowboarding, are always vying for recognition.

About 160 nations send thousands of male and female athletes to the Summer Olympics, and hundreds of millions watch the competition on television. The Winter Olympics are somewhat smaller, with about 60 nations participating.

## SYMBOLS

### *Olympic Flame*

The highlight of the opening ceremonies at both the Winter and Summer Olympics is the lighting of the Olympic flame, said to represent the "Olympic spirit" of competition. A cross-country relay runner carries a torch first lit at Olympia, Greece, and ignites the flame that burns throughout the 15 or 16 days of the games. Thousands of runners, representing each country between Greece and the host country, take part in the four-week torch relay. The lighting of the torch is followed by a spectacular production of fireworks, strobe lights, fly-overs, music, dance, and other entertainments.

## Further Reading

Henderson, Helene and Sue Ellen Thompson. *Holidays, Festivals, and Celebrations of the World Dictionary*, 2nd ed., 1997.

Van Straalen, Alice. *The Book of Holidays Around the World,* 1986.

# *Oshogatsu*
## *(New Year's Day in Japan)*

**Type of Holiday:** Calendar

**Date of Observation:** January 1

**Where Celebrated:** Japan

**Symbols:** Bells, Camellia, Crane and Tortoise, Daruma, Dreams, Gifts, Kadomatsu, Manzai, Mochi, Narcissus, Plum Bough, Rake, Shimenawa or Shimekazari, Utagaruta

**Related Holidays:** Chinese New Year

## ORIGINS

Oshogatsu or **NEW YEAR'S DAY** is the most important festival in the Japanese calendar. Schools, banks, and offices traditionally close from January 1 until January 3, a period during which people visit their friends, relatives, and superiors. Visits made during the first three days of the New Year are usually very brief, and they focus on relatives and superiors, as dictated by the rules of Japanese etiquette. Individuals of less importance may be visited anytime within the first two weeks.

*Shogatsu* means "standard month," a reference to the fact that the standards people set for their own behavior during the first few days of the year can influence their fortunes for the next 12 months. Businesses, clubs, and groups of friends get together and hold year-end parties, a good opportunity to promote good will and patch up any lingering quarrels or misunderstandings. All unfinished business is taken care of, debts are paid, and the house gets a thorough cleaning. The idea is to start the New Year with a clean slate.

The preparations for Oshogatsu are quite elaborate. They begin on the 23rd day of the 12th month with the burning of the Kitchen God's effigy. The Kitchen God is a minor deity who lives with the family all year and sets out on the 23rd day of the last month to file his annual report on the family's behavior, returning just before midnight on **NEW YEAR'S EVE**. The burning of his effigy releases the Kitchen God for his "ascent" to heaven. While he is gone, the house is cleaned. At one time, a symbolic house-cleaning was carried out with a green bamboo duster whose feathery twigs and leaves represented prosperity and good fortune. Nowadays, cleaning house includes recovering or replacing all tatami mats, repapering sliding doors and screens, and burning the old paper charms pasted up in the kitchen or bedroom and replacing them with new ones. There is an old Japanese saying that the New Year must be greeted with a swept garden, a mended roof, a new dress, a clean body, a clear conscience, and an honest purse (i.e., no debts).

The actual arrival of the New Year is announced by the ringing of BELLS in all the Buddhist temples. In the morning, *wakamizu* or "young water" is drawn from the well with a wooden bucket to ensure good health for the coming year. Family members rise early, wash in *wakamizu*, put on new clothing, and sit together at the table for the first meal of the year. *O-toso* or sweet, spiced wine is served before breakfast as a token of celebration, first to the youngest member of the family and last to the oldest. According to tradition, the family that drinks *o-toso* will have no sickness, for the drink has the power to destroy evil spirits and invigorate the human body. Pink and white rice cakes (see MOCHI) and many kinds of fruit are placed before the ancestral tablets in the family shrine. After the family feast is over, people toast each other and pay visits to their friends and relatives. Young girls and women play shuttlecock in long-sleeved kimonos, while men and boys fly kites and play with spinning tops.

Oshogatsu is believed to have evolved out of ancient Japanese rituals associated with seasonal changes, which were very important to farmers. The New Year celebration originally coincided with the **WINTER SOLSTICE**. It was believed that the dead visited the living at this time of year, and masked figures and troupes of dancers would go from house to house rattling bamboo sticks to scare off evil spirits. When the Western calendar was adopted in 1873, the New Year celebration was moved to January 1.

A number of special foods are served on Oshogatsu. The national dish of the New Year's festival is *o-zoni* (literally "boiled mixture"), a clear or bean-mash soup that might contain vegetables or bits of fish or chicken. Other foods served during the festival have symbolic value—for example, *kazu-no-ko* or herring roe ("many children"); *mame* or black beans ("good health"); *kachiguri* or hulled, baked chestnuts ("victory"); and *kombu* or kelp ("happiness").

## SYMBOLS

### Bells

The arrival of the New Year is announced by ringing the bells in Buddhist temples 108 times. The ringing of the *joya no kane* or "end-of-year bell" is said to represent the leaving behind of 108 worldly concerns of the old year. Some say that ringing the bell purges the 108 weaknesses described by Buddha's teaching.

### Camellia

The flower associated with the entire first month of the Japanese New Year is the *tsubaki* or camellia, which blossoms from December right through to March. A hardy perennial, it symbolizes a long and healthy life. But because the blossom can just as easily drop from its stem before the petals are withered, it also serves as a reminder of inconstancy. Among the warriors of feudal Japan, the camellia stood as a symbol of the Samurai's readiness to have his own head fall at the stroke of an enemy's sword.

### Crane and Tortoise

Both the crane (*tsuru*) and the tortoise (*kame*) are symbols of longevity. Cranes made by folding paper in a square are hung in homes at Oshogatsu or placed on trays of food as symbols of good fortune and long life. Crane-inspired designs can also be found on dishes, containers, and other household articles used during the New Year's festival.

A common song sung at New Year's in the Tokyo area is based on an early poem written by a Zen priest: "Cranes have a life of a thousand years;/Tortoises have the joy of ten thousand years./May your life prosper and continue/Longer than the cranes, tortoises, and bamboo."

## Daruma

The Daruma is a good-luck charm in the form of a doll. It takes its name from an Indian Buddhist priest named Bodhidharma, who sat facing a cliff in silent meditation for nine years. Because of this, he lost the use of his arms and legs. But he continued to travel throughout China, teaching people about Buddha. The Daruma doll therefore symbolizes inner strength and determination.

The Japanese purchase Daruma dolls during the New Year season in the hope that they will bring good fortune. Made of wood, clay, stone, or papier-mâché, the dolls have rounded bottoms, so that they'll return to an upright position if knocked over. They are usually painted red all over with the exception of the face. The eyes are very prominent and may be entirely blank or white. The purchaser of the doll can then paint in the iris while making a wish. When the wish comes true, the other iris is painted in.

## Dreams

According to Japanese belief, the first dream of the New Year (*hatsuyume*) foretells one's fate in the coming year. Someone who dreams about ships loaded with treasures will have a happy and prosperous year. Dreams about the rising sun are also symbolic of good fortune, as are dreams about sea voyages. Although dreams involving snakes and swords would not ordinarily be associated with good luck, on this particular night they indicate that wealth lies in store for the dreamer. Dreams about rain mean that worries can be expected, while dreams about moonlight mean that things will get better. Earthquake dreams foretell a change in residence, snow portends happiness, and ice signifies that an arranged marriage will take place.

## Gifts

Oshogatsu is a popular time for gift-giving, particularly among adults. Servants are given new kimonos and pocket money, while all employees receive at least an extra month's salary. Typical gifts include eggs (symbolizing the wish for a well-rounded, complete life), fruit (especially round fruit, which represents good luck), and dried cuttlefish (symbolizing numerous offspring). Among casual acquaintances, typical gifts exchanged might include printed cotton towels, folding fans, or even a packet of matches. Unless the gift is a single object, it must be given in sets of three, five, or nine, which are the most auspicious numbers. Seven is considered an unlucky number, as are all even numbers with the exception of ten and, in some cases, two.

Oshogatsu gifts are usually wrapped in paper and string that is half red, half white—colors that represent the *yin* and *yang* principles of Chinese philosophy and together represent "completeness." The ceremonial string or *mizuhiki* might have originated as a rain-charm. Under it there is a square of red and white paper folded into the shape of a lozenge with a tiny piece of seaweed in the middle, meant to convey the idea that "This gift is but a seaweed in the ocean of your prosperity."

The gifts are opened after the caller has left. If a particular gift is found to be useless, or is too similar to something that the person already owns, a fresh piece of paper is wrapped around it, a new string is tied, and the package is passed on to somebody else.

## Kadomatsu

First used in the seventeenth century, the *kadomatsu* is a decoration made from pine and bamboo that is placed at the front gate or on either side of the door to the house. It is put up at the start of the New Year season to ward off evil, promote growth and fertility, and bring blessings to the household. The pine (*matsu*) symbolizes constancy, morality, and the power to resist old age and adversity. Pine needles, which occur in pairs joined at the end, also symbolize married love and unity. Their sharp points are good for scaring off ghosts and evil spirits. The bamboo (*take*) symbolizes great strength under adversity, since it bends under a load of snow but springs back upright after shedding it. The bamboo is always cut on a slant so that any evil spirits will be snagged on its sharp points. Sometime the fern (*shida*) is added to the arrangement to symbolize vigor and progeny.

Like Christmas wreaths, kadomatsu can be either very simple or quite elaborate. Although some houses have only a cluster of pine boughs, larger houses have far more elegant arrangements consisting of pine, bamboo, and plum blossoms—all cold-weather plants as well as symbols of congratulations and good luck. The kadomatsu is placed in front of the house to express the hope that the New Year will bring vigor, long life, and strength to everyone in the family. It is left in place until the seventh day, when only a sprig of pine remains as a reminder of the holiday that has passed and as an omen of the future. All decorations come down around January 14, when they are burned in a huge community bonfire. In rural areas, the kadomatsu is often thrown into a stream or river so that it will carry off any lingering sins or illnesses.

Nowadays the kadomatsu is not complete without an orange. A mandarin orange is often used, but it should really be a *daidai*, which grows into a real tree. The fruit matures in winter and, if left on the branch, becomes green again the following spring, making it an apt symbol of rebirth. The *daidai's* many pips represent offspring, and its color and shape resemble that of the sun. The *daidai* must never be eaten, since this would be symbolic of destroying prosperity. Sometimes the orange is accompanied by a boiled crayfish or *ebi* (prawn), a reference to the ancient Japanese saying, "May you grow so old that your back becomes bent like an *ebi's!*" And because the prawn turns red when it is boiled, it also symbolizes rebirth into a more prosperous future.

## Manzai

*Manzai* are like Christmas carolers. Dressed in ancient costumes and wearing tall hats known as *eboshi,* the singers go from house to house during the New Year's season singing songs and beating their *tsuzumi* or hand drums. This custom originated more than 1,000 years ago, when artists from China danced and sang in the imperial court as a way of conveying the season's greetings. Most manzai today are professional groups who sing and dance in return for a nominal payment, although amateur manzai can often be found in rural areas.

The original manzai dancer was a semi-religious figure, called in by high-ranking noblemen to purify their houses by chanting good-luck songs. Then he evolved into an amusing beggar who sang and danced to the accompaniment of an hourglass-shaped drum shouting, *Manzai! Manzai!* meaning "ten thousand years!"—a good luck wish. The traditional manzai dancer wears a black-and-white striped hat with a red sun-disk on one side and a silver full moon on the other. His face is covered by a smiling mask, and he holds a folding fan that he uses to "blow in" good luck.

## Mochi

*Mochi* or pounded rice cakes are a traditional part of the Japanese New Year celebration. They are made from steamed rice that has been pounded into a sticky paste and shaped into small round buns. In earlier times, families would get together to make their own mochi, and traveling *mochi tsuki* men would come around with their special pounding equipment. Although mechanized pounding machines have taken over the task in most areas, some rural families continue to make mochi from scratch.

A *sambo* or raised wooden tray holds the mochi, which are made somewhat larger than usual for New Year's. Because of their circular shape, with a flat bottom and slightly convex top, they are often compared to a mirror. *Kagami mochi* or "mirrored mochi" consist of a large rice cake surmounted by a smaller one and placed on clean white paper in the center of a *sambo* stand. They are a symbol of the hope for a brighter and happier new year. Rather than being eaten, the kagami mochi stand in the alcove or household shrine as an offering to the gods. On January 11, they are removed from the alcove and, if they're not too hard, are cut up and served to family members.

Sometimes *kagami mochi* are embellished with other New Year's symbols: the fern for progeny; seaweed for joy; the lobster or prawn for longevity; the persimmon for fecundity and a happy family; and the *daidai* (see KADO-MATSU), a type of orange symbolizing many generations.

The custom of eating mochi at New Year's goes back to the early ninth century, when it was widely believed that for each mochi a person ate, one year would be added to his or her age.

## Narcissus

The *suisen* or narcissus is a symbol of purity and fertility (*sui* means "water") and of the life that lies beneath the frozen snow. It was the holy flower of the temple for the Hindus, and some of the Indian lore attached to it may have reached Japan via Buddhism. Because the narcissus blooms right around New Year's Day, it has always been associated with luck in the coming year. A spray of narcissus wrapped in folded paper and tied with a red and white string (see GIFTS) is a special emblem of the Oshogatsu festival.

## Plum Bough

The blossoming plum tree (*ume*) is considered a symbol of feminine beauty, charm, and chastity—the counterpart of the masculine pine. Because the plum blossoms while the ground is still covered with snow, it is also a symbol of courage.

The arrangement of pine, bamboo, and plum known as *shochikubai* appears frequently in Japanese art. It represents the beginning of a new year and the wish for happiness and fulfilled hopes. If the season is advanced enough, a plum bough may be added to the vase of pine branches in the entrance hall and main room during the Oshogatsu festival.

## Rake

One of the most popular objects purchased during Oshogatsu is a rake covered in trinkets. It stands as a symbol of "raking in" good fortune and prosperity during the New Year season.

## Shimenawa or Shimekazari

The *shimenawa* or rice-straw rope is one of the most important household decorations during the New Year's festival. It is hung over the front and back doors, barn door, around the well, and up over the roof or under the eaves to bring good luck and keep out evil. The use of the shimenawa can be traced back to an old myth about Amaterasu-omikami, the Sun Goddess. After being abused by her brother, the goddess withdrew into a rocky cave and refused to come out and shine. The world was plunged into darkness. To draw her out, the other gods and goddesses staged a dance and played music. When she came out of the cave to see where the music was coming from, they stretched a rice-straw rope across the entrance so she couldn't go back in. For hundreds of years, the shimenawa has been used to designate the boundaries of a sacred area, whether it be a shrine, a temple, a tree, or a home. It stands as a reminder that the place is sanctified and free of evil spirits.

The wisps of straw that are twisted into the rope are designed to prick intruders or demons, who are very susceptible to being hurt by sharp things. Other symbolic objects may be woven into the shimenawa or attached to it, such as fern-fronds (symbolic of expanding good fortune), a small orange (the word for which in Japanese sounds the same as the word meaning "generation to generation"), or a section of lobster (symbolizing old age because of its bent back). Some scholars theorize that the shimenawa is related to the sheaves of corn hung up in European homes and barns as a charm protecting the crops from disease.

Sometimes the shimenawa is twisted into a knot like a pretzel — knots and loops having magical powers in Japanese mythology. The name for this ornament is *shimekazari*. Shimekazari charms are hung up near every entrance and on the walls of stables and warehouses to bring prosperity and good luck.

Unlike a normal rope, the shimenawa is twisted from right to left. In Japan, anything done in reverse is considered good magic. While the shimenawa is used locally at all Shinto festivals, either draped around a shrine or to festoon the streets, only at Oshogatsu is it used in the home.

## Utagaruta

A traditional pastime among young people in Japan around this time of year is *utagaruta*, an unusual game based on the work of Fujiwara Sadaie, a poet who died in 1242. He collected what he considered to be the best poems of his time and published them as "Single Songs of a Hundred Poets." In the game of utagaruta, these poems are divided into two sets, each set having one half of each poem. The object of the game is to find the matching halves and put them together as quickly as possible. Expert players are able to find a match almost as soon as the first syllable of the poem has been read. Sometimes utagaruta games are broadcast on the radio.

## Further Reading

Araki, Nancy K., and Jane M. Horii. *Matsuri: Festival: Japanese-American Celebrations and Activities*, 1978.

Bauer, Helen, and Sherwin Carlquist. *Japanese Festivals*, 1965.

Casal, U. A. *The Five Sacred Festivals of Ancient Japan*, 1967.

Dobler, Lavinia. *Customs and Holidays Around the World*, 1962.

Heinberg, Richard. *Celebrate the Solstice: Honoring the Earth's Seasonal Rhythms through Festival and Ceremony*, 1993.

Henderson, Helene and Sue Ellen Thompson. *Holidays, Festivals, and Celebrations of the World Dictionary*, 2nd ed., 1997.

Ickis, Marguerite. *The Book of Festivals and Holidays the World Over*, 1970.

Purdy, Susan. *Festivals for You to Celebrate*, 1969.

# *Palm Sunday*
## *(Passion Sunday)*

**Type of Holiday:** Religious (Christian)

**Date of Observation:** Between March 15 and April 18 in the West; between March 28 and May 1 in the East; the Sunday preceding Easter

**Where Celebrated:** British Isles, Europe, United States, Mexico, Latin America, Scandinavia, and by Christians all over the world

**Symbols:** Palm Branches

**Colors:** Purple or violet is used throughout Holy Week to symbolize the passion or suffering of Christ.

**Related Holidays:** Ash Wednesday, Easter, Good Friday, Lent, Maundy Thursday

## ORIGINS

Palm Sunday commemorates the triumphant return of Jesus Christ to Jerusalem, where He received a hero's welcome from the people who had heard about the miracles He'd performed and regarded Him as the leader who would deliver them from the domination of the Roman Empire. He rode into the city on an ass, and the people greeted Him by waving PALM BRANCHES and strewing them in His path, shouting, "Hosanna: Blessed is the King of Israel that cometh in the name of the Lord" (John 12: 12, 13).

Although Jesus entered Jerusalem in triumph, later events proved that His popularity was largely superficial. The city was already filled with holiday pilgrims because it was the Jewish feast of **PASSOVER**, and it is likely that Jesus deliberately chose this time so that His final showdown with the Jewish authorities would take place in front of as many people as possible. The happy crowd of pilgrims, many of whom probably knew Jesus as a popular rabbi, made a special event of his arrival, cheering and throwing down palm branches for Him to ride over.

As a Christian observance, Palm Sunday dates back to the tenth century. But the persistence of ancient folk beliefs about the power of palm branches would seem to indicate a link with much earlier celebrations. At one time it was customary to use a wooden ass mounted on wheels with a human figure riding on it to represent Jesus. As soon as the ass passed over the willow or palm branches that had been strewn on the ground, people would rush to gather them up because they were regarded as protection against storms and lightning. Crosses made of woven palm were a popular charm against disease.

Probably the greatest present-day observance of Palm Sunday takes place in Rome, where the Pope, carried in St. Peter's Chair on the shoulders of eight men, comes out of St. Peter's Basilica to bless the palms. After the service, golden palm branches are distributed among the clergy and olive branches, a symbol of spiritual anointing, are given to the congregation. Then the thousands of worshippers who have gathered in St. Peter's Square march through the basilica and around the portico, emerging from one door and reentering through another to symbolize the entry of Jesus into Jerusalem. Some of the palm branches are saved and later burned to make ashes for the following year's **ASH WEDNESDAY**.

## SYMBOLS

### *Palm Branches*

The palm branch is a symbol of victory and a sign of reverence. In Europe, where palm branches are hard to find, branches of box, yew, or willow are often carried in procession on Palm Sunday to commemorate Jesus's triumphant entry into Jerusalem.

After the Reformation in the sixteenth century, Henry VII declared that carrying palms on Palm Sunday was a custom that should be maintained. By the nineteenth century in many parts of England, it was customary for young people to go "a-palming" on the Saturday before Palm Sunday—in other words, to go into the woods and gather willow twigs (in the absence of palms) and return with armloads of cuttings as well as sprigs of willow in their hats or buttonholes. Like the palm branches, the willow cuttings were collected and burned, and the ashes were set aside for the following **ASH WEDNESDAY**.

The belief that palm branches offered protection from disease and natural disasters can still be seen in the customs of some European countries. In Austria and the Bavarian region of Germany, for example, farmers make *Palmbuschen* by attaching holly leaves, willow boughs, and cedar twigs to the top of long poles. After these have been blessed in the local church on Palm Sunday, farmers set them up in their fields or barns to ward off illness and to protect their crops from hail and drought.

In the Netherlands, the *Palmpaas* is a stick to which a hoop has been attached. The hoop is covered with boxwood and decorated with paper flags, eggshells, sugar rings, oranges, figs, raisins, and chocolate eggs. Sometimes there is a figure of a swan or a cock on the top, made from baked dough. It is generally believed that the Palmpaas was originally a fertility symbol representing the arrival of spring and the resurgence of life after the long winter.

On Palm Sunday in Italy, the piazzas in front of most small churches are filled with people dressed up in new spring clothes and with vendors selling olive and palm branches. The olive branches may be gilded or painted silver, and the palms are often braided into crosses and decorated with roses, lilies, or other flowers. After the palms have been blessed in the church, they are often exchanged as peace offerings or as a sign of reconciliation between those who have quarreled.

In Czechoslovakia, the priests bless pussy willows. Farmers wave the willow branches over their fields of grain to protect them from hail or violent rainstorms. Sometimes pussy willow branches are placed on the roof to protect the house from fire.

## Further Reading

Chambers, Robert, ed. *The Book of Days*, 1864.

Dobler, Lavinia. *Customs and Holidays Around the World*, 1962.

Harper, Howard V. *Days and Customs of All Faiths*, 1957.

Henderson, Helene and Sue Ellen Thompson. *Holidays, Festivals, and Celebrations of the World Dictionary*, 2nd ed., 1997.

Ickis, Marguerite. *The Book of Festivals and Holidays the World Over*, 1970.

Metford, J. C. J. *The Christian Year*, 1991.

Monks, James L. *Great Catholic Festivals*, 1951.

Pike, Royston. *Round the Year with the World's Religions*, 1993.

Santino, Jack. *All Around the Year*, 1994.

# *Parilia*

**Type of Holiday:** Ancient or pagan

**Date of Observation:** April 21

**Where Celebrated:** Rome, Italy

**Symbols:** Bonfires, Foliage, Laurel, Olive

**Related Holidays:** Beltane, May Day, Midsummer Day, St. George's Day

## ORIGINS

The Parilia was an ancient Roman agricultural festival designed to purify and protect the flocks. Pales was the protector of shepherds and their sheep, an ancient god usually regarded as male, but sometimes as female. Shepherds would pray to Pales for forgiveness if they or their sheep had unwittingly trespassed on sacred ground and frightened the woodland deities, or if they disturbed the sacred fountains or cut the branches of sacred trees. They would also pray to Pales that their sheep be kept free of disease and not fall prey to wolves or dogs, that the rainfall and vegetation would be plentiful, that many lambs would be born, and that their wool would be thick and soft. They prepared for the Parilia by cleaning and sweeping out their folds with brooms made of LAUREL twigs, by decorating their stalls with FOLIAGE and green boughs, and by hanging wreaths over the entrances. Sometimes they would burn sulphur along with OLIVE wood, laurel, and rosemary, with the smoke passing through their sheepfolds and cattle sheds to purify their flocks and herds. Or they would drive their beasts through BONFIRES, then jump over the flames themselves three times to ensure the welfare of their flocks — a practice that was common throughout Europe on **EASTER, MAY DAY,** and **MIDSUMMER DAY**. The blood that had been preserved from the October Horse Sacrifice six months earlier was burned, as were bean shells and the ashes of the cattle sacrificed at the Fordicidia, the April 15 fertility festival in which unborn calves were torn from their mothers' wombs and burned. The festival would end with an open-air feast.

The Parilia was one of the oldest Roman festivals. One of the reasons why the festival remained so popular is that it fell on the day widely regarded as the birthday of the city of Rome, which was founded in 753 B.C.E. A public holiday known as the *Natalis urbis Romae* (birthday of the city of Rome) was observed with music, street dancing, and general revelry. **ST. GEORGE'S DAY,** which is believed to have been the medieval counterpart of the ancient Parilia, was also observed with revelry and dancing in the streets in honor of England's patron saint. But both of these observances had their roots in ancient fertility and purification rites involving turning the herds and flocks out to new pastures.

## SYMBOLS

### Bonfires

As a symbol of the sun, fire—in the form of bonfires, torches, burning embers, and even ashes—was believed to be capable of stimulating the growth of crops as well as the health and vigor of humans and animals. Ancient festivals observed, like the Parilia, with fire were designed to ensure the continued supply of light and heat from the sun as well as purification and the destruction of evil. As a symbol, fire combines both positive elements (heat, light) as well as negative (destruction, conflagration). To pass through the fire, as celebrants at the Parilia would do, symbolized transcending the human condition. Driving flocks through a bonfire was a well-known purification rite in ancient times, familiar from the celebration of **BELTANE** in Scotland and Ireland on May 1.

According to legend Romulus, the founder of Rome, played a significant role in conducting the purification rituals of the Parilia. This is probably why April 21 was set aside not only to honor the pastoral god Pales, but the founding of Rome.

### Foliage

The custom of decorating the enclosures where sheep and cattle were kept with green boughs and wreaths at the Parilia probably descended from the primitive rites used by ancient peoples to influence the gods of vegetation. It is still common to decorate houses by bringing leaves and branches indoors at certain special seasons—among them **MAY DAY, MIDSUM-MER DAY,** the harvest, and **CHRISTMAS.**

## *Laurel*

Laurel leaves were prized not only for their medicinal properties but also for their ability to cleanse the soul of guilt. In ancient Rome, laurel was believed to possess the power to purge those who had shed the blood of others, and according to legend, laurel was the one tree that was never struck by lightning. By using brooms made of laurel twigs to sweep out their sheep folds, the shepherds were carrying out a symbolic purification that would guarantee the health and safety of their sheep.

## *Olive*

For the Romans, the olive tree was associated with Pax, the goddess of peace. A messenger asking for peace of asylum often carried olive branches wrapped in wool, and wreaths made of olive or LAUREL were often used to crown the victors in military battles. As one of the ingredients in the purifying fires used on the Parilia to cleanse sheep folds and cattle stalls, olive wood was intended to protect the animals from danger and disease.

## Further Reading

Biedermann, Hans. *Dictionary of Symbolism: Cultural Icons and the Meanings Behind Them,* 1994.

Cirlot, J. E. *A Dictionary of Symbols,* 1962.

Fowler, W. Warde. *The Roman Festivals of the Period of the Republic,* 1925.

Frazer, Sir James G. *The Golden Bough: A Study in Magic and Religion,* 1931.

Hatch, Jane M. *The American Book of Days,* 1978.

Henderson, Helene and Sue Ellen Thompson. *Holidays, Festivals, and Celebrations of the World Dictionary,* 2nd ed., 1997.

James, E. O. *Seasonal Feasts and Festivals,* 1961.

Olderr, Steven. *Symbolism: A Comprehensive Dictionary,* 1986.

Scullard, H. H. *Festivals and Ceremonies of the Roman Republic,* 1981.

# *Paro Tsechu*

**Type of Holiday:** Religious (Buddhist)

**Date of Observation:** Early spring; tenth through 15th day of second month of Buddhist lunar calendar

**Where Celebrated:** Paro, Bhutan

**Symbols:** Thongdrel

## ORIGINS

One of the most popular festivals of Bhutan, a principality northeast of India in the Himalaya Mountains, is held in the town of Paro. *Tsechu* means "tenth day" and refers to the birth of the Buddha. It is also used in much the same way as "festival" is used in English.

The Paro festival commemorates the life and deeds of Padma Sambhava. Known in Bhutan as Guru Rinpoche, he was a mystic who brought Buddhism to Bhutan from Tibet. The purpose of the festival is to exorcise evil influences and to ensure good fortune in the coming year. The highlight of the five-day festival occurs before dawn on the final day, when a huge appliquéed scroll known as the THONGDREL is displayed at the local administrative and religious center known as the Dzong.

Dressed in their best clothes, people bring dried yak meat and *churra,* a puffed rice dish, to the Dzong, where they watch masked dancers perform. A series of dances, called *cham,* are performed for the festival. One of these, the Black Hat Dance, tells of the victory over a Tibetan king who tried to stamp out Buddhism. The Dance of the Four Stags commemorates the defeat of the god of the wind by Guru Rinpoche. Yet another dance, known as the Deer Dance, tells the story of how Guru Rinpoche taught Buddhism while traveling through the country on the back of a deer. The dances are performed by monks who play the roles of deities, heroes, and animals, dressed in brilliantly colored silks and brocades. They wear carved wooden or papier-mâché masks symbolizing the figures they portray. The dances are accompanied by the music of drums, bells, gongs, conch-shell trumpets, and horns—some of which are so long they touch the ground.

Other festival activities include folk dancing and singing, and performances by clowns called *atsaras.* Many of the dances and performances associated with Paro Tsechu are typical of Buddhist traditions observed in Tibet and the Ladakh area of India.

## SYMBOLS

### *Thongdrel*

The huge scroll known as the Thongdrel is unfurled from the top of the wall of the Dzong just before the first rays of the sun touch it. It is a type of *thangka* (a term that refers to a religious scroll of any size) and is so big that it covers the monastery's three-story-high wall. The Thongdrel is said to have the power to confer blessings and to provide an escape from the cycle of existence. It depicts various events in the life of Guru Rinpoche.

### Further Reading

Henderson, Helene and Sue Ellen Thompson. *Holidays, Festivals, and Celebrations of the World Dictionary*, 2nd ed., 1997.
Van Straalen, Alice. *The Book of Holidays Around the World,* 1986.

# *Paryushana*

**Type of Holiday:** Religious (Jain)
**Date of Observation:** Hindu month of Bhadrapada (August-September)
**Where Celebrated:** India
**Symbols:** Ten Cardinal Virtues

## ORIGINS

The followers of Jainism, also known as the Faith of the Conquerors, devote their lives to conquering themselves and their own human weaknesses. They adhere strictly to certain rules, the first of which (known as *ahimsa*) is that they cannot kill or hurt any living thing. This means that they can't eat meat or swat a mosquito. They can't go to war or retaliate against anyone who attacks them. They can't even be farmers, because plowing the fields would kill worms and insects. To avoid injuring living creatures, they often carry a small broom or brush with which they can sweep them out of harm's way.

The growth of Jainism and the scattering of its followers eventually led to a division over whether or not their monks should be allowed to wear clothing. One group believed that they should avoid any concession to human comfort, and that the body should not be protected from heat, cold, or rough surfaces. This group became known as the Digambaras, which means "clad in the four directions"—in other words, naked. The other group, known as the Svetambaras ("clad in white"), believed that a single white garment was permissible.

During the month of Bhadrapada in the Hindu calendar, the Jains observe an eight-day fast known as Paryushana. They confess their sins and ask forgiveness for any harm they might have caused, consciously or unconsciously, to any living thing. The fast, which allows them to eat only once a day, is observed by both the Svetambar and Digambar sects at different times. Svetambar Jains begin their fast on the 13th day of the waning half of the month, ending on the 5th day of the waxing half. Digambar Jains begin their observation on the 5th day of the waxing half and end on the 13th lunar day. They spend this period analyzing themselves and criticizing their own behavior. They beg forgiveness from one another for offenses they may have committed, whether deliberately or unknowingly, in the hope that they can restore lost friendships. They also worship the Tirthankaras or "crossing-makers"—the 24 great teachers of the Jain religion.

## SYMBOLS

### Ten Cardinal Virtues

A major focus of the self-examination that goes on during Paryushana is what are known as the Ten Cardinal Virtues: forgiveness, charity, simplicity, contentment, truthfulness, self-restraint, fasting, detachment, humility, and continence. Jain leaders lecture on the importance of pursuing these virtues and stress their cultivation. The process of cultivating the Ten Cardinal Virtues symbolizes man's emergence from an evil and depraved world to one of spiritual and moral refinement.

## Further Reading

Crim, Keith, ed. *The Perennial Dictionary of World Religions,* 1989.

Gaer, Joseph. *Holidays Around the World,* 1953.

Henderson, Helene and Sue Ellen Thompson. *Holidays, Festivals, and Celebrations of the World Dictionary,* 2nd ed., 1997.

Kelly, Aidan. *Religious Holidays and Calendars,* 1993.

MacDonald, Margaret R., ed. *The Folklore of World Holidays,* 1992.

# *Passover*
## *(Pesach)*

**Type of Holiday:** Religious (Jewish)

**Date of Observation:** Begins between March 27 and April 24; 15-21 (or 22) Nisan

**Where Celebrated:** Europe, United States, and by Jews all over the world

**Symbols:** Afikomen, Bitter Herbs, Egg, Elijah's Cup, Four Cups of Wine, Four Questions, Haggadah, Haroset, Karpas, Lamb Bone, Salt Water, Unleavened Bread (Matzoh)

## ORIGINS

According to the Bible, the Jews settled in Egypt, in the area around the Nile, at the invitation of Joseph. When the Pharoahs launched an ambitious building program, the Hebrews were forced into service and gradually became slaves. The Book of Exodus tells the story of their suffering and how their leader, Moses, brought them out of bondage and led them to the land that had been promised to their forefathers—an event considered to be the birth of the Jewish nation.

When the Pharoah referred to in Exodus (believed by scholars to be Ramses II) refused to let Moses lead the Jews out of Egypt, God sent nine plagues—including frogs, lice, locusts, fire, and hailstones—to change Pharoah's mind. But Pharoah remained unmoved, so God devised a tenth plague, sending the Angel of Death to kill the first-born son of every Egyptian household. The Jews, however, were warned ahead of time to sacrifice a lamb and sprinkle the blood on their doorposts so that the Angel of Death would "pass over" and spare their sons. Pharoah finally relented, and the Jews were allowed to leave.

Although Passover is an eight-day celebration of the Jews' deliverance from slavery in Egypt, it appears that its roots go back even further. The early inhabitants of the region known as Canaan (now Palestine) were farmers, and they held seasonal rites to honor their local gods. Their spring festival was known as Pesach, which in Hebrew meant "skipping" or "gamboling," and it apparently involved the sacrifice of lambs. When Moses led the Hebrew tribes out of slavery in Egypt and the people chose Jehovah to be their God—an event that occurred during the Hebrew month of Nisan (March-April)—the ancient spring festival of Pesach was reinterpreted to mean the "skipping over" or "passing over" of Jewish homes by the Angel of Death. Today, Pesach and Passover refer to the same holiday.

Passover is traditionally observed for seven days, from the 15th to the 21st of Nisan. Today, however, only the Jews of Israel and Reform Jews of other countries do this. Orthodox and Conservative Jews observe it for eight days, the first two of which are the most important. The primary activity is a special feast called the *Seder,* which means "order" and consists of several symbolic foods that are eaten in a particular sequence, including a hard-boiled EGG, a roasted LAMB BONE, parsley dipped in SALT WATER, BITTER HERBS, HAROSET, and matzoh or UNLEAVENED BREAD. The HAGGADAH, or story of the exodus from Egypt, is read aloud to explain the historical and religious meaning of the holiday. As the Seder comes to an end, people eat the last piece of matzoh, known as the AFIKOMEN, and thank God for the gift of their freedom.

Several features of the Seder and the accompanying narrative seem to indicate that these rituals have not been handed down intact from a particular age but have evolved from a number of different ages, providing a capsule history of the Jews. The custom of reclining on cushions while eating the meal, the preliminary dipping of parsley in salted water, and the eating of eggs as an hors d'oeuvre, for example, are all characteristic of a typical Roman banquet. Reciting the Haggadah may also have been modeled after the Roman practice of reading literary works aloud at mealtime.

The exact dates of the events related in the story of Passover are not known with any certainty. According to the Book of Exodus, some 600,000 Hebrews left Egypt after living there for 430 years. On the basis of this biblical account, scholars have calculated that they became slaves there in the fourteenth century B.C.E. and that they fled Egypt around 1270 B.C.E.

# SYMBOLS

## *Afikomen*

The *afikomen* is a piece broken off the middle of three matzoth traditionally placed under a special Pesach napkin on the Seder table. It serves both as a treat for the children and as a concluding bite for the adults. In order to keep the children awake and interested during the lengthy ritual of the Seder, the afikomen is hidden from them. At the end of the meal, they are asked to search for it, and the one who finds it is rewarded with a gift.

Another variation on this custom allows the children to "steal" the afikomen and exchange it at the end of the meal for a gift. When the afikomen gets back to the Seder table, it is broken in pieces and served to each participant as a dessert.

Little is known about the origins of the custom. The Talmud, a collection of writings about Jewish law and tradition, says that "men must not leave the paschal [Passover] meal *epikomin.*" This last word was the Greek *epi komon,* a popular expression for "going out on the town" to celebrate. This advice was later misinterpreted as "Men must not leave out the *afikomen* after the paschal meal," and this curious expression was taken to mean that some sort of special dessert had to be served at the conclusion of the Seder. This is probably where the custom of distributing small pieces of UNLEAVENED BREAD at the conclusion of the meal originated.

Another theory about the origin of the afikomen is that this piece of matzoh was a symbolic substitute for the sacrifice of a lamb at Passover, which was discontinued after the destruction of the second Temple in Jerusalem. The fact that the afikomen is usually wrapped in a napkin reminds Seder participants that the Hebrews left Egypt with their kneading troughs wrapped up in their clothes and carried on their shoulders.

### Bitter Herbs

The *maror* or bitter herbs, usually horseradish, eaten at the Seder symbolize the hardships endured by the Jews when they were slaves in Egypt. These are served in a "sandwich" between pieces of matzoh, thereby obeying the Bible's commandment (Exodus 12:8) that UNLEAVENED BREAD and bitter herbs be eaten together.

### Egg

The hard-boiled egg served at the Passover Seder represents the spiritual strength of the Jews. The fact that the egg is "roasted" serves as a reminder that in the days of the Temple in Jerusalem, animals were roasted (i.e., sacrificed) for God on this and other holidays.

Like the Easter egg in Christianity, the Seder egg also symbolizes the beginning of new life in the spring and recalls the holiday's agricultural origins.

### Elijah's Cup

In addition to the FOUR CUPS OF WINE traditionally drunk during the Passover meal, a fifth cup is filled but not drunk. Instead, the door is left

open for the prophet Elijah. According to tradition, Elijah will be the forerunner for the Messiah who will redeem Israel and the rest of the world.
He will arrive on the night of the Seder, dressed as a beggar to see how
people accept him, and will judge by their behavior whether or not they are
ready for the Messiah. After the fifth cup is filled with wine, therefore, the
children watch it eagerly to see if the level miraculously goes down, indicating that Elijah has visited their home.

The practice of leaving the door open for Elijah goes back to the Middle
Ages. Its original purpose may have been to disprove the belief that Jews
used the blood of Christian children to prepare matzoh. The door was left
open so that everyone could see exactly how it was made. Even today, leaving the door open expresses the spirit of freedom and safety that Jews feel
on this occasion, in spite of the false accusations they have had to endure.

## Four Cups of Wine

Four cups of red wine are supposed to be drunk during the Seder. But
because the Jews do not encourage or enjoy drunkenness, they usually
space out the designated drinking times and make sure that the wine is
accompanied by food or diluted with water.

Why four cups? The most popular explanation links them with the four
phrases in Exodus describing how God will redeem Israel: (1) "and I will
take you out;" (2) "and I will deliver you;" (3) "and I will redeem you;" and
(4) "and I will take you."

The custom is first mentioned in accounts dating from the middle of the
second century. Scholars trace it back to the destruction of the second Temple in Jerusalem, after which the Jews, under Roman rule, were exposed to
the customs of Roman banquets. The Romans would first drink wine while
eating vegetables dipped in vinegar (see KARPAS) or in fruit sauce (see
HAROSET). After these appetizers, they would move into the dining room for
the main course and a second glass of wine. They would have a third glass
following the meal. The fourth cup is the one drunk during the *Kiddush*, or
blessing over the wine, that is traditionally offered at Passover and other
Jewish holidays.

## Four Questions

The Seder begins with the chanting of the Kiddush prayer, the filling of the
wine glasses (see FOUR CUPS OF WINE), the breaking of the middle matzoh
(see AFIKOMEN), and the chanting of passages in either Hebrew or English

from the HAGGADAH. Then the youngest child present at the table asks the well-known Four Questions:

(1) Why is this night different from all other nights? On all other nights we may eat either leavened bread or unleavened. Why, on this night, do we eat only unleavened?

(2) On all other nights, we may eat all kinds of herbs. Why, on this night, do we eat only bitter herbs?

(3) On all other nights, we don't dip some foods into other foods. Why do we dip parsley into salt water and bitter herbs into haroset tonight?

(4) On all other nights, we may sit at table erect or leaning. Why on this night do we sit reclining?

The answers to these questions are also contained in the HAGGADAH, which is read aloud by the head of the family.

## Haggadah

The Haggadah is a compilation of stories, passages from the Bible, interpretations, benedictions, hymns, and instructions for conducting the Seder. Although portions of it are more than 2,000 years old, the basic text was put together by Rabbi Shimeon ben Gamaliel in the second century B.C.E. The story of Passover, which is read during the Seder, is introduced by a series of FOUR QUESTIONS asked by the youngest member of the family, beginning with "Why is this night different from all other nights?" Everything that follows constitutes the answer to this question. The Haggadah explains what each of the special Passover foods stands for and tells the story of how Moses led the Jewish slaves out of Egypt. The narrative is interspersed with expressions of gratitude to God for helping the Israelites escape and for guiding them on their journey to the Promised Land.

## Haroset

*Haroset* (or *charoset*) is a mixture of wine, chopped apples, nuts, sugar, and cinnamon. It symbolizes the clay used by the Jewish slaves to make bricks to build Pharoah's cities.

## Karpas

*Karpas* refers to a green vegetable, usually parsley, dipped in SALT WATER before being eaten. Because it is green, it symbolizes hope and new growth in the spring.

## Lamb Bone

The lamb bone is set on a special Seder plate, along with a roasted EGG and three matzoth (see UNLEAVENED BREAD). It symbolizes the lambs sacrificed by the Jews in Egypt, so that the blood could be painted on their doorposts and the Angel of Death would pass over their houses.

## Salt Water

The salt water in which parsley (see KARPAS) and other vegetables are dipped symbolizes the tears shed by the Hebrew slaves in Egypt.

## Unleavened Bread (Matzoh)

Unleavened bread is flat, because it is made without yeast. The unleavened bread that is served at Passover and other Jewish holidays is known as matzoh. It serves as a reminder of the Jews' hurried departure from Egypt, when there was no time to wait for the bread to rise. In addition to symbolizing the freedom gained by the Jews, matzoh also recalls the bread baked from the first grain harvested by the Jewish farmers in Palestine, thus recalling the festival's ancient agricultural roots.

Three pieces of matzoh are placed on the table at the start of the Seder. Together, they stand for unity. The top one represents the *Kohen* or priest, the middle one is called the Levite, and the bottom one is known as the Israelite — three of the earliest divisions among Jews. All Jews, the leader of the Seder explains, are brothers. Then he takes the middle of the three pieces and breaks it in half. One of these halves is the AFIKOMEN, which is spirited away from the table and hidden somewhere in the house, to be searched for later by the children. The afikomen is also the last thing eaten at the Seder, so that the taste of matzoh stays in everyone's mouth.

The best type of matzoh is made of only flour and water, without even salt to flavor it. This is the type of matzoh normally used at the Seder, and it is called the "bread of poverty" or "bread of affliction." The matzoth intended for use at Passover are usually labeled "Kosher for Pesach" on the box. While the original matzoh was round and soft, the invention of matzoh-making machines in the nineteenth century popularized the more brittle, rectangular matzoh that is eaten today.

## Further Reading

Cashman, Greer Fay. *Jewish Days and Holidays,* 1979.
Cuyler, Margery. *Jewish Holidays,* 1978.
Edidin, Ben. *Jewish Holidays and Festivals,* 1993.

Gaer, Joseph. *Holidays Around the World,* 1953.

Gaster, Theodor H. *Festivals of the Jewish Year,* 1953.

Henderson, Helene and Sue Ellen Thompson. *Holidays, Festivals, and Celebrations of the World Dictionary,* 2nd ed., 1997.

Ickis, Marguerite. *The Book of Festivals and Holidays the World Over,* 1970.

Purdy, Susan. *Festivals for You to Celebrate,* 1969.

Santino, Jack. *All Around the Year,* 1994.

# *Pentecost*
## *(Whitsunday)*

**Type of Holiday:** Religious (Christian)

**Date of Observation:** Seventh Sunday (50 days) after Easter

**Where Celebrated:** British Isles, Europe, United States, and throughout the Christian world

**Symbols:** Dew, Dove, Smoke Money, Rose

**Colors:** Pentecost is associated with the colors red and white—red for the tongues of fire that descended on the Apostles' heads, and white for the robes worn by the newly baptized.

**Related Holidays:** Easter, Shavuot

## ORIGINS

As recorded in the New Testament of the Bible, it was 50 days after **EASTER** that the Apostles gathered in Jerusalem to celebrate the Jewish festival of **SHAVUOT**. As they prayed together, the Holy Spirit descended on them in the form of "tongues of fire," enabling them to speak in other languages. Transformed from rather timid men into courageous missionaries, they immediately began to preach about Jesus Christ to the Jews from many nations who had flocked to Jerusalem for Shavuot. More than 3,000 were baptized, an event now considered to mark the birth of the Christian Church. According to tradition, this is also the day on which, centuries earlier, Moses received the Ten Commandments on Mt. Sinai, giving the Jewish religious community its start.

"Pentecost" comes from the Greek word meaning "fiftieth." Just as the Jewish feast of Shavuot comes 50 days after **PASSOVER**, Pentecost is observed 50 days after Easter. In the beginning, Pentecost included the entire 50-day period from Easter to the Descent of the Holy Spirit, although a special festival was observed on the last day. It was a period of continual rejoicing during which fasting was not permitted and prayers had to be offered while standing rather than kneeling, in honor of Christ's resurrection. The first mention of Pentecost as a separate feast occurred in the third century, when it became the second official date of the year (after Easter) when infants and catechumens (those who had been instructed in the basics of Christianity) could be baptized. The English called it Whitsunday (White Sunday), probably because of the white robes worn by the newly baptized. As the number of children left unchristened because their parents were waiting for Whitsuntide became too unwieldy, the rules regarding when people could be baptized were relaxed.

The period known as Whitsuntide (the week beginning on the Saturday before Whitsunday and ending the following Saturday) has traditionally been associated with the return of good weather and the emergence of green grass and spring flowers. A common way of observing Whitsuntide in many countries is to go out in the fields or woods and bring back green boughs to decorate a member of the village. Known variously as Green George, Jack-in-the-Green, the Leaf Man, and the Whitsuntide Lout, these woodland characters are believed to be a survival of pagan spring rites. In a game called "hunting the green man," children search for a young man dressed in leaves and moss.

In the early Christian Church, Pentecost was second in importance only to Easter. Nowadays no special ceremonies take place on this day in Roman Catholic churches, aside from the Saturday vigil and the Mass celebrated on Sunday with symbolic red vestments. In the Episcopal and Protestant churches, Pentecost is still a day for the confirmation and baptism of new members. All Christian churches celebrate Holy Communion on this day.

## SYMBOLS

### *Dew*

In rural areas of northern Europe, people still believe in the special healing power of the dew that falls during the night on the eve of Pentecost. They walk barefoot through the grass early on Sunday morning in the belief that the dew that touches their feet will cure their ills and protect them from harm. They also collect dew on pieces of bread and feed them to their pets and farm animals as protection against accidents and disease.

*Holiday Symbols*

## Dove

In both ancient and Christian art, the dove is a symbol of purity and peace. But since the earliest years of the Christian era, it has symbolized the Holy Ghost, based on the Bible's description of the descent of the Holy Spirit in John 1:32: "And John bore record, saying, I saw the spirit descending from heaven like a dove, and it abode upon him." Nowadays the dove can be seen on priestly vestments, on altars, sacred utensils, and in many religious paintings. It is customary to have a painted dove suspended over the altar during Mass on Pentecost, and some families hang a carved and painted dove over their dining room table during Whitsuntide.

Christians have come up with a number of ingenious ways of incorporating the dove into their celebration of Pentecost. At one time, real doves were often let loose during Pentecost services, or pieces of white wool were thrown down from the "Holy Ghost hole" in the church ceiling. Sometimes a slowly revolving disk bearing the figure of a white dove on a blue background would descend horizontally to announce the arrival of the Holy Spirit. In some central European countries, pieces of burning straw or wick were dropped from the hole to represent the tongues of fire (see ROSE). In France, trumpets were blown during Mass on Pentecost to signify the rushing wind that accompanied the Spirit's descent.

In Germany and Austria, it is customary to suspend a painted wooden dove over the altar on Pentecost. At Orvieto, Italy, a dove with extended wings runs along a wire in the great square in front of the cathedral, giving the illusion that the Holy Spirit is descending on the Apostles, who are gathered together on a platform set up in front of the cathedral doors.

## Smoke Money

In Scotland, Whitsunday was one of the so-called Quarter Days, the days on which rents and other payments fell due. In England, it was the day on which people paid their money to support the church. Because they were assessed on the basis of how many fireplaces they had in their houses, or according to the number of chimneys, the Whitsunday collection came to be known as "hearth" or "smoke" money.

## Rose

Just as the DOVE is a symbol of the Holy Spirit, the red rose has become a symbol for the tongues of fire that descended on the Apostles during the Holy Spirit's visit on Pentecost. Centuries ago, people used to shoot real flames from the church roof or use lit torches to represent the tongues of fire, but safety concerns eventually put a stop to the practice. Red roses became a less dangerous substitute for real flames, and huge quantities of them were often let down from the church ceiling during the Pentecost service.

In Germany, Pentecost is called Pfingsten, and the prevailing symbol of the feast is the pink and red peonies known as Pfingstrosen or "Whitsun roses."

### Further Reading

Appleton, LeRoy H., and Stephen Bridges. *Symbolism in Liturgical Art,* 1959.

Barz, Brigitte. *Festivals with Children,* 1989.

Chambers, Robert, ed. *The Book of Days,* 1864.

Dobler, Lavinia. *Customs and Holidays Around the World,* 1962.

Ferguson, George. *Signs and Symbols in Christian Art,* 1954.

Henderson, Helene and Sue Ellen Thompson. *Holidays, Festivals, and Celebrations of the World Dictionary,* 2nd ed., 1997.

Ickis, Marguerite. *The Book of Festivals and Holidays the World Over,* 1970.

Ickis, Marguerite. *The Book of Religious Holidays and Celebrations,* 1966.

Monks, James L. *Great Catholic Festivals,* 1951.

Spicer, Dorothy G. *The Book of Festivals,* 1990.

Spicer, Dorothy G. *Festivals of Western Europe,* 1994.

Urlin, Ethel L. *Festivals, Holy Days, and Saints' Days,* 1915.

Weiser, Francis X. *Handbook of Christian Feasts and Customs,* 1952.

# *Pitra Paksa Festival*
## *(Pitra Visarjana Amavasya)*

**Type of Holiday:** Religious (Hindu)

**Date of Observation:** Asvina (September-October)

**Where Celebrated:** India

**Symbols:** Kalasa, Rice, Vegetables

**Related Holidays:** All Souls' Day, Obon Festival

# ORIGINS

Hindus believe that the dead still need to be fed and clothed. They will become angry if they are not fed, and they need the clothing that is offered to them each year so they can gain admission to the resting place of dead souls, known as Swaraga, and avoid going to hell, or Naraka. If they aren't provided with what they need, accident, illness, or misfortune might befall their descendants. The two-week Pitra Paksa ("ancestors' fortnight") Festival observed in southern India is therefore one of the most important family rituals of the Hindu year, a time when people devote themselves to tending the needs of their deceased relatives.

Preparations for the festival include whitewashing houses, buying new clothes, and bathing. On the first day of the festival, one or two senior members of each family fast by avoiding all nonliquid foods, while the others eat only snacks. The floor of the area where the ancestor worship will take place—usually near the kitchen or front door—is cleaned carefully with cow dung, and *rangolli* designs are drawn on the floor with flour. A low wooden platform is placed on top of the design. A plantain leaf is laid on top of the platform (or directly on top of the rangolli design), some RICE is poured on the leaf, and the KALASA vessel is filled with water and set on top of the rice. Two butter-burning lamps are placed on either side.

The high point of the festival is the offering of a special meal to the deceased ancestors. It includes two meat dishes, no less than three VEGETABLE dishes, several kinds of snacks, and three or more (always an odd number) banana leaves filled with food. Three of these meals are prepared: One is placed on the roof, to be eaten by crows and sparrows, while the other two are consumed by humans. Sometimes Brahmans (members of the highest Hindu caste) are invited to partake of these special foods in the belief that they will ensure that the offerings reach the souls of departed family members. Occasionally one meal is fed to a cow in the belief that animals (as well as birds) are somehow connected to the ancestral spirits. During the entire two-week period, no male member of the family shaves, and no one is allowed to wear new clothes or cut his or her hair or nails. The eldest son usually performs the required religious ceremonies each day, which include offering water to the departed ancestors. On the last day of the two-week festival, known as *Amavasya*, or new moon, offerings are made to all ancestors whose day of death is unknown.

Brahmans and non-Brahmans honor the dead in quite different ways. Brahmans observe the lunar anniversaries of both parents' deaths, rather than attributing any particular importance to the Pitra Paksa fortnight. For non-Brahmans, however, the Pitra Paksa Festival is very similar to **ALL SOULS' DAY** for Christians, Day of the Dead for Mexicans, and the **OBON FESTIVAL** for Japanese Buddhists. It honors the ancestral spirits as a group, rather than individual family members who have died more recently.

## SYMBOLS

### Kalasa

The vessel known as the *kalasa* is either a new clay pot, which guarantees its purity, or one that has been cleaned thoroughly before being filled. There is no fixed rule determining who fills the kalasa with water; it may be the family member who is fasting, the head of the household, or the unmarried daughter. The water is drawn from a nearby river, irrigation channel, or well. A very specific procedure must be followed while filling the vessel, which includes chanting the name of the eldest female ancestor and placing some betel leaves and a coconut in the open top of the filled vessel.

Once the kalasa has been set in the place of worship, it is decorated with vermilion, a garland of yellow chrysanthemums (a symbol of life and prosperity), or necklaces. Sometimes it is wrapped in a sari as well. Most household shrines separate the male and female offerings that are set before the vessel. Male offerings, which might include a *pance* (waist-cloth), liquor, tobacco, and a towel, are placed on the right. Female offerings, including palm-leaf earrings and other items of jewelry, combs, and saris, are placed on the left.

The kalasa symbolizes the deceased ancestors to whom food, water, and clothing are being offered. Once the kalasa has been installed, decorated, clothed, and "fed," the family continues its worship throughout the two-week festival by burning incense and camphor.

### Rice

Rice plays an important part in this and other Hindu festivals. Raw rice is considered "hot," while cooked rice is "cool." Cooked rice is associated with funeral and mourning rituals, as well as with the spirits of the departed. Hindus of all castes put a small amount of raw rice in the corpse's mouth before it is cremated or buried. By the end of the ten-day period that is believed to mark the transition to a peaceful death, the deceased

Hindu's soul is considered to be as "cool," or as peaceful, as rice that has been cooked.

During the Pitra Paksa Festival, cooked rice is served in several different forms. *Khir,* or rice boiled in milk, is sometimes offered to Brahmans in the belief that whatever is given to them will also reach the souls of the departed. Some Hindus serve yogurt rice shaped into balls called "kalasa balls." Rice flour is also an important ingredient in several of the snacks and desserts eaten during the festival. Plain boiled rice is the main festival offering, symbolic of the ancestors' state of peaceful repose after having passed through all the stages of life. Cooked white rice is also a metaphor for their having given life to their descendants, and for the integrity of the family as a whole.

## Vegetables

Certain vegetables are a required element in the meal that is offered to the deceased ancestors, while others are taboo. This is because, as all Hindus know, the ancestors have their own preferences which must be catered to. Gourds and squashes feature prominently on the list of required vegetables because they are filled with seeds and grow on tendril-bearing vines, both of which symbolize the fertility and continuity of the family. Eggplant and potato are usually required as well, probably because they embody the principle of whiteness and purity. White is also the color of milk and of rice, and is therefore associated with nourishment and family ties. But other gourds, particularly those whose seeds are white when immature and then turn black when they're ready for planting, are strictly taboo.

Not every Hindu family has the same list of required vegetables for the ancestral feast. Some families might choose okra, for example, because it is filled with white seeds. But its skin is quite rough, and it lacks the pulpy white flesh that some other vegetables have. So while one family might be attracted to okra because of the white seeds, another family might reject it because of its rough skin and lack of white flesh. The list of vegetables offered to the ancestors at the festival is based on the characteristics of the vegetables themselves as well as on the habits and customs of each individual family.

Brahmans prepare a mixture called *saubhagya sunti* or "fortune-bestowing ginger," which they claim possesses the qualities of a thousand vegetables and can be used in the ancestors' meal to replace all other vegetables.

## Further Reading

Hanchett, Suzanne. *Coloured Rice: Symbolic Structure in Hindu Family Festivals,* 1988.

Henderson, Helene and Sue Ellen Thompson. *Holidays, Festivals, and Celebrations of the World Dictionary,* 2nd ed., 1997.

Kelly, Aidan. *Religious Holidays and Calendars,* 1993.

MacDonald, Margaret R., ed. *The Folklore of World Holidays,* 1992.

# *Pongal*
## *(Makara Sankranti)*

**Type of Holiday:** Religious (Hindu), Ancient or pagan
**Date of Observation:** Three days in mid-January
**Where Celebrated:** India
**Symbols:** Cow, Rice

## ORIGINS

One of the most colorful festivals observed in southern India, Pongal honors the sun, the earth, and the COW. Believed to be the survival of an ancient harvest festival because it falls around the time of the **WINTER SOLSTICE**, the three-day festival coincides with the harvest season and with the end of the monsoons. It is called Pongal in the state of Tamil Nadu; in Andhra Pradesh, Karnataka, and Gujarat, it is known as Makara Sankranti, because it takes place when the sun starts to move south in the zodiac from Cancer to the House of Makara (the Alligator), otherwise known as Capricorn (the Goat).

The first day, known as Bhogi Pongal, is observed as a family festival and is usually spent cleaning everything in the house. Shops, offices, and factories are cleaned as well—a symbolic washing-away of material sins. The second day is Surya Pongal, and it is set aside for worship of the Sun God, Surya. The third day, Mattu Pongal, is reserved for worshipping cattle (see COW). The fourth day, which is not always observed, is spent paying visits, reestablishing old relationships and forgotten connections.

Orthodox Hindus make a pilgrimage to Allahabad, the holy city where the Ganges and the Jumna Rivers meet, on Makara Sankranti. Sometimes as many as a million people arrive in this northern city to have their sins washed away by bathing in the Ganges. Because the festival is a time for banishing quarrels, it is common to serve visitors sugared sesamum seed, advising them to "Eat sweetly, speak sweetly." Chewing on raw sugar cane is another favorite pastime during the festival.

In some parts of India, women who want to have children take coconuts and secretly leave them in a Brahman home — or they bring gifts of betel nuts and spices to Brahman wives. Sometimes they take coconuts to their neighbors and exchange them for fruit, saying, "Take a boy and give a child."

In Ahmedabad in the state of Gujarat, Makara Sankranti is a time for competitive kite-flying. Kitemakers from other cities gather here to make their kites and see whose flies the highest. As darkness falls, the battle of the kites ends. But new kites, each carrying its own paper lamp, fill the sky with flickering lights.

## SYMBOLS

### Cow

The third day of Pongal is known as the Festival of the Cow. Cows and oxen are bathed, their horns are cleaned and polished, and garlands of flowers are hung around their necks. The main event in many Indian villages is bull-chasing: Bags of money are tied to the horns of ferocious bulls, who are allowed to stampede through the streets of the town. Young men try to catch a bull by the horns and claim the bag of money. Sometimes the horns have been sharpened and painted, which makes the chase even more dangerous and exciting.

Although bull-chasing is popular, Pongal is really a day to recognize the importance of cattle to the agricultural community. They are fed some of the newly harvested rice and showered with affection and attention. No cow is expected to work on Pongal; instead, they roam the countryside in all their flowers and finery.

### Rice

The most characteristic feature of Pongal in southern India, where rice is the staple food, is the cooking and eating of rice from the newly gathered harvest. On the second day of the festival, rice boiled in milk is offered to the Sun God, Surya — a symbolic expression of thanksgiving for the bounty of the harvest. Friends greet one another by asking, "Is it boiled?" The answer is always, "Yes, it is cooked." One of the literal meanings of *pongal,* in fact, refers to the foaming of milk without its boiling over, which is considered a very auspicious sign.

## Further Reading

Gaer, Joseph. *Holidays Around the World,* 1953.

Henderson, Helene and Sue Ellen Thompson. *Holidays, Festivals, and Celebrations of the World Dictionary,* 2nd ed., 1997.

Kelly, Aidan. *Religious Holidays and Calendars,* 1993.

MacDonald, Margaret R., ed. *The Folklore of World Holidays,* 1992.

Oki, Morihiro. *India: Fairs and Festivals,* 1989.

Sharma, Brijendra Nath. *Festivals of India,* 1978.

Thomas, Paul. *Festivals and Holidays in India,* 1971.

# Posadas, Las

**Type of Holiday:** Religious (Christian)
**Date of Observation:** December 16-24
**Where Celebrated:** Mexico, United States
**Symbols:** Piñata
**Related Holidays:** Christmas, Christmas Eve

## ORIGINS

Las Posadas is a Mexican tradition whose popularity is growing in the United States, especially southern California and the southwestern states. For nine nights, beginning on December 16, groups of friends and neighbors visit each other's houses and reenact Mary's and Joseph's search for shelter (Spanish *posada*) as they traveled from Nazareth to Bethlehem during the days preceding the birth of the infant Jesus. Each night the group knocks on someone's door, requests lodging, and is refused. Finally, on **CHRISTMAS EVE**, their request is granted. Once everyone is inside the house, there is feasting and merrymaking.

Las Posadas can take many different forms. Sometimes the processions are held in the streets and churches, with villagers carrying lighted candles and children pulling a wagon on which a nativity scene has been erected. There are also larger, more public presentations of *las posadas* that are open to townspeople and tourists. In some areas, *posadas* is synonymous with "parties," which are given on each of the nine nights leading up to CHRIST-MAS. Everyone gathers at a particular house on the ninth evening, and the search of Mary and Joseph for lodgings is reenacted at the door of each room. On the stroke of midnight, the hostess leads them to a room where a table has been prepared. Images of Mary and Joseph are placed on the table and the feasting begins. An essential element of the *posadas* party is a PIÑATA for the children.

Among the poor, it is customary for friends and neighbors to get together and share the expenses involved in celebrating Las Posadas. This is especially true in Mexico, where Christmas is more of a community than a family event. In the United States, one of the most famous Posadas celebrations takes place on Olvera Street in Los Angeles.

## SYMBOLS

### *Piñata*

The piñata—originally a clay or pottery container covered with papier-mâché and colored tissue paper to resemble an animal, bird, clown, ball, or some other playful object—originated in Italy during the Renaissance, where it was used as an entertainment at adult masquerade balls. But today it is primarily a party game for children. Blindfolded, they take turns trying to break the piñata, which is hung from a tree or a hook in the ceiling, with a stick. Once it shatters, everyone scrambles to collect the small toys and candy that have been concealed inside.

The last piñata of the Christmas season in Mexico is broken on Christmas Eve. After the final posada is held earlier in the evening and everyone has returned from midnight Mass, there is a big feast. The children get so excited trying to break open the piñata that they often start swinging the stick at each other.

## Further Reading

Crippen, T. G. *Christmas and Christmas Lore,* 1990.

Henderson, Helene and Sue Ellen Thompson. *Holidays, Festivals, and Celebrations of the World Dictionary,* 2nd ed., 1997.

MacDonald, Margaret R., ed. *The Folklore of World Holidays,* 1992.

Purdy, Susan. *Festivals for You to Celebrate,* 1969.

Santino, Jack. *All Around the Year,* 1994.

Spicer, Dorothy G. *The Book of Festivals,* 1990.

# Powamû Festival
### (Bean-Planting Festival)

**Type of Holiday:** Ethnic (Native American)

**Date of Observation:** Late January-early February for eight days

**Where Celebrated:** Arizona

**Symbols:** Bean Sprouts, Flogging, Masks, Soyokmana

**Related Holidays:** Hopi Snake Dance, Niman Katchina, Soyaluna

## ORIGINS

The Hopi Indians believe that for six months of the year, ancestral spirits called the Katchinas leave their mountain homes and visit the tribe, bringing health to the people and rain for their crops. The midwinter ceremony known as the Powamû celebrates their return, just as the **NIMAN KATCHINA** ceremony in July celebrates their departure.

Preparations for the ceremony include repainting the MASKS that will be worn by the individuals impersonating the Katchinas. On the third day, young men bring in baskets of wet sand, which they leave near the entrance to the kiva, or ceremonial meeting room. A hot fire burns throughout the eight days of the Powamû in the kiva of every Hopi village, and blankets are stretched across the opening so that the atmosphere inside is like that of a hothouse. Each man who enters the kiva during this period carries a basket or bowl of sand into it and plants a handful of beans, which sprout quickly in all the heat and humidity.

The Powamû culminates in a dance that takes place in the nine kivas that dot the mesa in northeastern Arizona. The dancers' bodies are painted red and white, and they wear squash blossoms — actually yucca fiber twisted into the shape of a squash blossom — in their hair. They put on white kilts and sashes and leggings with a fringe of shells tied down the side. The dance takes place in two lines facing each other, inside the sweltering kiva. When it is over, the dancers leave for the next village's kiva, and another group arrives. During the course of the night, each group dances at all nine kivas.

Wearing MASKS and painted bodies, the Katchinas arrive the next morning. They bring dolls and rattles for the girls, bows and arrows for the boys, and for both the green BEAN SPROUTS that have been growing in the overheated kivas. Clowns run around making jokes, tripping each other, and performing pantomimes for everyone's enjoyment. The festival concludes with a huge feast in which bean sprouts are the main ingredient. From this time until their departure in July, the Katchinas appear regularly in masked ceremonies performed in the Hopi villages.

## SYMBOLS

### Bean Sprouts

Sprouted beans are a symbol of fertility. Since the Hopis depend on the Katchinas to bring rain and other conditions essential to the growth of their crops, bean sprouts also symbolize the approaching spring.

### Flogging

Until the age of nine or ten, Hopi children believe that the Katchinas who appear at the Powamû and other ceremonial dances are superhuman. When they have matured, they are told that the real Katchinas no longer visit the earth but are impersonated by men wearing MASKS. The price for acquiring this knowledge, however, is participation in a ritual flogging or whipping ceremony. The children are never struck hard enough to cause real pain, and the ritual is not intended to be cruel. Sometimes a child who is particularly frightened is not actually flogged at all, but instead has a yucca whip whirled over his or her head. Occasionally an adult will be flogged as well, which is believed to promote healing.

On four successive mornings, the child who has been flogged is taken to a place on the mesa where he or she makes an offering at a shrine and casts meal toward the sun. During this period the child is not allowed to eat salt or meat, but on the fourth day, these restrictions are lifted. From this time onward, the child is allowed to look at the Katchinas without their masks and at other sacred objects in the kiva without incurring any punishment.

The flogging ceremony symbolizes the revelation of the secret of Hopi life: the knowledge that the Katchinas are not really spirits but men dressed to represent them.

## Masks

The masks worn by the men who impersonate the Katchinas during the Powamû Festival may vary from year to year, but some of the masks remain constant. Before the dance takes place, the masks are repainted and refurbished. They are designed to fit closely over the head, hiding it completely, with a ruff of feathers, fur, or spruce at the neck. The face usually resembles a bird, beast, monster, or man — or some combination thereof. Those who wear the Katchina masks usually carry an object associated with the being they represent — for example, a bow and arrow, a yucca whip, or feathers.

The female Katchinas, who are impersonated by men, wear wigs of long hair styled in the flat swirls over the ears known as squash blossoms, a symbol of virginity.

## Soyokmana

The group of Katchinas that visit each Hopi village during the Powamû Festival usually includes Soyokmana, a witch-like creature carrying a crook and a bloody knife. The group goes from house to house demanding food, receiving gifts, and presenting BEAN SPROUTS. When the food they are offered does not meet their standards, the Katchinas make hooting and whistling noises and refuse to leave until they have been properly fed. Sometimes Soyokmana uses her crook to hook a child around the neck and hold him or her there, screaming in terror. Parents tell their children that this is a punishment for being naughty.

## Further Reading

Cohen, Hennig, and Tristram Potter Coffin, eds. *The Folklore of American Holidays,* 2nd ed., 1991.

Fergusson, Erna. *Dancing Gods: Indian Ceremonials of New Mexico and Arizona,* 1931.

Fewkes, Jesse Walter. *Tusayan Katcinas and Hopi Altars,* 1990.

Henderson, Helene and Sue Ellen Thompson. *Holidays, Festivals, and Celebrations of the World Dictionary,* 2nd ed., 1997.

Leach, Maria, ed. *Funk & Wagnalls Standard Dictionary of Folklore, Mythology, & Legend,* 1984.

# Procession of the Swallow

**Type of Holiday:** Folkloric, Calendar
**Date of Observation:** March 1
**Where Celebrated:** Greece
**Symbols:** Ivy, Swallow
**Related Holidays:** Martenitza

## ORIGINS

The Procession of the Swallow is a Greek custom observed on March 1 in celebration of the arrival of spring. Children go from house to house in pairs, carrying a rod from which a basket full of IVY is hung. At the end of the rod is an effigy of a bird made of wood with tiny bells around its neck. This is the SWALLOW from which the festival takes its name.

As they proceed through the village, the children sing "swallow songs" that go back more than 2,000 years. The woman of the house takes a few ivy leaves from the basket and places them in her hen's nest in the hope that they will encourage the hen to lay more eggs. The children receive a few eggs in return, and they move on to the next house.

## SYMBOLS

### Ivy

Because it stays green all year long, the ivy that is carried from house to house during the Procession of the Swallow is a symbol of health and growth. It is believed to possess the power to keep hens and other domestic animals from succumbing to disease and to increase their fertility.

### Swallow

At one time it was widely believed that the swallow hibernated in the mud during the winter, reemerging with the advent of spring. For this reason it became a symbol for spring itself.

In Christian art, the swallow often appears in scenes of the Annunciation and of the Nativity, where it is usually shown nesting under the eaves or in holes in the wall. Just as it symbolized a rebirth from the death-like state of winter, it also became a symbol of the Resurrection of Christ.

## Further Reading

Ferguson, George. *Signs and Symbols in Christian Art,* 1954.

Henderson, Helene and Sue Ellen Thompson. *Holidays, Festivals, and Celebrations of the World Dictionary,* 2nd ed., 1997.

Ickis, Marguerite. *The Book of Festivals and Holidays the World Over,* 1970.

Leach, Maria, ed. *Funk & Wagnalls Standard Dictionary of Folklore, Mythology, & Legend,* 1984.

# *Purim*
## *(Feast of Lots)*

**Type of Holiday:** Religious (Jewish)

**Date of Observation:** Fourteenth day of Adar (February-March)

**Where Celebrated:** Europe, Israel, United States, and by Jews all over the world

**Symbols:** Hamantaschen, Kreplach, Megillah, Noisemakers, Purim Plays, Queen Esther, Shalachmanot

**Related Holidays:** Carnival, Halloween

## ORIGINS

Six hundred years before the Christian era, most of the Jews were slaves in Persia. Ahasuerus, the Persian king, had married the most beautiful girl he could find, Esther, without knowing that she was Jewish. Mordecai, her cousin and guardian, advised her not to reveal her identity as a Jew. After the marriage took place, Mordecai overheard two of the king's soldiers plotting to kill him. Their plans were foiled, and Mordecai was praised for having saved the king's life.

Mordecai's fortunes were reversed, however, when the king decided to appoint Haman as prime minister. Haman took a dislike to Mordecai, who refused to bow down before the new prime minister. Haman decided that Mordecai should be killed and persuaded the king to let him destroy the empire's entire Jewish population along with him. He cast lots (*pur* is the ancient Akkadian word for "lot") to find out which day would be the most auspicious for carrying out his evil plan. This means that he threw small sticks or stones on the ground, using them in much the same way that dice are used today to make a decision based on chance. The lots told him that things would go especially well on the 14th of Adar.

When Mordecai heard about Haman's plan, he rushed to tell Queen Esther, knowing that if she told the king she was Jewish, the slaughter would not take place. Esther was worried that her husband might be angry with her for concealing her background, and she told Mordecai she needed to summon her strength before she could confront the king. So Mordecai, Esther, and all the Persian Jews fasted and prayed for three days, at the end of which she felt brave enough to tell Ahasuerus the truth. Recalling that Mordecai had once saved his life, the king was grateful to Esther and Mordecai for revealing Haman's evil nature. Haman and his ten sons were hung from the gallows, and Mordecai became the new prime minister. In his first official act as the king's top adviser, Mordecai sent letters rolled into scrolls (see MEGILLAH) to everyone in the kingdom, telling them what had happened and declaring the next day a holiday.

Purim was not observed widely until the second century, when it was referred to as the Day of Mordecai or Day of Protection. But even the earliest celebrations included reciting the story of Esther and exchanging gifts (see SHALACHMANOT). It is customary to serve a large meal, known as the *Seudah,* in the afternoon rather than the evening. Turkey is a popular main dish at this meal, and there are usually KREPLACH in the soup. HAMAN-TASCHEN are the favorite Purim dessert.

Scholars have pointed out that the story of Esther cannot possibly be factual, since none of the Persian kings had a wife named Esther, and none had a prime minister named Haman. It is also highly unlikely that a Persian king could marry a Jewish bride without knowing it, since Persian kings were only allowed to marry into one of the seven leading families of the realm. How do they account, then, for the origin of Purim? Since the name of the holiday is similar to the Persian word meaning "first," some scholars think that Purim goes back to the old Persian New Year festival, which was celebrated around the time of the **VERNAL EQUINOX.**

Whatever its origins, Purim remains a happy occasion. Children dress up in costumes and put on PURIM PLAYS that tell the story of the holiday. It is also a time for sharing food with friends and for charity to the poor.

# SYMBOLS

## *Hamantaschen*

Hamantaschen are small pastries filled with a mixture of honey and poppy seeds. In Israel they are called *Oznei Haman,* which means "Haman's ears" and refers to the old European custom of cutting off a criminal's ears before hanging him. Elsewhere they are called "Haman's pockets," a reference to the fact that the legendary Haman's pockets were filled with money from all the bribes he had taken. Some claim that hamantaschen look like the three-cornered hat that Haman wore, but there is no evidence that such hats were in use at that time.

The custom of eating pastries filled with poppy seeds at Purim already existed in the Middle Ages. Sometimes the pastries are filled with prune jam, in commemoration of a plum merchant from Bohemia who, along with the rest of the Bohemian Jews, was saved from persecution in the early eighteenth century.

## *Kreplach*

On the eve of Purim, it is traditional among European Jews to eat kreplach, small pockets of dough filled with ground meat or cheese, boiled, and usually served in soup. For reasons that are not entirely clear, eating kreplach is also associated with beating and banging. They are eaten on the eve of **YOM KIPPUR** because people beat their breasts while reciting their sins. They are also eaten on the last day of **SUKKOT**, when the willow branches are beaten, and on Purim because of the banging that accompanies the mention of Haman's name (see PURIM PLAYS).

## *Megillah*

The Megillah is a scroll containing the Book of Esther, symbolic of the rolled letters that Mordecai sent throughout the Persian Empire, explaining how the Jews had been saved and declaring an official holiday. On Purim, the Megillah is read in the synagogue using a special melodic rhythm. Sometimes it is read in a comical way; for example, when the reader comes to the names of Haman's ten sons, it is common to read them very quickly so that they all blend together. Whenever Haman's name is mentioned, people boo and stamp their feet. The same spirit of celebration and merriment that is seen in the PURIM PLAYS and in the election of a QUEEN ESTHER carries over into the synagogue. Sometimes Haman's name is written in chalk on the soles of slippers so that the stomping and shuffling will make it wear off.

The Megillah is the only book of the Bible in which illustrations are permitted. The Jewish religion forbids drawing an image of God, but God's name is not mentioned in the Megillah, which has been illustrated by a number of artists over the centuries. The container in which the Megillah was traditionally kept was often decorated as well.

## Noisemakers

The *grager* (also spelled *gregger*) is the most popular noisemaker on Purim. It is used to drown out the sound of Haman's name during the reading of the MEGILLAH. Because the Bible instructs Jews to wipe out the memory of Amalek, the leader of the tribe from which Haman was descended, the use of noisemakers symbolically eliminates the evil prime minister who was nearly responsible for wiping out the Persian Jews. In Israel, children often use pop guns or cap guns as their noisemakers.

Haman was so universally detested that in some Jewish communities, making noise was not enough. The people also made effigies of Haman and burned them.

## Purim Plays

During the Middle Ages, the celebration of Purim included masquerades, jesters, musicians, and actors. It was, in fact, the Jewish counterpart of the Christian **CARNIVAL** celebration. But Purim plays didn't really become popular until the sixteenth century. Young men and women dressed in costumes would go from house to house in the Jewish community, parodying the characters described in the MEGILLAH. Ahasuerus, for example, might resemble the local sheriff, and Haman was often modeled after the town drunkard. They also poked fun at other Biblical figures and at contemporary Jewish life. A surefire way to get laughs was to mock the rabbi's recital of the prayer known as the Kiddush by reeling off a meaningless string of Hebrew words or by chanting obscure verses from the Bible that had nothing to do with one another. In return for the entertainment they provided, the players received money or treats.

This kind of door-to-door theater eventually gave way to actual stage performances and folklore plays. Up until World War II, such plays were common in Germany and eastern Europe during the month of Adar. Although they were more formal, these Purim plays still retained their burlesque character, often degenerating into vulgarity and even obscenity. They were tolerated rather than encouraged by the Jewish authorities — and, in some cases, prohibited.

In western Europe, North America, and Israel, the plays gave way to masquerade parties for adults and children, and to beauty contests held to select a QUEEN ESTHER. Masquerading remains especially popular in Israel, where Purim is an official school holiday and children roam the streets in all kinds of costumes, much as they do on **HALLOWEEN** in the United States.

## Queen Esther

Just as the celebration of **TWELFTH NIGHT** involved the crowning of a mock "king," a young boy was crowned Purim King, a custom that dates back to the fourteenth century. In modern times, especially in the United States and at the Purim Carnival in Tel Aviv, the winner of a beauty contest is crowned as Queen Esther.

Scholars believe that these mock kings and queens who are chosen to reign for just the brief period of the festival are actually a survival of a very ancient custom, which was to install a temporary monarch during the brief period between the end of one year and the beginning of the next.

## Shalachmanot

*Shalachmanot* is the word used to describe the Purim gifts that parents give to children, and friends and relatives exchange with each other. Gifts are also made to rabbis and teachers. Donating to the poor and the needy is part of the Purim tradition as well. In the United States, it usually takes the form of presenting Purim baskets to poor families and making contributions to various Jewish funds.

Cakes, candies, and fruit have always been popular Shalachmanot items, along with books, clothing, and other useful items. Sephardic children (the descendants of Jews from Spain and Portugal) prefer cakes baked in the shape of the MEGILLAH, QUEEN ESTHER, or Mordecai riding on a horse. Jewish bakers in Jerusalem and other communities compete with one another to see who can make the most interesting Purim cakes.

## Further Reading

Cashman, Greer Fay. *Jewish Days and Holidays,* 1979.

Crim, Keith, ed. *The Perennial Dictionary of World Religions,* 1989.

Cuyler, Margery. *Jewish Holidays,* 1978.

Edidin, Ben. *Jewish Holidays and Festivals,* 1993.

Gaer, Joseph. *Holidays Around the World,* 1953.

Gaster, Theodor H. *Festivals of the Jewish Year,* 1953.

Henderson, Helene and Sue Ellen Thompson. *Holidays, Festivals, and Celebrations of the World Dictionary*, 2nd ed., 1997.

MacDonald, Margaret R., ed. *The Folklore of World Holidays,* 1992.

# *Raksha Bandhan*
## *(Janai Purnima, Brother and Sister Day)*

**Type of Holiday:** Religious (Hindu, Buddhist)
**Date of Observation:** July-August; Hindu month of Sravana
**Where Celebrated:** India, Nepal
**Symbols:** Rakhi

## ORIGINS

Raksha Bandhan is a day for brothers and sisters to reaffirm their bonds of affection. It is observed by the Hindus in northern India and by both Hindus and Buddhists in Nepal, where members of both religions often celebrate in each other's temples. Sisters tie colorful threads or amulets (see RAKHI) on their brothers' wrists and put dots of vermilion paste on their brothers' foreheads while praying for them to live a long life. Brothers, in turn, give their sisters gifts—usually a piece of jewelry or clothing, or perhaps some money—while promising to protect them throughout their lives. In families where there are only boys or only girls, a friend or relative is asked to act as a brother or sister during the festival.

In Nepal, the Brahmins (members of the highest caste) put golden threads around everyone's wrists while reciting a mantra or sacred word to give the thread the power to protect its wearer. The *Janai* or "sacred threads" which all Brahmins wear around their necks are also changed at this time. This three-stringed thread necklace is said to symbolize the Hindu trinity of Brahma, Vishnu, and Siva.

## SYMBOLS

### Rakhi

Usually made from a few colorful cotton or silk threads, or sometimes from silver and gold threads, the *rakhi* symbolizes protection against evil during the coming year. According to legend, when Sultan Babar, the Mohammedan Emperor at Delhi, received a portion of a silken bracelet from the Rajputanan princess who was in grave danger, he immediately rushed to help her. Such a relationship was considered to be like that of brother and sister, and it became customary in India for men who had received *rakhis* to risk their lives, if necessary, to help their "sisters" and rescue them from danger.

Another legend says that Sachi, the consort of the Hindu god Indra, tied such a thread bracelet around the right wrist of her husband when he was disgraced in battle by the demon forces. Indra fought the demons again and was victorious this time.

Old, worn-out *rakhis* must be discarded in the water of a pool, sacred tank, or river.

## Further Reading

Henderson, Helene and Sue Ellen Thompson. *Holidays, Festivals, and Celebrations of the World Dictionary*, 2nd ed., 1997.
Kelly, Aidan. *Religious Holidays and Calendars*, 1993.
MacDonald, Margaret R., ed. *The Folklore of World Holidays*, 1992.
Spicer, Dorothy Gladys. *The Book of Festivals*, 1990.

# Ramadan

**Type of Holiday:** Religious (Islamic)
**Date of Observation:** Ninth month of the Islamic lunar calendar
**Where Celebrated:** Africa, Egypt, India, Indonesia, Iran, Iraq, Jordan,

Lebanon, Malaya, Morocco, Pakistan, Saudi Arabia, Syria, Thailand, Turkey, and throughout the Muslim world

**Symbols:** Fasting, Five Pillars, Iftar, New Moon, Sahur

**Related Holidays:** Hajj, Id al-Fitr, Laylat al-Qadr

# ORIGINS

Ramadan is the ninth month of the Islamic year, and it marks the anniversary of more than one significant event. It was during Ramadan that the Koran was first revealed to the Prophet Muhammad (see **LAYLAT AL-QADR**). According to legend, as Muhammad sat alone in the wilderness, the angel Gabriel came to him with a golden tablet in his hands and told the Prophet to read what was written on it. This was the essence of the Koran, just as the Tablets of the Law received by Moses on Mt. Sinai were the essence of the Old Testament. The Battle of Badr—the first battle between the idol worshippers of Mecca and the Muslims of Medina—also occurred during Ramadan, resulting in a glorious victory for the Muslims.

FASTING during the holy month of Ramadan is one of the FIVE PILLARS or requirements of the Islamic faith. It begins with the sighting of the NEW MOON, usually on the 28th day of the previous month. In many Islamic countries, the start of Ramadan is announced with the firing of a gun or cannon on the eve of the first day, since the Islamic "day" begins at sunset. Cannon fire is also used to signal the beginning and end of each day's fast. The morning hours are typically spent reciting the Koran, while the remainder of the day is spent sleeping, reading, and praying. As sunset approaches, Muslims gather in the mosque to chant the Koran and pray. When the gun announcing the end of the fast is fired, they return home to eat. It is compulsory for every Muslim over the age of 12 to observe the fast. Children learn to fast by doing so gradually, until they are old enough to do so without injuring their health.

Because the Islamic calendar is lunar, the observation of Ramadan moves through the year, eventually occurring in each of the seasons. When it falls at the height of summer, the fast is even more difficult to observe. The days can be nearly 16 hours long, and although Muslims are permitted to hold water in their mouths for a moment, they cannot drink any until the sun goes down.

Like the Christian **LENT** or the period between **ROSH HASHANAH** and **YOM KIPPUR** for Jews, Ramadan is a time for self-examination and increased religious devotion. The fast ends when the new moon is again sighted and the month of Shawwal begins. It is followed by the **ID AL-FITR** or Festival of Breaking Fast, which lasts for three days and is marked by feasting and the exchange of gifts.

## SYMBOLS

### Fasting

The rules regarding the Ramadan fast are very stringent. No food or drink is permitted between sunrise and sunset; kissing, smoking, bathing, sexual intercourse, and receiving injections are forbidden as well. Some Muslims even try to avoid swallowing their saliva or opening their mouths more than is absolutely necessary to draw in fresh air. Only travellers, mothers with young babies, young children, the aged, and those who are very ill are excused from the requirements of the fast. Menstruating women are also exempt, but they must make up for the lost fast days at some point during the year. The same rule applies to days lost for health or travel reasons.

While the days are spent fasting, each night the fast is broken with a feast. It is customary to begin with a white soup made of wheat broiled in meat broth. This is followed later by a regular dinner of meat, rice, and vegetables. The rule is that when it becomes light enough outside to distinguish a white thread from a black one, the fast must be resumed. Muslims believe that whoever observes the fast faithfully and with pure intentions will have his or her sins forgiven. Fasting during Ramadan is said to be 30 times more effective than doing so at any other time of year.

The purpose of fasting is to teach the self-discipline that is needed to prepare for the suffering that Muslims may have to face in the course of obeying their God. It is also a powerful means of defeating Satan, because the passions that are Satan's weapons are strengthened by eating and drinking. Finally, fasting is a communal experience that makes everyone more aware of what it is like to feel hunger.

According to the Prophet, there are five things that will undo the good that has been acquired through fasting: telling a lie, denoucing someone behind his or her back, slander, a false oath, and greed or covetousness.

### Five Pillars

The Five Pillars of Islam are the fundamental tenets or requirements that are accepted by all branches of the Muslim faith. They are as follows:

(1) *Shahadah:* The duty to recite the creed of Islam: "There is no god but Allah, and Muhammad is His Prophet."

(2) *Salah:* The duty to worship God with prayer five times each day.

(3) *Zakah:* The duty to be charitable, to distribute alms, and to help the needy.

(4) *Sawm:* The observance of the Fast of Ramadan.

(5) *Hajj:* The duty to make a pilgrimage to Mecca at least once in a lifetime.

Fasting during Ramadan is the Fourth Pillar, although the first two Pillars are considered the most essential (i.e., no one who disregards them can be considered a Muslim).

## Iftar

When the fast ends at sunset each day during Ramadan, the meal that is taken to break the fast is called *iftar.* It is a happy occasion in most Muslim families. Foods that have been prepared at home or purchased at the market are spread out on a table while everyone sits around and waits for the sun to go down.

The timing of iftar is usually announced on radio and television, but the old tradition is to listen for the call from the minarets of the mosque. Muslims usually break their fast by first eating a date or taking a drink of water—in imitation of the Prophet, who broke his fast in a similar manner.

## New Moon

The Islamic calendar is lunar, which means that each month begins with the appearance of the new moon. In Muslim countries, everyone comes out of the house to see the new moon of Ramadan. Many climb up on their roofs or go to the tops of nearby hills to get a better view. Once the new moon has been sighted, everyone congratulates each other and hurries back inside to prepare for the early morning meal (see SAHUR).

If the weather is cloudy and the moon is difficult to see, Islamic countries broadcast the news of its sighting. Once the appearance of the new moon is confirmed by at least two people, the news is announced on radio and television. Before these means of communication were invented, it was traditionally announced by firing a cannon.

## Sahur

The *sahur* is a meal taken just before dawn and the start of the day's fast during the month of Ramadan. In cities and towns, many people walk through the streets in the early morning hours, beating drums and playing flutes or calling out to let people know that it is time to partake of the pre-dawn meal.

If Ramadan falls during the winter, when the nights are long and people have plenty of time to rest, sahur is a full meal. But on short summer nights, because of the limited amount of time between IFTAR and sahur, the early morning meal is very light and simple. After it is over, everyone pre-pares for morning prayer, worshipping either at the mosque or at home.

## Further Reading

Ahsan, M. M. *Muslim Festivals,* 1987.

Crim, Keith, ed. *The Perennial Dictionary of World Religions,* 1989.

Gaer, Joseph. *Holidays Around the World,* 1953.

Glassé, Cyril. *The Concise Encyclopedia of Islam,* 1989.

Henderson, Helene and Sue Ellen Thompson. *Holidays, Festivals, and Cele-brations of the World Dictionary,* 2nd ed., 1997.

Pike, Royston. *Round the Year with the World's Religions,* 1993.

Von Grunebaum, G. D. *Muhammadan Festivals,* 1988.

# Rath Yatra
## *(Jagannatha Festival, Car Festival)*

**Type of Holiday:** Religious (Hindu)

**Date of Observation:** Hindu month of Asadha (June-July)

**Where Celebrated:** India

**Symbols:** Chariot

## ORIGINS

Jagannatha, whose name means "Lord of the World," is a form of the Hindu god Krishna worshipped primarily in the state of Orissa, India. The Jagannatha Temple in Puri, one of the largest Hindu temples in India, is a pilgrimage site for his worshippers and the focus of a major festival observed at the end of June. Wooden images of Jagannatha, his brother

Balabhadra, and his sister Subhadra are carried in procession in three huge CHARIOTS or carts that resemble temples and are called *raths*. Jagannatha's is the largest—as high as a three-story building—and all three chariots are drawn along the processional route by thousands of devotees.

Early on the morning of the festival, 108 pitchers of water are drawn from a well reserved for the occasion, and the images of Jagannatha and his siblings are washed with reverence and placed in their respective chariots. These huge, ornate vehicles are then dragged from the temple to Gundicha Mandir, the god's summer house, a distance of about a mile and a half. Seven days later, the chariots return to the temple, where they are disassembled and their materials used to make religious relics.

At one time, worshippers would throw themselves under the wheels of the chariot as it moved forward in the belief that they would be guaranteed a holy death. Nowadays this practice has been forbidden, but people still flock to Puri to take part in the procession and the feast that follows. Similar festivals are held in other Indian cities where there are temples dedicated to Jagannatha, but participation in the procession at Puri is considered to be the greatest honor.

The Jagannatha Festival is very popular because distinctions among the castes are suspended on this day. All Hindus are considered equal, and everyone has to eat the food prepared at the shrine by low caste men.

## SYMBOLS

### *Chariot*

The main chariot containing the image of Jagannatha has a yellow-and-orange striped canopy 45 feet high, with 16 wheels seven feet in diameter. As it is pulled through the city along the established processional path, devotees have an opportunity for *darsana* or "sight" of the god. They may toss flowers, break coconuts, or sprinkle the image with water as the cart passes before them. Because the moving chariot represents an inexorable force that can crush anything in its path, Jagannatha's name has entered the English language as the word "juggernaut."

The journey of the huge chariot commemorates Krishna's journey from the village of Gokul, where he had been raised by cowherds, back to Mathura, the city of his birth, where his divine mission was to kill the wicked king, Kamsa.

## Further Reading

Crim, Keith, ed. *The Perennial Dictionary of World Religions,* 1989.

Eliade, Mircea. *The Encyclopedia of Religion,* 1897.

Gaer, Joseph. *Holidays Around the World,* 1953.

Henderson, Helene and Sue Ellen Thompson. *Holidays, Festivals, and Celebrations of the World Dictionary,* 2nd ed., 1997.

Kelly, Aidan. *Religious Holidays and Calendars,* 1993.

Leach, Maria, ed. *Funk & Wagnalls Standard Dictionary of Folklore, Mythology, & Legend,* 1984.

# *Rocket Festival*
### *(Boun Bang Fay, Bun Bang Fai)*

**Type of Holiday:** Folkloric, Religious (Buddhist)

**Date of Observation:** April-May; full moon day of Vaisakha

**Where Celebrated:** Laos, Thailand, United States

**Symbols:** Rocket

**Related Holidays:** Vesak

## ORIGINS

The Festival of the Rockets in Laos marks the coming of the rainy season. It provides people with an excuse to get together and celebrate during a time when the weather makes almost any work impossible. Known as Bun Bang Fai (*bun* means "festival" in Laos), the festival was originally intended to guarantee good crops. But with the arrival of Buddhism, it also became a commemoration of the birth, enlightenment, and death of Buddha.

The festival takes its name from the main event: a contest among *wat* (temple) communities to see which can build and launch the most successful ROCKET. After the religious ceremonies associated with the festival are over, people dress in traditional costumes and gather outdoors. The rockets are traditionally bamboo poles up to 20 feet in length, decorated with dragons and colored streamers and filled with a special gunpowder mix. They are judged not only on the basis of how far they fly when launched, but on how beautifully they are decorated. Buddhist monks are generally the best rocket makers.

The Rocket Festival was brought to the United States by Laotians who immigrated in the 1970s and 1980s. Since there is no rainy season in the United States, Bun Bang Fai is observed there primarily for nostalgic reasons, and to introduce Americans to Laotian culture.

## SYMBOLS
### *Rocket*

Bun Bang Fai dates back to a time when Laotians believed in many gods, and would fire rockets in hopes of persuading them to send the rain needed for the rice harvest. The rocket was seen as a much more immediate way of communicating with the gods than the traditional methods of prayer and sacrifice.

The rocket contests that are held today have less to do with religion and agriculture than with competition among neighborhoods and between civic and military groups. Officials judging the contest usually watch from a grandstand and give prizes for the most brilliant, the fastest, and the highest rocket.

### Further Reading

Henderson, Helene and Sue Ellen Thompson. *Holidays, Festivals, and Celebrations of the World Dictionary*, 2nd ed., 1997.
MacDonald, Margaret R., ed. *The Folklore of World Holidays*, 1992.
Van Straalen, Alice. *The Book of Holidays Around the World*, 1986.

# *Rosh Hashanah*
## *(Jewish New Year, Day of Remembrance)*

**Type of Holiday:** Religious (Jewish)
**Date of Observation:** 1 and 2 Tishri; between September 6 and October 4
**Where Celebrated:** By Jews all over the world

**Symbols:** Book of Life, Challah, Honey, Kittel, Shanah Tovah Cards, Shofar, Tashlikh Ceremony

**Colors:** Many Jews wear white clothing on Rosh Hashanah to remind themselves of the holiness and purity of the festival.

**Related Holidays:** New Year's Day, Yom Kippur

# ORIGINS

The Jewish year begins around the time of the autumn equinox (September 21-23), at the beginning of the month of Tishri. The first ten days of the month are known as the High Holy Days. The New Year celebration, Rosh Hashanah, is observed on the first and second of these days, when God opens the sacred BOOK OF LIFE and judges people on the basis of their actions over the past year. The next several days are known as the Days of Penitence, a period during which Jews can influence their fate by making amends for the wrongs they have committed during the year. The tenth and last of the High Holy Days is **YOM KIPPUR**, the Day of Atonement or the day on which their fates for the coming year are inscribed and sealed.

Unlike the secular observance of **NEW YEAR'S DAY**, Rosh Hashanah marks the start of a very solemn season. The story of Abraham is read in the synagogue, and the blowing of the SHOFAR serves as a call to penitence and a reminder of Abraham's willingness to obey God. Jews ponder their behavior and think about what they can do to make themselves better people. All debts from the past year are supposed to be settled before Rosh Hashanah, and many Jews ask forgiveness from their friends and families for any slights or transgressions they may have committed.

Rosh Hashanah is observed for two days in countries outside of Palestine. Back in the days when travel was dangerous and difficult, and messages often failed to arrive on time, Jews living in foreign countries weren't sure exactly when certain holidays should be celebrated. In such instances they would observe two days, because one of them was bound to be correct. This gave rise to the custom of observing Rosh Hashanah, **PASSOVER, SHAVUOT,** and **SUKKOT** over a two-day period. This custom was retained for Jews living outside Palestine, while Reform Jews and those living in Palestine observe only one day.

The turning of the year was closely related to the turning of the seasons. At one time, the three great Jewish festivals (Rosh Hashanah, Yom Kippur, and Sukkot) may have been one great harvest festival. But today they are distinct.

# SYMBOLS

## Book of Life

The Book of Life is divided into three sections: one for the wicked, one for the righteous, and one for those who fall in between. The names of the righteous are immediately inscribed in the Book of Life for good fortune in the coming year, while the wicked are condemned to death. Judgments about those who fall in between is made on Yom Kippur, which gives them time to repent and change their ways. It is for this reason that Jews often wish each other not only "Happy New Year" but "Have a good signature."

## Challah

Challah is a special bread served on Rosh Hashanah that is braided and baked in a circular shape, symbolizing the roundness of the year and the cycle of the seasons. Sometimes it is shaped like a ladder, a bird, or a crown. The ladder serves as a reminder that people are judged on this day, and that some are destined to climb and prosper while others will descend and suffer. The bird is a symbol of God's mercy, which extends to even the smallest of animals. The crown is a symbol of the kingship of God, which Rosh Hashanah emphasizes.

## Honey

It is customary at Rosh Hashanah to eat pieces of CHALLAH dipped in honey, which is symbolic of sweet life in the new year. It is also customary to eat a new fruit of the year, such as apples, dipped in honey, and to have honey cake for dessert.

## Kittel

During the morning service at Rosh Hashanah, it is customary for rabbis, cantors, and some adult male worshippers to wear a long white robe known as a kittel. It stands as a symbol of purity and a reminder of the white linen robe that the high priest used to wear in the Temple of Jerusalem. Very pious Jews are married and buried in a kittel, which is also worn on Yom Kippur and at the Seder on Passover.

## Shanah Tovah Cards

Just as Christians exchange Christmas and New Year's cards, Jews send out Shanah Tovah greeting cards that say "Leshanah Tovah Tikatevu," or "May you be written down for a good year." Although the custom of extending good wishes at Rosh Hashanah started among German Jews during medieval times, these wishes weren't expressed in writing until the fifteenth century, when Jews both in and outside Germany started ending their letters and notes with such messages during the month preceding the holiday. The custom of sending New Year's cards evolved from this practice.

Shanah Tovah cards are sent to rabbis, relatives, friends, and teachers, as well as to business associates and community leaders. Some Jews print their own personal cards, while others buy them at a stationery store. Schoolchildren often make their own. In Israel, they can be purchased from stalls set up in the streets. The cards often feature figures from comic strips, portraits of political and military figures, and sometimes planes, tanks, and guns, symbolic of the violence that has plagued the Middle East in recent decades.

## Shofar

Rosh Hashanah is also known as the Day of Blowing the Shofar or Ram's Horn. It recalls the story of Abraham, who was willing to sacrifice his son, Isaac, to prove the strength of his faith in God. At the last minute, he heard God's voice telling him not to harm his son but to sacrifice an animal instead. Miraculously, he saw a ram caught by its horns in a nearby thicket.

The shofar is also associated with other important events in Jewish history. It sounded when Moses called the Israelites together to give them the Ten Commandments on Mt. Sinai, and when the Temple in Jerusalem was destroyed. The shofar is still used in Israel to announce the arrival of the Sabbath on Friday afternoons and during the swearing-in of a new president.

The shofar makes three distinct sounds: *Shevarim,* which consists of three broken notes said to resemble sobbing; *Teruah,* or nine short notes resembling wailing; and *Tekiah,* a long, unbroken sound. These three tones, which honor Abraham, Isaac, and Jacob, are repeated several times in different sequences. Blowing this ancient instrument properly on Rosh Hashanah requires a trained expert; the notes are prescribed by tradition, and their order cannot be changed in any way. Its call summons worshippers to search their consciences and to repent before it is too late.

Although the shofar is usually made from a ram's horn, it can be the horn of any kosher (clean) animal, with the exception of cows, which might remind people of the disgraceful incident involving the Golden Calf (Exodus 32). A curved horn is preferred because it symbolizes the natural posture of the humble, or man bowing in submission to God.

Primitive peoples regarded the New Year as a time when demons were likely to be roaming about. To scare them away, it was customary to make noise by beating drums, sounding gongs, blowing trumpets, and cracking whips. The blowing of the shofar is probably related to this ancient custom, but it is regarded today as a symbol of the history and faith of the Jewish people.

## Tashlikh Ceremony

Orthodox Jews, whose ancestors came from northern Europe, observe the ceremony of *Tashlikh* ("you will cast"), a symbolic throwing away of one's sins into a body of water. On the afternoon of the first day of the New Year (or the second day, if the first day is the Sabbath), they go to the nearest body of flowing water and recite in Hebrew the closing words of the Book of Micah: "He will turn again, he will have compassion upon us; he will subdue our iniquities; and thou wilt cast all their sins into the depths of the sea." As these words are being recited, people empty their pockets of lint and bread crumbs, throwing them into the water so their sins will be carried away. If flowing water is not available, the ceremony can take place by a well, or facing in the direction of a distant body of water.

Some scholars think that the origin of this custom can be found in the ancient Roman practice of throwing offerings to the river spirits at certain critical times of the year.

## Further Reading

Cashman, Greer Fay. *Jewish Days and Holidays,* 1979.

Cuyler, Margery. *Jewish Holidays,* 1978.

Edidin, Ben. *Jewish Holidays and Festivals,* 1993.

Gaer, Joseph. *Holidays Around the World,* 1953.

Gaster, Theodor H. *Festivals of the Jewish Year,* 1953.

Henderson, Helene and Sue Ellen Thompson. *Holidays, Festivals, and Celebrations of the World Dictionary,* 2nd ed., 1997.

Ickis, Marguerite. *The Book of Festivals and Holidays the World Over,* 1970.

Purdy, Susan. *Festivals for You to Celebrate,* 1969.

Renberg, Dalia H. *The Complete Family Guide to Jewish Holidays,* 1985.

Santino, Jack. *All Around the Year,* 1994.

# St. Barbara's Day

**Type of Holiday:** Religious (Christian)

**Date of Observation:** December 4

**Where Celebrated:** Czech Republic, France, Germany, Poland, Syria, and by Christians throughout the world

**Symbols:** Barbara Branch, St. Barbara's Grain

**Related Holidays:** Christmas

## ORIGINS

According to legend, St. Barbara's father, a wealthy pagan, was so afraid that his daughter would fall in love and leave him that he locked her up in a richly furnished tower. She heard about Christianity, however, and arranged to receive a visit from a Christian disciple disguised as a physician. She was eventually converted to Christianity and baptized. One day, while her father was away, she had some workmen install a third window in her tower, which only had two. When she confessed her new faith to her father, she explained that the Christian soul received its light through three windows: the Father, the Son, and the Holy Ghost. At the time, Christianity was considered a criminal offense. Her father was so angry that he took her before a judge, who sentenced her to death by beheading. One version of the story says that Barbara's father carried out the sentence himself, but was killed by lightning on his way home. Another says that he was struck by lightning just as he was about to behead her. In any case, St. Barbara today is usually represented by a tower with three windows, for which reason she is somewhat inaccurately known as the patron saint of forts and of artillerymen. She is also called upon to protect people from lightning, storms, and sudden death.

In parts of France, Germany, and Syria, St. Barbara's Day is considered the beginning of the **CHRISTMAS** season. In Poland, St. Barbara's Day is associated with prophecies concerning the weather. If it rains on December 4, it will be cold and icy on Christmas Day; if it's cold and icy on St. Barbara's Day, Christmas will be warmer and rainy.

## SYMBOLS

### *Barbara Branch*

It was customary among Czechs and Slovaks, as well as other central Europeans, to break a branch off a cherry tree on St. Barbara's Day. It was placed in a pot of water in the kitchen and kept warm. If the girl who tended the twig was successful in making it bloom on **CHRISTMAS EVE**, it was considered an omen that she would find a good husband within a year.

The custom of cutting a dormant branch of the flowering cherry and bringing it indoors on St. Barbara's Day in the hope that it will bloom in time for Christmas is once again regaining its popularity among western Christians. The cherry blossom is a symbol of spring as well as of spiritual or feminine beauty. The sweet fruit of the cherry symbolizes the sweetness of character that is derived from good works. In some countries, Barbara branches are cut from apple, plum, almond, forsythia, jasmine, or horse chestnut trees.

### *St. Barbara's Grain*

In southern France, particularly Provence, it is customary to set out dishes with grains of wheat soaked in water on sunny window sills. There is a folk belief that if the "St. Barbara's grain" grows quickly, it means a good year for crops. But if it withers and dies, the crops will be ruined.

On Christmas Eve, the grain is placed near the crèche as a symbol of the coming harvest.

## Further Reading

Barz, Brigitte. *Festivals with Children,* 1989.
Eliade, Mircea. *The Encyclopedia of Religion,* 1897.

Ferguson, George. *Signs and Symbols in Christian Art,* 1954.

Harper, Howard V. *Days and Customs of All Faiths,* 1957.

Henderson, Helene and Sue Ellen Thompson. *Holidays, Festivals, and Celebrations of the World Dictionary,* 2nd ed., 1997.

Olderr, Steven. *Symbolism: A Comprehensive Dictionary,* 1986.

Weiser, Francis X. *Handbook of Christian Feasts and Customs,* 1952.

# *St. Bridget's Day*

**Type of Holiday:** Religious (Christian)
**Date of Observation:** February 1
**Where Celebrated:** England, Ireland, Scotland
**Symbols:** Bridie Doll, Fire, Rush Cross
**Related Holidays:** Imbolc, St. Patrick's Day

## ORIGINS

St. Bridget (or Bride) is the female patron saint of Ireland. She was an Irish princess who converted to Christianity and became the first Irish nun. In 585 she built a cell for herself under a large oak that may have been the site of pagan ceremonies in earlier times. Her hermitage there was known as Kill-Dara, or "the cell of the oak." She established a convent there, around which the Irish city of Kildare eventually grew.

The customs associated with St. Bridget's Day resemble in many ways those of the ancient Celtic festival of **IMBOLC**, observed at the same time of year and considered to mark the first day of spring and the beginning of the planting season. Bridget was therefore associated with a number of legends and superstitions regarding the weather and agricultural prosperity. For example, every other day between St. Bridget's Day and **ST. PATRICK'S DAY** (March 17) is supposed to be fair, according to Irish folklore. After that, every day is supposed to be fair. And like the groundhog on **CANDLEMAS**, the hedgehog's behavior on St. Bridget's Day is believed to predict the upcoming weather.

The custom of having women propose marriage to men during Leap Year (see **LEAP YEAR DAY**) can be traced back to St. Bridget, who complained to St. Patrick about the fact that men always took the initiative. She persuaded him to grant women the right to propose to men one year out of every four. Then Bridget proposed to Patrick, who turned her down but softened his refusal by giving her a kiss and a silk gown.

# SYMBOLS

## *Bridie Doll*

"Bride" or "Bridie" is another form of "Bridget." Bridie dolls were small figures made of straw and decorated with flowers. Women would bring them to the door on St. Bridget's Day and call out, "Let Bride come in!" The doll was then placed in a cradle inside the house with a wand of birch, broom, or willow beside it to represent Bride's husband.

The custom of displaying Bridie dolls originated in Scotland but has recently been revived in the area around Glastonbury, England. Irish children still go from door to door carrying a large doll, which they call "St. Bridget's baby," and ask for money to buy candles for the saint.

## *Fire*

The pagan sun god in Ireland had a daughter named Brighit, usually shown with a child in her arms. Her chief temple, in what later became known as Kildare, was served by virgins of noble birth called "the daughters of fire." It was their duty to keep Brighit's sacred fire burning without interruption. When the temple later became the site of St. Bridget's Christian convent, the nuns continued to tend the fire that had originally been dedicated to the pagan goddess, whose name was close enough to the Christian saint's name to be easily confused.

Brighit was associated with fire because *breo* is Irish for a firebrand or torch, and *breoch* means "glowing." St. Bridget's fire continued to burn for several hundred years, but it was suppressed by an order from the Archbishop of Dublin in the year 1220, perhaps because of its pagan origins. But the custom of lighting a fire on St. Bridget's Day survived for many years in Scotland, where schoolchildren would build a "Candlemas blaze" on the first of February.

## *Rush Cross*

In some parts of Ireland, children are still sent out on St. Bridget's Eve to pull up rushes, which cannot be cut with a knife. When the rushes are brought into the house, everyone gathers around the fire and makes crosses from them, which are then sprinkled with holy water. The wife or eldest daughter prepares tea and pancakes, and a plate of pancakes is laid on top of the rush crosses. After the food has been eaten, the crosses are hung up over doors and beds to bring good luck.

The rush crosses are probably a survival of a pre-Christian custom associated with a pagan demigoddess who was considered to be a patroness of the Irish bards. They were adapted by the Christian missionaries, for whom the cross was a symbol of Jesus Christ.

## Further Reading

Brewster, H. Pomeroy. *Saints and Festivals of the Christian Church,* 1990.

Crippen, T. G. *Christmas and Christmas Lore,* 1990.

Henderson, Helene and Sue Ellen Thompson. *Holidays, Festivals, and Celebrations of the World Dictionary,* 2nd ed., 1997.

King, John. *The Celtic Druids'Year: Seasonal Cycles of the Ancient Celts,* 1995.

Santino, Jack. *All Around the Year,* 1994.

Urlin, Ethel L. *Festivals, Holy Days, and Saints' Days,* 1915.

# *St. Christopher's Day*

**Type of Holiday:** Religious (Christian)

**Date of Observation:** July 25 in the West; May 9 or 22 in the East

**Where Celebrated:** Nesquehoning, Pennsylvania, and by Christians all over the world

**Symbols:** Blessing of the Cars, Staff, St. Christopher Medal

## ORIGINS

Very little is known for sure about the man whose Christian name was Christopher, aside from the fact that he was martyred in Asia Minor around 250 C.E. during a series of persecutions ordered by Emperor Decius. By the sixth century, however, his following was well established in the East, and it had spread to the West by the ninth century.

The most popular legend concerning St. Christopher is that he started out as a pagan named Offerus, who lived in Canaan and was so proud of his strength that he vowed to serve only the most powerful man he could find. He started out serving the Emperor, who turned out to be afraid of the Devil. Then he served the Devil, who turned out to be afraid of a cross. Finally he was converted to Christianity by a hermit, who baptized him with the name "Christopher" and suggested that the best way for him to serve God was to perform the earthly work for which he was best suited. So he became a ferryman, carrying pilgrims on his strong shoulders across a swift-moving river while using a STAFF to maintain his balance.

One day a young child approached and asked to be ferried across the stream. Halfway across, the weight of the child became so great that he feared they wouldn't make it. When they finally arrived safely on the other side, the child explained that he had been carrying the weight of the sins of the world. Christopher knew then that he had been carrying Christ, and that he'd met the all-powerful god for whom he'd been searching. The name "Christopher" means "Christ-bearer," and he is usually shown supporting the Christ child on his shoulders.

Although the Roman Catholic church removed his name from its universal calendar in 1969—largely because of the lack of reliable information about his life—St. Christopher's reputation has not diminished. As the patron saint of motorists, travelers, pilgrims, sailors, and ferrymen, his popularity extends beyond the walls of any one church and even beyond Christianity. Statues of St. Christopher can often be seen on car dashboards (see BLESS-ING OF THE CARS), and ST. CHRISTOPHER MEDALS often appear on car sun-visors and key chains.

## SYMBOLS

### *Blessing of the Cars*

In Nesquehoning, Pennsylvania, St. Christopher's Day is the occasion for the Blessing of the Cars. The custom began in 1933, when the pastor of Our Lady of Mount Carmel Church started blessing automobiles after he himself had been involved in three serious car accidents.

Sometimes it takes an entire week to bless all the cars that arrive in Nesquehoning from throughout Pennsylvania and other nearby states. In recent years, other Catholic churches have taken up the custom and perform their own blessing ceremonies.

## *Staff*

According to legend, after St. Christopher carried the Christ child safely to the far side of the river, he was told to plant his staff in the ground, whereupon it immediately turned into a tree and put forth leaves and fruit. It was this miracle that convinced him of his passenger's true identity and confirmed his vow to spend the rest of his life in the service of God.

The staff has more than one symbolic meaning in relation to St. Christopher. On the one hand, it is a symbol for travelers and pilgrims. But it is also a symbol of Christ's strength and power, since its miraculous transformation into a tree proved beyond any doubt that God was more powerful than the emperor or the devil.

## *St. Christopher Medal*

In the Middle Ages, there was a widespread belief that whoever looked upon a picture or statue of St. Christopher would be free from harm for the rest of the day. This led to the practice of hanging his picture or image across from the church doors, where everyone who entered would gaze upon it. The popularity of St. Christopher medals today, particularly among soldiers and travelers, is an extension of this custom.

## Further Reading

Chambers, Robert, ed. *The Book of Days,* 1864.

Cohen, Hennig, and Tristram Potter Coffin, eds. *The Folklore of American Holidays,* 2nd ed., 1991.

Harper, Howard V. *Days and Customs of All Faiths,* 1957.

Hatch, Jane M. *The American Book of Days,* 1978.

Henderson, Helene and Sue Ellen Thompson. *Holidays, Festivals, and Celebrations of the World Dictionary,* 2nd ed., 1997.

Jobes, Gertrude. *Dictionary of Mythology, Folklore, and Symbols,* 1962.

Urlin, Ethel L. *Festivals, Holy Days, and Saints' Days,* 1915.

# St. David's Day

**Type of Holiday:** Religious (Christian)
**Date of Observation:** March 1
**Where Celebrated:** Wales
**Symbols:** Leek

## ORIGINS

The patron saint of Wales, St. David was a monk, an ascetic, and a bishop who founded or restored many monasteries and greatly influenced religious life in Wales. Although his dates are not known for certain, he may have died around the late sixth century. Although he died on March 1 in the Pembrokeshire town where he'd founded his first monastery, known today as St. David's, his remains were later moved to the Abbey of Glastonbury.

St. David's Day is observed not only in Wales but by Welsh groups all over the world. It has been observed in the United States since very early times, due to the extensive migration of Welsh people to Pennsylvania at the end of the seventeenth century. Their presence eventually led to the establishment of the St. David's Society (sometimes called the Welsh Society), whose members are known for wearing LEEKS in their hats on St. David's Day and who have worked hard to preserve Welsh history and traditions. Such groups exist in Ohio, Wisconsin, and Florida as well as in New York City, where the St. David's Society has held an annual banquet on March 1 since 1835. This is a popular day on which to hold *Eisteddfodau,* which are traditional Welsh festivals involving competition in singing and literature. Another popular way to observe St. David's Day is with choral singing, for which the Welsh are noted.

## SYMBOLS

### Leek

The leek is an herb similar to an onion and is also the floral emblem of Wales. The association of St. David with the leek is said to date back to a battle fought in the seventh century between the Welsh and the Saxons. St. David suggested that the Welsh wear a leek in their caps so they could recognize one another and avoid killing their own men. He is also said to have lived for many years on the site of what would later become one of his monasteries, eating only bread, water, and wild leeks.

To this day, new Welsh army recruits must eat ritual leeks on March 1.

### Further Reading

Chambers, Robert, ed. *The Book of Days,* 1864.

Cohen, Hennig, and Tristram Potter Coffin, eds. *The Folklore of American Holidays,* 2nd ed., 1991.

Dunkling, Leslie. *A Dictionary of Days,* 1988.

Harper, Howard V. *Days and Customs of All Faiths,* 1957.

Hatch, Jane M. *The American Book of Days,* 1978.

Henderson, Helene and Sue Ellen Thompson. *Holidays, Festivals, and Celebrations of the World Dictionary,* 2nd ed., 1997.

Leach, Maria, ed. *Funk & Wagnalls Standard Dictionary of Folklore, Mythology, & Legend,* 1984.

MacDonald, Margaret R., ed. *The Folklore of World Holidays,* 1992.

Urlin, Ethel L. *Festivals, Holy Days, and Saints' Days,* 1915.

# *St. Francis of Assisi, Feast of*

**Type of Holiday:** Religious (Christian)
**Date of Observation:** October 4
**Where Celebrated:** Italy, United States
**Symbols:** Blessing of the Animals
**Related Holidays:** Christmas

## ORIGINS

St. Francis was the son of a wealthy family who lived in the Italian town of Assisi. When he was about 20, he was held prisoner for a year as the result of a war between two neighboring towns. This experience, combined with a serious illness he suffered at about the same time, prompted him to reexamine his life. He ended up forsaking any claim to his family's fortune and going off to live in a hut, where he spent his time ministering to the poor and the sick. A group of his boyhood friends left their homes and joined him. These were the first Franciscans, as the members of the religious order started by St. Francis eventually came to be known. In the beginning, however, they were called the Penitents of Assisi.

The Penitents were known for their high spirits and appreciation of the simple things in life. Like St. Francis, their leader, they were troubadours who went around singing about God's goodness. Their numbers increased rapidly, and they made their headquarters at the Portiuncula, a small chapel of the church of Santa Maria degli Angeli. Even though the Franciscans were ragged and underfed, they all shared the joy and enthusiasm that had originally drawn them to St. Francis. They spent much of their time renovating churches that had fallen into disrepair and taking care of lepers and other outcasts.

Although St. Francis died when he was only in his 40s, he is believed to have been responsible for instituting two widespread **CHRISTMAS** traditions. He gave instructions for building the first crèche, in the town of Greccio, so that he could see with his own eyes the scene that must have surrounded the infant Jesus as He lay in the manger. St. Francis is also credited with the custom of caroling, since it was the Franciscans who composed and sang the first Italian Christmas carols.

The Feast of St. Francis is one of the most important festivals of the year in Assisi, Italy. For two days, the entire town is illuminated by oil lamps burning consecrated oil brought from a different Italian town each year. A parchment in St. Francis's handwriting, believed to be the saint's deathbed blessing to his follower, Brother Leo, is taken to the top of the Santa Maria degli Angeli basilica, and the people are blessed by a representative of the Pope.

## SYMBOLS

### *Blessing of the Animals*

St. Francis loved animals because they were God's creatures. He instituted the custom of showing special kindness to animals at Christmastime, urging farmers to provide their oxen and asses with extra corn and hay in commemoration of the night when the infant Jesus lay between an ox and an ass in the manger. he also encouraged people to scatter grain and corn on the streets so that the birds would have enough to eat. He had a great fondness for songbirds, especially larks.

In the United States, it is not uncommon for children to bring their pets to the church to be blessed on St. Francis's feast day. The annual blessing of the animals held at the Cathedral of St. John the Divine in New York City on this day has turned into quite a spectacle. Among the animals that have come there to be blessed are a camel, an 8,000-pound elephant, a macaw with a 30-word vocabulary, and a turtle that was rescued from a Chinese restaurant, where it was about to be made into a soup.

## Further Reading

Brewster, H. Pomeroy, *Saints and Festivals of the Christian Church,* 1990.

Cohen, Hennig, and Tristram Potter Coffin, eds. *The Folklore of American Holidays,* 2nd ed., 1991.

Dobler, Lavinia. *Customs and Holidays Around the World,* 1962.

Harper, Howard V. *Days and Customs of All Faiths,* 1957.

Hatch, Jane M. *The American Book of Days,* 1978.

Henderson, Helene and Sue Ellen Thompson. *Holidays, Festivals, and Celebrations of the World Dictionary,* 2nd ed., 1997.

# St. George's Day
## (Georgemas)

**Type of Holiday:** Religious (Christian), National

**Date of Observation:** April 23 (February 25)

**Where Celebrated:** England, United States, Republic of Georgia

**Symbols:** Armor, Blessing of the Horses, Cross, Dragon, Green George, Lance

**Colors:** St. George's Day is associated with the colors scarlet and blue. Scarlet can be seen in the banner of the Church of England, which has a red CROSS on a white background in honor of the country's patron saint. It was also the custom in England on St. George's Day for men of fashion to wear a blue coat, perhaps in imitation of the blue mantle worn by the Knights of the Garter, the highest order of British knighthood. In the April 23 service held in St. Paul's Cathedral in London, members of the Order of St. Michael and St. George still dress in blue capes lined with scarlet.

**Related Holidays:** May Day, Parilia

# ORIGINS

The patron saint of England, St. George is best known for slaying the vicious DRAGON who had terrorized a village in Cappadocia, a country in Asia Minor that became a Roman province in 17 C.E. After demanding to be fed two sheep a day, the dragon started asking for human victims. Lots were drawn to determine who would be sacrificed, and eventually the lot fell to the king's daughter. Dressed as a bride, the princess was led to the dragon's lair. St. George, an officer in the Roman army, happened to be riding by at the time and, in the name of Christ, stopped to help the princess. Making the sign of the CROSS, he engaged in combat and finally succeeded in pinning the dragon to the ground with his LANCE and then slaying it with his sword. In another version of the legend, he made a leash out of the princess's sash and led the dragon back to the city like a pet dog. The king and all his people were so impressed by St. George's victory that they were converted to the Christian faith.

Most Romans were still pagan at this time, and Christians were routinely persecuted. After killing the dragon, St. George continued on his journey to Palestine. There he defied the Roman emperor Diocletian's decree outlawing Christianity, refusing to give up his faith. He was seized and tortured, and eventually beheaded on April 23 in the year 300 C.E. By the Middle Ages he had become the model for Christian soldiers and warriors everywhere. He was made the patron saint of England around 1344.

St. George's Day, sometimes referred to as Georgemas, has been observed as a religious feast as well as a holiday since the thirteenth century. In the United States, there are St. George's Societies in Philadelphia; New York City; Charleston, South Carolina; and Baltimore, Maryland dedicated to charitable causes who hold their annual dinner on April 23. In the former Soviet Union, St. George's Day is celebrated on February 25 as the national day of the Georgian Republic. In the Alps, shepherds pay special homage to St. George, probably because his feast day coincides with the time of year when they move their flocks up to mountain pastures (see **PARILIA**).

# SYMBOLS

## *Armor*

St. George was a favorite subject among Renaissance artists. He is usually represented as a young knight in shining armor emblazoned with a red CROSS, riding on his horse. Armor is a symbol not only of chivalry but of the Christian faith as a safeguard against evil. In Ephesians 6:11-17, St. Paul says, "Put on the whole armor of God, that ye may be able to stand against the wiles of the devil . . . having on the breastplate of righteousness . . . the shield of faith . . . the helmet of salvation, and the sword of the Spirit, which is the word of God."

## Blessing of the Horses

In Germany, St. George is the protector of horses and their riders. On April 23 in the villages of upper Bavaria, people bring their horses to church and the parish priest blesses the animals and their masters, sprinkling both with holy water. In the Swiss Canton of Valais, farmers lead their donkeys, mules, and horses to church on April 23 to be blessed, believing that the ceremony will protect their animals from disease and accident throughout the year.

In parts of Greece, St. George's Day is observed with games and horse races. The prize for the winner is often a saddle or harness.

## Cross

The cross known as St. George's Cross is the one that appears on the banner of the Church of England. The cross is red on a white background, in imitation of the red cross popularly shown on St. George's ARMOR.

In the former Soviet Union, this festival honors the patron of the Military Order of St. George's Cross. It is observed with special church services and reunions among military officers. Celebratory dinners are held for military men of all ranks.

## Dragon

The dragon is an imaginary animal that combines characteristics from various other aggressive and dangerous animals, such as crocodiles, lions, and snakes. Found in the majority of the world's cultures, the dragon usually stands as a symbol of the primordial enemy who must be confronted in combat as a supreme test of one's power or faith. In Christianity, the dragon often symbolizes the Devil or Satan. He is usually depicted as a devouring monster who destroys his victims in an attempt to get even with God for casting him out of heaven.

In stark contrast to Western ideas about the dragon, the Chinese dragon is a benign, good-natured creature symbolizing fertility and male vigor (see **DOUBLE FIFTH**).

## *Green George*

The gypsies of Transylvania and Romania celebrate the festival of Green George on April 23. On the eve of St. George's Day, a young willow tree is cut down, set in the ground, and decorated with leaves and garlands. Pregnant women place a piece of their clothing under the tree and leave it there overnight. If they find a leaf lying on the garment the following morning, they know they will have an easy delivery. Sick and elderly people visit the tree as well, spitting on it and asking for a long life.

On the morning of St. George's Day, a young man dressed from head to toe in green leaves and blossoms appears. He is known as Green George, the human double of the willow tree. While the power of granting an easy delivery to pregnant women and vital energy to the sick and elderly belongs to the willow, Green George throws a few handfuls of grass to the farm animals so they won't lack fodder during the year. It is also Green George's responsibility to gain the favor of the water spirits. He does this by taking three iron nails and, after knocking them into the willow, pulling them out and throwing them into a running stream. Sometimes a puppet version of Green George is thrown into the stream as well. This is supposed to ensure the rain that will be needed to make the fields and meadows green in summer.

Like other tree spirits, the appearance of Green George in April is seen as necessary to the regeneration that is taking place in the natural world. His counterpart in England is known as Jack-of-the-Green (see **MAY DAY**).

## *Lance*

According to the legend of St. George and the dragon, the saint pierced the dragon with his lance, which then broke, forcing him to kill the dragon with his sword. A symbol of war—in this case, the struggle between the Christian spirit and evil—the lance is considered an earthly weapon, in contrast to the spiritual implications of the sword. The broken lance is considered a symbol of St. George and also of the Passion, since it was a lance that was used to pierce the side of Christ as He hung on the Cross.

## **Further Reading**

Brewster, H. Pomeroy. *Saints and Festivals of the Christian Church,* 1990.
Cirlot, J. E. *A Dictionary of Symbols,* 1962.
Dobler, Lavinia. *Customs and Holidays Around the World,* 1962.

Ferguson, George. *Signs and Symbols in Christian Art,* 1954.

Frazer, Sir James G. *The Golden Bough: A Study in Magic and Religion,* 1931.

Henderson, Helene and Sue Ellen Thompson. *Holidays, Festivals, and Celebrations of the World Dictionary,* 2nd ed., 1997.

Ickis, Marguerite. *The Book of Festivals and Holidays the World Over,* 1970.

Leach, Maria, ed. *Funk & Wagnalls Standard Dictionary of Folklore, Mythology, & Legend,* 1984.

Olderr, Steven. *Symbolism: A Comprehensive Dictionary,* 1986.

Urlin, Ethel L. *Festivals, Holy Days, and Saints' Days,* 1915.

# St. Joseph's Day
### *(Dia de San Guiseppe, Fallas)*

**Type of Holiday:** Religious (Christian)

**Date of Observation:** March 19 in the West; July 29 in the East

**Where Celebrated:** Italy, Sicily, Spain, United States, and by Christians all over the world

**Symbols:** Breads, Fruits, and Grains; Fish; Flowering Rod

## ORIGINS

Joseph, husband of the Virgin Mary and foster-father of Jesus, has been honored as a saint since the earliest days of the Christian Church. But very little is known about his life, or even the exact date of his death, which is believed to have occurred when Jesus Christ was 18.

St. Joseph's Day is widely celebrated in Italy as a day of feasting and sharing with the poor, of whom he is the patron saint. Each village prepares a "table of St. Joseph" by contributing money, candles, flowers, and food (see FISH). Then they invite three guests of honor—representing Mary, Joseph, and Jesus—to join in their feast, as well as others representing the 12 Apostles. They also invite the orphans, widows, beggars, and poor people of the village to eat with them. The food is blessed by the village priest and by the child chosen to represent Jesus; then it is passed from one person to the next. Dia de San Guiseppe, as the day is known, is celebrated by Italians in the United States and in other countries as well.

In Valencia, Spain, it is a week-long festival (March 12-19) called Fallas de San Jose (Bonfires of St. Joseph). Its roots can be found in medieval times, when the carpenters' guild (of whom Joseph was the patron saint) made a huge bonfire on St. Joseph's Eve out of the wood shavings that had accumulated over the winter. This was considered the end of the winter and the last night on which candles and lamps would have to be lighted. In fact, the carpenters often burned the *parot,* or wooden candelabrum, in front of their shops.

In Valencia nowadays the *parots* have become *fallas,* or huge floats of intricate scenes made of wood and papier-mâché, satirizing everything from the high cost of living to political personalities. On St. Joseph's Eve, March 18, the *fallas* parade through the streets. At midnight on March 19, the celebration ends with a spectacular ceremony known as the *crema,* when all the *fallas* are set on fire.

Among Sicilian Catholics living in the United States, St. Joseph's Day is a major event — the equivalent of **ST. PATRICK'S DAY** among Irish-Americans. This is particularly true in New Orleans, Milwaukee, and other cities where there are large Sicilian populations. In Southern California, a custom similar to the Hispanic **POSADAS** takes place on St. Joseph's Day: Mary's and Joseph's search for shelter is reenacted by children, who go from house to house requesting lodging for the night. When they reach the third house, they are greeted by a large St. Joseph's Altar and an elaborate meal.

## SYMBOLS

### *Breads, Fruits, and Grains*

Cards exchanged by Roman Catholics on St. Joseph's Day often show specially baked breads, fruits, and grains along with images of the saint. They are a symbol of fertility and abundance, although now the day is more of an ethnic festival than a celebration of spring.

### *Fish*

The tables or altars set up in Sicilian homes on St. Joseph's Day are often used to display the special foods associated with the holiday. Fish is a favorite choice, probably because this holy day falls during **LENT**, when meat is forbidden. But it may also have something to do with fish as a fertility symbol (see BREADS, FRUITS, AND GRAINS) and a symbol of Christianity. The fish often stands for Christ in Christian art and literature because the five Greek letters forming the word "fish" are the initial letters of the five words, "Jesus Christ God's Son Savior." The fish is also a symbol of baptism: Just as the fish cannot live out of the water, the true Christian cannot live except through the waters of baptism.

### Flowering Rod

Mary didn't choose Joseph to be her husband. According to legend, the priest Zacharius was told by an angel to gather together all the widowers, instructing them to bring their rods (or staffs) with them. Joseph appeared with the rest, and their rods were placed in the temple overnight in the hope that God would provide a sign to indicate which of them he favored. The next morning, it was discovered that Joseph's rod had burst into flower, and a white dove flew out of it. This was taken to be a clear sign of God's intentions for him. In paintings of the subject, the rejected suitors are often shown breaking their rods with expressions of envy and disgust. Joseph's rod is usually shown in the form of a stalk of lilies — the lily being a symbol of purity and the flower most often associated with the Virgin Mary.

### Further Reading

Appleton, LeRoy H., and Stephen Bridges. *Symbolism in Liturgical Art,* 1959.

Biedermann, Hans. *Dictionary of Symbolism: Cultural Icons and the Meanings Behind Them,* 1994.

Brewster, H. Pomeroy. *Saints and Festivals of the Christian Church,* 1990.

Ferguson, George. *Signs and Symbols in Christian Art,* 1954.

Henderson, Helene and Sue Ellen Thompson. *Holidays, Festivals, and Celebrations of the World Dictionary,* 2nd ed., 1997.

Santino, Jack. *All Around the Year,* 1994.

# St. Lucy's Day
## (Luciadagen)

**Type of Holiday:** Religious (Christian)
**Date of Observation:** December 13
**Where Celebrated:** Denmark, Finland, Norway, Sweden, United States
**Symbols:** Candles, Eyes, Lucia Cats

**Colors:** St. Lucy's Day is associated with the colors white and red. In Scandinavia, it is traditional to observe this day by dressing the oldest daughter in the family in a white robe tied with a crimson sash.

**Related Holidays:** Winter Solstice

# ORIGINS

According to tradition, St. Lucy or Santa Lucia was born in Syracuse, Sicily, in the third century. She was so beautiful that she attracted the unwanted attentions of a pagan nobleman, to whom she was betrothed against her will. In an attempt to end the affair, she cut out her EYES, which her suitor claimed "haunted him day and night." But God restored them as a reward for her sacrifice. She then gave away her entire dowry to the poor people of Syracuse. This made her lover so angry that he tried to force her to perform a sacrifice to his pagan gods. She refused and was taken off to prison. There she was again ordered to perform the sacrifice or be condemned to death. But when the soldiers tried to move her to the place of execution, they could not budge her. They lit a fire on the floor around her, used ropes and pulleys, and finally stabbed her in the neck with a dagger. For this reason she is the patron saint for protection from throat infections.

According to the Julian or Old Style calendar, St. Lucy blinded herself on the **WINTER SOLSTICE**—the shortest, darkest day of the year. When the Vikings were converted to Christianity, they adopted the Italian saint as the day's patroness because her name, Lucia, meant "light." To the sun-starved inhabitants of Sweden, Norway, Finland, and Denmark, this was the joyful day after which winter began yielding to spring, and they brought to it many of their pagan light and fire customs (see CANDLES). Their belief in the saint's power to break winter's spell gave rise to the popular folk custom of writing her name on doors and fences, along with the drawing of a girl, in the hope that Lucia would drive winter away.

In Sweden, where St. Lucy's Day is known as Luciadagen, it marks the official start of the **CHRISTMAS** season. Before sunrise on December 13, the oldest (or, in some cases, the prettiest) girl in the house goes among the sleeping family members dressed in a white robe with a red sash and wearing a metal crown covered with whortleberry (sometimes lingonberry) leaves and encircled by nine lighted CANDLES. The younger girls also dress in white and wear haloes of glittering tinsel. The boys—known as *Starngossar* or Star Boys—wear white robes and tall cone-shaped hats made of silver paper, and they carry star-topped scepters. The "Lucia Bride," as she is called, leads the Star Boys and younger girls through the house, awakening the rest of the family by singing a special song and bringing them coffee and buns (see LUCIA CATS).

The Lucy celebrations were brought to the United States by Swedish immigrants, whose customs survive in Swedish-American communities throughout the country. Chicago holds a major citywide festival on the afternoon of December 13 each year at the downtown Chicago Civic Center. A similar celebration takes place in Philadelphia, with Swedish Christmas songs, folk dances, and a procession of Lucia brides.

# SYMBOLS

## Candles

The bonfires traditionally kindled on the **WINTER SOLSTICE** were designed to encourage the return of the sun at the darkest time of year. Even after the arrival of Christianity and the New Style calendar, light and fire were considered an essential part of St. Lucy's Day observations. The candles that the Lucia bride wears in her crown are one of the forms of light associated with this holiday. It was also common at one time for people to keep candles burning in their homes all day on December 13. Although St. Lucy's Day now falls several days before the solstice, it is still associated with light and the lengthening days.

## Eyes

St. Lucy is often shown carrying her eyes on a platter, although there is no support for this in early accounts of her life. The eyes are a familiar symbol associated with the saint, however, and they serve as a good example of how a symbolic idea can be converted into a fact. Her name in Latin, Lucia, comes from *lux*, meaning "light." St. Lucy was often invoked by the blind for this reason, and eventually this gave rise to the story that she blinded herself by gouging out her eyes. Both the eyes and the lamp that Lucy is often shown carrying symbolize her divine light and wisdom.

## Lucia Cats

Special buns are served on the morning of December 13. Although they come in a variety of shapes, the most popular are the *Lussekatter* or "Lucia cats," with raisins for eyes and baked dough that curls up at either end.

Cats have been a symbol of good luck since ancient times. They were also used as a sign to keep the devil out of the house, because he was believed to appear in the form of a cat.

### Further Reading

Appleton, LeRoy H., and Stephen Bridges. *Symbolism in Liturgical Art,* 1959.

Brewster, H. Pomeroy. *Saints and Festivals of the Christian Church,* 1990.

Dobler, Lavinia. *Customs and Holidays Around the World,* 1962.

Ferguson, George. *Signs and Symbols in Christian Art,* 1954.

Henderson, Helene and Sue Ellen Thompson. *Holidays, Festivals, and Celebrations of the World Dictionary,* 2nd ed., 1997.

Miles, Clement A. *Christmas in Ritual and Tradition,* 1990.

Purdy, Susan. *Festivals for You to Celebrate,* 1969.

Santino, Jack. *All Around the Year,* 1994.

Weiser, Francis X. *Handbook of Christian Feasts and Customs,* 1952.

# *St. Mennas's Day*

**Type of Holiday:** Religious (Orthodox Christian)
**Date of Observation:** November 11
**Where Celebrated:** Greece
**Symbols:** Scissors

## ORIGINS

The name Mennas means "messenger, revealer." It is believed that St. Mennas has the power to reveal where lost or stolen items lie hidden. He is therefore very important to shepherds who have lost their sheep or who wish to protect them against wolves. In Greece, his day is observed by the many shepherds who must guide their sheep through the rough, mountainous terrain.

There are actually two different saints by the name of Mennas. One was a camel driver in Egypt who enlisted in the Roman army. When his legion reached Phrygia, he discovered that the Roman emperor, Diocletian, had started persecuting Christians. He left the army and hid in a mountain cave there to avoid persecution. But then, during the annual games held in the arena at Cotyaeum, he boldly entered the arena and announced that he was a Christian — an act of courage for which he was beheaded in 295 C.E. The other St. Mennas was a Greek from Asia Minor who became a hermit in the Abruzzi region of Italy and died in the sixth century.

There is an old proverb that says winter announces its arrival on St. Mennas's Day, November 11, and arrives on St. Philip's Day, November 15.

## SYMBOLS

### *Scissors*

In Greece, shepherds' wives refrain from using scissors on St. Mennas's Day. Instead, they wind a thread around the points of their scissors—a symbolic action designed to keep the jaws of wolves closed and the mouths of the village gossips shut.

## Further Reading

Henderson, Helene and Sue Ellen Thompson. *Holidays, Festivals, and Celebrations of the World Dictionary*, 2nd ed., 1997.

Ickis, Marguerite. *The Book of Festivals and Holidays the World Over*, 1970.

MacDonald, Margaret R., ed. *The Folklore of World Holidays*, 1992.

# *St. Patrick's Day*

**Type of Holiday:** Religious (Christian)

**Date of Observation:** March 17

**Where Celebrated:** Ireland, United States

**Symbols:** Bonfires, Drinking, Harp, Leprechaun, Parades, Shamrock, Shillelagh

**Colors:** St. Patrick's Day is associated with the colors green, white, and orange. In addition to being a symbol of spring and fertility, green has been Ireland's national color since the nineteenth century. Whether they're Irish or not, many Americans wear something green on this day. In Ireland, young girls wear green hair ribbons, and boys often wear a green badge with a golden HARP on it. Everyone wears sprigs of green SHAMROCK on St. Patrick's Day.

The three broad stripes on the flag of the Republic of Ireland are green, white, and orange: green for the Gaelic and Catholic majority, orange for

Ireland's Protestants (after William of Orange, the Protestant son-in-law of the British King James II), and white for peace between the two groups.

**Related Holidays:** Beltane, St. Bridget's Day, Vernal Equinox

# ORIGINS

St. Patrick, the patron saint of Ireland, was not actually Irish. He was born on this day around 385 somewhere in Roman Britain, possibly near Dumbarton in Scotland. At the age of 16 he was captured by Irish raiders looking for slaves and carried off to Ireland, where he spent much of his time tending his master's sheep. He was lonely and homesick there, but he believed that he deserved to be punished for ignoring God's commandments.

After six years of slavery, he heard a voice telling him, "Thy ship is ready for thee." He ran away, heading for the coast, and was taken aboard a ship as a crew member. He ended up deserting his shipmates and wandering through southern Gaul (France) and Italy. After spending several years in Europe making up for the education he'd never received, he had a vision from God telling him to return to Ireland and convert the pagans to Christianity.

St. Patrick landed in County Wicklow, south of what is now Dublin, around 432. He made his way through the country as a missionary, visiting the Irish chieftains and telling them about the new religion he represented. Although his life was in constant danger, he somehow managed to survive to old age and when he died in 464, the entire country went into mourning. He is probably best remembered for ordering all the snakes to leave Ireland—an event that, according to legend, occurred on the mountain later known as Croagh Patrick. On the last Sunday in July every year, hundreds of pilgrims gather there to commemorate their patron saint.

The first St. Patrick's Day celebration in the United States was held in Boston in 1737. The potato famine of 1845-49 brought many Irish immigrants to the United States, where St. Patrick's Day became an opportunity to express pride in their national heritage. In cities like Boston, New York, Philadelphia, and Los Angeles, it was observed with PARADES, banquets, speeches, and Irish plays, pageants, and dancing. People wore green and displayed the SHAMROCK and the green Irish flag with the gold HARP.

Today, there are more people of Irish descent in the United States than there are in Ireland, and the holiday has become a time for the Irish everywhere to show their unity and express their feelings about freedom—particularly freedom from British rule. In Ireland, it is a far less rowdy and commercial event than it is in the United States. People attend sporting events or stay home and watch the New York St. Patrick's Day Parade on television, but they don't drink green beer, wear green derbies (an English invention), or put green carnations in their lapels.

Popular foods served on St. Patrick's Day include corned beef and cabbage, mulligatawny soup, Irish stew, and Irish soda bread. In Ireland, the preferred dish is colcannon, made from mashed potatoes combined with shredded kale or cabbage, minced onion, and melted butter.

## SYMBOLS

### *Bonfires*

According to legend, St. Patrick was driven out of County Wicklow not long after he arrived. He sailed north and ended up in Tara, the legendary seat of Ireland's high kings. He arrived just as **BELTANE** was being celebrated, and all the fires had to be extinguished until the king had kindled his fire on the hill of Tara. St. Patrick lit his own campfire, and the flames were spotted by the king, Laoghaire. Outraged at this show of disrespect, he took a group of Druids to St. Patrick's camp to confront the missionary. But the Druids were afraid of Patrick's power and advised the king not to enter the camp. Instead, Patrick came out and settled the dispute, delivering a sermon during which he picked a SHAMROCK and used it to demonstrate the concept of the Holy Trinity.

St. Patrick was wise enough not to try to eliminate pagan rites and customs altogether. Instead, he tried to find a way to combine them with Christian customs. Since the Irish had traditionally honored their gods with bonfires on the hilltops in the spring, St. Patrick instituted the custom of lighting **EASTER** fires as a symbol for the Christian faith, which could never be extinguished.

### *Drinking*

Drinking is a popular activity on St. Patrick's Day. St. Patrick is said to have brought the art of distilling spirits to Ireland, and the traditional cottage dweller's drink known as *poteen,* made from Irish white potatoes, has long been regarded as a way of warding off the ills associated with the country's damp climate. In the traditional custom known as "drowning the Shamrock," families with servants would put SHAMROCKS in a bowl and cover them with Irish whiskey, giving the remainder of the bottle to the servants. Nowadays, pub-crawling has become a popular way to spend the holiday.

Although the Irish are only moderately heavy drinkers by European standards (Belgians and Germans both consume more beer), the stereotype of the drunken Irishman remains a popular one in America. In Ireland, both the churches and the government have tried to discourage the custom in recent years by putting more emphasis on the religious aspects of the holiday.

## Harp

The harp is a symbol of St. Patrick's Day and of Ireland itself. It appears on Irish coins and on some Irish flags. It is also part of the national coat of arms, the presidential flag, and the royal arms of the United Kingdom. Harp music is often played in Irish castles that are open to the public, as well as in hotels and other public places. One of the world's oldest musical instruments, the harp has a long history in Irish mythology and legend.

The old Irish harp, known as the *clarsach*, was relatively small, with a sound box carved from a solid block of wood. The harpist held it on his or her knee and plucked the heavy brass strings with the fingernails of the other hand. Irish stone carvings and early Christian metal work often show people playing harps, so it is likely that the harp was a popular instrument by the time St. Patrick arrived in Ireland. Kings, church officials, princes, and poets often gathered to recite tales about Ireland to the accompaniment of harp music. The well-known Irish song, "The Harp That Once Through Tara's Halls," written by the Irish poet Thomas Moore, describes such a gathering in the hall of the Irish kings at Tara, a hill in County Meath.

## Leprechaun

The legendary creatures known in Ireland as leprechauns were part of a group of fairies known as *Luchorpan,* which means "the wee ones." Over the years, the name luchorpan became confused with an Irish word meaning "one-shoemaker." Since shoemakers had a reputation for living alone and having a grumpy nature, the leprechaun was depicted as a solitary creature, usually working on a single shoe rather than a pair. He was a wizened, bearded dwarf who wore a green suit and cap and worked day and night mending the shoes of the other fairies.

The Irish were generally afraid of fairies, who could kidnap brides and snatch babies from their cradles. They believed that listening to fairy music could make a person lose all sense of human sympathy, after which the person might become a seer, a great poet, or a musician. Some scholars believe that fairies were the gods of ancient Ireland and that when the Christian gods took their place, they dwindled in both status and size to the miniature beings they are today.

## *Parades*

The St. Patrick's Day Parade is largely an American invention. It was well established in Boston, Philadelphia, Atlanta, Cleveland, and many other American cities by the 1850s; by the 1870s, there were enough Irish living in Los Angeles to make the parade there an annual event. Today there are parades on March 17 in at least 30 states.

The largest takes place in New York City. It began in 1763, when small groups of Irish settlers banded together and followed the cobblestone streets to celebrate at their local taverns. Such informal marches became more organized after the Revolutionary War, when a veterans' group called the Friendly Sons of St. Patrick began advertising their ancestry on March 17. The growing number of Irish immigrants who poured into New York following the 1840s potato famine gave rise to religious and political tensions, particularly with British Protestants, and the St. Patrick's Day parade often erupted in fights and violence. It was the Ancient Order of Hibernians who finally converted the parade from a rough, informal social outing to a large, well-organized civil rights demonstration. As the Irish became more influential in New York City politics, the parade gradually quieted down. But even today the parade often provokes controversy, as it did when gay and lesbian Irish-Americans wanted to march as a group up Fifth Avenue.

No matter where the parades take place, they usually feature marching bands, fife and drum corps, and musicians wearing kilts and playing such favorite Irish songs as "Danny Boy," "The Minstrel Boy," and "Garryowen." Local dignitaries in morning coats and top hats wear green, white, and orange sashes and carry SHILLELAGHS. There are green hats, green banners, and green carnations everywhere.

## *Shamrock*

Shamrock is an English name for the plant known in Gaelic as *seamrog.* It is a small, three-leaved plant similar to clover. The ancient Druids associated it with the coming of spring and the rebirth of the natural world at the **VERNAL EQUINOX**. Even today, it is customary in Ireland to plant something new in the garden each day during "Patrick's Week," the week following March 17.

St. Patrick is said to have used the shamrock when he explained the theological doctrine of the Holy Trinity (three persons in one God) to the unconverted Irish pagans, pointing out that the shamrock has three separate leaves but is a single plant with a single stem. This legend may have arisen after the fact to justify the high esteem in which the shamrock was traditionally held by the Irish people.

The shamrock still grows freely all over Ireland, where the mild climate keeps it green all year. Although it started out as a symbol of St. Patrick and his teachings, over the centuries it became symbolic of the way the Irish felt about their country. In the nineteenth and twentieth centuries, it became an emblem of Irish rebellion and, more than ever, a symbol of national pride.

## *Shillelagh*

*Shillelagh* is an old Irish word for a short, stout club or cudgel made of oak. It is also the name of a famous oak forest that once stood in County Wicklow. A club or cudgel cut from one of these oaks was referred to as a "sprig of shillelagh." Eventually the name was used to describe any cudgel made of oak, and it served as an apt symbol of the staunch spirit of the Irish.

The shillelagh was often used as a weapon. Ancient feuds between families were often fought with shillelaghs at county fairs. Sometimes two of the clubs were used, so that the fighter could strike with one hand and fend off his opponent with the other. The typical Irishman is often depicted swinging a shillelagh, even though a real shillelagh was never swung but grasped in the middle.

When the English cut down most of Ireland's oak trees, Irishmen started cutting their clubs or walking sticks from blackthorn hedges. Tourists today bring back mock shillelaghs made of blackthorn bound with green ribbons as souvenirs. In St. Patrick's Day PARADES, officials often carry blackthorn walking sticks, while children in the crowd wave toy shillelaghs made of green plastic.

## Further Reading

Appleton, LeRoy H., and Stephen Bridges. *Symbolism in Liturgical Art,* 1959.

Barth, Edna. *Shamrocks, Harps, and Shillelaghs: The Story of the St. Patrick Day Symbols,* 1977.

Cohen, Hennig, and Tristram Potter Coffin, eds. *The Folklore of American Holidays,* 2nd ed., 1991.

Crim, Keith, ed. *The Perennial Dictionary of World Religions,* 1989.

Harper, Howard V. *Days and Customs of All Faiths,* 1957.

Hatch, Jane M. *The American Book of Days,* 1978.

Henderson, Helene and Sue Ellen Thompson. *Holidays, Festivals, and Celebrations of the World Dictionary,* 2nd ed., 1997.

Ickis, Marguerite. *The Book of Festivals and Holidays the World Over,* 1970.

Kelly, Aidan. *Religious Holidays and Calendars,* 1993.

MacDonald, Margaret R., ed. *The Folklore of World Holidays,* 1992.

Santino, Jack. *All Around the Year,* 1994.

Tuleja, Tad. *Curious Customs: The Stories Behind 296 Popular American Rituals,* 1987.

Urlin, Ethel L. *Festivals, Holy Days, and Saints' Days,* 1915.

Weiser, Francis X. *Handbook of Christian Feasts and Customs,* 1952.

# St. Stephen's Day
### (Boxing Day)

**Type of Holiday:** Religious (Christian)

**Date of Observation:** December 26

**Where Celebrated:** Australia, Austria, Canada, England, Germany, Ireland, Poland, Sweden, and other Christian nations

**Symbols:** Christmas Box, Horse, Wren

**Related Holidays:** Christmas

## ORIGINS

St. Stephen became the first Christian martyr on this day somewhere between 31 and 35 C.E. According to the New Testament book of Acts, Stephen was chosen by the Apostles as one of the first seven deacons of the church in Jerusalem. He was later denounced as a blasphemer by the Sanhedrin, the Jewish council in ancient Palestine, and stoned to death outside the gate of Jerusalem that now bears his name. Stephen's death is considered an example of the highest class of martyrdom, because he intentionally gave his life for Christ.

In England, Australia, Canada, and many other countries, the day after **CHRISTMAS** is Boxing Day. There are a number of theories about where this holiday got its name. Some point to the church alms-box, the contents of which were not dispensed until the day after Christmas. The most popular explanation is that it was named after the earthenware CHRISTMAS BOXES that servants and tradespeople used to carry around to collect tips and end-of-the-year bonuses. Some people believe that it comes from the Arabic *backsheesh,* meaning "gratuity." Crusaders brought this word back with them, and it became common for anyone who had rendered service to another person during the year to expect *backsheesh* at Christmas.

# SYMBOLS

## *Christmas Box*

At one time, every ship that went off on a long voyage kept a box on board for donations to the priest who, in return, was expected to offer masses for the safety of the ship and its sailors. The box was not to be opened until the vessel returned. If the voyage had been rough, it was usually quite full. Because mass at that time was called Christ-mass, the boxes kept to pay for it were called "Christmass Boxes."

A relic of these ancient boxes can be seen in the earthenware or wooden boxes with slits in the top used by servants and children in nineteenth-century England to gather money during the Christmas season, giving rise to the name Boxing Day. Servants, apprentices, and tradespeople, especially in London, broke their boxes open as soon as Christmas was over. Christmas boxes were also associated with the custom of "doling," in which bands of young, poor, and often rowdy people went around demanding gifts of money and food from the wealthy and privileged. In the 1820s and 1830s, the English custom of Christmas boxes was transformed into the Victorian custom of exchanging Christmas gifts.

The earthen savings box can still be found in the Netherlands, where it is commonly made in the shape of a pig, much like the American piggy bank. It is considered bad luck to break open this box, known as "The Feast Pig," before Christmas.

## *Horse*

St. Stephen is the patron saint of horses. According to a Swedish legend, he had five of them. As he made his rounds preaching the Word of God and one of his horses got tired, he simply mounted the next. After his death, his body was tied to the back of an unbroken colt, which brought him back to his hometown, Norrala, to be buried. The church that was later built on the site of his grave became a place of pilgrimage to which owners brought their sick animals, particularly horses, for healing. Some scholars think that this legendary Swedish St. Stephen is a mythical figure rather than the New Testament martyr, and that the legend surrounding him and his horses was an attempt to account for the folk customs that were already well established on this day.

In England at one time, horses were bled on St. Stephen's Day in the belief that it would benefit them — a custom that is still carried out in some parts of Austria. During St. Stephen's Day services in Munich, Germany, it was customary for more than 200 men on horseback to ride three times around the interior of a church, a practice that wasn't abolished until 1876. Horse races are common on this day, and horses are often fed consecrated salt or bread as a good-luck charm.

The customs associated with horses on this day appear to be non-Christian in origin. It is possible that horses were sacrificed or slaughtered on this day in pagan times, and that the horse races that often took place were a prelude to some kind of purification ceremony for houses and fields.

## Wren

In England and Ireland it was the custom on the day after Christmas to "hunt the wren." Young men and boys would dress up in leaves and branches to go out hunting, and after they had killed a bird, they fastened it to the top of a long pole and went from house to house collecting money. In some areas, a feather from the wren was exchanged for a small donation and then kept as protection against shipwreck during the coming year. After all the houses in the village had been visited, the wren was laid out on a funeral bier and carried to the churchyard, where it was buried with great solemnity. Sometimes the bird was boiled and eaten.

Known as "the king of birds," the wren was probably once regarded as sacred. Hunting it at Christmastime may have been all that remained of the primitive custom of slaying the divine animal. Carrying its body from door to door was apparently intended to convey to each house a portion of the bird's virtues. Eating the bird may have originally been some sort of communion feast.

## Further Reading

Brewster, H. Pomeroy. *Saints and Festivals of the Christian Church,* 1990.

Crippen, T. G. *Christmas and Christmas Lore,* 1990.

Henderson, Helene and Sue Ellen Thompson. *Holidays, Festivals, and Celebrations of the World Dictionary,* 2nd ed., 1997.

Hervey, Thomas K. *The Book of Christmas,* 1888.

Miles, Clement A. *Christmas in Ritual and Tradition,* 1990.

Santino, Jack. *All Around the Year,* 1994.

Schmidt, Leigh Eric. *Consumer Rites: The Buying and Selling of American Holidays,* 1995.

Urlin, Ethel L. *Festivals, Holy Days, and Saints' Days,* 1915.

# St. Sylvester's Day

**Type of Holiday:** Religious (Christian)

**Date of Observation:** December 31

**Where Celebrated:** Austria, Belgium, France, Germany, Hungary, Switzerland

**Symbols:** Bells, Pig

**Related Holidays:** New Year's Eve

## ORIGINS

St. Sylvester was Pope in the year 325 C.E., when the Emperor Constantine declared that the pagan religion of Rome would be replaced by Christianity as the official religion of the Empire. Although it is unclear exactly what role, if any, St. Sylvester played in this important event, he is usually given at least some of the credit for stamping out paganism. A number of European countries—including Belgium, Germany, and Switzerland—observe a holiday on the anniversary of Pope Sylvester's death in 335.

In Belgium, the last girl or boy to get out of bed on December 31 is nicknamed "Sylvester" and must pay a fine to his or her sisters and brothers—which means that most young people get up very early in the morning on this day. There is a superstition that the young girl who does not finish her work by sunset will not have any marriage prospects in the coming year.

In Switzerland, there is an old folk tradition that the spirits of darkness are out and about on the last night of the year. These demons must be frightened away by ringing bells and lashing whips. For centuries men and boys have dressed up as "Sylvesterklause" in costumes made from twigs, mosses, and other natural things. They walk through the countryside, stopping at every farmhouse to yodel a greeting and to receive coins and mulled wine. They perform dances designed to scare off demons and ring the huge bells they carry before moving on to the next house. Because St. Sylvester's Day is also **NEW YEAR'S EVE,** the Swiss celebrate by lighting bonfires in the mountains and ringing church bells to signal the passing of the old year and the beginning of the new. In some Swiss villages, grain is threshed on specially constructed platforms to ensure a plentiful harvest in the coming year.

In Germany, it is considered lucky to eat the traditional St. Sylvester's day carp, and to keep a few of the fish scales as a New Year's charm.

## SYMBOLS
### Bells

The custom of making noise — in this case, by ringing bells — to scare off evil demons can be traced back to very ancient times, long before the arrival of Christianity. The Sylvesterklause who go from house to house on this day in Switzerland wear costumes that include enormous bells, and church bells are rung in every village. In Geneva, Switzerland, a huge crowd gathers in front of the Gothic Cathedral of St. Pierre to listen to the midnight chiming of the bells, especially "La Clémence," believed to be the oldest and most beautiful bell in all of Europe.

### Pig

In Austria and Hungary, it is not uncommon in restaurants and cafés for the owner to set a pig loose at midnight on St. Sylvester's Day. Everyone tries to touch it because it is considered a symbol of good luck. In private homes, a pig made of marzipan might be hung from the ceiling or chandelier, with a gold piece placed in its mouth to symbolize the wish for wealth. At midnight, everyone touches the pig for good luck. In Vienna, people sometimes lead young pigs by pink satin leashes along fashionable city streets on St. Sylvester's Day.

### Further Reading

Brewster, H. Pomeroy. *Saints and Festivals of the Christian Church,* 1990.

Dobler, Lavinia. *Customs and Holidays Around the World,* 1962.

Hatch, Jane M. *The American Book of Days,* 1978.

Henderson, Helene and Sue Ellen Thompson. *Holidays, Festivals, and Celebrations of the World Dictionary,* 2nd ed., 1997.

Spicer, Dorothy G. *The Book of Festivals,* 1990.
Spicer, Dorothy G. *Festivals of Western Europe,* 1994.
Van Straalen, Alice. *The Book of Holidays Around the World,* 1986.

# *Samhain*

**Type of Holiday:** Ancient or pagan
**Date of Observation:** November 1
**Where Celebrated:** British Isles
**Symbols:** Bonfires, Harp, Swan
**Related Holidays:** All Souls' Day, Beltane, Halloween, Imbolc, Lughnasa

## ORIGINS

Samhain (pronounced *sah-win*) is an Irish word meaning "summer's end." Along with **IMBOLC** (February 1), **BELTANE** (May 1), and **LUGHNASA** (August 1), it was one of the four major Celtic festivals observed in ancient times. Samhain was the Celtic **NEW YEAR'S DAY**, a time of transition between the old and new year, when the souls of those who had died during the previous year gathered to travel to the land of the dead. The festival actually began at sundown on October 31, and many of the symbols now associated with **HALLOWEEN** — including witches, ghosts, and goblins— derived from the pagan belief that the gates to the underworld were opened on this day, and that the spirits of the dead were free to roam the earth. Since Samhain was also a harvest festival, people made offerings of fruits and vegetables to honor the dead.

Some of the customs associated with Samhain — and later with Halloween — can be traced back to the ancient Roman festival dedicated to Pomona, the goddess of fruit, held at around the same date. When the Romans conquered Britain, they brought these customs with them. The tradition of bobbing for apples, for example, probably comes from the Roman games played during Pomona's festival.

The early Christian missionaries particularly disliked Samhain's emphasis on the supernatural, and they tried to convince people that the spirits of the dead were actually delusions sent by the devil. Due largely to their efforts, the Celtic underworld eventually became associated with the Christian hell, and the concept of honoring the benevolent spirits of the dead gradually gave way to fears about evil spirits and witchcraft.

Although Samhain is widely regarded as the Celtic New Year's Day, some scholars believe that the Celts actually began their year in midsummer, somewhere between Beltane and Lughnasa.

## SYMBOLS

### Bonfires

In pagan times, the Druids in Ireland gathered to make human sacrifices to the gods on the eve of Samhain. All fires had to be extinguished, and they could only be rekindled from the sacrificial fire. Although such sacrifices no longer take place, it is still common in parts of Ireland and Scotland to extinguish the peat fires on Halloween and relight them from the bonfires that burn on the hilltops.

Bonfires were also a way of illuminating the path for the souls of the dead as they wandered from the world of the living back to the Celtic under-world. Some people hoped that their fires would scare off any spirits that meant them harm.

In addition to lighting bonfires, special lanterns were carved out of gourds or turnips. These were meant to symbolize the life-giving energy of the sun and to encourage its regeneration at a time of year when the days were growing shorter. Although carving and displaying pumpkins at Halloween is often assumed to be an American tradition, it is likely that the custom goes back much further.

### Harp

An old Irish legend associated with Samhain tells the story of the annual destruction of Tara, the magical hill which was also the ancestral seat of the gods. Every year at Samhain a goblin called Aillen played the harp so skill-fully that everyone was charmed into sleep, allowing him to set fire to the palace. A hero named Finn finally overcame Aillen's magic by holding the sharp point of a spear against his own forehead. The pain kept him awake while everyone else fell asleep.

As a symbol, the harp is regarded as a bridge between heaven and earth. This is why heroes often requested that a harp be buried with them, to facilitate their access to heaven. Along with the SWAN, the harp is consid-ered one of the essential symbols of the journey from the world of the liv-ing to the world of the dead.

## *Swan*

According to Irish folklore, a god named Oenghus fell in love with a young girl names Caer (also known as Rhiannon), who was capable of taking on the form of a swan at the festival of Samhain. Because her father would not let Oenghus woo Caer, the only way he could be with her was to wait for the festival and then transform himself into a swan. United at last, the pair flew three times around a lake, putting everyone else into a dream-sleep that lasted three days and three nights, giving the lovers an opportunity to fly off to the god's palace.

Along with the HARP, the swan is symbolically associated with the journey to the land of the dead, and it is often shown harnessed to funerary wagons. The festival of Samhain may have celebrated, through the legend of people and gods shape-shifting into swans, the transformation of life from one state to another. There is also some evidence that swan-dances were held at Samhain.

### Further Reading

Cirlot, J. E. *A Dictionary of Symbols,* 1962.

Heinberg, Richard. *Celebrate the Solstice: Honoring the Earth's Seasonal Rhythms through Festival and Ceremony,* 1993.

Henderson, Helene and Sue Ellen Thompson. *Holidays, Festivals, and Celebrations of the World Dictionary,* 2nd ed., 1997.

King, John. *The Celtic Druids'Year: Seasonal Cycles of the Ancient Celts,* 1995.

Leach, Maria, ed. *Funk & Wagnalls Standard Dictionary of Folklore, Mythology, & Legend,* 1984.

Santino, Jack. *All Around the Year,* 1994.

# *Saturnalia*

**Type of Holiday:** Ancient or pagan

**Date of Observation:** December 17-23

**Where Celebrated:** Rome, Italy

**Symbols:** Candles, Clay Dolls (Sigillaria), Holly and Ivy, Mock King

**Related Holidays:** Christmas, Feast of Fools, Twelfth Night, Winter Solstice

# ORIGINS

The ancient Roman **WINTER SOLSTICE** festival known as the Saturnalia was held in honor of Saturn, the god of agriculture and mythical king of Italy during its fabled "Golden Age." For seven days, all social distinctions and public business were suspended: The law courts and schools closed down, wars were interrupted or postponed, and slaves exchanged places with their masters. They sat down at the table, wearing their masters' clothes and the *pilleus* or badge of freedom. They could drink as much as they wanted and exhibit behavior that would normally have been punished by death or imprisonment. This temporary reversal of the social order was typical of ancient New Year's rites, which celebrated the "turning" of the year. It was often accompanied by masquerading or change of dress between the sexes, drinking, gambling, and other forms of frivolity and self-indulgence. The idea was to recapture "the good old days," when Saturn ruled and everyone was happy.

Although the festivities lasted for only seven days, the entire month leading up to the kalends (first day) of January was dedicated to Saturn. There were thanksgiving ceremonies at shrines and temples, public feasting, and private family feasts. People exchanged gifts, often in the form of artificial fruit (a symbol of fertility), CLAY DOLLS, or CANDLES. The most popular foods to serve at this time of year were figs, dates, plums, pears, and apples; fresh pomegranates and melons; sweet breads, cakes, and pastries in the shape of stars; nuts; and cider or mulled wine—all of which is now associated with **CHRISTMAS**. In fact, the date of Jesus Christ's birth was deliberately set to coincide with this pagan festival, which had degenerated over the centuries into a week-long spree of debauchery and crime. It is for this reason that the term "saturnalia" is now used to describe a period of unrestrained license and revelry.

# SYMBOLS

## Candles

The Saturnalia was a fire festival, when homes were decorated with candles and colored lanterns. One of the gifts frequently exchanged at the Saturnalia was wax tapers (*cerei*), believed to be a survival of the fires that traditionally burned at the **WINTER SOLSTICE**, the darkest time of the year. Much like the Yule log in northern Europe, burning candles was a means of bringing fire—symbol of the blessings of the sun god—into the house. Burning candles at the time of the solstice was also meant to symbolize— and perhaps to ensure—the return of the sun's power.

## Clay Dolls (Sigillaria)

Part of the celebration of the Saturnalia was a fair known as the *sigillario-rum celebritas,* at which people could buy the small clay images they later gave away as gifts. At one time there was actually a separate festival called the Sigillaria or Feast of Dolls, held on December 22. But it was eventually absorbed into the seven days of the Saturnalia.

Although there is no hard evidence that these earthenware dolls had symbolic value or that they served as more than playthings, some scholars believe that the little clay figures of the Holy Family—Mary, Joseph, and Jesus—traditionally sold in Rome's Piazza Navona at Christmastime are the modern-day counterparts of the *sigillaria* exchanged as gifts during the pagan Saturnalia.

## Holly and Ivy

The two plants associated with the Christmas season, holly and ivy, are also associated with the Saturnalia. Saturn's club was made from holly wood, and his sacred bird, the gold-crested wren, made its nest in ivy. The advent of Christianity, however, linked holly (spelled "holi" in Middle English) with Jesus. The berry and leaf of the holly became symbols for the blood of Christ and the crown of thorns that Jesus wore when He was crucified.

## Mock King

In the early days of the Saturnalia, a mock king was chosen by drawing lots. His role was to preside over the revels, which often included making ridiculous demands of his subjects—such as asking them to dance naked. It is possible that his behavior represented the last relic of a very ancient custom, which was to have a young man take on the role of Saturn for the duration of the festival and then, when his brief reign ended, be killed or sacrifice himself on the altar by cutting his own throat. Although this bloodshed was supposed to symbolize the renewal of life at the **WINTER SOLSTICE**, it is also possible that the mock king acted as a scapegoat—that is, by taking his own life, he took with him the offenses of the community as a whole. But as Roman society became more civilized, this human sacrifice was no longer considered acceptable. The mock king or Lord of Misrule survived, however, and can still be found in modern-day celebrations of **CARNIVAL** and **TWELFTH NIGHT**, as well as in the medieval **FEAST OF FOOLS**.

## Further Reading

Crippen, T. G. *Christmas and Christmas Lore,* 1990.

Frazer, Sir James G. *The Golden Bough: A Study in Magic and Religion,* 1931.

Heinberg, Richard. *Celebrate the Solstice: Honoring the Earth's Seasonal Rhythms through Festival and Ceremony,* 1993.

Henderson, Helene and Sue Ellen Thompson. *Holidays, Festivals, and Celebrations of the World Dictionary,* 2nd ed., 1997.

James, E. O. *Seasonal Feasts and Festivals,* 1961.

King, John. *The Celtic Druids'Year: Seasonal Cycles of the Ancient Celts,* 1995.

Leach, Maria, ed. *Funk & Wagnalls Standard Dictionary of Folklore, Mythology, & Legend,* 1984.

Miles, Clement A. *Christmas in Ritual and Tradition,* 1990.

Santino, Jack. *All Around the Year,* 1994.

# Shab-i-Barat
### *(Shaaban, Laylat Al-Bara'ah, Night of Forgiveness)*

**Type of Holiday:** Religious (Islamic)

**Date of Observation:** Night of the 15th of Sha'ban

**Where Celebrated:** Egypt, India, Iran, Pakistan, and throughout the Islamic world

**Symbols:** Fireworks, Lotus Tree

**Related Holiday:** Ramadan

## ORIGINS

The night of the 15th of Sha'ban, known as Shab-i-Barat in Pakistan and India, is a time when Muslims ask God to forgive the people they know who have died. They often visit graveyards to pray for the souls of deceased friends and relatives. Muslims also believe that this is the night when God reviews all the good and bad things they have done during the year and fixes their destinies for the coming year. In some countries, this is an occasion for celebration; in others, the night is spent in the mosque, praying and reading the Koran or Islamic holy book so that God will ordain good things.

Although the first day of Muharram marks the official beginning of the Islamic New Year, the 15th of Sha'ban, which falls in the middle of the eighth month, is in many ways more characteristic of a New Year's festival. FIREWORKS displays are common in some Muslim countries, and it is a popular time for people to ponder their future. Because it occurs right before the long fast of **RAMADAN**, Sha'ban is considered a very holy month. The Prophet Muhammad used to fast for several days during Sha'ban, offering prayers each night that grew more intense on the night following the 14th. In imitation of Muhammad, Muslims offer extra prayers on this night, asking forgiveness for their sins and God's blessings on the coming year.

## SYMBOLS

### Fireworks

In Iran, the 15th of Sha'ban is similar to the **FOURTH OF JULY** in America. It commemorates the marriage of Caliph Ali, the Prophet's cousin and one of the first converts to Islam, and Fatimah, the Prophet's daughter. Fatimah had many suitors, but her father wanted her to marry a blood relative. He decreed that only the man whose house had been struck by a falling star would be allowed to have his daughter. Because Ali was the Prophet's favorite, his house was hit by a falling star.

In honor of this legendary event, Muslims gather in the streets or go up on the rooftops to watch fireworks, symbolic of the falling star that struck Ali's house.

### Lotus Tree

In Egypt, it is believed that the Lotus Tree at the Boundary, which the Koran describes as standing at the extremity of Paradise, is shaken a little after sunset on the night of the 14th of Sha'ban (the Islamic day runs from sunset to sunset). The tree has as many leaves as there are human beings in the world, and each leaf has the name of a person written on it. If a leaf falls, it means that the person whose name is inscribed on it is destined to die in the coming year.

## Further Reading

Ahsan, M. M. *Muslim Festivals*, 1987.
Glassé, Cyril. *The Concise Encyclopedia of Islam,* 1989.

Henderson, Helene and Sue Ellen Thompson. *Holidays, Festivals, and Celebrations of the World Dictionary,* 2nd ed., 1997.

MacDonald, Margaret R., ed. *The Folklore of World Holidays,* 1992.

Von Grunebaum, G. D. *Muhammadan Festivals,* 1988.

# *Shalako Ceremony*

**Type of Holiday:** Ethnic (Native American)

**Date of Observation:** Late November-early December

**Where Celebrated:** New Mexico

**Symbols:** Shalako

**Related Holidays:** Winter Solstice

## ORIGINS

The Shalako Ceremony is the most important event of the year for the Zuni Indians of New Mexico. It takes place in the early winter, after the crops are in, and the timing is crucial. In former days, it was the duty of the Sun Priest to ensure that the Shalako Ceremony coincided as closely as possible with both the **WINTER SOLSTICE** and the full moon. During the eight days preceding the solstice, the Sun Priest would pray and fast, making pilgrimages to the sacred Thunder Mountain to commune with the Sun Father. On the ninth morning, he announced the approach of the solstice with a low, mournful call.

Nowadays everyone knows when the Shalako Ceremony will be held, and it attracts more outside visitors than any other Zuni festival. Preparations begin a full year in advance. Each of the SHALAKO must be housed and entertained during the festival — an expense that can take a family years to recover from. Although other members of the village help each host bring in his crop and fix up his house, the brunt of the expense falls to the individual. Sometimes a new house must be built to accommodate the Shalako dancers. At the very least, the existing house must be replastered.

About eight days before the ceremony, the Mudheads — clown-like figures wearing mud-daubed masks that resemble deformed human faces —

announce the arrival of the Shalako. Early on the morning of the ceremony, the "impersonators of the gods" and their attendants leave the village quietly, carrying their masks and other paraphernalia hidden under their blankets. The Fire God — usually a young boy with his body painted black and spotted with red, yellow, blue, and white — and his ceremonial father visit each house where the Shalako will be staying and leave two prayer-plumes, symbolizing the original man and woman, in a box. The Council of the Gods arrives next, making the same rounds that the Fire God has made and pausing in front of each house to dance and shake bunches of deer bones. The Council includes Sayatasha, the Rain God of the North, and Hu-tu-tu, the Rain God of the South. They enter the house designated for Sayatasha through a hatchway in the roof and are greeted by the host and his family, who sprinkle them with sacred meal. Food is put out for the Council members, and everyone eats.

By the time the Council of the Gods disappears, it is sunset and time for the Shalako to appear and perform their dance. Spectators gather behind a barbed-wire fence set up in an open field. The Shalako appear just at dusk — six huge figures who tower above their attendants, wearing headdresses with eagle feathers that fan out like the rays of the sun. They carry their masks on long poles hidden under blankets, and the same man who carries the pole manipulates the mask's bulging eyes and clacks its wooden beak. Each Shalako has two attendants: a manager and a man who will relieve him when he tires of dancing while maneuvering the heavy superstructure. The switch in dancers takes place behind blankets so that no one will see what is going on and the children won't know that these images aren't really gods. The dancers take great pride in balancing their masks and never missing a step as they bend their knees, dip their heads, and then right themselves. At the end of the ceremony, each Shalako enters the house that has been prepared for him, and a welcoming ceremony is performed there.

More dancing begins at midnight in the Shalako houses, where the men take turns handling the heavy, swaying masks. The departure of the gods takes place around noon, with the Fire God followed by the Council of the Gods and finally the Shalako themselves. Long lines of spectators watch them leave, with their peculiar swooping motion and clacking wooden beaks. Since the Shalako act as messengers to the gods, their departure is the final prayer for rain to fill the rivers, wells, and springs before summer arrives.

## SYMBOLS

### *Shalako*

According to Zuni legend, their ancestors emerged from the underworld to the earth's surface and searched for their "center," where they would find water and security. The Water Spider led them to an anthill, which he proclaimed was the center of the earth, instructing them to build their village there.

The Shalako, who are believed to have first appeared at Zuni around 1840, retrace the wanderings of the Zunis from the center of the earth to the modern pueblo. Since they are the couriers of the gods, they run back and forth all year carrying messages, bringing moisture and rain when it is needed. When they leave, they carry the Zunis' prayers for rain with them.

### Further Reading

Fergusson, Erna. *Dancing Gods: Indian Ceremonials of New Mexico and Arizona*, 1931.

Heinberg, Richard. *Celebrate the Solstice: Honoring the Earth's Seasonal Rhythms through Festival and Ceremony*, 1993.

Henderson, Helene and Sue Ellen Thompson. *Holidays, Festivals, and Celebrations of the World Dictionary*, 2nd ed., 1997.

Kelly, Aidan. *Religious Holidays and Calendars*, 1993.

Leach, Maria, ed. *Funk & Wagnalls Standard Dictionary of Folklore, Mythology, & Legend*, 1984.

# *Shavuot*
## *(Feast of Weeks)*

**Type of Holiday:** Religious (Jewish)

**Date of Observation:** Sixth day of Sivan; between May 16 and June 13

**Where Celebrated:** Europe, Israel, Palestine, United States, and by Jews all over the world

**Symbols:** Bikkurim, Milk and Honey, Roses

**Related Holidays:** Lag Ba-Omer, Passover, Sukkot

# ORIGINS

Shavuot — which means "weeks" in Hebrew — originated as an agricultural festival that took its name from the seven weeks between Pesach (or **PASSOVER**), when the first sheaf of barley was brought to the Temple in Jerusalem, and the beginning of the wheat harvest. Because the Jews had no written calendar, the exact date of Shavuot would be determined by counting seven weeks from the second day of Passover, with the holiday taking place on the 50th day. When a fixed calendar was later adopted, the 6th of Sivan was designated as the date of the harvest festival.

Every housewife would grind some fresh flour from the new grain and bake cakes and loaves of bread for the family feast. At the Temple in Jerusalem, there was a ceremonial sacrifice of two loaves baked from the new wheat crop. Pilgrims would come from all parts of the country to participate in the harvest ceremonies at the Temple, often bringing an offering of wheat as well as grapes, figs, and pomegranates (see BIKKURIM). Sometimes families would gather in each farming village and walk to Jerusalem together, forming a long column as they approached the temple. At the front of these processions there would be an ox whose horns were painted gold and decorated with olive branches. Behind the ox there would be musicians playing tambourines, flutes, and other instruments. They would bring their offerings to the Temple, where the priests would bless them.

After the Second Temple was destroyed, the Jews no longer had a place to perform this annual ritual. The rabbis looked for a way to preserve the holiday and give it new meaning. In the middle of the second century, they designated Shavuot as the anniversary of the day on which the Ten Commandments were given to the children of Israel at Mount Sinai. The agricultural and spiritual aspects of the festival formed a meaningful parallel: Just as Shavuot marked the end of seven weeks' collaboration between God and man in gathering the harvest, it also celebrated the end of a spiritual harvest, which began with the deliverance of the Jews from Egypt and reached its climax with the Covenant (or contract) between God and the people of Israel that was made on Mt. Sinai.

Many Shavuot customs are related to the Torah, or Jewish Bible, the contents of which were also revealed to Moses on Mt. Sinai. On the eve of the holiday, many pious Jews wash in the *mikvah* or ritual bath and put on new clothes so that they will be clean when they receive the Torah. They dedicate the evening to studying portions of the Torah and the Talmud, a collection of writings that constitute Jewish civil and religious law. The Book of Ruth is a popular selection to read on Shavuot because it manages to combine both the holiday's agricultural and religious roots. It tells the story of a pagan woman who was converted to Judaism, but the events take place against the background of the barley harvest.

Shavuot's agricultural roots have not been entirely forgotten. Houses and synagogues are decorated with flowers (see ROSES) and greenery; in Israel, children fill baskets with vegetables and fruits from their garden and carry them to school, where they are donated to charity.

## SYMBOLS

### *Bikkurim*

The Mishnah or first part of the Talmud describes how the *bikkurim* or first fruits used in the celebration of Shavuot are selected: "When a man comes down to his field and sees a ripe fig, or a ripe cluster of grapes, or a ripe pomegranate, he ties each with a red thread, saying, 'These are bikkurim.'"

In modern Israel, many kibbutzim (community settlements) and other agricultural communities have revived the bikkurim ceremony. Fresh produce is brought to a designated place by tractors, carts, and wheelbarrows that have been decorated with flowers and greenery. There is singing, folk dancing to the music of ancient instruments, and poetry reading. Sometimes there are pageants that re-create the traditional pilgrimage and ceremony at the Temple of Jerusalem.

One of the most colorful bikkurim ceremonies is held in Haifa, where Jews from the Sharon, Emek, and Jordan valleys gather to offer their first fruits to the Jewish National Fund (Keren Kayemet). There is a procession of young people carrying decorated baskets filled with ripe fruits and vegetables, sheaves of fresh-cut barley and wheat, jugs of honey (see MILK AND HONEY), and young fowl or lambs. After handing over the first fruits to the Keren Kayemet, everyone takes a seat in the open-air theater to enjoy the pageant known as *Hatene* or "The Basket," which is a reenactment of ancient bikkurim ceremonies.

In the United States, an impressive bikkurim festival is held annually in one of the city parks of Chicago.

### *Milk and Honey*

Cheese and dairy dishes are often served at Shavuot because, according to legend, the Israelites were too exhausted after witnessing the revelation on Mt. Sinai to slaughter an animal and cook its meat. It is also said that when they returned to their tents after spending all day at Mt. Sinai and discovered that their milk had gone sour, they turned it into cheese. Modern Jews eat cheese blintzes (pancakes filled with cottage cheese), ice cream, and cheese-filled kreplach (dumplings). Any food made from milk is considered symbolic, for milk plays the same role in physical growth that the Torah plays in moral and spiritual growth.

Honey, usually in the form of honey cakes, is also eaten on Shavuot. According to Jewish scholars, this is because the Torah is as sweet as honey and as nourishing as milk to those who study and live by its teachings.

## Roses

Flowers and greenery are used to decorate homes and synagogues at Shavuot for two reasons. Like **SUKKOT**, it originated as a celebration of the harvest. The flowers and green branches are symbols of the farming life that the Jewish people led in ancient times. It is also said that Mt. Sinai was unusually green on the day that Moses received the Ten Commandments. According to one version of the events of that day, the mountain was actually covered in roses. The custom of decorating with roses, either fresh or cut out of paper, was so prevalent at one time that the Persian Jews referred to Shavuot as the Feast of the Flowers, while Italian Jews called it the Feast of the Roses.

## Further Reading

Cohen, Hennig, and Tristram Potter Coffin, eds. *The Folklore of American Holidays,* 2nd ed., 1991.

Crim, Keith, ed. *The Perennial Dictionary of World Religions,* 1989.

Edidin, Ben. *Jewish Holidays and Festivals,* 1993.

Gaer, Joseph. *Holidays Around the World,* 1953.

Gaster, Theodor H. *Festivals of the Jewish Year,* 1953.

Harper, Howard V. *Days and Customs of All Faiths,* 1957.

Hatch, Jane M. *The American Book of Days,* 1978.

Henderson, Helene and Sue Ellen Thompson. *Holidays, Festivals, and Celebrations of the World Dictionary,* 2nd ed., 1997.

Ickis, Marguerite. *The Book of Festivals and Holidays the World Over,* 1970.

Kelly, Aidan. *Religious Holidays and Calendars,* 1993.

MacDonald, Margaret R., ed. *The Folklore of World Holidays,* 1992.

Renberg, Dalia H. *The Complete Family Guide to Jewish Holidays,* 1985.

Urlin, Ethel L. *Festivals, Holy Days, and Saints' Days,* 1915.

# *Shichi-Go-San*
## *(Seven-Five-Three Festival)*

**Type of Holiday:** Religious (Shinto)

**Date of Observation:** November 15

**Where Celebrated:** Japan

**Symbols:** Guardian Bag, Thousand-Year Candy, Toy Dog

**Colors:** Red is the most popular color for girls to wear on this day. Boys usually dress in gray and black.

## ORIGINS

It has long been traditional in Japan to take girls aged seven, boys of five, and all three-year-olds, dressed in their finest, to the neighborhood Shinto shrine on November 15 to invoke the blessings of the family's guardian gods. Three-year-old girls wear their hair fully dressed for the first time in the style worn by their mothers. Five-year-old boys put on traditional skirt-like trousers, and seven-year-old girls wear their first *obi,* or wide kimono sash.

After the young children have assembled at the shrine where they were registered at birth, the priest performs an old Shinto ritual in which he waves a branch in circles high over the children's heads. At the close of the brief ceremony, the priest's attendants come out, carrying white box-like trays with pyramids of small white paper packages, two for each child. One contains cakes in the form of the Shinto emblems — the mirror, the sword, and the jewel—while the other contains a small quantity of uncooked rice, which is considered sacred because it has been in front of the altar. The mothers take the rice home and mix it with the rice they serve at the evening meal, where family members offer their congratulations to the child before lifting their chopsticks to eat.

Seven, five, and three are considered lucky numbers in Japan, and the most fortunate mother of all is the one who has three children of the appropriate ages and sexes. Fathers often videotape their children as they receive the priest's blessings and a bag of THOUSAND-YEAR CANDY.

The Shichi-Go-San festival is believed to have originated back in the days when children often died young, and parents wanted to express their gratitude for those who had survived.

## SYMBOLS

### Guardian Bag

Many children carry a bag made of brocade or some other brightly colored cloth. It often contains a piece of writing that the priest gave to the child on his or her first visit to the shrine as an infant. Both boys and girls carry these so-called guardian bags, which are considered a symbolic protection against evil.

### Thousand-Year Candy

When they get to the shrine, the children who have come to celebrate the Seven-Five-Three festival are given sacks full of pink candy known as "Thousand-Year Candy." It is supposed to bring them good luck and a long life.

### Toy Dog

Almost every child carries a toy dog to the shrine. These dogs are usually black-and-white, with a cape-like red collar or a red band with a tiny bell. Friends and relatives give the toy dogs to the children as gifts on the festival, and some children are burdened with so many dogs that they must have help carrying them. The dogs, which can range in size from very small to 18 or more inches high, are considered to be good luck guardians for small children.

## Further Reading

Bauer, Helen, and Sherwin Carlquist. *Japanese Festivals,* 1965.

Dobler, Lavinia. *Customs and Holidays Around the World,* 1962.

Henderson, Helene and Sue Ellen Thompson. *Holidays, Festivals, and Celebrations of the World Dictionary,* 2nd ed., 1997.

MacDonald, Margaret R., ed. *The Folklore of World Holidays,* 1992.

Van Straalen, Alice. *The Book of Holidays Around the World,* 1986.

# Shick-Shack Day
## (Royal Oak Day, Restoration Day)

**Type of Holiday:** Historic

**Date of Observation:** May 29

**Where Celebrated:** England

**Symbols:** Oak Sprig

**Related Holidays:** May Day

## ORIGINS

Also known as Restoration Day, Shick-Shack Day commemorates the restoration of King Charles II to the throne in 1660, ending the Puritan Commonwealth that had been introduced in 1649. After his defeat by the English Parliamentarians (also known as Roundheads, because they wore their hair cut short), Charles II hid in an oak tree near Boscobel to escape the soldiers who were pursuing him. He was forced to remain there all day, unable to speak or shift his position for fear of being discovered.

This event occurred in September of 1651. He was restored to the throne in 1660, much to the relief of most of the English people. He is particularly remembered at the Royal Hospital in Chelsea, founded in 1682 as a refuge for old soldiers no longer able to earn a living. They celebrate their Founders' Day on May 29 by parading in his honor, by covering the statue of Charles II that stands in the center of the main courtyard with oak boughs, and by wearing a sprig of oak in their lapels.

Although it occurs at the end of May, Shick-Shack Day has much in common with **MAY DAY**. Maypoles are displayed along the streets of many English villages, and people dance around them much as they do elsewhere on May 1. Young women often bathe their faces in the early morning dew, and children bring branches and blossoms in from the woods—both popular May Day customs.

The *Oxford English Dictionary* suggests that this day takes its name from a corruption of *shitsack,* a derogatory name for the Nonconformists, Protestants who did not follow the doctrines and practices of the established Church of England. The term was later applied to anyone who didn't wear an oak leaf or oak-apple in memory of Charles II on May 29, and nowadays refers to the OAK SPRIG itself.

444

There are a number of local names for Shick-Shack Day. In some areas it is known as Oak Apple Day because people wear oak-apples as well as sprigs of oak leaves, and children gather twigs with oak-apples still attached and try to sell them in the streets. In the town of Ulverston, it is known as Bobby Ack Day—"bobby" referring to the knob-like oak-apple, and "ack" representing an older pronunciation of "oak." In other towns it is called Nettle Day, because children punish those who forget to wear an oak sprig by pushing them into a bed of nettles.

"The Royal Oak" is one of the most popular names for pubs in England today. The signs usually show Charles II peering through the leaves of an oak tree, looking more like a boy who's been caught stealing apples than a king escaping his enemies.

## SYMBOLS

### *Oak Sprig*

The sprig of oak worn by people on Shick-Shack Day is a symbol of the oak tree that concealed King Charles II when he was under attack by the Roundheads. The oak sprig also recalls the king himself, who was one of the most popular English monarchs and is still remembered for his many good deeds.

## Further Reading

Chambers, Robert, ed. *The Book of Days,* 1864.
Dunkling, Leslie. *A Dictionary of Days,* 1988.
Henderson, Helene and Sue Ellen Thompson. *Holidays, Festivals, and Celebrations of the World Dictionary,* 2nd ed., 1997.
Hole, Christina. *English Custom and Usage,* 1941.
MacDonald, Margaret R., ed. *The Folklore of World Holidays,* 1992.

# *Shrove Tuesday*

**Type of Holiday:** Religious (Christian)

**Date of Observation:** Between February 3 and March 9; day before Ash Wednesday

**Where Celebrated:** England, Europe, Scandinavia, United States, and by
Christians all over the world

**Symbols:** Games, Pancakes, Shrovetide Bear

**Related Holidays:** Ash Wednesday, Carnival, Lent

## ORIGINS

The verb "to shrive" originally meant "to write." In medieval England, a
priest would hear someone's confession and write down or prescribe an
appropriate penance. After absolution, the person was said to have been
"shriven." The last three days before **ASH WEDNESDAY** were referred to
as "Shrovetide," traditionally a period of penitence. The final day, Shrove
Tuesday, was the last opportunity for Christians to confess their sins before
the start of **LENT**.

Also known as Fat Tuesday (*Mardi Gras* in French) or Pancake Tuesday,
Shrove Tuesday was also a time for merrymaking. Back in the days when
Lent required wearing dark clothing, eating meals without meat, and ban-
ning all forms of pleasure and entertainment for 40 days, it was customary
for people to have a good time on the day before these restrictions went
into effect. Because they had to use up all the fat, eggs, and butter in the
house, housewives used these ingredients to make doughnuts, PANCAKES,
and other rich foods. In England, Shrove Monday was sometimes referred
to as Collop Monday for the same reason—a *collop* being a slice of meat. In
addition to eating more than usual, people would play GAMES and hold costume parades. The Mardi Gras celebration in New Orleans is typical of the
masquerades and dancing in the streets that still take place in many countries on this day.

## SYMBOLS

### Games

It was customary to hold seasonal games and contests on Shrove Tuesday
in England and elsewhere in Europe. Such activities may originally have
been designed to promote fertility and conquer the forces of evil at the
beginning of spring. In England, it was customary for parishes to divide
themselves into two opposing groups and engage in "rough and tumbles"
or a game of football. The earliest recorded game of Shrove Tuesday football took place at Chester in 1533. By the eigtheenth century, Shrovetide
games had become considerably more brutal, and often involved cockfight-
ing or hen-thrashing. Even the football games had a tendency to get out of

hand, resulting in broken legs and other injuries. As many as a thousand or more people would congregate at these events, and many would end up dunking each other in the nearest river. Shop windows were often shattered by tugs-of-war going on in the streets.

Although Shrovetide games were a widespread form of pre-Lenten celebration, they eventually died out in most areas because they were too dangerous and caused too much damage. They survived in a few small towns, however, up until the present century.

## Pancakes

Shrove Tuesday is believed to be a survival of the ancient Roman Fornacalia, or Feast of Ovens, which took place around February 17. A movable feast that lasted a week, it involved making an offering of *far*, a flour made from the oldest kind of Italian wheat, which was then roasted in the oven and crushed in a primitive mill and served in the form of cakes.

Centuries later, Shrove Tuesday became associated with frying pancakes, which gave housewives an opportunity to use up their leftover lard before the Lenten fast. Before the Reformation, eating anything made with fats or butter was strictly forbidden during Lent, and making pancakes (called *bannocks* in Scotland), doughnuts, or sweet buns was a form of thrift as well as self-indulgence. The typical menu served on this day in many European countries is still pancakes with sausages, bacon, or meat scraps.

Because so many pancakes were made on this day, they also featured prominently in the GAMES that were played. The most famous is the Pancake Race held since 1445 in Olney, England. The participants must wear a skirt, an apron, and a headscarf and flip their pancakes in the air three times as they run the 415-yard course.

## Shrovetide Bear

In Western Europe, especially in rural areas, it was traditional at one time to dramatize the "death" of **CARNIVAL** on Shrove Tuesday by condemning to death a scarecrow or strawman dressed in an old pair of trousers and known as the Shrovetide Bear or *Fastnachtsbär*. The effigy would often be beheaded, laid in a coffin, and buried in the churchyard on **ASH WEDNESDAY**. Sometimes it would be hanged, burned, drowned, or thrown in the village dump. In some areas, it was believed that if the last woman to marry jumped over the fire in which the Shrovetide Bear was burned, it would make her fertile.

In Bohemia in the eastern Czech Republic, a person in a mask or disguise, known as the "Oats Goat," is led from house to house on Shrove Tuesday. He dances with the women and, in return, receives food, money, and drink. Like the Shrovetide Bear, the Oats Goat is dressed in straw and wears horns on his head. He is also associated with fertility, because at one time it was believed that dancing with him ensured the growth of crops. Women would pluck bits of straw from him and put them in their hens' nests to guarantee a good supply of eggs.

## Further Reading

Allan, Philip. *The Folklore Calendar,* 1990.

Dobler, Lavinia. *Customs and Holidays Around the World,* 1962.

Frazer, Sir James G. *The Golden Bough: A Study in Magic and Religion,* 1931.

Harper, Howard V. *Days and Customs of All Faiths,* 1957.

Henderson, Helene and Sue Ellen Thompson. *Holidays, Festivals, and Celebrations of the World Dictionary,* 2nd ed., 1997.

Hole, Christina. *English Custom and Usage,* 1941.

Ickis, Marguerite. *The Book of Festivals and Holidays the World Over,* 1970.

James, E. O. *Seasonal Feasts and Festivals,* 1961.

Jobes, Gertrude. *Dictionary of Mythology, Folklore, and Symbols,* 1962.

Metford, J. C. J. *The Christian Year,* 1991.

Urlin, Ethel L. *Festivals, Holy Days, and Saints' Days,* 1915.

Weiser, Francis X. *Handbook of Christian Feasts and Customs,* 1952.

# *Simhat Torah*
### *(Festival of Rejoicing in the Law)*

**Type of Holiday:** Religious (Jewish)

**Date of Observation:** Twenty-third day of Tishri; between September 28 and October 26

**Where Celebrated:** Europe, Israel, United States, and by Jews all over the world

**Symbols:** Candles or Flags, Hakafot, Torah

**Related Holidays:** Shemini Aztaret, Sukkot

# ORIGINS

Simhat Torah, which follows **SUKKOT**, celebrates the annual completion of the public reading of the Jewish holy book known as the TORAH, which consists of the first five books of the Old Testament. In Hebrew, *Simhat Torah* means "rejoicing in the law," since the Torah is often referred to as "the Law" of the Jewish faith.

Unlike other major Jewish holidays, Simhat Torah is of relatively recent origin. The observance was established in Western Europe around the eleventh century. In ancient times, the public reading of the Torah took place on a three-year cycle, and it wasn't until the fourteenth century that the custom of reading the beginning of the Torah immediately after its completion was made official. To be chosen as the "Bridegroom of the Law," who reads the final verses of the last book (Deuteronomy), or the "Bridegroom of the Beginning," who reads the opening verses of the first book (Genesis), is considered a great honor. After the final portion has been read and special prayers have been recited, members of the congregation take the scrolls in their arms and dance in circles around the synagogue (see HAKAFOT).

In Israel and among Reform Jews, this festival is observed on the 22nd day of Tishri, concurrently with Shemini Aztaret (see **SUKKOT**). All other Jews celebrate Simhat Torah separately on the 23rd day. Israelis also hold a second HAKAFOT or procession around the synagogue on the night after Simhat Torah, frequently accompanied by bands and choirs.

Simhat Torah customs have varied from country to country. In Afghanistan, all the scrolls are taken out of their Arks and heaped in a pyramid that reaches almost to the synagogue's roof. In Cochin, China, a carpet was traditionally laid on the courtyard flagstones, coconut oil lamps were stacked up in a pyramid in front of the synagogue entrance, and the Scrolls of the Law were carried around the outside of the synagogue. One synagogue in Calcutta, India, has 50 scrolls, and the women go from scroll to scroll, kissing them. Young Yemeni children are taken to the synagogue for the first time on this holiday.

In southern France, two mourners stand on either side of the reader, crying bitterly as the death of Moses is related. The Bridegroom of the Law in Holland is escorted home in a torchlight parade accompanied by music. A crown was placed on the head of every reader in medieval Spain, and in some places in Eastern Europe, the reader wore a large paper hat decorated with bells and feathers.

# SYMBOLS

## *Candles or Flags*

The procession in which the scrolls of the TORAH are carried around the synagogue is usually led by children waving FLAGS and carrying poles topped by scooped-out apples in which candles have been inserted. These candles are considered symbolic of the Law or Torah itself, which is said to "enlighten the eyes."

In former times, the children leading the procession around the synagogue carried dried willow branches left over from **SUKKOT** and used them as torches. Concern for their safety prompted rabbis to prohibit this practice and ask children to substitute small candles. But some rabbis considered any form of fire unsafe and replaced the candles with flags topped with apples or beets in which candles have been inserted before being lighted, or flags topped with candles that remain unlit. During the eighteenth century, special Simhat Torah flags were introduced for the purpose of making the holiday more fun for children and encouraging their participation. These flags often display the Hebrew words meaning "Flag of the camp of Judah."

## *Hakafot*

The highlight of the evening service held on Simhat Torah is the series of seven ceremonial processions around the synagogue in which people take turns carrying the Torah scrolls. Known as *hakafot* or "encirclements," the custom is designed to be an expression of joy. A similar custom characterizes the traditional Jewish wedding, which includes walking seven times around the bridal couple in order to "close the circle" and protect the bride and groom from the demons believed to be hovering around them. The service held in the synagogue on Simhat Torah is really an imitation of the Jewish wedding service, symbolizing the "marriage" of Israel to the Law.

As a part of the Simhat Torah celebration, the hakafot custom began in the late sixteenth century, probably as an adaptation of the procession that already took place on **SUKKOT** with palm and willow branches. In Israel, where the celebration of Simhat Torah often continues well into the night, there is often a public hakafot with bands, singing, and dancing in public squares.

## *Torah*

The Jewish holy book is divided into three parts: (1) the Torah (The Law); (2) the Nevi'im (The Prophets); and (3) the Ketuvim (The Writings). While

450

all three are considered sacred, it is the Torah that receives the most reverence. It consists of the first five books of the Old Testament in the Christian Bible, written by Moses and often referred to as the Pentateuch: Genesis, Exodus, Leviticus, Numbers, and Deuteronomy.

The essential element and symbol of Simhat Torah, the Torah scroll is made of parchment (from the hides of kosher animals) attached at each end to a wooden roller. The scribe who copies the Torah onto the parchment, using a quill from a kosher bird and special black ink, cannot make a mistake when writing any words that refer to God or he must throw away the entire sheet. Mistakes in any other words can be erased with a pumice stone. After he has finished writing on the parchment, the sheets are sewn together with special threads made from the foot-tendons of a kosher animal.

The rollers are usually topped with silver ornaments called *rimonim,* which is Hebrew for "pomegranates"—perhaps a reference to their original form. When the Torah is rolled up, it is put inside an embroidered silk or velvet cover for protection, usually topped by an ornamental silver crown. A silver breastplate or *hoshen* is hung by chains on the cover of the Torah and decorated with pictures of various Jewish motifs. A silver pointer (*yad*) , usually in the shape of a hand with one finger extended, is used while reading the Torah because the parchment may not be touched.

## Further Reading

Cashman, Greer Fay. *Jewish Days and Holidays,* 1979.

Cohen, Hennig, and Tristram Potter Coffin, eds. *The Folklore of American Holidays,* 2nd ed., 1991.

Crim, Keith, ed. *The Perennial Dictionary of World Religions,* 1989.

Gaer, Joseph. *Holidays Around the World,* 1953.

Gaster, Theodor H. *Festivals of the Jewish Year,* 1953.

Hatch, Jane M. *The American Book of Days,* 1978.

Henderson, Helene and Sue Ellen Thompson. *Holidays, Festivals, and Celebrations of the World Dictionary,* 2nd ed., 1997.

MacDonald, Margaret R., ed. *The Folklore of World Holidays,* 1992.

Renberg, Dalia H. *The Complete Family Guide to Jewish Holidays,* 1985.

# *Songkran*
## *(Water Festival, New Year's Day in Thailand)*

**Type of Holiday:** Calendar, Religious (Buddhist)
**Date of Observation:** April 13-15
**Where Celebrated:** Thailand
**Symbols:** Water
**Related Holidays:** Holi

## ORIGINS

Songkran is the traditional New Year's Day celebration in Thailand, observed near the time of the **VERNAL EQUINOX**. The festivities, which are religious as well as secular, take place over a three-day period and include colorful processions and traditional games. The most widespread custom on this day, however, is throwing or sprinkling WATER on images of the Buddha, a traditional purification rite which usually leads to people throwing water at each other. Water-filled plastic bags are sold everywhere, so that everyone—even tourists—can join in the celebration. Not surprisingly, the most popular gift on this holiday is a towel.

Although the tendency among young people to douse each other with water can often get out of hand, people are careful to show respect to their elders by sprinkling water on their hands or feet. Monks, too, are shown respect by bringing them offerings of rice, meat, and fruit and by blessing them with a small amount of water.

## SYMBOLS

### *Water*

It is considered a blessing to be soaked with water on Songkran because it symbolizes the washing away of all the old year's evils and the giving of new life. For the same reason, it is common for people to release pet birds from their cages and to pour fish from their fishbowls into the river.

The custom of throwing water at one another is believed to have derived from the Hindu celebration of **HOLI**. It should also be remembered that while New Year's Day in the United States falls at the coldest time of year, in Thailand it can be extremely hot in April, which makes the water-splashing custom more welcome than it might be elsewhere.

## Further Reading

Henderson, Helene and Sue Ellen Thompson. *Holidays, Festivals, and Celebrations of the World Dictionary*, 2nd ed., 1997.

Ickis, Marguerite. *The Book of Festivals and Holidays the World Over*, 1970.

Kelly, Aidan. *Religious Holidays and Calendars*, 1993.

MacDonald, Margaret R., ed. *The Folklore of World Holidays*, 1992.

Shemanski, Frances. *A Guide to World Fairs and Festivals*, 1985.

Van Straalen, Alice. *The Book of Holidays Around the World*, 1986.

# *Soyaluna*
## *(Soyal, Soyala, Sol-ya-lang-eu)*

**Type of Holiday:** Ethnic (Native American)

**Date of Observation:** December 22

**Where Celebrated:** Arizona

**Symbols:** Plumed Snake, Sun Shield

**Related Holidays:** Hopi Snake Dance, Niman Katchina, Powamû Festival

## ORIGINS

Sun worship was very common among primitive peoples. In North America, the Hopi Indians observed the sun rising and setting at different points on the horizon. They also noticed that it reached its most vertical position in the sky in summer, and that when it rose lower in the sky, the weather was cold and the earth was barren. In midsummer, when they imagined the sun close to the earth, the Hopis performed their Snake Dance (see **HOPI SNAKE DANCE**), asking the snake to bring their request for rain to the gods of the underworld. But when the sun started to withdraw, their attention shifted to preventing it from forsaking them altogether. At the time of the **WINTER SOLSTICE** in December, they believed that the Sun God had traveled as far from the earth as he ever did. It required the most powerful humans—in this case, the warriors—to persuade the Sun God to turn around and come back to the pueblo. The purpose of the Soyaluna ceremony, which is still held among the Hopi today, is to prevent the disappearance of the sun at the time of year when the days are at their shortest.

Preparations for the ceremony begin with cutting pieces of cotton string and tying feathers and pinyon needles to the end. These are exchanged among friends and relatives during the day, and are sometimes tied in the recipient's hair. When the person who made the feathered string presents it to a friend, he says, "May all the Katchinas grant you your wishes tomorrow"—the Katchinas being the spirits of the Hopi ancestors. Then the giver holds his or her gift vertically and moves it back and forth horizontally. At night, everyone takes a willow branch and attaches all the strings that he or she has received to it. The sticks are carried to the *kiva* or ceremonial meeting room and placed in the rafters, making the room look like a bower of feathers and pinyon needles.

The main celebration takes place in the kiva. The chief of the resident Hopi society wears a headdress decorated with symbols of rain clouds and carries a shield on which the sun appears. Representatives of other societies carry shields on which a star, an antelope, or other symbolic objects have been drawn. Someone carries an effigy of Palulukonuh, the PLUMED SNAKE, carved from the woody stalk of the agave plant.

The shield bearers enter the kiva and take turns stamping on the *sipapu,* a shallow hole covered by a board, which is the symbolic entrance to the underworld. Then they arrange themselves into two separate groups—one on the north and one on the south side of the room—and start singing, while the bearer of the SUN SHIELD rushes to one side and then to the other. He is driven back by the shield bearers on both sides, whose movements symbolize the attack of hostile powers on the sun. It is not uncommon for one or more of the participants in this mock struggle to faint from the heat and exhaustion.

On the west wall of the kiva, there is an altar consisting of a stack of corn, two or more ears of which have been contributed by each family in the pueblo, surrounded by stalks and husks. There is also a large gourd with an opening in it, from which the head of the Plumed Snake effigy protrudes. Manipulated by someone behind the altar, the snake's head rises slowly to the center of the opening and makes a roaring noise. The shield bearers throw meal to the effigy and in response to each offering, the snake roars again. During the ceremony the Hopi priest sprinkles sand on the floor of the kiva. When the Sun God's footprints appear in the sand, everyone knows that he has been persuaded to return.

One of the most sacred ceremonies held by the Hopi, Soyaluna means "Prayer-Offering Ceremony." It is a time for saying prayers for the New Year and for wishing each other prosperity and health.

## SYMBOLS

### Plumed Snake

The effigy of the Plumed (or Plumed-Head) Snake that appears in the kiva during the Soyaluna ceremony is painted black, with a tongue-like appendage protruding from its mouth. The snake symbolizes the evil influences that are driving the sun away. The assembled chiefs make their offerings of prayer and meal to the Plumed Snake to persuade him not to "swallow" the sun, as he does when there is an eclipse.

### Sun Shield

The Hopis have their own explanation for why the days grow shorter in winter and longer in summer. They envision the sun as being driven away by hostile forces and then, after a considerable struggle, persuaded to return. Without the Soyaluna ceremony, the sun might never return, bringing the warmer weather that is needed for growing corn and other food. The bearer of the Sun Shield, therefore, represents the Hopi Sun God, whose favors are crucial to the tribe's survival.

## Further Reading

Fewkes, Jesse Walter. *Tusayan Katcinas and Hopi Altars,* 1990.

Heinberg, Richard. *Celebrate the Solstice: Honoring the Earth's Seasonal Rhythms through Festival and Ceremony,* 1993.

Henderson, Helene and Sue Ellen Thompson. *Holidays, Festivals, and Celebrations of the World Dictionary,* 2nd ed., 1997.

Leach, Maria, ed. *Funk & Wagnalls Standard Dictionary of Folklore, Mythology, & Legend,* 1984.

# *Sukkot*
## *(Sukkoth, Succoth)*

**Type of Holiday:** Religious (Jewish)

**Date of Observation:** 15-21 Tishri (begins between September 20 and October 18)

**Where Celebrated:** Europe, Israel, United States, and by Jews all over the world

**Symbols:** Beating the Willow, Four Species, Sukkah, Water Libation Ceremony

**Related Holidays:** Simhat Torah, Yom Kippur

## ORIGINS

The Jewish holiday of Sukkot can be traced back to an ancient Canaanite holiday held after the grape harvest, around the time of the autumn equinox. Jewish farmers made little booths or SUKKAHS from the branches of fruit trees and evergreens and lived in them throughout the seven days of the celebration. It was primarily a festival of thanksgiving, a time to celebrate the fruit harvest — as opposed to **SHAVUOT**, which marked the end of the grain harvest. Many farmers collected some of their produce, gathered up their families, and made a pilgrimage to Jerusalem for the festival. Often referred to as the Feast of the Ingathering because of its associations with the gathering of the harvest and the close of the agricultural year, Sukkot also involved the performance of special ceremonies designed to induce rainfall.

After the Jews were released from slavery in Egypt, they wandered for 40 years before entering the Promised Land. During this period they lived in tents or booths (called *succot* or *sukkot*), which they pitched wherever they happened to stop for the night. When they finally reached the Promised Land, most of them became farmers. Because the fields were so far from their homes, they would often live in the fields for the entire period of the harvest, once again building *succot* to protect themselves from the sun during the day and the cold wind at night. The holiday that originally celebrated the ingathering of the harvest, therefore, took on added significance as the Feast of Tabernacles or the Feast of Booths, commemorating the period in Jewish history when the *sukkah* was the only home that the Jews knew.

Sukkot begins at sundown on the 14th day of Tishri. On the first two days, people build small huts out of branches to recall the sukkot in which their ancestors lived. The inside is hung with apples, grapes, corn, pomegranates, and other fruits and vegetables to commemorate the harvest. In the synagogue, Jews give thanks to God for the plants He has created by waving the FOUR SPECIES in all directions. The seventh day is more of a holiday than the third through sixth days, which are considered half-holidays. According to tradition, this is the last possible day on which one can seek and obtain forgiveness for the sins of the previous year — an extension of the Day of Atonement or **YOM KIPPUR**. Pious Jews stay up half the night chanting psalms and reading sacred books. Most try to stay awake until midnight, when they believe that the heavens open up. Children in particular believe that if they make a wish at the moment the skies open, it is certain to come true.

The eighth day of Sukkot, known as Shemini Aztaret, is the Day of Solemn Assembly. A more serious mood prevails on this day, and it is customary to eat meals in the SUKKAH. Special services for people who have died are held in the synagogue, and prayers are offered for rain in Israel. No matter where they live, Jews pray for rain in their homeland during this season because it is needed there to ensure a good spring harvest. The afternoon of Shemini Aztaret is spent visiting and receiving friends and relatives. The following day, known as **SIMHAT TORAH**, celebrates the completion of the reading of the Torah, which immediately begins again. Simhat Torah is now celebrated as a separate holiday by Orthodox and Conservative Jews.

Sukkot has remained a major festival throughout the centuries. Ceremonies that were originally held in the Temple have been moved to the synagogue and the home, but the holiday has retained both its agricultural and historical significance. But of all the Jewish festivals, Sukkot has suffered the most from the changes brought about by modern life. It is difficult to build a sukkah in many modern cities, and because the festival is based on events that occurred more than 3,000 years ago, modern Jews have found it difficult to identify with the customs and hardships they are commemorating.

## SYMBOLS

### *Beating the Willow*

On the last day of Sukkot, willow twigs (see FOUR SPECIES) are beaten against the altar until all the leaves fall off. The usual explanation for this custom is that it symbolizes the fragility of human life, which fades and falls like autumn leaves. Some say that the falling leaves are also symbolic of sins that have been cast away.

The tradition is probably rooted in the primitive belief that the willow is a symbol of fertility and that beating people with willow branches ensures potency and fertility. The beating of the willow branches on the seventh day of Sukkot is not unlike the "Easter smacks" used in some European countries to promote fertility.

## *Four Species*

In the religious services held each morning during Sukkot, Jews engage in a thanksgiving ritual involving four symbolic plants: the *lulav* or date palm, the myrtle, the willow, and the *etrog*, a fragrant citrus fruit that resembles a large lemon. Three myrtle twigs and two willow branches are tied around a long branch of lulav, while the etrog is taken out of its special, well-padded box. As prayers are said, the lulav and the etrog are waved in all directions, and the worshippers thank God for the good things that come from the earth. Because Sukkot has its roots in farming, harvesting, and the world of nature, these prayers usually include a plea for rain to help the crops grow.

These four fruits or "species" were chosen because they were abundant in ancient Israel and would last throughout the seven-day festival without wilting. But over the years, they have accumulated symbolic meaning as well. Some say they stand for the four most important bodily organs: the heart (etrog), the spine (lulav), the eye (myrtle), and the lips or mouth (willow). Another interpretation is that they stand for four different types of people: The etrog represents the person who possesses both beauty and character; the lulav is the person who is beautiful but has no character; the myrtle is the person with character who lacks beauty; and the willow is the person who lacks both. Yet another theory is that they symbolize the four periods of Jewish history: The stately lulav recalls the period of kings and prophets; the fragrant myrtle is a reminder of the Talmudic era of learning and wisdom; the drooping willow symbolizes the Jews' period of exile and wandering; and the etrog, which is both beautiful and fragrant, symbolizes their hope for the future.

A simpler explanation is that the Four Species represent all forms of vegetation. The etrog tree, whose fruit resembles an oversize lemon, is fragrant but needs human attention to help it grow. The lulav or date palm, which has no scent, represents those fruit-bearing trees that can survive on rainwater alone. The myrtle is a pleasant-smelling, ornamental shrub that does not yield edible fruit. And the willow, which needs a great deal of water to grow, has neither fruit nor fragrance but is useful for building things and for making fires.

In the synagogue, there is a procession in which the lulav and the etrog are waved in unison each day during Sukkot. On the seventh day, the procession is repeated seven times. After the service, the lulav is given to the children, who weave rings, bracelets, and baskets from strips of palm leaf.

## Sukkah

Building a sukkah in the backyard—or on a terrace or rooftop—is the primary tradition associated with Sukkot. It must have at least two standing walls, and the roof must be made of leaves and twigs so that the stars can shine through and people will be reminded of God in heaven. Some Jews avoid using nails when they build the sukkah because metal is associated with the tools of war.

The sukkah represents the huts in which Jewish farmers traditionally lived during the harvest season in Palestine and the tents in which the exiled Jews were sheltered during their desert wanderings. It also stands as a symbol of the brevity and insecurity of human life. For modern Jews, it serves as a reminder of the lack of safety and security experienced by millions of Jews in Germany, Italy, Poland, Rumania, Hungary, and other countries. According to the Talmud, the sukkah's frail roof should remind people not to put too much trust in the power of man.

Traditionally, all meals are eaten in the sukkah throughout the festival. But since it is often impossible to do this in modern cities, the rules have been modified to require that at least one meal be taken in the booth each day and each night of the festival. Since building a sukkah may be impossible for those who live in apartment buildings, the usual solution is a communal sukkah set up in the courtyard of the synagogue. The greens, fruits, and flowers with which it is decorated are more likely to come from the local florist or grocery store, and a perfunctory visit to the sukkah after the synagogue service often substitutes for spending the night in it.

The task of building the sukkah, as well as eating and sleeping in it, usually falls to the male members of the family. The mother and girls are responsible for decorating it, typically with the seven Israeli farm products mentioned in the Bible (grapes, figs, pomegranates, wheat, barley, olives, and honey). In Europe, the decorations often include cutout paper chains and lanterns, pictures of holy men and places, and birds made out of egg shells and feathers.

## Water Libation Ceremony

At one time, the second day of Sukkot marked the ancient water-drawing (or water-pouring) ceremony described in the Talmud. A golden pitcher was filled with water from a spring outside Jerusalem. The person who carried the pitcher was greeted by three blasts of the shofar (or ram's horn) and by shouts of joy from several thousand pilgrims who had gathered at the city's Water Gate. They joined the procession to the altar, where the priest took the golden vase and poured water over the altar while the pilgrims sang. That night, the Temple court was illuminated with candles and torches, and people danced and sang around the pillars. At a given signal, they formed a huge procession and marched to the eastern gate of the city accompanied by harps, lutes, cymbals, and trumpets.

The water libation ceremony is based on "sympathetic magic," the ancient notion that the things men do may induce similar actions on nature's part. Pouring water, for example, was probably designed to induce rain, and lighting candles and torches might originally have been a magical rite that would rekindle the sun at the time of the autumn equinox.

Nowadays, the once elaborate water-pouring ceremony has dwindled to a special celebration in the synagogue on the night of the second day. Psalms are chanted and the evening is spent eating, drinking, and being entertained. Jewish organizations often organize special parties on this evening, which they call Simhat Bet Hashoevah gatherings.

## Further Reading

Cashman, Greer Fay. *Jewish Days and Holidays,* 1979.

Cuyler, Margery. *Jewish Holidays,* 1978.

Edidin, Ben. *Jewish Holidays and Festivals,* 1993.

Gaer, Joseph. *Holidays Around the World,* 1953.

Gaster, Theodor H. *Festivals of the Jewish Year,* 1953.

Henderson, Helene and Sue Ellen Thompson. *Holidays, Festivals, and Celebrations of the World Dictionary,* 2nd ed., 1997.

Ickis, Marguerite. *The Book of Festivals and Holidays the World Over,* 1970.

Penner, Lucille Recht. *The Thanksgiving Book,* 1986.

Purdy, Susan. *Festivals for You to Celebrate,* 1969.

Renberg, Dalia H. *The Complete Family Guide to Jewish Holidays,* 1985.

Santino, Jack. *All Around the Year,* 1994.

# *Summer Solstice*

**Type of Holiday:** Ancient or pagan, Calendar

**Date of Observation:** June 21 or 22 in the Northern Hemisphere; December 21 or 22 in the Southern Hemisphere

**Where Celebrated:** Modern observances of the Summer Solstice are rare, but in ancient times it was observed throughout Europe, the British Isles, China, Egypt, North Africa, and Scandinavia.

**Symbols:** Bonfires, Herbs, Midsummer Bride, Mock Funerals

**Related Holidays:** Winter Solstice, Midsummer Day, Incwala, Inti Raymi Festival

## ORIGINS

Few celebrations can be traced back as far as the Summer Solstice, the day when the sun is at its furthest point from the equator. It reaches its northernmost point around June 21, which is the longest day of the year for those living north of the equator, and its southernmost point around December 22, which is the longest day for those living in the Southern Hemisphere. The word "solstice" comes from the Latin *solstitium* meaning "sun-stopping," because the point in the sky where the sun appears to rise and set stops and reverses direction after this day.

One of the oldest celebrations of the Summer Solstice took place in ancient Egypt at the Temple of Amen-Ra at Karnak, whose foundations date back to about 3700 B.C.E. On the day of the solstice, a beam of light would illuminate a sanctuary in the temple's interior for about two to three minutes, during which the brightness would reach a peak and then begin to subside. This dramatic spotlighting effect enabled the Egyptian priests to calculate the length of the solar year with a high degree of accuracy.

A similar phenomenon was observed at Stonehenge in the Wiltshire plain of southwest England. Built by pre-Celtic peoples over a period of many centuries, beginning around 2800 B.C.E., this ancient monument composed of enormous stone arches was a gathering place for ancient tribes throughout southern England at the time of the Summer Solstice. If one stands at the center of the monument and faces northeast along its axis, the 35-ton Heel Stone appears 256 feet away, marking the approximate place on the horizon where the sun rises on the Summer Solstice. In recent years, astronomers have discovered at least two dozen other solar and lunar alignments that the ancient builders of Stonehenge incorporated into its structure.

The earliest Chinese emperors observed the Summer Solstice in ways designed to stimulate the earthy, feminine *yin* forces. The solstice rites took place on the Altar of the Earth just north of the Forbidden City. Unlike the Round Mound used to observe the **WINTER SOLSTICE**, the altar was square and had a stairway leading in each of the four cardinal directions (north, south, east, and west). While the human sacrifice that took place at the Winter Solstice was burned, in summer the sacrificial victim was buried, thus maintaining a healthy balance in the earth's natural rhythms.

If the Winter Solstice is an occasion for hope, when the days begin to grow longer, the Summer Solstice is often tinged with sadness. Although it is a time of warmth, abundance, and fertility, when the days are long and nature is at her peak, it is also the point after which the days begin to get shorter and the darkness increases. While Winter Solstice traditions can still be found in modern **CHRISTMAS** and **NEW YEAR'S DAY** celebrations, the ancient Summer Solstice rites have virtually disappeared. In the United States, it is usually "New Age" groups who continue to celebrate the June solstice. One of the largest celebrations is held in Belfast, Maine, home of the Institute of Advanced Thinking, which has been described as "the world's oldest think tank." People arrive in Belfast from five countries and as many as 20 different states the night before the solstice. They set up their tents and sleeping bags outdoors and rise at dawn to greet and worship the sun with prayers and ritual chants.

## SYMBOLS

### *Bonfires*

Lighting bonfires was one of the most universal of ancient midsummer rites—one that still survives in some northern European countries. In Denmark and Norway, the fires were believed to prevent cattle from being struck by disease. The Germans looked into the fire through branches of larkspur in the belief that this would keep their eyes healthy. In Scotland, cowherds walked around their cattle three times carrying burning torches in order to purify and protect the animals.

Solstice bonfires were also associated with fertility and courtship. In Bohemia, girls and boys would stand on opposite sides of the fire and look at one another through wreaths they'd made to see whether they would be true to one another and who would marry whom. Then the girls would throw their wreaths across the flames toward their sweethearts. The singed wreaths were taken home afterward and kept in the house, in the belief that they offered protection from illness and thunderstorms throughout the year. When the fire had burned down a little, the couples would join hands and leap across the embers three times.

At San Pedro Manrique in Spain, people still build a bonfire and light it at six o'clock on Midsummer Eve. At midnight, they spread its coals into a carpet and walk barefoot across the glowing path, each carrying another person on his or her back. Midsummer bonfires are also common in North Africa, even though the Islamic calendar is lunar and therefore independent of the seasons. This would seem to suggest that the custom of lighting fires is even older than the arrival of Islam.

## Herbs

The Summer Solstice was associated with the earth's feminine energies. Since most healers in preindustrial Europe were women and most of their healing was accomplished with herbs, the solstice was considered the best time of year to gather the herbs that would cure diseases and offer protection against evil. When the Christian Church tried to draw attention away from the pagan rites of the solstice by making June 24 St. John the Baptist's Day, these herbs were referred to as "St. John's herbs."

*Mugwort* was gathered at the solstice and made into garlands. Herbalists still use mugwort to cure rheumatism, fevers, and ague. When sewn into a pillow, its dried leaves are said to induce vivid dreams. In France, mugwort is known as the "herb of St. John"—a clear attempt to Christianize an old pagan remedy.

*Verbena*, also referred to as *vervain*, was gathered after sunset on Midsummer Eve and soaked overnight in water, or dried and worn around the neck. It was highly valued for its ability to strengthen the nervous system and relieve stress. The ancients used it as an aphrodisiac.

*St. John's wort* blooms around the time of the Summer Solstice, putting out masses of bright yellow flowers that resemble the sun. Its oil is still used to relieve sunburn, and the ancients believed that one whiff of this strong-scented plant would send evil spirits running.

Among Christians, *Hawkweed* or *Mouse-ear* root was believed to contain the blood of St. John. But the ancients valued the milky, reddish juice of the plant as a remedy for whooping cough and respiratory diseases.

Ancient peoples believed that *ferns* bloomed at midnight on Midsummer Eve. Whoever saw the blooming take place would be endowed with miraculous knowledge and power. But if the magical flower was touched by a human hand, it would vanish instantly.

Other herbs associated with the Summer Solstice and midsummer in general include chamomile, geranium, thyme, rue, chervil seed, giant fennel, and pennyroyal, all of which were prized for the aromas they gave off when they were thrown on BONFIRES.

## Midsummer Bride

Because it marked the peak of the summer season, the solstice was associated with fertility and sexuality. Even today, June remains the most popular month for weddings, although most people know nothing about the ancient ceremonies involving symbolic marriage that once took place at midsummer.

In Sweden, each village chose a Midsummer Bride, who in turn selected a mock-bridegroom. Young men of the village also took advantage of the season to choose temporary brides. In Sardinia, these summer solstice couples were known as "Sweethearts of St. John," and the celebration featured pots of sprouting wheat and barley that suggested a symbolic link between human sexuality and the fertility of nature.

These marriage rituals were more than play-acting; they were designed to make the crops grow and the flowers bloom. The ancients believed that human sexual intercourse exercised a harmonizing influence on nature and society—an influence that was particularly needed at the solstices, when Heaven and Earth were at their extremes.

## Mock Funerals

The Summer Solstice was the point after which the days grew shorter and the light declined. Many of the ancient rites that took place at the solstice were designed to postpone the sun's decline by celebrating life and fertility, or to mourn its passing. Midsummer was therefore a popular time for both weddings (see MIDSUMMER BRIDE) and funerals. In Tsarist Russia, midsummer was celebrated by dressing a straw man in women's clothes and decorating it with a crown of flowers. Young people would take this effigy in their arms and leap over a bonfire; on the following day, it would be stripped and thrown into a stream. In some areas, the straw figure was attacked and torn to bits, after which its "death" would be loudly mourned. Sometimes it was carried in a coffin through the streets.

The point of these mock-funeral rites was to mourn the "death" of the sun and the beginning of the cycle of decay in the natural world. Both weddings and funerals were seen as moments of transformation, when energy was released and Heaven and Earth were momentarily reunited.

## Further Reading

Frazer, Sir James G. *The Golden Bough: A Study in Magic and Religion*, 1931.

Heinberg, Richard. *Celebrate the Solstice: Honoring the Earth's Seasonal Rhythms through Festival and Ceremony*, 1993.

Henderson, Helene and Sue Ellen Thompson. *Holidays, Festivals, and Celebrations of the World Dictionary*, 2nd ed., 1997.

King, John. *The Celtic Druids'Year: Seasonal Cycles of the Ancient Celts*, 1995.

# *Sun Dance*

**Type of Holiday:** Ethnic (Native American)

**Date of Observation:** Late June-Early July (full moon closest to the summer solstice)

**Where Celebrated:** North America

**Symbols:** Buffalo, Sage, Sun Pole, Willow

**Colors:** The Sun Dance is associated with the colors red (symbol of the sunset), yellow (forked lightning), white (light), and black (night).

**Related Holidays:** Summer Solstice

## ORIGINS

Seasonal and celestial cycles were very important to the nomadic Native Americans who at one time inhabited the Great Plains of North America. Most of the tribes, particularly the Sioux, participated in a common ceremonial event known as the Sun Dance, traditionally held at the time of the full moon closest to the **SUMMER SOLSTICE**. The entire ceremony lasted 16 days: Eight days were spent in preparation, the performance itself took four days, and there were four days of abstinence. It was a time of renewal and healing, and it was crucial that it take place at midsummer, when the SAGE plant was succulent and when the sun was at its highest point in the sky.

The participants did not eat or drink during the dance itself. They took a sweat bath in the morning on the first day and painted their bodies in the symbolic colors of red, blue, yellow, white, and black (see "Colors"). They dressed in a deerskin apron, wristlets and anklets made of rabbit fur, and a feather in their hair. Members of tribes from many miles around would set up their tipis to form a circular dance enclosure around the SUN POLE, which had been cut and painted in advance. To the accompaniment of a large drum and special ceremonial songs, the dancers circled in procession and paid homage to the sun.

Pain and self-sacrifice were an essential part of life to many Native American tribes, and the Sun Dance provided them with an opportunity to renew themselves and give thanks to the sun by sacrificing their own flesh. Certain participants in the dance, known as "pledgers," would have wooden skewers (or sometimes eagle claws) inserted under the skin of their chests. The skewers were then attached to a strong rope and tied to the Sun Pole. The dancers formed a circle around the pole, and after going toward it four times to place their hands on it and pray, they would pull back as hard as they could until the skewers were torn free. An alternative method was to have two skewers inserted under the skin of the shoulder blades. Heavy buffalo skulls (see BUFFALO) would be hung from the skewers by thongs and dragged around until their weight eventually tore the skewers loose. Yet another variation was for the dancers to suspend themselves from the pole with ropes attached to the skewers or tie the ropes to a horse. The dancers would continue this way until they fell unconscious from the pain or tore themselves loose, after which they believed they would receive a divine vision. Although such self-inflicted tortures sound barbaric today, at the time the participants had the moral support of the entire tribe. The ceremony was popular at one time among the Kiowa, Bungi, Mandan, Hidatsa, Arapaho, Cheyenne, Blackfoot, and Crow. The Shoshone, Ute, Comanche, and other tribes performed the dance without the self-torture.

Many Indian tribes believe that the sun "died" after the solar eclipse of August 7, 1869. The Sioux performed their last Sun Dance in 1881. The torture elements of the dance were widely misunderstood, which resulted in its being condemned in many areas. It survives, however, among some of the northern and western tribes, particularly the Southern Utes and the Arapaho, who hold their Sun Dance without any sacrifice of flesh.

## SYMBOLS

### Buffalo

The buffalo head is a symbol of plenty, because at one time Native Americans killed and ate the animals and used their skins for clothing. The buffalo also symbolizes strength and comfort. It was often featured in the Sun

Dance because the buffalo feeds on SAGE and WILLOW, which means that it ultimately depends on the sun.

The buffalo figures prominently in the Sun Dance held by the Arapaho Indians on the Wind River Reservation near Fort Washakie, Wyoming. A huge center pole (see SUN POLE) with a buffalo head on top and 12 outer poles surrounding it form a circular enclosure within which the dance is performed. The buffalo head faces west, toward the Rocky Mountains, and freshly picked SAGE is placed on its nose. The dancers approach the pole and then step back, always keeping their eyes on the buffalo head.

## Sage

Sage was often placed on the nose of the buffalo head that surmounted the central SUN POLE in the dance enclosure. Since sage is known for its strong scent and was a common symbol for healing as well as breathing, placing it on the buffalo's nose made it seem as though the buffalo were still alive and able to breathe.

## Sun Pole

The tall pole, usually cottonwood, that occupies the center of the circular enclosure in which the Sun Dance is performed is both a phallic symbol and a symbol of the sun. Among the Sioux, it represented *Wakan-Tanka,* the all-pervading power of the universe. The ceremonial cutting of the Sun Pole was conducted by four young virgins, two male and two female. Among some tribes, a sword or stick was substituted.

## Willow

Both the Ute and the Cheyenne fastened a willow branch in the fork at the top of the cottonwood SUN POLE. In fact, the Northern Cheyenne refer to the ceremony as the Willow Dance, ignoring the sun worship aspect of the dance altogether. The willow is a symbol of water and of growing things.

## Further Reading

Dobler, Lavinia. *Customs and Holidays Around the World,* 1962.

Heinberg, Richard. *Celebrate the Solstice: Honoring the Earth's Seasonal Rhythms through Festival and Ceremony,* 1993.

Henderson, Helene and Sue Ellen Thompson. *Holidays, Festivals, and Celebrations of the World Dictionary*, 2nd ed., 1997.

Leach, Maria, ed. *Funk & Wagnalls Standard Dictionary of Folklore, Mythology, & Legend*, 1984.

# *Tanabata*
## *(Star Festival)*

**Type of Holiday:** Folkloric

**Date of Observation:** July 7

**Where Celebrated:** Japan

**Symbols:** Bamboo, Kusudama, Magpies, Mulberry Leaves

**Colors:** The colored strips of paper that are used to decorate the BAMBOO branches that are displayed during the Tanabata festival come in five colors: green, yellow, red, white, and dark blue (or purple) as a substitute for black. They were originally colored threads representing the cloth that the Weaving Girl in the legend used to make for the gods.

## ORIGINS

Tanabata, which means "Weaving Loom Festival," is a Japanese festival based on an old Chinese legend about two lovers who were parted. The daughter of the celestial emperor, Tentei, lived on the eastern bank of the River of Heaven (also known as the Milky Way), where she spent her days weaving the cloth needed by the gods who lived in her father's mansion. Known as Shokujo or the Weaving Girl, she was betrothed to Kengyu, a simple cowherd. Their honeymoon lasted so long that they neglected their other duties: Kengyu's cows grew thin, and the gods complained that they didn't have enough clothing. In a fit of anger, Tentei punished the couple by forcing them to live on opposite sides of the River of Heaven, allowing them to see each other only once a year, on the seventh night of the seventh moon. Since there was no bridge across the river, a flock of MAGPIES extended their wings to form a bridge that the Weaving Girl could walk across. The lovers wept so hard when they were forced to leave each other that it provided the fields with abundant summer rain.

There are many versions of this legend throughout China and Korea. It may have been linked to an ancient fertility rite, and several generations ago it was still common in rural parts of Japan for young men and women to climb a nearby mountain on the night of Tanabata and sleep there together. The fact that the hero of the legend is a cowherd would appear to support this theory, since cows and bulls were a well-established symbol of fertility. In rural areas, the Tanabata festival was observed by planting young trees in fields and gardens, where they could protect the crops from harmful insects.

The Japanese took over what had been essentially a Chinese festival in 755 C.E., and eventually it was declared one of the five most important festivals of Japan, along with **OSHOGATSU** or New Year's Day, **HINA MATSURI** (Doll Festival), Tango No Sekku (Boys' Festival), and the **CHRYSANTHEMUM FESTIVAL**. Today it is primarily a women's and children's festival, since the Weaving Girl is the patroness of women and of needlework. At one time the festival was observed with embroidery contests and needlethreading competitions: Only a superior needlewoman could thread a needle while holding it under a table or while sitting in a room lit only by a glowing ember or by moonlight. But today the primary activity is laying out offerings to the Star Goddess or Weaving Girl, consisting usually of watermelons, cakes, and various feminine toilet articles such as combs, mirrors, and rouge-pots. Unmarried girls typically lay out their offerings in sets of seven, one for the Weaver Princess and the others for her six sisters. In more educated households, there may be a *koto* (harp) and a flute laid out with the rest of the offerings to symbolize the "harmony" of music and of a happy marriage. In cities and towns, people often go to the theater to see a special play, "Crossing the Milky Way," which is performed only on this holiday.

Tanabata was observed on the seventh day of the seventh lunar month until use of the Gregorian calendar transposed it to July 7. Those who observe the festival believe that if the night is cloudy or rainy, the magpies will not form their bridge, and the celestial lovers must wait another year.

# SYMBOLS

## *Bamboo*

The Japanese consider bamboo a sacred plant, admired for its ability to bend and withstand adversity. But it is also a womanly plant, full of grace and capable of being influenced by wind or soil.

It is customary to stick branches of freshly cut bamboo in the ground in front of the house or to attach them to the doors or the eaves on the day of the Tanabata festival. These bamboo branches were originally decorated with multicolored threads in honor of the Weaver Princess. Today these threads have been replaced by strips of paper in many different colors, which are believed to scare off evil spirits by fluttering in the wind. Love poems may be written on some of the strips, or poems in praise of the Weaver Princess. Children sit around the table on the eve of the festival and, with their parents' help, try to compose these poems, although sometimes they are copied out of anthologies. Other symbolic items may be hung in the bamboo branches as well, such as a crane (for long life), a brush (for improvement of calligraphy), a net (for good crops and a bountiful catch), a kimono (for protection of the body), a lottery basket (for luck), and a money pouch (for the spirit of saving).

Like other forms of greenery associated with spring and rebirth, the branches serve as a reminder of the life-giving qualities of bamboo, which spreads very rapidly. On the day after the festival, the branches are taken down and thrown in the nearest river, where they are allowed to float away with the current.

## *Kusudama*

*Kusudama* are balls or pompoms made from paper, cloth, or celluloid with long tassels of many colors. The original kusudama were medicinal balls made of herbs and used to get rid of evil spirits and ward off illnesses. The emperor would give them to his guests and noblemen, but eventually they became common household ornaments and were often used as playthings for children.

In the Japanese city of Sendai, where Tanabata is a very elaborate celebration observed a month later than usual (August 6-8), colorful kusudama are hung all along the streets and in train stations, a testament to the Japanese love of papercraft.

## *Magpies*

Crows, magpies, and ravens were interchangeable in China and Japan. These birds were all regarded as messengers of the gods, and they possessed supernatural powers enabling them to predict the future. Although all three are considered birds of ill omen, under certain circumstances they can prophesy happiness as well. The magpie in particular is associated with good news or the arrival of a guest. The joy it symbolizes is often associated with marital bliss, due to its role in the legend of the cowherd and the weaver.

According to legend, magpies cannot be seen in the trees after the hour of noon on the day of the Tanabata festival. If any are spotted, children throw stones at them to punish them for not doing their duty. They are supposed to be up in heaven, helping to build a bridge across the Milky Way for the thwarted lovers.

## *Mulberry Leaves*

On the night of Tanabata, people used to dip leaves from a mulberry tree in a large bowl of water while standing outdoors and studying the reflection of the stars on the water's surface. The way the leaves behaved and the appearance of the water were then interpreted as omens regarding marriage, offspring, and prospects for the rice crop. Since the mulberry tree was connected with the making of silk in China (silkworms feed on mulberry leaves), it was a natural symbol to use on a day devoted to a weaver of cloth.

The custom of "reading" mulberry leaves on Tanabata is rarely practiced nowadays. It survives only in very rural areas of Japan.

## Further Reading

Araki, Nancy K, and Jane M. Horii. *Matsuri: Festival: Japanese-American Celebrations and Activities,* 1978.

Bauer, Helen, and Sherwin Carlquist. *Japanese Festivals,* 1965.

Bredon, Juliet, and Igor Mitrophanow. *The Moon Year: A Record of Chinese Customs and Festivals,* 1966.

Casal, U. A. *The Five Sacred Festivals of Ancient Japan,* 1967.

Eberhard, Wolfram. *A Dictionary of Chinese Symbols: Hidden Symbols in Chinese Life and Thought,* 1986.

Gaer, Joseph. *Holidays Around the World,* 1953.

Henderson, Helene and Sue Ellen Thompson. *Holidays, Festivals, and Celebrations of the World Dictionary*, 2nd ed., 1997.

Stepanchuk, Carol, and Charles Wong. *Mooncakes and Hungry Ghosts: Festivals of China*, 1991.

# *Terminalia*

**Type of Holiday:** Ancient or pagan
**Date of Observation:** February 23
**Where Celebrated:** Rome, Italy
**Symbols:** Boundary Stones

## ORIGINS

The worship of Terminus, the god of boundaries, was established by Numa, the second king of Rome, who founded a public festival to correspond with farmers' private worship of the spirits that inhabited the BOUNDARY STONES marking their property's borders. The Terminalia, as the celebration was called, was probably the basis for a number of later ceremonies that involved marking boundaries, such as Common Ridings Day in Scotland, Beating the Bounds in England, and the Boundary Walk Festivals (Grenzumgang) held in many German towns.

The terminus or boundary stones marking the outer limits of ancient Rome stood between the fifth and sixth milestones on the road to Laurentum. During the observance of the Terminalia, property owners would gather there or at the boundary stones marking their private lands. Each landowner decorated his side of the stone and helped to build the altar on which a fire would be kindled and sacrifices made. Someone would throw corn from a basket into the fire three times while the others, dressed in white, looked on in silence. The stone was then sprinkled with blood. Afterward, there would be singing and socializing among family members and servants.

On the Capitoline Hill in Rome, an ancient boundary stone was located in the temple of Jupiter. The stone was placed under an opening in the roof so that it could be worshipped under an open sky as farmers had traditionally done. How Terminus came to be associated with Jupiter is uncertain. But according to legend, when Jupiter was to be introduced into the Capitoline Temple, all of the gods made way for him except Terminus, who insisted on sharing Jupiter's space. Another theory is that the temple was erected on the site of an ancient boundary stone that was so sacred it couldn't be moved.

## SYMBOLS

### Boundary Stones

The stones that marked the boundaries of privately owned property in ancient Rome were regarded as the dwelling place of *numina,* spirits that can be traced back to very primitive times. These spirits helped to promote good relationships among neighbors and to keep strong territorial feelings under control. Their purpose can perhaps best be summarized by a line from the American poet Robert Frost: "Good fences make good neighbors."

Certain rites were carried out every time a boundary stone was put in place. Fruits of the earth, honey, and wine, along with the bones, ashes, and blood of a lamb or a suckling pig, were placed in a hole located where property owned by two or three farmers converged. A stone or a stump of wood was then rammed down on top of these offerings and fixed in place. The fact that sacrificial blood was considered essential to the ritual indicates just how important it was.

## Further Reading

Fowler, W. Warde. *The Roman Festivals of the Period of the Republic,* 1925.

Henderson, Helene and Sue Ellen Thompson. *Holidays, Festivals, and Celebrations of the World Dictionary,* 2nd ed., 1997.

Hole, Christina. *English Custom and Usage,* 1941.

James, E. O. *Seasonal Feasts and Festivals,* 1961.

*Lemprière's Classical Dictionary,* 3rd ed., 1984.

Scullard, H. H. *Festivals and Ceremonies of the Roman Republic,* 1981.

# *Tet*

**Type of Holiday:** Calendar

**Date of Observation:** First to seventh day of first lunar month (usually late January or early February)

**Where Celebrated:** Vietnam

**Symbols:** Cay Neu, Peach Tree

**Colors:** It is customary at Tet to give children red envelopes with money in them. The color red is symbolic of happiness.

**Related Holidays:** Chinese New Year

## ORIGINS

"Tet" is an abbreviation for *Tet Nguyen Dan,* which means "first day" in Vietnamese. It is the most important festival of the year in Vietnam, signifying both the beginning of the year and the arrival of spring. People wear new clothes, settle their old debts and quarrels, clean and repaint their houses, and visit their friends and relatives. Tet is also a time for making sacrifices and setting out special foods for the family's deceased ancestors, who are invited to come back for a few days and share in the festivities with the living members of the family.

The seven days of Tet officially begin with a ceremony bidding farewell to the kitchen god or spirit of the household, who leaves at midnight on the last day of the old year to travel to the celestial court of the Jade Emperor and report on the family's affairs. After he has left, firecrackers are set off to usher in the new year. Because the first visitor to arrive at the house after midnight is believed to influence the family's happiness and well-being for the entire year, many families invite certain guests to drop by early and encourage others, who might be unlucky, to come later. If a rich man should be the first caller, for example, it means that the family's fortunes will increase during the coming year. Whatever happens on the first day of Tet is believed to set the "tone" for the rest of the year, so everyone tries to be as polite, cheerful, and optimistic as possible.

On the first day of the new year, the adults of the household get up early and set up an altar to honor the departed ancestors. Twice a day, special foods are prepared and placed on the family altar for the ancestors who come back to visit. The second day is spent visiting friends and relatives, and the third day is spent visiting one's teachers. The ancestors are believed to depart on the fourth day of Tet, after which most people return to work, and life resumes a more normal pace. This is also a popular day to visit graveyards, where family members escort their departing relatives back to the land of the dead.

Tet became known all over the world in 1968 for the "Tet Offensive" of the Vietnam War. The lunar New Year truce was shattered on January 31 by attacks from North Vietnam and the National Liberation Front against more than 100 South Vietnamese cities. The attacks were repulsed, and the United States and South Vietnam claimed victory. But television viewers who had seen the ferocity of the attack knew otherwise, and the Tet Offensive led to increased pressure from Americans to end the war.

## SYMBOLS

### Cay Neu

The Cay Neu is a high bamboo pole set up in front of the house on the last day of the old lunar year. Various items are placed on top, including red paper with special inscriptions and a small basket containing various gifts for the good spirits of the household—including betel and areca nuts, wind chimes, a small square of woven bamboo (a symbolic barrier to stop evil spirits), and cock feathers for decoration. The Vietnamese believe that since the good spirits of the household must report to heaven during Tet, special precautionary measures must be taken to scare off the evil spirits, who might otherwise take advantage of the situation. But even the Cay Neu cannot stop a bad spirit, so many families take the added precaution of scattering lime powder around the house and using it to draw a bow and arrow in front of the threshold—a symbolic weapon to drive away evil.

### Peach Tree

It is very common to place a flowering branch of the peach tree in a vase for the duration of the Tet holiday. A symbol of longevity and immortality, the peach boughs placed in and around the house at the new year are believed to drive away evil spirits.

Certain Vietnamese villages specialize in cultivating peach trees particularly for this purpose. But factories in Hanoi also make artificial peach tree branches that resemble the real thing and last much longer.

## Further Reading

Cohen, Hennig, and Tristram Potter Coffin, eds. *The Folklore of American Holidays,* 2nd ed., 1991.

Eberhard, Wolfram. *A Dictionary of Chinese Symbols,* 1983.

Henderson, Helene and Sue Ellen Thompson. *Holidays, Festivals, and Celebrations of the World Dictionary,* 2nd ed., 1997.

Ickis, Marguerite. *The Book of Festivals and Holidays the World Over,* 1970.

MacDonald, Margaret R., ed. *The Folklore of World Holidays,* 1992.

Santino, Jack. *All Around the Year,* 1994.

# *Thaipusam*
## *(Thai Poosam)*

**Type of Holiday:** Religious (Hindu)

**Date of Observation:** January-February for three days

**Where Celebrated:** India, Malaya, Sri Lanka, Singapore, South Africa, Mauritius

**Symbols:** Kavadi (Kavadee)

## ORIGINS

One of the most dramatic Hindu festivals, Thaipusam marks the birthday of Lord Subramaniam (Subramanya), second son of the goddess Parvati. Hindus show their devotion to Subramaniam in a number of ways on this day, many of which involve testing their ability to withstand physical pain (see KAVADI).

In Malaya, the highlight of the festival is the procession from Kuala Lumpur to the Batu Caves about eight miles away. The statue of Subramanya is decorated with jewels and finery and placed on an elaborately carved chariot drawn by bullocks. The devotees who join in the procession through the main streets of the city to the caves chant the slogan, *vel-vel, vetri-vel*—a reference to the lance (*vel*) that Parvati gave to her son. The statue is later carried up the 272 steps to the cave and placed beside the permanent statue kept there. The next day, about 200,000 people begin to pay homage, while movies, carousels, and other entertainments are provided for their amusement. Temporary sheds are erected to house the worshippers who have traveled a great distance and must stay there during the three-day festival.

Self-inflicted torture is part of the celebration of Thaipusam in other countries as well, particularly among the Tamil people in Mauritius and in Durban, South Africa.

## SYMBOLS

### Kavadi (Kavadee)

The most extreme way of showing devotion to Subramanya during Thaipusam is known as "kavadi-carrying." A *kavadi* is a wooden arch on a wooden base, decorated with flowers, peacock feathers, and paper. It is carried on the devotee's shoulders, with various food offerings tied to the arch or balanced on the base. The *kavadi* bearers prepare for their ordeal by abstaining from all meat and sex during the ten days preceding the festival. Before they begin their journey, they undergo a special ceremony to put them in a trance-like state. Then they subject themselves to various degrees of physical torture, which may include having their upper bodies symmetrically pierced with *vels* (lances) and skewers thrust through their cheeks and tongues.

The procession begins, with the devotees carrying the *kavadis* on their shoulders. Some draw a small chariot behind them by means of chains fixed to hooks dug into their sides; others wear sandals studded with nails. In some areas, as many as 600-800 *kavadis* appear in the procession, and the people carrying them are usually in a state of utter frenzy or exhaustion by the time they deposit their burdens at the feet of the statue of Subramanya.

Some Hindus believe that carrying the *kavadi* washes away sins through self-inflicted suffering. Others see it as a symbol of the triumph of good over evil. Most Hindus who choose to carry the *kavadi* during this festival do so to achieve a desired objective or to pay back the gods for helping them avoid a calamity. Someone who has recently recovered from a life-threatening illness, or who has finally given birth to a child, for example, may take a vow to bear *kavadi* on Thaipusam day.

## Further Reading

Henderson, Helene and Sue Ellen Thompson. *Holidays, Festivals, and Celebrations of the World Dictionary*, 2nd ed., 1997.

MacDonald, Margaret R., ed. *The Folklore of World Holidays*, 1992.

Shemanski, Frances. *A Guide to World Fairs and Festivals*, 1985.

# *Thanksgiving*

**Type of Holiday:** Historic

**Date of Observation:** Fourth Thursday in November (United States); second Monday in October (Canada)

**Where Celebrated:** Canada, United States

**Symbols:** Corn Dolly, Cornucopia, Indian Corn, Parades, Pilgrims, Plymouth Rock, Turkey

**Colors:** The colors of the autumn harvest—orange, brown, and gold—can be seen in Thanksgiving decorations and table settings. Because it is not strictly a religious festival, there are no liturgical colors associated with the day.

**Related Holidays:** Sukkot

## ORIGINS

The autumn harvest has always been a cause for celebration. The ancient Greeks honored Demeter, their corn goddess, at the annual festival known as the Thesmophoria in October, when the seeds for the next year's crop were about to be planted. The Romans had their Cerealia, held each year on October 4 in honor of the grain goddess, Ceres. They offered her the first fruits of the harvest and paraded through the field, participating in games and sports and sharing a huge thanksgiving feast. The Jews observed **SUKKOT**, or the Feast of Tabernacles, in the autumn as well. They hung the walls of the small huts built for this festival with apples, grapes, corn, pomegranates, and other fruits and vegetables. Both the North American and South American Indians celebrated the harvest as well. All of these early thanksgiving ceremonies were social as well as religious occasions, providing those whose work in the fields was completed with an opportunity to sing, dance, feast, and play games.

Even in America, there were at least two Thanksgiving celebrations before the one that took place at Plymouth in 1621. In 1607, a group of English settlers led by Captain George Popham met with a group of Abnaki Indians near the mouth of the Kennebec River to share a harvest feast and prayer meeting. On December 14, 1619, there was a celebration in Virginia led by Captain John Woodleaf and 39 colonists who had traveled up the James River from Jamestown to a place called Berkeley Hundred, where they went ashore and gave thanks.

Most Americans, however, think of the first "official" Thanksgiving as being the one that took place at Plymouth Colony in October 1621, a year after the PILGRIMS first landed on the New England coast (see PLYMOUTH ROCK). They were joined in their three-day feast by Massasoit, the chief of the Wampanoag tribe, and about 90 of his fellow tribesmen. Only 50 of the original 100 Pilgrims had survived the first winter, and those who did owed their survival to the Indians. The feast they shared with them in 1621 was primarily a harvest celebration rather than a religious one.

During the next several years, no one specific day was set aside in the American colonies for giving thanks. A day would be named when there was a special reason to be thankful, such as a bumper crop or escape from an epidemic. It was largely due to the efforts of a women's magazine editor named Sarah Hale that Thanksgiving came to be a national holiday. She petitioned presidents and government officials for more than 20 years to establish a national day of thanksgiving. On October 3, 1863, President Abraham Lincoln finally proclaimed the fourth Thursday in November as Thanksgiving Day. President Franklin D. Roosevelt moved it up a week to stimulate the economy by allowing more time for Christmas shopping. But the tradition was already so well established that the change created an uproar. Finally, Congress ruled in 1941 that the fourth Thursday in November would be the legal federal holiday. Canadians celebrate their Thanksgiving Day on the second Monday in October.

The Pilgrims' Thanksgiving can be traced back to the English Harvest Home celebration and Dutch thanksgiving traditions, which some Pilgrims learned about during the ten years they spent in the city of Leyden before coming to America. Today, Thanksgiving is a time for family reunions, most of which center around the preparation of an elaborate meal featuring TURKEY and a dozen or so accompanying dishes. Although some people go to special church services on Thanksgiving Day, far more line the streets to watch PARADES or sit in front of the television watching football games. In many American cities and towns, the day after Thanksgiving marks the official start of the **CHRISTMAS** shopping season.

## SYMBOLS

### *Corn Dolly*

Many rituals were associated with the cutting of the last sheaf of corn at the harvest. At one time, people believed that the corn spirit or corn goddess ran from plant to plant, just ahead of the advancing sickles. Sometimes farmers "caught" the corn spirit by making the last sheaf into a doll, who was believed to possess magical powers. The corn doll was then decorated with ribbons or crowned with a wreath of flowers and hung up on the farmhouse wall until it was time to plow for the next year's crops. Then the farmer's wife would cut the doll into pieces and bring it to the fields as food for the horses. Or she would burn it, and the farmer would plow the ashes back into the earth as a way of ensuring a plentiful harvest. In some places, the corn doll would be thrown into a river in the hope that it would guarantee sufficient rainfall.

At the traditional English festival known as Harvest Home, the last of the corn was piled on a cart decorated with flowers, ribbons, and green branches. A "lord" and "lady" of the harvest were chosen to ride in the cart, and as it passed, people hiding in the bushes would throw buckets of water at it — another rain charm.

In America today, small dolls made from corn husks are a popular household decoration at Thanksgiving.

### *Cornucopia*

Also known as the "horn of plenty," the cornucopia is not only a harvest symbol but a symbol of early America, with its seemingly endless supply of game and produce. In ancient Rome, a goat's horn overflowing with fruit and other foods was an attribute of both Flora, the goddess of flowers, and Fortuna, the goddess of fortune. In Greece, it was associated with Amalthea, a nymph in the form of a goat who nursed the infant Zeus in a cave on the island of Crete. According to legend, Amalthea broke off one of her horns and filling it with fruits and flowers, gave it to Zeus. To show his gratitude, Zeus set the goat's image in the sky as the constellation Capricorn. In another version of the myth, the grateful young Zeus breaks off a goat's horn and gives it to Amalthea, his foster mother, telling her it will supply her with whatever she needs.

Cornucopia—from the Latin *cornu copiae,* meaning "horn of plenty"—is a longstanding symbol of fruitfulness and abundance. Americans often place cornucopia baskets on their Thanksgiving tables to symbolize their gratitude for the feast they are about to share.

## Indian Corn

The Pilgrims didn't know about corn when they first arrived in America, but the Indians showed them how to plant the kernels and fertilize the mounds with fish. Because they didn't want the Indians to know how many of the original settlers had died that first winter, the Pilgrims planted corn over the graves to disguise them. The ears of maize or Indian corn, as it was known, were small and knobby, with red, yellow, blue, green, and blackish kernels. Sometimes they were roasted and eaten, but more often they were dried and pounded into cornmeal for cornbread and cornmeal mush.

Although it is not part of the traditional Thanksgiving menu, Indian corn is a favorite household decoration at this time of year. Although corn is an ancient symbol of fertility, prosperity, and growth, the irregularly shaped and colored Indian corn is a more recent American symbol of the harvest.

## Parades

In ancient Greece and Rome, harvest celebrations often included farm wagons decorated with sheaves of grain. Today, many Americans celebrate Thanksgiving with parades featuring floats reminiscent of these early harvest wagons. In fact, some scholars see the harvest queens who ride in modern-day Thanksgiving parades as the descendants of the pagan corn goddesses.

The oldest Thanksgiving Day parade, which dates back to 1920, is the one held by Gimbel's department store in Philadelphia. Macy's department store in New York held its first parade in 1924. Today the Macy's parade features characters from story books, movies, television, and toyland. It attracts more than two million spectators, while another 80 million Americans watch it on television. In Hollywood, television and movie stars parade through the streets on floats.

## Pilgrims

Originally the Pilgrims were called Puritans because they wanted to "purify" the Church of England, which they felt was too concerned with ritual and with telling people what to believe. They met secretly in homes to study the Bible and listen to sermons. Those who were prepared to leave the Church of England and set up their own church—without bishops, altars, candles, incense, or organ music—were known as Separatists. Because the English church and government were one and the same in the 1600s, separating from the church was considered an act of treason. One group of Separatists, under the leadership of William Brewster, decided to move to Holland. They lived in Leyden for ten years, but worried about their children forgetting English language and customs. Fifty or 60 of these, along with other passengers who had their own reasons for wanting to leave—102 in all—decided to make the journey to the New World on board the *Mayflower*. Among the best-known Pilgrims are Miles Standish and John Alden, who were not Separatists at all but who became famous as characters in Henry Wadsworth Longfellow's 1858 poem, "The Courtship of Miles Standish."

The Pilgrims as seen today—on Thanksgiving posters, greeting cards, paper tablecloths and napkins, and in the form of candles or figurines—wear gray, black, or dun-colored clothing with white collars and cuffs. They have tall black hats with broad brims and a silver buckle in front; their shoes have silver buckles as well. The women and girls usually wear long dresses in drab colors with white aprons and caps. In reality, however, Pilgrim women often wore red, purple, bright blue, or green dresses colored with vegetable dyes. The ornamental buckles seen on the Pilgrims' hats and shoes weren't introduced until later in the seventeenth century.

The figures of Pilgrims seen at Thanksgiving today are a symbol of the bravery and determination of America's earliest settlers. They are often portrayed as male-female couples because they represent the "parents" of the American people.

## Plymouth Rock

Perhaps the most famous landmark in America today is the granite boulder on which the Pilgrims first stepped when they came ashore at Plymouth, Massachusetts. But until just before the American Revolution, it was simply another rock. During the next century it was moved first to Plymouth's town square, then to a local museum known as Pilgrim Hall. Finally it was brought back to the waterfront and placed under a stone canopy with a box believed to contain Pilgrim bones. Eventually, to prevent souvenir-hunters from chipping off pieces, the rock was placed in a pit surrounded by an iron railing, with a portico overhead to shelter visitors from the weather.

Whether or not the Pilgrims actually stepped ashore on this rock is not known with any certainty. Apparently there was a huge boulder about 40 feet from shore along the sandy coast of Massachusetts in 1620. But since there is no documentation about exactly where the Pilgrims landed, there is no way of knowing whether this rock provided them with a stepping-stone. Some historians have theorized that the Pilgrims used the rock as a landmark to help guide them into the harbor.

Plymouth Rock has long symbolized America's freedom. During the Revolutionary War, the residents of Plymouth took it as a good omen rather than a coincidence when the rock split in two while being pried from its bed for use as a pedestal for a liberty pole: Shortly after, the colonies officially split from England. The two halves were eventually reunited under a protective canopy at the foot of Coles Hill, where it now sits. Although originally estimated to have measured 12 feet in diameter and to have weighed seven or eight tons, over the years the rock has been whittled down considerably by souvenir-hunters and the difficulties of moving it.

## Turkey

There is no record of what was eaten at the Pilgrims' first Thanksgiving feast. The Indians who had been sent out to hunt probably returned with wild geese and ducks, but there is no way of knowing whether they brought back a turkey—a large, stately bird with greenish-bronze feathers that was native to North America. Because of their size (20-30 pounds) and because they were relatively easy to catch, however, wild turkeys quickly became an important source of food for the early American settlers.

Some say the turkey was named by the late sixteenth-century European explorers, who confused it with the European turkey cock, a completely different bird. Others claim that the word comes from the Hebrew *tukki,* meaning "big bird," which is what the doctor on Columbus's ship shouted when he saw one for the first time. In any case, the turkey did not become an American Thanksgiving tradition until the 1860s. After World War II, an aggressive marketing campaign by the poultry industry and the development of larger, hybrid turkeys combined to make the stuffed bird a symbol of American abundance and the traditional main course at Thanksgiving dinner.

The custom of snapping the turkey's wishbone, bringing luck to the person who gets the larger half, can be traced back to the Romans. It was certainly a well-established tradition in England by the time the Pilgrims brought it to America. Some word historians believe that the bone-snapping custom gave rise to the popular expression, "to get a lucky break."

Today, Americans eat more than 535 million pounds of turkey every Thanksgiving, accompanied by such traditional American dishes as cranberries, squash, sweet potatoes, pumpkin pie, and stuffing (which the Pilgrims referred to as "pudding in the belly"). After the United States won its independence, Congress debated the choice of a national bird. Benjamin Franklin thought the bald eagle was a bird of "bad moral character" and advocated the turkey as a "true, original Native of North America."

## Further Reading

Barth, Edna. *Turkeys, Pilgrims, and Indian Corn: The Story of the Thanksgiving Symbols,* 1975.

Biedermann, Hans. *Dictionary of Symbolism: Cultural Icons and the Meanings Behind Them,* 1994.

Cirlot, J. E. *A Dictionary of Symbols,* 1962.

Graham-Barber, Lynda. *Gobble!: The Complete Book of Thanksgiving Words,* 1991.

Henderson, Helene and Sue Ellen Thompson. *Holidays, Festivals, and Celebrations of the World Dictionary,* 2nd ed., 1997.

Penner, Lucille Recht. *The Thanksgiving Book,* 1986.

Purdy, Susan. *Festivals for You to Celebrate,* 1969.

Santino, Jack. *All Around the Year,* 1994.

Tuleja, Tad. *Curious Customs: The Stories Behind 296 Popular American Rituals,* 1987.

# *Thesmophoria*

**Type of Holiday:** Ancient or pagan
**Date of Observation:** October
**Where Celebrated:** Greece
**Symbols:** Pigs

## ORIGINS

The ancient Greek festival known as the Thesmophoria was observed only by women for three days in October (some say between the 11th and the 13th; others say between the 14th and the 16th), at a time of year when the ground was being prepared for the autumn sowing of crops. It was held in honor of the corn goddess and earth mother Demeter, who was sometimes referred to as Thesmophorus. According to Greek mythology, Demeter's daughter Kore, the corn maiden, was gathering flowers near Eleusis one day when she was abducted by Pluto, god of the underworld, and taken away to his subterranean kingdom. By lowering PIGS into chasms in the earth, the women chosen to participate in the rituals of the Thesmophoria commemorated the abduction of Kore.

In Athens and other Greek cities, women dressed in white robes and observed a period of strict chastity for several days before and during the ceremony. They would strew their beds with herbs that were supposed to ward off venereal diseases and sit on the ground to promote the fertility of the corn that had just been sown. Although the festival itself was taken very seriously, it was not uncommon for the women to joke among themselves, as if in doing so they could cheer up the goddess Demeter, who suffered greatly over the loss of her daughter.

Scholars believe that the Thesmophoria can be traced back to an even more ancient festival that celebrated the bringing up of the corn from the underground silos in which it was stored after being threshed in June. During the four months when the grain was concealed in the earth, the fields were barren and parched by the sun. It wasn't until the winter rains began in October that they could be plowed and sown again, so this was an appropriate time to hold a festival celebrating the earth's fertility. The Romans had a similar festival in honor of Ceres, called the Cerealia.

## SYMBOLS

### Pigs

Pigs were considered sacred to Demeter because, according to legend, when the earth opened up and Pluto emerged in his chariot to abduct Kore, the herdsman Eubouleus and his pigs were swallowed up as well.

To commemorate this event, pigs were let down into caves or clefts in the earth, together with cakes and the branches of pine trees. Each year at the Thesmophoria, women who had undergone special purification rituals for the purpose went down into these underground chasms and brought up the putrefied remains of the pigs that had been thrown in there the previous year. The rotted flesh was placed on altars and mixed with seed-corn, which was then sown in the fields as a kind of magical fertilizer to ensure a good crop.

The pigs are not only symbolic of Kore, the corn maiden, but of the corn itself, which was at one time stored in underground silos. Bringing the pig-flesh up out of the earth symbolizes the return of the earth's fertility at the beginning of the winter rainy season.

## Further Reading

Henderson, Helene and Sue Ellen Thompson. *Holidays, Festivals, and Cele-brations of the World Dictionary*, 2nd ed., 1997.

James, E. O. *Seasonal Feasts and Festivals*, 1961.

*L'Emprière's Classical Dictionary of Proper Names Mentioned in Ancient Authors*, 3rd ed., 1984.

Scullard, H. H. *Festivals and Ceremonies of the Roman Republic*, 1981.

# Tisha be-Av
## (Fast of Av)

**Type of Holiday:** Religious (Jewish)

**Date of Observation:** Ninth day of Av; between July 17 and August 14

**Where Celebrated:** Europe, Israel, United States, and by Jews throughout the world

**Symbols:** Eggs and Ashes, Wailing Wall

**Colors:** Because it is observed as a day of mourning, Tisha be-Av is associated with the color black. In many synagogues, the ark housing the Torah or Jewish holy book is covered with a black cloth on this day.

**Related Holidays:** Lag Ba-Omer

## ORIGINS

Tisha be-Av is a 24-hour period of fasting, lamentation, and prayer in memory of the destruction of both the First and Second Temples in Jerusalem, two events that took place on the same day several centuries apart. The First Temple, built by King Solomon, was destroyed in 586 B.C.E. by the Babylonians under King Nebuchadnezzar, who sold many of the

Jews into slavery and exiled thousands of others. When they were finally permitted to return to their land about 70 years later, the first thing they did was to build a new temple on the site of the first one. The Second Temple was in use for almost 600 years, although at one point the Greeks nearly ruined it by erecting statues of Zeus and other Greek gods in the temple and making it unholy. The Romans under Titus finally burned it down in 70 C.E., an even greater tragedy than the destruction of the First Temple in terms of lost life and property. The only piece of the temple that still remains standing is part of the western wall that surrounded it, also known as the WAILING WALL.

Other sad events have taken place on this day as well. In 132 C.E., the Romans plowed over the holy places of Jerusalem and started building their own city, ending any hopes the Jews might have had of rebuilding their temple. It was also on the 9th of Av in 135 C.E. that the town of Bethar, the last stronghold of Bar Kochva and his rebels, fell to the Romans (see **LAG BA-OMER**). In 1492, all Spanish Jews were ordered to leave the country on Tisha be-Av; in 1670, the Jews of Vienna were expelled from the city on this day.

Tisha be-Av marks the end of a three-week period of national mourning that begins on the 17th of Tammuz, the day on which, about 2,000 years ago, the Roman threat to Jerusalem became so menacing that sacrifices could no longer be offered in the Holy Temple. Any kind of festivity or entertainment is forbidden during this three-week period. No new clothes may be worn, no hair cut, no music played, and no weddings held. Celebration is only permitted on the Sabbath and on days of special events—a Bar Mitzvah, for example. Many Jews visit the cemetery during these weeks to pay their respects to friends and relatives who have died.

The feeling of mourning intensifies as the three weeks pass, culminating on Tisha be-Av. No flags are flown, no parades are held, and no bands are allowed to play on this day. Most Jews spend the day quietly in prayer and fasting. The principal feature of the service held in the synagogue is the recital of the Book of Lamentations. Believed to have been written by the prophet Jeremiah, Lamentations is really a collection of five dirges (mournful tales) on the subject of the Temple's destruction in 586 B.C.E. and the subsequent scattering of the Jewish people. The synagogue is lit only by candles, and worshippers take off their shoes and sit on the floor or on low benches. Like mourners, they do not greet one another. If Tisha be-Av falls on the Sabbath, the fast is postponed until the following day.

## SYMBOLS

### Eggs and Ashes

The last meal eaten before the Fast of Av includes eggs and a pinch of ashes. Eggs are served, according to one Jewish poet, because "eggs have no mouth and our grief is too strong for words." Ashes are used as a symbol of mourning. Eggs and ashes are traditionally served to Jewish mourners when they return from a funeral.

### Wailing Wall

Huge crowds of Jews assemble at the Wailing Wall in Jerusalem — believed to be the last remaining portion of the wall that once surrounded the Second Temple — on the 9th of Av. For many years following the Temple's destruction in 70 C.E., Jews could not visit the Wailing Wall (sometimes called the Western Wall) because the land on which it stood was ruled by Arabs, who would not permit the Jews to go there. But this part of Jerusalem was retaken by the Israeli army in 1967. Since that time, anyone who wants to can cry or pray at the wall. Some people have left notes with special prayers to God in the cracks between the stones.

## Further Reading

Edidin, Ben. *Jewish Holidays and Festivals,* 1993.

Gaster, Theodor H. *Festivals of the Jewish Year,* 1953.

Henderson, Helene and Sue Ellen Thompson. *Holidays, Festivals, and Celebrations of the World Dictionary,* 2nd ed., 1997.

Renberg, Dalia H. *The Complete Family Guide to Jewish Holidays,* 1985.

# *Tori-no-ichi*
## *(Bird Fair)*

**Type of Holiday:** Religious (Shinto)
**Date of Observation:** November
**Where Celebrated:** Japan
**Symbols:** Eagle, Rake

# ORIGINS

The Bird Fair held at Shinto shrines in Japan every November takes its name not only from the sacred crow that perched on the long-bow of the first Mikado (emperor) and guided him out of the wilderness by the light shining from its wings, but also from a play on the Japanese words signifying financial gain. This may be because most of the members of the Shinto sect that observe this festival are wealthy merchants and speculators.

The most visible feature of the celebration are the bamboo RAKES that everyone buys at the fair. Other good luck emblems that are often used for advertising or decoration purposes during the fair include the income book, gold and silver coins, the magic key that is believed to unlock the door of fate, and the hammer that has the ability to pound out whatever it is that a person wishes to obtain from the fortune bag carried by the god of wealth.

# SYMBOLS

## *Eagle*

Tori-no-ichi is observed at shrines dedicated to "The Great Bird" or sacred crow in Shinto mythology. The eagle is symbolic of good fortune because it is stronger and flies higher than any other bird. It is for this reason that nowadays the Bird Shrine Fair is often called the Eagle Market.

## *Rake*

The bamboo rakes that are sold and displayed everywhere during the Eagle Market are symbolic of the ability to attract good fortune because they resemble the outstretched claws of the *kumade* or "bear's paw." In the lore of the market, the *kumade* is believed to give its possessor the power to attract any treasure he or she may desire.

The rakes seen during the Eagle Market are similar to those used in the garden, but they are usually decorated with many good luck emblems and, in the center, the smiling mask of Okame, the so-called "laughing goddess" or goddess of good nature. Tiny rakes are also worn as hair ornaments and tucked in the sashes or necklines of women's dresses.

# Further Reading

Henderson, Helene and Sue Ellen Thompson. *Holidays, Festivals, and Celebrations of the World Dictionary*, 2nd ed., 1997.

MacDonald, Margaret R., ed. *The Folklore of World Holidays*, 1992.

# *Tu Bishvat*
## *(Bi-Shevat, Tu B'Shevat, New Year of the Trees)*

**Type of Holiday:** Religious (Jewish)

**Date of Observation:** Fifteenth day of Shevat; between January 16 and February 13

**Where Celebrated:** Israel, Palestine, United States, and by Jews throughout the world

**Symbols:** Trees

**Related Holidays:** Arbor Day

## ORIGINS

Tu Bishvat is a minor Jewish holiday honoring TREES, similar to the American observation of Arbor Day. It originated in Israel, where the 15th of Shevat comes at the beginning of spring when the buds on the trees are beginning to open. The ancient Jews loved trees and treasured them for the fruit, shade, and lumber they provided. They assigned many trees special symbolic meanings (see TREES) and compared the Torah, their holy book, to "a tree of life." In fact, most of the forests seen in Palestine today were originally planted by Jewish colonists.

It is said that the sap begins to rise in the fruit trees of the Holy Land on the 15th day of Shevat. It is customary, therefore, to sit up late the previous evening and recite passages from the Bible dealing with trees, fruits, and the fertility of the earth. Israeli schoolchildren go outside with shovels and hoes and plant trees on Tu Bishvat, singing songs about trees and flowers as they work and dancing around the trees they have planted. Because there are relatively few trees in Israel, the task of planting them on this day is considered crucial to preserving the soil.

Tu Bishvat is primarily a children's holiday in Europe. They bring figs, dates, raisins, almonds, and other fruits native to Palestine into their classrooms, where the teacher divides the supply equally so there will be no distinctions between rich and poor. In the United States and other countries, Tu Bishvat is often celebrated as Palestine Day with special assemblies, classroom parties, and entertainment for parents. Refreshments usually include fruits that grow in Palestine, such as dates, figs, carobs, and Jaffa oranges. In some countries, Jewish children buy Jewish National Fund tree certificates, which can be purchased for the modest cost of a sapling and its planting, in honor of their parents, while parents often buy the certificates as educational gifts for their children. Many Jews in the United States have donated money for trees in honor of famous Americans, such as George Washington, Harry S. Truman, Eleanor Roosevelt, and Chief Justice Louis Brandeis.

Because Tu Bishvat is primarily a nature festival without any specific religious ceremonies, it is surprising that it was remembered after the Jews left Palestine. That it survived and is still observed in Western countries where there is often frost and snow during the month of Shevat shows how deeply Jews have longed for their homeland.

# SYMBOLS

## Trees

There was a long-standing Jewish tradition, revived recently in Israel, of planting a cedar tree, symbolic of courage and strength, when a baby boy was born and a cypress, which is smaller and more fragrant, to honor the birth of a girl. When the child grew up, the wood of this tree was used to make the *huppa* or wedding canopy.

Because trees were associated with two of the most important events in a person's life, birth and marriage, Jewish children were raised with a great reverence for trees. Different types of trees were used to symbolize human characteristics: for example, the olive (wisdom), the grapevine (joy and childbearing), and the palm (beauty and stateliness). Planting trees to celebrate births and setting aside a day specifically for tree-planting has kept the Jewish homeland wooded from one generation to the next.

Tu Bishvat is also known as Rosh Hashanah Leilanot, or New Year of the Trees. It is widely believed to be the day on which trees are "judged"; in other words, it is the day on which each tree's fate is decided. This determines which trees will flourish and grow tall; which will wither and die; which will suffer from lightning, strong winds, or insects; and which will be strong enough to withstand all danger.

# Further Reading

Cirlot, J. E. *A Dictionary of Symbols,* 1962.

Dobler, Lavinia. *Customs and Holidays Around the World,* 1962.

Edidin, Ben. *Jewish Holidays and Festivals,* 1993.

Ferguson, George. *Signs and Symbols in Christian Art,* 1954.

Gaer, Joseph. *Holidays Around the World,* 1953.

Gaster, Theodor H. *Festivals of the Jewish Year,* 1953.

Henderson, Helene and Sue Ellen Thompson. *Holidays, Festivals, and Celebrations of the World Dictionary,* 2nd ed., 1997.

Renberg, Dalia H. *The Complete Family Guide to Jewish Holidays,* 1985.

# Twelfth Night
### (Epiphany Eve)

**Type of Holiday:** Religious (Christian)

**Date of Observation:** January 5 or 6

**Where Celebrated:** Great Britain, Europe, United States

**Symbols:** Fire, Lord of Misrule, Twelfth Night Pageants

**Related Holidays:** Christmas, Epiphany

## ORIGINS

As the last of the traditional Twelve Days of Christmas, Twelfth Night marks the end of the Christmas season. Why 12 days? The custom of extending **CHRISTMAS** may have derived from the pagan custom of marking the **WINTER SOLSTICE** for a number of days—a widespread tradition in Europe, particularly England, from the eleventh century onwards. But the exact day on which this season ends remains ambiguous. To some people, Twelfth Night means the evening before the Twelfth Day, or January 5. To others, it means the evening *of* the Twelfth Day, or January 6. In any case, it is often observed on the night of **EPIPHANY** rather than the night before.

Twelfth Night has been observed since the Middle Ages with games, masquerades, and other revelries. Elaborate pageants, processions, and pantomimes, combined with singing, dancing, and feasting, took place under the direction of a LORD OF MISRULE, a mock official assisted by a "fool" or jester. In rural parts of England, Twelfth Night celebrations included bonfires (see FIRE), masques, and the curious custom of "wassailing" the fruit trees, which meant carrying jugs of cider to the orchards and offering toasts to the apple trees to ensure a good yield. In France, Germany, and the Low Countries, young boys would dress up in exotic costumes and paper crowns. Representing the Three Kings or Magi, they would go begging from house to house, carrying paper star lanterns on long poles.

By the eighteenth century, the lavish celebrations that had been associated with Twelfth Night began to lose their appeal; by the nineteenth century, they had practically died out, although remnants of the ancient festivities survived in some areas. The King of the Bean (see LORD OF MISRULE) is still a popular Twelfth Night tradition in Belgium, Portugal, England, France, Germany, and the Netherlands. In the United States, TWELFTH NIGHT PAGEANTS are still popular, including masked figures, costumed musicians, and the performance of traditional English dances like the Abbots Bromley Antler Dance or Horn Dance. In New Orleans, Twelfth Night marks the beginning of the **CARNIVAL** season, which ends on Mardi Gras, the day before **ASH WEDNESDAY**.

January 5 is also referred to as Old Christmas Eve, because according to the Old Style or Julian Calendar, Christmas fell on January 6. The inhabitants of some remote areas of Great Britain continue to observe ancient customs associated with Old Christmas Eve.

## SYMBOLS

### Fire

At one time in England, it was customary to light 12 small fires and one large one in a field sown with wheat as a means of protecting it from disease. In Ireland, a sieve full of oats was set up as high as possible, and 12 lighted candles were set in the grain, with a larger one in the middle. Although the meaning of these customs has been largely forgotten, some say that the fires were intended to symbolize Jesus Christ and His 12 Apostles. Others see them as a survival of heathen sun worship.

A similar Twelfth Night custom survived in Westmoreland. A holly bush or young ash tree would have torches fastened to the branches. The torches were lit and the tree was carried around the village to the accompaniment of music. When the torches had burned out, two rival groups would scramble for the remains of the tree, and the rest of the night would be spent in merrymaking.

In the United States, it is traditional to take down the Christmas tree and other greenery used to decorate the house, pile it up outdoors, and burn it on Twelfth Night. In fact, the custom of lighting bonfires on Twelfth Night seems to be gaining in popularity.

## Lord of Misrule

The custom of electing a king to rule over the festivities on Twelfth Night can be traced back to the reign of Edward II in England. The usual custom was to prepare a special cake, known as the Kings' Cake (*Gâteau des Rois* in France), and to conceal a bean (sometimes a pea or a coin) inside. The cake would be cut into as many pieces as there were guests at the Twelfth Night feast. The youngest member of the family would distribute the pieces, and whoever got the piece with the bean inside was crowned "King of the Bean" or "Lord of Misrule." If a woman got the bean, she would choose a king. A mock court would be assembled by drawing slips of paper from a hat, and these assumed characters would have to be maintained throughout the evening. The custom lasted far into the nineteenth century, but it was eventually discontinued because so many coarse and offensive characters had been introduced. Elaborately decorated Twelfth Cakes remained popular until late Victorian times, and are still served in some parts of Europe today.

## Twelfth Night Pageants

For hundreds of years, miracle plays about the Three Kings had been staged at this time of year, originally in church sanctuaries and then later, when the performances had become too secular, outside the church. Religious dramas were eventually joined by the staging of popular tragedies, comedies, and historical dramas. William Shakespeare's comedy *Twelfth Night* is believed to have been first presented for Queen Elizabeth I at Whitehall Palace in 1601.

The Twelfth Night pageants performed in the United States today are usually far more modest than the elaborate productions of Elizabethan England. But many of the dances and characters incorporated into these modern performances can be traced back to medieval times.

## Further Reading

Chambers, Robert, ed. *The Book of Days,* 1864.

Cohen, Hennig, and Tristram Potter Coffin, eds. *The Folklore of American Holidays,* 2nd ed., 1991.

Crippen, T. G. *Christmas and Christmas Lore,* 1990.

Hatch, Jane M. *The American Book of Days*, 1978.

Henderson, Helene and Sue Ellen Thompson. *Holidays, Festivals, and Celebrations of the World Dictionary*, 2nd ed., 1997.

Kelly, Aidan. *Religious Holidays and Calendars*, 1993.

MacDonald, Margaret R., ed. *The Folklore of World Holidays*, 1992.

Miles, Clement A. *Christmas in Ritual and Tradition*, 1990.

Spicer, Dorothy Gladys. *The Book of Festivals*, 1990.

Urlin, Ethel L. *Festivals, Holy Days, and Saints' Days*, 1915.

# Vaisakh
## (Baisakh, Baisakhi)

**Type of Holiday:** Religious (Sikh), Calendar
**Date of Observation:** First day of Vaisakha (April 13)
**Where Celebrated:** India, Malaysia
**Symbols:** Akhand Path, Five K's, Pahul Ceremony

## ORIGINS

Among the Sikhs who live in Malaysia and the region of northwestern India known as the Punjab, where the Sikh religion was founded, the first day of the month of Vaisakha is New Year's Day. Because the date is based on the solar calendar used in this part of the country, it normally coincides with April 13, although once every 36 years it falls on April 14.

Aside from being the first day of the year, Vaisakh is also the anniversary of several important historical events. It is the day on which Guru Gobind Singh, the tenth and last of the gurus whose teachings are central to Sikhism, founded the militant Khalsa brotherhood in 1699. And it was on this day in 1747 that the Sikhs decided to build a permanent fortress at Amritsar, which is why this city has become a focal point for their worship. On Vaisakh in 1919, the British lieutenant governor of the Punjab tried to prevent the Sikhs from gathering there. They assembled anyway and were fired on by the army, an act that resulted in the deaths of 337 men, 41 boys, and a baby.

Because of the day's historical and religious significance, all Sikhs are required to visit the largest and most important *gurdwara* (public place of worship) they can get to. If possible, they should visit the Golden Temple in Amritsar, where a continuous reading of the *Granth Sahib* (see AKHAND PATH) and certain other rituals are held. After the religious ceremonies are over, there is feasting and folk dancing. Thousands of Sikhs visit the Golden Temple in Amritsar every year and bathe in the Pool of Immortality.

Viasakh is also a harvest festival in northern India, particularly in the Punjab, where most of the country's grain is grown. People dance the strenuous folk dance known as the *bhangra,* which involves movements that re-enact the entire agricultural process: plowing, sowing, weeding, reaping, and winnowing. The final sequence of the dance shows the farmer celebrating the harvest.

## SYMBOLS

### *Akhand Path*

The main religious event that takes place on Vaisakh is the reading of the *Granth Sahib,* the Sikh holy book, from beginning to end. This takes approximately 48 hours and begins two days before the holiday so that the reading will end at dawn on the first of Vaisakha. It begins with the preparation of *karah parshad,* the "gift of God to his devotees," prepared in an iron bowl (*karah*) and made of equal portions of flour, sugar, and ghee (clarified butter). Then the Ardas, a three-part prayer, is recited by the entire congregation, standing with their palms pressed together facing the throne of the Guru Granth Sahib. Then the holy book is opened at random, a verse is read for spiritual guidance, and the akhand path begins with the *Japji,* written by Guru Nanak, the first guru.

Members of the community visit the gurdwara whenever they can during the two days during which the scripture is being read. A number of readers participate in the round-the-clock reading of the scripture, each reading for about two hours before the next one takes over. At the end, everyone gathers at the gurdwara and shares some karah parshad. Then the Granth Sahib is carried in a procession to the accompaniment of religious music. Five leaders of the congregation walk in front of the Granth with drawn swords in memory of the *panj pyares* (see PAHUL CEREMONY below) of Guru Gobind Singh.

## Five K's

Members of the Khalsa or militant brotherhood of the Sikh religion distinguish themselves by the wearing of five symbols: the *kesh* (uncut hair), *khanga* (comb), *kirpan* (sword), *kara* (steel wrist band), and *kacch* (a pair of breeches that must not reach below the knee). The *kesh* and the *khanga* symbolize an orderly form of spirituality, since unlike other religious groups that wear uncut hair, the Sikhs are instructed to wash their hair regularly and comb it twice a day. The *kacch* symbolizes modesty and moral restraint. The *kara*, worn on the right wrist, is also a symbol of restraint, although some believe that it was originally a means of protecting the wrist from the bowstring. But the circular shape of the wristband serves as a reminder of the Sikh's unity with God and with the other members of the Khalsa. The sword or *kirpan* symbolizes dignity and self-respect. Khalsa members are supposed to be ready to fight, but only in self-defense or to protect the weak and the oppressed.

## Pahul Ceremony

Pahul means "baptism," and the initiation ceremony for new members of the Khalsa that frequently takes place on Vaisakh recalls the "baptism of the sword" used by Guru Gobind Singh to select the first members of this militant brotherhood in 1699. Since it was customary for Sikhs to gather on Vaisakh, Guru Gobind Singh took advantage of the annual gathering to remind his followers of the dangerous times in which they lived and the importance of being a strong, unified people. Then, drawing his sword, he asked any man who was willing to sacrifice his head as a show of faith to step forward. There was a prolonged silence during which no one responded. Then one man came forward and was taken into the Guru's tent. When the Guru reappeared with a bloody sword in his hand, four more men followed. After the last of the *panj pyares* ("beloved five") had disappeared into the tent, the Guru emerged with his small band of dedicated followers. To celebrate their courage, he gave them nectar (*amrit*) made from water and sugar crystals prepared in an iron bowl and stirred with a double-edged sword.

Although new members may be initiated into the Khalsa at any time of year, Viasakh is the most popular season for doing so. Initiates must be at least 14 years of age and must possess the five symbols of their faith (see FIVE K'S above) and be devout members of the Sikh community. The initiation ceremony begins with an explanation of the principles of the Sikh faith, readings from the scriptures, and the preparation of amrit. Five men representing the original *panj pyares* kneel around an iron bowl and take turns stirring its contents with a double-edged sword (*khanda*). When the nectar is ready, the *panj pyares* lift up the bowl and offer a prayer. One by one the initiates come forward and are given a handful of amrit to drink. Then the remaining nectar is sprinkled five times on their hair and eyes. The initiation ceremony ends with the reading of a passage of scripture chosen at random and the sharing of *karah parshad*—flour, sugar, and ghee mixed in equal proportions in an iron bowl, symbolic of the equality and brotherhood of the Sikh faith.

## Further Reading

Cole, William Owen, and Piara Singh Sambhi. *The Sikhs: Their Religious Beliefs and Practices,* 1978.

Crim, Keith, ed. *The Perennial Dictionary of World Religions,* 1989.

Henderson, Helene and Sue Ellen Thompson. *Holidays, Festivals, and Celebrations of the World Dictionary,* 2nd ed., 1997.

MacDonald, Margaret R., ed. *The Folklore of World Holidays,* 1992.

# *Valentine's Day*

**Type of Holiday:** Folkloric

**Date of Observation:** February 14

**Where Celebrated:** Primarily Britain and the United States, although Valentine's Day was at one time celebrated widely in Italy, France, Austria, Hungary, Germany, and Spain

**Symbols:** Cupid, Heart and Arrow, Lovebirds, Valentine Cards

**Colors:** Valentine's Day is associated with red and white—the colors of blood and milk, both of which were central to the ancient Roman **LUPERCALIA**. Because it is the color of the human heart, red is a symbol of warmth and feeling. White stands for purity; some think that the bridal veil was the inspiration for the white lace traditionally used on VALENTINE CARDS. White is also a symbol of faith—in this case, the faith between two lovers.

**Related Holidays:** Candlemas, Lupercalia

# ORIGINS

What is known as Valentine's Day descended from the ancient Roman celebration known as the **LUPERCALIA,** held on February 15. Although it
started out as a fertility ritual, the Lupercalia quickly took on the character of
a lovers' holiday. Roman boys chose their partners for the celebration by
drawing girls' names from a box or urn; then the couple would exchange
gifts on the day of the festival. When the Roman armies invaded what is
now France and Britain, they brought their Lupercalia customs with them —
including the drawing of names for partners or sweethearts. But the advent
of Christianity in the fourth century necessitated putting a Christian face on
what was essentially a pagan celebration. So in 469 C.E., Pope Gelasius set
aside February 14 to honor St. Valentine, a young Roman who was martyred
by Emperor Claudius II on this day in 270 C.E. for refusing to give up Christianity. Because of the proximity of the two dates, many customs associated
with the Lupercalia were carried over to the Feast of St. Valentine.

One legend describes St. Valentine as a third-century priest who defied the
Roman emperor's ban on marriages and engagements by marrying young
people in secret and who was eventually arrested and put to death. Another story tells of a man named Valentine who was imprisoned for helping
Christians who were being persecuted. While serving time in jail, he converted the jailer and his family to Christianity and restored the sight of the
jailer's blind daughter, with whom he fell in love. On the morning of his
execution, he sent her a farewell message signed, "From your Valentine."

There was a spring festival observed in Italy during the Middle Ages at
which young people gathered in groves and gardens to listen to love poetry
and romantic music. Afterward, they would pair off and stroll among the
trees and flowers. Similar pairing-off customs were popular in France as
well, but they often led to hard feelings and trouble, and were finally
banned in 1776. Valentine's Day customs survived, however, in the British
Isles, where young men were drawing names for "valentines" or sweethearts for centuries after the departure of the Roman armies. In England,
young people played a popular game in which they would write down the
names of all the young women on pieces of paper, roll them up tightly, and
place them in a bowl. The young men, blindfolded, would then take turns
drawing a name from the bowl. The girl whose name was drawn would be
that boy's "Valentine" for the coming year.

Because it occurs seven weeks after the **WINTER SOLSTICE** and marks
the progression from winter to spring, mid-February has traditionally been
regarded as a time of fertility. In the Middle Ages, it was said that birds
chose their mates on February 14 (see LOVEBIRDS). This was also the day on

which Groundhog Day was originally observed (see **CANDLEMAS**), heralding the approach of spring.

## SYMBOLS

### *Cupid*

Cupid, the Roman god of love, is a favorite symbol for VALENTINE CARDS, party decorations, and candy boxes. He was originally depicted as a young man carrying a bow and a quiver full of arrows. Over the years, Cupid's form was gradually altered, and the handsome youth of ancient mythology became a pudgy baby. This transformation of a god who was said to have sharpened his arrows on a grindstone whetted with blood to a helpless infant got a boost during the Victorian era, when merchants were eager to promote Valentine's Day as a holiday more suitable for women and children.

Cupid was the son of Venus, the Roman goddess of love and beauty. To the Romans, he was a symbol of passionate, playful, or tender love. His arrows were invisible, and his victims, who included gods as well as humans, would not be aware that they had been shot until they suddenly fell in love.

### *Heart and Arrow*

A red or pink heart pierced by an arrow is the best known and most enduring symbol of Valentine's Day. It can be seen in VALENTINE CARDS and decorations as well as in candies, cookies, and cakes served on this day. The heart itself symbolizes vulnerability as well as love: By sending someone a Valentine, one is taking a risk that he or she will be rejected. The arrow that pierces the heart is a symbol of death and the vulnerability of the unprotected heart. Together, the heart and the arrow also represent the merging of the male and female principles.

As early as the twelfth century, the heart was considered the seat of love and affection. But the conventional heart shape, which is symmetrical and tapers to a point at the bottom, doesn't look anything like a real heart. Some scholars speculate that it was designed by a casual doodler to represent the human buttocks, a female torso with prominent breasts, or even the imprint that a woman wearing lipstick makes when she presses her lips against a piece of paper.

In the early 1800s, young British and American men sometimes wore slips of paper with their girlfriends' names written on them pinned to their sleeves for several days, thus giving rise to the expression "to wear one's heart on one's sleeve."

In the United States, the American Heart Association holds its "Save a Sweet Heart" program during Valentine's week. It is an anti-smoking campaign that uses the symbol of the heart to educate high school students about the health risks involved in smoking.

## Lovebirds

The popular medieval folk belief that birds chose their mates on February 14 made doves a favorite symbol for VALENTINE CARDS. The dove was sacred to Venus and other love deities and had a reputation for choosing a lifelong mate. Known for their "billing and cooing," doves have long been a symbol of romantic love.

When printed Valentines first began to appear, many of them featured lovebirds. Toward the end of the nineteenth century, some even had a stuffed hummingbird or bird of paradise mounted on a satin cushion. The lovebirds that appear on today's Valentines are usually tiny parrots with brilliant feathers. In the wild, they are known for living in pairs and keeping to themselves, much like couples in love.

## Valentine Cards

The custom of exchanging love notes on Valentine's Day can be traced back to the ancient Roman **LUPERCALIA**, when boys drew the names of girls from a box and escorted the girl whose name they had drawn to the festival. The Christian church tried to downplay the holiday's sexual aspects by initiating the custom of drawing saints' names from a box. The participants would then be expected to emulate the saint whose name they had drawn for the rest of the year. Needless to say, the idea never really caught on, and Valentine's Day remains an occasion for exchanging love messages.

One of the first Valentine cards was created by Charles, Duke of Orleans. Imprisoned in the Tower of London for several years following the Battle of Agincourt in 1415, he sent Valentine poems to his wife in France from his jail cell. Commercially made Valentines didn't appear in England until almost 1800, although handmade cards had been popular for some time. In the nineteenth century, "penny dreadfuls" took the place of romantic Valentines. These were insulting and sometimes cruel cards, meant to be funny and usually sent anonymously.

In America, handmade Valentines began to appear around 1740. They were sealed with red wax and left secretly on a lover's doorstep or sent by mail. They were often quite elaborate, with cutout or pinprick designs resembling lace. Another popular handmade Valentine was the "puzzle purse," which had verses hidden within its folds that had to be read in a certain order. Commercially made cards began to take over in the 1880s.

"Valentine" meant the person whose name was picked from the box, or who was chosen to be one's sweetheart, by 1450. By 1533, it meant the folded piece of paper with the name on it; by 1610 it referred to a gift given to the special person; and by 1824 it referred to the verse, letter, or message sent to that person. Some say that the word "Valentine" doesn't come from St. Valentine at all, but rather from the Old French *galantine,* meaning "a lover or gallant."

## Further Reading

Barth, Edna. *Hearts, Cupids, and Red Roses: The Story of the Valentine Symbols,* 1974.

Buday, George. *The History of the Christmas Card,* 1971.

Gaer, Joseph. *Holidays Around the World,* 1953.

Henderson, Helene and Sue Ellen Thompson. *Holidays, Festivals, and Celebrations of the World Dictionary,* 2nd ed., 1997.

Ickis, Marguerite. *The Book of Festivals and Holidays the World Over,* 1970.

Purdy, Susan. *Festivals for You to Celebrate,* 1969.

Santino, Jack. *All Around the Year,* 1994.

Schmidt, Leigh Eric. *Consumer Rites: The Buying and Selling of American Holidays,* 1995.

Tuleja, Tad. *Curious Customs: The Stories Behind 296 Popular American Rituals,* 1987.

# *Vata Savitri*

**Type of Holiday:** Religious (Hindu)

**Date of Observation:** Last three days (or last day) of the bright half of Jyestha (May-June)

**Where Celebrated:** India

**Symbols:** Banyan Tree

# ORIGINS

Vata Savitri is a fast observed by Hindu women who want to avoid widowhood. During the Middle Ages, being left a widow was the most dreaded misfortune that could befall a Hindu woman. Even now, orthodox Hindu women all hope to die before their husbands. On Vata Savitri, therefore, they perform special ceremonies designed to promote the health and longevity of their husbands.

Savitri was the daughter of King Ashvapati. When she was old enough to marry, her father told her she could choose the man she wanted as her husband. She chose Satyavan, a hermit who lived in the jungle. The seer Narad warned Savitri that Satyavan was destined to die within a year. But she refused to let this knowledge change her mind and married him anyway. She got rid of all her jewels and fancy dresses and wore the coarse garments of a hermit. During the last three days of his life, she vowed to fast. Then, on his final day, she followed him as he went out to cut wood. He was so tired he lay down with his head in her lap and fell asleep.

There are several versions of what happened next. One says that the branch of a tree fell on his head, while another claims he was bitten by a snake. In any case, when Yama, the god of death, appeared to snatch his soul out of his body, Savitri chose to follow. Yama was so impressed by her devotion that he restored her husband to life and blessed them with a hundred sons.

Savitri is regarded as a symbol of marital fidelity. The festival held in her honor takes its name from the *vata* or BANYAN TREE, which she worshipped on the day of her husband's death. Hindu women get up early on this day and, after bathing, go out in groups to worship the banyan tree. They water the tree, sprinkle vermilion (red powder) on it, wrap raw cotton threads around its trunk, and then circle it seven times. They also observe a fast and make an offering of sugar and ghee (clarified butter). Women who are unable to get to a banyan tree worship a twig of it at home and distribute sweets to their family members and neighbors. They also pray for their husbands' prosperity and good health.

# SYMBOLS

## Banyan Tree

The banyan tree, also known as the Indian fig tree, is a symbol of immortality because it never dies. Its aerial roots support new branches, and it can go on growing for hundreds of years. Savitri is usually shown holding a branch of the banyan in one hand and the tree's aerial root in the other. An offshoot of the banyan tree can be seen growing over her head.

Hindu women believe that worshipping the banyan tree on Vata Savitri will guarantee a long life for their husbands.

### Further Reading

Gupte, Rai Bahadur B. A. *Hindu Holidays and Ceremonials,* 1916.

Henderson, Helene and Sue Ellen Thompson. *Holidays, Festivals, and Celebrations of the World Dictionary,* 2nd ed., 1997.

Kelly, Aidan. *Religious Holidays and Calendars,* 1993.

MacDonald, Margaret R., ed. *The Folklore of World Holidays,* 1992.

Spicer, Dorothy G. *The Book of Festivals,* 1990.

# *Vernal Equinox*

**Type of Holiday:** Calendar, Ancient or pagan

**Date of Observation:** On or about March 21

**Where Celebrated:** All over the world

**Symbols:** Flowers

**Related Holidays:** Arbor Day, Easter, May Day, New Year's Day, Passover, Walpurgis Night

## ORIGINS

The vernal equinox—from the Latin *vernalis,* meaning "of spring," and *equinoxium,* meaning "time of equal days and nights"—is one of two times during the year (the other being the autumnal equinox) when day and night are of equal length all over the world. This occurs because the ecliptic, or the sun's path through the sky, and the earth's equator intersect, with the sun above the equator. At this precise moment, known as the equinox, exactly one-half of the earth is illuminated by the sun's rays while the other half is in darkness, producing a day and a night that are both 12 hours long.

In ancient times, the vernal equinox marked the beginning of the year and the point from which the 12 constellations of the zodiac were calculated.

For this reason, the vernal equinox was sometimes referred to as the "first point of Aries," because at one time spring began when the sun entered the zodiac sign of Aries. But because of a phenomenon known as the "precession of the equinoxes," which refers to a cyclical wobbling in the earth's axis of rotation, the vernal equinox has shifted westward over the centuries, and spring now begins when the sun is in Pisces, the next constellation to the west.

In terms of earthly weather, the astronomical seasons mean nothing. In many parts of the United States, for example, where spring is widely identified with the months of March, April, and May, winter weather can persist well into April and even into May. In Great Britain, on the other hand, spring is popularly thought to include February, March, and April. In the Southern Hemisphere, of course, the seasons are reversed: There, spring begins around September 23 and ends about December 21.

As the season of planting and germination, when life and light replaced the darkness and death of the winter season, spring had a profound influence on ancient peoples and played an important role in their folklore, mythology, and art. Most ancient New Year rites taking place around the time of the vernal equinox involved one or more of the following elements: (1) fasting; (2) purgation, usually involving fire, the ringing of bells, and the cleansing of houses and temples; (3) invigoration, often in the form of a mock combat between the forces of life and death or the release of sexual energy; and (4) jubilation in the form of feasting and merriment.

The people of Bali, for example, celebrate the vernal equinox and the New Year by driving the devils out of their villages and then observing a day of stillness, known as Nyepí. After luring the evil spirits out of their hiding places with an elaborate offering of food, drink, and money, with samples of every kind of seed, fruit, and animal found on the island arranged in the shape of an eight-pointed star, the demons are driven out of the village by people running through the streets lighting firecrackers and banging on drums and tin cans. The following day, Nyepí, is observed as a day of absolute stillness: no cooking or fires, sexual intercourse, or work of any kind is permitted.

The early Christians, who regarded the seasons as symbolic of the course of human life, identified spring with rebirth and resurrection. The Christian festival of **EASTER**, which takes its name from Eostre, the Teutonic goddess of spring and fertility, is a joyful celebration of the resurrection of Christ observed on the Sunday after the first full moon following the vernal equinox. Even the Jewish feast of **PASSOVER** is rooted in ancient agricultural customs associated with spring and planting.

## SYMBOLS

### *Flowers*

Ancient sculptors and artists often depicted spring as a female figure carrying flowers. Flowers are a traditional symbol not only of spring but of the transitory beauty associated with this season. Flowers in a field are a popular Christian symbol of the Virgin Mary and the Church, and white flowers in particular are associated with the Virgin.

In the United States and other countries, spring remains a popular time for flower festivals and garden tours. Just as seeds are planted in the spring, it is also a time for other kinds of beginnings, including graduations and weddings.

### Further Reading

Chambers, Robert, ed. *The Book of Days,* 1864.

Hatch, Jane M. *The American Book of Days,* 1978.

Heinberg, Richard. *Celebrate the Solstice: Honoring the Earth's Seasonal Rhythms through Festival and Ceremony,* 1993.

Henderson, Helene and Sue Ellen Thompson. *Holidays, Festivals, and Celebrations of the World Dictionary,* 2nd ed., 1997.

Leach, Maria, ed. *Funk & Wagnalls Standard Dictionary of Folklore, Mythology, & Legend,* 1984.

MacDonald, Margaret R., ed. *The Folklore of World Holidays,* 1992.

Olderr, Steven. *Symbolism: A Comprehensive Dictionary,* 1986.

# *Vesak*
### (Wesak, Buddha's Birthday)

**Type of Holiday:** Religious (Buddhist)

**Date of Observation:** Full moon of Vaisakha (April-May)

**Where Celebrated:** China, India, Indonesia, Japan, Korea, Nepal, Singapore, Sri Lanka, Thailand, Tibet, and by Buddhists all over the world

**Symbols:** Bathing the Buddha, Bodhi Tree

**Related Holidays:** Hana Matsuri

# ORIGINS

For Buddhists, this is the holiest day of the year, celebrating the Buddha's birth, enlightenment, and death, or attainment of Nirvana. While these anniversaries are observed in all Buddhist countries, they are not always celebrated on the same day. Theravada Buddhists, who practice the oldest form of their religion and can be found primarily in Southeast Asia, observe all three anniversaries on the full moon of the sixth month. In Japan and other Mahayana Buddhist countries, these three events are celebrated on separate days: the Buddha's birth on April 8, his enlightenment on December 8, and his death on February 15.

Although the celebration differs from country to country, activities generally center on the Buddhist temples, where people gather to listen to sermons on the life of Buddha. In the evening, there are candlelight processions around the temples, while homes are decorated with paper lanterns and oil lamps. Because it's considered important to practice the virtues of kindness to all living things, it's traditional in some countries to free caged birds on this day, or to set up booths to dispense food to the poor.

Siddhartha Gautama, who came to be called the Buddha ("the Enlightened"), was born about 563 B.C.E. into an aristocratic family. At the age of 29, distressed by the misery of mankind, he renounced his life of luxury and left his wife and infant son to become a wandering ascetic. For six years he practiced the most severe austerities, eating little and meditating regularly. But then he realized that self-deprivation wasn't leading him to what he sought. One morning in 528 B.C.E. while sitting in deep meditation under the BODHI TREE, he experienced a wider vision of his own existence and derived from that vision his blueprint for religious life. In the years that followed, he laid down rules of ethics and condemned the caste system. He taught that the aim of religion is to free oneself of worldly concerns in order to attain enlightenment or Nirvana. The Buddha trained large numbers of disciples to continue his work. He died in about 483 B.C.E.

In Japan, Buddha's birthday is known as Hana Matsuri or Flower Festival because it marks the beginning of the cherry blossom season. The image of Buddha is covered by a miniature unwalled shrine called the *hana-mido* or "flowery temple." Sometimes the flower-decked temple is drawn through the streets by a horse or ox. In China, *sutras* (sermons of Buddha) are chanted to the accompaniment of drums and bells, brass cymbals, and tiny gongs. The fish, a symbol of watchfulness, appears in the form of wooden fish heads, which are struck with small sticks. In Ceylon, where the great festival of Wesak is held on the first full moon in May, people sit out in the moonlight in little shanties made of flowers and greenery, and listen to the long sermons of the Bikkhus (priests), which tell stories from the life of Buddha.

# SYMBOLS

## *Bathing the Buddha*

The tradition of bathing images of the Buddha on Vesak seems to have derived from an episode in the story of the life in which the two serpents, Nanda and Upananda, bathe him after his birth. Today, the bathing ritual takes many different forms. In China, his image is carried out of the temple and into the courtyard, where it is sprinkled with water that is exceptionally pure. Sometimes the image of Buddha is placed in a big jar of water, and believers take a spoonful of water and sprinkle it over his head as they pass through the courtyard.

In Japan, Buddha's image is bathed with *ama-cha,* a sweet tea prepared from hydrangea leaves that have been steamed and dried. The statue of the Buddha usually shows him with one hand raised high toward heaven and the other directed toward the earth. This posture is derived from the story of his birth, soon after which he raised his right hand and lowered his left, declaring, "I am my own Lord throughout heaven and earth." Worshippers take some of the tea home with them so their faith and good health will be perpetuated.

## *Bodhi Tree*

The tree under which the Buddha was enlightened in 528 B.C.E. was a type of ficus or Asian fig tree that can grow as high as 100 feet. Like the banyan tree, it branches indefinitely and has thick "prop" roots that support the extended branches.

There are actually two points in Gautama's life where a tree plays a significant role. The first was when he was a boy and he slipped naturally into a trance while sitting under a rose-apple tree. When Gautama abandoned the ascetic life at the age of 35, he recalled that early experience and again sought refuge under a tree to compose his thoughts and await enlightenment. The tree that sheltered him throughout the night came to be known as the Bodhi Tree — *bodhi* meaning "enlightenment" or "awakening."

When King Asoka of India sent his daughter to Sri Lanka as a Buddhist missionary, she took a branch of the famous Bodhi Tree with her. According to legend, the branch took root, a symbol of the new religion.

## Further Reading

Bauer, Helen, and Sherwin Carlquist. *Japanese Festivals,* 1965.

Bredon, Juliet, and Igor Mitrophanow. *The Moon Year: A Record of Chinese Customs and Festivals,* 1966.

Crim, Keith, ed. *The Perennial Dictionary of World Religions,* 1989.

Eberhard, Wolfram. *A Dictionary of Chinese Symbols,* 1986.

Eliade, Mircea. *The Encyclopedia of Religion,* 1897.

Henderson, Helene and Sue Ellen Thompson. *Holidays, Festivals, and Celebrations of the World Dictionary,* 2nd ed., 1997.

Ickis, Marguerite. *The Book of Festivals and Holidays the World Over,* 1970.

Pike, Royston. *Round the Year with the World's Religions,* 1993.

# Veterans' Day
## *(Remembrance Day)*

**Type of Holiday:** Historic
**Date of Observation:** November 11
**Where Celebrated:** Canada, England, France, United States
**Symbols:** Poppy, Tomb of the Unknown Soldier

## ORIGINS

The armistice that ended the fighting in World War II was signed in Marshal Ferdinand Foch's railroad car in the Forest of Compiègne, France, on November 11, 1918. There were huge public celebrations in Paris, London, and New York City, where more than a million Americans jammed Broadway, danced in the streets, and hurled ticker tape out their windows.

During the 1920s, the annual observance of the armistice became a tradition on both sides of the Atlantic. It was known as Remembrance Day in England and Canada, and Armistice Day in the United States, or sometimes Victory Day. The United States started honoring its war dead in 1921 (SEE TOMB OF THE UNKNOWN SOLDIER), but November 11 didn't become a legal federal holiday until 1938.

One of the reasons the armistice was such a cause for celebration is that people believed that the death and destruction of the First World War would never be repeated. But the advent of World War II changed all that, and for many years afterward, celebrations of the 1918 ceasefire received little attention. Veterans' groups urged that November 11 be set aside to pay tribute to all those who had served in the armed forces — in other words, those who had fought in World War II and the Korean War as well. In 1954 President Dwight Eisenhower signed a bill specifying that Armistice Day would thereafter be commemorated as Veterans' Day.

Veterans' Day observances take place all over the United States, particularly in places associated with the American war effort — for example, the USS *North Carolina* Battleship Memorial, a restored World War II ship docked in Wilmington, North Carolina. The celebrations usually include parades, speeches, military balls, and religious services. In many places, the 11th day of the 11th month is celebrated by observing a two-minute silence at 11:00 in the morning, the hour at which the hostilities ceased.

## SYMBOLS

### Poppy

The poppy is a small red flower that grows wild in the fields of Europe where many of those who died in the First World War are buried. It was popularized by the famous war poem written by John McCrae, whose most famous lines are, "In Flanders fields the poppies blow/ Between the crosses, row on row." Flanders was the sight of heavy fighting during the war, and for many, the poppy came to symbolize both the beauty of the landscape and the blood that was shed there.

Artificial paper poppies are sold by veterans' organizations in most countries on November 11. Poppies are also used to decorate the graves of those who died fighting in World War I.

### Tomb of the Unknown Soldier

The United States didn't really start honoring its war dead on November 11 until 1921, when the remains of an unidentified American soldier who had died fighting in France were disinterred and transported back to the United States. The remains of the "unknown soldier," as he came to be called, lay in state in the rotunda of the Capitol in Washington, D.C., for three days before being moved to their final resting place at Arlington National Cemetery in Virginia.

The principal observation of Veterans' Day in the United States still takes place at the Tomb of the Unknown Soldier, which symbolizes the nation's desire to honor its war dead. Throughout the year, sentries maintain a constant vigil at the grave site. Since 1960, a flaming torch that was lighted in Antwerp, Belgium, and then brought to the United States, has burned there to honor all those who have died while serving their country. Taps are sounded at the tomb on November 11 at exactly 11:00 a.m., and the President or his representative places a wreath on the shrine. Afterward, representatives of the armed forces and several thousand spectators listen to an address by a prominent public figure in the amphitheater behind the tomb.

## Further Reading

Dunkling, Leslie. *A Dictionary of Days,* 1988.

Hatch, Jane M. *The American Book of Days,* 1978.

Henderson, Helene and Sue Ellen Thompson. *Holidays, Festivals, and Celebrations of the World Dictionary,* 2nd ed., 1997.

Spicer, Dorothy G. *The Book of Festivals,* 1990.

Van Straalen, Alice. *The Book of Holidays Around the World,* 1986.

# Walpurgis Night
## (Walpurgisnacht)

**Type of Holiday:** Folkloric

**Date of Observation:** April 30

**Where Celebrated:** Austria, Germany, Scandinavia

**Symbols:** Bonfires, Witches

**Related Holidays:** Beltane, May Day

## ORIGINS

April 30, the eve of **MAY DAY**, is named for St. Walpurga, an English missionary who became an abbess in Germany, where she died in 780 C.E. On the eve of May 1, her remains were moved from Heidenheim to Eichstätt, where her shrine became a popular place of pilgrimage. Legend has it that the rocks at Eichstätt give off a miraculous oil possessing curative powers. Walpurga is known as the saint who protects against magic.

The traditions associated with St. Walpurga's Day can be traced back to pre-Christian celebrations on the eve of **BELTANE**, one of the four major festivals of the ancient Celts who once inhabited much of the European continent. The people who lived in the Harz Mountains of Germany believed for many centuries that WITCHES rode across the sky on the eve of St. Walpurga's Day to hold a coven or gathering on Brocken Mountain. To frighten them off, they rang church bells, banged pots and pans, and lit torches topped with hemlock, rosemary, and juniper. The legend of Walpurgis Night is still celebrated in Germany, Austria, and Scandinavia with BONFIRES and other festivities designed to welcome spring by warding off demons, disaster, and darkness.

Although Walpurgis Night is not widely observed in the United States, many Scandinavian clubs and associations, particularly in cities with large Swedish or Norwegian populations, hold celebrations on April 30 consisting primarily of BONFIRES, speeches, folk dancing, and music.

## SYMBOLS

### Bonfires

Bonfires have been lit to scare off witches and other evil creatures since ancient times. The fires that were lit on the eve of **BELTANE** were designed to promote fertility and to ward off bad luck and disease. They represented the life-giving power of the sun, and leaping through the flames or over the glowing embers was a way of sharing the sun's power.

It is still customary in parts of Sweden to build huge bonfires on Walpurgis Night and light them by striking two flints together. Every large village has its own fire, often built on a hilltop, and young people dance around it in a ring. If the flames blow toward the north, it means that the spring will be cold and slow to arrive; if they incline to the south, it will be mild. People leap over the glowing embers in a ceremony called "Burning the Witches." There is a widespread folk belief that the fields will be blessed for as far as the light of the bonfire reaches.

### Witches

Witches symbolize the evil that is everywhere in the world and that must be guarded against. Because witches were believed to be out riding their broomsticks to a gathering on the tallest peak of Germany's Harz Mountains on Walpurgis Night, people tried to make light of their own fears by wearing costumes and holding parties. Straw effigies of witches were often paraded through the streets and burned in BONFIRES.

## Further Reading

Frazer, Sir James G. *The Golden Bough: A Study in Magic and Religion,* 1931.

Hatch, Jane M. *The American Book of Days,* 1978.

Heinberg, Richard. *Celebrate the Solstice: Honoring the Earth's Seasonal Rhythms through Festival and Ceremony,* 1993.

Henderson, Helene and Sue Ellen Thompson. *Holidays, Festivals, and Celebrations of the World Dictionary*, 2nd ed., 1997.

James, E. O. *Seasonal Feasts and Festivals,* 1961.

King, John. *The Celtic Druids'Year: Seasonal Cycles of the Ancient Celts,* 1995.

Santino, Jack. *All Around theYear,* 1994.

# *Washington's Birthday*
### *(Presidents' Day, Washington-Lincoln Day)*

**Type of Holiday:** Historic

**Date of Observation:** February 22 or third Monday in February

**Where Celebrated:** United States

**Symbols:** Cherry Tree

**Colors:** Washington's Birthday is often associated with the colors red, white, and blue, symbolic of the American flag and of patriotism in general. These colors can be seen not only in the flags and bunting that decorate public streets and buildings on this day, but also in advertisements promoting Presidents' Day sales.

**Related Holidays:** Lincoln's Birthday

## ORIGINS

As commander-in-chief of the Continental Army during the American Revolution and as the first president of the United States, George Washington has always played an important role in American literature and legend. People started celebrating his birthday while he was still alive, particularly during his two terms as president (1789-96). But they usually held their observances on February 11. The date wasn't shifted to February 22 until 1796, some years after the New Style or Gregorian calendar was adopted.

Richmond, Virginia, was the first town to sponsor a public celebration of George Washington's birthday in 1782. Celebrations became more popular during his first term as president, then began to wane with the development of two political parties, the Federalists (with whom Washington sympathized) and the Jeffersonian Democratic-Republicans, who found such celebrations offensive. Partisan feelings weren't set aside until after Washington's death in 1799, when Congress passed a resolution calling on the nation to observe February 22, 1800, with appropriate activities.

The observance of Washington's Birthday didn't really take hold until 1832, the centennial of his birth. One of the most memorable celebrations was held in Los Angeles in 1850. The town's leading citizens decided to mark the occasion with a fancy ball, but some of the community's less refined members were excluded. They retaliated by firing a cannon into the ballroom, killing several men and wounding others.

While the third Monday in February is observed as Washington's Birthday by the federal government and most states, some combine it with the February birthday of another famous American president, Abraham Lincoln, calling it Washington-Lincoln Day or Presidents' Day. Today it is primarily a commercial event, as store owners take advantage of the holiday weekend to empty their shelves of midwinter stock.

## SYMBOLS

### Cherry Tree

Stories about George Washington's precocious adolescence were largely the invention of his biographers. Probably the most popular is the legend of how he chopped down one of his father's cherry trees and then owned up to his mistake by saying to his father, "I cannot tell a lie." There appears to be no historic basis for this tale, which first appeared in the 1806 edition of *The Life and Memorable Actions of George Washington,* by Parson Mason Weems. The cherry tree, along with the hatchet that chopped it down, has nevertheless come to represent the honesty and forthrightness for which Washington was revered.

Ironically, this and the other popular legend concerning George Washington — how he threw a silver dollar across the Potomac River — are remembered today primarily by merchandisers. Their advertisements often employ phrases like, "We're chopping our prices for you!" or "Silver Dollar Days" to lure shoppers into America's malls during the holiday weekend.

## Further Reading

Chambers, Robert, ed. *The Book of Days,* 1864.
Dunkling, Leslie. *A Dictionary of Days,* 1988.

Hatch, Jane M. *The American Book of Days,* 1978.

Henderson, Helene and Sue Ellen Thompson. *Holidays, Festivals, and Celebrations of the World Dictionary,* 2nd ed., 1997.

Schaun, George and Virginia. *American Holidays and Special Days,* 1986.

Tuleja, Tad. *Curious Customs: The Stories Behind 296 Popular American Rituals,* 1987.

# *Wianki Festival of Wreaths*

**Type of Holiday:** Folkloric

**Date of Observation:** June 23

**Where Celebrated:** Washington, D.C.

**Symbols:** Wreath

**Related Holidays:** Midsummer Day, Midsummer Eve

## ORIGINS

The Wianki Festival of Wreaths (*wianki* means "wreath" in Polish) is observed by Polish-American young people in Washington, D.C., on St. John's Eve, June 23. Girls make wreaths out of fresh greens, put a lit candle in the center, and set them afloat in the reflecting pool in front of the Lincoln Memorial. Young men gather around the pool in the hope that the wind will blow their girlfriends' wreaths toward them.

The origins of this festival can be traced back to pagan times. For centuries in Poland it has been customary for girls to wear a garland of wildflowers on St. John's Eve, decorate it with ribbons, and fasten a lighted candle to the center. Then they throw their wreaths far out into a moving river or stream. If the wreath drifts to shore, it is taken as a sign that the girl will never marry; it if sinks, she will die within the year; if it floats downstream, she will definitely be married. According to superstition, the boy who catches a wreath will marry the girl to whom it belongs. So the boys hide in boats along the river banks and try to capture their sweethearts' garlands. At the end of the festival, the boys take the girls upstream in their boats.

A very similar festival took place in pre-Revolutionary Russia. Known as Semik—meaning "seventh," because it was held on the seventh Thursday after **EASTER**—it involved young girls throwing wreaths into the water or hanging them on trees as an offering to the god of the woods. The fate of the wreath was regarded as evidence of the young girl's fate.

## SYMBOLS

### *Wreath*

The myrtle wreath is traditionally considered to be the symbol of a bride, and the wreath in general has been used to symbolize immortality, victory, and mourning. The wreaths that young Polish and Polish-American girls set afloat on the water can therefore be seen as symbolic of the several different paths their lives may take: They may die within the year, they may marry, etc.

## Further Reading

Henderson, Helene and Sue Ellen Thompson. *Holidays, Festivals, and Celebrations of the World Dictionary*, 2nd ed., 1997.
MacDonald, Margaret R., ed. *The Folklore of World Holidays*, 1992.
Olderr, Steven. *Symbolism: A Comprehensive Dictionary*, 1986.
Spicer, Dorothy G. *The Book of Festivals*, 1990.

# *Winter Solstice*

**Type of Holiday:** Ancient or pagan, Calendar

**Date of Observation:** December 21 or 22 in the Northern Hemisphere; June 21 or 22 in the Southern Hemisphere

**Where Celebrated:** Modern observances of the Winter Solstice are rare, but in ancient times it was observed throughout Europe, the British Isles, China, India, and Scandinavia

**Symbols:** Fire, Tree

**Related Holidays:** Christmas, Saturnalia, Summer Solstice

# ORIGINS

The word "solstice" comes from the Latin *sol stetit,* which means, "The sun stood still." In the Northern Hemisphere, the sun rises and sets further south on the horizon as the Winter Solstice approaches; it rises and sets further north as the **SUMMER SOLSTICE** approaches. For a period of about six days in late December and again in late June, the sun appears to rise and set in almost exactly the same place, giving the solstices their name.

The ancient Romans celebrated the Winter Solstice with a festival dedicated to Saturn, the god of agriculture (see **SATURNALIA**). When Emperor Constantine declared in the early fourth century that Christianity would be the new faith of the Roman Empire, the holiday was given an entirely new name and meaning: It became the birthday of Jesus of Nazareth, also known as Christ Mass or **CHRISTMAS.** Many familiar Yuletide customs — including the Christmas TREE and the Yule log (see FIRE) — actually have more to do with the Winter Solstice than with Christian doctrine. Even Santa Claus may originally have been a "solstice shaman" who officiated at the rites that took place on the Winter Solstice.

The ancient Chinese people believed that at sunrise on the Winter Solstice, the *yang* or masculine principle was born into the world and began a six-month period of ascendancy. The Hindus, even though their calendar was based on lunar cycles, held festivals on the solstices and equinoxes as well. In northern India, for example, people greeted the Winter Solstice with a ceremonial clanging of bells and gongs to frighten off evil spirits. In the British Isles, the Druids celebrated the overthrow of the old god, Bran, by the new god, Bel, at the time of the December solstice.

The Winter Solstice was marked by the victory of light over darkness, the end of the cycle of death and decay and the beginning of a new cycle of light and growth. It has traditionally been a time for people to celebrate the gradual lengthening of the days and the regeneration of the earth.

# SYMBOLS

## *Fire*

The Winter Solstice was traditionally celebrated by lighting fires, symbolic of the sun, whose powers would increase as the days grew longer. The midwinter tradition of lighting a Yule log, for example, was an ancient Celtic fire ritual performed at the time of the December solstice. To bring the log indoors and burn it was symbolically to bring the blessing of the Sun God into the house. The log had to burn steadily without being extinguished, or else bad luck would follow. Sometimes wine, cider, ale, or corn was sprinkled over the log before it was lit. In southern England, particularly Cornwall, the figure of a man was drawn in chalk on the log—perhaps a survival of what was originally a human sacrifice by fire. Part of the log was kept and used to ignite the new log a year later.

The Yule candle lit in many churches at the beginning of the Christmas season is another example of how pagan solstice rites were gradually absorbed by Christianity. At one time only the head of the household was allowed to light or extinguish the flame, and an unused remnant was preserved as protection against thunder and lightning. In some countries, tallow from the Yule candle was rubbed on the farmers' plow to promote fertility in the fields. The electric candles that are displayed in so many American homes at Christmastime today reflect this ancient Celtic reverence for the candle as a symbol of light during the darkest time of the year.

## Tree

Tree worship was central to the religious beliefs of the Teutons and the Druids, who built their temples in the woods. Trees were regarded as possessing spirits, and they were only cut down out of necessity. The ancient Norsemen and the people of Central Asia saw the tree as a symbol for the universe. Native Americans and the early people of India and China held similar ideas.

The Christmas tree probably derived from customs associated with pre-Christian tree worship. The Romans decorated evergreen trees and wreaths at the **SATURNALIA**, and an evergreen shrub called the "herb of the sun" was especially favored at the time of the Winter Solstice. Nowadays, the popularity of cut Christmas trees has been challenged by those whose concern for the environment favors the idea of planting a living tree around Christmas or the Winter Solstice.

# Further Reading

Gaer, Joseph. *Holidays Around the World,* 1953.

Hatch, Jane M. *The American Book of Days,* 1978.

Heinberg, Richard. *Celebrate the Solstice: Honoring the Earth's Seasonal Rhythms through Festival and Ceremony,* 1993.

Henderson, Helene and Sue Ellen Thompson. *Holidays, Festivals, and Cele-brations of the World Dictionary*, 2nd ed., 1997.

Kelly, Aidan. *Religious Holidays and Calendars*, 1993.

King, John. *The Celtic Druids'Year: Seasonal Cycles of the Ancient Celts,* 1995.

MacDonald, Margaret R., ed. *The Folklore of World Holidays,* 1992.

Urlin, Ethel L. *Festivals, Holy Days, and Saints' Days,* 1915.

# Yom Kippur
## (Day of Atonement, Day of Judgment)

**Type of Holiday:** Religious (Jewish)

**Date of Observation:** Tenth day of Tishri; between September 15 and October 13

**Where Celebrated:** Europe, Israel, Palestine, United States, and by Jews all over the world

**Symbols:** Kapparot Ceremony, Kol Nidre, Scapegoat, Shofar

**Colors:** Yom Kippur is associated with the color white. The rabbi, cantor, and married men of the congregation wear the *kittel* or long white robe of purity. It is also customary to drape the scrolls of the Torah in white, to cover the ark or closet in which the scrolls are kept with a white curtain, and to spread white cloths over the cantor's reading desk and the pulpit. For this reason, Yom Kippur is sometimes known as "the White Fast."

**Related Holidays:** Rosh Hashanah, Sukkot

## ORIGINS

The ten-day period of penitence in the Jewish calendar between **ROSH HASHANAH**, the Jewish New Year, and Yom Kippur, or the Day of Atonement, is typical of similar periods in other cultures marking the transition between the old year and the new. It was a period during which all normal activities were suspended. It was regarded as being "outside time," because extra days were often inserted between the end of one year and the beginning of the next to bring the lunar and solar calendars into harmony. In Judaism, this ten-day period was dedicated to examining the soul.

The last of the ten High Holy Days, Yom Kippur is the most solemn day in the Jewish calendar. It is the day on which God examines people's lives and writes down His final decision concerning their future in the Book of Life, which is then sealed until the following year. Because it is their last chance to acknowledge their sins and ask God to forgive them, Jews often spend the entire 24 hours at the synagogue, where five services are held. They also abstain from food and water during this period, which keeps their minds clear for prayer and repentance.

God is said to open three books on Rosh Hashanah. The first contains the names of the virtuous, whose lives will be blessed during the next 12 months. The second contains the names of the wicked, who are doomed to death and disaster. In the third, however, are the names of those who still have a chance to redeem themselves and determine their own fates, because this book isn't sealed until twilight on Yom Kippur. If a person is genuinely sorry for what he or she has done and asks God to forgive and correct his or her wrongdoing, God will put a "good signature" next to the person's name and the coming year will be a happy one. When Jews meet each other in the synagogue on this day, they often say, "May you end this day with a good signature."

The celebration of Yom Kippur begins in the evening at the synagogue, where the prayer known as the KOL NIDRE is recited. Worshippers then read prayers from the Yom Kippur prayer book and spend the entire period of the holiday praying that they will be forgiven for their sins and thinking about how they might become better people. Many of these prayers are said out loud, with everyone in the synagogue joining in. On the afternoon of Yom Kippur, the story of the prophet Jonah and the whale is read from the Bible as a reminder that God is eager for people to repent. The end of the service is marked by a long blast from the SHOFAR or ram's horn, after which people go home to eat their first meal following the day-long fast.

The *challah* or bread baked on Yom Kippur is often made in special shapes—usually a ladder, symbolic of the hope that Yom Kippur prayers will reach heaven, or wings, because the scriptures read on Yom Kippur compare men to angels.

# SYMBOLS

## *Kapparot Ceremony*

In a very ancient ceremony held on the day before Yom Kippur and known as the *Kapparah* or *Kapparot,* it was customary to take a chicken (a rooster for a man, a hen for a woman) and swing it around one's head three times while reciting verses from the Psalms and the Book of Job. The chicken served as a kind of SCAPEGOAT: It took on the individual's sins and absorbed any punishment that he or she deserved. The custom of Kapparot is normally practiced only by very pious Jews. Today, many people observe it by swinging money tied in a handkerchief over their heads and then giving it to charity.

The act of making circles appears in many other Jewish customs as well as in those of other ancient cultures. Making a "magic ring" was originally believed to ward off evil spirits. Some Jewish authorities have condemned the Kapparot ceremony as a display of heathen superstition, but it remains popular among Orthodox Jews.

## *Kol Nidre*

On the eve of Yom Kippur, there is a service at the synagogue known as the Kol Nidre ("All Vows"). It dates back to the sixth century when, during the Spanish Inquisition, Jews were forced to become Christians. They tried to follow their religious beliefs in secret, asking God to forgive them for breaking vows they could not keep because of events beyond their control. The Kol Nidre prayer has also been used during other times in history when Jews have been forced, in one way or another, to abandon the practice of their religion.

To many Jews the Kol Nidre prayer is synonymous with Yom Kippur. Modern Reform Jews no longer recite the Kol Nidre because it has been criticized for providing a "loophole" by which they might avoid fulfilling their obligations. But the haunting melody to which the words of the Kol Nidre are sung, composed between the mid-fifteenth and mid-sixteenth centuries, can be very moving, and many people have tears in their eyes when they listen to it.

## *Scapegoat*

A scapegoat is someone or something that bears the blame for the wrongs committed by others. The idea of using a scapegoat to atone for human sins goes back to the most primitive societies. The ancient Babylonians included in their ten-day New Year celebration a *Kapparu* day—a day for the cleansing of sins. They would kill a ram and rub its body against the walls of the temple so that any impurities would be absorbed. The next day, they would designate a criminal to act as a human scapegoat for the sins of the community. This unfortunate person would be paraded in the streets and beaten over the head. When the Jews took over this ceremony, it became more than an act of purgation; people had to be purified not just for their own sakes, but for the sake of their God. Sin was regarded as an obstacle not only to their material welfare but to the fulfillment of their duty to God. In fact, Yom Kippur gets its name from *kippurim,* which refers to the various procedures used to remove the taint of sin.

Why a scape*goat?* The male goat for pre-Christians was a symbol of virility and unbridled lust. But as sexuality became more and more repressed, the goat's status was reduced to that of an "impure, stinking" creature who only cared about gratifying its own appetites. In portrayals of the Last Judgment, the goat is used to symbolize those who are damned. This is based upon a passage in the Bible describing how Christ on Judgment Day will separate the believers from the nonbelievers as the shepherd separates the sheep from the goats.

In ancient times, two scapegoats were chosen. After special ceremonies were held transferring the sins of the community to the goats, one of them was sacrificed and the other was driven into the wilderness. When the Second Temple in Jerusalem was destroyed in 70 C.E., animal sacrifices were discontinued, and Yom Kippur underwent a profound change. The sins that used to be removed by the ritual of the scapegoat now had to be purged by each individual through confession and absolution. At the same time, atoning for one's sins by attending synagogue services on Yom Kippur remains a community experience.

## *Shofar*

In Jerusalem, it was customary to signal the end of Yom Kippur by blowing the shofar or ram's horn at the Western Wall, also known as the Wailing Wall (see **TISHA BE-AV**). After the Arabs rioted against the Jewish population of Palestine in 1919, the British administrators ordered the Jews to stop the custom. Defying threats from both Arabs and the British police, certain dedicated Jews continued the practice; many were imprisoned for doing so.

In June of 1967, after the old city of Jerusalem was freed from Jordanian control, one of the first things that the Chief Rabbi of the Israeli Defense

Force did was to blow the shofar at the Western Wall. Since that time, the custom has been restored. Every year on Yom Kippur, thousands of Israelis gather at the wall to listen.

# Further Reading

Biedermann, Hans. *Dictionary of Symbolism: Cultural Icons and the Meanings Behind Them,* 1994.

Cashman, Greer Fay. *Jewish Days and Holidays,* 1979.

Edidin, Ben. *Jewish Holidays and Festivals,* 1993.

Ferguson, George. *Signs and Symbols in Christian Art,* 1954.

Frazer, Sir James G. *The Golden Bough: A Study in Magic and Religion,* 1931.

Gaer, Joseph. *Holidays Around the World,* 1953.

Gaster, Theodor H. *Festivals of the Jewish Year,* 1953.

Henderson, Helene and Sue Ellen Thompson. *Holidays, Festivals, and Celebrations of the World Dictionary,* 2nd ed., 1997.

Purdy, Susan. *Festivals for You to Celebrate,* 1969.

Renberg, Dalia H. *The Complete Family Guide to Jewish Holidays,* 1985.

# General Index

# Symbols Index

3 1161 00642 7937